Philosophy in Ar
Primary Readings
Volume I

Nancy A. Stanlick
University of Central Florida

Bruce S. Silver
University of South Florida

PEARSON
Prentice
Hall

Upper Saddle River, NJ 07458

Library of Congress Cataloging-in-Publication Data

Philosophy in America: selected readings/[edited by] Nancy A. Stanlick, Bruce S. Silver.
   p. cm.
Includes bibliographical references.
ISBN 0-13-095037-8
   1. Philosophy, American—History. I. Stanlick, Nancy A. II. Silver, Bruce S.

B851.P49 2004
191—dc21   2002193123

VP, Editorial Director: *Charlyce Jones Owen*
Acquisitions Editor: *Ross Miller*
Assistant Editor: *Wendy Yurash*
AVP, Director of Production and Manufacturing: *Barbara Kittle*
Editorial/Production Supervision and Interior Design: *Harriet Tellem*
Prepress and Manufacturing Manager: *Nick Sklitsis*
Prepress and Manufacturing Buyer: *Brian Mackey*
Marketing Manager: *Chris Ruel*
Editorial Assistant: *Carla Worner*

PEARSON
Prentice
Hall

©2004 by Pearson Education, Inc.
Upper Saddle River, New Jersey 07458

This book was set in 10/12 Palatino by Interactive Composition Corporation,
and was printed and bound by RR Donnelley Harrisonburg.
The cover was printed by Phoenix Color Corp.

Printed in the United States of America

10 9 8 7 6 5 4 3 2 1

ISBN 0-13-095037-8

Pearson Education Ltd., *London*
Pearson Education Australia, Pty, Limited, *Sydney*
Pearson Education Singapore, Pte. Ltd.
Pearson Education North Asia Ltd., *Hong Kong*
Pearson Education Canada, Ltd., *Toronto*
Pearson Educación De Mexico, S.A. De C.V.
Pearson Education—Japan, *Tokyo*
Pearson Education Malaysia, Pte. Ltd.
Pearson Education, Upper Saddle River, *New Jersey*

Contents

Preface

Why assemble an anthology in American philosophy? The answer is straight-forward: there is a need for one. Some of the fine earlier collections are out of print. Some of the anthologies that remain take as their emphasis middle nineteenth-century pragmatism and what comes in its wake. We think that there is a need for a collection, the one we have put together, that captures at least some of the principal figures, philosophers, and speculative thinkers who wrote before there was a United States and after the great pragmatists had come and gone. We believe, in short, that philosophy in America was alive well before the 1860s and that it continues to live into the very early years of the twenty-first century. We hope that this anthology ratifies our beliefs.

Philosophy in America: Primary Readings is more a collection of spirited arguments and development of ideas than it is a focus on a single notion or project. From the Calvinism of Jonathan Edwards to the feminism of Marilyn Frye, from Thomas Paine's arguments against monarchy and John Adams's brief for a balance of powers to John Rawls's treatment of justice, and from Ralph Waldo Emerson's intuitionism to John Dewey's instrumentalism, we find that the history of American philosophy is too rich and varied to limit to immutable categories.

A dim measure of optimism lurks throughout the often grim writings of Jonathan Edwards, even with his pessimism about chances for salvation and God's often violent, always "incensed," wrath over the sins of humanity. Edwards develops a kind of theodicy, a view that everything must work out as God foresaw it and that divine justice is a manifestation of the beauty, bounty, and order of the universe. Even those who are damned to suffer the eternal and unspeakable torments of hell are all too briefly aware of the beauty and balance that surround them in the present life.

American thought takes a hard turn after the first Great Awakening, especially in the work of Paine, a staunch advocate of all that is good in the world and an equally vigorous opponent of what he saw as the hopelessly flawed and sinister nature of traditional Christianity. Paine looked to reason, observation, and the sciences as he indicted established religions as sources of hatred, cruelty, and fear.

The New England Transcendentalists and pragmatists go beyond Paine's impatience with conventional religion. Ralph Waldo Emerson said that "to be great is to be misunderstood" and that intellectual and moral obligations reflect one's place in the universe as a "part and particle of God." In the reflections of Emerson and Henry David Thoreau, a preoccupation with human depravity and sinfulness lost out to more generous sentiments. Threats of eternal damnation were replaced by melioristic philosophies and by exhortations to recognize the potential for human progress here and now. Human dignity, not depravity, was often the assumption of philosophers at home in this young nation that experimented and succeeded with its unprecedented formulas for justice and a republican political order.

William James is among the philosophical activists at work during America's Gilded Age. His position in "What Makes a Life Significant" embodies a promising philosophy that celebrates the value of human life. Living has a purpose whether the scope of our interests is getting by day to day or recognizing that life can be meaningful and heroic beyond our most extravagant expectations. Whether optimism is expressed in the claims of C. S. Peirce, as he defends the scientific method of inquiry, or in Rawls's conviction that human beings can agree to live by principles of justice and fairness, American philosophy frequently celebrates progress, good character, productive knowledge, and noble values. Optimism is at work and at home in the writings, ideas, and actions of the American civil rights and women's rights movements. From Frederick Douglass's impassioned speech "What to the Slave Is the Fourth of July?" to Elizabeth Cady Stanton's Emersonian attitude of self-sovereignty in "Solitude of Self," we find—even among the problems of oppression and unfairness that characterize the lives of marginalized peoples—an undying spirit of hope.

Individualism, not so much the kind that we acquire from dime novel versions of the Wild West but the kind that sees the individual as an important member of the human community, persists as an element of American philosophy. Paine and Jefferson develop their versions of praise for individualism in a kind of populist confidence that human beings, using their own intellect and power, can find their way to truth and happiness. Paine raises his own position to its zenith by proclaiming that "my mind is my church" and by his steadfast determination to demonstrate the goodness of God and the ability of reflective people to make a difference in their own lives. Emerson's exhortation in "Self-Reliance" to trust oneself and to act autonomously is another, much more metaphysical and broader rendering of what Paine so vigorously defends in rational religion and benign government.

Thoreau makes his version of individualism come alive in both *Walden* and *Civil Disobedience*, especially when he asserts his wish to be as much a good neighbor as a bad subject. He understands the place of the individual in the community and yet insists that there must also be a private sphere for contemplation, creativity, and quietly reveling in life itself. He finds or demands the right, perhaps even the obligation, to live by convictions that no one else can rightfully threaten. John Dewey, like his contemporary Josiah Royce, raises the place of the individual in society to a different kind of height. He maintains, in something like the spirit of Jefferson, that the Great Society can become the

Great Community only where the freedom to acquire and disseminate information is understood and exercised, and where a citizen's influence in a democratic society is manifest in informed opinion and legitimate influence on the community of which he is inseparably a part.

The ability of individual human beings to make a difference in combating the evils of racism and sexism is represented in the works of civil rights and women's rights activists such as Angelina Grimké in her "Appeal to the Christian Women of the South." Grimké expresses the conviction that although it is a difficult road to travel, the individual has an obligation to work toward reform of official policies and customs regarding the enslavement and treatment of African Americans. She argues that this difficult task is to begin with individuals taking care to be mindful of the plight of slaves and to act individually to help realize their emancipation. Such individualism, again in the form of understanding the place of the individual in the community, is present in the work of E. C. Stanton, echoing the Constitution, but adding significant resonance to the words when, in the Seneca Falls "Declaration of Sentiments and Resolutions," she expresses the revolutionary idea that all men *and* women are created equal. Those two words ("and women") are an exhortation to recognize the value of human beings, not simply of idealized men, living and working together in the moral and political world. The notion that women are important and significant players in the ethical and political thought of any society, that to ignore their contributions, abilities, and viewpoints is a travesty to be rectified, is also a major component of the work of contemporary American feminist philosophers.

That reform also has a place among the ideas and ideals of American philosophers is undeniable. Reform and optimism are reciprocally related since belief in the power of the individual and society to achieve reform is a necessary prerequisite for reform itself. But occasional reform is not the goal. Reform for the purpose of inspiring further progress, which leads to even more enduring reform, is the end in view. Whether we address religion, epistemological theory, metaphysical speculation, moral concepts, or political ideals, there is nothing so sacred in the American philosophical landscape that it is off limits to change, reformulation, and novel applications. Even the Constitution, one of the most remarkable documents in world history, was approved with the understanding that laws and political institutions change. What, after all, are constitutional amendments if not mutations in the law that match changing times and needs? This hallowed guarantee of individual rights and protections, as well as its implicit statements of the possibility for unimpeded social progress and individual opportunity, is itself subject to criticism and reform, but all the while it is an eternal light through which American thought, expectations, and progress find their embodiment.

Perhaps Dewey's conception of the true nature of democracy, informed by scientific method and the idea of progress, is one of the clearest and most complete expressions of the American conception of reform. This conception, which had currency before Dewey, is one in which a vision of absolute truth is set aside insofar as a "quest for certainty" ends in failure, and a metaphysically minded search for absolutes of any kind does nothing for us in the present or the future. We are far wiser, as American pragmatists see matters, to look toward the future, toward goals and productive ambitions, toward theories that "will do," toward action and the "cash value" of our ideas. Lamenting or venerating the past, like looking toward an otherworldly eternity, amounts to squandering the present and the future that are filled with opportunities for anyone who is prepared to act today and to take risks for a better tomorrow.

The women's rights and civil rights movements in the United States are perhaps the crowning achievements of the American spirit of reform and its realization in action, not simply in theory. Martin Luther King, Jr., points out in "The Letter from the Birmingham Jail" that too many people have advised the African-American community to wait, to let time take its course and to believe that change will occur. Dr. King knew all too well that time does nothing of the sort. Change must be caused and the action to take is the kind that is decisive and revolutionary. American feminists see action combined with reasoned, but impassioned, argumentation and appeal to the dignity of men and women as the means by which social change may be effected. Again, optimism regarding the place of the individual, and the individual's ability to make a difference in society, must not be underrated or understated.

The American philosophers included in this anthology do not, on the whole, believe that problems will be solved by simple faith in the possibility of progress, but by faith joined with determinate action. Happiness, much less greatness, does not come to those who passively await it. Here at least Transcendentalists, proto-pragmatists, pragmatists, and idealists meet at a common center. Chauncey Wright, Peirce, James, and Dewey, Royce and Stanton, like Benjamin Franklin before them and Martin Luther King, Jr., and Marilyn Frye after them, ask what we can become and what we should do. These philosophers refuse to surrender to despair by contriving doctrines about what lies outside our knowledge and power. Mythic realms that in principle exceed our reach rarely find a place anywhere within the scope of American philosophy. What we are and what we can do, the people we can become, the knowledge we have and continue to gain, the self-reliance that independent thought and autonomous activity beget, are the benchmarks of America's philosophers and sages.

We do not pretend that the selections in this volume are a comprehensive look at the entire history of American philosophy. We have selected works that represent some of the persistent trends in the development of American thought. These trends are historically significant and important as they point to the development of ideals and expectations that characterize the American experience. There are, of course, unavoidable omissions, and for some readers these omissions might represent gaps in any effort to capture the marrow of American philosophy. Because we stress assorted themes, we believe that our choices lead to an enriched, not an antecedently defined, understanding of American philosophy. We concede that our selections will not satisfy every reader, and we grant that our task is incomplete. We have omitted some philosophers and readings to make room for others. That our effort is incomplete reflects the American experience as incomplete. In a real sense, completeness would undermine the nature of what we wish to present in this work. There is, to borrow liberally from William James, no final truth in American philosophy, nor will there be until the last Americans have lived and have had their say. We earnestly hope that there will be no last Americans and that there will be no end, no final theory, that constitutes the whole of American philosophy.

We have arranged this anthology both historically and thematically. Part I covers some major works in American epistemology, metaphysics, and the philosophy of religion. Part II covers works in American ethics, social and political philosophy. In each part, we have tried in almost every case to arrange writings chronologically. The division of this work into two parts reflects partially our different specialties in the history of American philosophy.

At the beginning of each chapter, we provide a brief introductory essay. Chapters include relevant works from a particular period or style of American philosophy. A short section of review questions and a modest list of suggested readings close each chapter. We have intentionally avoided long, critical introductions so that individual instructors may use this text in a way most consistent with their own pedagogical styles and preferences, and so that this collection can be appropriately augmented by *Philosophy in America: Interpretative Essays, Volume II*, a collection of our interpretive chapters on individual philosophers, themes, and leading ideas in the development of American philosophy.

No book of this sort is the creation of only one or two authors. Thank you to the following reviewers: John R. Shook, Oklahoma State University; Scott Bartlett, Southern Methodist University; Jacquelyn A. Kegley, California State University-Bakersfield; and Kenneth Stikkers, Southern Illinois University-Carbondale. We gratefully acknowledge the help of Ross Miller, Wendy Yurash, Harriet Tellem, and Carla Worner, all with Prentice Hall. Their warm and detailed responses to our many questions throughout this project have been invaluable. For the many conversations about American philosophy and the development of ideas and themes in this book, we thank our colleagues and students. Their lively discussions and searching comments helped to shape the final published work. For support and patience, we thank our families, who perhaps have wondered at times exactly what it is we have been doing and whether our project would ever end.

We are grateful to Prentice Hall for a grant to aid in acquiring materials for this book. To Shelley Park of the University of Central Florida we extend our thanks for making helpful comments on some of our introductory essays; and to Stephen Turner from the University of South Florida we extend appreciation for his comments about John Dewey and contemporary communitarianism. We also express our thanks to Jennifer Pumo, our student assistant from the University of Central Florida, for putting her philosophical talents to work in helping us with the production of this book. Her patience in checking references, compiling bibliographical entries, and making copies is almost legendary. We, the editors, are of course responsible for whatever errors or omissions remain.

NAS.
B.S.S.

Part I
American Metaphysics and Epistemology

Chapter 1

Jonathan Edwards
The Great Awakening and Beyond

Jonathan Edwards (1703–1758), America's first important philosopher, was born in East Windsor, Connecticut, the only son among ten children. He entered Yale College in 1716 and earned his A.B. Having trained for the clergy, he preached for a year at a Scottish Presbyterian church in New York City. Following his stay in New York and having earned his M.A. after another two years at Yale, Edwards was invited to Northampton, Massachusetts, where he was ordained and, soon afterward, married Sarah Pierpoint. He was attached to the same church for almost twenty-five years when, in 1750 his parishioners, showing little enthusiasm for strict Calvinism, dismissed him. From Northampton Edwards went to Stockbridge, where he served for seven years as a missionary to the Houssatunnuck Indians. In Stockbridge he also found time to devote himself to philosophy and writing. In 1757 Edwards accepted an invitation to become president of the College of New Jersey (Princeton). Seeking protection from an outbreak of smallpox in New Jersey, Edwards was inoculated but died of a secondary infection before he could take up the duties of his new post.

The selections that follow reflect Edwards's evangelic mysticism during the first Great Awakening of the 1740s ("A Divine and Supernatural Light" and "Sinners in the Hands of an Angry God") and his talents as a careful, analytic philosopher whose *Freedom of the Will* (1754) is the first true classic in 250 years of American philosophy and speculative thought.

Although each of these selections represents a distinct facet of Edwards's thought, religious prepossessions, and philosophy, there is a constant that connects them. Whether Edwards describes the source of authentic religious character, the sins of fallen men, or the compatibility between rigid determinism (secured by divine foreknowledge and foreordination of all that occurs) and responsibility for our choices, his faith in God and his demand that men venerate God every day and at every turn in their lives is bedrock. One can never

1

successfully separate Edwards from his religious calling or from the depths of his convictions. Whether as an active preacher trying to rekindle beliefs that God is sovereign and that sinners depend for their being and salvation on God's mercy, or as a careful philosophical analyst trying to resolve paradoxes that have plagued thinkers since at least the time of Saint Augustine, Edwards's appeal to divine power and authority is always at the center and circumference of his sermons and essays. For him, at least, talk of human independence and autonomy, a touchstone for the later unfolding of American philosophy, is misplaced. Perhaps we are, and should be, independent of other human beings, but in the most important sense we are utterly dependent upon God and upon all that God has in store for us. Human dependence on an angry God and the consequence that God is our only hope for a blissful eternity that none of us deserves—these are the unyielding facts of Edwards's philosophy.

A Divine and Supernatural Light (1734)

*And Jesus answered and said unto him, Blessed art thou, Simon Bar-jona: for flesh and blood hath not revealed it unto thee, but my Father which is in heaven.—*Matt. xvi.17

Christ addresses these words to Peter upon occasion of his professing his faith in him as the Son of God. Our Lord was inquiring of his disciples, whom men said that he was; not that he needed to be informed, but only to introduce and give occasion to what follows. They answer, that some said he was John the Baptist, and some Elias, and others Jeremias, or one of the prophets. When they had thus given an account whom others said that he was, Christ asks them, whom they said that he was? Simon Peter, whom we find always zealous and forward, was the first to answer: he readily replied to the question, *Thou art Christ, the Son of the living God.*

Upon this occasion, Christ says as he does *to* him and *of* him in the text: in which we may observe,

1. That Peter is pronounced blessed on this account.—*Blessed art thou—* "Thou art an happy man, and thou art not ignorant of this, that I am *Christ, the Son of the living God.* Thou art distinguishingly happy. Others are blinded, and have dark and deluded apprehensions, as you have now given an account, some thinking that I am Elias, and some that I am Jeremias, and some one thing, and some another; but none of them thinking right, all of them are misled. Happy art thou, that art so distinguished as to know the truth in this matter."
2. The evidence of this his happiness declared, *viz.* That God, and he *only*, had *revealed it* to him. This is an evidence of his being *blessed.*

First, As it shews how peculiarly favoured he was of God above others: *q. d.* "How highly favoured art thou, that others, wise and great men, the

Scribes, Pharisees, and rulers, and the nation in general, are left in darkness, to follow their own misguided apprehensions; and that thou shouldst be singled out, as it were, by name, that my heavenly Father should thus set his love on *thee, Simon Bar-jona.*—This argues thee *blessed*, that thou shouldst thus be the object of God's distinguishing love."

Secondly, It evidences his blessedness also, as it intimates that this knowledge is above any that *flesh* and *blood* can *reveal*. "This is such knowledge as only my *Father which is in heaven* can give. It is too high and excellent to be communicated by such means as other knowledge is. Thou art *blessed*, that thou knowest what God alone can teach thee."

The original of this knowledge is here declared, both negatively and positively. *Positively*, as God is here declared the author of it. *Negatively*, as it is declared, that *flesh* and *blood* had *not revealed it*. God is the author of all knowledge and understanding whatsoever. He is the author of all moral prudence, and of the skill that men have in their secular business. Thus it is said of all in Israel that were *wise-hearted*, and skilled in embroidering, that God had *filled* them *with the spirit of wisdom*. Exod. xxviii, 3.

God is the author of such knowledge; yet so that *flesh and blood reveals it*. Mortal men are capable of imparting the knowledge of human arts and sciences, and skill in temporal affairs. God is the author of such knowledge by those means: *flesh and blood* is employed as the *mediate* or *second* cause of it; he conveys it by the power and influence of natural means. But this spiritual knowledge, spoken of in the text, is what God is the author of, and none else: he *reveals it*, and *flesh and blood reveals it not*. He imparts this knowledge immediately, not making use of any intermediate natural causes, as he does in other knowledge.

What had passed in the preceding discourse naturally occasioned Christ to observe this; because the disciples had been telling how others did not know him, but were generally mistaken about him, divided and confounded in their opinions of him: but Peter had declared his assured faith, that he was the *Son of God*. Now it was natural to observe, how it was not *flesh and blood* that had *revealed it to him*, but God; for if this knowledge were dependent on natural causes or means, how came it to pass that they, a company of poor fishermen, illiterate men, and persons of low education, attained to the knowledge of the truth; while the Scribes and Pharisees, men of vastly higher advantages, and greater knowledge and sagacity in other matters, remained in ignorance? This could be owing only to the gracious distinguishing influence and revelation of the Spirit of God. Hence, what I would make the subject of my present discourse from these words, is this DOCTRINE.

That there is such a thing as a spiritual and divine light, immediately imparted to the soul by God, of a different nature from any that is obtained by natural means. And on this subject I would, I. Shew what this divine light is. II. How it is given immediately by God, and not obtained by natural means. III. Shew the truth of the doctrine.

And then conclude with a brief improvement.

I would shew what this spiritual and divine light is. And in order to it would shew,

First, In a few things what it is not. And here,

Those convictions that natural men may have of their sin and misery, is not this spiritual and divine light. Men in a natural condition may have convictions of this guilt that lies upon them, and of the anger of God, and of their danger of divine vengeance. Such convictions are from the light of truth. That some sinners have a greater conviction of their guilt, and misery than others, is because some have more light, or more of an apprehension of truth than others. And this light and conviction may be from the Spirit of God; the Spirit convinces men of sin: but yet nature is much more concerned in it than in the communication of that spiritual and divine light that is spoken of in the doctrine; it is from the Spirit of God only as assisting natural principles, and not as infusing any new principles. Common grace differs from special, in that it influences only by assisting of nature; and not by imparting grace, or bestowing any thing above nature. The light that is obtained is wholly natural, or of no superior kind to what mere nature attains to, though more of that kind be obtained than would be obtained, if men were left wholly to themselves; or, in other words, common grace only assists the faculties of the soul to do that more fully which they do by nature, as natural conscience or reason will by mere nature make a man sensible of guilt, and will accuse and condemn him when he has done amiss. Conscience is a principle natural to men; and the work that it doth naturally, or of itself, is to give an apprehension of right and wrong and to suggest to the mind the relation that there is between right and wrong and retribution. The Spirit of God, in those convictions which unregenerate men sometimes have, assist conscience to do this work in a further degree than it would do if they were left to themselves. He helps it against those things that tend to stupefy it, and obstruct its exercise. . . . Not only are remaining principles assisted to do their work more freely and fully, but those principles are restored that were utterly destroyed by the fall; and the mind thenceforward habitually exerts those acts that the dominion of sin had made it as wholly destitute of as a dead body is of vital acts.

The Spirit of God acts in a very different manner in the one case, from what he doth in the other. He may indeed act upon the mind of a natural man, but he acts in the mind of a saint as an indwelling vital principle. He acts upon the mind of an unregenerate person as an extrinsic occasional agent; for in acting upon them, he doth not unite himself to them: for notwithstanding all his influences that they may possess, they are still sensual, having not the Spirit. Jude 19. But he unites himself with the mind of a saint, takes him for his temple, actuates and influences him as a new supernatural principle of life and action. There is this difference, that the Spirit of God, in acting in the soul of a godly man, exerts and communicates himself there in his own proper nature. Holiness is the proper nature of the Spirit of God. The Holy Spirit operates in the minds of the godly, by uniting himself to them, and living in them, and exerting his own nature in the exercise of their faculties. The Spirit of God may act upon a creature, and yet not in acting communicate itself. ... [H]e acts in a way of peculiar communication of himself; so that the subject is thence denominate spiritual.

This spiritual and divine light does not consist in any impression made upon the imagination. It is no impression upon the mind, as though one saw any thing with the bodily eyes. It is no imagination or idea of an outward light or glory, or any beauty of form or countenance, or a visible luster or brightness of any object. The imagination may be strongly impressed with such things; but this is not spiritual light. Indeed when the mind has a lively discovery of spiritual things, and is greatly affected by the power of divine light, it may ... much affect the imagination; so that impressions of an outward beauty or brightness may *accompany* those spiritual discoveries. But spiritual light is not that impression upon the imagination, but an exceedingly different thing. Natural men may have lively impressions on their imaginations; and we cannot determine but that the devil, who transforms himself into an angel of light, may cause imaginations ... ; but these are things of a vastly inferior nature to spiritual light.

This spiritual light is not the suggesting of any new truths or propositions not contained in the word of God. This suggesting of new truths or doctrines to the mind, independent of any antecedent revelations of those propositions, either in word or writing, is inspiration. ... But his spiritual light that I am speaking of, is quite a different thing from inspiration. It reveals no new doctrine, it suggests no new proposition to the mind, it teaches no new thing of God, or Christ, or another world, not taught in the Bible, but only gives a due apprehension of those things that are taught in the word of God.

It is not every affecting view that men have of religious things that is this spiritual and divine light. Men by mere principles of nature are capable of being affected with things that have a special relation to religion as well as other things. A person by mere nature, for instance, may be liable to be affected with the story of Jesus Christ, and the sufferings he underwent, as well as by any other tragical story. He may be the more affected with it from the interest he conceives mankind to have in it. Yea, he may be affected with it without believing it. ... A person therefore may have affecting views of the things of religion, and yet be very destitute of spiritual light. Flesh and blood may be the author of this: One man may give another an affecting view of divine things with but common assistance; but God alone can give a spiritual discovery of them.—But I proceed to shew,

Secondly, Positively what this spiritual and divine light is.

And it may be thus described: A true sense of the divine excellency of the things revealed in the world of God, and a conviction of the truth and reality of them thence arising. The spiritual light primarily consists in the former of these, *viz.* a real sense and apprehension of the divine excellency of things revealed in the word of God. A spiritual and saving conviction of the truth and reality of these things, arises from such a sight of their divine excellency and glory; so that this conviction of their truth is an effect and natural consequence of this sight of their divine glory. There is therefore in this spiritual light, 1. A true sense of the divine and superlative excellency of the things of religion; a real sense of the excellency of God and Jesus Christ, and of the work of redemption, and the ways and works of God revealed in the gospel.

There is a twofold knowledge of good of which God has made the mind of man capable. The first, that which is merely notional; as when a person only speculatively judges that any thing is, which, by the agreement of mankind, is called good or excellent, *viz.* that which is most to general advantage, and between which and a reward there is a suitableness,—and the like. And the other is, that which consists in the sense of the heart; as when the heart is sensible of pleasure and delight in the presence of the idea of it. In the former is exercised merely the speculative faculty, or the understanding, in distinction from the will or disposition of the soul. In the latter, the will, or inclination, or heart, are mainly concerned.

Thus there is a difference between having an *opinion*, that God is holy and gracious, and having a *sense* of the loveliness and beauty of that holiness and grace. There is a difference between having a rational judgment that honey is sweet, and having a sense of its sweetness. A man may have the former, that knows not how honey tastes; but a man cannot have the latter unless he has an idea of the taste of honey in his mind. So there is a difference between believing that a person is beautiful, and having a sense of his beauty. The former may be obtained by hearsay, but the latter only by seeing the countenance. When the heart is sensible of the beauty and amiableness of a thing, it necessarily feels pleasure in the apprehension. It is implied in a person's being heartily sensible of the loveliness of a thing, that the idea of it is pleasant to his soul; which is a far different thing from having a rational opinion that it is excellent. 2. There arises from this sense of the divine excellency of things contained in the word of God, a conviction of the truth and reality of them; and that either indirectly or directly.

First, Indirectly, and that in two ways: 1. As the prejudices of the heart, against the truth of divine things, are hereby removed; so that the mind becomes susceptive of the due force of rational arguments for their truth. The mind of man is naturally full of prejudices against divine truth. It is full of enmity against the doctrines of the gospel; which is a disadvantage to those arguments that prove their truth, and causes them to lose their force on the mind. But when a person has discovered to him the divine excellency of Christian doctrines, this destroys the enmity, removes those prejudices, sanctifies reason, and causes it to lie open to the force of arguments and their truth. . . .

It not only removes the hindrances of reason, but positively helps reason. It makes even the speculative notions more lively. It engages the attention of the mind, with more fixedness and intenseness to that kind of objects; which causes it to have a clearer view of them. . . .

The mind being sensible of the excellency of divine objects, dwells upon them with delight; and the powers of the soul are more awakened and enlivened to employ themselves in the contemplation of them, and exert themselves more fully and much more to the purpose. . . .

Secondly, A true sense of the divine excellency of the things of God's word doth more directly and immediately convince us of their truth; and that because the excellency of these things is so superlative. . . . When there is an actual and lively discovery of this beauty and excellency, it will not allow of any such thought as that it is the fruit of men's invention. This is a kind of intuitive and immediate evidence. . . .

I proceed now to the *second* thing proposed, *viz.* to shew how this light is immediately given by God, and not obtained by natural means. And here, 1. It is not intended that the natural faculties are not used in it. They are the subject of this light; and in such a manner, that they are not merely passive, but active in it. God, in letting in this light into the soul, deals with man according to his nature, and makes use of his rational faculties. But yet this light is not the less immediately from God for that; the faculties are made use of as the subject, and not as the cause. And the use we make of our eyes in beholding various objects, when the sun arises, is not the cause of the light that discovers those objects to us. 2. It is not intended that outward means have no concern in this affair. It is not in this affair, as in inspiration, where new truths are suggested: for, by this light is given only a due apprehension of the same truths that are revealed in the word of God; and therefore it is not given without the word. The gospel is employed in this affair. . . . 3. When it is said that this light is given immediately by God, and not obtained by natural means, HEREBY IS INTENDED THAT IT IS GIVEN BY God without making use of any means that operate by their own power or natural force. . . .

To shew the truth of the doctrine; that is, to shew that there is such a thing as that spiritual light that has been described, thus immediately let into the mind by God. And here I would shew briefly, that this doctrine is both *scriptural* and *rational*.

First, It is scriptural. My text is not only full to the purpose, but it is a doctrine with which the Scripture abounds. We are there abundantly taught, that the saints differ from the ungodly in this, that they have the knowledge of God, and a sight of God, and of Jesus Christ. . . . This knowledge, or sight of God and Christ, cannot be a mere speculative knowledge; because it is spoken of as that wherein they differ from the ungodly. And by these scriptures it must not only be a different knowledge in degree and circumstances, and different in its effects; but it must be entirely different in nature and in kind. . . .

Secondly, This doctrine is rational.

It is rational to suppose, that there is really such an excellency in divine things—so transcendent and exceedingly different from what is in other things—that, if it were seen, would most evidently distinguish them. We cannot rationally doubt but that things divine, which appertain to the supreme Being, are vastly different from things that are human; that there is a high, glorious, and god-like excellency in them, that does most remarkably difference them from the things that are of men; insomuch that if the difference were but seen, it would have a convincing, satisfying influence upon any one, that they are divine. . . .

If Christ should now appear to any one as he did on the mount at his transfiguration; or if he should appear to the world in his heavenly glory, as he will do at the day of judgment; without doubt, his glory and majesty would be such as would satisfy everyone, that he was a divine person, and that his religion was true: and it would be a most reasonable, and well-grounded conviction too. . . . Would it not be rational to suppose, that (God's) speech would be exceeding different from men's speech, that there should be such an excellency and sublimity in his word, such a stamp of wisdom, holiness, majesty, and other divine perfections, that the word of men, yea of the wisest of men, should appear mean and base in comparison of it? Doubtless it would be thought rational to expect this, and unreasonable to think otherwise. When a wise man speaks in the exercise of his wisdom, there is something in every thing he says, that is very distinguishable from the talk of a little child. So, without doubt, and much more is the speech of God, to be distinguished from that of the wisest of men.

If there be such a distinguishing excellency in divine things; it is rational to suppose that there may be such a thing as seeing it. What should hinder but what it may be seen? It is no argument, that there is no such distinguishing excellency, or that it cannot be seen, because some do not see it, though they may be discerning men in temporal matters. It is not rational to suppose, if there be any such excellency in divine things, that wicked men would see it. It is rational to suppose, that those whose minds are full of spiritual pollution, and under the power of filthy lusts, should have any relish or sense of divine beauty or excellency; or that their minds should be susceptive of that light that is in is own nature so pure and heavenly? . . .

It is rational to suppose, that this knowledge should be given immediately by God, and not be obtained by natural means. Upon what account should it seem unreasonable, that there should be any immediate communication between God and the creature? It is strange that men should make any matter of difficulty of it. . . .

It is rational to suppose, that it should be beyond man's power to obtain this light by the mere strength of natural reason; for it is not a thing that belongs to reason, to see the beauty and loveliness of spiritual things; it is not a speculative thing, but depends on the sense of the heart. Reason indeed is necessary in order to it, as it is by reason only that we are become the subjects of the means of it; which means I have already shewn to be necessary in order to it, though they have no proper causal influence in the affair. It is by reason that we become possessed of a notion of those doctrines that are the subject matter of this divine light, or knowledge; and reason may many ways be indirectly and remotely an advantage to it. Reason has also to do in the acts that are immediately consequent on this discovery: for seeing the truth of religion from hence, is by reason; though it be but by one step, and the inference be immediate. So reason has to do in that accepting of, and trusting in Christ, *that* is consequent on it. . . .

Sinners in the Hands of an Angry God (1741)

Their foot shall slide in due time.—Deut. xxxii.35

In this verse is threatened the vengeance of God on the wicked unbelieving Israelites, who were God's visible people, and who lived under the means of grace; but who, notwithstanding all God's wonderful works towards them, remained (as ver. 28.) void of counsel, having no understanding in them. Under all the cultivations of heaven, they brought forth bitter and poisonous fruit; as in the two verses next preceding the text.—The expression I have chosen for my text, *Their foot shall slide in due time*, seems to imply the following things, relating to the punishment and destruction to which these wicked Israelites were exposed.

That they were always exposed to *destruction*; as one that stands or walks in slippery places is always exposed to fall. This is implied in the manner of their destruction coming upon them, being represented by their foot sliding. The same is expressed, Psalm lxxiii.18. "Surely thou didst set them in slippery places; thou castedst them down into destruction."

It implies, that they were always exposed to sudden unexpected destruction. As he that walks in slippery places is every moment liable to fall, he cannot foresee one moment whether he shall stand or fall the next; and when he does fall, he falls at once without warning: Which is also expressed in Psalm lxxiii.18, 19. "Surely thou didst set them in slippery places; thou castedst them down into destruction: How are they brought into desolation as in a moment!"

Another thing implied is, that they are liable to fall *of themselves*, without being thrown down by the hand of another; as he that stands or walks on slippery ground needs nothing but his own weight to throw him down.

That the reason why they are not fallen already, and do not fall now, is only that God's appointed time is not come. For it is said, that when that due time, or appointed time comes, *their foot shall slide*. Then they shall be left to fall, as they are inclined by their own weight. God will not hold them up in these slippery places any longer, but will let them go; and then, at that very instant, they shall fall into destruction; as he that stands on such slippery declining ground, on the edge of a pit, he cannot stand alone, when he is let go he immediately falls and is lost.

The observation from the words that I would not insist upon is this.— "There is nothing that keeps wicked men at any one moment out of hell, but the mere pleasure of God: "—By the *mere* pleasure of God, I mean his *sovereign* pleasure, his arbitrary will, restrained by no obligation, hindered by no manner of difficulty, any more than if nothing else but God's mere will had in the least degree, or in any respect whatsoever, any hand in the preservation of the wicked men one moment.—The truth of this observation may appear by the following considerations.

There is no want of *power* in God to cast wicked men into hell at any moment. Men's hands cannot be so strong when God rises up: The strongest have no power to resist him, nor can any deliver out of his hands.—He is not only able to cast wicked men into hell, but he can most easily do it. Sometimes an earthly prince meets with a great deal of difficulty to subdue a rebel, who has found means to fortify himself, and has made himself strong by the numbers of his followers. But it is not so with God. There is no fortress that is any defence from the power of God. Though hand join in hand, and vast multitudes of God's enemies combine and associate themselves, they are easily broken in pieces. They are as great heaps of light chaff before the whirlwind; or large quantities of dry stubble before devouring flames. We find it easy to tread on and crush a worm that we see crawling on the earth; so it is easy for us to cut or singe a slender thread that any thing hangs by; thus easy is it for God, when he pleases, to cast his enemies down to hell. What are we, that we should think to stand before him, at whose rebuke the earth trembles, and before whom the rocks are thrown down?

They *deserve* to be cast into hell; so that divine justice never stands in the way, it makes no objection against God's using his powers at any moment to destroy them. Yea, on the contrary, justice calls aloud for an infinite punishment of their sins. Divine justice says of the tree that brings forth such grapes of Sodom, "Cut it down, why cumbereth it the ground?" Luke xiii.7. The sword of divine justice is every moment brandished over their heads, and it is nothing but the hand of arbitrary mercy, and God's mere will, that holds it back.

They are already under a sentence of *condemnation* to hell. They do not only justly deserve to be cast down thither, but the sentence of the law of God, that eternal and immutable rule of righteousness that God has fixed between him and mankind, is gone out against them, and stands against them; so that they are bound over already to hell. John iii.18. "He that believeth not is condemned already." So that every unconverted man properly belongs to hell; that is his place; from thence he is. John viii.23. "Ye are from beneath:" And thither he is bound; it is the place that justice, and God's word, and the sentence of his unchangeable law, assign to him.

They are now the objects of that very same *anger* and wrath of God, that is expressed in the torments of hell. And the reason why they do not go down to hell at each moment, is not because God, in whose power they are, is not then very angry with them; as he is with many miserable creatures now tormented in hell, who there feel and bear the fierceness of his wrath. Yea, God is a great deal more angry with great numbers that are now on earth; yea, doubtless, with many that are now in this congregation, who it may be are at ease, than he is with many of those who are now in the flames of hell.

So that it is not because God is unmindful of their wickedness, and does not resent it, that he does not let loose his hand and cut them off. God is not altogether such an one as themselves, though they may imagine him to be so. The wrath of God burns against them, their damnation does not slumber; the pit is prepared, the fire is made ready, the furnace is now hot, ready to receive them; the flames do now rage and glow. The glittering sword is whet, and held over them, and the pit hath opened its mouth under them.

The *devil* stands ready to fall upon them, and seize them as his own, at what moment God shall permit him. They belong to him, he has their souls in his possession, and under his dominion. The scripture represents them as his goods, Luke xi.12. The devils watch them; they are ever by them, at their right hand; they stand waiting for them, like greedy hungry lions that see their prey, and expect to have it, but are for the present kept back. If God should withdraw his hand, by which they are restrained, they would in one moment fly upon their poor souls. The old serpent is gaping for them; hell opens its mouth wide to receive them; and if God should permit it, they would be hastily swallowed up and lost.

There are in the souls of wicked men those hellish *principles* reigning, that would presently kindle and flame out into hell fire, if it were not for God's restraints. There is laid in the very nature of carnal men, a foundation for the torments of hell. There are those corrupt principles, in reigning power in them, and in full possession of them, that are the seeds of hell fire. These principles are active and powerful, exceeding violent in their nature, and if it were not for the restraining hand of God upon them, they would soon break out, they would flame out after the same manner as the same corruptions, the same enmity does in the hearts of the damned souls, and would beget the same torments as they do in them. The souls of the wicked are in scripture compared to the troubled sea, Isaiah lvii.20. For the present, God restrains their wickedness by his mighty power, as he does the raging waves of the troubled sea, saying, "Hitherto shalt thou come, but no further;" but if God should withdraw that restraining power, it would soon carry all before it. Sin is the ruin and misery of the soul; it is destructive in its nature; and if God should leave it without restraint, there would need nothing else to make the soul perfectly miserable. The corruption of the heart of man is immoderate and boundless in its fury; and while wicked men live here, it is like fire pent up by God's restraints, whereas if it were let loose, it would set on fire the course of nature; and as the heart is now a sink of sin, so, if sin was not restrained, it would immediately turn the soul into a fiery oven, or a furnace of fire and brimstone.

It is no security to wicked men for one moment, that there are no visible means of death at hand. It is no security to a natural man, that he is now in health, and that he does not see which way he should now immediately go out of the world by any accident, and that there is no visible danger in any respect in his circumstances. The manifold and continual experience of the world in all ages, shews this is no evidence, that a man is not on the very brink of eternity, and that the next step will not be into another world. The unseen, unthought-of ways and means of persons going suddenly out of the world are innumerable and inconceivable. Unconverted men walk over the pit of hell on a rotten covering, and there are innumerable places in this covering so weak that they will not bear their weight, and these places are not seen. The arrows of death fly unseen at noon-day; the sharpest sight cannot discern them. God has so many different unsearchable ways of taking wicked men out of the world and sending them to hell, that there is nothing to make it appear, that

God had need to be at the expence of a miracle, or go out of the ordinary course of his providence, to destroy any wicked man, at any moment. All the means that there are of sinners going out of the world, are so in God's hands, and so universally and absolutely subject to his power and determination, that it does not depend at all the less on the mere will of God, whether sinners shall at any moment go to hell, than if means were never made use of, or at all concerned in the case. . . .

But the foolish children of men miserably delude themselves in their own schemes, and in confidence in their own strength and wisdom; they trust to nothing but a shadow. The greater part of those who heretofore have lived under the same means of grace, and are now dead, are undoubtedly gone to hell; and it was not because they were not as wise as those who are now alive; it was not because they did not lay out matters as well for themselves to secure their own escape. If we could speak with them, and inquire of them, one by one, whether they expected, when alive, and when they used to hear about hell, ever to be the subjects of that misery; we, doubtless, should hear one and another reply, "No, I never intended to come here: I had laid out matters otherwise in my mind; I thought I should contrive well for myself: I thought my scheme good. I intended to take effectual care; but it came upon me unexpected; I did not look for it at that time, and in that manner; it came as a thief: Death outwitted me: God's wrath was too quick for me. Oh, my cursed foolishness! I was flattering myself, and pleasing myself with vain dreams of what I would do hereafter; and what I was saying, Peace and safety, then sudden destruction came upon me."

God has laid himself under *no obligation*, by any promise to keep any natural man out of hell one moment. God certainly has made no promises either of eternal life, or of any deliverance or preservation from eternal death, but what are contained in the covenant of grace, the promises that are given in Christ, in whom all the promises are yea and amen. But surely they have no interest in the promises of the covenant of grace who are not the children of the covenant, who do not believe in the promises, and have no interest in the Mediator of the covenant. . . .

So that, thus it is that natural men are held in the hand of God, over the pit of hell; they have deserved the fiery pit, and are already sentenced to it; and God is dreadfully provoked, his anger is as great towards them as to those that are actually suffering the executions of the fierceness of his wrath in hell, and they have done nothing in the least to appease or abate that anger, neither is God in the least bound by any promise to hold them up one moment; the devil is waiting for them, hell is gaping for them, the flames gather and flash about them, and would fain lay hold on them, and swallow them up; the fire pent up in their own hearts is struggling to break out; and they have no interest in any Mediator, there are no means within reach that can be any security to them. In short, they have no refuge, nothing to take hold of; all that preserves them every moment is the mere arbitrary will, and uncovenanted, unobliged forbearance of an incensed God.

APPLICATION

The use of this awful subject may be for awakening unconverted persons in this congregation. This that you have heard is the case of everyone of you that are out of Christ.—That world of misery, that lake of burning brimstone, is extended abroad under you. There is the dreadful pit of the glowing flames of the wrath of God; there is hell's wide gaping mouth open; and you have nothing to stand upon, nor anything to take hold of; there is nothing between you and hell but the air; it is only the power and mere pleasure of God that holds you up. . . .

Your wickedness makes you as it were heavy as lead, and to tend downwards with great weight and pressure towards hell; and if God should let you go, you would immediately sink and swiftly descend and plunge into the bottomless gulf, and your healthy constitution, and your own care and prudence, and best contrivance, and all your righteousness, would have no more influence to uphold you and keep you out of hell, than a spider's web would have to stop a falling rock. Were it not for the sovereign pleasure of God, the earth would not bear you for one moment; for you are a burden to it; the creation groans with you; the creature is made subject to the bondage of your corruption, not willingly; the sun does not willingly shine upon you to give you light to serve sin and Satan; the earth does not willingly yield her increase to satisfy your lusts; nor is it willingly a stage for your wickedness to be acted upon; the air does not willingly serve you for breath to maintain the flame of life in your vitals, while you spend your life in the service of God's enemies. God's creatures are good, and were made for men to serve God with, and do not willingly subserve to any other purpose, and groan when they are abused to purposes so directly contrary to their nature and end. And the world would spew you out, were it not for the sovereign hand of him who hath subjected it in hope. There are the black clouds of God's wrath now hanging directly over your heads, full of the dreadful storm, and big with thunder; and were it not for the restraining hand of God, it would immediately burst forth upon you. . . .

The wrath of God is like great waters that are dammed for the present. . . . If God should only withdraw his hand from the flood-gate, it would immediately fly open, and the fiery floods of the fierceness and wrath of God, would rush forth with inconceivable fury. . . .

The bow of God's wrath is bent, and the arrow made ready on the string, and justice bends the arrow at your heart, and strains the bow, and it is nothing but the mere pleasure of God, and that of an angry God, without any promise or obligation at all, that keeps the arrow one moment from being made drunk with your blood. Thus all you that never passed under a great change of heart, by the mighty power of the Spirit of God upon your souls; all you that were never born again, and made new creatures, and raised from being dead in sin, to a state of new, and before altogether unexperienced light and life, are in the hands of an angry God. . . .

The God that holds you over the pit of hell, much as one holds a spider, or some loathsome insect over the fire, abhors you, and is dreadfully provoked. . . . You have offended him infinitely more than ever a stubborn rebel did his prince; and yet it is nothing but his hand that holds you from falling into the fire every moment. It is to be ascribed to nothing else, that you did not go to hell the last night; that you was [sic] suffered to awake again in this world, after you closed your eyes to sleep. . . .

O sinner! Consider the fearful danger you are in: it is a great furnace of wrath, a wide and bottomless pit, full of the fire of wrath, that you are held over in the hand of God. . . . You hang by a slender thread, with the flames of divine wrath flashing about it, and ready every moment to singe it, and burn it asunder. . . .

Freedom of the Will (1754)

CONCERNING THE NATURE OF THE WILL

It may possibly be thought, that there is no great need of going about to define or describe the *Will*; this word being generally well understood as any other words we can use to explain it: and so perhaps it would be, had not philosophers, metaphysicians and polemic divines brought the matter into obscurity by the things they have said of it. But since it is so, I think it may be of some use . . . to say a few things concerning it.

And therefore I observe, that the *Will* (without any metaphysical refining) is, *That by which the mind chooses any thing*. The faculty of the *Will*, is that power, or principle of mind, by which it is capable of *choosing*: an act of the *Will* is the same as an act of *choosing* or choice.

If any think it is a more perfect definition of the Will, to say, that it is that by which the soul either *chooses* or *refuses*; I am content with it: though I think, it enough to say, It is that by which the soul chooses. . . . [I]n every act of refusal, the mind chooses the absence of the thing refused; the positive and the negative are set before the mind for its choice, and it chooses the negative; and the mind's making its choice in that case is properly the act of the Will: the Will's determining between the two, is a voluntary determination; but that is the same thing as making a choice. . . . For the soul to act *voluntarily*, is evermore to act *electively*. . . .

. . . I trust it will be allowed by all, that in every act of *will* there is an act of *choice*; that in every *volition* there is a *preference*, or a prevailing inclination of the soul, whereby, at that instant, it is out of a state of perfect indifference, with respect to the direct object of the volition. So that in every act, or going forth of the Will, there is some preponderation of the mind, one way rather than another; and the soul had rather *have* or *do* one thing, than another, or than *not* to have or do that thing; and that where there is absolutely no preferring or choosing, but a perfect, continuing equilibrium, there is no volition.

CONCERNING THE DETERMINATION OF THE WILL

By *determining* the Will, if the phrase be used with any meaning, must be intended, *causing* that the act of the Will or Choice should be thus, and not otherwise: and the Will is said to be *determined*, when, in consequence of some action, or influence, its choice is directed to, and fixed upon a particular object. As when we speak of the determination of motion, we mean causing the motion of the body to be in such a direction, rather than another.

The Determination of the Will, supposes an effect, which must have a cause. If the Will be determined, there is a Determiner. This must be supposed to be intended even by them that say, the Will determines itself. If it be so, the Will is both Determiner and determined; it is a cause that acts and produces effects upon itself, and is the object of its own influence and action.

With respect to that grand enquiry, "What determines the Will (and) Whether the Will always follows the last dictate of the understanding?" It is sufficient to my present purpose to say, *It is that motive, which, as it stands in the view of the mind, is the strongest, that determines the Will. . . .*

By *motive*, I mean the whole of that which moves, excites, or invites the mind to volition, whether that be one thing singly, or many things conjunctly. Many particular things may concur, and unite their strength, to induce the mind; and when it is so, all together are as one complex motive. And when I speak of the *strongest* motive, I have respect to the strength of the whole that operates to induce a particular act to volition, whether that be the strength of one thing alone, or of many together.

Whatever is objectively a motive, in this sense, must be something that is *extant in the view or apprehension of the understanding*, or perceiving faculty. Nothing can induce or invite the mind to will or act any thing, any further than it is perceived, or is some way or other in the mind's view; for what is wholly unperceived and perfectly out of the mind's view, cannot affect the mind at all. It is most evident, that nothing is in the mind, or reaches it, or takes any hold of it, any otherwise than as it is perceived or thought of.

And I think it must also be allowed by all, that every thing that is properly called a motive, excitement, or inducement to a perceiving, willing agent, has some sort and degree of *tendency* or *advantage* to move or excite the Will, previous to the effect, or the act of the Will excited. This previous tendency of the motive is what I call the *strength* of the motive. That motive which has a less degree of previous advantage, or tendency to move the Will, or which appears less inviting, as it stands in the view of the mind, is what I call a *weaker* motive. On the contrary, that which appears most inviting, and has, by what appears concerning it to the understanding or apprehension, the greatest degree of previous tendency to excite and induce the choice, is what I call the *strongest* motive. And in this sense, I suppose the will is always determined by the strongest motive.

Things that exist in the view of the mind have their strength, tendency, or advantage to move, or excite its Will, from many things appertaining to the nature and circumstances of the *thing viewed*, the nature and circumstances of the *mind that views*, and the degree and manner of its *view*. . . . But . . . whatever is perceived or apprehended by an intelligent and voluntary agent, which has the nature and influence of a motive to volition or choice, is considered or viewed as *good*. . . . And therefore it must be true, in some sense, that *the Will always is, as the greatest apparent good is*. . . .

I have . . . chosen to express myself thus, "that the Will always is as the greatest apparent good," or "as what appears most agreeable," than to say that the Will *is determined by* the greatest apparent good," or "by what seems most agreeable;" because an appearing most agreeable to the mind, and mind's preferring, seem scarcely distinct. . . .

CONCERNING THE MEANING OF THE TERMS NECESSITY, IMPOSSIBILITY, INABILITY, &C. AND OF CONTINGENCE

The words *necessary, impossible, &c.* are abundantly used in controversies about Free-Will and Moral Agency; and therefore the sense in which they are used, should be clearly understood.

Here I might say, that a thing is then said to be *necessary*, when it *must* be, and cannot be otherwise. But this would not properly be a definition of Necessity, any more than if I explained the word *must*, by the phrase, there being a Necessity. The words *must, can,* and *cannot*, need explication. . . .

The word *necessary*, as used in common speech, is a relative term; and relates to some supposed opposition made to the existence of a thing, which opposition is overcome, or proves insufficient to hinder or alter it. That is necessary, in the original and proper sense of the word, which is, or will be, not withstanding all supposable opposition. To say, that a thing is necessary, is the same thing as to say, that it is impossible, it should not be. But the word *impossible* is manifestly a relative term, and has reference to supposed power exerted to bring a thing to pass, which is insufficient for the effect; as the word *unable* is relative, and has relation to ability, or endeavour, which is insufficient. Also the word *irresistible* is relative, and has always reference to resistance which is made, or may be made, to some force or power tending to an effect, and is insufficient to withstand the power, or hinder the effect. The common notion of Necessity and Impossibility implies something that frustrates endeavour or desire. . . .

As the word *Necessity*, in its vulgar . . . use, is relative, and has always a reference to some supposable insufficient opposition; so when we speak of anything as necessary *to us*, it is with relation to some supposable opposition of *our Wills*, or some voluntary exertion or effort of ours to the contrary. . . . Things are said to be what must be, or *necessarily are, as to us*, when they are, or will be, though we desire or endeavour the contrary, or try to prevent or remove their existence. . . .

It is manifest that all such like words and phrases, as vulgarly used, are understood in this manner. A thing is said to be *necessary*, when we cannot help it, let us do what we will. So any thing is said to be *impossible* to us, when we would do it, or would have it brought to pass, and endeavour it; or at least may be supposed to desire and seek it; but all our desires and endeavours are, or would be vain. And that is said to be *irresistible*, which overcomes all our opposition, resistance, and endeavour to the contrary. And we are said to be *unable* to do a thing, when our supposable desires and endeavours are insufficient.

. . . Such ideas, and these words, are so associated, that they unavoidably go together; one suggests the other, and never can be easily separated . . . yet, unless we are exceedingly circumspect, we shall insensibly slide into the vulgar use of them, and so apply the words in a very inconsistent manner, which will deceive and confound us in our reasonings and discourses. . . .

It appears from what has been said, that these terms . . . are often used by philosophers and metaphysicians in a sense quite diverse from their common and original signification; for they apply them to many cases in which no opposition is supposable. Thus they use them with respect to God's existence before the creation of the world, when there was no other being; with regard to many of the dispositions and acts of the divine Being, such as his loving himself, his loving righteousness, hating sin, &c. . . .

Metaphysical or *Philosophical* Necessity is nothing different from their certainty. I speak not now of the certainty of knowledge, but the certainty that is in things in themselves, which is the foundation of the certainty of the knowledge, or that wherein lies the ground of the infallibility of the proposition which affirms them.

What is sometimes given as the definition of philosophical Necessity, namely, *"That by which a thing cannot but be,"* or *"whereby it cannot be otherwise,"* fails of being a proper explanation of it, on two accounts: *First*, the words *can*, or *cannot*, need explanation as much as the word necessity, and the former may as well be explained by the latter, as the latter by the former. And *Secondly*, this definition is liable to the forementioned great inconvenience; that words *cannot*, or *unable*, are properly relative, and have relation to power exerted, or that may be exerted, in order to the things spoken of; to which as I have now observed, the word *Necessity*, as used by philosophers has no reference.

Philosophical Necessity is really nothing else than the FULL AND FIXED CONNECTION BETWEEN THE THINGS SIGNIFIED BY THE SUBJECT AND PREDICATE OF A PROPOSITION which affirms something to be true. When there is such a connection, then the thing affirmed in the proposition is necessary, in a philosophical sense; whether any opposition, or contrary effort be supposed or no. . . . When the subject and predicate of the proposition, which affirms the existence of any thing . . . have a full and CERTAIN CONNECTION, then the existence or being of that thing is said to be *necessary* in a metaphysical sense. And in this sense I use the word *Necessity*, in the following discourse, when I endeavour to prove *that Necessity is not inconsistent with Liberty*. . . .

What has been said to show the meaning of the terms *necessary* and *Necessity*, may be sufficient for the explaining of the opposite terms, *impossible* and *impossibility*. For there is no difference, but only the latter are negative, and the former positive. . . .

The same may be observed concerning the words *unable* and *Inability*. . . .

As the words *necessary, impossible, unable*, &c. are used by polemic writers, in a sense diverse from their common signification, the like has happened to the term *contingent*. Any thing is said to be contingent, or to come to pass by chance or accident, in the original meaning of such words, when its connection with its causes or antecedents, according to the established course of things, is *not discerned*; and so is what we have no means of foreseeing. And especially is any thing said to be contingent, or accidental, with regard to us, when it comes to pass without our foreknowledge, and beside our design and scope. . . .

OF THE DISTINCTION OF NATURAL AND MORAL NECESSITY, AND INABILITY

. . . The phrase, *moral Necessity*, is used variously: sometimes it is used for a Necessity of moral obligation. So we say, a man is under Necessity, when he is under bonds of *duty* and conscience, from which he cannot be discharged. Again, the word *Necessity* is often used for great obligation in point of *interest*. Sometimes by moral Necessity is meant that apparent connection of things, which is the ground of *moral evidence*; and so is distinguished from *absolute Necessity*, or that sure connection of things, that is a foundation for *infallible certainty*. In this sense, moral Necessity signifies much the same as that high degree of *probability*, which is ordinarily sufficient to satisfy mankind . . . as they would consult their own safety and interest, and treat others properly as members of society. And sometimes by moral Necessity is meant that Necessity of connection and *consequence*, which arises from such *moral causes*, as the strength of inclination, or motives, and the connection which there is in many cases between these, and such certain volitions and actions. And it is in *this* sense, that I use the phrase, *moral Necessity*, in the following discourse.

By *natural Necessity*, as applied to men, I mean such Necessity as men are under though the force of natural causes; as distinguished from what are called moral causes, such as habits and dispositions of the heart, and moral motives and inducements. Thus men placed in certain circumstances, are the subjects of particular sensations by Necessity: they feel pain when their bodies are wounded; they see the objects presented before them in a clear light, when their eyes are opened: so they assent to the truth of certain propositions, as soon as the terms are understood. . . .

Moral Necessity may be as *absolute*, as natural Necessity. That is, the effect may be as perfectly connected with its moral cause, as a natural, necessary effect is with its moral cause. Whether the Will in every case is necessarily determined by the strongest motive, or whether the Will ever makes any resistance to such a motive, or can ever oppose the strongest present inclination, or not; if that matter should be controverted, yet I suppose none will deny, but that . . . a previous bias and inclination . . . may be so powerful, that the act of the Will may be certainly and indissolubly connected therewith. When motives or previous bias are very strong, all will allow that there is some *difficulty* in going against them. And if they were yet stronger, the difficulty would still be greater. And therefore, if more were still added to their strength, to a certain degree, it would make the difficulty so great, that it would be wholly *impossible* to surmount it; . . . because whatever power men may be supposed to have to surmount difficulties, yet that power is not infinite. . . . As therefore it must be allowed, that there may be such a thing as a *sure* and *perfect* connection between moral causes and effects; so this only is what I call by the name of *moral Necessity.* . . .

I suppose, that Necessity which is called *natural* in distinction from *moral* necessity, is so called, because *mere nature* as the word is vulgarly used, is concerned, without any thing of *choice.* The word *nature* is often used in opposition to *choice*; but not because nature has indeed never any hand in our choice; but, probably, because we first get our notion of nature from that obvious course of events, which we observe in many things where our choice has no concern. . . . But where we do not readily discern the rule and connection, (though there be a connection, according to an established law, truly taking place) we signify the manner of the event by some other name. . . . So men make a distinction between nature and choice; as if they were completely and universally distinct. Whereas, I suppose none will deny but that choice, *in many cases*, arises from nature, as truly as other events. But the connection between acts of choice, and other causes, according to established laws, is not so obvious. And we observe that choice is . . . a new principle of motion and action, different from that established order of things which is most obvious, and seen especially in corporeal things. The choice also often interposes, interrupts, and alters the chain of events in these external objects, and causes them to proceed otherwise than they would do, if let alone. Hence it is spoken of as if it were a principle of motion entirely distinct from nature, and properly set in opposition to it. . . .

CONCERNING THE NOTION OF LIBERTY, AND OF MORAL AGENCY

The plain and obvious meaning of the words *Freedom* and *Liberty*, in common speech, is *The power, opportunity, or advantage, that any one has, to do as he pleases.* Or in other words, his being free from hinderance or impediments in the way of doing . . . as he wills. And the contrary to Liberty . . . is a person's being hindered or unable to conduct as he will, or being necessitated to do otherwise.

If this . . . be the meaning of the word Liberty . . . then it will follow, neither Liberty, nor its contrary, can properly be ascribed to any being or thing, but that which has such a faculty, power or property, as is called will. For that which is possessed of no *will*, cannot have any *power* or *opportunity* of doing *according to its will*, nor be necessitated to act *contrary to its will*, nor be re-trained from acting agreeably to it. And therefore to talk of Liberty, or the con-trary, as belonging to the very *will itself*, is not to speak good sense. . . . For the *will itself* is not an Agent that *has a will*; the power of choosing, itself, has not a power of choosing. That which has the power of volition is the man, or the soul, and not the power of volition itself. And he that has the Liberty of doing according to his will, is the Agent who is possessed of the will; and not the will which he is possessed of. . . . To be free is the property of an Agent, who is possessed of powers and faculties, as much as to be cunning, valiant, bounti-ful, or zealous. But these qualities are the properties of persons; and not the properties of properties.

There are two things contrary to what is called Liberty in common speech. One is *constraint*; otherwise called *force, compulsion* and *coaction* which is a person's being necessitated to do a thing *contrary* to his will. The other is *restraint*; which is . . . not having the power to do *according* to his will. But that which has no will, cannot be the subject of these things.—I need say the less on this head, Mr. LOCKE having set the same thing forth, with so great clearness, in his *Essay on the Human Understanding*.

But one thing more I would observe concerning what is vulgarly called *Liberty*; namely, that power and opportunity for one to do and conduct as he will, or according to his choice, is all that is meant by it; without taking into the meaning of the word, any thing of the *cause* of that choice; or at all consid-ering how the person came to have such a volition. . . . Let the person come by his choice any how, yet, if he is able, and there is nothing in the way to hinder his pursuing and executing his will, the man is perfectly free, according to the primary and common notion of freedom.

What has been said may be sufficient to shew what is meant by *Liberty*, according to the common notion of mankind . . . ; but the word, as used by *Arminians, Pelagians* and others, who oppose the *Calvinists*, has an entirely dif-ferent signification.—These several things belong to their notion of Liberty. 1. That it consists in a *self-determining power* of the will, or a certain sovereign-ty the will has over itself, and its own acts, whereby it determines its own vo-litions; so as not to be dependent in its determinations, on any cause without itself, nor determined by any thing prior to its own acts. 2. *Indifference* belongs to Liberty in their notion of it, or that the mind, previous to the act of volition, be, *in equilibrium*. 3. *Contingence* is another thing that belongs and is essential to it; not in the common acceptation of the word . . . but as opposed to all *necessity*, or any fixed and certain connection with some previous ground or reason of its existence. They suppose the essence of Liberty so much to consist in these things, that unless the will of man be free in this sense, he has no real freedom, how much soever he may be at Liberty to act according to his will.

A *moral Agent* is a being that is capable of those actions that have a *moral* quality, and which can properly be denominated good or evil in a moral sense, virtuous or vicious, commendable or faulty. To moral Agency belongs a *moral faculty*, or sense of moral good and evil, or of such a thing as desert or worthiness, of praise or blame, reward or punishment; and a capacity which an Agent has of being influenced in his actions by moral inducements or motives, exhibited to the view of understanding and reason, to engage in conduct agreeable to the moral faculty. . . .

SHEWING THE MANIFEST INCONSISTENCE OF THE ARMINIAN NOTION OF LIBERTY OF WILL, CONSISTING IN THE WILL'S SELF-DETERMINING POWER

. . . I proceed to consider the *Arminian* notion of the *Freedom of the Will*, and the supposed necessity of it in order to moral agency, or in order to any one's being capable of virtue or vice, and properly the subject of command or counsel, praise or blame, promises or threatenings, rewards or punishments. . . .

. . . [F]irst of all, I shall consider the notion of a *self-determining Power* in the will: wherein, according to the *Arminians*, does most essentially consist the Will's Freedom; and shall particularly enquire, whether it be not plainly absurd, and a manifest inconsistence, to suppose that the *will itself determines all the free acts of the will.*

Here I shall not insist on the great impropriety of such ways of speaking, as *the Will determining itself;* because actions are to be ascribed to agents, and not properly to the powers of agents; which improper way of speaking leads to many mistakes and much confusion, as Mr. Locke observes. But I shall suppose that the *Arminians,* when they speak of the Will's determining itself, do by the *Will* mean the *soul willing.* I shall take it for granted, that when they speak of the Will, as the determiner, they mean *the soul in the exercise of a power of willing,* or acting voluntarily. I shall suppose this to be their meaning, because nothing else can be meant, without the grossest and plainest absurdity. . . . So when it is said, the will decides or determines, the meaning must be, that the person in the exercise of a Power of willing and chusing, or the soul acting voluntarily, determines.

Therefore, if the Will determines all its own free acts, the *soul* determines them in the exercise of a Power of willing and choosing; or, which is the same thing, it determines them of choice; it *determines* its own acts, by *choosing* its own acts. If the Will determines the Will, then choice orders and determines the choice: and acts of choice are subject to the decision, and follow the conduct of *other* acts of choice. And therefore if the Will determines all its own free acts, then every free act of choice is determined by a preceding act of choice, choosing that act. And if that preceding act of the Will be also a free act, then by these principles . . . the Will is self-determined: that is, this, in like manner, is an act that the soul voluntarily chooses; or, which is the same thing, it is an act determined still by a preceding act of the Will, choosing that. Which brings us directly to a contradiction: for it supposes an act of the Will preceding the first act of the whole train, directing and determining the rest; or a free act of the Will, before the first free act of the Will. Or else we must come at last to an act of the Will, determining the consequent acts, wherein the Will is not self-determined, and so is not a free act, in this notion of freedom: but if the first act in the train, determining and fixing the rest, be not free, none of them all can be free; as is manifest at first view. . . .

. . . [I]f that first volition is not determined by any preceding act of the Will, then that act is not determined by the Will, and so is not free in the *Arminian* notion of freedom, which consists in the Will's self-determination. And if that first act of the Will which determines and fixes the subsequent acts, be not free, none of the following acts, which are determined by it can be free. . . . If the will be not free in the first act, which causes the next, then neither is it free in the next, which is caused by that first act: for though indeed the will caused it, yet it did not cause it freely; because the preceding act, by which it was caused, was not free. . . . Thus, this *Arminian* notion of Liberty of the Will, consisting in the Will's *Self-determination*, is repugnant to itself, and shuts itself wholly out of the world. . . .

WHETHER ANY EVENT WHATSOEVER, AND VOLITION IN PARTICULAR, CAN COME TO PASS WITHOUT A CAUSE OF ITS EXISTENCE

. . . I would explain how I would be understood, when I use the word *Cause* in this discourse; since, for want of a better word, I shall have occasion to use it in a sense which is more extensive, than that in which it is sometimes used. The word is often used in so restrained a sense as to signify only that which has a *positive efficiency* or influence *to produce* a thing, or bring it to pass. But there are many things which have no such positive productive influence; which yet are Causes in this respect, that they have truly the nature of a reason why some things are, rather than others; or why they are thus, rather than otherwise. . . .

It may be further observed, that when I speak of *connection of Causes and Effects*, I have respect to *moral* Causes, as well as those that are called *natural* in distinction from them. Moral Causes may be Causes in a proper sense, as any Causes whatsoever; may have as real an influence, and may as truly be the ground and reason of an Event's coming to pass.

Therefore I sometimes use the word *Cause*, in this enquiry, to signify any *antecedent*, either natural or moral, positive or negative, on which an Event, either a thing, or the manner and circumstance of a thing, so depends, that it is the ground and reason, either in whole, or in part, why it is, rather than not; or why it is as it is, rather than otherwise. . . .

. . . I assert, that nothing ever comes to pass without a Cause. What is self-existent must be from eternity, and must be unchangeable: but as to all things that *begin to be*, they are not self-existent, and therefore must have some foundation of their existence without themselves.—That whatsoever begins to be, which before was not, must have a Cause why it then begins to exist, seems to be the first dictate of the common and natural sense which God hath implanted in the minds of all mankind, and the main foundation of all our reasonings about the existence of things. . . .

If this grand principle of common sense be taken away, all arguing from effects to Causes ceaseth, and so all knowledge of any existence, besides what we have by the most direct and immediate intuition, particularly all our proof of the beginning of God ceases. . . .

Indeed, I will not affirm, that there is in the nature of things no foundation for the knowledge of the Being of God, without any evidence of it from his works. I do suppose there is a great absurdity in denying Being in general, and imagining an eternal, absolute, universal nothing: and therefore that there would be, in the nature of things, a foundation of intuitive evidence, that there must be an eternal, infinite, most perfect Being; if we had strength and comprehension of mind sufficient, to have a clear idea of general and universal Being. But then we should not properly come to the knowledge of the Being of God by arguing; our evidence would be intuitive. . . . If we had as clear an idea of universal, infinite entity, as we have of these other things, I suppose we should most intuitively see the absurdity of supposing such Being not to be. . . . But we have not that strength and extent of mind, to know this certainly and this intuitive, independent manner: but the way that mankind come to the knowledge of the Being of God, is that which the apostle speaks of, Rom. i.20. *The invisible things of him, from the creation of the world, are clearly seen; being understood by the things that are made; even his eternal power and Godhead.* . . .

But if once this grand principle of common sense be given up, that what is not necessary in itself, must have a Cause; and we begin to maintain, that things which heretofore have not been, may come into existence, and begin to be of themselves, without any cause; all our means of ascending in our arguing from the creature to the Creator, and all our evidence of the Being of God, is cut off at one blow. . . .

Yes, if once it should be allowed, that things may come to pass without a Cause, we should not only have no proof of the Being of God, but we should be without evidence of the existence of any thing whatsoever, but our own immediately present ideas and consciousness. For we have no way to prove any thing else, but by arguing from effects to Causes. . . .

And indeed, according to the hypothesis I am opposing, of the acts of the will coming to pass without a Cause, it is the cause in fact, that millions of Events are continually coming into existence *contingently* without any Cause or reason why they do so, all over the world, every day and hour, through all ages. So it is in a constant succession, in every moral agent. This contingency, this efficient nothing, this effectual No-Cause, is always ready at hand, to produce this sort of effects, as long as the agent exists, and as often as he has occasion.

If it were so, that things only of one kind, *viz.* acts of the will, seemed to come to pass of themselves; and it were an event that was continual, and that happened in a course, wherever were found subjects capable of such events; this very thing would demonstrate that there was some Cause of them, which made such a difference between this Event and others, and that they did not really happen contingently. For contingence is blind, and does not pick and choose a particular sort of Events. Nothing has no choice. . . .

If any should imagine, there is something in the sort of Event that renders it possible for it to come into existence without a Cause, and should say, that the free acts of the will are existences of an exceeding *different nature* from other things; by reason of which they may come into existence without any previous ground or reason of it, though other things cannot: if they make this objection in good earnest, it would be an evidence of their strangely forgetting themselves; for they would be giving an account of some ground of the existence of a thing, when at the same time they would maintain there is no ground of its existence. . . .

So that it is indeed as repugnant to reason, to suppose that an act of the will should come into existence without a cause, as to suppose the human soul, or an angel, or the globe of the earth, or the whole universe, should come into existence without a cause. . . .

LIBERTY OF INDIFFERENCE . . . INCONSISTENT WITH THE ARMINIAN NOTIONS OF LIBERTY AND MORAL AGENCY

To suppose such a freedom of will, as *Arminians* talk of, to be requisite to Virtue and Vice, is many ways contrary to common sense.

If indifference belong to Liberty of Will, as *Arminians* suppose, and it be essential to a virtuous action, that it be performed in a state of Liberty, as they also suppose; it will follow, that it is essential to a virtuous action, that it be performed in a *state* of Indifference: and if it be performed in a *state* of Indifference, then doubtless it must be performed in a *time* of Indifference. And so it will follow, that in order to the virtue of an act, the heart must be indifferent in the time of performance of that act, and the more indifferent and cold the heart is with relation to the act performed, so much the better; because the act is performed with so much greater Liberty. But is this agreeable to the light of nature? Is it agreeable to the notions which mankind in all ages, have of Virtue, that it lies in what is contrary to Indifference, even in the *Tendency* and *Inclination* of the heart to virtuous action; and that the stronger the Inclination, and the further from Indifference, the more virtuous the *heart*, and so much the more praiseworthy the *act* which proceeds from it?

And besides, the actions that are done in a state of Indifference, or that arise immediately out of such a state, cannot be virtuous, because, by the supposition, they are not determined by any preceding choice. . . . But those acts which are not determined by preceding choice, cannot be virtuous or vicious, by *Arminian* principles, because they are not determined by the will. So that neither one way, nor the other, can any actions be virtuous or vicious, according to those principles. If the action *be determined* by a preceding act of choice, it cannot be virtuous; because the action is not done in a state of Indifference, nor does immediately arise from such a state; and so it is not done in a state of Liberty. If the action be *not determined* by a preceding act of choice, then it cannot be virtuous; because then the will is not self-determined in it. So that it is made certain, that neither Virtue nor Vice can ever find any place in the Universe!

Moreover, that it is necessary to a virtuous action that it be performed in a state of Indifference, under a notion of that being a state of Liberty, is contrary to common sense; as it is a dictate of common sense, that Indifference itself, in many cases, is vicious, and so to a high degree. As if when I see my neighbour or near friend, and one who has in the highest degree merited of me, in extreme distress, and ready to perish, I find an Indifference in my heart with respect to any thing proposed to be done, which I can easily do, for his relief. ...

MORAL NECESSITY CONSISTENT WITH PRAISE AND BLAME, REWARD AND PUNISHMENT

... [T]his (praising, blaming, rewarding, punishing) is not at all inconsistent with the natural apprehensions of mankind, and that sense of things which is found every where in the common people who are furthest from having their thoughts perverted from their natural channel, by metaphysical and philosophical subtilties; but, on the contrary, altogether agreeable *to*, and the very voice and dictate *of* this natural and vulgar Sense.

This will appear, if we consider what the vulgar Notion of *blameworthiness* is. The idea which the common people ... have of faultiness, I suppose to be plainly this: *a person being or doing wrong, with his own will and pleasure*; containing these two things; 1. *His doing wrong, when he does as he pleases*. 2. *His pleasure being wrong*. Or, in other words. ... a person *having his heart wrong, and doing wrong from his heart*. And this is the sum total of the matter.

The common people do not ascend up in their reflections and abstractions to the metaphysical sources, relations and dependencies of things, in order to form their Notion of faultiness or blameworthiness. ... All the ground they go upon, consists in these two things; *experience* and a *natural sensation* of a certain fitness or agreeableness, which there is in uniting such moral evil as is above described, *viz. a being or doing wrong with the will*, and resentment in others, and pain inflicted on the person in whom this moral evil is. Which *natural Sense* is what we call by the name of *conscience*.

It is true, the common people and children. ... do suppose that it is the person's *own act and deed*. But this is all that belongs to what they understand by a thing being a person's *own deed or action*; even that it is something done by him of *choice*. That some exercise or motion should begin of itself, does not belong to their Notion of *an action*, or *doing*. If so, it would belong to their Notion of it, that it is the cause of its own beginning; and that is as much as to say, that it is before it begins to be. Nor is their Notion of an *action* some motion or exercise, that begins accidentally, without any cause or reason; for that is contrary to one of the prime dictates of common Sense, namely, that everything that begins to be, has some cause or reason why it is.

The common people . . . have no Notion of liberty consisting in the will first acting, and so causing its own acts; determining, and so causing its own determinations; or choosing, and so causing its own choice. Such a Notion of liberty is what none have, but those that have darkened their own minds with confused metaphysical speculation, and abstruse and ambiguous terms. . . . Nor have men commonly any notion of freedom consisting of indifference. For if so, then it would be agreeable to their Notion, that the greater indifference men act with, the more freedom they act with; whereas, the reverse is true. . . .

If it were inconsistent with the common Sense of mankind, that men should be either blamed or commended in any volitions, in the case of moral necessity or impossibility; then it would surely also be agreeable to the same Sense and reason of mankind, that the nearer the case approaches to such a moral necessity or impossibility—either through a strong antecedent moral propensity . . . or a great antecedent opposition and difficulty . . . the nearer does it approach to a person being neither blameable nor commendable; so that acts exerted with such preceding propensity, would be worthy of proportionably less praise; and when omitted, the act being attended with such difficulty, the omission would be worthy of the less blame. . . . And if it were as much a dictate of common Sense, that moral necessity of doing, or impossibility of avoiding, takes away *all* praise and blame, as that natural necessity or impossibility does; then, by a perfect parity of reason, it would be as much the dictate of common Sense, that an *approach* of moral necessity of doing, or impossibility of avoiding, *diminishes* praise and blame. . . . It is equally the voice of common Sense, that persons are *excusable in part*, in neglecting things *difficult* against their wills, as that they are *excusable wholly* in neglecting things *impossible* against their wills. . . .

But it is apparent, that the reverse of these things is true. If there be an approach to a moral necessity in a man's exertion of good acts of will, they being the exercise of a strong propensity to good, and a very powerful love to virtue; it is so far from being the dictate of common Sense, that he is less virtuous, and the less to be esteemed, loved and praised; that it is agreeable to the natural Notions of all mankind, that he is so much the better man, worthy of greater respect, and higher commendation. And the stronger the inclination is, and the nearer it approaches to necessity in that respect; or to impossibility of neglecting the virtuous act, or of doing a vicious one; still the more virtuous, and worthy of higher commendation. And, on the other hand, if a man exerts evil acts of mind; as, for instance, acts of pride or malice from a rotted and strong habit or principle of haughtiness and maliciousness, and a violent propensity of heart to such acts; according to the natural Sense of men, he is so far from being the less hateful and blameable on that account, that he is so much the more worthy to be detested and condemned, by all that observe him. . . .

. . . Whereas . . . men do not think a good act to be the less praiseworthy, for the agent being much determined in it by a good inclination or a good motive, but the more. And if good inclination, or motive, has but little influence in determining the agent, they do not think his act so much the more virtuous, but the less. And so concerning evil acts, which are determined by evil motives or inclinations.

Yea, if it be supposed, that good or evil dispositions are implanted in the hearts of men, by nature itself (which, it is certain, is vulgarly supposed in innumerable cases) yet it is not commonly supposed, that men are worthy of no praise or dispraise for such dispositions; although what is natural, is undoubtedly necessary, nature being prior to all acts of the will whatsoever. . . . Yea . . . vile natural dispositions . . . will commonly be mentioned rather as an *aggravation* of the wicked acts, that come from such a fountain, than an extenuation of them. It being natural for men to act thus, is often observed by men in the height of their indignation: they will say, "It is his very nature: he is of a vile natural temper; it is as natural to him to act so, as it is to breathe; he cannot help serving the devil, &c." But it is not thus with regard to hurtful mischievous things, that any are the subjects or occasions of, by *natural necessity*, against their inclinations. In such a case, the necessity, by the common voice of mankind, will be spoken of as a full excuse.—Thus it is very plain, that common Sense makes a vast difference between these two kinds of necessity, as to the judgment it makes of their influence on the moral quality and desert of men's actions. . . .

Upon the whole, I presume there is no person of good understanding, who impartially considers these things, but will allow, that it is not evident, from the dictates of common sense, or natural notions, that moral necessity is inconsistent with praise and blame. . . .

Study Questions

1. In the sermon, "A Divine and Supernatural Light," Edwards argues that a truly religious person possesses a special sense or faculty that other people lack. How, according to Edwards, does one come by this faculty, and what changes does it make in those who have it? Explain, and defend your answer.

2. Throughout Edwards's most famous sermon, "Sinners in the Hands of an Angry God," we read of human depravity and inattention to the religious life. We also learn that no one deserves to be saved. Given the human condition and our countless demerits, why does Edwards's sovereign, angry God choose to save some of us? Explain, and defend your answer.

3. What is the principal task that Edwards sets for himself in *Freedom of the Will*? Be specific. How, given this task, does Edwards go about trying to argue for it and against his Arminian critics? Does Edwards succeed or fail in his effort to defend his position? Explain.

4. In *Freedom of the Will*, does Edwards make it clear that he is a determinist? What are the defining features of determinism as Edwards understands it, and how do these features differ from what Arminians believe? Be specific, and defend your claims.

Suggestions for Further Reading

Chai, Leon. *Jonathan Edwards and the Limits of Enlightenment Philosophy.* Oxford: Oxford University Press, 1998.

Cherry, Conrad. *The Theology of Jonathan Edwards: a Reappraisal.* New York: Anchor Books, 1966.

Conkin, Paul. "Jonathan Edwards: Theology." In *Puritans and Pragmatists: Eight Eminent American Thinkers.* New York: Dodd, Mead & Co., 1968.

Edwards, Jonathan. *Freedom of the Will.* Edited by Paul Ramsey. New Haven: Yale University Press, 1957.

Edwards, Jonathan. *Jonathan Edwards: Representative Selections.* Edited by C. H. Faust and T. H. Johnson, revised edition. New York: American Book Co., 1962.

Edwards, Jonathan. *A Jonathan Edwards Reader.* Edited by John E. Smith, Harry S. Stout, and Kenneth P. Minkema. New Haven: Yale University Press, 1995.

Fiering, Norman. *Jonathan Edwards's Moral Thought and Its British Context.* Chapel Hill: University of North Carolina Press, 1981.

Howe, Daniel Walker. "Benjamin Franklin, Jonathan Edwards, and the Problem of Human Nature." *Making the American Self: Jonathan Edwards to Abraham Lincoln.* Cambridge, Mass.: Harvard University Press, 1997.

Lee, Sang Hyun. *The Philosophical Theology of Jonathan Edwards*, expanded edition. Princeton: Princeton University Press, 2000.

Miller, Perry. "Jonathan Edwards and the Great Awakening." *Errand into the Wilderness.* Cambridge, Mass.: Belknap Press of Harvard University Press, 1956.

Miller, Perry. *Jonathan Edwards.* New York: Meridian Books, 1959.

Wainwright, William J. "Jonathan Edwards and the Heart." *Reason and the Heart: A Prolegomenon to a Critique of Passional Reason.* Ithaca: Cornell University Press, 1995.

White, Morton. "Jonathan Edwards: the Doctrine of Necessity and the Sense of the Heart." *Science and Sentiment in America.* New York: Oxford University Press, 1972.

Chapter 2

Benjamin Franklin and Thomas Paine
The Enlightenment in America

More than anyone else, Benjamin Franklin (1706–1790) is the epitome of the self-made American. Born without distinction in Boston, he dropped out of school at age twelve. Initially apprenticed to his half-brother as a printer, he moved to Philadelphia in 1723 to seek more profitable opportunities. There too he worked as a printer and also managed to acquire encouraging and influential friends. By 1729, the young Franklin had begun publishing *The Pennsylvania Gazette*, his own newspaper. Four years later he began writing and publishing the remarkably successful and durable *Poor Richard's Almanac* (1733–1758).

Before he had turned forty, Franklin proposed and helped to establish the American Philosophical Society, which was formed in Philadelphia and still exists to advance knowledge of all kinds. By age forty-two, Franklin was able to retire from commerce and from the need for gainful employment. During the second half of his life, he devoted himself to the advancement of education as one of the founders of the University of Pennsylvania, articulated a pre-Revolutionary Plan of the Union at the Albany Conference (1754) to unite the American colonies for defensive purposes, opposed and argued the case against the notorious Stamp Act of 1765, served as a delegate to the Second Continental Congress and as America's minister to France, and helped to negotiate the formal end to the Revolutionary War (Treaty of Paris, 1783). At the close of his long life he participated in meetings of the Constitutional Convention of 1787.

None of this includes Franklin's inventive and speculative side. His electrical theories and experiments made him the scientific giant of colonial America. He was invited to join the Royal Society of London, then and now the most prestigious scientific organization in the world. The lightning rod, Franklin stove, bifocal lenses, and glass harmonica are among his most famous inventions. Franklin was a Renaissance man. He was a genius who came from the "unripe side" of the globe and who enjoyed a reputation that equaled or exceeded the reputations of eighteenth-century Europeans who themselves made enduring contributions to technology and the theoretical sciences.

These selections from Franklin's voluminous writings reveal the man, his aspirations and attitudes toward topics as various as the value of self-reliance, the constructive approach to a productive life, and effective strategies for improving moral character. The "philosophy" distributed throughout *The Autobiography* (1771–1789) maps Franklin's views on maturity, autonomy, integrity, happiness, and responsibility. He expresses his views retrospectively. They are an old man's recollections of what he was and became between his earliest years and late maturity. His "Articles of Belief and Acts of Religion" (1728) are a window into the rational theology that was in vogue among the *intelligentsia* of eighteenth-century Europe and, to a lesser extent, America. That Franklin was a devout theist seems certain. Whether he was also a Christian is less clear.

It is obvious that assorted themes are abundant in Franklin's works. If, however, one were pressed to explain why he fits into a selection of writings in American philosophy, the most obvious response is that Franklin praises the self-made human being and provides details that, taken together, tell us what constitutes autonomy, personal identity, and the good life. And if one objects that demands and methods for self-improvement did not begin with Franklin, the reposte is that Franklin, throughout his own life and in *The Autobiography*, helped to make almost canonical the position that to be American and to be self-reliant, to become independent and upwardly mobile, are inseparable outcomes. For Franklin, as against Edwards and his moribund Calvinism, autonomy and happiness are also inseparable. From the last decades of the eighteenth century forward, self-improvement and self-liberation became the indispensable bedrock on which so much American philosophy takes its stand.

There is little in Thomas Paine's formative years to suggest that he would become both an advocate of rational religion (deism) or a key spokesman for the coming American Revolution. Born in England in 1737, he did not leave for America until he was nearly forty years old. In England he had practiced many talents, including those of a staymaker, sailor, and teacher. In America he worked briefly as a journalist and clerk of the Pennsylvania Assembly. Following the successful revolution, he returned to England and later left for France. There he was imprisoned for a time because of his vocal objections to the execution of Louis XVI. Set free in November 1794 at James Monroe's request, he decided in 1802 to return to America. He died June 8, 1809, and was buried in New Rochelle, New York.

A persistent trust in reason and reverence for nature punctuate Paine's political tracts, which are taken up later in this volume, and *The Age of Reason, Part I* (1794), a scathing indictment of Christianity and its earthly institutions but also a brief for a religion based upon the revelations of objective reason. Throughout this brief tract, Paine enumerates the excesses of Christianity as it is practiced throughout the eighteenth century. He includes among his complaints the ties between Christianity and corrupt governments, the Bible as little more than a collection of groundless prophecies and obscene stories, revelations and miracles as highly doubtful claims of gullible zealots and enthusiasts, and so-called mysteries of the faith as thinly veiled admissions of ignorance.

The remedy, as far as Paine is concerned, for the half-truths, blind conviction, and duplicity that are inseparable from institutional Christianity, is its rejection, not the rejection of legitimate religious beliefs. These for Paine are the beliefs that satisfy the criteria of settled rationality and that can be verified by observation or, even better, by the careful study of nature. The guiding principle of the positive content in *The Age of Reason, Part I*, is that the creation itself, not the Bible, is the book of God and, therefore, is the only volume that enables us to discover that God exists, that God is benevolent, and that God's knowledge, like his power, is immeasurable.

Reading this book of nature—that is, observing its regularities, discovering the laws that govern its orderly changes, and noting the extraordinary adaptations of means to ends in living beings or in intricate organ like the eye—enables us to infer that the universe is a series of effects that are caused by an extra-mundane, wise, and artful designer. This designer, the cosmic architect we call by the name "God," does not retreat from human understanding or hide behind the language of confusing prophecies. He is evident to anyone who is willing to employ reason judiciously and to learn the course of nature in the manner of an empirical scientist.

Moreover, as Paine sees things, we can learn from God's own generosity and benevolence to treat others with liberality and compassion. Here too Paine's reasoning is simple or, some might wish to claim, simplistic. His inference is based on an analogy. Even as God gives us life and what we need to enjoy it, so too are we, as God's most intelligent creatures, obligated to do for others as He had done for us. If benevolence and charity are hallmarks of divine goodness, as Paine believes they are, then they should be the hallmarks of our character as well.

That there are problems with Paine's version of the argument from design and, for that matter, with rational religion is undeniable. Indeed, one of the consequences of Darwin's theory is that it became possible and feasible to account for apparent design and divine craftsmanship by looking to the principle of natural selection as it is explained and defended in *Origin of Species*. Even before Darwin, philosophers such as Spinoza, Kant, and Hume had used reason to show why and how the arguments of rational theologians miscarry. So it is probably fair to say that by the time Paine wrote *The Age of Reason, Part I*, rational religion was nearly moribund and that his pamphlet was a philosophical anachronism.

Nonetheless, the kind of thinking and arguments Paine used managed to retain some fashion in pre- and post-Revolutionary America. Ethan Allen and Benjamin Franklin adopted and defended the principles of rational religion. George Washington rejected organized religion and worshiped in several churches, as well as at least one synagogue, but faith did not play a prominent role in his life as a general, president, or gentleman farmer. Much the same can be said about the doubts and beliefs of Alexander Hamilton and Thomas Jefferson. Their attitudes toward religion may be about all that Hamilton and Jefferson held in common.

The Age of Reason, Part I has a place in this anthology, then, because it provides at least some information about the Enlightenment that found its way from Europe to America. We choose Paine, rather than some less prominent religious rationalist or deist, because he managed, without starting out as an American, to ignite the Revolution and to announce many of the ideas and ideals that induced cautious colonists to become committed revolutionaries. There is no doubt that reason in the service of true religion and reason in the cause of revolution present arguments appropriate to different tasks. In the end, however, it is the productive use of reason, not passive hopes and comfortable faith, that drives Paine and makes him a dominant voice at the time that British America struggled to become the United States.

The Autobiography (1793)

Benjamin Franklin

Dear Son: . . . Imagining it may be . . . agreeable to you to know the circumstances of my life, . . . I sit down to write them for you. To which I have besides some other inducements. Having emerged from the poverty and obscurity in which I was born and bred, to a state of affluence and some degree of reputation in the world, and having gone so far through life with a considerable share of felicity, the conducing means I made use of, which with the blessing of God so well succeeded, my posterity may like to know, as they may find some of them suitable to their own situations, and therefore fit to be imitated. . . .

Before I enter upon my public appearance in business, it may be well to let you know the then state of my mind with regard to my principles and morals, that you may see how far those influence'd the future events of my life. My parents had early given me religious impressions, and brought me through my childhood piously in the Dissenting way. But I was scarce fifteen, when, after doubting by turns of several points, as I found them disputed in the different books I read, I began to doubt of Revelation itself. Some books against Deism fell into my hands; they were said to be the substance of sermons preached at Boyle's Lectures. It happened that they wrought an effect on me quite contrary to what was intended by them; for the arguments of the Deists, which were quoted to be refuted, appeared to me much stronger than the refutations; in short, I soon became a thorough Deist. . . . I began to suspect that this doctrine, tho' it might be true, was not very useful. My London pamphlet, which had for its motto these lines of Dryden:

From *The Writings of Benjamin Franklin*, ed. A. H. Smyth. (New York: Haskell House Publishers, 1970), Vol. II, pp. 91–95, 97–100, 386–96. Reprinted with permission of the publisher.

"Whatever is, is right. Though purblind man
Sees but a part o'; the chain, the nearest link:
His eyes not carrying to the equal beam,
That poises all above."

And from the attributes of God, his infinite wisdom, goodness and power, concluded that nothing could possibly be wrong in the world, and that vice and virtue were empty distinctions, no such things existing, appear'd now not so clever a performance as I once thought; and I doubted whether some error had not insinuated itself unperceiv'd into my argument, so as to infect all that follow'd, as is common in metaphysical reasonings.

I grew convinc'd that *truth, sincerity* and *integrity* in dealings between man and man were of the utmost importance to the felicity of life; and I form'd written resolutions, which still remain in my journal book, to practice them ever while I lived. Revelation had indeed no weight with me, as such; but I entertain'd an opinion that, though certain actions might not be bad *because* they were forbidden by it, or good *because* it commanded them, yet probably these actions might be forbidden *because* they were bad for us, or commanded *because* they were beneficial to us, in their own natures, all the circumstances of things considered. . . .

I had been religiously educated as a Presbyterian; and tho' some of the dogmas of that persuasion, such as *the eternal decrees of God, election, reprobation, etc.*, appeared to me unintelligible, others doubtful, and I early absented myself from the public assemblies of the sect, Sunday being my studying day, I never was without some religious principles. I never doubted, for instance, the existence of the Deity; that he made the world, and govern'd it by his Providence; that the most acceptable service of God was the doing good to man; that our souls are immortal; and that all crime will be punished, and virtue rewarded, either here or hereafter. These I esteem'd the essentials of every religion; and, being to be found in all the religions we had in our country, I respected them all, tho' with different degrees of respect, as I found them more or less mix'd with other articles, which, without any tendency to inspire, promote, or confirm morality, serv'd principally to divide us, and make us unfriendly to one another. . . .

. . . I conceived the bold and arduous project of arriving at moral perfection. I wish'd to live without committing any fault at any time; I would conquer all that either natural inclination, custom, or company might lead me into. As I knew, or thought I knew, what was right and wrong, I did not see why I might not always do the one and avoid the other. But I soon found I had undertaken a task of more difficulty than I had imagined. While my care was employ'd in guarding against one fault, I was often surprised by another; habit took the advantage of inattention; inclination was sometimes too strong for reason. I concluded, at length, that the mere speculative conviction that it was our interest to be completely virtuous, was not sufficient to prevent our slipping; and that the contrary habits must be broken, and good ones acquired and established, before we can have any dependence on a steady, uniform rectitude of conduct. For this purpose I therefore contrived the following method.

In the various enumerations of the moral virtues I had met with in my reading, I found the catalogue more or less numerous, as different writers included more or fewer ideas under the same name. Temperance, for example, was by some confined to eating and drinking, while by others it was extended to mean the moderating every other pleasure, appetite, inclination, or passion, bodily or mental, even to our avarice and ambition. I propos'd to myself, for the sake of clearness, to use rather more names, with fewer ideas annex'd to each, than a few names with more ideas; and I included under thirteen names of virtues all that at that time occur'd to me as necessary or desirable, and annexed to each a short precept, which fully express'd the extent I gave to its meaning.

These names of virtues, with their precepts, were:

1. TEMPERANCE. Eat not to dullness; drink not to elevation.
2. SILENCE. Speak not but what may benefit others or yourself; avoid trifling conversation.
3. ORDER. Let all your things have their places; let each part of your business have its time.
4. RESOLUTION. Resolve to perform what you ought; perform without fail what you resolve.
5. FRUGALITY. Make no expense but to do good to others or yourself; *i.e.*, waste nothing.
6. INDUSTRY. Lose no time; be always employ'd in something useful; cut off all unnecessary actions.
7. SINCERITY. Use no hurtful deceit; think innocently and justly, and, if you speak, speak accordingly.
8. JUSTICE. Wrong none by doing injuries, or omitting the benefits that are your duty.
9. MODERATION. Avoid extreams; forbear resenting injuries so much as you think they deserve.
10. CLEANLINESS. Tolerate no uncleanliness in body, cloaths, or habitation.
11. TRANQUILLITY. Be not disturbed at trifles, or accidents common or unavoidable.
12. CHASTITY. Rarely use venery but for health or offspring, never to dullness, weakness, or the injury of your own or another's peace or reputation.
13. HUMILITY. Imitate Jesus and Socrates.

My intention being to acquire the *habitude* of all these virtues, I judg'd it would be well not to distract my attention by attempting the whole at once, but to fix it on one of them at a time; and, when I should be master of that, then to proceed to another, and so on, till I should have gone thro' the thirteen; and, as the previous acquisition of some might facilitate the acquisition of certain others, I arrang'd them with that view, as they stand above. Temperance first, as it tends to procure that coolness and clearness of head, which is so necessary where constant vigilance was to be kept up, and guard maintained against the unremitting attraction of ancient habits, and the force of perpetual temptations. This being acquir'd and establish'd, Silence would be more easy; and my desire being to gain knowledge at the same time that I improv'd in virtue, and considering that in conversation it was obtain'd rather by the use of the ears than of the tongue, and therefore wishing to break a habit I was getting into of prattling, punning, and joking, which only made me acceptable to trifling company, I gave *Silence* the second place. This and the next, *Order*, I expected would allow me more time for attending to my project and my studies. *Resolution*, once become habitual, would keep me firm in my endeavours to obtain all the subsequent virtues; *Frugality* and Industry freeing me from my remaining debt, and producing affluence and independence, would make more easy the practice of Sincerity and Justice, etc., etc. Conceiving then, that, agreeably to the advice of Pythagoras in his Golden Verses, daily examination would be necessary, I contrived the following method for conducting that examination.

I made a little book, in which I allotted a page for each of the virtues. I rul'd each page with red ink, so as to have seven columns, one for each day of the week, marking each column with a letter for the day. I cross'd these columns with thirteen red lines, marking the beginning of each line with the first letter of one of the virtues, on which line, and in its proper column, I might mark, by a little black spot, every fault I found upon examination to have been committed respecting that virtue upon that day. . . .

I determined to give a week's strict attention to each of the virtues successively. Thus, in the first week, my great guard was to avoid every the least offence against *Temperance*, leaving the other virtues to their ordinary chance, only marking every evening the faults of the day. Thus, if in the first week I could keep my first line, marked T, clear of spots, I suppos'd the habit of that virtue so much strengthen'd, and its opposite weaken'd, that I might venture extending my attention to include the next, and for the following week keep both lines clear of spots. Proceeding thus to the last, I could go thro' a course compleat in thirteen weeks, and four courses in a year. And like him who, having a garden to weed, does not attempt to eradicate all the bad herbs at once, which would exceed his reach and his strength, but works on one of the beds at a time, and, having accomplish'd the first, proceeds to a second, so I should have, I hoped, the encouraging pleasure of seeing on my pages the progress I made in virtue, by clearing successively my lines of their spots, till in the end, by a number of courses, I should be happy in viewing a clean book, after a thirteen weeks' daily examination. . . .

The precept of *Order* requiring that *every part of my business should have its allotted time*, one page in my little book contain'd the following scheme of employment for the twenty-four hours of a natural day.

THE MORNING *Question:* What good shall I do this day?	5 6 7	Rise, wash, and address *Powerful Goodness!* Contrive day's business, and take the resolution of the day; prosecute the present study, and breakfast.
	8 9 10 11	Work.
NOON	12 1	Read, or overlook my accounts, and dine.
	2 3 4 5	Work.
EVENING *Question:* What good have I done to-day?	6 7 8 9	Put things in their places. Supper. Music or diversion, or conversation. Examination of the day.
NIGHT	10 11 12 1 2 3 4	Sleep.

I enter'd upon the execution of this plan for self-examination, and continu'd it with occasional intermissions for some time. I was surpris'd to find myself so much fuller of faults than I had imagined; but I had the satisfaction of seeing them diminish. To avoid the trouble of renewing now and then my little book, which, by scraping out the marks on the paper of old faults to make room for new ones in a new course, became full of holes, I transferr'd my tables and precepts to the ivory leaves of a memorandum book, on which the lines were drawn with red ink, that made a durable stain, and on those lines I mark'd my faults with a black-lead pencil, which marks I could easily wipe out with a wet sponge. After a while I went thro' one course only in a year, and afterward only one in several years, till at length I omitted them entirely, being employ'd in voyages and business abroad, with a multiplicity of affairs that interfered; but I always carried my little book with me. ...

In truth, I found myself incorrigible with respect to Order; and now I am grown old, and my memory bad, I feel very sensibly the want of it. But, on the whole, tho' I never arrived at the perfection I had been so ambitious of obtaining, but fell far short of it, yet I was, by the endeavour, a better and a happier man than I might otherwise should have been if I had not attempted it; as those who aim at perfect writing by imitating the engraved copies, tho' they never reach the wish'd-for excellence of those copies, their hand is mended by the endeavour, and is tolerable while it continues fair and legible. ...

It will be remark'd that, tho' my scheme was not wholly without religion, there was in it no mark of any of the distinguishing tenets of any particular sect. I had purposely avoided them; for, being fully persuaded of the utility and excellency of my method, and that it might be serviceable to people in all religions, and intending some time or other to publish it, I would not have any thing in it that should prejudice any one, of any sect, against it. I purposed writing a little comment on each virtue, in which I would have shown the advantages of possessing it, and the mischiefs attending its opposite vice; and I should have called my book THE ART OF VIRTUE, because it would have shown the means and manner of obtaining virtue, which would have distinguished it from the mere exhortation to be good, that does not instruct and indicate the means, but is like the apostle's man of verbal charity, who only without showing to the naked and hungry how or where they might get clothes or victuals, exhorted them to be fed and clothed.—James ii.15, 16. ...

FIRST PRINCIPLES

I believe there is one supreme, most perfect Being, Author and Father of the Gods themselves. For I believe that Man is not the most perfect Being but one, rather that as there are many Degrees of Beings his Inferiors, so there are many Degrees of Beings superior to him.

Also, when I stretch my Imagination thro' and beyond our System of Planets, beyond the visible fix'd Stars themselves, into that Space that is every Way infinite, and conceive it fill'd with Suns like ours, each with a Chorus of Worlds forever moving round him, then this little Ball on which we move, seems, even in my narrow Imagination, to be almost Nothing, and myself less than nothing, and of no sort of Consequence.

When I think thus, I imagine it great Vanity in me to suppose, that the *Supremely Perfect* does in the least regard such an inconsiderable Nothing as Man. More especially, since it is impossible for me to have any positive clear idea of that which is infinite and incomprehensible, I cannot conceive otherwise than that he *the Infinite Father* expects or requires no Worship or Praise from us, but that he is even infinitely above it.

But, since there is in all Men something like a natural principle, which inclines them to DEVOTION, or the Worship of some unseen Power;

And since Men are endued with Reason superior to all other Animals, that we are in our World acquainted with;

Therefore I think it seems required of me, and my Duty as a Man, to pay Divine Regards to SOMETHING.

I conceive then, that the INFINITE has created many beings or Gods, vastly superior to Man, who can better conceive his Perfections than we, and return him a more rational and glorious Praise.

As, among Men, the Praise of the Ignorant or of Children is not regarded by the ingenious Painter or Architect, who is rather honour'd and pleas'd with the approbation of Wise Men & Artists.

It may be that these created Gods are immortal; or it may be that after many Ages, they are changed, and others Supply their Places.

Howbeit, I conceive that each of these is exceeding wise and good, and very powerful; and that Each has made for himself one glorious Sun, attended with a beautiful and admirable System of Planets.

It is that particular Wise and good God, who is the author and owner of our System, that I propose for the object of my praise and adoration.

For I conceive that he has in himself some of those Passions he has planted in us, and that, since he has given us Reason whereby we are capable of observing his Wisdom in the Creation, he is not above caring for us, being pleas'd with our Praise, and offended when we slight Him, or neglect his Glory.

I conceive for many Reasons, that he is a *good* Being; and as I should be happy to have so wise, good, and powerful a Being my Friend, let me consider in what manner I shall make myself most acceptable to him.

Next to the Praise resulting from and due to his Wisdom, I believe he is pleas'd and delights in the Happiness of those he has created; and since without Virtue Man can have no Happiness in this World, I firmly believe he delights to see me Virtuous, because he is pleased when he sees Me Happy.

And since he has created many Things, which seem purely design'd for the Delight of Man, I believe he is not offended, when he sees his Children solace themselves in any manner of pleasant exercises and Innocent Delights; and I think no Pleasure innocent, that is to Man hurtful.

I *love* him therefore for his Goodness. And I *adore* him for his Wisdom.

Let me then not fail to praise my God continually, for it is his Due, and it is all I can return for his many Favours and great Goodness to me; and let me resolve to be virtuous, that I may be happy, that I may please Him, who is delighted to see me happy. Amen!

The Age of Reason, Part I (1794)

Thomas Paine

. . .The circumstance that has now taken place in France of the total abolition of the whole national order of priesthood, and of everything appertaining to compulsive systems of religions, and compulsive articles of faith, has not only precipitated my intention, but rendered a work of this kind exceedingly necessary, lest, in the general wreck of superstition, of false systems of government and false theology, we lose sight of morality, of humanity, and of the theology that is true. . . .

I believe in one God, and no more; and I hope for happiness beyond this life.

I believe in the equality of man, and I believe that religious duties consist in doing justice, loving mercy, and endeavoring to make our fellow creatures happy.

But, lest it should be supposed that I believe in many other things in addition to these, I shall . . . declare the things I do not believe, and my reasons for not believing them.

I do not believe in the creed professed by the Jewish church, by the Roman church, by the Greek church, by the Turkish church, by the Protestant church, nor by any church that I know of. My own mind is my own church.

All national institutions of churches . . . appear to me no other than human inventions set up to terrify and enslave mankind, and monopolize power and profit. . . .

It is impossible to calculate the moral mischief . . . that mental lying has produced in society. When a man has so far corrupted and prostituted the chastity of his mind, as to subscribe his professional belief to things he does not believe, he has prepared himself for the commission of every other crime. He takes up the trade of a priest for the sake of gain, and, in order to qualify himself for that trade, he begins with a perjury. Can we conceive anything more destructive to morality than this?

Soon after I had published the pamphlet *Common Sense*, in America, I saw the exceeding provability that a revolution in the system of government would be followed by a revolution in the system of religion. The adulterous connection of church and state . . . had so effectually prohibited, by pains and penalties, every discussion upon established creeds, and upon first principles of religion, that until the system of government should be changed, those subjects could not be brought fairly and openly before the world; but that whenever this should be done, a revolution in the system of religion would follow. Human inventions and priestcraft would be detected; and man would return to the pure, unmixed, and unadulterated belief of one God, and no more.

From Thomas Paine, *The Age of Reason, Part I.* (New York: The Modern Library) © 1925, pp. 185–271.

Every national church or religion has established itself by pretending some special mission from God, communicated to certain individuals . . . as if the way to God was not open to every man alike. . . .

Each . . . (church) accuse(s) the other of unbelief; and, for my own part, I disbelieve them all.

As it is necessary to affix right ideas to words, I will . . . offer some observations on the word "revelation." Revelation when applied to religion, means something communicated *immediately* from God to man.

No one will deny or dispute the power of the Almighty to make such a communication if he pleases. But admitting, for the sake of a case, that something has been revealed to a certain person, and not revealed to any other person, it is revelation to that person only. . . . It is revelation to the first person only, and hearsay to every other, and, consequently they are not obliged to believe it.

It is a contradiction in terms and ideas to call anything a revelation that comes to us at second hand, either verbally or in writing. Revelation is necessarily limited to the first communication. After this, it is only an account of something which that person says was a revelation made to him; and though he may find himself obliged to believe it, it cannot be incumbent on me to believe it in the same manner, for it was not a revelation made to me, and I have only his word for it that it was to him.

When Moses told the children of Israel that he received the two tables of the Commandments from the hand of God, they were not obliged to believe him, because they had no other authority for it than his telling them so; and I have no other authority for it than some historian telling me so; the commandments carrying no internal evidence of divinity with them. They contain some good moral precepts such as any man qualified to be a lawgiver or a legislator could produce himself, without having recourse to supernatural intervention. . . .

It is curious to observe how the theory of what is called the Christian church, sprung out of the tail of the heathen mythology. . . . The Christian theory is little else than the idolatry of the ancient mythologists, accommodated to the purposes of power and revenue, and it yet remains to reason and philosophy to abolish the amphibious fraud.

Nothing that is here said can apply, even with the most distant disrespect, to the *real* character of Jesus Christ. He was a virtuous and an amiable man. The morality that he preached and practiced was of the most benevolent kind; and though similar systems of morality had been preached by Confucius, and by some of the Greek philosophers, many years before, by the Quakers since, and by many good men in all ages, it has not been exceeded by any.

Jesus Christ wrote no account of himself, of his birth, parentage, or anything else. Not a line of what is called the New Testament is of his writing. The history of him is altogether the work of other people; and as to the account of his resurrection and ascension, it was the necessary counterpart to the story of his birth. His historians, having brought him into the world in a supernatural manner, were obliged to take him out again in the same manner, or the first part of the story must have fallen to the ground. . . .

(T)he resurrection of a dead person from the grave, and his ascension through the air, is a thing very different, as to the evidence it admits of, the invisible conception of a child in the womb. The resurrection and ascension, supposing them to have taken place, admitted of public and ocular demonstration, like that of the ascension of a balloon, or the sun at noonday, to all Jerusalem at least. A thing which everybody is required to believe, requires that the proof and evidence of it should be equal to all, and universal; and as the public visibility of this last related act was the only evidence that could give sanction to the former part, the whole of it falls to the ground because that evidence was never given.

It is in vain to attempt to palliate or disguise this matter. The story, so far as relates to the supernatural part, has every mark of fraud and imposition stamped upon the face of it. Who were the authors of it is as impossible for us now to know, as it is for us to be assured that the books in which the account is related were written by the persons whose names they bear. The best surviving evidence we now have respecting this affair is the Jews. They are regularly descended from the people who lived in the time this resurrection and ascension is said to have happened, and they say, *it is not true.* . . .

That such a person as Jesus Christ existed, and that he was crucified, which was the mode of execution at that day, are historical relations strictly within the limits of probability. . . .

(But) these Christian mythologists bring the two ends of their fable together. They represent this virtuous and amiable man, Jesus Christ, to be at once both God and man, and also the Son of God, celestially begotten, on purpose to be sacrificed, because they say that Eve in her longing had eaten an apple.

Putting aside everything that might excite laughter by its absurdity, or detestation by its prophaneness, and confining ourselves merely to an examination of the parts, it is impossible to conceive a story more derogatory to the Almighty, more inconsistent with his wisdom, more contradictory to his power, than this story is.

In order to make for it a foundation to rise upon, the inventors were under the necessity of giving to the being whom they call Satan a power equally as great, if not greater, than they attribute to the Almighty. . . .

They represent (Satan) as having compelled the Almighty to the *direct necessity* either of surrendering the whole of the creation to the government and sovereignty of this Satan, or of capitulating for its redemption by coming down upon earth, and exhibiting himself upon a cross in the shape of a man.

Had the inventors of this story told it the contrary way, that is, had they represented the Almighty as compelling Satan to exhibit *himself* on a cross, in the shape of a snake, as a punishment for his new transgression, the story would have been less absurd, less contradictory. But, instead of this they make the transgressor triumph, and the Almighty fall. . . .

But if objects for gratitude and admiration are our desire, do they not present themselves every hour to our eyes? Do we not see a fair creation prepared to receive us the instant we are born—a world furnished to our hands, that cost us nothing? Is it we that light up the sun; that pour down the rain; and fill the earth with abundance? Whether we sleep or wake, the vast machinery of the universe still goes on. Are those things, and the blessings they indicate in future, nothing to us? Can our gross feelings be excited by no other subjects than tragedy and suicide? Or is the gloomy pride of man become so intolerable, that nothing can flatter it but a sacrifice of the Creator? . . .

Whenever we read the obscene stories, the voluptuous debaucheries, the cruel and torturous executions, the unrelenting vindictiveness, with which more than half the Bible is filled, it would be more consistent that we called it the word of a demon, than the Word of God. It is a history of wickedness, that has served to corrupt and brutalize mankind; and, for my own part, I sincerely detest it, as I detest everything that is cruel. . . .

Thus much for the Bible; I now go on to the book called the New Testament. The *New Testament*! that is, the new Will, as if there could be two wills of the Creator. . . .

The manner in which (Jesus) was apprehended shews that he was not much known at that time; and it shews also that the meetings he then held with his followers were in secret; and that he had given over or suspended preaching publicly. Judas could no otherways betray him than by giving information where he was, and pointing him out to the officers that went to arrest him; and the reason for employing and paying Judas to do this could arise only from the causes already mentioned, that of his not being much known, and living concealed.

The idea of his concealment, not only agrees very ill with his reputed divinity, but associates with it something of pusillanimity; and his being betrayed, or in other words, his being apprehended, on the information of one of his followers, shews that he did not intend to be crucified. . . .

If Jesus Christ was the being which those mythologists tell us he was, and that he came into this world to *suffer*, which is a word they sometimes use instead of to die, the only real suffering he would have endured would have been *to live*. His existence here was a state of exilement or transportation from heaven, and the way back to his original country was to die. In fine, everything in this strange system is the reverse of what it pretends to be. It is the reverse of truth, and I become so tired of examining into its inconsistencies and absurdities, that I hasten to the conclusion of it, in order to proceed to something better. . . .

(T)he internal evidence is, that the theory or doctrine of redemption has for its basis an idea of pecuniary justice, and not that of moral justice.

If I owe a person money, and cannot pay him, and he threatens to put me in prison, another person can take the debt upon himself, and pay it for me. But if I have committed a crime, every circumstance of the case is changed. Moral justice cannot take the innocent for the guilty even if the innocent would offer itself. To suppose justice to do this, is to destroy the principle of its existence, which is the thing itself. It is then no longer justice. It is indiscriminate revenge.

This single reflection will shew that the doctrine of redemption is founded on a mere pecuniary idea corresponding to that of a debt which another person might pay; and as this pecuniary idea corresponds again with the system of second redemptions, obtained through the means of money given to the Church for pardons, the probability is that the same persons fabricated both the one and the other of those theories; and that, in truth, there is no such thing as redemption; that it is fabulous; and that man stands in the same relative condition with his Maker he ever did stand, since man existed; and that it is his greatest consolation to think so.

(In the case of devoutness, the Christian) consumes his life in grief, or the affectation of it. His prayers are reproaches. His humility is ingratitude. He calls himself a worm, and the fertile earth a dunghill; and all the blessings of life by the thankless name of vanities. He despises the choicest gift of God to man, the *gift of reason*; and having endeavored to force upon himself the belief of a system against which reason revolts, he ungratefully calls it *human reason*, as if man could give reason to himself. ...

It is only in the creation that all our ideas and conceptions of a *WORD of God can unite*. ... It does not depend upon the will of man whether it shall be published or not; it publishes itself from one end of the earth to the other. It preaches to all nations and to all worlds; and this *word of God* reveals to man all that is necessary for man to know of God.

Do we want to contemplate his power? We see it in the immensity of the creation. Do we want to contemplate his wisdom? We see it in the unchangeable order by which the incomprehensible Whole is governed. Do we want to contemplate his munificence? We see it in the abundance with which he fills the earth. Do we want to contemplate his mercy? We see it in his not withholding that abundance even from the unthankful. In fine, do we want to know what God is? Search not the book called the scripture, which any human hand might make, but the scripture called the Creation.

The only idea man can affix to the name of God, is that of a *first cause*, the cause of all things. And, incomprehensibly difficult as it is for a man to conceive what a first cause is, he arrives at the belief of it, from the tenfold greater difficulty of disbelieving it. ...

In like manner of reasoning, everything we behold carries in itself the internal evidence that it did not make itself. Every man is an evidence to himself, that he did not make himself; neither could his father make himself, nor his grandfather, nor any of his race. ...

It is only by the exercise of reason, that man can discover God. Take away that reason, and he would be incapable of understanding anything; and in this case it would be just as consistent to read even the book called the Bible to a horse as to a man. How then is it that those people pretend to reject reason?

Almost the only parts in the book called the Bible, that convey to us any idea of God, are some chapters in Job, and the 19th Psalm; I recollect no other. Those parts are true *deistical* compositions, for they treat of the *Deity* through his works. They take the book of Creation as the word of God; they refer to no other book; and all the inferences they make are drawn from that volume. . . .

As to the Christian system of faith, it appears to me as a species of atheism; a sort of religious denial of God. It professes to believe in a man rather than in God. It is a compound made up chiefly of manism with but little deism, and is as near to atheism as twilight is to darkness. It introduces between man and his Maker an opaque body, which it calls a redeemer, as the moon introduces her opaque self between the earth and the sun, and it produces by this means a religious or an irreligious eclipse of light. It has put the whole orbit of reason into shade. . . .

That which is now called natural philosophy, embracing the whole circle of science, of which astronomy occupies the chief place, is the study of the works of God, and of the power and wisdom of God in his works, and is the true theology.

As to the theology that is now studied in its place, it is the study of human opinions and of human fancies *concerning* God. It is not the study of God himself in the works that he has made, but in the works or writings that man has made; and it is not among the least of the mischiefs that the Christian system has done to the world, that it has abandoned the original and beautiful system of theology, like a beautiful innocent, to distress and reproach, to make room for the hag of superstition. . . .

It is a fraud of the Christian system to call the sciences *human invention*; it is only the application of them that is human. Every science has for its basis a system of principles as fixed and unalterable as those by which the universe is regulated and governed. Man cannot make principles, he can only discover them. . . .

All the properties of a triangle exist independently of the figure, and existed before any triangle was drawn or thought of by man. Man had no more to do in the formation of these properties or principles, than he had to do in making the laws by which the heavenly bodies move; and therefore the one must have the same divine origin as the other.

In the same manner as, it may be said, that man can make a triangle, so also, may it be said, he can make the mechanical instrument called a lever. But the principle by which the lever acts, is a thing distinct from the instrument, and would exist if the instrument did not; it attaches itself to the instrument after it is made; the instrument, therefore, can act no otherwise than it does act; neither can all the efforts of human invention make it act otherwise. That which, in all such cases, man calls the *effect* is no other than the principle itself rendered perceptible to the senses.

Since, then, man cannot make principles, from whence did he gain a knowledge of them, so as to be able to apply them, not only to things on earth, but to ascertain the motion of bodies so immensely distant from him as all the heavenly bodies are? From whence, I ask, *could* he gain that knowledge but from the study of the true theology?

It is the structure of the universe that has taught this knowledge to man. That structure is an ever-existing exhibition of every principle upon which every part of mathematical science is founded. . . .

The Almighty lecturer, by displaying the principles of science in the structure of the universe, has invited man to study and to imitation. It is as if he had said to the inhabitants of this globe that we call ours, "I have made an earth for man to dwell upon, and I have rendered the starry heavens visible, to teach him science and the arts. He can now provide for his own comfort AND LEARN FROM MY MUNIFICENCE TO ALL TO BE KIND TO EACH OTHER."

Of what use is it, unless it be to teach man something, that his eye is endowed with the power of beholding, to an incomprehensible distance, an immensity of worlds revolving in the ocean of space? . . .

It is only by contemplating what he calls the starry heavens, as the book and school of science, that he discovers any use in their being visible to him, or any advantage resulting from his immensity of vision. But when he contemplates the subject in this light, he sees an additional motive for saying, that *nothing was made in vain*; for in vain would be this power of vision if it taught man nothing. . . .

. . . It is in the knowledge of the things that science and philosophy teach that learning consists. . . .

. . . It is . . . true that the age of ignorance commenced with the Christian system. There was more knowledge in the world before that period, than for many centuries afterwards; and as to religious knowledge, the Christian system, as already said, was only another species of mythology; and the mythology to which it succeeded, was a corruption of an ancient system of theism. . . .

It is an inconsistency scarcely possible to be credited, that anything should exist, under the name of a religion, that held it to be *irreligious* to study and contemplate the structure of the universe that God had made. But the fact is too well established to be denied. The event that served more than any other to break the first link in this long chain of despotic ignorance, is that known by the name of the Reformation by Luther. From that time, though it does not appear to have made any part of the intention of Luther, or of those who are called Reformers, the Sciences began to revive, and Liberality, their natural associate, began to appear. This was the only public good the Reformation did; for, with respect to religious good, it might as well not have taken place. The mythology still continued the same; and a multiplicity of National Popes grew out of the downfall of the Pope of Christendom. . . .

It seems as if parents of the christian profession were ashamed to tell their children anything about the principles of their religion. They sometimes instruct them in morals, and talk to them of the goodness of what they call Providence. . . . But the christian story of God the Father putting his son to death, or employing people to do it, (for that is the plain language of the story,) cannot be told by a parent to a child; and to tell him that it was done to make mankind happier and better, is making the story still worse; as if mankind could be improved by the example of murder; and to tell him that all this is a mystery, is only making an excuse for the incredibility of it.

How different is this to the pure and simple profession of Deism! The true Deist has but one Deity; and his religion consists in contemplating the power, wisdom, and benignity of the Deity in his works, and in endeavouring to imitate him in everything moral, scientifical, and mechanical. . . .

But, in the midst of those reflections (concerning the possibility that there might be a plurality of worlds created by God), what are we to think of the christian system of faith that forms itself upon the idea of only one world, and that of no greater extent, as is before shewn, than twenty-five thousand miles. An extent which a man, walking at the rate of three miles an hour for twelve hours in the day, could he keep on in a circular direction, would walk entirely round in less than two years. Alas! what is this to the mighty ocean of space, and the almighty power of the Creator!

From whence then could arise the solitary and strange conceit that the Almighty, who had millions of worlds equally dependent on his protection, should quit the care of all the rest, and come to die in our world, because, they say, one man and one woman had eaten an apple! And on the other hand, are we to suppose that every world in the boundless creation had an Eve, an apple, a serpent, and a redeemer? In this case, the person who is irreverently called the Son of God, and sometimes God himself, would have nothing else to do than travel from would to world, in an endless succession of death with scarcely a momentary interval of life. . . .

Having thus shewn the irreconcilable inconsistencies between the real word of God existing in the universe, and that which is called *the word of God*, as shewn to us in a printed book that any man might make, I proceed to speak of the three principal means that have been employed in all ages, and perhaps in all countries, to impose upon mankind.

Those three means are Mystery, Miracle, and Prophecy. The two first are incompatible with true religion, and the third ought always to be suspected.

With respect to Mystery, every thing we behold is, in one sense, a mystery to us. Our own existence is a mystery: the whole vegetable world is a mystery. We cannot account how it is that an acorn, when put into the ground, is made to develop itself and become an oak. We know not how it is that the seed we sow unfolds and multiplies itself, and returns to us such an abundant interest for so small a capital.

The fact however, as distinct from the operating cause, is not a mystery, because we see it; and we know also the means we are to use, which is no other than putting the seed in the ground. We know, therefore, as much as in necessary for us to know; and that part of the operation that we do not know, and which if we did, we could not perform, the Creator takes upon himself and performs it for us. We are, therefore, better off than if we had been let into the secret and left to do it for ourselves.

But though every created thing is, in this sense, a mystery, the word mystery cannot be applied to a *moral truth*, any more than obscurity can be applied to light. The God in whom we believe is a God of moral truth, and not a God of mystery or obscurity. Mystery is the antagonist of truth. It is a fog of human invention that obscures truth, and represents it in distortion. Truth never involps *itself* in mystery; and the mystery in which it is at any time enveloped, is the work of its antagonist, and never of itself.

Religion, therefore, being the belief of a God, and the practice of moral truth, cannot have connection with mystery. The belief of a God, so far from having anything of mystery in it, is of all beliefs the most easy, because it arises to us, as is before observed, out of necessity. And the practice of moral truth, or, in other words, a practical imitation of the moral goodness of God, is no other than our acting towards each other as he acts benignly towards all. We cannot *serve* God in the manner we serve those who cannot do without such service; and, therefore, the only idea we can have of serving God, is that of contributing to the happiness of the living creation that God has made. This cannot be done by retiring ourselves from the society of the world and spending a recluse life in selfish devotion.

The very nature and design of religion, if I may so express it, prove even to demonstration that it must be free from every thing of mystery, and unincumbered with every thing that is mysterious. . . .

In the same sense that everything may be said to be a mystery, so also may it be said that everything is a miracle, and that no one thing is a greater miracle than another. . . . To an almighty power it is no more difficult to make (one thing) than another, and no more difficult to make a million worlds than to make one. Every thing, therefore, is a miracle, in one sense; whilst, in the other sense, there is no such thing as a miracle. It is a miracle when compared to our power, and to our comprehension. It is not a miracle compared to the power that performs it. . . .

Of all the modes of evidence that ever were invented to obtain belief to any system or opinion to which the name of religion has been given, that of miracle, however successful the imposition may have been, is the most inconsistent. For, in the first place, whenever recourse is had to show, for the purpose of procuring that belief (for a miracle, under any idea of the word, is a show) it implies a lameness or weakness in the doctrine that is preached. And, in the second place, it is degrading the Almighty into the character of a showman, playing tricks to amuse and make the people stare and wonder. It is also the most equivocal sort of evidence that can be set up; for the belief is not to depend upon the thing called a miracle, but upon the credit of the reporter, who says that he saw it; and, therefore, the thing, were it true, would have no better chance of being believed than if it were a lie. . . .

. . . We have never seen, in our time, nature go out of her course; but we have good reason to believe that millions of lies have been told in the same time; it is, therefore, at least millions to one, that the reporter of a miracle tells a lie.

The story of the whale swallowing Jonah, though a whale is large enough to do it, borders greatly on the marvellous; but it would have approached nearer to the idea of a miracle, if Jonah had swallowed the whale. In this, which may serve for all cases of miracles, the matter would decide itself as before stated, namely, Is it more probable that a man should have swallowed a whale, or told a lie? . . .

If by a prophet we are to suppose a man to whom the Almighty communicated some event that it would take place in future, either there were such men, or there were not. If there were, it is consistent to believe that the event so communicated would be told in terms that could be understood, and not related in such a loose and obscure manner as to be out of the comprehension of those that heard it, and so equivocal as to fit almost any circumstance, that might happen afterwards. It is conceiving very irreverently of the Almighty, to suppose that he would deal in the jesting manner with mankind; yet all the things called prophecies in the book of the Bible come under this description.

But it is with Prophecy as it is with Miracle. It could not answer the purpose even if it were real. Those to whom a prophecy should be told could not tell whether the man prophesied or lied, or whether it had been revealed to him, or whether he conceited it; and if the thing that he prophesied, or pretended to prophesy, should happen, or something like it, among the multitude of things that are daily happening, nobody could again know whether he foreknew it, or guessed at it, or whether it was accidental. A prophet, therefore, is a character useless and unnecessary; and the safe side of the case is to guard against being imposed upon, by not giving credit to such relations.

Upon the whole, Mystery, Miracle, and Prophecy, are appendages that belong to fabulous and not to true religion.

Study Questions

1. To what evidence can you point in Franklin's *Autobiography* to support the familiar claim that he is the quintessential example of the American self-made man or woman? Be specific.

2. Critics and interpreters of *The Autobiography* sometimes complain that Franklin does very little to reveal much about his "inner" self. What does this complaint mean, and is Franklin guilty as charged? Explain, and support your answer.

3. Describe Franklin's religious beliefs. In what sense are these beliefs congruent with those of eighteenth-century American Christians? In what sense are his beliefs different? Develop and defend your answer.

4. Does Franklin's reputation for thrift and industry square with his decision to retire from labor and commerce at age forty-two? Explain, and defend your position.

5. What are Thomas Paine's fundamental objections in *The Age of Reason, Part I,* to appeals to Christians to miracles and prophecies? Explain, and defend your answer.

6. Why does Paine discount revelation as evidence of God's presence and activities in the world and affairs of human beings? Explain, and defend your answer.

7. Paine describes himself as a deist or advocate for rational religion. In what ways are Paine's religious beliefs based on reason and on what he finds in the natural world? Be specific and defend your answer.

Suggestions for Further Reading

Aldridge, A. Owen. *Thomas Paine's American Ideology*. Newark: University of Delaware Press, 1984.

Allen, Ethan. *Reason the only Oracle of Man*. Introduction by John Pell. New York: Kraus Reprints, 1970.

Brands, H. W. *The First American: the Life and Times of Benjamin Franklin*. New York: Doubleday, 2000.

Breitwieser, Mitchell Robert. *Cotton Mather and Benjamin Franklin: The Price of Representative Personality*. Cambridge: Cambridge University Press, 1984.

Cohen, I. B. *Benjamin Franklin: Scientist and Statesman*. New York: Charles Scribner's Sons, 1975.

Cohen, I. B. "Benjamin Franklin: A Scientist in the World of Public Affairs." In *Science and the Founding Fathers: Science in the Political Thought of Jefferson, Franklin, Adams, and Madison*. New York: W.W. Norton, 1995.

Conkin, Paul K. "Benjamin Franklin: Science and Morals." In *Puritans and Pragmatists: Eight Eminent Thinkers*. New York: Dodd, Mead & Company, 1968.

Conner, Paul W. *Poor Richard's Politicks: Benjamin Franklin and His New American Order*. New York: Oxford University Press, 1965.

Dennett, Daniel C. *Darwin's Dangerous Idea: Evolution and the Meanings of Life*. New York: Simon and Schuster, 1995.

Franklin, Benjamin. *The Autobiography and Other Writings*. Edited by L. Jesse Lemisch. New York: Signet Classic, 1961.

Franklin, Benjamin. *The Autobiography of Benjamin Franklin*. Edited by Leonard W. Labaree, Ralph L. Ketcham, Helen C. Boatfield, and Helene H. Fineman. New Haven: Yale University Press, 1964.

Franklin, Benjamin. "Criticism." In *Benjamin Franklin's Autobiography*. Edited by J. A. Leo Lemay and P. M. Zall, New York: W.W. Norton, 1986.

Fruchtman, Jack, Jr. *Thomas Paine and the Religion of Nature*. Baltimore: Johns Hopkins University Press, 1993.

Gay, Peter. *The Enlightenment: An Interpretation, The Rise of Modern Paganism.* New York: Alfred A. Knopf, 1966.

Hume, David. *Dialogues Concerning Natural Religion,* second edition. Edited by Richard H. Popkin. Indianapolis, Ind.: Hackett Publishing, 1998.

Lawrence, D. H. "Benjamin Franklin." In *Studies in Classic American Literature.* New York: T. Seltzer, 1923.

Paine, Thomas. *The Age of Reason, Part I,* second edition. Edited by Aulburey Castell. Indianapolis, Ind.: Library of Liberal Arts, 1957.

Van Doren, Carl. *Benjamin Franklin.* New York: Viking Press, 1938.

Chapter 3

The New England Transcendentalists
Ralph Waldo Emerson and Henry David Thoreau

Although there were several men and women who are counted among the New England Transcendentalists of the 1830s and 1840s, the two whose reputations endure are Ralph Waldo Emerson (1803–1882) and Henry David Thoreau (1817–1862). Emerson was born in Boston. After his father's death, the burden of taking care of their mother and sister fell to the eight-year-old Emerson and his four brothers. Emerson became a student at Harvard College and Divinity School (1817–1829), and following his graduation became pastor of Boston's Second Unitarian Church. In the same year (1829) he married Ellen Tucker, who died in 1831. Deeply affected by Ellen's early death and perhaps by the loss of traditional Christian faith, Emerson resigned his position in 1832 and spent a year traveling in Europe. After returning to the United States, he became a prominent and successful public lecturer and remarried in 1835. He and Lydia Jackson settled in Concord and reared four children, although their first son Waldo died before his sixth birthday.

From 1842 to 1844, Emerson edited *The Dial*, the publication of the New England Transcendental Club; however, neither *The Dial* nor the Club itself lasted very long. Common philosophical views and attitudes, not meetings and editorial responsibilities, tied Emerson to others. He spent the balance of his life writing essays and poetry, lecturing, traveling, and concerning himself with social reform—including, especially, the entrenched problem of slavery. His last decade was a period of deepening senility. Emerson died at home of pneumonia, April 27, 1882.

Because many themes emerge from carefully reading Emerson's principal essays and lectures, one is pressed to claim that any single set of them constitutes the essence of his philosophical thought. But that said, one can still suggest a few features that are never far from the particular message of any major lecture or essay. Whether, therefore, one reads Emerson's *Nature* (1836), "The American Scholar" (1837), the "Divinity School Address" (1838), "Self-Reliance" (1841), or almost any of his other philosophical writings, he or she finds an emphasis on individual value and dignity, a vigorous plea for personal independence, hints or declarations that every human being, as part of the Over-Soul, is divine and thus able to enjoy unerring intuitions of ultimate facts and values. These facts and values, revealed to us through Emersonian Reason, show us what lurks deep behind the world of appearances, that is, a world in which most of us perpetually dwell and a world that cannot exhibit—because it does not include—the truth, goodness, and beauty that make life worth living. This world, which bombards our conventional senses and which makes ordinary demands on it, is the place that philosophical empiricists, notably John Locke, call home. Emerson's approach to empiricism (the realm of practical understanding and activity, not metaphysical intuition) was always adversarial. As he saw things, because empiricists were convinced that there is nothing in the intellect that does not first confront our five senses, they routinely reject as nonsense the realm that Reason alone discerns.

Beyond metaphysical themes, Emerson also believed that the potential of every human being, as divine and as capable of remarkable insights and attainments, must show itself in independent thought and action. This is the clarion call that helps us to situate Emerson in the development of American philosophy. In a direct and uncomplicated sense, Emerson insists that we as individuals and as citizens of a young and vigorous new nation must free ourselves from dependence on the past and on traditional models of European "excellence." His recurrent lament, expressed so forcefully in the opening paragraph of *Nature*, is that we have yet to emancipate ourselves culturally and artistically from England and the rest of Western Europe. He wonders why we have not yet demanded of ourselves and of the United States an intellectual, aesthetic, and religious independence that matches the successful demand for political and economic independence of July 4, 1776.

The irony in Emerson's philosophy is that as he insists upon freedom from the past and from the Old World, a good deal of his thinking was shaped by what he was able to glean from reading the works of Europeans such as Immanuel Kant, Samuel Taylor Coleridge, William Wordsworth, and the mystical Swedenborg. One cannot, however, indict the content of a philosophy simply on the grounds that it is in some measure derivative. If, therefore, Emerson is not always able in practice to act on what he preaches, his message of self-reliance at the individual and national levels stands at the center of what makes him and other New England Transcendentalists, such as Thoreau, so important to understanding the character and history of American philosophy and speculative thought.

Thoreau (1817–1862) spent most of his life in Concord. He studied at Harvard and worked for a while with his father as a pencil manufacturer. Later he worked briefly as a kind of handyman for Emerson and for Emerson's brother William as a tutor to his children. Thoreau was drawn to Transcendentalism during his senior year at Harvard (1837) and participated in the activities of the Transcendental Club. He also wrote occasional essays for *The Dial*. Thoreau's interests, apart from his (frustrated) efforts to marry Ellen Sewall, were maintaining the untrammeled beauty and interpreting the unspoken message of nature, objecting to governmental intrusions in one's private life and, like Emerson, speaking out against America's unresolved injustices, especially slavery and the imposition of onerous taxes.

Even though Thoreau kept a journal, to which he regularly contributed entries from 1837 to 1861, he is clearly best known as the author of *Walden* (1854). It is probably safe to say that many know Thoreau only as its author and far fewer have ever read his "Resistance to Civil Government" (1849). That *Walden* is a classic piece of American literature and reflective prose is indisputable. That "Resistance to Civil Government" is a pioneering document in American libertarianism is also the case. Still, one can fairly wonder how a literary classic and insistence upon strictly limited government, which was far from unique in the middle decades of the nineteenth century, justifies including Thoreau in an anthology on American philosophy. The answer is reasonably simple.

The setting for *Walden* is the now famous pond not far from Concord. Thoreau's account is of the two years (1845–1847) he lived on the fringes of the pond, not geographically remote from civilization but socially, practically, intellectually, and emotionally "far from the madding crowd." *Walden* is, then, a literary embodiment of a New England Transcendentalist's determination to do more than chant a litany to self-mastery, independence, and proximity to nature as a manifestation of God. More than that, *Walden* is not only a directive to become self-reliant or to exhibit independence by retreating from society and the help of those with whom one is socially involved. Nor is it merely Thoreau's record of a prolonged stay in the Massachusetts woods; rather, it is a "how-to" book that answers the question, "How can I do more than celebrate the virtues of an autonomous and authentic life; how do I live it?" Thoreau's answer is to live the life of a mostly solitary man who seeks comfort and happiness on the frontiers of civilization. But the more general answer that applies to all of us is that a self-sufficient life—a life in which we respect nature rather than react to it as an acquisitive adversary—can be practiced by those who take the trouble to chart their own course.

In the end, therefore, the appeal of *Walden* is intended to reach beyond its sturdy and elegant prose. This book artfully integrates a number of messages, but the overriding message is populist and democratic. Everyone who wishes and also strives to be human, in the fullest sense of the term "human," can manage the task. The key, however, is to recognize that the first step in the process is also its consummation, since one cannot be truly human unless one becomes and remains independent. At the same time, one cannot become independent merely by acting out past, even inspirational, models from history and literature. Here, as in so many other instances that wed them philosophically, Thoreau and Emerson concur.

One must, on the assumption that Thoreau has something to offer throughout *Walden*, act on one's own, trust one's insights, and shape a unique path that emancipates the essential man or woman from the artifice, expectations, and suffocating impositions of society. This can happen in the woods or wilderness of a vast continent, in a remote corner of a ship sailing the high seas, or in the self-protecting and hard-won privacy of a cacophonous city. The shores of Walden Pond were Thoreau's choice for discovering and remaking himself. His readers are left to make their own choices. Far less important than choice of an exterior place to begin their inner journey is the choice to begin and to see the task of self-discovery or self-recovery to its close. Perhaps this, more than anything else, is the salient message of *Walden*, a piece of American pastoral literature whose narrative reaches far beyond the peaceful woods of New England.

The American Scholar (1837)

RALPH WALDO EMERSON

... [T]here is One Man,—present to all particular men only partially, or through one faculty; and ... you must take the whole society to find the whole man. Man is not a farmer or a professor, or an engineer, but he is all. Man is priest, and scholar, and statesman, and producer, and soldier. In the *divided* or social state these functions are parcelled out to individuals, each of whom aims to do his stint of the joint work, whilst each other performs his. The fable implies that the individual, to possess himself, must sometimes return from his own labor to embrace all the other laborers. But, unfortunately, this original unit, this fountain of power, has been so distributed to multitudes, has been so minutely subdivided and peddled out, that it is spilled into drops, and cannot be gathered. The state of society is one in which the members have suffered amputation from the trunk, and strut about so many walking monsters,—a good finger, a neck, a stomach, an elbow, but never a man.

Man is thus metamorphosed into a thing, into many things. The planter, who is Man sent out into the field to gather food, is seldom cheered by any idea of the true dignity of his ministry. He sees his bushel and his cart, and nothing beyond, and sinks into the farmer instead of Man on the farm. The tradesman scarcely ever gives an ideal worth to his work, but is ridden by the routine of his craft, and the soul is subject to dollars. The priest becomes a form; the attorney a statute-book; the mechanic a machine; the sailor a rope of the ship.

In this distribution of functions the scholar is the delegated intellect. In the right state he is *Man Thinking*. In the degenerate state, when the victim of society, he tends to become a mere thinker, or still worse, the parrot of other men's thinking.

In this view of him, as Man Thinking, the theory of his office is contained. Him Nature solicits with all her placid, all her monitory pictures; him the past instructs; him the future invites. ... In life, too often, the scholar errs with mankind and forfeits his privilege. Let us see him in his school, and consider him in reference to the main influences he receives.

The first in time and the first in importance of the influences upon the mind is that of nature. ... Every day, men and women, conversing—beholding and beholden. The scholar is he of all men whom this spectacle most engages. He must settle its value in his mind. What is nature to him? There is never a beginning, there is never an end, to the inexplicable continuity of this web of God, but always circular power returning into itself. Therein it resembles his own spirit, whose beginning, whose ending, he never can find,—so entire, so boundless. . . .

. . . He shall see that nature is the opposite of the soul, answering to it part for part. One is seal and one is print. Its beauty is the beauty of his own mind. Its laws are the laws of his own mind. Nature then becomes to him the measure of his attainments. So much of nature as he is ignorant of, so much of his own mind does he not yet possess. And, in fine, the ancient precept, "Know thyself," and the modern precept, "Study nature," become at last one maxim.

II. The next great influence into the spirit of the scholar is the mind of the Past,—in whatever form, whether of literature, of art, of institutions, that mind is inscribed. Books are the best type of the influence of the past, and perhaps we shall get at the truth,—learn the amount of this influence more conveniently,—by considering their value alone.

The theory of books is noble. The scholar of the first age received into him the world around; brooded thereon; gave it the new arrangement of his own mind, and uttered it again. It came into him life; it went out from him truth. It came to him short-lived actions; it went out from him immortal thoughts. It came to him business; it went from him poetry. It was dead fact; now, it is quick thought. It can stand, and it can go. It now endures, it now flies, it now inspires. Precisely in proportion to the depth of mind from which it issued, so high does it soar, so long does it sing.

. . . But none is quite perfect. . . . Each age, it is found, must write its own books; or rather, each generation for the next succeeding. The books of an older period will not fit this.

Yet hence arises a grave mischief. The sacredness which attaches to the act of creation, the act of thought, is transferred to the record. The poet chanting was felt to be a divine man: henceforth the chant is divine also. The writer was a just and wise spirit: henceforward it is settled the book is perfect; as love of the hero corrupts into worship of his statue. Instantly the book becomes noxious: the guide is a tyrant. The sluggish and perverted mind of the multitude, slow to open to the incursions of Reason, having once so opened, having once received this book, stands upon it, and makes an outcry if it is disparaged. Colleges are built on it. Books are written on it by thinkers, not by Man Thinking; by men of talent, that is, who start wrong, who set out from accepted dogmas, not from their own sight of principles. Meek young men grow up in libraries, believing it their duty to accept the views which Cicero, which Locke, which Bacon, have given; forgetful that Cicero, Locke, and Bacon were only young men in libraries when they wrote these books.

Hence, instead of Man Thinking, we have the bookworm. Hence the book-learned class, who value books, as such; not as related to nature and the human constitution, but as making a sort of Third Estate with the world and the soul. Hence the restorers of readings, the emendators, the bibliomaniacs of all degrees.

Books are the best of things, well used; abused, among the worst. What is the right use? What is the one end which all means go to effect? They are for nothing but to inspire. I had better never see a book than to be warped by its attraction clean out of my own orbit, and made a satellite instead of a system. The one thing in the world, of value, is the active soul. This every man is entitled to; this every man contains within him, although in almost all men obstructed and as yet unborn. The soul active sees absolute truth and utters truth, or creates. In this action it is genius. . . . In its essence it is progressive. The book, the college, the school of art, the institution of any kind, stop with some past utterance of genius. This is good, say they, let us hold by this. They pin me down. They look backward and not forward. But genius looks forward: the eyes of man are set in his forehead, not in his hindhead: man hopes: genius creates. . . .

Undoubtedly there is a right way of reading, so it be sternly subordinated. Man Thinking must not be subdued by his instruments. Books are for the scholar's idle times. When he can read God directly, the hour is too precious to be wasted in other men's transcripts of their readings. But when the intervals of darkness come, as come they must,—when the sun is hid and the stars withdraw their shining,—we repair to the lamps which were kindled by their ray, to guide our steps to the East again, where the dawn is. . . .

Of course there is a portion of reading quite indispensable to a wise man. History and exact science he must learn by laborious reading. Colleges, in like manner, have their indispensable office,—to teach elements. But they can only highly serve us when they aim not to drill, but to create. . . .

III. There goes in the world a notion that the scholar should be a recluse, a valetudinarian,—as unfit for any handiwork or public labor as a penknife for an axe. The so-called "practical men" sneer at speculative men, as if, because they speculate or *see*, they could do nothing. I have heard it said that the clergy,—who are always, more universally than any other class, the scholars of their day,—are addressed as women; that the rough, spontaneous conversation of men they do not hear, but only a mincing and diluted speech. They are often virtually disfranchised; and indeed there are advocates for their celibacy. As far as this is true of the studious classes it is not just and wise. Action is with the scholar subordinate, but it is essential. Without it he is not yet man. Without it thought can never ripen into truth. . . . Inaction is cowardice, but there can be no scholar without the heroic mind. . . . Only so much do I know, as I have lived. Instantly we know whose words are loaded with life, and whose not.

The world,—this shadow of the soul, or *other me*,—lies wide around. Its attractions are the keys which unlock my thoughts and make me acquainted with myself. I run eagerly into this resounding tumult. . . . So much only of life as I know by experience, so much of the wilderness have I vanquished and planted, or so far have I extended my being, my dominion. I do not see how any man can afford, for the sake of his nerves and his nap, to spare any action in which he can partake. It is pearls and rubies to his discourse. Drudgery, calamity, exasperation, want, are instructors in eloquence and wisdom. The true scholar grudges every opportunity of action past by, as a loss of power. . . .

If it were only for a vocabulary, the scholar would be covetous of action. Life is our dictionary. Years are well spent in country labors; in town; in the insight into trades and manufactures; in frank intercourse with many men and women; in science; in art; to the one end of mastering in all their facts a language by which to illustrate and embody our perceptions. I learn immediately from any speaker how much he has already lived, through the poverty or the splendor of his speech. . . .

. . . Character is higher than intellect. Thinking is the function. Living is the functionary. . . . This is a total act. Thinking is a partial act. Let the grandeur of justice shine in his affairs. Let the beauty of affection cheer his lowly roof. . . .

I hear therefore with joy whatever is beginning to be said of the dignity and necessity of labor to every citizen. There is virtue yet in the hoe and the spade, for learned as well as for unlearned hands. And labor is everywhere welcome; always we are invited to work; only be this limitation observed, that a man shall not for the sake of wider activity sacrifice any opinion to the popular judgments and modes of action.

I have now spoken of the education of the scholar by nature, by books, and by action. It remains to say somewhat of his duties.

They are such as become Man Thinking. They may all be comprised in self-trust. The office of the scholar is to cheer, to raise, and to guide men by showing them facts amidst appearances. He plies the slow, unhonored, and unpaid task of observation. . . . In the long period of his preparation he must betray often all ignorance and shiftlessness in popular arts, incurring the disdain of the able who shoulder him aside. Long he must stammer in his speech; often forego the living for the dead. Worse yet, he must accept—how often!—poverty and solitude. . . . He is one who raises himself from private considerations and breathes and lives on public and illustrious thoughts. He is the world's eye. He is the world's heart. He is to resist the vulgar prosperity that retrogrades ever to barbarism, by preserving and communicating heroic sentiments, noble biographies, melodious verse, and the conclusions of history. . . .

These being his functions, it becomes him to feel all confidence in himself, and to defer never to the popular cry. He and he only knows the world. The world of any moment is the merest appearance. . . . For the instinct is sure, that prompts him to tell his brother what he thinks. He then learns that in going down into the secrets of his own mind he has descended into the secrets of all minds. . . .

In self-trust all the virtues are comprehended. Free should the scholar be,—free and brave. Free even to the definition of freedom, "without any hindrance that does not arise out of his own constitution." Brave; for fear is a thing which a scholar by his very function puts behind him. Fear always springs from ignorance. It is a shame to him if his tranquillity, amid dangerous times, arise from the presumption that like children and women his is a protected class; or if he seek a temporary peace by the diversion of his thoughts

from politics or vexed questions, hiding his head like an ostrich in the flowering bushes, peeping into microscopes, and turning rhymes, as a boy whistles
to keep his courage up. So is the danger a danger still; so is the fear worse.
Manlike let him turn and face it. . . .

. . . I believe man has been wronged; he has wronged himself. He has almost lost the light that can lead him back to his prerogatives. Men are become
of no account. Men in history, men in the world of to-day, are bugs, are spawn,
and are called "the mass" and "the herd." . . . They sun themselves in the great
man's light, and feel it to be their own element. They cast the dignity of man
from their downtrod selves upon the shoulders of a hero, and will perish to
add one drop of blood to make that great heart beat, those giant sinews combat and conquer. . . .

Men, such as they are, very naturally seek money or power; and power
because it is as good as money,—the "spoils," so called, "of office." And why
not? for they aspire to the highest, and this, in their sleep-walking, they dream
is highest. Wake them and they shall quit the false good and leap to the true,
and leave governments to clerks and desks. This revolution is to be wrought
by the gradual domestication of the idea of Culture. The main enterprise of the
world for splendor, for extent, is the upbuilding of a man. Here are the materials strewn along the ground. The private life of one man shall be a more illustrious monarchy, more formidable to its enemy, more sweet and serene in its
influence to its friend, than any kingdom in history. For a man, rightly viewed,
comprehendeth the particular natures of all men. Each philosopher, each bard,
each actor has only done for me, as by a delegate, what one day I can do for
myself. . . . It is one soul which animates all men.

. . . I ought not to delay longer to add what I have to say of nearer reference to the time and to this country. . . .

. . . If there is any period one would desire to be born in, is it not the age
of Revolution; when the old and the new stand side by side and admit of
being compared; when the energies of all men are searched by fear and by
hope; when the historic glories of the old can be compensated by the rich possibilities of the new era? This time, like all times, is a very good one, if we but
know what to do with it.

I read with some joy of the auspicious signs of the coming days, as they
glimmer already through poetry and art, through philosophy and science,
through church and state.

. . . The literature of the poor, the feelings of the child, the philosophy of
the street, the meaning of household life, are the topics of the time. It is a great
stride. It is a sign—is it not?—of new vigor when the extremities are made active, when currents of warm life run into the hands and the feet. . . . I embrace
the common, I explore and sit at the feet of the familiar, the low. Give me insight into to-day, and you may have the antique and future worlds. . . .

. . . Man is surprised to find that things near are not less beautiful and
wondrous than things remote. The near explains the far. The drop is a small
ocean. A man is related to all nature. . . .

Another sign of our times, also marked by an analogous political movement, is the new importance given to the single person. Every thing that tends to insulate the individual,—to surround him with barriers of natural respect, so that each man shall feel the world is his, and man shall treat with man as a sovereign state with a sovereign state,—tends to true union as well as greatness. ... Mr. President and Gentlemen, this confidence in the unsearched might of man belongs, by all motives, by all prophecy, by all preparation, to the American Scholar. We have listened too long to the courtly muses of Europe. The spirit of the American freeman is already suspected to be timid, imitative, tame. Public and private avarice make the air we breathe thick and fat. The scholar is decent, indolent, complaisant. See already the tragic consequence. The mind of this country, taught to aim at low objects, eats upon itself. There is no work for any but the decorous and the complaisant. ... Is it not the chief disgrace in the world, not to be an unit;—not to be reckoned one character;—not to yield that peculiar fruit which each man was created to bear, but to be reckoned in the gross, in the hundred, or the thousand, of the party, the section, to which we belong; and our opinion predicted geographically, as the north, or the south? Not so. ... We will walk on our own feet; we will work with our own hands; we will speak our own minds. The study of letters shall be no longer a name for pity, for doubt, and for sensual indulgence. The dread of man and the love of man shall be a wall of defence and a wreath of joy around all. A nation of men will for the first time exist, because each believes himself inspired by the Divine Soul which also inspires all men.

An Address, Divinity College (1838)

RALPH WALDO EMERSON

. . . One is constrained to respect the perfection of this world, in which our senses converse. How wide, how rich, what invitation from every property it gives to every faculty of man. . . .

But when the mind opens, and reveals the laws which traverse the universe, and makes things what they are, then shrinks the great world at once into a mere illustration and fable of his mind. What am I? and What is? asks the human spirit with a curiosity new-kindled, but never to be quenched. . . .

A more secret, sweet, and overpowering beauty appears to man when his heart and mind open to the sentiment of virtue. . . .

The sentiment of virtue is a reverence and delight in the presence of certain divine laws. It perceives that this homely game of life we play, covers, under what seem foolish details, principles that astonish. The child amidst his baubles is learning the action of light, motion, gravity, muscular force; and in the game of human life, love, fear, justice, appetite, man and God interact. These laws refuse to be adequately stated. They will not be written out on paper, or spoken by the tongue. They elude our persevering thought; yet we read them hourly in each other's faces, in each other's actions, in our own remorse. The moral traits which are all globed into every virtuous act and thought,—in speech, we must sever, and describe or suggest by painful enumeration of many particulars. Yet, as this sentiment is the essence of all religion, let me guide your eye to the precise objects of the sentiment, by an enumeration of some of those classes of facts in which this element is conspicuous.

The intuition of the moral sentiment is an insight of the perfection of the laws of the soul. These laws execute themselves. They are out of time, out of space, and not subject to circumstance. Thus, in the soul of man there is a justice whose retributions are instant and entire. He who does a good deed is instantly ennobled. He who does a mean deed is by the action itself contracted. He who puts off impurity, thereby puts on purity. If a man is at heart just, then in so far is he God; the safety of God, the immortality of God, the majesty of God, do enter into that man with justice. . . .

This sentiment is divine and deifying. It is the beatitude of man. It makes him illimitable. Through it the soul first knows itself. It corrects the capital mistake of the infant man, who seeks to be great by following the great, and hopes to derive advantages *from another*, by showing the fountain of all good to be in himself, and that he, equally with every man, is an inlet into the deeps of Reason. When he says, "I ought"; when love warns him; when he chooses, warned from on high, the good and the great deed,—then deep melodies wander through his soul from Supreme Wisdom. Then he can worship, and be enlarged by his worship; for he can never go behind this sentiment. . . .

This sentiment lies at the foundation of society, and successively creates all forms of worship. The principle of veneration never dies out. Man fallen into superstition, into sensuality, is never quite without the visions of the moral sentiment. In like manner all the expressions of this sentiment are sacred and permanent in proportion to their purity. The expressions of this sentiment affect us more than all other compositions. . . .

Meantime . . . it is guarded by one stern condition; this namely, it is an intuition. It cannot be received at second hand. Truly speaking, it is not instruction, but provocation, that I can receive from another soul. What he announces, I must find true in me, or wholly reject; and on his word, or as his second, be he who he may, I can accept nothing. On the contrary, the absence of this primary faith is the presence of degradation. As is the flood, so is the ebb. Let this faith depart, and the very words it spake, and the things it made, become false and hurtful. Then falls the church, the state, art, letters, life. The doctrine of the divine nature being forgotten, a sickness infects and dwarfs the constitution. Once man was all; now he is an appendage, a nuisance. And because the indwelling Supreme Spirit cannot wholly be got rid of, the doctrine of it suffers this perversion, that the divine nature is attributed to one or two persons, and denied to all the rest, and denied with fury. The doctrine of inspiration is lost: the base doctrine of the majority of voices usurps the place of the doctrine of the soul. Miracles, prophecy, poetry; the ideal of life, the holy life, exist as ancient history merely; they are not in the belief nor in the aspiration of society; but, when suggested, seem ridiculous. Life is comic or pitiful as soon as the high ends of being fade out of sight, and man becomes near-sighted, and can only attend to what addresses the senses. . . .

Jesus Christ belonged to the true race of prophets. He saw with open eye the mystery of the soul. Drawn by its severe harmony, ravished with its beauty, he lived in it, and had his being there. Alone in all history, he estimated the greatness of man. One man was true to what was in you and me. He saw that God incarnates himself in man, and evermore goes forth anew to take possession of his world. He said, in this jubilee of sublime emotion:—"I am divine. Through me, God acts; through me, speaks. Would you see God, see me; or, see thee, when thou also thinkest as I now think." But what distortion did his doctrine and memory suffer in the same, in the next, and the following ages! There is no doctrine of the Reason which will bear to be taught by the Understanding. The understanding caught this high chant from the poet's lips, and said, in the next age:—"This was Jehovah come down out of heaven. I will kill you if you say he was a man." The idioms of his language and the figures of his rhetoric have usurped the place of his truth; and churches are not built on his principles, but on his tropes. Christianity became a Mythus, as the poetic teaching of Greece and of Egypt, before. He spoke of miracles; for he felt that man's life was a miracle, and all that man doth, and he knew that this daily miracle shines, as the character ascends. But the word "miracle," as pronounced by Christian churches, gives a false impression; it is "monster." . . .

He felt respect for Moses and the prophets; but no unfit tenderness at postponing their initial revelations to the hour and the man that now is, to the eternal revelation in the heart. Thus was he a true man. Having seen that the law in us is commanding he would not suffer it to be commanded. . . . Thus is he, as I think, the only soul in history who has appreciated the worth of a man.

In this point of view we become very sensible of the first defect of historical Christianity. Historical Christianity has fallen into the error that corrupts all attempts to communicate religion. As it appears to us, and as it has appeared for ages, it is not the doctrine of the soul, but an exaggeration of the personal, the positive, the ritual. It has dwelt, it dwells, with noxious exaggeration about the *person* of Jesus. The soul knows no persons. It invites every man to expand to the full circle of the universe, and will have no preferences but those of spontaneous love. But by this Eastern monarchy of a Christianity, which indolence and fear have built, the friend of man is made the injurer of man. The manner in which his name is surrounded with expressions, which were once sallies of admiration and love, but are now petrified into official titles, kills all generous sympathy and liking. All who hear me, feel that the language that describes Christ to Europe and America is not the style of friendship and enthusiasm to a good and noble heart, but is appropriated and formal,—paints a demigod. . . .

That is always best which gives me to myself. The sublime is excited in me by the great stoical doctrine. Obey thyself. That which shows God in me, fortifies me. That which shows God out of me, makes me a wart and a wen. There is no longer a necessary reason for my being. Already the long shadows of untimely oblivion creep over me, and I shall decease forever. . . .

. . . To aim to convert a man by miracles is a profanation of the soul. A true conversion, a true Christ, is now, as always, to be made by the reception of the beautiful sentiments. . . . The time is coming when all men will see that the gift of God to the soul is not a vaunting, overpowering, excluding sanctity, but a sweet, natural goodness, a goodness like thine and mine, and that so invites thine and mine to be and to grow.

The injustice of the vulgar tone of preaching is not less flagrant to Jesus than to the souls which it profanes. The preachers do not see that they make his gospel not glad, and shear him of the locks of beauty and the attributes of heaven. . . . Now, do not degrade the life and dialogues of Christ out of the circle of his charm, by insulation and peculiarity. Let him lie as they befell, alive and warm, part of human life, and of the landscape, and of the cheerful day.

The second defect of the traditionary and limited way of using the mind of Christ is a consequence of the first; this, namely, that the Moral Nature, that law of laws, whose revelations introduce greatness, yea, God himself, into the open soul, is not explored as the fountain of the established teaching in society. Men have come to speak of the revelation as somewhat long ago given and done, as if God were dead. The injury to faith throttles the preacher, and the goodliest of institutions becomes an uncertain and inarticulate voice.

It is very certain that it is the effect of conversation with the beauty of the soul, to beget a desire and need to impart to others the knowledge and love. If utterance is denied, the thought lies like a burden on the man. Always the seer is a sayer. Somehow his dream is told; somehow he publishes it with solemn joy. . . .

The man enamored of this excellency becomes its priest or poet. The office is coeval with the world. But observe the condition, the spiritual limitation of the office. The spirit only can teach. . . . The man on whom the soul descends, through whom the soul speaks, alone can teach. Courage, piety, love, wisdom, can teach; and every man can open his door to these angels, and they shall bring him the gift of tongues. But the man who aims to speak as books enable, as synods use, as the fashion guides, and as interest commands, babbles. Let him hush. . . .

It is time that this ill-suppressed murmur of all thoughtful men against the famine of our churches; this moaning of the heart because it is bereaved of the consolation, the hope, the grandeur, that come alone out of the culture of the moral nature,—should be heard through the sleep of indolence and over the din of routine. This great and perpetual office of the preacher is not discharged. Preaching is the expression of the moral sentiment in application to the duties of life. In how many churches, by how many prophets . . . is man made sensible that he is an infinite soul; that the earth and heavens are passing into his mind; that he is drinking forever the soul of God? . . .

But now the priest's Sabbath has lost the splendor of nature; it is unlovely; we are glad when it is done; we can make, we do make, even sitting in our pews, a far better, holier, sweeter, for ourselves.

Wherever the pulpit is usurped by a formalist, then is the worshipper defrauded and disconsolate. We shrink as soon as the prayers begin, which do not uplift, but smite and offend us. . . .

Certainly there have been periods when, from the inactivity of the intellect on certain truths, a greater faith was possible in names and persons. The Puritans in England and America found in the Christ of the Catholic Church, and in the dogmas inherited from Rome, scope for their austere piety and their longings for civil freedom. But their creed is passing away, and none arises in its room. I think no man can go with his thoughts about him into one of our churches, without feeling that what hold the public worship had on men is gone, or going. It has lost its grasp on the affection of the good and the fear of the bad. . . . It is already beginning to indicate character and religion to withdraw from the religious meetings. . . .

My friends, in these two errors I think I find the causes of a decaying church and a wasting unbelief. And what greater calamity can fall upon a nation than the loss of worship? Then all things go to decay. Genius leaves the temple, to haunt the senate or the market. Literature becomes frivolous. Science is cold. The eye of youth is not lighted by the hope of other worlds, and age is without honor. Society lives to trifles, and when die we do not mention them.

. . . What in these desponding days can be done by us? The remedy is already declared in the ground of our complaint of the Church. We have contrasted the Church with the Soul. In the soul, then, let the redemption be sought. Wherever a man comes, there comes revolution. The old is for slaves. When a man comes, all books are legible, all things transparent, all religions are forms. He is religious. Man is the wonderworker. He is seen amid miracles. . . . The stationariness of religion; the assumption that the age of inspiration is past, that the Bible is closed; the fear of degrading the character of Jesus by representing him as a man,—indicate with sufficient clearness the falsehood of our theology. It is the office of a true teacher to show us that God is, not was; that He speaketh, not spake. The true Christianity—a faith like Christ's in the infinitude of man—is lost. . . .

Let me admonish you . . . to go alone; to refuse the good models, even those which are sacred in the imagination of men, and dare to love God without mediator or veil. . . . The imitator dooms himself to hopeless mediocrity. The inventor did it, because it was natural to him, and so in him it has a charm. In the imitator, something else is natural, and he bereaves himself of his own beauty, to come short of another man's.

Yourself a new-born bard of the Holy Ghost,—cast behind you all conformity, and acquaint men at first hand with Deity. Look to it first and only, that fashion, custom, authority, pleasure, and money are nothing to you . . . but live with the privilege of the immeasurable mind. . . . By trusting your own heart, you shall gain more confidence in other men. For all our penny-wisdom, for all our soul-destroying slavery to habit, it is not to be doubted that all men have sublime thoughts; that all men value the few real hours of life; they love to be heard; they love to be caught up into the vision of principles. . . . Discharge to men the priestly office, and, present or absent, you shall be followed with their love as by an angel. . . .

And now let us do what we can to rekindle the smouldering, nigh quenched fire on the altar. The evils of the Church that now is are manifest. The question returns, what shall we do? I confess, all attempts to project and establish a Cultus with new rites and forms seem to me in vain. Faith makes us, and not we it, and faith makes its own forms. All attempts to contrive a system are as cold as the new worship introduced by the French to the goddess of Reason. . . . Rather let the breath of new life be breathed by you through the forms already existing. For, if once you are alive, you shall find they shall become plastic and new. The remedy to their deformity is, first, Soul, and second, Soul, and evermore, Soul. . . .

Self-Reliance (1841)

Ralph Waldo Emerson

. . . To believe your own thought, to believe that what is true for you in your private heart is true for all men,—that is genius. Speak your latent conviction, and it shall be the universal sense; for always the inmost becomes the outmost—and our first thought is rendered back to us by the trumpets of the Last Judgment. Familiar as the voice of the mind is to each, the highest merit we ascribe to Moses, Plato and Milton is that they set at naught books and traditions, and spoke not what men, but what they thought. A man should learn to detect and watch that gleam of light which flashes across his mind from within, more than the luster of the firmament of bards and sages. Yet he dismisses without notice his thought, because it is his. In every work of genius we recognize our own rejected thoughts; they come back to us with a certain alienated majesty. Great works of art have no more affecting lesson for us than this. They teach us to abide by our spontaneous impression with good-humored inflexibility then most when the whole cry of voices is on the other side. Else to-morrow a stranger will say with masterly good sense precisely what we have thought and felt all the time, and we shall be forced to take with shame our own opinion from another. . . .

Trust thyself: every heart vibrates to that iron string. Accept the place the divine providence has found for you, the society of your contemporaries, the connexion of events. Great men have always done so, and confided themselves childlike to the genius of their age, betraying their perception that the Eternal was stirring at their heart, working through their hands, predominating in all their being. And we are now men, and must accept in the highest mind the same transcendent destiny; and not pinched in a corner, not cowards fleeing before a revolution, but redeemers and benefactors, pious aspirants to the noble clay under the Almighty effort let us advance on Chaos and the Dark. . . .

Whoso would be a man, must be a nonconformist. He who would gather immortal palms must not be hindered by the name of goodness, but must explore if it be goodness. Nothing is at last sacred but the integrity of your own mind. Absolve you to yourself, and you shall have the suffrage of the world. I remember an answer which when quite young I was prompted to make to a valued adviser who was wont to importune me with the dear old doctrines of the church. On my saying, What I have to do with the sacredness of traditions, if I live wholly from within? My friend suggested—"But these impulses may be from below, not from above." I replied, "They do not seem to me to be such; but if I am the devil's child, I will live then from the devil." No law can be sacred to me but that of my nature. Good and bad are but names very readily transferable to that or this; the only right is what is after my constitution; the only wrong what is against it. A man is to carry himself in the presence of all opposition as if every thing were titular and ephemeral but he. I am ashamed to think how easily we capitulate to badges and names, to large societies and dead institutions. Every decent and well-spoken individual affects and sways me more than is right. I ought to go upright and vital, and speak the rude truth in all ways. . . .

What I must do is all that concerns me, not what the people think. This rule, equally arduous in actual and in intellectual life, may serve for the whole distinction between greatness and meanness. It is the harder because you will always find those who think they know what is your duty better than you know it. It is easy in the world to live after the world's opinion; it is easy in solitude to live after our own; but the great man is he who in the midst of the crowd keeps with perfect sweetness the independence of solitude.

The objection to conforming to usages that have become dead to you is that it scatters your force. It loses your time and blurs the impression of your character. If you maintain a dead church, contribute to a dead Bible Society, vote with a great party either for the Government or against it, spread your table like base housekeepers,—under all these screens I have difficulty to detect the precise man you are. And of course so much force is withdrawn from your proper life. But do your thing, and I shall know you. Do your work, and you shall reinforce yourself. A man must consider what a blindman's-bluff is the game of conformity. If I know your sect I anticipate your argument. I hear a preacher announce for his text and topic the expediency of one of the institutions of his church. Do I not know beforehand that not possibly can he say a new and spontaneous word? Do I not know that with all this ostentation of examining the grounds of the institution he will do no such thing? Do I not know that he is pledged to himself not to look but at one side, the permitted side, not as a man, but as a parish minister? He is a retained attorney, and these airs of the bench are the emptiest affectation. Well, most men have bound their eyes with one or another handkerchief, and attached themselves to some one of these communities of opinion. This conformity makes them not false in a few particulars, authors of a few lies, but false in all particulars. Their every truth is not quite true. . . .

The other terror that scares us from self-trust is our consistency; a reverence for our past act or word because the eyes of others have no other data for computing our orbit than our past acts, and we are loath to disappoint them.

But why should you keep your head over your shoulder? Why drag about this monstrous corpse of your memory, lest you contradict somewhat you have stated in this or that public place? Suppose you should contradict yourself; what then? It seems to be a rule of wisdom never to rely on your memory alone, scarcely even in acts of pure memory, but to bring the past for judgment into the thousand-eyed present, and live ever in a new day. Trust your emotion. In your metaphysics you have denied personality to the Deity, yet when the devout motions of the soul come, yield to them heart and life, though they should clothe God with shape and color. Leave your theory, as Joseph his coat in the hand of the harlot, and flee.

A foolish consistency is the hobgoblin of little minds, adored by little statesmen and philosophers and divines. He may as well concern himself with his shadow on the wall. Out upon your guarded lips! Sew them up with pack-thread, do. Else if you would be a man speak what you think to-day in words as hard as cannon balls, and tomorrow speak what to-morrow thinks in hard words again, though it contradict every thing you said to-day. Ah, then, ex-claim the aged ladies, you shall be sure to be misunderstood! Misunderstood! It is a right fool's word. Is it so bad then to be misunderstood? Pythagoras was misunderstood, and Socrates, and Jesus, and Luther, and Copernicus, and Galileo, and Newton, and every pure and wise spirit that ever took flesh. To be great is to be misunderstood. . . .

I hope in these days we have heard the last of conformity and consisten-cy. Let the words be gazetted and ridiculous henceforward. . . . Every true man is a cause, a country, and an age; requires infinite spaces and numbers and time fully to accomplish his thought;—and posterity seems to follow his steps as a procession. A man Caesar is born, and for ages after we have a Roman Empire. Christ is born, and millions of minds so grow and cleave to his genius that he is confounded with virtue and the possible of man. . . .

The magnetism which all original action exerts is explained when we in-quire the reason of self-trust. Who is the Trustee? What is the aboriginal Self, on which a universal reliance may be rounded? What is the nature and power of that science-baffling star, without parallax, without calculable elements, which shoots a ray of beauty even into trivial and impure actions, if the least mark of independence appear? The inquiry leads us to that source, at once the essence of genius, the essence of virtue, and the essence of life, which we call Spontaneity or Instinct. We denote this primary wisdom as Intuition, whilst all later teachings are tuitions. In that deep force, the last fact behind which analysis cannot go, all things find their common origin. For the sense of being which in calm hours rises, we know not how, in the soul, is not diverse from things, from space, from light, from time, from man, but one with them and proceedeth obviously from the same source whence their life and being also proceedeth. We first share the life by which things exist and afterwards see them as appearances in nature and forget that we have shared their cause. Here is the fountain of action and the fountain of thought. . . .

The relation of the soul to the divine spirit is so pure that it is profane to seek to interpose helps. It must be that when God speaketh he should commu-nicate, not one thing, but all things; should fill the world with his voice; should scatter forth light, nature, time, souls, from the center of the present thought; and new date and new create the whole. Whenever a mind is simple and re-ceives a divine wisdom, then old things pass away,—means, teachers, texts, temples fall; it lives now, and absorbs past and future into the present hour. All things are made sacred by relation to it,—one thing as much as another. All things are dissolved to their center by their cause, and in the universal miracle petty and particular miracles disappear. This is and must be. If therefore a man claims to know and speak of God and carries you backward to the phraseolo-gy of some old mouldered nation in another country, in another world, believe him not. Is the acorn better than the oak which is its fullness and completion?

Is the parent better than the child into whom he has cast his ripened being? Whence then this worship of the past? The centuries are conspirators against the sanity and majesty of the soul. Time and space are but physiological colors which the eye maketh, but the soul is light; where it is, is day; where it was, is night; and history is an impertinence and an injury if it be any thing more than a cheerful apologue or parable of my being and becoming.

Man is timid and apologetic; he is no longer upright; he dares not say "I think," "I am," but quotes some saint or sage. . . . He cannot be happy and strong until he too lives with nature in the present, above time.

This should be plain enough. Yet see what strong intellects dare not yet hear God himself unless he speaks the phraseology of I know not what David, or Jeremiah, or Paul. We shall not always set so great a price on a few texts, on a few lives. We are like children who repeat by rote the sentences of grand-dames and tutors, and, as they grow older, of the men of talents and character they chance to see,—painfully recollecting the exact words they spoke; after-wards, then they come into the point of view which those had who uttered these sayings, they understand them and are willing to let the words go; for at any time they can use words as good when occasion comes. So was it with us, so will it be, if we proceed. If we live truly, we shall see truly. It is as easy for the strong man to be strong, as it is for the weak to be weak. When we have new perception, we shall gladly disburthen the memory of its hoarded trea-sures as old rubbish. When a man lives with God, his voice shall be as sweet as the murmur of the brook and the rustle of the corn.

And now at last the highest truth on this subject remains unsaid; proba-bly cannot be said; for all that we say is the far off remembering of the intu-ition. That thought, by what I can now nearest approach to say it, is this. When good is near you, when you have life in yourself,—it is not by any known or appointed way; you shall not discern the footprints of any other; you shall not see the face of man; you shall not hear any name;—the way, the thought, the good, shall be wholly strange and new. . . .

It is for want of self-culture that the idol of Travelling, the idol of Italy, of England, of Egypt, remains for all educated Americans. They who made England, Italy, or Greece venerable in the imagination, did so not by rambling round creation as a moth round a lamp, but by sticking fast where they were, like an axis of the earth. In manly hours we feel that duty is our place and that the merry men of circumstance should follow as they may. The soul is no trav-eler: the wise man stays at home with the soul, and when his necessities, his duties, on any occasion call him from his house, or into foreign lands, he is at home still and is not gadding abroad from himself, and shall make men sensi-ble by the expression of his countenance that he goes, the missionary of wis-dom and virtue, and visits cities and men like a sovereign and not like an interloper or a valet. . . .

Travelling is a fool's paradise. We owe to our first journeys the discovery that place is nothing. At home I dream that at Naples, at Rome, I can be intox-icated with beauty and lose my sadness. I pack my trunk, embrace my friends, embark on the sea and at last wake up in Naples, and there beside me is the stern Fact, the sad self, the unrelenting, identical, that I fled from. I seek the Vatican and the palaces. I affect to be intoxicated with sights and suggestions, but I am not intoxicated. My giant goes with me wherever I go.

But the rage of traveling is itself only a symptom of a deeper unsoundness affecting the whole intellectual action. The intellect is vagabond, and the universal system of education fosters restlessness. Our minds travel when our bodies are forced to stay at home. We imitate; and what is imitation but the traveling of the mind? Our houses are built with foreign taste; our shelves are garnished with foreign ornaments; our opinions, our tastes, our whole minds, lean, and follow the Past and the Distant, as the eyes of a maid follow her mistress. The soul created the arts wherever they have flourished. It was in his own mind that the artist sought his model. It was an application of his own thought to the thing to be done and the condition to be observed. And why need we copy the Doric or the Gothic model? Beauty, convenience, grandeur of thought and quaint expression are as near to us as to any, and if the American artist will study with hope and love the precise thing to be done by him, considering the climate, the soil, the length of the day, the wants of the people, the habit and form of the government, he will create a house in which all these will find themselves fitted, and taste and sentiment will be satisfied also. . . .

As our Religion, our Education, our Art look abroad, so does our spirit of society. All men plume themselves on the improvement of society, and no man improves.

Society never advances. It recedes as fast on one side as it gains on the other. Its progress is only apparent like the workers of a treadmill. It undergoes continual changes; it is barbarous, it is civilized, it is christianized, it is rich, it is scientific; but this change is not amelioration. For every thing that is given something is taken. Society acquires new arts and loses old instinct. What a contrast between the well-clad, reading, writing, thinking American, with a watch, a pencil and a bill of exchange in his pocket, and the naked New Zealander, whose property is a club, a spear, a mat and an undivided twentieth of a shed to sleep under. But compare the health of the two men and you shall see that his aboriginal strength, the white man has lost. If the traveler tell us truly, strike the savage with a broad axe and in a day or two the flesh shall unite and heal as if you struck the blow into soft pitch, and the same blow shall send the white man to his grave.

The civilized man has built a coach, but has lost the use of his feet. He is supported on crutches, but lacks so much support of muscle. He has got a fine Geneva watch, but he has lost the skill to tell the hour by the sun. A Greenwich nautical almanac he has, and so being sure of the information when he wants it, the man in the street does not know a star in the sky. The solstice he does not observe; the equinox he knows as little; and the whole bright calendar of the year is without a dial in his mind. His note-books impair his memory: his libraries overload his wit; the insurance-office increases the number of accidents; and it may be a question whether machinery does not encumber;

whether we have not lost by refinement some energy, by a Christianity entrenched in establishments and forms some vigor or wild virtue. ...

And so the reliance on Property, including the reliance on governments which protect it, is the want of self-reliance. Men have looked away from themselves and at things so long that they have come to esteem what they call the soul's progress, namely, the religious, learned and civil institutions as guards of property, and they deprecate assaults on these, because they feel them to be assaults on property. They measure their esteem of each other by what each has, and not by what each is. ...

Walden (1854)

Economy

Henry David Thoreau

When I wrote the following pages, or rather the bulk of them, I lived alone, in the woods, a mile from any neighbor, in a house which I had built myself, on the shore of Walden Pond, in Concord, Massachusetts, and earned my living by the labor of my hands only. I lived there two years and two months. At present I am a sojourner in civilized life again.

I should not obtrude my affairs so much on the notice of my readers if very particular inquiries had not been made by my townsmen concerning my mode of life, which some would call impertinent, though they do not appear to me at all impertinent, but, considering the circumstances, very natural and pertinent. Some have asked what I got to eat; if I did not feel lonesome; if I was not afraid; and the like. Others have been curious to learn what portion of my income I devoted to charitable purposes; and some, who have large families, how many poor children I maintained. I will therefore ask those of my readers who feel no particular interest in me to pardon me if I undertake to answer some of these questions in this book. In most books, the *I*, or first person, is omitted; in this it will be retained; that, in respect to egotism, is the main difference. We commonly do not remember that it is, after all, always the first person that is speaking. I should not talk so much about myself if there were anybody else whom I knew as well. Unfortunately, I am confined to this theme by the narrowness of my experience. Moreover, I, on my side, require of every writer, first or last, a simple and sincere account of his own life, and not merely what he has heard of other men's lives; some such account as he would send to his kindred from a distant land; for if he has lived sincerely, it must have been in a distant land to me. Perhaps these pages are more particularly addressed to poor students. As for the rest of my readers, they will accept such

Courtesy of Houghton Mifflin Company, New York.

portions as apply to them. I trust that none will stretch the seams in putting on the coat, for it may do good service to him whom it fits. . . .

I see young men, my townsmen, whose misfortune it is to have inherited farms, houses, barns, cattle, and farming tools; for these are more easily acquired than got rid of. Better if they had been born in the open pasture and suckled by a wolf, that they might have seen with clearer eyes what field they were called to labor in. Who made them serfs to the soil? Why should they eat their sixty acres, when man is condemned to eat only his peck of dirt? Why should they begin digging their graves as soon as they are born? They have got to live a man's life, pushing all these things before them, and get on as well as they can. How many a poor immortal soul have I met well nigh crushed and smothered under its load, creeping down the road of life, pushing before it a barn seventy-five feet by forty, its augean stables never cleansed, and one hundred acres of land, tillage, mowing, pasture, and wood-lot! The portionless, who struggle with no such unnecessary inherited encumbrances, find it labor enough to subdue and cultivate a few cubic feet of flesh.

But men labor under a mistake. The better part of the man is soon ploughed into the soil for compost. By a seeming fate, commonly called necessity, they are employed, as it says in an old book, laying up treasures which moth and rust will corrupt and thieves break through and steal. It is a fool's life, as they will find when they get to the end of it, if not before. . . .

Most men, even in this comparatively free country, through mere ignorance and mistake, are so occupied with the factitious cares and superfluously coarse labors of life that its finer fruits cannot be plucked by them. Their fingers, from excessive toil, are too clumsy and tremble too much for that. Actually, the laboring man has not leisure for a true integrity day by day; he cannot afford to sustain the manliest relations to men; his labor would be depreciated in the market. . . . The finest qualities of our nature, like the bloom on fruits, can be preserved only by the most delicate handling. Yet we do not treat ourselves nor one another thus tenderly. . . .

The mass of men lead lives of quiet desperation. What is called resignation is confirmed desperation. From the desperate city you go into the desperate country, and have to console yourself with the bravery of minks and muskrats. A stereotyped but unconscious despair is concealed even under what are called the games and amusements of mankind. There is no play in them, for this comes after work. But it is a characteristic of wisdom not to do desperate things. . . .

Let us consider for a moment what most of the trouble and anxiety which I have referred to is about, and how much it is necessary that we be troubled, or at least careful. It would be some advantage to live a primitive and frontier life, though in the midst of an outward civilization, if only to learn what are the gross necessaries of life and what methods have been taken to obtain them. . . .

By the words, *necessary of life,* I mean whatever, of all that man obtains by his own exertions has been from the first, or from long use has become, so important to human life that few, if any, whether from savageness, or poverty, or philosophy, ever attempt to do without it. . . .

The grand necessity, then, for our bodies, is to keep warm, to keep the vital heat in us. What pains we accordingly take, not only with our Food, and Clothing, and Shelter, but with our beds, which are our night-clothes, robbing the nests and breasts of birds to prepare this shelter within a shelter, as the mole has its bed of grass and leaves at the end of its burrow! The poor man is wont to complain that this is a cold world; and to cold, no less physical than social, we refer directly a great part of our ails. The summer, in some climates, makes possible to man a sort of Elysian life. Fuel, except to cook his Food, is then unnecessary; the sun is his fire, and many of the fruits are sufficiently cooked by its rays; while Food generally is more various, and more easily obtained, and Clothing and Shelter are wholly or half unnecessary. At the present day, and in this country, as I find by my own experience, a few implements, a knife, an axe, a spade, a wheelbarrow, etc., and for the studious, lamplight, stationery, and access to a few books, rank next to necessaries, and can all be obtained at a trifling cost. . . .

Most of the luxuries, and many of the so-called comforts of life, are not only not indispensable, but positive hindrances to the elevation of mankind. . . . None can be an impartial or wise observer of human life but from the vantage ground of what *we* should call voluntary poverty. Of a life of luxury the fruit is luxury, whether in agriculture, or commerce, or literature, or art. There are nowadays professors of philosophy, but not philosophers. Yet it is admirable to profess because it was once admirable to live. To be a philosopher is not merely to have subtle thoughts, nor even to found a school, but so to love wisdom as to live according to its dictates, a life of simplicity, independence, magnanimity, and trust. It is to solve some of the problems of life, not only theoretically, but practically. The success of great scholars and thinkers is commonly a courtier-like success, not kingly, not manly. They make shift to live merely by conformity, practically as their fathers did, and are in no sense the progenitors of a nobler race of men. But why do men degenerate ever? What makes families run out? What is the nature of the luxury which enervates and destroys nations? Are we sure that there is none of it in our own lives? The philosopher is in advance of his age even in the outward form of his life. He is not fed, sheltered, clothed, warmed, like his contemporaries. How can a man be a philosopher and not maintain his vital heat by better methods than other men? . . .

Finding that my fellow-citizens were not likely to offer me any room in the court house, or any curacy or living anywhere else, but I must shift for myself, I turned my face more exclusively than ever to the woods, where I was better known. I determined to go into business at once, and not wait to acquire the usual capital, using such slender means as I had already got. My purpose in going to Walden Pond was not to live cheaply nor to live dearly there, but to transact some private business with the fewest obstacles; to be hindered from accomplishing which for want of a little common sense, a little enterprise and business talent, appeared not so sad as foolish. . . .

I have thought that Walden Pond would be a good place for business, not solely on account of the railroad and the ice trade; it offers advantages which it may not be good policy to divulge; it is a good port and a good foundation. No Neva marshes to be filled; though you must everywhere build on piles of your own driving. It is said that a flood-tide, with a westerly wind, and ice in the Neva, would sweep St. Petersburg from the face of the earth.

As this business was to be entered into without the usual capital, it may not be easy to conjecture when those means, that will still be indispensable to every such undertaking, were to be obtained. As for Clothing, to come at once to the practical part of the question, perhaps we are led oftener by the love of novelty and a regard for the opinions of men, in procuring it, than by a true utility. Let him who has work to do recollect that the object of clothing is, first, to retain the vital heat, and secondly, in this state of society, to cover naked-ness, and he may judge how much of any necessary or important work may be accomplished without adding to his wardrobe. . . .

On the whole, I think that it cannot be maintained that dressing has in this or any country risen to the dignity of an art. At present men make shift to wear what they can get. Like shipwrecked sailors, they put on what they can find on the beach, and at a little distance, whether of space or time, laugh at each other's masquerade. Every generation laughs at the old fashions, but fol-lows religiously the new. . . .

As for shelter, I will not deny that this is now a necessary of life, though there are instances of men having done without it for long periods in colder countries than this. . . . But, probably, man did not live long on the earth with-out discovering the convenience which there is in a house, the domestic com-forts, which phrase may have originally signified the satisfactions of the house more than of the family; though these must be extremely partial and occasion-al in those climates where the house is associated in our thoughts with winter or the rainy season chiefly, and two thirds of the year, except for a parasol, is unnecessary. In our climate, in the summer, it was formerly almost solely a covering at night. In the Indian gazettes a wigwam was the symbol of a day's march, and a row of them cut or painted on the bark of a tree signified that so many times they had camped. Man was not made so large limbed and robust but that he must seek to narrow his world, and wall in a space such as fitted him. He was at first bare and out of doors; but though this was pleasant enough in serene and warm weather, by daylight, the rainy season and the winter, to say nothing of the torrid sun, would perhaps have nipped his race in the bud if he had not made haste to clothe himself with the shelter of a house. Adam and Eve, according to the fable, wore the bower before other clothes. Man wanted a home, a place of warmth, or comfort, first of physical warmth, then the warmth of the affections.

We may imagine a time when, in the infancy of the human race, some en-terprising mortal crept into a hollow in a rock for shelter. . . . From the cave we have advanced to roofs of palm leaves, of bark and boughs, of linen woven and stretched, of grass and straw, of boards and singles, of stones and tiles. At last, we know not what it is to live in the open air, and our lives are domestic in more sense than we think. From the hearth the field is a great distance. It would be well, perhaps, if we were to spend more of our days and nights without any obstruction between us and the celestial bodies, if the poet did not speak so much from under a roof, or the saint dwell there so long. Birds do not sing in caves, nor do doves cherish their innocence in dovecots.

However, if one designs to construct a dwelling house, it behooves him to exercise a little Yankee shrewdness, lest after all he find himself in a work-house, a labyrinth without a clue, a museum, an almshouse, a prison, or a splendid mausoleum instead. Consider first how slight a shelter is absolutely necessary. I have seen Penobscot Indians, in this town, living in tents of thin cotton cloth, while the snow was nearly a foot deep around them, and I thought that they would be glad to have it deeper to keep out the wind. Formerly, when how to get my living honestly, with freedom left for my proper pursuits, was a question which vexed me even more than it does now, for unfortunately I am become somewhat callous, I used to see a large box by the railroad, six feet long by three wide, in which the laborers locked up their tools at night; and it suggested to me that every man who was hard pushed might get such a one for a dollar, and, having bored a few auger holes in it, to admit the air at least, get into it when it rained and at night, and hook down the lid, and so have freedom in his love, and in his soul be free. This did not appear the worst, nor by any means a despicable alternative. You could sit up as late as you pleased, and, whenever you got up, go abroad without any landlord or house-lord dogging you for rent. Many a man is harassed to death to pay the rent of a larger and more luxurious box who would not have frozen to death in such a box as this. I am far from jesting. Economy is a subject which admits of being treated with levity, but it cannot so be disposed of. A comfortable house for a rude and hardy race, that lived mostly out of doors, was once made here almost entirely of such materials as Nature furnished ready to their hands. ... The Indians had advanced so far as to regulate the effect of the wind by a mat suspended over the hole in the roof and moved by a string. Such a lodge was in the first instance constructed in a day or two at most, and taken down and put up in a few hours; and every family owned one, or its apartment in one.

In the savage state every family owns a shelter as good as the best, and sufficient for its coarser and simpler wants; but I think that I speak within bounds when I say that, though the birds of the air have their nests, and the foxes their holes, and the savages their wigwams, in modern civilized society not more than one half the families own a shelter. In the large towns and cities, where civilization especially prevails, the number of those who own a shelter is a very small fraction of the whole. The rest pay an annual tax for this outside garment of all become indispensable summer and winter, which would buy a village of Indian wigwams, but now helps to keep them poor as long as they live. ... But how happens it that he who is said to enjoy these things is so commonly a *poor* civilized man, while the savage, who has them not, is rich as a savage? If it is asserted that civilization is a real advance in the condition of man,—and I think that it is, though only the wise improve their advantages,—

it must be shown that it has produced better dwellings without making them more costly; and the cost of a thing is the amount of what I will call life which is required to be exchanged for it, immediately or in the long run. An average house in this neighborhood costs perhaps eight hundred dollars, and to lay up this sum will take from ten to fifteen years of the laborer's life, even if he is not encumbered with a family,—estimating the pecuniary value of every man's labor at one dollar a day, for if some receive more, others receive less;—so that he must have spent more than half his life commonly before *his* wigwam will be earned. If we suppose him to pay a rent instead, this is but a doubtful choice of evils. Would the savage have been wise to exchange his wigwam for a palace on these terms? . . .

The very simplicity and nakedness of man's life in the primitive ages imply this advantage, at least, that they left him still but a sojourner in nature. When he was refreshed with food and sleep he contemplated his journey again. He dwelt, as it were, in a tent in this world, and was either threading the valleys, or crossing the plains, or climbing the mountain tops. But lo! Men have become the tools of their tools. The man who independently plucked the fruits when he was hungry is become a farmer; and he who stood under a tree for shelter, a housekeeper. We now no longer camp as for a night, but have settled down on earth and forgotten heaven. We have adopted Christianity merely as an improved method of *agri*-culture. We have built for this world a family mansion, and for the next a family tomb. The best works of art are the expression of man's struggle to free himself from this condition, but the effect of our art is merely to make this low state comfortable and that higher state to be forgotten. There is actually no place in this village for a work of *fine* art, if any had come down to us, to stand, for our lives, our houses and streets, furnish no proper pedestal for it. There is not a nail to hang a picture on, nor a shelf to receive the bust of a hero or a saint. When I consider how our houses are built and paid for, or not paid for, and their internal economy managed and sustained, I wonder that the floor does not give way under the visitor while he is admiring the gewgaws upon the mantelpiece, and let him through into the cellar, to some solid and honest though earthy foundation. I cannot but perceive that this so-called rich and refined life is a thing jumped at, and I do not get on in the enjoyment of the *fine* arts which adorn it, my attention being wholly occupied with the jump; for I remember that the greatest genuine leap, due to human muscles alone, on record, is that of certain wandering Arabs, who are said to have cleared twenty-five feet on level ground. Without factitious support, man is sure to come to earth again beyond that distance. The first question which I am tempted to put to the proprietor of such great impropriety is, Who bolsters you? Are you one of the ninety-seven who fall, or the three who succeed? Answer me these questions, and then perhaps I may look at your bawbles and find them ornamental. . . .

. . . It is not the tailor alone who is the ninth part of a man; it is as much the preacher, and the merchant, and the farmer. Where is this division of labor to end? And what object does it finally serve? No doubt another *may* also think for me; but it is not therefore desirable that he should do so to the exclusion of my thinking for myself. . . .

. . . The most interesting dwellings in this country, as the painter knows, are the most unpretending, humble log huts and cottages of the poor commonly; it is the life of the inhabitants whose shells they are, and not any peculiarity in their surfaces merely, which makes them *picturesque*; and equally interesting will be the citizen's suburban box, when his life shall be as simple and as agreeable to the imagination, and there is as little straining after effect in the style of his dwelling. A great proportion of architectural ornaments are literally hollow, and a September gale would strip them off, like borrowed plumes, without injury to the substantials. . . .

Study Questions

1. Although scholars and preachers usually have different interests and callings, Emerson's objections to traditional scholars and preachers arise from the same sources. What are these sources, and how do they affect and limit these traditionalists and formalists? Explain, and defend your answer.
2. In what sense or senses is it useful to read Emerson as a philosopher or speculative thinker who seeks a cultural revolution in America to match the economic and political revolution that commenced on July 4, 1776? Defend your answer.
3. What are the points of convergence and divergence between Thoreau's treatment of self-sufficiency in *Walden* and Emerson's insistence upon the value of independence in "Self Reliance"? Develop, and defend your answer.
4. Do you find any evidence in *Walden* that Thoreau might be divided about the value of nonconformity and the rewards of solitude? Explain, and defend your answer.

Suggestions for Further Reading

Baker, Carlos. *Emerson among the Eccentrics.* New York: Viking, 1996.

Burbick, Joan. *Thoreau's Alternative History: Changing Perspectives on Nature, Culture, and Language.* Philadelphia: University of Pennsylvania Press, 1987.

Cavell, Stanley. *The Senses of Walden*, revised edition. San Francisco: North Point Press, 1981.

Cavell, Stanley. *Conditions Handsome and Unhandsome: The Constitution of Emersonian Perfectionism.* Chicago: University of Chicago Press, 1990.

Emerson, Ralph Waldo. *The Portable Emerson.* Edited by Carl Bode with Malcolm Cowley. Harmondsorth: Penguin Books, 1981.

Emerson, Ralph Waldo. *Essays and Poems.* Edited by Tony Tanner. London: Everyman, 1995.

Emerson, Ralph Waldo. *Prose and Poetry.* Edited by Joel Porte and Saundra Morris. New York: W.W. Norton, 2001.

Gilmore, Michael. *American Romanticism and the Marketplace.* Chicago: University of Chicago Press, 1985.

Howe, Irving. *The American Newness: Culture and Politics in the Age of Emerson.* Cambridge, Mass.: Harvard University Press, 1986.

Marx, Leo. *The Machine in the Garden: Technology and the Pastoral Ideal in America.* Oxford: Oxford University Press, 1964.

Nash, Roderick. *Wilderness and the American Mind*, third edition. New Haven: Yale University Press, 1982.

Neufeldt, Leonard N. *The Economist: Henry Thoreau and Enterprise.* New York: Oxford University Press, 1989.

Peck, H. Daniel. *Thoreau's Morning Work: Memory and Perception in the Concord and Merrimack Rivers, the Journal, and Walden.* New Haven: Yale University Press, 1990.

Richardson, Robert D. Jr. *Thoreau: A Life of the Mind.* Berkeley: University of California Press, 1986.

Richardson, Robert D. Jr. *Emerson: The Mind on Fire.* Berkeley: University of California Press, 1995.

Tanner, Tony. "The Unconquered Eye and the Enchanted Circle." In *Romanticism: Critical Essays in American Literature.* Edited by James Barbour and Thomas Quirk. New York: Garland Publishing, 1986.

Thoreau, Henry David. "Walking." In *The American Transcendentalists: Their Prose and Poetry.* Edited by Perry Miller. Garden City, N.Y.: Doubleday Anchor Books, 1957.

Thoreau, Henry David. *Walden and Resistance to Civil Government*, second edition. Edited by William Rossi. New York: W.W. Norton, 1992.

West, Cornell. *The American Evasion of Philosophy: A Genealogy of Pragmatism.* Madison: University of Wisconsin Press, 1989.

White, Morton, and White, Lucia. *The Intellectual versus the City: From Thomas Jefferson to Frank Lloyd Wright.* Cambridge, Mass.: Harvard University Press and MIT Press, 1962.

Chapter 4

Chauncey Wright
Positivist and Precursor to Pragmatism

For many years, Chauncey Wright (1830–1875) was one of America's best-kept philosophical secrets. Occasionally, a student of American pragmatism recognizes Wright as the founder of what was to be called "The Metaphysical Club," a club of distinguished thinkers that included C. S. Peirce, William James, and Oliver Wendell Holmes, Jr. These and other members gathered informally in Cambridge, Massachusetts, for about nine months in 1872. Besides his role in the Metaphysical Club, we know that Wright was a Harvard-trained mathematician who lectured at Harvard in psychology (1870) and later in mathematical physics (1874). We also know that Wright was one of Darwin's foremost American defenders and that in 1872 he actually visited Darwin in England. In his role as defender, he wrote a number of pro-Darwinian articles for the *Nation* and *North American Review*.

Although Wright was born into an established old-line family, his pedigree did not come with a stipend. He had some income from working for a federal agency that produced charts for accurate navigation. He also drank too much and spoke far better among his friends than to his few students. At forty-five, Wright suffered a fatal stroke. Henry James, the American novelist and brother of William, was at his side when he died.

We can regret Wright's poverty, excesses, and poor health, but what concerns us here are ideas that outlived him. In his posthumously published *Philosophical Discussions* (1877) and *Letters* (1878), we find the assembled strands of Wright's philosophy. From these we learn that Wright, as an avid and doctrinaire Darwinian, accepted only those scientific hypotheses that were truly scientific, in other words, those that were verifiable through experience and experimentation. He obviously believed that Darwin's *The Origin of Species* (1859) was well-founded science and that religious hypotheses about the creation of the world *ex nihilo* were baseless. But this did not entail for Wright a need to reject religious beliefs. Since such beliefs have more to do with feeling and faith than with thinking and reason, we are entitled to accept them on emotional grounds. We are not, however, entitled to characterize them as "scientific," nor are we justified in suggesting that science and religion must endlessly oppose each other. So long as scientists adhere to their method and demands for public verification, they do no harm. And so long as theists, which might include some scientists when they are off duty, do not try to subvert scientific facts with religious convictions and texts, no harm follows.

Wright also objected vigorously to Darwinians who tried to expand Darwinism to explain behavior, occurrences, and states of affairs that Darwinian biology was never intended to explain. Here the celebrated culprit was the English philosopher Herbert Spencer (1820–1903), a prominent philosopher throughout the nineteenth century and one who is uniformly neglected in our own day. Spencer thought that the principles of Darwin's theory were sufficiently plastic to account for the evolution of the heavens, societies, and progress of every sort. Wright had no sympathy for Spencer or for any other Darwinian who treated evolution as the far more general "evolutionism." In his view, not Spencer's, this remarkable theory applied to the multiplication of plant and animal species and to the demise of other plant and animal species. To expect this or any other theory to range over variables that fall outside its scope is to misunderstand and to misappropriate the sciences.

One might expect that Wright, who was no friend to metaphysics and to highly speculative hypotheses, would try hard to avoid speculation and articulating theories for which he could find no evidence. Still, he was persuaded by Darwin, or by his interpretation of Darwin, that self-consciousness was uniquely human but was prefigured in less complex and earlier animal species. Wright's desire was to deny what in his opinion so many unscientific men and women believed, namely that self-consciousness is a supernatural capacity that is situated in a separate, immaterial soul. His desire notwithstanding, the argument he develops for the evolutionary origins of self-consciousness is no less conjectural, hence no less incompatible with the requirements of serious scientists, than the metaphysical and religious hypotheses to which he objects.

An assessment of Wright as an important philosopher will depend to some degree upon where the reader's sympathies lie. A skeptic or agnostic is likely to be impressed with Wright's criticism of the excursions that theists sometimes make into the sciences. A serious theist will object that Wright, despite his disclaimers, thinks of religion as the remnant of an early and benighted age. In either case, a serious reader will not be able to deny Wright's influence on the emergence and development of pragmatism. This alone makes him too important to neglect.

Natural Theology as a Positive Science (1865)

Natural history and anatomy have hitherto furnished the principal grounds to the theologian for the speculation of final causes, since these sciences exhibit many instances of a complex combination of causes in the structures and habits of organic bodies, and at the same time a distinct and peculiar class of effects, namely, those which constitute the well-being and perfection of organic life; and from these causes and effects, regarded as means and ends in the order of nature, the arguments and illustrations of natural theology have been chiefly drawn. The facts of these sciences are not merely the most useful to the theologian; they are indeed indispensable, and occupy a peculiar position in his argument, since they alone afford the class of effects on which, assumed as ends, the speculation of final causes ultimately rests.

It is only by assuming human welfare, or with this the welfare also of other sentient beings, as the end for which the universe exists, that the doctrine of final causes has hitherto found any support in natural science.

Though it is still maintained by theologians that the arguments for design are properly inductive arguments, yet the physical proofs of natural theology are not regarded by many modern writers as having any independent weight; and it is in mental and moral science that the facts are sought which will warrant the induction of design from the general phenomena of nature. It is hardly considered logical, even by the theological writers of our day, to conclude, with Paley, "that the works of nature proceed from intelligence and design; because, in the properties of relation to a purpose, subserviency to a use, they resemble what intelligence and design are constantly producing, and what nothing [which we know] except intelligence and design ever produce at all." For it is denied by the physical philosopher that causes and effects in natural phenomena can be interpreted into the terms of natural theology by any key which science itself affords. By what criterion, he would ask, can we distinguish among the numberless effects, that are also causes, and among the causes that may, for aught we can know, be also effects,—how can we distinguish which are the means and which are the ends? What effects are we warranted by observation in calling final, or final causes, or the ends for which the others exist? The belief on other grounds that there *are* final causes, that the universe exists for some purpose, is one thing; but the belief that science discloses, or even that science can disclose, what this purpose is, is quite a different thing. . . . The analogy of natural production to human contrivance fails . . . at the very outset; and the interpretation of natural causes and effects as means and ends, virtually assumes the conclusion of the argument, and is not founded on any natural evidence. These considerations are overlooked by most writers on this subject, who, in addition to a legitimate faith in final causes, assume the dogma that these causes are manifest or discoverable. They begin with the definition, sometimes called an argument, "that a combination of means conspiring to a particular end implies intelligence," and they then assume that the causes which science discovers are means, or exist for the sake of the effects which science accounts for; and from the relation of means to ends, thus assumed, they infer intelligence.

This definition we have quoted contains, however, more than is really implied in this argument, since the relation of means to ends in itself, and without further qualification, implies intelligence, while a combination of means conspiring to a particular end implies a high degree of intelligence; and it is with this, the degree of intelligence manifested in the phenomena of nature, that scientific discourses on the natural evidences are really dealing, though sometimes unconsciously. These discourses really aim, not so much to prove the existence of design in the universe, as to show the wisdom of certain designs which are assumed to be manifest. But for this purpose it is requisite to translate the facts of science, and those combinations of causes which are discovered to be the conditions of particular effects, into the terms of the argument, and to show that these combinations are means, or exist for the sake of particular effects, for which, as ends, the universe itself must be shown to exist,—a task for which science is obviously incompetent. . . .

It is essential to the validity of Paley's argument, that "design," or the determination of effects by the intelligence of an agent, be shown to be not merely the only known cause of such effects, but also to be a real cause, or an independent determination by an efficient agent. If intelligence itself be a product, if the human powers of contrivance are themselves effects, it follows that designed effects should be ascribed, not to intelligence, but to the causes of intelligence; and the same objection will hold against the theologian's use of the word "design," which he urges against the physicist's use of the word "law." "It is a perversion of language," says Paley, "to assign any law as the efficient operative cause of anything. A law presupposes an agent, for it only is the mode according to which the agent proceeds; it implies a power, for it is the order according to which this power acts. Without this agent, without this power, which are both distinct from itself, the "law" does nothing, is nothing." By substituting the word "design" for the word "law" in this quotation, we have the materialist's objection to the theologian's perversion of language. This objection was entirely overlooked by Paley, who seems to have thought it sufficient for the purposes of his argument to consider only the phenomena of the visible material universe. But later writers have seen the necessity of basing the argument for design on the psychological doctrine that intelligence is a free, undetermined power, and that design is the free, undetermined act of this power. Without this assumption, which indeed Paley himself virtually makes, it would be as unphilosophical to refer the course of nature to the determination of intelligence, as it is to refer it to the determination of the abstraction which the materialist prefers, or to the "agency of law."

"That intelligence stands first in the absolute order of existence,—in other words, that final preceded efficient causes,—and that the universe is governed by moral laws," are the two propositions, the proof of which, says Sir William Hamilton, is the proof of a God; and this proof "establishes its foundation exclusively on the phenomena of mind." Without this psychological proof, the order of adaptation cannot be logically referred to the order of design; and the resemblance of human contrivances to the adaptations of nature can only warrant the conclusion that both proceed from similar conditions, and by a power of whose efficiency human intelligence and physical laws are alike manifestations, but whose nature neither human intelligence comprehends nor physical laws can disclose.

Even such a result, which is all that the unaided physical sciences can compass, is not altogether barren of religious interest, though it is made so by the materialist's attempt to define the nature of power by assigning to physical forces an absolute efficiency. The spiritualist, on the other hand, if we allow his psychological proof that intelligence stands first in the absolute order of existence, and is a free, undetermined power, is logically competent to interpret the order of nature as a designed order. Yet to him physical proofs of design have little or no value, and can only serve as obscure and enigmatical illustrations of what is far more clearly apparent in the study of mind. And though logically competent to interpret the order of design, if his spiritual doctrine be true, yet the difficulties which we first mentioned, and waived for the nonce, are difficulties as insuperable to the psychologist as to the physicist. He gains no criterion from his studies by which to distinguish, in the order of natural phenomena, which are the means and which are the ends, or where the relation of means to ends is to be found, among the infinite successions of effects which are also causes, and of causes which may, for aught he can know, be also effects. His faith in final causes is not a guide by which he can determine what the final causes are by which he believes the order of nature to be determined. ...

Not only do the peculiar doctrines of natural theology add nothing to the grounds of a faith in final causes; they, in effect, narrow this faith to ideas which scarcely rise in dignity above the rank of superstitions. If to believe that God is what we can think him to be is blasphemy, [what shall we call the attempt] to discover his intentions and to interpret his plans in nature? ... It is from the illegitimate pretensions of natural theology that the figment of a conflict between science and religion has arisen; and the efforts of religious thinkers to counteract the supposed atheistical tendencies of science, and to give a religious interpretation to its facts, have only served to deepen the false impression that such a conflict actually exists, so that revolutions in scientific theories have been made to appear in the character of refutations of religious doctrines.

That there is a fundamental distinction between the natures of scientific and religious ideas ought never to be doubted; but that contradiction can arise, except between religious and superstitious ideas, ought not for a moment to be admitted. Progress in science is really a progress in religious truth, not because any new reasons are discovered for the doctrines of religion, but because the advancement in knowledge frees us from the errors both of ignorance and of superstition, exposing the mistakes of a false religious philosophy, as well as those of a false science. If the teachings of natural theology are liable to be refuted or corrected by progress in knowledge, it is legitimate to suppose, not that science is irreligious, but that these teachings are superstitious; and whatever evils result from the discoveries of sciences are attributable to the rashness of the theologian, and not to the supposed irreligious tendencies of science. When a proof of special design is invalidated by the discovery that a particular effect in the operations of nature, which previously appeared to result from a special constitution and adjustment of certain forces, is really a consequent of the general properties of matter,—when, for example, the laws of planetary motion were shown to result from the law of universal gravitation, and the mathematical plan of the solar system was seen to be a consequent of a single universal principle,—the harm, if there be any, results from the theologian's mistakes, and not from the corrections of science. He should refrain from attributing any special plan or purpose to the creation, if he would find in science a constant support to religious truth. But this abstinence does not involve a withdrawal of the mind from the proper religious interests of natural science, nor weaken a legitimate faith in final causes. Even the Newtonian mechanism of the heavens, simple, primordial, and necessary as it seems, still discloses to the devout mind evidence of a wisdom unfathomable, and of a design which transcends interpretation; and when, in the more complicated order of organic life, surprising and beautiful adaptations inspire in the naturalist the conviction that purpose and intelligence are manifested in them,—that they spring from a nature akin to the devising power of his own mind,—there is nothing in science or philosophy which can legitimately rebuke his enthusiasm,—nothing, unless it be the dogmatism which would presumptuously interpret as science what is only manifest to faith, or would require of faith that it shall justify itself by proofs.

The progress of science has indeed been a progress in religious truth, but in spite of false theology, and in a way which narrow theologians have constantly opposed. It has defined with greater and greater distinctness the boundary between what can be discovered and what cannot. It has purified religious truth by turning back the moral consciousness to discover clearly in itself what it had obscurely divined from its own interpretations of nature. It has impressed on the mind of the cautious inquirer the futility, as well as the irreverence, of attempting a philosophy which can at best be but a finer sort of superstition, a real limitation to our conceptions of final causes, while apparently an extension of them.

But instead of learning these lessons from the experience of repeated failures, theologians have constantly opposed new hypotheses in science, until proof has compelled a tardy assent, and even then they have retreated to other regions of science, as if these were the only refuge of a persecuted faith.

Humility and cautiousness, and that suspension of judgment in matters about which we really know so little . . . in view of the pending controversy on the origin of organic species and adaptations, are virtues, which, had they been generally cultivated by theologians, would have rendered this controversy harmless at least, if not unnecessary.

Evolution of Self-Consciousness (1873)

It has come to be understood, and very generally allowed, that the conception of the origin of man as an animal race, as well as the origin of individual men within it, in accordance with the continuity of organic development maintained in the theory of evolution, does not involve any very serious difficulties, or difficulties so great as are presented by any other hypothesis of this origin, not excepting that of "special creation";—if that can be properly called a hypothesis, which is, in fact, a resumption of all the difficulties of natural explanation, assuming them to be insuperable and summarizing them under a single positive name. Yet in this evolution, the birth of self-consciousness is still thought by many to be a step not following from antecedent conditions in "nature," except in an incidental manner, or in so far only as "natural" antecedents have prepared the way for the "supernatural" advent of the self-conscious soul.

Independently of the form of expression, and of the false sentiment which is the motive of the antithesis in this familiar conception, or independently of its mystical interest, which has given to the words "natural" and "supernatural" their commonly accepted meanings, there is a foundation of scientific truth in the conception. For the word "evolution" conveys a false impression to the imagination, not really intended in the scientific use of it. It misleads by suggesting a continuity in the *kinds* of powers and functions in living beings, that is, by suggesting transition by insensible steps from one *kind* to another, as well as in the *degrees* of their importance and exercise at different stages of development. The truth is, on the contrary, that according to the theory of evolution, new uses of old powers arise discontinuously both in the bodily and mental natures of the animal, and in its individual developments, as well as in the development of its race, although, at their rise, these uses are small and of the smallest importance to life. They seem merged in the powers to which they are incident, and seem also merged in the special purposes or functions in which, however, they really have no part, and which are no parts of them. Their services or functions in life, though realized only incidentally at first, and in the feeblest degree, are just as distinct as they afterwards come to appear in their fullest development. The new uses are related to older powers only as *accidents*, so far as the special services of the older powers are concerned, although, from the more general point of view of natural law, their relations to older uses have not the character of accidents, since these relations are, for the most part, determined by universal properties and laws, which are not specially related to the needs and conditions of living beings. Thus the uses of limbs for swimming, crawling, walking, leaping, climbing, and flying are distinct uses, and are related to each other only through the general mechanical principles of locomotion, through which some one use, in its first exercise, may be incident to some other, though, in its full exercise and perfection of special service, it is independent of the other, or has only a common dependence with the other more general conditions.

Many mental as well as bodily powers thus have mixed natures, or independent uses; as, for example, the powers of the voice to call and allure. To warn and repel, and its uses in music and language; or the numerous uses of the human hand in services of strength and dexterity. And, on the contrary, the same uses are, in some cases, realized by independent organs as, for example, respiration in water and in the air by gills and lungs, or flight by means of fins, feathers, and webs. The appearance of a really new power in *nature* (using this word in the wide meaning attached to it in science), the power of flight in the first birds, for example, is only involved potentially in previous phenomena. In the same way, no act of self-consciousness, however elementary, may have been realized before man's first self-conscious act in the animal world; yet the act may have been involved potentially in pre-existing powers or causes. The derivation of this power, supposing it to have been observed by a finite angelic (not animal) intelligence, could not have been foreseen to be involved in the mental causes, on the conjunction of which it might, nevertheless, have been seen to depend. The angelic observation would have been a purely empirical one. The possibility of a subsequent analysis of these causes by the self-conscious animal himself, which would afford an explanation of their agency, by referring it to a rational combination of simpler elements in them, would not alter the case to the angelic intelligence, just as a rational explanation of flight could not be reached by such an intelligence as a consequence of known mechanical laws; since these laws are also animal conditions, or rather are more general and material ones, of which our angelic, spherical intelligence is not supposed to have had any experience. . . .

As soon, then, as the progress of animal intelligence through an extension of the range in its powers of memory, or in revived impressions, together with a corresponding increase in the vividness of these impressions, has reached a certain point . . . it becomes possible for such an intelligence to fix its attention on a vivid outward sign, without losing sight of, or dropping out of distinct attention, an image or revived impression; which latter would only serve, in case of its spontaneous revival in imagination, as a sign of the same thing, or the same event. Whether the vivid outward sign be a real object or event, of which the revived image is the counterpart, or whether it be a sign in a stricter meaning of the term,—that is, some action, figure, or utterance, associated either naturally or artificially with all similar objects or events, and, consequently, with the revived and representative image of them,—whatever the character of this outward sign may be, provided the representative image, or inward sign, still retains, in distinct consciousness, its power as such, then the outward sign may be consciously recognized as a substitute for the inward one, and a consciousness of simultaneous internal and external suggestion, or significance, might be realized; and the contrast of thoughts and things, at least in their power of suggesting that of which they may be coincident signs, could, for the first time, be perceptible. This would plant the germ of the distinctively human form of self-consciousness. . . .

. . . Thought, henceforward, may be an object to thought in its distinct contrast, as an inward sign, with the outward and more vivid sign of that which they both suggest, or revive from memory. This contrast is heightened if the outward one is more strictly a sign; that is, is not the perception of an object or event, of which the inward and representative image is a counterpart, but is of a different nature, for instance some movement or gesture or vocal utterance, or some graphic sign, associated by contiguity with the object or event, or, more properly, with its representative image. The "concept" so formed is not a thing complete in itself, but is essentially a cause, or step, in mental trains. The outward sign, the image, or inward sign, and the suggested thought, or image, form a train, like a train which might be wholly within the imagination. This train is present, in all its three constituents, to the first, or immediate, consciousness, in all degrees of intelligence; but in the revival of it, in the inferior degrees of intelligence, the middle term is obliterated, as in the trains of thought above considered. The animal has in mind only an image of the sign, previously present in perception, followed now immediately by an image of what was suggested through the obliterated mental image. But the latter, in the higher degrees of intelligence, is distinctly recalled as a middle term. In the revival of past trains, which were first produced through outward signs, the dumb animal has no consciousness of there having been present more than one of the two successive signs, which, together with the suggested image, formed the actual train in its first occurrence. The remembered outward sign is now a thought, or image, immediately suggesting or recalling that which was originally suggested by a feebler intermediate step. . . .

When a thought, or an outward expression, acts in an animal's mind or in a man's, in the capacity of a sign, it carries forward the movements of a train, and directs attention away from itself to what it signifies or suggests; and consciousness is concentrated on the latter. But being sufficiently vivid in itself to engage distinct attention, it determines a new kind of action, and a new faculty of observation, of which the cerebral hemispheres appear to be the organs. From the action of these, in their more essential powers in memory and imagination, the objects or materials of reflection are also derived. Reflection would thus be, not what most metaphysicians appear to regard it, a fundamentally new faculty in man, as elementary and primordial as memory itself, or the power of abstractive attention, or the function of signs and representative images in generalization; but it would be determined in its contrasts with other mental faculties by the nature of its objects. On its subjective side it would be composed of the same mental faculties—namely, memory, attention, abstraction—as those which are employed in the primary use of the senses. It would be engaged upon what these senses have furnished to memory; but would act as independently of any orders of grouping and succession presented by them, as the several senses themselves do of one another. To this extent, reflection is a distinct faculty, and though, perhaps, not peculiar to man, is in him so prominent and marked in its effects on the development of the individual mind, that it may be regarded as his most essential and elementary mental distinction in kind. For differences of degrees in causes may make differences of kinds in effects. . . .

. . . Command of language is an important condition of the effective cognition of a sign as such. It is highly probable that the dog not only cannot utter the sound "fox," but cannot revive the sound as heard by him. The word cannot, therefore, be of aid to him in fixing his attention in reflection on the mental image of the fox as seen or smelt by him. But the latter, spontaneously arising, would be sufficient to produce a lively train of thoughts, or a vivid dream. It by no means follows from his deficiencies of vocal and auditory imagination that the dog has not, in some directions, aid from outward signs, and some small degree of reflective power, though this, probably, falls far short of the clear division of the two worlds realized in the cognition of "cogito."

Command of signs, and, indeed, all the volitional or active powers of an animal, including attention in perception, place it in relation to outward things in marked contrast with its passive relations of sensation and inattentive or passive perception. The distinctness, or prominence, in consciousness given by an animal's attention to its perceptions, and the greater energy given by its intentions or purposes to its outward movements, *cannot fail to afford a ground of discrimination between these* as causes, both of inward and outward events, and those outward causes which are not directly under such control, but form an independent system, or several distinct systems, of causes. This would give rise to a form of self-consciousness more immediate and simple than the intellectual one, and is apparently realized in dumb animals. They, probably, do not have, or have only in an indistinct and ineffective form, the intellectual cognitions of *cogito* and *sum*; but having reached the cognition of a contrast in subject and object as *causes* both in inward and outward events, they have already acquired a form of subjective consciousness, or a knowledge of the *ego*. That they do not, and cannot, name it, at least by a general name, or understand it by the general name of "I" or *ego*, comes from the absence of the attributes of *ego* which constitute the intellectual self-consciousness. . . .

Not only the dog and other intelligent dumb animals, but some of the least advanced among human beings, also, are unable to arrive at a distinct abstraction of what is expressed by "to be," or "to exist." . . .

Study Questions

1. According to Chauncey Wright, the Darwinian theory is sustained by evidence. What kind of evidence does he have in mind? Explain, and defend your answer.

2. Wright is sometimes characterized as a philosophical "positivist," in other words, as one of those philosophers who dismiss as meaningless any claim that cannot be verified in fact or in principle. Is this a correct characterization of Wright's philosophic approach to traditional issues in philosophy? Be specific, and defend your analysis.

3. In "The Evolution of Self-Consciousness," Wright tries to establish that human self-consciousness evolved over time from the rude seeds of consciousness in more primitive organisms. How does Wright try to argue for this particular evolutionary hypothesis? Is his argument appropriately scientific? Explain, and defend your position.

Suggestions for Further Reading

Madden, Edward H. *Chauncey Wright and the Foundations of Pragmatism.* Seattle: University of Washington Press, 1963.

Menand, Lewis. *The Metaphysical Club: A Story of Ideas in America.* New York: Farrar, Straus & Giroux, 2001.

White, Morton. *Science and Sentiment in America: Philosophical Thought from Jonathan Edwards to John Dewey*. New York: Oxford University Press, 1972.

Wiener, Philip P. *Evolution and the Founders of Pragmatism*. Cambridge, Mass.: Harvard University Press, 1949.

Wright, Chauncey. *Philosophical Discussions*. Edited by Charles Eliot Norton. New York: H. Holt, 1877.

Wright, Chauncey. *Letters*. Edited by James Bradley Thayer. Cambridge, Mass.: John Wilson and Son, 1878.

Wright, Chauncey. *The Philosophical Writings of Chauncey Wright: Representative Selections*. Edited by Edward H. Madden. New York: Liberal Arts Press, 1958.

Chapter 5

Charles Sanders Peirce, William James, and John Dewey
Pragmatism, a Philosophy Made in America

Although several American thinkers became philosophical pragmatists, the unquestionable giants of the movement were Charles Sanders Peirce, William James, and John Dewey. Taking shape in the 1870s and lasting in some form into the present, pragmatism is the one philosophy that was developed and refined by a cluster of original American thinkers.

Peirce was born in 1839 and reared in Cambridge, Massachusetts. His father Benjamin was Harvard's most distinguished mathematician. He constantly encouraged Charles to employ his wide-ranging talents. Charles described himself as having "inhabited a laboratory from the age of six until long past maturity." Unfortunately, he had lapses of character as well as health problems that offset his mental gifts. He suffered throughout his life from painful neurological deficits and took powerful addictive drugs to deal with his discomfort. All of this, and his own volatility, made him a burden to himself and to others.

In 1862 Peirce married Harriet Fay. Despite her own shortcomings, she managed to bring a measure of peace and stability into Peirce's otherwise tortured life, but infrequent periods of relative tranquility were not enough to enable him to find employment that matched his prodigious ability. He found work in 1861 and managed to remain employed until 1887 as a mathematician for the federal government. After his retirement, he continued to write and to refine his version of pragmatism. Peirce died in 1914. His legacy was his influence on other pragmatists, including—but by no means limited to—James and Dewey.

William James (1842–1910) was born in New York City and became the star of the pragmatist show. The best known of the grand American triumvirate, he was also a stylist of the highest water and, like Peirce, was at home in the sciences—especially experimental psychology and medicine—and in philosophy. He and Henry, an American world-class novelist, are almost certainly the most distinguished brothers in American history. Their father, Henry James, Sr., was an eccentric whose interests extended from religious philosophy and mystical writings of Emanuel Swedenborg.

William's attainments were prodigious. He entered Harvard in 1861 and graduated with a medical degree in 1869; however, disciplines in which he had no formal training interested him most. After briefly teaching anatomy and physiology at Harvard, he turned to philosophy and psychology, and in 1880 he was named assistant professor of philosophy. In 1878 he married Alice Howe Gibbons and was the father of five children.

Like Peirce, but not to the same unfortunate degree, James suffered from his own demons. He seems to have had serious bouts of depression and a persistent sense of inadequacy. Enjoying a duplex reputation as a psychologist and philosopher of the first order seems never to have satisfied him. But what matters for understanding the history of American philosophy is how others see James, not how James saw himself. The prevailing view of James's colleagues, successors, and readers, including many who did not and do not see themselves as pragmatists, is that he stands near the summit of what is worth celebrating in American philosophy. Perhaps it was with James that Emerson's wish for a cultural declaration of independence found its actualization in philosophy. More than any other philosopher before him, James was proof that original and serious thought, no less than the machinery, technology, and capitalist ingenuity of the late nineteenth century, could emerge from American sources and genius.

John Dewey was born in Burlington, Vermont, the same year that Darwin published *The Origin of Species*, and he died in 1952. Following his graduation from the University of Vermont, Dewey spent two years teaching high school in Oil City, Pennsylvania. He returned to Vermont where he taught in a small school and wrote some essays that he submitted to the *Journal of Speculative Philosophy*. Encouraged by his first formal steps in philosophy, he entered Johns Hopkins University to do graduate work. There he studied logic under Peirce but was more interested in the philosophy of Hegel, which was briefly in vogue in a few American universities. After receiving his Ph.D., Dewey became an instructor at the University of Michigan. He remained in Ann Arbor for ten years and there married Alice Chipman, by whom he became the father of six children.

From Michigan he moved in 1894 to accept a professorship and to head the Department of Philosophy and Psychology at the newly founded University of Chicago. From Chicago, which he left in 1904, Dewey joined the faculty of Columbia University and remained there until he retired from teaching in 1930. But retirement from life as a university professor did not prefigure retirement from the philosophical life. Living in New York until his death, Dewey continued to write, lecture, and involve himself in assorted social and political causes. Among the books Dewey wrote after his retirement are *Philosophy and Civilization* (1931), *Art as Experience* (1935), *Liberalism and Social Action* (1935), and *Logic: The Theory of Inquiry* (1938).

There is no simple way to characterize pragmatism, although in the selections that follow we will see efforts to do just that. When Peirce, James, and Dewey write about topics as diverse as using the scientific method outside the sciences, overcoming doubt and acquiring knowledge, solving philosophical disputes, and closing the traditional gap between theory and practice, we begin to acquire an understanding of what it meant to be a pioneering pragmatist.

We learn, for example, that first-generation pragmatists were, like Chauncey Wright, aware that Darwinism provided an instructive model for understanding the relations and tensions between human beings and their environment. We also learn that despite their general distaste for metaphysical excesses, the pragmatists—especially Peirce and James—found places in their philosophies for speculative and unverifiable metaphysical assertions, religious prepossessions, and an investment in hypotheses that make a difference to some people but make no sense to others. We find that phrases like "sensible effects," "cash value," and "making a difference" are indispensable to getting at what pragmatists have in mind and wish to promote.

These three empiricists believe that traditional empiricism—that is, the view that what we can know is ultimately tethered to experience—must be enriched to satisfy the pressing needs and desires of people who truly need a philosophy. James and Dewey are populists who insist that a viable philosophy has to address the urgent, if sometimes unremarkable, concerns of men and women who are not themselves highly trained philosophers. In this respect, they look to and demand consequences from philosophical inquiry and reflection. Indeed, "consequences" and "action" may be the two words at the center of diverse versions of pragmatism. None of these philosophers settles for a philosophy that refused to sully itself in the give and take of daily life. Each of them in his own way echoes the positions of philosophers as different from each other as Francis Bacon, Thomas Hobbes, and Karl Marx: It is never enough that philosophers know the world. They must also do what they can to expand possibilities for human well-being. The American pragmatists tend to dismiss philosophers who deny the value of change, turn away from this world and toward some mythic order of being, or value abstract reflection over purposeful action.

Whether pragmatism could have developed outside the United States and at a different point in history is a question worth pondering and one that histories of the pragmatic movement often address. Some philosophers, including Bertrand Russell, believe that pragmatism mirrors the vigor, muscle, and can-do nature of post-Civil War American industry and commerce. There may be something to this, but efforts to account for an entire movement in terms of a few facts and features are invariably flawed. This kind of reductionism rarely tells the entire story or answers every question. Perhaps, therefore, the wise course is to ask readers of these selections to decide for themselves whether pragmatism, that philosophy that came into being and matured under North American skies, is inevitably or accidentally American.

The Fixation of Belief (1877)

C. S. PEIRCE

I

. . . Few persons care to study logic, because everybody conceives himself to be proficient enough in the art of reasoning already. But I observe that this satisfaction is limited to one's own ratiocination, and does not extend to that of other men.

We come to the full possession of our power of drawing inferences, the last of all our faculties; for it is not so much a natural gift as a long and difficult art. . . . The medieval schoolmen, following the Romans, made logic the earliest of a boy's studies after grammar, as being very easy. So it was as they understood it. Its fundamental principle, according to them, was, that all knowledge rests either on authority or reason; but that whatever is deduced by reason depends ultimately on a premiss derived from authority. Accordingly, as soon as a boy was perfect in the syllogistic procedure, his intellectual kit of tools was held to be complete.

II

The object of reasoning is to find out, from the consideration of what we already know, something else which we do not know. Consequently, reasoning is good if it be such as to give a true conclusion from true premisses, and not otherwise. Thus, the question of validity is purely one of fact and not of thinking. A being the facts stated in the premisses and B being that concluded, the question is, whether these facts are really so related that if A were B would generally be. If so, the inference is valid; if not, not. It is not in the least the question whether, when the premisses are accepted by the mind, we feel an impulse to accept the conclusion also. It is true that we do generally reason correctly by nature. But that is an accident; the true conclusion would remain true if we had no impulse to accept it; and the false one would remain false, though we could not resist the tendency to believe in it. . . .

That which determines us, from given premisses, to draw one inference rather than another, is some habit of mind, whether it be constitutional or acquired. The habit is good or otherwise, according as it produces true conclusions from true premisses or not; and an inference is regarded as valid or not, without reference to the truth or falsity of its conclusion specially, but according as the habit which determines it is such as to produce true conclusions in general or not. The particular habit of mind which governs this or that inference may be formulated in a proposition whose truth depends on the validity of the inferences which the habit determines; and such a formula is called a

From *Popular Science Monthly*, 1878.

guiding principle of inference. Suppose, for example, that we observe that a rotating disk of copper quickly comes to rest when placed between the poles of a magnet, and we infer that this will happen with every disk of copper. The guiding principle is, that what is true of one piece of copper is true of another. Such a guiding principle with regard to copper would be much safer than with regard to many other substances—brass, for example. . . .

III

We generally know when we wish to ask a question and when we wish to pronounce a judgment, for there is a dissimilarity between the sensation of doubting and that of believing.

But this is not all which distinguishes doubt from belief. There is a practical difference. Our beliefs guide our desires and shape our actions. The Assassins, or followers of the Old Man of the Mountain, used to rush into death at his least command, because they believed that obedience to him would insure everlasting felicity. Had they doubted this, they would not have acted as they did. So it is with every belief, according to its degree. The feeling of believing is a more or less sure indication of there being established in our nature some habit which will determine our actions. Doubt never has such an effect.

Nor must we overlook a third point of difference. Doubt is an uneasy and dissatisfied state from which we struggle to free ourselves and pass into the state of belief, while the latter is a calm and satisfactory state which we do not wish to avoid, or to change to a belief in anything else. On the contrary, we cling tenaciously, not merely to believing, but to believing just what we do believe.

Thus, both doubt and belief have positive effects upon us, though very different ones. Belief does not make us act at once, but puts us into such a condition that we shall behave in some certain way, when the occasion arises. Doubt has not the least such active effect, but stimulates us to inquiry until it is destroyed. This reminds us of the irritation of a nerve and the reflex action produced thereby; while for the analogue of belief, in the nervous system, we must look to what are called nervous associations—for example, to that habit of the nerves in consequence of which the smell of a peach will make the mouth water.

IV

The irritation of doubt causes a struggle to attain a state of belief. I shall term this struggle *inquiry,* though it must be admitted that this is sometimes not a very apt designation.

The irritation of doubt is the only immediate motive for the struggle to attain belief. It is certainly best for us that our beliefs should be such as may truly guide our actions so as to satisfy our desires; and this reflection will make us reject every belief which does not seem to have been so formed as to insure this result. But it will only do so by creating a doubt in the place of that belief. With the doubt, therefore, the struggle begins, and with the cessation of doubt it ends. Hence, the sole object of inquiry is the settlement of opinion. We may fancy that this is not enough for us, and that we seek, not merely an opinion, but a true opinion. But put this fancy to the test, and it proves groundless; for as soon as a firm belief is reached we are entirely satisfied, whether the belief be true or false. And it is clear that nothing out of the sphere of our knowledge can be our object, for nothing which does not affect the mind can be the motive for mental effort. The most that can be maintained is, that we seek for a belief that we shall *think* to be true. But we think each one of our beliefs to be true, and, indeed, it is mere tautology to say so.

That the settlement of opinion is the sole end of inquiry is a very important proposition. It sweeps away, at once, various vague and erroneous conceptions of proof. A few of these may be noticed here.

1. Some philosophers have imagined that to start an inquiry it was only necessary to utter a question whether orally or by setting it down upon paper, and have even recommended us to begin our studies with questioning everything! But the mere putting of a proposition into the interrogative form does not stimulate the mind to any struggle after belief. There must be a real and living doubt, and without this all discussion is idle.

2. It is a very common idea that a demonstration must rest on some ultimate and absolutely indubitable propositions. These, according to one school, are first principles of a general nature; according to another, are first sensations. But, in point of fact, an inquiry, to have that completely satisfactory result called demonstration, has only to start with propositions perfectly free from all actual doubt. If the premisses are not in fact doubted at all, they cannot be more satisfactory than they are.

3. Some people seem to love to argue a point after all the world is fully convinced of it. But no further advance can be made. When doubt ceases, mental action on the subject comes to an end; and, if it did go on, it would be without a purpose.

V

If the settlement of opinion is the sole object of inquiry, and if belief is of the nature of a habit, why should we not attain the desired end, by taking as answer to a question any we may fancy, and constantly reiterating it to ourselves, dwelling on all which may conduce to that belief, and learning to turn with contempt and hatred from anything that might disturb it? This simple and direct method is really pursued by many men. I remember once being entreated not to read a certain newspaper lest it might change my opinion upon free-trade. "Lest I might be entrapped by its fallacies and misstatements," was the form of expression. "You are not," my friend said, "a special student of political economy. You might, therefore, easily be deceived by fallacious arguments upon the subject. You might, then, if you read this paper, be led to believe in protection. But you admit that free-trade is the true doctrine; and you do not wish to believe what is not true." I have often known this system to be deliberately adopted. Still oftener, the instinctive dislike of an undecided state of mind, exaggerated into a vague dread of doubt, makes men cling spasmodically to the views they already take. The man feels that, if he only holds to his belief without wavering, it will be entirely satisfactory. Nor can it be denied that a steady and immovable faith yields great peace of mind. It may, indeed, give rise to inconveniences, as if a man should resolutely continue to believe that fire would not burn him, or that he would be eternally damned if he received his *ingesta* otherwise than through a stomach-pump. But then the man who adopts this method will not allow that its inconveniences are greater than its advantages. He will say, "I hold steadfastly to the truth, and the truth is always wholesome." And in many cases it may very well be that the pleasure he derives from his calm faith overbalances any inconveniences resulting from its deceptive character. Thus, if it be true that death is annihilation, then the man who believes that he will certainly go straight to heaven when he dies, provided he have fulfilled certain simple observances in this life, has a cheap pleasure which will not be followed by the least disappointment. A similar consideration seems to have weight with many persons in religious topics, for we frequently hear it said, "Oh, I could not believe so-and-so, because I should be wretched if I did." When an ostrich buries its head in the sand as danger approaches, it very likely takes the happiest course. It hides the danger, and then calmly says there is no danger; and, if it feels perfectly sure there is none, why should it raise its head to see? A man may go through life, systematically keeping out of view all that might cause a change in his opinions, and if he only succeeds—basing his method, as he does, on two fundamental psychological laws—I do not see what can be said against his doing so. It would be an egotistical impertinence to object that his procedure is irrational, for that only amounts to saying that his method of settling belief is not ours. He does not propose to himself to be rational, and, indeed, will often talk with scorn of man's weak and illusive reason. So let him think as he pleases.

But this method of fixing belief, which may be called the method of tenacity, will be unable to hold its ground in practice. The social impulse is against it. The man who adopts it will find that other men think differently from him, and it will be apt to occur to him, in some saner moment, that their opinions are quite as good as his own, and this will shake his confidence in his belief. This conception, that another man's thought or sentiment may be equivalent to one's own, is a distinctly new step, and a highly important one. It arises from an impulse too strong in man to be suppressed, without danger of destroying the human species. Unless we make ourselves hermits, we shall necessarily influence each other's opinions; so that the problem becomes how to fix belief, not in the individual merely, but in the community.

Let the will of the state act, then, instead of that of the individual. Let an institution be created which shall have for its object to keep correct doctrines before the attention of the people, to reiterate them perpetually, and to teach them to the young; having at the same time power to prevent contrary doctrines from being taught, advocated, or expressed. Let all possible causes of a change of mind be removed from men's apprehensions. Let them be kept ignorant, lest they should learn of some reason to think otherwise than they do. Let their passions be enlisted, so that they may regard private and unusual opinions with hatred and horror. Then, let all men who reject the established belief be terrified into silence. Let the people turn out and tar-and-feather such men, or let inquisitions be made into the manner of thinking of suspected persons, and when they are found guilty of forbidden beliefs, let them be subjected to some signal punishment. When complete agreement could not otherwise be reached, a general massacre of all who have not thought in a certain way has proved a very effective means of settling opinion in a country. If the power to do this be wanting, let a list of opinions be drawn up, to which no man of the least independence of thought can assent, and let the faithful be required to accept all these propositions, in order to segregate them as radically as possible from the influence of the rest of the world.

This method has, from the earliest times, been one of the chief means of upholding correct theological and political doctrines, and of preserving their universal or catholic character. In Rome, especially, it has been practised from the days of Numa Pompilius to those of Pius Nonus. This is the most perfect example in history; but wherever there is a priesthood—and no religion has been without one—this method has been more or less made use of. Wherever there is an aristocracy, or a guild, or any association of a class of men whose interests depend, or are supposed to depend, on certain propositions, there will be inevitably found some traces of this natural product of social feeling. Cruelties always accompany this system; and when it is consistently carried out, they become atrocities of the most horrible kind in the eyes of any rational man. Nor should this occasion surprise, for the officer of a society does not feel justified in surrendering the interests of that society for the sake of mercy, as he might his own private interests. It is natural, therefore, that sympathy and fellowship should thus produce a most ruthless power.

In judging this method of fixing belief, which may be called the method of authority, we must, in the first place, allow its immeasurable mental and moral superiority to the method of tenacity. Its success is proportionately greater; and, in fact, it has over and over again worked the most majestic results. The mere structures of stone which it has caused to be put together—in Siam, for example, in Egypt, and in Europe—have many of them a sublimity hardly more than rivaled by the greatest works of Nature. And, except the geological epochs, there are no periods of time so vast as those which are measured by some of these organized faiths. If we scrutinize the matter close-ly, we shall find that there has not been one of their creeds which has remained always the same; yet the change is so slow as to be imperceptible during one person's life, so that individual belief remains sensibly fixed. For the mass of mankind, then, there is perhaps no better method than this. If it is their high-est impulse to be intellectual slaves, then slaves they ought to remain.

But no institution can undertake to regulate opinions upon every subject. Only the most important ones can be attended to, and on the rest men's minds must be left to the action of natural causes. This imperfection will be no source of weakness so long as men are in such a state of culture that one opinion does not influence another—that is, so long as they cannot put two and two togeth-er. But in the most priest-ridden states some individuals will be found who are raised above that condition. These men possess a wider sort of social feeling; they see that men in other countries and in other ages have held to very differ-ent doctrines from those which they themselves have been brought up to be-lieve; and they cannot help seeing that it is the mere accident of their having been taught as they have, and of their having been surrounded with the man-ners and associations they have, that has caused them to believe as they do and not far differently. Nor can their candour resist the reflection that there is no reason to rate their own views at a higher value than those of other nations and other centuries; thus giving rise to doubts in their minds.

They will further perceive that such doubts as these must exist in their minds with reference to every belief which seems to be determined by the caprice either of themselves or of those who originated the popular opinions. The willful adherence to a belief, and the arbitrary forcing of it upon others, must, therefore, both be given up. A different new method of settling opinions must be adopted, that shall not only produce an impulse to believe, but shall also decide what proposition it is which is to be believed. Let the action of nat-ural preferences be unimpeded, then, and under their influence let men, con-versing together and regarding matters in different lights, gradually develop beliefs in harmony with natural causes. This method resembles that by which conceptions of art have been brought to maturity. The most perfect example of it is to be found in the history of metaphysical philosophy. Systems of this sort have not usually rested upon any observed facts, at least not in any great de-gree. They have been chiefly adopted because their fundamental propositions seemed "agreeable to reason." This is an apt expression; it does not mean that which agrees with experience, but that which we find ourselves inclined to be-lieve. Plato, for example, finds it agreeable to reason that the distances of the celestial spheres from one another should be proportional to the different lengths of strings which produce harmonious chords. Many philosophers have been led to their main conclusions by considerations like this; but this is the lowest and least developed form which the method takes, for it is clear that another man might find Kepler's theory, that the celestial spheres are pro-portional to the inscribed and circumscribed spheres of the different regular solids, more agreeable to *his* reason. But the shock of opinions will soon lead men to rest on preferences of a far more universal nature. Take, for example, the doctrine that man only acts selfishly—that is, from the consideration that acting in one way will afford him more pleasure than acting in another. This rests on no fact in the world, but it has had a wide acceptance as being the only reasonable theory.

This method is far more intellectual and respectable from the point of view of reason than either of the others which we have noticed. But its failure has been the most manifest. It makes of inquiry something similar to the development of taste; but taste, unfortunately, is always more or less a matter of fashion, and accordingly metaphysicians have never come to any fixed agreement, but the pendulum has swung backward and forward between a more material and a more spiritual philosophy, from the earliest times to the latest. And so from this, which has been called the *a priori* method, we are driven, in Lord Bacon's phrase, to a true induction. We have examined into this *a priori* method as something which promised to deliver our opinions from their accidental and capricious element. But development, while it is a process which eliminates the effect of some casual circumstances, only magnifies that of others. This method, therefore, does not differ in a very essential way from that of authority. The government may not have lifted its finger to influence my convictions; I may have been left outwardly quite free to choose, we will say, between monogamy and polygamy, and, appealing to my conscience only, I may have concluded that the latter practice is in itself licentious. But when I come to see that the chief obstacle to the spread of Christianity among a people of as high culture as the Hindoos has been a conviction of the immorality of our way of treating women, I cannot help seeing that, though governments do not interfere, sentiments in their development will be very greatly determined by accidental causes. Now, there are some people, among whom I must suppose that my reader is to be found, who, when they see that any belief of theirs is determined by any circumstance extraneous to the facts, will from that moment not merely admit in words that that belief is doubtful, but will experience a real doubt of it, so that it ceases to be a belief.

To satisfy our doubts, therefore, it is necessary that a method should be found by which our beliefs may be determined by nothing human, but by some external permanency—by something upon which our thinking has no effect. Some mystics imagine that they have such a method in a private inspiration from on high. But that is only a form of the method of tenacity, in which the conception of truth as something public is not yet developed. Our external permanency would not be external, in our sense, if it was restricted in its influence to one individual. It must be something which affects, or might affect, every man. And, though these affections are necessarily as various as are individual conditions, yet the method must be such that the ultimate conclusion of every man shall be the same. Such is the method of science. Its fundamental hypothesis, restated in more familiar language, is this: There are Real things, whose characters are entirely independent of our opinions about them; those Reals affect our senses according to regular laws, and, though our sensations are as different as are our relations to the objects, yet, by taking advantage of the laws of perception, we can ascertain by reasoning how things really and truly are; and any man, if he have sufficient experience and he reason enough about it, will be led to the one True conclusion. The new conception here involved is that of Reality. It may be asked how I know that there are any Reals. If this hypothesis is the sole support of my method of inquiry, my method of inquiry must not be used to support my hypothesis. The reply is this: 1. If investigation cannot be regarded as proving that there are Real things, it at least does not lead to a contrary conclusion; but the method and the conception on which it is based remain ever in harmony. No doubts of the method, therefore, necessarily arise from its practice, as is the case with all the others. 2. The feeling which gives rise to any method of fixing belief is a dissatisfaction at two repugnant propositions. But here already is a vague concession that there is some *one* thing which a proposition should represent. Nobody, therefore, can really doubt that there are Reals, for, if he did, doubt would not be a source of dissatisfaction. The hypothesis, therefore, is one which every mind admits. So that the social impulse does not cause men to doubt it. 3. Everybody uses the scientific method about a great many things, and only ceases to use it when he does not know how to apply it. 4. Experience of the method has not led us to doubt it, but, on the contrary, scientific investigation has had the most wonderful triumphs in the way of settling opinion. These afford the explanation of my not doubting the method or the hypothesis which it supposes; and not having any doubt, nor believing that anybody else whom I could influence has, it would be the merest babble for me to say more about it. If there be anybody with a living doubt upon the subject, let him consider it. . . .

This is the only one of the four methods which presents any distinction of a right and a wrong way. If I adopt the method of tenacity, and shut myself out from all influences, whatever I think necessary to doing this, is necessary according to that method. So with the method of authority: the state may try to put down heresy by means which, from a scientific point of view, seem very ill-calculated to accomplish its purposes; but the only test *on that method* is what the state thinks; so that it cannot pursue the method wrongly. So with the *a priori* method. The very essence of it is to think as one is inclined to think. All metaphysicians will be sure to do that, however they may be inclined to judge each other to be perversely wrong. . . . But with the scientific method the case is different. I may start with known and observed facts to proceed to the unknown; and yet the rules which I follow in doing so may not be such as investigation would approve. The test of whether I am truly following the method is not an immediate appeal to my feelings and purposes, but, on the contrary, itself involves the application of the method. Hence it is that bad reasoning as well as good reasoning is possible; and this fact is the foundation of the practical side of logic.

How to Make Our Ideas Clear (1878)

C. S. PEIRCE

I

. . . The very first lesson that we have a right to demand that logic shall teach us is, how to make our ideas clear; and a most important one it is, depreciated only by minds who stand in need of it. To know what we think, to be masters of our own meaning, will make a solid foundation for great and weighty thought. It is most easily learned by those whose ideas are meagre and restricted; and far happier they than such as wallow helplessly in a rich mud of conceptions. A nation, it is true, may, in the course of generations, overcome the disadvantage of an excessive wealth of language and its natural concomitant, a vast, unfathomable deep of ideas. We may see it in history, slowly perfecting its literary forms, sloughing at length its metaphysics, and, by virtue of the untirable patience which is often a compensation, attaining great excellence in every branch of mental acquirement. The page of history is not yet unrolled that is to tell us whether such a people will or will not in the long run prevail over one whose ideas (like the words of their language) are few, but which possesses a wonderful mastery over those which it has. For an individual, however, there can be no question that a few clear ideas are worth more than many confused ones. A young man would hardly be persuaded to sacrifice the greater part of his thoughts to save the rest; and the muddled head is the least apt to see the necessity of such a sacrifice. Him we can usually only commiserate, as a person with a congenital defect. Time will help him, but intellectual maturity with regard to clearness is apt to come rather late. This seems an unfortunate arrangement of Nature, inasmuch as clearness is of less use to a man settled in life, whose errors have in great measure had their effect, than it would be to one whose path lay before him. It is terrible to see how a single unclear idea, a single formula without meaning, lurking in a young man's head, will sometimes act like an obstruction of inert matter in an artery, hindering the nutrition of the brain, and condemning its victim to pine away in the fullness of his intellectual vigor and in the midst of intellectual plenty. . . .

II

The principles set forth in the first part of this essay lead, at once, to a method of reaching a clearness of thought of higher grade than the "distinctness" of the logicians. It was there noticed that the action of thought is excited by the

From *Chance, Love, and Logic: Philosophical Essays* by Charles Sanders Peirce. Published by University of Nebraska Press, Lincoln, NE.

irritation of doubt, and ceases when belief is attained; so that the production of belief is the sole function of thought. All these words, however, are too strong for my purpose. It is as if I had described the phenomena as they appear under a mental microscope. Doubt and Belief, as the words are commonly employed, relate to religious or other grave discussions. But here I use them to designate the starting of any question, no matter how small or how great, and the resolution of it. If, for instance, in a horse-car, I pull out my purse and find a five-cent nickel and five coppers, I decide, while my hand is going to the purse, in which way I will pay my fare. To call such a question Doubt, and my decision Belief, is certainly to use words very disproportionate to the occasion. To speak of such a doubt as causing an irritation which needs to be appeased, suggests a temper which is uncomfortable to the verge of insanity. Yet, looking at the matter minutely, it must be admitted that, if there is the least hesitation as to whether I shall pay the five coppers or the nickel (as there will be sure to be, unless I act from some previously contracted habit in the matter), though irritation is too strong a word, yet I am excited to such small mental activity as may be necessary to deciding how I shall act. Most frequently doubts arise from some indecision, however momentary, in our action. Sometimes it is not so. I have, for example, to wait in a railway-station, and to pass the time I read the advertisements on the walls. I compare the advantages of different trains and different routes which I never expect to take, merely fancying myself to be in a state of hesitancy, because I am bored with having nothing to trouble me. Feigned hesitancy, whether feigned for mere amusement or with a lofty purpose, plays a great part in the production of scientific inquiry. However the doubt may originate, it stimulates the mind to an activity which may be slight or energetic, calm or turbulent. Images pass rapidly through consciousness, one incessantly melting into another, until at last, when all is over—it may be in a fraction of a second, in an hour, or after long years—we find ourselves decided as to how we should act under such circumstances as those which occasioned our hesitation. In other words, we have attained belief.

In this process we observe two sorts of elements of consciousness, the distinction between which may best be made clear by means of an illustration. In a piece of music there are the separate notes, and there is the air. A single tone may be prolonged for an hour or a day, and it exists as perfectly in each second of that time as in the whole taken together; so that, as long as it is sounding, it might be present to a sense from which everything in the past was as completely absent as the future itself. But it is different with the air, the performance of which occupies a certain time, during the portions of which only portions of it are played. It consists in an orderliness in the succession of sounds which strike the ear at different times; and to perceive it there must be some continuity of consciousness which makes the events of a lapse of time present to us. We certainly only perceive the air by hearing the separate notes; yet we cannot be said to directly hear it, for we hear only what is present at the instant, and an orderliness of succession cannot exist in an instant. These two sorts of objects, what we are *immediately* conscious of and what we are *mediately* conscious of, are found in all consciousness. Some elements (the sensations) are completely present at every instant so long as they last, while others (like thought) are actions having beginning, middle, and end, and consist in a congruence in the succession of sensations which flow through the mind. They cannot be immediately present to us, but must cover some portion of the past or future. Thought is a thread of melody running through the succession of our sensations. . . .

And what, then, is belief? It is the demi-cadence which closes a musical phrase in the symphony of our intellectual life. We have seen that it has just three properties: First, it is something that we are aware of; second, it appeases the irritation of doubt; and, third, it involves the establishment in our nature of a rule of action, or, say for short, a *habit*. As it appeases the irritation of doubt, which is the motive for thinking, thought relaxes, and comes to rest for a moment when belief is reached. But, since belief is a rule for action, the application of which involves further doubt and further thought, at the same time that it is a stopping-place, it is also a new starting-place for thought. That is why I have permitted myself to call it thought at rest, although thought is essentially an action. The *final* upshot of thinking is the exercise of volition, and of this thought no longer forms a part; but belief is only a stadium of mental action, an effect upon our nature due to thought, which will influence future thinking.

The essence of belief is the establishment of a habit; and different beliefs are distinguished by the different modes of action to which they give rise. If beliefs do not differ in this respect, if they appease the same doubt by producing the same rule of action, then no mere differences in the manner of consciousness of them can make them different beliefs, any more than playing a tune in different keys is playing different tunes. Imaginary distinctions are often drawn between beliefs which differ only in their mode of expression;— the wrangling which ensues is real enough, however. To believe that any objects are arranged among themselves as in Fig. 1, and to believe that they are arranged in Fig. 2, are one and the same belief; yet it is conceivable that a man

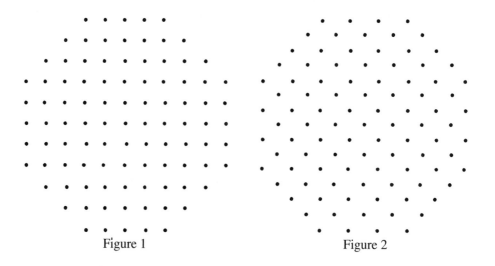

Figure 1   Figure 2

should assert one proposition and deny the other. Such false distinctions do as much harm as the confusion of beliefs really different, and are among the pitfalls of which we ought constantly to beware, especially when we are upon metaphysical ground. One singular deception of this sort, which often occurs, is to mistake the sensation produced by our own unclearness of thought for a character of the object we are thinking. Instead of perceiving that the obscurity is purely subjective, we fancy that we contemplate a quality of the object which is essentially mysterious; and if our conception be afterward presented to us in a clear form we do not recognize it as the same, owing to the absence of the feeling of unintelligibility. So long as this deception lasts, it obviously puts an impassable barrier in the way of perspicuous thinking; so that it equally interests the opponents of rational thought to perpetuate it, and its adherents to guard against it. . . .

From all these sophisms we shall be perfectly safe so long as we reflect that the whole function of thought is to produce habits of action; and that whatever there is connected with a thought, but irrelevant to its purpose, is an accretion to it, but no part of it. If there be a unity among our sensations which has no reference to how we shall act on a given occasion, as when we listen to a piece of music, why we do not call that thinking. To develop its meaning, we have, therefore, simply to determine what habits it produces, for what a thing means is simply what habits it involves. Now, the identity of a habit depends on how it might lead us to act, not merely under such circumstances as are likely to arise, but under such as might possibly occur, no matter how improbable they may be. What the habit is depends on *when* and *how* it causes us to act. As for the *when*, every stimulus to action is derived from perception; as for the *how*, every purpose of action is to produce some sensible result. Thus, we come down to what is tangible and conceivably practical, as the root of every real distinction of thought, no matter how subtle it may be; and there is no distinction of meaning so fine as to consist in anything but a possible difference of practice.

To see what this principle leads to, consider in the light of it such a doctrine as that of transubstantiation. The Protestant churches generally hold that the elements of the sacrament are flesh and blood only in a tropical sense; they nourish our souls as meat and the juice of it would our bodies. But the Catholics maintain that they are literally just meat and blood; although they possess all the sensible qualities of wafercakes and diluted wine. But we can have no conception of wine except what may enter into a belief, either—

1. That this, that, or the other, is wine; or,
2. That wine possesses certain properties.

Such beliefs are nothing but self-notifications that we should, upon occasion, act in regard to such things as we believe to be wine according to the qualities which we believe wine to possess. The occasion of such action would be some sensible perception, the motive of it to produce some sensible result. Thus our action has exclusive reference to what affects the senses, our habit has the same bearing as our action, our belief the same as our habit, our conception the same as our belief; and we can consequently mean nothing by wine but what has certain effects, direct or indirect, upon our senses; and to talk of something as having all the sensible characters of wine, yet being in reality blood, is senseless jargon. Now, it is not my object to pursue the theological question; and having used it as a logical example I drop it, without caring to anticipate the theologian's reply. I only desire to point out how impossible it is that we should have an idea in our minds which relates to anything but conceived sensible effects of things. Our idea of anything *is* our idea of its sensible effects; and if we fancy that we have any other we deceive ourselves, and mistake a mere sensation accompanying the thought for a part of the thought itself. It is absurd to say that thought has any meaning unrelated to its only function. It is foolish for Catholics and Protestants to fancy themselves in disagreement about the elements of the sacrament, if they agree in regard to all their sensible effects, here and hereafter.

It appears, then, that the rule for attaining the third grade of clearness of apprehension is as follows: Consider what effects, that might conceivably have practical bearings, we conceive the object of our conception to have. Then, our conception of these effects is the whole of our conception of the object.

III

Let us illustrate this rule by some examples; and, to begin with the simplest one possible, let us ask what we mean by calling a thing *hard*. Evidently that it will not be scratched by many other substances. The whole conception of this quality, as of every other, lies in its conceived effects. There is absolutely no difference between a hard thing and a soft thing so long as they are not brought to the test. Suppose, then, that a diamond could be crystallized in the midst of a cushion of soft cotton, and should remain there until it was finally burned up. Would it be false to say that that diamond was soft? This seems a foolish question, and would be so, in fact, except in the realm of logic. There such questions are often of the greatest utility as serving to bring logical principles into sharper relief than real discussions ever could. In studying logic we must not put them aside with hasty answers, but must consider them with attentive care, in order to make out the principles involved. We may, in the present case, modify our question, and ask what prevents us from saying that all hard bodies remain perfectly soft until they are touched, when their hardness increases with the pressure until they are scratched. Reflection will show that the reply is this: there would be no *falsity* in such modes of speech. They would involve a modification of our present usage of speech with regard to the words hard and soft, but not of their meanings. For they represent no fact to be different from what it is; only they involve arrangements of facts which would be exceedingly maladroit. This leads us to remark that the question of what would occur under circumstances which do not actually arise is not a question of fact, but only of the most perspicuous arrangement of them. For example, the question of free-will and fate in its simplest form, stripped of verbiage, is something like this: I have done something of which I am ashamed; could I, by an effort of the will, have resisted the temptation, and done otherwise? The philosophical reply is, that this is not a question of fact, but only of the arrangement of facts. Arranging them so as to exhibit what is particularly pertinent to my question—namely, that I ought to blame myself for having done wrong—it is perfectly true to say that, if I had willed to do otherwise than I did, I should have done otherwise. On the other hand, arranging the facts so as to exhibit another important consideration, it is equally true that, when a temptation has once been allowed to work, it will, if it has a certain force, produce its effect, let me struggle how I may. There is no objection to a contradiction in what would result from a false supposition. The *reductio ad absurdum* consists in showing that contradictory results would follow from a hypothesis which is consequently judged to be false. Many questions are involved in the free-will discussion, and I am far from desiring to say that both sides are equally right. On the contrary, I am of opinion that one side denies important facts, and that the other does not. But what I do say is, that the above single question was the origin of the whole doubt; that, had it not been for this question, the controversy would never have arisen; and that this question is perfectly solved in the manner which I have indicated. ...

IV

Let us now approach the subject of logic, and consider a conception which particularly concerns it, that of *reality*. Taking clearness in the sense of familiarity, no idea could be clearer than this. Every child uses it with perfect confidence, never dreaming that he does not understand it. As for clearness in its second grade, however, it would probably puzzle most men, even among those of a reflective turn of mind, to give an abstract definition of the real. Yet such a definition may perhaps be reached by considering the points of difference between reality and its opposite, fiction. A figment is a product of somebody's imagination; it has such characters as his thought impresses upon it. That those characters are independent of how you or I think is an external reality. There are, however, phenomena within our own minds, dependent upon our thought, which are at the same time real in the sense that we really think them. But though their characters depend on how we think, they do not depend on what we think those characters to be. Thus, a dream has a real existence as a mental phenomenon, if somebody has really dreamt it; that he dreamt so and so, does not depend on what anybody thinks was dreamt, but is completely independent of all opinion on the subject. On the other hand, considering, not the fact of dreaming, but the thing dreamt, it retains its peculiarities by virtue of no other fact than that it was dreamt to possess them.

Thus we may define the real as that whose characters are independent of what anybody may think them to be.

But, however satisfactory such a definition may be found, it would be a great mistake to suppose that it makes the idea of reality perfectly clear. Here, then, let us apply our rules. According to them, reality, like every other quality, consists in the peculiar sensible effects which things partaking of it produce. The only effect which real things have is to cause belief, for all the sensations which they excite emerge into consciousness in the form of beliefs. . . .

. . . [A]ll the followers of science are animated by a cheerful hope that the processes of investigation, if only pushed far enough, will give one certain solution to each question to which they apply it. One man may investigate the velocity of light by studying the transits of Venus and the aberration of the stars; another by the oppositions of Mars and the eclipses of Jupiter's satellites; a third by the method of Fizeau; a fourth by that of Foucault; a fifth by the motions of the curves of Lissajoux; a sixth, a seventh, an eighth, and a ninth, may follow the different methods of comparing the measures of statical and dynamical electricity. They may at first obtain different results, but, as each perfects his method and his processes, the results are found to move steadily together toward a destined centre. So with all scientific research. Different minds may set out with the most antagonistic views, but the progress of investigation carries them by a force outside of themselves to one and the same conclusion. This activity of thought by which we are carried, not where we wish, but to a fore-ordained goal, is like the operation of destiny. No modification of the point of view taken, no selection of other facts for study, no natural bent of mind even, can enable a man to escape the predestinate opinion. This great hope is embodied in the conception of truth and reality. The opinion which is *fated* to be ultimately agreed to by all who investigate, is what we mean by the truth, and the object represented in this opinion is the real. That is the way I would explain reality.

But it may be said that this view is directly opposed to the abstract definition which we have given of reality, inasmuch as it makes the characters of the real depend on what is ultimately thought about them. But the answer to this is that, on the one hand, reality is independent, not necessarily of thought in general, but only of what you or I or any finite number of men may think about it; and that, on the other hand, though the object of the final opinion depends on what that opinion is, yet what that opinion is does not depend on what you or I or any man thinks. Our perversity and that of others may indefinitely postpone the settlement of opinion; it might even conceivably cause an arbitrary proposition to be universally accepted as long as the human race should last. Yet even that would not change the nature of the belief, which alone could be the result of investigation carried sufficiently far; and if, after the extinction of our race, another should arise with faculties and disposition for investigation, that true opinion must be the one which they would ultimately come to. "Truth crushed to earth shall rise again," and the opinion which would finally result from investigation does not depend on how anybody may actually think. But the reality of that which is real does depend on the real fact that investigation is destined to lead, at last, if continued long enough, to a belief in it.

But I may be asked what I have to say to all the minute facts of history, forgotten never to be recovered, to the lost books of the ancients, to the *buried secrets*.

> *Full many a gem of purest ray serene*
> *The dark, unfathomed caves of ocean bear;*
> *Full many a flower is born to blush unseen,*
> *And waste its sweetness on the desert air.*

Do these things not really exist because they are hopelessly beyond the reach of our knowledge? And then, after the universe is dead (according to the prediction of some scientists), and all life has ceased forever, will not the shock of atoms continue though there will be no mind to know it? To this I reply that, though in no possible state of knowledge can any number be great enough to express the relation between the amount of what rests unknown to the amount of the known, yet it is unphilosophical to suppose that, with regard to any given question (which has any clear meaning), investigation would not bring forth a solution of it, if it were carried far enough. Who would have said, a few years ago, that we could ever know of what substances stars are made whose light may have been longer in reaching us than the human race has existed? Who can be sure of what we shall not know in a few hundred years? Who can guess what would be the result of continuing the pursuit of science for ten thousand years, with the activity of the last hundred? And if it were to go on for a million, or a billion, or any number of years you please, how is it possible to say that there is any question which might not ultimately be solved?

But it may be objected, "Why make so much of these remote considerations, especially when it is your principle that only practical distinctions have a meaning?" Well, I must confess that it makes very little difference whether we say that a stone on the bottom of the ocean, in complete darkness, is brilliant or not—that is to say, that it *probably* makes no difference, remembering always that that stone *may* be fished up tomorrow. But that there are gems at the bottom of the sea, flowers in the untraveled desert, etc., are propositions which, like that about a diamond being hard when it is not pressed, concern much more the arrangement of our language than they do the meaning of our ideas.

It seems to me, however, that we have, by the application of our rule, reached so clear an apprehension of what we mean by reality, and of the fact which the idea rests on, that we should not, perhaps, be making a pretension so presumptuous as it would be singular, if we were to offer a metaphysical theory of existence for universal acceptance among those who employ the scientific method of fixing belief. However, as metaphysics is a subject much more curious than useful, the knowledge of which, like that of a sunken reef, serves chiefly to enable us to keep clear of it, I will not trouble the reader with any more Ontology at this moment. I have already been led much further into that path than I should have desired; and I have given the reader such a dose of mathematics, psychology, and all that is most abstruse, that I fear he may already have left me, and that what I am now writing is for the compositor and proof-reader exclusively. . . .

What Pragmatism Is (1905)

C. S. Peirce

. . . Much as the writer has gained from the perusal of what other pragmatists have written, he still thinks there is a decisive advantage in his original conception of the doctrine. From this original form every truth that follows from any of the other forms can be deduced, while some errors can be avoided into which other pragmatists have fallen. The original view appears, too, to be a more compact and unitary conception than the others. But its capital merit, in the writer's eyes, is that it more readily connects itself with a critical proof of its truth. Quite in accord with the logical order of investigation, it usually happens that one first forms an hypothesis that seems more and more reasonable the further one examines into it, but that only a good deal later gets crowned with an adequate proof. The present writer, having had the pragmatist theory under consideration for many years longer than most of its adherents, would naturally have given more attention to the proof of it. At any rate, in endeavoring to explain pragmatism, he may be excused for confining himself to that form of it that he knows best. In the present article there will be space only to explain just what this doctrine (which, in such hands as it has now fallen into, may probably play a pretty prominent part in the philosophical discussions of the next coming years) really consist in. . . .

The bare definition of pragmaticism could convey no satisfactory comprehension of it to the most apprehensive of minds, but requires the commentary to be given below. Moreover, this definition takes no notice of one or two other doctrines without the previous acceptance (or virtual acceptance) of which pragmaticism itself would be a nullity. They are included as a part of the pragmatism of Schiller, but the present writer prefers not to mingle different propositions. The preliminary propositions had better be stated forthwith.

The difficulty in doing this is that no formal list of them has ever been made. They might all be included under the vague maxim, "Dismiss make-believes." Philosophers of very diverse stripes propose that philosophy shall take its start from one or another state of mind in which no man, least of all a beginner in philosophy, actually is. One proposes that you shall begin by doubting everything, and says that there is only one thing that you cannot doubt, as if doubting were "as easy as lying." Another proposes that we should begin by observing "the first impressions of sense," forgetting that our very percepts are the results of cognitive elaboration. But in truth, there is but one state of mind from which you can "set out," namely, the very state of mind in which you actually find yourself at the time you do "set out"—a state in which you are laden with an immense mass of cognition already formed, of which you cannot divest yourself if you would; and who knows whether, if you could, you would not have made all knowledge impossible to yourself? Do you call it *doubting* to write down on a piece of paper that you doubt? If so, doubt has nothing to do with any serious business. But do not make believe; if pedantry has not eaten all the reality out of you, recognize, as you must, that there is much that you do not doubt, in the least. Now that which you do not at all doubt, you must and do regard as infallible, absolute truth. Here breaks in Mr. Make Believe: "What! Do you mean to say that one is to believe what is not true, or that what a man does not doubt is *ipso facto* true?" No, but unless he can make a thing white and black at once, *he* has to regard what he does not doubt as absolutely true. Now you, *per hypothesiu*, are that man. "But you tell me there are scores of things I do not doubt. I really cannot persuade myself that there is not some one of them about which I am mistaken." You are adducing one of your make-believe facts, which, even if it were established, would only go to show that doubt has a *limen*, that is, is only called into being by a certain finite stimulus. You only puzzle yourself by talking about this metaphysical "truth" and metaphysical "falsity," that you know nothing about. All you have any dealings with are your doubts and beliefs, with the course of life that forces new beliefs upon you and gives you power to doubt old beliefs. If your terms "truth" and "falsity" are taken in such senses as to be definable in terms of doubt and belief and the course of experience (as for example they would be if you were to define the "truth" as that to a belief in which belief would tend if it were to tend indefinitely toward absolute fixity), well and good: in that case, you are only talking about doubt and belief. But if by truth and falsity you mean something not definable in terms of doubt and belief in any way, then you are talking of entities of whose existence you can know nothing, and which Ockham's razor would clean shave off. Your problems would be greatly simplified if, instead of saying that you want to know the "Truth," you were simply to say that you want to attain a state of belief unassailable by doubt.

Belief is not a momentary mode of consciousness; it is a habit of mind essentially enduring for some time, and mostly (at least) unconscious; and like other habits, it is (until it meets with some surprise that begins its dissolution) perfectly self-satisfied. Doubt is of an altogether contrary genus. It is not a habit, but the privation of a habit. Now a privation of a habit, in order to be anything at all, must be a condition of erratic activity that in some way must get superseded by a habit.

Among the things which the reader, as a rational person, does not doubt is that he not merely has habits, but also can exert a measure of self-control over his future actions; which means, however, *not* that he can impart to them any arbitrarily assignable character, but on the contrary, that a process of self-preparation will tend to impart to action (when the occasion for it shall arise) one fixed character, which is indicated and perhaps roughly measured by the absence (or slightness) of the feeling of self-reproach, which subsequent reflection will induce. Now, this subsequent reflection is part of the self-preparation for action on the next occasion. Consequently, there is a tendency, as action is repeated again and again, for the action to approximate indefinitely toward the perfection of that fixed character, which would be marked by entire absence of self-reproach. The more closely this is approached, the less room for self-control there will be; and where no self-control is possible there will be no self-reproach.

These phenomena seem to be the fundamental characteristics which distinguish a rational being. Blame, in every case, appears to be a modification, often accomplished by a transference, or "projection," of the primary feeling of self-reproach. Accordingly, we never blame anybody for what had been beyond his power of previous self-control. Now, thinking is a species of conduct which is largely subject to self-control. In all their features (which there is no room to describe here), logical self-control is a perfect mirror of ethical self-control—unless it be rather a species under that genus. In accordance with this, what you cannot in the least help believing is not, justly speaking, wrong belief. In other words, for you it is the absolute truth. True, it is conceivable that you cannot help believing today, you might find you thoroughly disbelieve tomorrow. But then there is a certain distinction between things you "cannot" do, merely in the sense that nothing stimulates you to the great effort and endeavors that would be required, and things you cannot do because in their own nature they are insusceptible of being put into practice. In every stage of your excogitations, there is something of which you can only say, "I cannot think otherwise," and your experientially based hypothesis is that the impossibility is of the second kind.

There is no reason why "thought," in what has just been said, should be taken in that narrow sense in which silence and darkness are favorable to thought. It should rather be understood as covering all rational life, so that an experiment shall be an operation of thought. Of course, that ultimate state of habit to which the action of self-control ultimately tends, where no room is left for further self-control, is, in the case of thought, the state of fixed belief, or perfect knowledge. . . .

What Pragmatism Means (1907)

WILLIAM JAMES

Some years ago, being with a camping party in the mountains, I returned from a solitary ramble to find everyone engaged in a ferocious metaphysical dispute. The *corpus* of the dispute was a squirrel—a live squirrel supposed to be clinging to one side of a tree-trunk; while over against the tree's opposite side a human being was imagined to stand. This human witness tries to get sight of the squirrel by moving rapidly round the tree, but no matter how fast he goes, the squirrel moves as fast in the opposite direction, and always keeps the tree between himself and the man, so that never a glimpse of him is caught. The resultant metaphysical problem now is this: *Does the man go round the squirrel or not?* He goes round the tree, sure enough, and the squirrel is on the tree; but does he go round the squirrel? In the unlimited leisure of the wilderness, discussion had been worn threadbare. Everyone had taken sides, and was obstinate; and the numbers on both sides were even. Each side, when I appeared, therefore appealed to me to make it a majority. Mindful of the scholastic adage that whenever you meet a contradiction you must make a distinction, I immediately sought and found one, as follows: "Which party is right," I said, "depends on what you *practically mean* by 'going round' the squirrel. If you mean passing from the north of him to the east, then to the south, then to the west, and then to the north of him again, obviously the man does go round him, for he occupies these successive positions. But if on the contrary you mean being first in front of him, then on the right of him then behind him, then on his left, and finally in front again, it is quite as obvious that the man fails to go round him, for by the compensating movements the squirrel makes, he keeps his belly turned towards the man all the time, and his back turned away. Make the distinction, and there is no occasion for any farther dispute. You are both right and both wrong according as you conceive the verb 'to go round' in one practical fashion or the other." . . .

I tell this trivial anecdote because it is a peculiarly simple example of what I wish now to speak of as *the pragmatic method*. The pragmatic method is primarily a method of settling metaphysical disputes that otherwise might be interminable. Is the world one or many?—fated or free?—material or spiritual?—here are notions either of which may or may not hold good of the world; and disputes over such notions are unending. The pragmatic method in such cases is to try to interpret each notion by tracing its respective practical consequences. What difference would it practically make to anyone if this notion rather than that notion were true? If no practical difference whatever can be traced, then the alternatives mean practically the same thing, and all dispute is

From *The Writings of William James*, edited by John J. McDermott (New York, NY: Random House, Inc.) © Copyright 1967.

idle. Whenever a dispute is serious, we ought to be able to show some practical difference that must follow from one side or the other's being right.

A glance at the history of the idea will show you still better what pragmatism means. The term is derived from the same Greek word *pragma*, meaning action, from which our words 'practice' and 'practical' come. It was first introduced into philosophy by Mr. Charles Peirce in 1878 (in) an article entitled 'How to Make Our Ideas Clear,' in the *Popular Science Monthly* for January of that year. Mr. Peirce, after pointing out that our beliefs are really rules for action, said that, to develop a thought's meaning, we need only determine what conduct it is fitted to produce: that conduct is for us its sole significance. And the tangible fact at the root of all our thought-distinctions, however subtle, is that there is no one of them so fine as to consist in anything but a possible difference of practice. To attain perfect clearness in our thoughts of an object, then, we need only consider what conceivable effects of a practical kind the object may involve—what sensations we are to expect from it, and what reactions we must prepare. Our conception of these effects, whether immediate or remote, is then for us the whole of our conception of the object, so far as that conception has positive significance at all. . . .

To take in the importance of Peirce's principle, one must get accustomed to applying it to concrete cases. I found a few years ago that Ostwald, the illustrious Leipzig chemist, had been making perfectly distinct use of the principle of pragmatism in his lectures on the philosophy of science, tho he had not called it by that name.

"All realities influence our practice," he wrote me, "and that influence is their meaning for us. I am accustomed to put questions to my classes in this way: In what respects would the world be different if this alternative or that were true? If I can find nothing that would become different, then the alternative has no sense."

That is, the rival views mean practically the same thing, and meaning, other than practical, there is for us none. Ostwald in a published lecture gives this example of what he means. Chemists have long wrangled over the inner constitution of certain bodies called 'tautomerous.' Their properties seemed equally consistent with the notion that an instable hydrogen atom oscillates inside of them, or that they are instable mixtures of two bodies. Controversy raged; but never was decided. "It would never have begun," says Ostwald, "if the combatants had asked themselves what particular experimental fact could have been made different by one or the other view being correct. For it would then have appeared that no difference of fact could possibly ensue; and the quarrel was as unreal as if, theorizing in primitive times about the raising of dough by yeast, one party should have invoked a 'brownie,' while another insisted on an 'elf' as the true cause of the phenomenon."

It is astonishing to see how many philosophical disputes collapse into insignificance the moment you subject them to this simple test of tracing a concrete consequence. There can *be* no difference anywhere that doesn't *make* a difference elsewhere—no difference in abstract truth that doesn't express itself in a difference in concrete fact and in conduct consequent upon that fact, imposed on somebody, somehow, somewhere and somewhen. The whole function of philosophy ought to be to find out what definite difference it will make to you and me, at definite instants of our life, if this world-formula or that world-formula be the true one. . . .

Pragmatism represents a perfectly familiar attitude in philosophy, the empiricist attitude, but it represents it, as it seems to me, both in a more radical and in a less objectionable form than it has ever yet assumed. A pragmatist turns his back resolutely and once for all upon a lot of inveterate habits dear to professional philosophers. He turns away from abstraction and insufficiency, from verbal solutions, from bad *a priori* reasons, from fixed principles, closed systems, and pretended absolutes and origins. He turns towards concreteness and adequacy, towards facts, towards action, and towards power. That means the empiricist temper regnant, and the rationalist temper sincerely given up. It means the open air and possibilities of nature, as against dogma, artificiality and the pretence of finality in truth.

At the same time it does not stand for any special results. It is a method only. But the general triumph of that method would mean an enormous change in what I called in my last lecture the 'temperament' of philosophy. Teachers of the ultra-rationalistic type would be frozen out, much as the courtier type is frozen out in republics, as the ultramontane type of priest is frozen out in protestant lands. Science and metaphysics would come much nearer together, would in fact work absolutely hand in hand. . . .

Metaphysics has usually followed a very primitive kind of quest. You know how men have always hankered after unlawful magic, and you know what a great part, in magic, words have always played. . . . So the universe has always appeared to the natural mind as a kind of enigma, of which the key must be sought in the shape of some illuminating or power-bringing word or name. That word names the universe's *principle,* and to possess it is, after a fashion, to possess the universe itself 'God,' 'Matter,' 'Reason,' 'the Absolute,' 'Energy,' are so many solving names. You can rest when you have them. You are at the end of your metaphysical quest.

But if you follow the pragmatic method, you cannot look on any such word as closing your quest. You must bring out of each word its practical cash-value, set it at work within the stream of your experience. It appears less as a solution, then, than as a program for more work, and more particularly as an indication of the ways in which existing realities may be *changed.*

Theories thus become instruments, not answers to enigmas, in which we can rest. We don't lie back upon them, we move forward, and, on occasion, make nature over again by their aid. Pragmatism unstiffens all our theories, limbers them up and sets each one at work. Being nothing essentially new, it harmonizes with many ancient philosophic tendencies. It agrees with nominalism for instance, in always appealing to particulars; with utilitarianism in emphasizing practical aspects; with positivism in its disdain for verbal solutions, useless questions, and metaphysical abstractions.

All these, you see, are *anti-intellectualist* tendencies. Against rationalism as a pretension and a method, pragmatism is fully armed and militant. But, at the outset, at least, it stands for no particular results. It has no dogmas, and no doctrines save its method. . . .

No particular results then, so far, but only an attitude of orientation, is what the pragmatic method means. *The attitude of looking away from first things, principles, 'categories,' supposed necessities; and of looking towards last things, fruits, consequences, facts.*

So much for the pragmatic method! You may say that I have been praising it rather than explaining it to you, but I shall presently explain it abundantly enough by showing how it works on some familiar problems. Meanwhile the word pragmatism has come to be used in a still wider sense, as meaning also a certain *theory of truth. I* mean to give a whole lecture to the statement of that theory, after first paving the way, so I can be very brief now. But brevity is hard to follow, so I ask for your redoubled attention for a quarter of an hour. If much remains obscure, I hope to make it clearer in the later lectures.

One of the most successfully cultivated branches of philosophy in our time is what is called inductive logic, the study of the conditions under which our sciences have evolved. Writers on this subject have begun to show a singular unanimity as to what the laws of nature and elements of fact mean, when formulated by mathematicians, physicists and chemists. When the first mathematical, logical and natural uniformities, the first *laws*, were discovered, men were so carried away by the clearness, beauty and simplification that resulted, that they believed themselves to have deciphered authentically the eternal thoughts of the Almighty. His mind also thundered and reverberated in syllogisms. He also thought in conic sections, squares and roots and ratios, and geometrized like Euclid. He made Kepler's laws for the planets to follow; he made velocity increase proportionally to the time in falling bodies; he made the law of the sines for light to obey when refracted; he established the classes, orders, families and genera of plants and animals, and fixed the distances between them. He thought the archetypes of all things, and devised their variations; and when we rediscover any one of these his wondrous institutions, we seize his mind in its very literal intention.

But as the sciences have developed farther, the notion has gained ground that most, perhaps all, of our laws are only approximations. The laws themselves, moreover, have grown so numerous that there is no counting them; and so many rival formulations are proposed in all the branches of science that investigators have become accustomed to the notion that no theory is absolutely a transcript of reality, but that any one of them may from some point of view be useful. Their great use is to summarize old facts and to lead to new ones. They are only a man-made language, a conceptual shorthand, as someone calls them, in which we write our reports of nature; and languages, as is well known, tolerate much choice of expression and many dialects. . . .

Riding now on the front of this wave of scientific logic Messrs. Schiller and Dewey appear with their pragmatistic account of what truth everywhere signifies. Everywhere, these teachers say, 'truth' in our ideas and beliefs means the same thing that it means in science. It means, they say, nothing but this, *that ideas (which themselves are but parts of our experience) become true just in so far as they help us to get into satisfactory relation with other parts of our experience,* to summarize them and get about among them by conceptual short-cuts instead of following the interminable succession of particular phenomena. Any idea upon which we can ride, so to speak; any idea that will carry us prosperously from any one part of our experience to any other part, linking things satisfactorily, working securely, simplifying, saving labor; is true for just so much, true in so far forth, true *instrumentally*. . . .

Messrs. Dewey, Schiller and their allies, in reaching this general conception of all truth, have only followed the example of geologists, biologists and philologists. In the establishment of these other sciences, the successful stroke was always to take some simple process actually observable in operation—as denudation by weather, say, or variation from parental type, or change of dialect by incorporation of new words and pronunciations—and then to generalize it, making it apply to all times, and produce great results by summating its effects through the ages.

The observable process which Schiller and Dewey particularly singled out for generalization is the familiar one by which any individual settles into new opinions. The process here is always the same. The individual has a stock of old opinions already, but he meets a new experience that puts them to a strain. Somebody contradicts them; or in a reflective moment he discovers that they contradict each other; or he hears of facts with which they are incompatible; or desires arise in him which they cease to satisfy. The result is an inward trouble to which his mind till then had been a stranger, and from which he seeks to escape by modifying his previous mass of opinions. He saves as much of it as he can, for in this matter of belief we are all extreme conservatives. So he tries to change first this opinion, and then that (for they resist change very variously), until at last some new idea comes up which he can graft upon the ancient stock with a minimum of disturbance of the latter, some idea that mediates between the stock and the new experience and runs them into one another most felicitously and expediently.

This new idea is then adopted as the true one. It preserves the older stock of truths with a minimum of modification, stretching them just enough to make them admit the novelty, but conceiving that in ways as familiar as the case leaves possible. An *outrée* explanation, violating all our preconceptions, would never pass for a true account of a novelty. We should scratch round industriously till we found something less excentric. The most violent revolutions in an individual's beliefs leave most of his old order standing. Time and space, cause and effect, nature and history, and one's own biography remain untouched. New truth is always a go-between, a smoother-over of transitions. It marries old opinion to new fact so as ever to show a minimum of jolt, a maximum of continuity. We hold a theory true just in proportion to its success in solving this 'problem of maxima and minima.' But success in solving this problem is eminently a matter of approximation. We say this theory solves it on the whole more satisfactorily than that theory; but that means more satisfactorily to ourselves, and individuals will emphasize their points of satisfaction differently. To a certain degree, therefore, everything here is plastic.

The point I now urge you to observe particularly is the part played by the older truths. Failure to take account of it is the source of much of the unjust criticism leveled against pragmatism. Their influence is absolutely controlling. Loyalty to them is the first principle—in most cases it is the only principle; for by far the most usual way of handling phenomena so novel that they would make for a serious rearrangement of our preconceptions is to ignore them altogether, or to abuse those who bear witness for them.

You doubtless wish examples of this process of truth's growth, and the only trouble is their superabundance. The simplest case of new truth is of course the mere numerical addition of new kinds of facts, or of new single facts of old kinds, to our experience—an addition that involves no alteration in the old beliefs. Day follows day, and its contents are simply added. The new contents themselves are not true, they simply *come* and *are*. Truth is *what we say about* them, and when we say that they have come, truth is satisfied by the plain additive formula. . . .

I need not multiply instances. A new opinion counts as 'true' just in proportion as it gratifies the individual's desire to assimilate the novel in his experience to his beliefs in stock. It must both lean on old truth and grasp new fact; and its success (as I said a moment ago) in doing this, is a matter for the individual's appreciation. When old truth grows, then, by new truth's addition, it is for subjective reasons. We are in the process and obey the reasons. That new idea is truest which performs most felicitously its function of satisfying our double urgency. It makes itself true, gets itself classed as true, by the way it works; grafting itself then upon the ancient body of truth, which thus grows much as a tree grows by the activity of a new layer of cambium.

Now Dewey and Schiller proceed to generalize this observation and to apply it to the most ancient parts of truth. They also once were plastic. They also were called true for human reasons. They also mediated between still earlier truths and what in those days were novel observations. Purely objective truth, truth in whose establishment the function of giving human satisfaction in marrying previous parts of experience with newer parts played no rôle whatever, is nowhere to be found. The reasons why we call things true is the reason why they *are* true, for 'to be true' *means* only to perform this marriage-function.

The trail of the human serpent is thus over everything. Truth independent; truth that we *find* merely; truth no longer malleable to human need; truth incorrigible, in a word; such truth exists indeed superabundantly—or is supposed to exist by rationalistically minded thinkers; but then it means only the dead heart of the living tree, and its being there means only that truth also has its paleontology and its 'prescription,' and may grow stiff with years of veteran service and petrified in men's regard by sheer antiquity. But how plastic even the oldest truths nevertheless really are has been vividly shown in our day by the transformation of logical and mathematical ideas, a transformation which seems even to be invading physics. The ancient formulas are reinterpreted as special expressions of much wider principles, principles that our ancestors never got a glimpse of in their present shape and formulation.

Mr. Schiller still gives to all this view of truth the name of 'Humanism,' but, for this doctrine too, the name of pragmatism seems fairly to be in the ascendant, so I will treat it under the name of pragmatism in these lectures.

Such then would be the scope of pragmatism—first, a method; and second, a genetic theory of what is meant by truth. And these two things must be our future topics. . . .

The Will to Believe (1896)

WILLIAM JAMES

. . . I have brought with me tonight something like a sermon on justification by faith to read to you,—I mean an essay in justification *of* faith, a defence of our right to adopt a believing attitude in religious matters, in spite of the fact that our merely logical intellect may not have been coerced. 'The Will to Believe,' accordingly, is the title of my paper.

I have long defended to my own students the lawfulness of voluntarily adopted faith; but as soon as they have got well imbued with the logical spirit, they have as a rule refused to admit my contention to be lawful philosophically, even though in point of fact they were personally all the time chock-full of some faith or other themselves. . . .

I

Let us give the name of *hypothesis* to anything that may be proposed to our belief; and just as the electricians speak of live and dead wires, let us speak of any hypothesis as either live or dead. A live hypothesis is one which appeals as a real possibility to him to whom it is proposed. If I ask you to believe in the Mahdi, the notion makes no electric connection with your nature,—it refuses to scintillate with any credibility at all. As an hypothesis it is completely dead. To an Arab, however (even if he be not one of the Mahdi's followers), the hypothesis is among the mind's possibilities: it is alive. This shows that deadness and liveness in an hypothesis are not intrinsic properties, but relations to the individual thinker. They are measured by his willingness to act. The maximum of liveness in hypothesis means willingness to act irrevocably. Practically, that means belief; but there is some believing tendency wherever there is willingness to act at all.

From *The Writings of William James*, edited by John J. McDermott (New York, NY: Random House, Inc.) © Copyright 1967.

Next, let us call the decision between two hypotheses an option. Options may be of several kinds. They may be—1, *living* or *dead*; 2, *forced* or *avoidable*; 3, *momentous* or *trivial*; and for our purposes we may call an option a *genuine* option when it is of the forced, living, and momentous kind.

1. A living option is one in which both hypotheses are live ones. If I say to you: "Be a theosophist or be a Mohammedan," it is probably a dead option, because for you neither hypothesis is likely to be alive. But if I say: "Be an agnostic or be Christian," it is otherwise: trained as you are, each hypothesis makes some appeal, however small, to your belief.

2. Next, if I say to you: "Choose between going out with your umbrella or without it," I do not offer you a genuine option, for it is not forced. You can easily avoid it by not going out at all. Similarly, if I say, "Either love me or hate me," "Either call my theory true or call it false," your option is avoidable. You may remain indifferent to me, neither loving nor hating, and you may decline to offer any judgment as to my theory. But if I say, "Either accept this truth or go without it," I put on you a forced option, for there is no standing place outside of the alternative. Every dilemma based on a complete logical disjunction, with no possibility of not choosing, is an option of this forced kind.

3. Finally, if I were Dr. Nansen and proposed to you to join my North Pole expedition, your option would be momentous; for this would probably be your only similar opportunity, and your choice now would either exclude you from the North Pole sort of immortality altogether or put at least the chance of it into your hands. He who refuses to embrace a unique opportunity loses the prize as surely as if he tried and failed. Per contra, the option is trivial when the opportunity is not unique, when the stake is insignificant, or when the decision is reversible if it later prove unwise. Such trivial options abound in the scientific life. A chemist finds an hypothesis live enough to spend a year in its verification: he believes in it to that extent. But if his experiments prove inconclusive either way, he is quit for his loss of time, no vital harm being done. . . .

II

The next matter to consider is the actual psychology of human opinion. When we look at certain facts, it seems as if our passional and volitional nature lay at the root of all our convictions. When we look at others, it seems as if they could do nothing when the intellect had once said its say. Let us take the latter facts up first.

Does it not seem preposterous on the very face of it to talk of our opinions being modifiable at will? Can our will either help or hinder our intellect in its perceptions of truth? Can we, by just willing it, believe that Abraham Lincoln's existence is a myth, and that the portraits of him in McClure's Magazine are all of some one else? Can we, by any effort of our will, or by any strength of wish that it were true, believe ourselves well and about when we are roaring with rheumatism in bed, or feel certain that the sum of the two one-dollar bills in our pocket must be a hundred dollars? We can say any of these things, but we are absolutely impotent to believe them; and of just such things is the whole fabric of the truths that we do believe in made up,—matters of fact, immediate or remote, as Hume said, and relations between ideas, which are either there or not there for us if we see them so, and which if not there cannot be put there by any action of our own.

In Pascal's Thoughts there is a celebrated passage known in literature as Pascal's wager. In it he tries to force us into Christianity by reasoning as if our concern with truth resembled our concern with the stakes in a game of chance. Translated freely his words are these: You must either believe or not believe that God is—which will you do? Your human reason cannot say. A game is going on between you and the nature of things which at the day of judgment will bring out either heads or tails. Weigh what your gains and your losses would be if you should stake all you have on heads, or God's existence: if you win in such case, you gain eternal beatitude; if you lose, you lose nothing at all. If there were an infinity of chances, and only one for God in this wager, still you ought to stake your all on God; for though you surely risk a finite loss by this procedure, any finite loss is reasonable, even a certain one is reasonable, if there is but the possibility of infinite gain. . . .

You probably feel that when religious faith expresses itself thus, in the language of the gaming-table, it is put to its last trumps. Surely Pascal's own personal belief in masses and holy water had far other springs; and this celebrated page of his is but an argument for others, a last desperate snatch at a weapon against the hardness of the unbelieving heart. We feel that a faith in masses and holy water adopted willfully after such a mechanical calculation lack the inner soul of faith's reality; and if we were of the Deity, we should probably take pleasure in cutting off believers from their infinite reward. It is evident that unless there be some pre-existing tendency to believe in masses and holy water, the option offered to the will by Pascal is not a living option. . . .

The talk of believing by our volition seems, then, from one point of view, simply silly. From another point of view it is worse than silly, it is vile. . . .

III

. . . As a rule we disbelieve all facts and theories for which we have no use. . . . Why do so few 'scientists' even look at the evidence for telepathy, so called? Because they think . . . that even if such a thing were true, scientists ought to band together to keep it suppressed and concealed. It would undo the uniformity of Nature and all sorts of other things without which scientists cannot carry on their pursuits. But if this very man had been shown something which as a scientist he might do with telepathy, he might not only have examined the evidence, but even have found it good enough. This very law which the logicians would impose upon us—if I may give the name of logicians to those who would rule out our willing nature here—is based on nothing but their own natural wish to exclude all elements for which they, in their professional quality of logicians, can find no use.

Evidently, then, our non-intellectual nature does influence our convictions. There are passional tendencies and volitions which run before and others which come after belief, and it is only the latter that are too late for the fair; and they are not too late when the previous passional work has been already in their own direction. Pascal's argument, instead of being powerless, then seems a regular clincher. . . . The state of things is evidently far from simple; and pure insight and logic, whatever they might do ideally, are not the only things that really do produce our creeds.

IV

. . . The thesis I defend is, briefly stated, this: *Our passional nature not only lawfully may, but must, decide an option between propositions, whenever it is a genuine option that cannot by its nature be decided on intellectual grounds; for to say, under such circumstances, "Do not decide, but leave the question open," is itself a passional decision,—just like deciding yes or no,—and is attended with the same risk of losing the truth.* . . .

VII

. . . There are two ways of looking at our duty in the matter of opinion,—ways entirely different, and yet ways about whose difference the theory of knowledge seems hitherto to have shown very little concern. *We must know the truth;* and *we must avoid error,*—these are our first and great commandments as would-be knowers; but they are not two ways of stating an identical commandment, they are two separable laws. Although it may indeed happen that when we believe the truth *A*, we escape as an incidental consequence from believing the falsehood *B*, it hardly ever happens that by merely disbelieving *B* we necessarily believe *A*. We may in escaping *B* fall into believing other falsehoods, *C* or *D*, just as bad as *B*; or we may escape *B* by not believing anything at all, not even *A*.

Believe truth! Shun error!—these, we see, are two materially different laws; and by choosing between them we may end by coloring differently our whole intellectual life. We may regard the chase for truth as paramount, and the avoidance of error as secondary; or we may, on the other hand, treat the avoidance of error as more imperative, and let truth take its chance. . . . You . . .

may think that the risk of being in error is a very small matter when compared with the blessings of real knowledge, and be ready to be duped many times in your investigation rather than postpone indefinitely the chance of guessing true. . . . We must remember that these feelings of our duty about either truth or error are in any case only expressions of our passional life. Biologically considered, our minds are as ready to grind out falsehood as veracity, and he who says, "Better go without belief forever than believe a lie!" merely shows his own preponderant private horror of becoming a dupe. He may be critical of many of his desires and fears, but this fear he slavishly obeys. He cannot imagine any one questioning its binding force. For my own part, I have also a horror of being duped; but I can believe that worse things than being duped may happen to a man in this world. . . . It is like a general informing his soldiers that it is better to keep out of battle forever than to risk a single wound. Not so are victories either over enemies or over nature gained. Our errors are surely not such awfully solemn things. In a world where we are so certain to incur them in spite of all our caution, a certain lightness of heart seems healthier than this excessive nervousness on their behalf. At any rate, it seems the fittest thing for the empiricist philosopher.

VIII

. . . I fear here that some of you my hearers will begin to scent danger, and lend an inhospitable ear. Two first steps of passion you have indeed had to admit as necessary,—we must think so as to avoid dupery, and we must think so as to gain truth; but the surest path to those ideal consummations, you will probably consider, is from now onwards to take no further passional step.

Well, of course, I agree as far as the facts will allow. Wherever the option between losing truth and gaining it is not momentous, we can throw the chance of gaining truth away, and at any rate save ourselves from any chance of believing falsehood, by not making up our minds at all till objective evidence has come. In scientific questions, this is almost always the case; and even in human affairs in general, the need of acting is seldom so urgent that a false belief to act on is better than no belief at all. . . . But in our dealings with objective nature we obviously are recorders, not makers, of the truth; and decisions for the mere sake of deciding promptly and getting on to the next business would be wholly out of place. Throughout the breadth of physical nature facts are what they are quite independently of us, and seldom is there any such hurry about them that the risks of being duped by believing a premature theory need be faced. The questions here are always trivial options, the hypotheses are hardly living (at any rate not living for us spectators), the choice between believing truth or falsehood is seldom forced. The attitude of sceptical balance is therefore the absolutely wise one if we would escape mistakes. . . .

I speak, of course, here of the purely judging mind. For purposes of discovery such indifference is to be less highly recommended, and science would be far less advanced than she is if the passionate desires of individuals to get their own faiths confirmed had been kept out of the game. . . . The most useful investigator, because the most sensitive observer, is always he whose eager interest in one side of the question is balanced by an equally keen nervousness lest he become deceived. Science has organized this nervousness into a regular technique, her so-called method of verification; and she has fallen so deeply in love with the method that one may even say she has ceased to care for truth by itself at all. It is only truth as technically verified that interests her. The truth of truths might come in merely affirmative form, and she would decline to touch it. . . . Human passions, however, are stronger than technical rules. . . . Let us agree, however, that wherever there is no forced option, the dispassionately judicial intellect with no pet hypothesis, saving us, as it does, from dupery at any rate, ought to be our ideal.

The question next arises: Are there not somewhere forced options in our speculative questions, and can we . . . always wait with impunity till the coercive evidence shall have arrived? It seems *a priori* improbable that the truth should be so nicely adjusted to our needs and powers as that. . . .

X

In truths dependent on our personal action, then, faith based on desire is certainly a lawful and possibly an indispensable thing.

But now, it will be said, these are all childish human cases, and have nothing to do with great cosmic matters, like the question of religious faith. Let us then pass on to that. Religions differ so much in their accidents that in discussing the religious question we must make it very generic and broad. What then do we now mean by the religious hypothesis? Science says things are; morality says some things are better than other things; and religion says essentially two things.

First, she says that the best things are the more eternal things, the overlapping things, the things in the universe that throw the last stone, so to speak, and say the final word. . . .

The second affirmation of religion is that we are better off even now if we believe her first affirmation to be true.

Now, let us consider what the logical elements of this situation are *in case the religious hypothesis in both its branches be really true*. . . . So proceeding, we see, first that religion offers itself as a momentous option. We are supposed to gain, even now, by our belief, and to lose by our nonbelief, a certain vital good. Secondly, religion is a forced option, so far as that good goes. We cannot escape the issue by remaining sceptical and waiting for more light, because, although we do avoid error in that way if religion be untrue, we lose the good, if it be true, just as certainly as if we positively chose to disbelieve. It is as if a man should hesitate indefinitely to ask a certain woman to marry him because he was not perfectly sure that she would prove an angel after he brought her home. Would he not cut himself off from that particular angel-possibility as decisively as if he went and married some one else? Scepticism, then, is not avoidance of option; it is option of a certain particular kind of risk. Better risk loss of truth than chance of error,—that is your faith-vetoer's exact position. He is actively playing his stake as much as the believer is; he is backing the field against the religious hypothesis, just as the believer is backing the religious hypothesis against the field. To preach scepticism to us as a duty until 'sufficient evidence' for religion be found, is tantamount therefore to telling us, when in presence of the religious hypothesis, that to yield to our fear of its being error is wiser and better than to yield to our hope that it may be true. It is not intellect against all passions, then; it is only intellect with one passion laying down its law. And by what, forsooth, is the supreme wisdom of this passion warranted? Dupery for dupery, what proof is there that dupery through hope is so much worse than dupery through fear? I, for one, can see no proof; and I simply refuse obedience to the scientist's command to imitate his kind of option, in a case where my own stake is important enough to give me the right to choose my own form of risk. If religion be true and the evidence for it be still insufficient, I do not wish, by putting your extinguisher upon my nature (which feels to me as if it had after all some business in this matter), to forfeit my sole chance in life of getting upon the winning side,—that chance depending, of course, on my willingness to run the risk of acting as if my passional need of taking the world religiously might be prophetic and right.

All this is on the supposition that it really may be prophetic and right, and that, even to us who are discussing the matter, religion is a live hypothesis which may be true. Now, to most of us religion comes in a still further way that makes a veto on our active faith even more illogical. The more perfect and more eternal aspect of the universe is represented in our religions as having personal form. The universe is no longer a mere *It* to us, but a *Thou*, if we are religious; and any relation that may be possible from person to person might be possible here. . . . This feeling, forced on us we know not whence, that by obstinately believing that there are gods (although not to do so would be so easy both for our logic and our life) we are doing the universe the deepest service we can, seems part of the living essence of the religious hypothesis. If the hypothesis were true in all its parts, including this one, then pure intellectualism, with its veto on our making willing advances, would be an absurdity; and some participation of our sympathetic nature would be logically required. I, therefore, for one, cannot see my way to accepting the agnostic rules for truth-seeking, or wilfully agree to keep my willing nature out of the game. I cannot do so for this plain reason, that *a rule of thinking which would absolutely prevent me from acknowledging certain kinds of truth if those kinds of truth were really there, would be an irrational rule.* . . .

I confess I do not see how this logic can be escaped. But sad experience makes me fear that some of you may still shrink from radically saying with me, *in abstracto*, that we have the right to believe at our own risk any hypothesis that is live enough to tempt our will. I suspect, however, that if this is so, it is because you have got away from the abstract logical point of view altogether, and are thinking (perhaps without realizing it) of some particular religious hypothesis which for you is dead. The freedom to 'believe what we will' you apply to the case of some patent superstition; and the faith you think of is the faith defined by the schoolboy when he said, "Faith is when you believe something that you know ain't true." I can only repeat that this is misapprehension. *In concreto*, the freedom to believe can only cover living options which the intellect of the individual cannot by itself resolve; and living options never seem absurdities to him who has them to consider. When I look at the religious question as it really puts itself to concrete men, and when I think of all the possibilities which both practically and theoretically it involves, then this command that we shall put a stopper on our heart, instincts, and courage, and wait—acting of course meanwhile more or less as if religion were *not* true . . . till doomsday, or till such time as our intellect and senses working together may have raked in evidence enough,—this command, I say, seems to me the queerest idol ever manufactured in the philosophic cave. . . . Indeed we may wait if we will,—I hope you do not think that I am denying that,—but if we do so, we do so at our peril as much as if we believed. In either case we act, taking our life in our hands. No one of us ought to issue vetoes to the other, nor should we bandy words of abuse. We ought, on the contrary, delicately and profoundly to respect one another's mental freedom: then only shall we bring about the intellectual republic; then only shall we have that spirit of inner tolerance without which all our outer tolerance is soulless, and which is empiricism's glory; then only shall we live and let live, in speculative as well as in practical things. . . .

The Dilemma of Determinism (1884)

WILLIAM JAMES

A common opinion prevails that the juice has ages ago been pressed out of the free-will controversy, and that no new champion can do more than warm up stale arguments which every one has heard. This is a radical mistake. I know of no subject less worn out, or in which inventive genius has a better chance of breaking open new ground,—not, perhaps, of forcing a conclusion or of coercing assent, but of deepening our sense of what the issue between the two parties really is, of what the ideas of fate and of free-will imply. At our very side almost, in the past few years, we have seen falling in rapid succession from the press works that present the alternative in entirely novel lights. . . .

. . . The arguments I am about to urge all proceed on two suppositions: first, when we make theories about the world and discuss them with one another, we do so in order to attain a conception of things which shall give us subjective satisfaction; and, second, if there be two conceptions, and the one seems to us, on the whole, more rational than the other, we are entitled to suppose that the more rational one is the truer of the two. I hope that you are all willing to make these suppositions with me; for I am afraid that if there be any of you here who are not, they will find little edification in the rest of what I have to say. I cannot stop to argue the point; but I myself believe that all the magnificent achievements of mathematical and physical science—our doctrines of evolution, of uniformity of law, and the rest—proceed from our indomitable desire to cast the world into a more rational shape in our minds than the shape into which it is thrown there by the crude order of our experience. The world has shown itself, to a great extent, plastic to this demand of ours for rationality. How much farther it will show itself plastic no one can say. Our only means of finding out is to try; and I, for one, feel as free to try conceptions of moral as of mechanical or of logical rationality. If a certain formula for expressing the nature of the world violates my moral demand, I shall feel as free to throw it overboard, or at least to doubt it, as if it disappointed my demand for uniformity in sequence, for example; the one demand being, so far as I can see, quite as subjective and emotional as the other is. The principle of causality, for example,—what is it but a postulate, an empty name covering simply a demand that the sequence of events shall some day manifest a deeper kind of belonging of one thing with another than the mere arbitrary juxtaposition which now phenomenally appears? . . . All our scientific and philosophic ideals are altars to unknown gods. Uniformity is as much so as is free-will. If this be admitted, we can debate on even terms. . . .

To begin, then, I suppose you acquainted with all the usual arguments on the subject. I cannot stop to take up the old proofs from causation, from statistics,

From *The Writings of William James*, edited by John J. McDermott (New York, NY: Random House, Inc.) © Copyright 1967.

from the certainty with which we can foretell one another's conduct, from the fixity of character, and all the rest. But there are two *words* which usually encumber these classical arguments, and which we must immediately dispose of if we are to make any progress. One is the eulogistic word *freedom*, and the other is the opprobrious word *chance*. The word 'chance' I wish to keep, but I wish to get rid of the word 'freedom.' Its eulogistic associations have so far overshadowed all the rest of its meaning that both parties claim the sole right to use it, and determinists to-day insist that they alone are freedom's champions. Old-fashioned determinism was what we may call *hard* determinism. It did not shrink from such words as fatality, bondage of the will, necessitation, and the like. Nowadays, we have a *soft* determinism which abhors harsh words, and, repudiating fatality, necessity, and even predetermination, says that its real name is freedom; for freedom is only necessity understood, and bondage to the highest is identical with true freedom. . . .

. . . Freedom in all these senses presents simply no problem at all. No matter what the soft determinist means by it,—whether he mean the acting without external constraint; whether he mean the acting rightly, or whether he mean the acquiescing in the law of the whole,—who cannot answer him that sometimes we are free and sometimes we are not? But there *is* a problem, an issue of fact and not of words, an issue of the most momentous importance, which is often decided without discussion in one sentence,—nay, in one clause of a sentence,—by those very writers who spin out whole chapters in their efforts to show what 'true' freedom is; and that is the question of determinism. . . .

Fortunately, no ambiguities hang about this word or about its opposite, indeterminism. Both designate an outward way in which things may happen, and their cold and mathematical sound has no sentimental associations that can bribe our partiality either way in advance. Now, evidence of an external kind to decide between determinism and indeterminism is . . . strictly impossible to find. Let us look at the differences between them and see for ourselves. What does determinism profess?

It professes that those parts of the universe already laid down absolutely appoint and decree what the other parts shall be. The future has no ambiguous possibilities hidden in its womb: the part we call the present is compatible with only one totality. Any other future complement than the one fixed from eternity is impossible. The whole is in each and every part, and welds it with the rest into an absolute unity, an iron block, in which there can be no equivocation or shadow of turning. . . .

Indeterminism, on the contrary, says that the parts have a certain amount of loose play on one another, so that the laying down of one of them does not necessarily determine what the other shall be. It admits that possibilities may be in excess of actualities, and that things not yet revealed to our knowledge may really in themselves be ambiguous. Of two alternative futures which we conceive, both may now be really possible; and the one become impossible only at the very moment when the other excludes it by becoming real itself.

Indeterminism thus denies the world to be one unbending unit of fact. It says there is a certain ultimate pluralism in it; and, so saying, it corroborates our ordinary unsophisticated view of things. To that view, actualities seem to float in a wider sea of possibilities from out of which they are chosen; and, *somewhere*, indeterminism says, such possibilities exist, and form a part of truth.

Determinism, on the contrary, says that they exist *nowhere*, and that necessity on the one hand and impossibility on the other are the sole categories of the real. Possibilities that fail to get realized are, for determinism, pure illusions: they never were possibilities at all. There is nothing inchoate, it says, about this universe of ours, all that was or is or shall be actual in it having been from eternity virtually there. The cloud of alternatives our minds escort this mass of actuality withal is a cloud of sheer deceptions, to which 'impossibilities' is the only name that rightfully belongs.

This issue . . . is a perfectly sharp one, which no eulogistic terminology can smear over or wipe out. The truth *must* lie with one side or the other, and its lying with one side makes the other false.

The question relates solely to the existence of possibilities, in the strict sense of the term, as things that may, but need not, be. Both sides admit that a volition, for instance, has occurred. The indeterminists say another volition might have occurred in its place: the determinists swear that nothing could possibly have occurred in its place. Now, can science be called in to tell us which of these two point-blank contradicters of each other is right? Science professes to draw no conclusions but such as are based on matters of fact, things that have actually happened; but how can any amount of assurance that something actually happened give us the least grain of information as to whether another thing might or might not have happened in its place? Only facts can be proved by other facts. With things that are possibilities and not fact, facts have no concern. If we have no other evidence than the evidence of existing facts, the possibility-question must remain a mystery never to be cleared up.

And the truth is that facts practically have hardly anything to do with making us either determinists or indeterminists. Sure enough, we make a flourish of quoting facts this way or that; and if we are determinists, we talk about the infallibility with which we can predict one another's conduct; while if we are indeterminists, we lay great stress on the fact that it is just because we cannot foretell one another's conduct, either in war or statecraft or in any of the great and small intrigues and businesses of men, that life is so intensely anxious and hazardous a game. . . . What fills up the gaps in our minds is something not objective, not external. What divides us into possibility men and anti-possibility men is different faiths or postulates,—postulates of rationality. To this man the world seems more rational with possibilities in it,—to that man more rational with possibilities excluded; and to talk as we will about having to yield to evidence, what makes us monists or pluralists, determinists or indeterminists, is at bottom always some sentiment like this.

The stronghold of the deterministic sentiment is the antipathy to the idea of chance. As soon as we begin to talk indeterminism to our friends, we find a number of them shaking their heads. This notion of alternative possibility, they say, this admission that any one of several things may come to pass, is, after all, only a roundabout name for chance; and chance is something the notion of which no sane mind can for an instant tolerate in the world. What is it, they ask, but barefaced crazy unreason, the negation of intelligibility and law? And if the slightest particle of it exist anywhere, what is to prevent the whole fabric from falling together, the stars from going out, and chaos from recommencing her topsy-turvy reign? . . .

The sting of the word 'chance' seems to lie in the assumption that it means something positive, and that if anything happens by chance, it must needs be something of an intrinsically irrational and preposterous sort. Now, chance means nothing of the kind. It is a purely negative and relative term, giving us no information about that of which it is predicated, except that it happens to be disconnected with something else,—not controlled, secured, or necessitated by other things in advance of its own actual presence. As this point is the most subtle one of the whole lecture, and at the same time the point on which all the rest hinges, I beg you to pay particular attention to it. What I say is that it tells us nothing about what a thing may be in itself to call it 'chance.' . . .

This negativeness, however, and this opacity of the chance-thing when thus considered *ab extra*, or from the point of view of previous things or distant things, do not preclude its having any amount of positiveness and luminosity from within, and at its own place and moment. All that its chance-character asserts about it is that there is something in it really of its own, something that is not the unconditional property of the whole. If the whole wants this property, the whole must wait till it can get it, if it be a matter of chance. That the universe may actually be a sort of joint-stock society of this sort, in which the sharers have both limited liabilities and limited powers, is of course a simple and conceivable notion. . . .

And this at last brings us within sight of our subject. We have seen what determinism means: we have seen that indeterminism is rightly described as meaning chance; and we have seen that chance, the very name of which we are urged to shrink from as from a metaphysical pestilence, means only the negative fact that no part of the world, however big, can claim to control absolutely the destinies of the whole. But although in discussing the word 'chance,' I may at moments have seemed to be arguing for its real existence, I have not meant to do so yet. We have not yet ascertained whether this be a world of chance or no; at most, we have agreed that it seems so. And I now repeat what I said at the outset, that, from any strict theoretical point of view, the question is insoluble. To deepen our theoretic sense of the *difference* between a world with chances in it and a deterministic world is the most I can hope to do. . . .

I wish first of all to show you just what the notion that this is a deterministic world implies. The implications I call our attention to are all bound up with the fact that it is a world in which we constantly have to make what I shall . . . call judgments of regret. Hardly an hour passes in which we do not wish that something might be otherwise. . . .

Now, it is undeniable that most of these regrets are foolish. . . . Wise men therefore regret as little as they can. But still some regrets are pretty obstinate and hard to stifle,—regrets for acts of wanton cruelty or treachery, for example, whether performed by others or by ourselves. Hardly any one can remain *entirely* optimistic after reading the confession of the murderer at Brockton the other day: how, to get rid of the wife whose continued existence bored him, he inveigled her into a desert spot, shot her four times, and then, as she lay on the ground and said to him, "You didn't do it on purpose, did you, dear?" replied, "No, I didn't do it on purpose," as he raised a rock and smashed her skull. Such an occurrence, with the mild sentence and self-satisfaction of the prisoner, is a field for a crop of regrets. . . . We feel that, although a perfect mechanical fit to the rest of the universe, it is a bad moral fit, and that something else would really have been better in its place.

But for the determinist philosophy the murder, the sentence, and the prisoner's optimism were all necessary from eternity. . . . To admit such a chance, the determinist tells us, would be to make a suicide of reason; so we must steel our hearts against the thought. And here our plot thickens, for we see the first of those difficult implications of determinism and monism which it is my first purpose to make you feel. If this . . . murder was called for by the rest of the universe, if it had to come at its preappointed hour, and if nothing else would have been consistent with the sense of the whole, what are we to think of the universe? Are we . . . to stick to our judgment of regret, and say, though it *couldn't* be, yet it *would* have been a better universe with something different . . . in it? That, of course, seems the natural and spontaneous thing for us to do; and yet it is nothing short of deliberately espousing a kind of pessimism. The judgment of regret calls the murder bad. Calling a thing bad means, if it mean anything at all, that the thing ought not to be, that something else ought to be in its stead. Determinism, in denying that anything else can be in its stead, virtually defines the universe as a place in which what ought to be is impossible,— in other words, as an organism whose constitution is afflicted with an incurable taint, an irremediable flaw. . . . Regret for the murder must transform itself, if we are determinists and wise, into a larger regret. It is absurd to regret the murder alone. Other things being what they are, *it* could not be different. What we should regret is that whole frame of things of which the murder is one member. I see no escape whatever from this pessimistic conclusion, if, being determinists, our judgment of regret is to be allowed to stand at all.

The only deterministic escape from pessimism is everywhere to abandon the judgment of regret. That this can be done, history shows to be not impossible. The devil, *quoad existentiam*, may be good. That is, although he be a *principle* of evil, yet the universe, with such a principle in it, may practically be a better universe than it could have been without. On every hand . . . we find that a certain amount of evil is a condition by which a higher form of good is bought. . . . An optimism *quand même* a systematic and infatuated optimism like that ridiculed by Voltaire in his Candide, is one of the possible ideal ways in which a man may train himself to look upon life. Bereft of dogmatic hardness to lift up with the expression of a tender and pathetic hope, such an optimism has the grace of some of the most religious characters that ever lived. . . .

Thus, our deterministic pessimism may become a deterministic optimism at the price of extinguishing our judgments of regret.

But does this not immediately bring us into a curious logical predicament? Our determinism leads us to call our judgments of regret wrong, because they are pessimistic in implying what is impossible yet ought to be. But how then about the judgments of regret themselves? If they are wrong, other judgments, judgments of approval presumably, ought to be in their place. But as they are necessitated, nothing else *can* be in their place; and the universe is just what it was before,—namely, a place in which what ought to be appears impossible. We have got one foot out of the pessimistic bog, but the other one sinks all the deeper. We have rescued our actions from the bonds of evil, but our judgments are now held fast. When murders and treacheries cease to be sins, regrets are theoretic absurdities and errors. . . . Murder and treachery cannot be good without regret being bad: regret cannot be good without treachery and murder being bad. Both, however, are supposed to have been foredoomed; so something must be fatally unreasonable, absurd, and wrong in the world. . . . From this dilemma there seems at first sight no escape. Are we then so soon to fall back into the pessimism from which we thought we had emerged? And is there no possible way by which we may, with good intellectual consciences, call the cruelties and the treacheries, the reluctances and the regrets, *all* good together?

Certainly there is such a way, and you are probably most of you ready to formulate it yourselves. But, before doing so, remark how inevitably the question of determinism and indeterminism slides us into the question of optimism and pessimism, or, as our fathers called it, 'the question of evil.' The theological form of all these disputes is the simplest and the deepest, and the form from which there is the least escape. . . .

But this brings us right back . . . to the question of indeterminism and to the conclusion of all I came here to say to-night. For the only consistent way of representing a pluralism and a world whose parts may affect one another through their conduct being either good or bad is the indeterministic way. What interest, zest, or excitement can there be in achieving the right way, unless we are enabled to feel that the wrong way is also a possible and a natural way,—nay, more, a menacing and imminent way? And what sense can there be in condemning ourselves for taking the wrong way, unless we need have done nothing of the sort, unless the right way was open to us as well. I cannot understand the willingness to act, no matter how we feel, without the belief that acts are really good and bad. I cannot understand the belief that an act is bad, without regret at its happening. I cannot understand regret without the admission of real, genuine possibilities in the world. . . .

Let me . . . say just this. The world is enigmatical enough in all conscience, whatever theory we may take up toward it. The indeterminism I defend, the free-will theory of popular sense based on the judgment of regret, represents that world as vulnerable, and liable to be injured by certain of its parts if they act wrong. And it represents their acting wrong as a matter of possibility or accident, neither inevitable nor yet to be infallibly warded off. In all this, it is a theory devoid either of transparency or of stability. It gives us a pluralistic, restless universe, in which no single point of view can ever take in the whole scene; and to a mind possessed of the love of unity at any cost, it will, no doubt, remain forever unacceptable. . . .

. . . When, for example, I imagine such carrion as the Brockton murder, I cannot conceive it as an act by which the universe, as a whole, logically and necessarily expresses its nature without shrinking from complicity with such a whole. And I deliberately refuse to keep on terms of loyalty with the universe by saying blankly that the murder, since it does flow from the nature of the whole, is not carrion. There are *some* instinctive reactions which I, for one, will not tamper with. . . .

. . . If some of the members of the pluralism are bad, the philosophy of pluralism, whatever broad views it may deny me, permits me, at least, to turn to the other members with a clean breast of affection and an unsophisticated moral sense. And if I still wish to think of the world as totality, it lets me feel that a world with a *chance* in it of being altogether good, even if the chance never comes to pass, is better than a world with no such chance at all. That 'chance' whose very notion I am exhorted and conjured to banish from my view of the future as the suicide of reason concerning it, that 'chance' is—what? Just this,—the chance that in moral respects the future may be other and better than the past has been. This is the only chance we have any motive for supposing to exist. Shame, rather, on its repudiation and its denial! For its presence is the vital air which lets the world live, the salt which keeps it sweet. . . .

The Influence of Darwinism on Philosophy (1909)

JOHN DEWEY

I

That the publication of the "Origin of Species" marked an epoch in the development of natural sciences is well known to the layman. That the combination of the very words origin and species embodied an intellectual revolt and introduced a new intellectual temper is easily overlooked by the expert. The conceptions that had reigned in the philosophy of nature and knowledge for two thousand years, the conceptions that had become the familiar furniture of the mind, rested on the assumption of the superiority of the fixed and final; they rested upon treating change and origin as signs of defect and unreality. In laying hands upon the sacred arc of absolute permanency, in treating the forms that had been regarded as types of fixity and perfection as originating and passing away, the "Origin of Species" introduced a mode of thinking that in the end was bound to transform the logic of knowledge, and hence the treatment of morals, politics, and religion.

No wonder, then, that the publication of Darwin's book, a half century ago, precipitated a crisis. The true nature of the controversy is easily concealed from us, however, by the theological clamor that attended it. The vivid and popular features of the anti-Darwinian row tended to leave the impression that the issue was between science on the one side and theology on the other. Such was not the case—the issue lay primarily within science itself, as Darwin himself early recognized. The theological outcry he discounted from the start, hardly noticing it. . . .

Religious considerations lent fervor to the controversy, but they did not provoke it. . . . Although the ideas that rose up like armed men against Darwinism owed their intensity to the religious associations, their origin and meaning are to be sought in science and philosophy, not religion.

II

Few words in our language foreshorten intellectual history as much as does the word species. The Greeks, in initiating the intellectual life of Europe, were impressed by characteristic traits of the life of plants and animals; so impressed indeed that they made these traits the key to defining nature and to explaining mind and society. And truly, life is so wonderful that a seemingly successful reading of its mystery might well lead men to believe that the key to the secrets of heaven and earth was in their hands. The Greek rendering of this mystery, the Greek formulation of the aim and standard of knowledge, was in the course of time embodied in the word species, and it controlled philosophy for two thousand years. To understand the intellectual face-about expressed in the phrase "Origin of Species," we must, then, understand the long dominant idea against which it is a protest.

Consider how men were impressed by the facts of life. Their eyes fell upon certain things slight in bulk, and frail in structure. To every appearance, these perceived things were inert and passive. Suddenly, under certain circumstances, these things—henceforth known as seeds or eggs or germs—begin to change, to change rapidly in size, form, and qualities. Rapid and extensive changes occur, however, in many things—as when wood is touched by fire. But the changes in the living thing are orderly; they are cumulative; they tend constantly in one direction; they do not, like other changes, destroy or consume, or pass fruitless into wandering flux; they realize and fulfill. Each successive stage, no matter how unlike its predecessor, preserves its net effect and also prepares the way for a fuller activity on the part of its successor. In living beings, changes do not happen as they seem to happen elsewhere, any which way; the earlier changes are regulated in view of later results. This progressive organization does not cease till there is achieved a true final term, a *telos*, a completed, perfected end. This final form exercises in turn a plenitude of functions, not the least noteworthy of which is production of germs like those from which it took its own origin, germs capable of the same cycle of self-fulfilling activity.

But the whole miraculous tale is not yet told. The same drama is enacted to the same destiny in countless myriads of individuals so sundered in time, so severed in space, that they have no opportunity for mutual consultation and no means of interaction. . . .

This formal activity which operates throughout a series of changes and holds them to a single course; which subordinates their aimless flux to its own perfect manifestation; which, leaping the boundaries of space and time, keeps individuals distant in space and remote in time to a uniform type of structure and function: this principle seemed to give insight into the very nature of reality itself. To it Aristotle gave the name, *eidos*. This term the scholastics translated as *species*.

The force of this term was deepened by its application to everything in the universe that observes order in flux and manifests constancy through change. From the causal drift of daily weather, through the uneven recurrence of seasons and unequal return of seed time and harvest, up to the majestic sweep of the heavens—the image of eternity in time—and from this to the unchanging pure and contemplative intelligence beyond nature lies one unbroken fulfillment of ends. Nature as a whole is a progressive realization of purposes strictly comparable to the realization of purpose in any single plant or animal.

The conception of *eidos*, species, a fixed form and final cause, was the central principle of knowledge as well as of nature. Upon it rested the logic of science. Change as change is mere flux and lapse; it insults intelligence. Genuinely to know is to grasp a permanent end that realizes itself through changes, holding them thereby within the metes and bounds of fixed truth.

Completely to know is to relate all special forms to their one single end and good: pure contemplative intelligence. Since, however, the scene of nature which directly confronts us in the change, nature as directly and practically experienced does not satisfy the condition of knowledge. Human experience is in flux, and hence the instrumentalities of sense-perception and of inference based upon observation are condemned in advance. Science is compelled to aim at realities lying behind and beyond the processes of nature, and to carry on its search for these realities by means of rational forms transcending ordinary modes of perception and influence.

There are, indeed, but two alternative courses. We must either find the appropriate objects and organs of knowledge in the mutual interactions of changing things; or else, to escape the infection of change, we *must* seek them in some transcendent and supernal region. The human mind, deliberately as it were, exhausted the logic of the changeless, the final, and the transcendent, before it essayed adventure on the pathless wastes of generation and transformation. We dispose all too easily of the efforts of the schoolmen to interpret nature and mind in terms of real essences, hidden forms, and occult faculties, forgetful of the seriousness and dignity of the ideas that lay behind. We dispose of them by laughing at the famous gentleman who accounted for the fact that opium put people to sleep on the ground it had a dormitive faculty. But the doctrine, held in our own day, that knowledge of the plant that yields the poppy consists in referring the peculiarities of an individual to a type, to a universal form, a doctrine so firmly established that any other method of knowing was conceived to be unphilosophical and unscientific, is a survival of precisely the same logic. This identity of conception in the scholastic and anti-Darwinian theory may well suggest greater sympathy for what has become unfamiliar as well as greater humility regarding the further unfamiliarities that history has in store. . . .

III

The exact bearings upon philosophy of the new logical outlook are, of course, as yet, uncertain and inchoate. We live in the twilight of intellectual transition. One must add the rashness of the prophet to the stubbornness of the partizan to venture a systematic exposition of the influence upon philosophy of the Darwinian method. At best, we can but inquire as to its general bearing—the effect upon mental temper and complexion, upon that body of half-conscious, half-instinctive intellectual aversions and preferences which determine, after all, our more deliberate intellectual enterprises. In this vague inquiry there happens to exist as a kind of touchstone a problem of long historic currency that has also been much discussed in Darwinian literature. I refer to the old problem of design *versus* chance, mind *versus* matter, as the causal explanation, first or final, of things.

As we have already seen, the classic notion of species carried with it the idea of purpose. In all living forms, a specific type is present directing the earlier stages of growth to the realization of its own perfection. Since this purposive regulative principle is not visible to the senses, it follows that it must be an ideal or rational force. Since, however, the perfect form is gradually approximated through the sensible changes, it also follows that in and through a sensible realm a rational ideal force is working out its own ultimate manifestation. These inferences were extended to nature: (a) She does nothing in vain; but all for an ulterior purpose. (b) Within natural sensible events there is therefore contained a spiritual causal force, which as spiritual escapes perception, but is apprehended by an enlightened reason. (c) The manifestation of this principle brings about a subordination of matter and sense to its own realization, and this ultimate fulfillment is the goal of nature and of man. The design argument thus operated in two directions. Purposefulness accounted for the intelligibility of nature and the possibility of science, while the absolute or cosmic character of this purposefulness gave sanction and worth to the moral and religious endeavors of man. Science was underpinned and morals authorized by one and the same principle, and their mutual agreement was eternally guaranteed.

This philosophy remained, in spite of skeptical and polemic outbursts, the official and the regnant philosophy of Europe for over two thousand years. The expulsion of fixed first and final causes from astronomy, physics, and chemistry had indeed given the doctrine something of a shock. But, on the other hand, increased acquaintance with the details of plant and animal life operated as counterbalance and perhaps even strengthened the argument from design. The marvelous adaptations of organisms to their environment . . . were increasingly recognized with the progress of botany, zoology, paleontology, and embryology. Together, they added such prestige to the design argument that by the late eighteenth century it was, as approved by the sciences of organic life, the central point of theistic and idealistic philosophy.

The Darwinian principle of natural selection cut straight under this philosophy. If all organic adaptations are due simply to constant variation and the elimination of those variations which are harmful in the struggle for existence that is brought about by excessive reproduction, there is no call for a prior intelligent causal force to plan and preordain them. Hostile critics charged Darwin with materialism and with making chance the cause of the universe.

Some naturalists, like Asa Gray, favored the Darwinian principle and attempted to reconcile it with design. Gray held to what may be called design on the installment plan. If we conceive the "stream of variations" to be itself intended, we may suppose that each successive variation was designed from the first to be selected. In that case, variation, struggle, and selection simply define the mechanism of "secondary causes" through which the "first cause" acts; and the doctrine of design is none the worse off because we know more of its *modus operandi*.

Darwin could not accept this mediating proposal. He admits or rather he asserts that it is "impossible to conceive this immense and wonderful universe including man with his capacity for looking far backwards and far into futurity as the result of blind chance or necessity."[1] But nevertheless he holds that since variations are in useless as well as useful directions, and since the latter are sifted out simply by the stress of the conditions of struggle for existence, the design argument as applied to living beings is unjustifiable; and its lack of support there deprives it of scientific value as applied to nature in general. . . .

IV

So much for some of the more obvious facts of the discussion of design *versus* chance, as causal principles of nature and of life as a whole. . . . What does our touchstone indicate as to the bearing of Darwinian ideas upon philosophy? In the first place, the new logic outlaws, flanks, dismisses—what you will—one type of problems and substitutes for it another type. Philosophy forswears inquiry after absolute origins and absolute finalities in order to explore specific values and the specific conditions that generate them.

Darwin concluded that the impossibility of assigning the world to chance as a whole and to design in its parts indicated the insolubility of the question. Two radically different reasons, however, may be given as to why a problem is insoluble. One reason is that the problem is too high for intelligence; the other is that the question in its very asking makes assumptions that render the question meaningless. The latter alternative is unerringly pointed to in the celebrated case of design *versus* chance. Once admit that the sole verifiable or fruitful object of knowledge is the particular set of changes that generate the object of study together with the consequences that then flow from it, and no intelligible question can be asked about what, by assumption, lies outside. To assert—as is often asserted—that specific values of particular truth, social bonds and forms of beauty, if they can be shown to be generated by concretely knowable conditions, are meaningless and in vain; to assert that they are justified only when they and their particular causes and effects have all at once been gathered up into some inclusive first cause and some exhaustive final goal, is intellectual atavism. Such argumentation is reversion to the logic that explained the extinction of fire by water through the formal essence of aqueousness and the quenching of thirst by water through the final cause of aqueousness. Whether used in the case of the special event or that of life as a whole, such logic only abstracts some aspect of the existing course of events in order to reduplicate it as a petrified eternal principle by which to explain the very changes of which it is the formalization. . . .

---

[1]"Life and Letters," Vol. I, p. 282; cf. 285.

In the second place, the classic type of logic inevitably set philosophy upon proving that life *must* have certain qualities and values—no matter how experience presents the matter—because of some remote cause and eventual goal. The duty of wholesale justification inevitably accompanies all thinking that makes the meaning of special occurrences depend upon something that once and for all lies behind them. The habit of derogating from present meanings and uses prevents our looking the facts of experience in the face; it prevents serious acknowledgment of the evils they present and serious concern with the goods they promise but do not as yet fulfill. . . .

Finally, the new logic introduces responsibility into the intellectual life. To idealize and rationalize the universe at large is after all a confession of inability to master the courses of things that specifically concern us. As long as mankind suffered from this impotency, it naturally shifted a burden of responsibility that it could not carry over to the more competent shoulders of the transcendent cause. But if insight into specific conditions of value and into specific consequences of ideas is possible, philosophy must in time become a method of locating and interpreting the more serious of the conflicts that occur in life, and a method of projecting ways for dealing with them; a method of moral and political diagnosis and prognosis. . . .

Doubtless I seem to have violated the implied promise of my earlier remarks and to have turned both prophet and partizan. But in anticipating the direction of the transformations in philosophy to be wrought by the Darwinian genetic and experimental logic, I do not profess to speak for any save those who yield themselves consciously or unconsciously to this logic. No one can fairly deny that at present there are two effects of the Darwinian mode of thinking. On the one hand, there are making many sincere and vital efforts to revise our traditional philosophic conceptions in accordance with its demands. On the other hand, there is as definitely a recrudescence of absolutistic philosophies; an assertion of a type of philosophic knowing distinct from that of the sciences, one which opens to us another kind of reality from that to which the sciences give access; an appeal through experience to something that essentially goes beyond experience. This reaction affects popular creeds and religious movements as well as technical philosophies. The very conquest of the biological sciences by the new ideas has led many to proclaim an explicit and rigid separation of philosophy of science.

Old ideas give way slowly; for they are more than abstract logical forms and categories. They are habits, predispositions, deeply engrained attitudes of aversion and preference. Moreover, the conviction persists—though history shows it to be a hallucination—that all the questions that the human mind has asked are questions that can be answered in terms of the alternatives that the questions themselves present. But in fact intellectual progress usually occurs through sheer abandonment of questions together with both of the alternatives they assume—an abandonment that results from their decreasing vitality and a change of urgent interest. We do not solve them: we get over them. . . . Doubtless the greatest dissolvent in contemporary thought of old questions, the greatest precipitant of new methods, new intentions, new problems, is the one effected by the scientific revolution that found its climax in the "Origin of Species."

Nature, Life and Body-Mind (1925)

John Dewey

. . . Every "mind" that we are empirically acquainted with is found in connection with some organized body. Every such body exists in a natural medium to which it sustains some adaptive connection: plants to air, water, sun, and animals to these things and also to plants. Without such connections, animals die; the "purest" mind would not continue without them. An animal can live only as long as it draws nutriment from its medium, finds there means of defence, and ejects into it waste and superfluous products of its own making. Since no particular organism lasts forever, life in general goes on only as an organism reproduces itself; and the only place where it can reproduce itself is in the environment. In all higher forms reproduction is sexual; that is, it involves the meeting of two forms. The medium is thus one which contains similar and conjunctive forms. At every point and stage, accordingly, a living organism and its life processes involve a world or nature temporally and spatially "external" to itself but "internal" to its functions.

The only excuse for reciting such commonplaces is that traditional theories have separated life from nature, mind from organic life, and thereby created mysteries. Restore the connection, and the problem of how a mind can know an external world or even know that there is such a thing, is like the problem of how an animal eats things external to itself; it is the kind of problem that arises only if one assumes that a hibernating bear living off its own stored substance defines the normal procedure, ignoring moreover the question where the bear got its stored material. . . .

Body-mind designates an affair with its own properties. A large part of the difficulty in its discussion—perhaps the whole of the difficulty in general apart from detailed questions—is due to vocabulary. Our language is so permeated with consequences of theories which have divided the body and mind from each other, making separate existential realms out of them, that we lack words to designate the actual existential fact. The circumlocutions we are compelled to resort to—exemplified in the previous discussion—thus induce us to think that analogous separations exist in nature, which can also only be got around by elaborate circuitous arrangements. But body-mind simply designates what actually takes place when a living body is implicated in situations of discourse, communication and participation. In the hyphenated phrase

From John Dewey, *Experience and Nature* (New York: Dover Publications, 1958) pp. 277–285.

body-mind, "body" designates the continued and conserved, the registered and cumulative operation of factors continuous with the rest of nature, inanimate as well as animate; while "mind" designates the characters and consequences which are differential, indicative of features which emerge when "body" is engaged in a wider, more complex and interdependent situation. ...

The Quest for Certainty

JOHN DEWEY

Chapter I

ESCAPE FROM PERIL

Man who lives in a world of hazards is compelled to seek for security. He has sought to attain it in two ways. One of them began with an attempt to propitiate the powers which environ him and determine his destiny. It expressed itself in supplication, sacrifice, ceremonial rite and magical cult. In time these crude methods were largely displaced. The sacrifice of a contrite heart was esteemed more pleasing than that of bulls and oxen; the inner attitude of reverence and devotion more desirable than external ceremonies. If man could not conquer destiny he could willingly ally himself with it; putting his will, even in sore affliction, on the side of the powers which dispense fortune, he could escape defeat and might triumph in the midst of destruction.

The other course is to invent arts and by their means turn the powers of nature to account; man constructs a fortress out of the very conditions and forces which threaten him. He builds shelters, weaves garments, makes flame his friend instead of his enemy, and grows into the complicated arts of associated living. This is the method of changing the world through action, as the other is the method of changing the self in emotion and idea. It is a commentary on the slight control man has obtained over himself by means of control over nature, that the method of action has been felt to manifest dangerous pride, even defiance of the powers which be. People of old wavered between thinking arts to be the gift of the gods and to be an invasion of their prerogatives. Both versions testify to the sense of something extraordinary in the arts, something either superhuman or unnatural. The souls who have predicted that by means of the arts man might establish a kingdom of order, justice and beauty through mastery of nature's energies and laws have been few and little heeded.

Men have been glad enough to enjoy the fruits of such arts as they possess, and in recent centuries have increasingly devoted themselves to their multiplication. But this effort has been conjoined with a profound distrust of the arts as a method of dealing with the serious perils of life. Doubt as to the truth of this statement will be dispelled if one considers the disesteem in which the idea of practice has been held. Philosophers have celebrated the method of change in personal ideas, and religious teachers that of change in the affections of the heart. These conversions have been prized on their own account, and only incidentally because of a change in action which would ensue. The latter has been esteemed as an evidence of the change in thought and sentiment, not as a method of transforming the scene of life. The places in which the use of the arts has effected actual objective transformation have been regarded as inferior, if not base, and the activities connected with them as menial. The disparagement attending the idea of the material has seized upon them. The honorable quality associated with the idea of the "spiritual" has been reserved for change in inner attitudes.

The depreciation of action, of doing and making, has been cultivated by philosophers. But while philosophers have perpetuated the derogation by formulating and justifying it, they did not originate it. They glorified their own office without doubt in placing theory so much above practice. But independently of their attitude, many things conspired to the same effect. Work has been onerous, toilsome, associated with a primeval curse. It has been done under compulsion and the pressure of necessity, while intellectual activity is associated with leisure. On account of the unpleasantness of practical activity, as much of it as possible has been put upon slaves and serfs. Thus the social dishonor in which this class was held was extended to the work they do. There is also the age-long association of knowing and thinking with immaterial and spiritual principles, and of the arts, of all practical activity in doing and making, with matter. For work is done with the body, by means of mechanical appliances and is directed upon material things. The disrepute which has attended the thought of material things in comparison with immaterial thought has been transferred to everything associated with practice.

One might continue in this strain. The natural history of conceptions about work and the arts if it were traced through a succession of peoples and cultures would be instructive. But all that is needed for our purpose is to raise the question: Why this invidious discrimination? A very little reflection shows that the suggestions which have been offered by way of explanation themselves need to be explained. Ideas derived from social castes and emotional revulsions are hardly reasons to be offered in justification of a belief, although they may have a bearing on its causation. Contempt for matter and bodies and glorification of the immaterial are affairs which are not self-explanatory. And, as we shall be at some pains to show later in the discussion, the idea which connects thinking and knowing with some principle or force that is wholly separate from connection with physical things will not stand examination, especially since the whole-hearted adoption of experimental method in the natural sciences.

The questions suggested have far-reaching issues. What is the cause and the import of the sharp division between theory and practice? Why should the latter be disesteemed along with matter and the body? What has been the effect upon the various modes in which action is manifested: industry, politics, the fine arts, and upon morals conceived of as overt activity having consequences, instead of as mere inner personal attitude? How has the separation of intellect from action affected the theory of knowledge? What has been in particular the effect upon the conception and course of philosophy? What forces are at work to break down the division? What would the effect be if the divorce were annulled, and knowing and doing were brought into intrinsic connection with one another? What revisions of the traditional theory of mind, thought and knowing would be required, and what change in the idea of the office of philosophy would be demanded? What modifications would ensue in the disciplines which are concerned with the various phases of human activity?

These questions form the theme of this book, and indicate the nature of the problems to be discussed. In this opening chapter we shall consider especially some historic grounds for the elevation of knowledge above making and doing. This phase of the discussion will disclose that exaltation of pure intellect and its activity above practical affairs is fundamentally connected with the quest for a certainty which shall be absolute and unshakeable. The distinctive characteristic of practical activity, one which is so inherent that it cannot be eliminated, is the uncertainty which attends it. Of it we are compelled to say: Act, but act at your peril. Judgment and belief regarding actions to be performed can never attain more than a precarious probability. Through thought, however, it has seemed that men might escape from the perils of uncertainty.

Practical activity deals with individualized and unique situations which are never exactly duplicable and about which, accordingly, no complete assurance is possible. All activity, moreover, involves change. The intellect, however, according to the traditional doctrine, may grasp universal Being, and Being which is universal is fixed and immutable. Wherever there is practical activity we human beings are involved as partakers in the issue. All the fear, disesteem and lack of confidence which gather about the thought of ourselves, cluster also about the thought of the actions in which we are partners. Man's distrust of himself has caused him to desire to get beyond and above himself; in pure knowledge he has thought he could attain this self-transcendence.

There is no need to expatiate upon the risk which attends overt action. The burden of proverbs and wise saws is that the best laid plans of men as of mice gang agley. Fortune rather than our own intent and act determines eventual success and failure. The pathos of unfulfilled expectation, the tragedy of defeated purpose and ideals, the catastrophes of accident, are the commonplaces of all comment on the human scene. We survey conditions, make the wisest choice we can; we act, and we must trust the rest to fate, fortune or providence. Moralists tell us to look to the end when we act and then inform us that the end is always uncertain. Judging, planning, choice, no matter how thoroughly conducted, and action no matter how prudently executed, never are the sole determinants of any outcome. Alien and indifferent natural forces, unforeseeable conditions enter in and have a decisive voice. The more important the issue, the greater is their say as to the ulterior event.

Hence men have longed to find a realm in which there is an activity which is not overt and which has no external consequences. "Safety first" has played a large rôle in effecting a preference for knowing over doing and making. With those to whom the process of pure thinking is congenial and who have the leisure and the aptitude to pursue their preference, the happiness attending knowing is unalloyed; it is not entangled in the risks which overt action cannot escape. Thought has been alleged to be a purely inner activity, intrinsic to mind alone; and according to traditional classic doctrine, "mind" is complete and self-sufficient in itself. Overt action may follow upon its operations but in an external way, a way not intrinsic to its completion. Since rational activity is complete within itself it needs no external manifestation. Failure and frustration are attributed to the accidents of an alien, intractable and inferior realm of existence. The outer lot of thought is cast in a world external to it, but one which in no way injures the supremacy and completeness of thought and knowledge in their intrinsic natures.

Thus the arts by which man attains such practical security as is possible of achievement are looked down upon. The security they provide is relative, ever incomplete, at the risk of untoward circumstance. The multiplication of arts may even be bemoaned as a source of new dangers. Each of them demands its own measures of protection. Each one in its operation brings with it new and unexpected consequences having perils for which we are not prepared. The quest for certainty is a quest for a peace which is assured, an object which is unqualified by risk and the shadow of fear which action casts. For it is not uncertainty *per se* which men dislike, but the fact that uncertainty involves us in peril of evils. Uncertainty that affected only the detail of consequences to be experienced provided they had a warrant of being enjoyable would have no sting. It would bring the zest of adventure and the spice of variety. Quest for complete certainty can be fulfilled in pure knowing alone. Such is the verdict of our most enduring philosophic tradition.

While the tradition has, as we shall see later, found its way into all themes and subjects, and determines the form of current problems and conclusions regarding mind and knowledge, it may be doubted whether if we were suddenly released from the burden of tradition, we should, on the basis of present experience take the disparaging view of practice and the exalted view of knowledge apart from action which tradition dictates. For man, in spite of the new perils in which the machinery of his new arts of production and transportation have involved him, has learned to play with sources of danger. He even seeks them out, weary of the routine of a too sheltered life. The enormous change taking place in the position of women is itself, for example, a commentary on a change of attitude toward the value of protection as an end in itself. We have attained, at least subconsciously, a certain feeling of confidence; a feeling that control of the main conditions of fortune is to an appreciable degree passing into our own hands. We live surrounded with the protection of thousands of arts and we have devised schemes of insurance which mitigate and distribute the evils which accrue. Barring the fears which war leaves in its train, it is perhaps a safe speculation that if contemporary western man were completely deprived of all the old beliefs about knowledge and actions he would assume, with a fair degree of confidence, that it lies within his power to achieve a reasonable degree of security in life.

This suggestion is speculative. Acceptance of it is not needed by the argument. It has its value as an indication of the earlier conditions in which a felt need for assurance was the dominant emotion. For primitive men had none of the elaborate arts of protection and use which we now enjoy and no confidence in his own powers when they were reinforced by appliances of art. He lived under conditions in which he was extraordinarily exposed to peril, and at the same time he was without the means of defense which are to-day matters of course. Most of our simplest tools and utensils did not exist; there was no accurate foresight; men faced the forces of nature in a state of nakedness which was more than physical; save under unusually benign conditions he was beset with dangers that knew no remission. In consequence, mystery attended experiences of good and evil; they could not be traced to their natural causes and they seemed to be the dispensations, the gifts and the inflictions, of powers beyond possibility of control. The precarious crises of birth, puberty, illness, death, war, famine, plague, the uncertainties of the hunt, the vicissitudes of climate and the great seasonal changes, kept imagination occupied with the uncertain. Any scene or object that was implicated in any conspicuous tragedy or triumph, in no matter how accidental a way, got a peculiar significance. It was seized upon as a harbinger of good or as an omen of evil. Accordingly, some things were cherished as means of encompassing safety just as a good artisan to-day looks after his tools; others were feared and shunned because of their potencies for harm.

As a drowning man is said to grasp at a straw, so men who lacked the instruments and skills developed in later days, snatched at whatever, by any stretch of imagination, could be regarded as a source of help in time of trouble. The attention, interest and care which now go to acquiring skill in the use of appliances and to the invention of means for better service of ends, were devoted to noting omens, making irrelevant prognostications, performing ritualistic ceremonies and manipulating objects possessed of magical power over natural events. In such an atmosphere primitive religion was born and fostered. Rather this atmosphere *was* the religious disposition.

Search for alliance with means which might promote prosperity and which would afford defense against hostile powers was constant. While this attitude was most marked in connection with the recurrent crises of life, yet the boundary line between these crucial affairs with their extraordinary risks and everyday acts was shadowy. The acts that related to common-place things and everyday occupations were usually accompanied, for good measure of security, by ritual acts. The making of a weapon, the molding of a bowl, the weaving of a mat, the sowing of seed, the reaping of a harvest, required acts different in kind to the technical skills employed. These other acts had a special solemnity and were thought necessary in order to ensure the success of the practical operations used.

While it is difficult to avoid the use of the word supernatural, we must avoid the meaning the word has for us. As long as there was no defined area of the *natural*, that which is over and beyond the natural can have no significance. The distinction, as anthropological students have pointed out, was between ordinary and extraordinary; between the prosaic, usual run of events and the crucial incident or irruption which determined the direction which the average and expected course of events took. But the two realms were in no way sharply demarcated from each other. There was a no-man's land, a vague territory, in which they overlapped. At any moment the extraordinary might invade the commonplace and either wreck it or clothe it with some surprising glory. The use of ordinary things under critical conditions was fraught with inexplicable potentialities of good and evil.

The two dominant conceptions, cultural categories one might call them, which grew and flourished under such circumstances were those of the holy and the fortunate, with their opposites, the profane and the unlucky. As with the idea of the supernatural, meanings are not to be assigned on the basis of present usage. Everything which was charged with some extraordinary potency for benefit or injury was holy; holiness meant necessity for being approached with ceremonial scruples. The holy thing, whether place, object, person or ritual appliance, has its sinister face; "to be handled with care" is written upon it. From it there issues the command: *Noli me tangere*. Tabus, a whole set of prohibitions and injunctions, gather about it. It is capable of transmitting its mysterious potency to other things. To secure the favor of the holy is to be on the road to success, while any conspicuous success is proof of the favor of some overshadowing power—a fact which politicians of all ages have known how to utilize. Because of its surcharge of power, ambivalent in quality, the holy has to be approached not only with scruples but in an attitude of subjection. There are rites of purification, humiliation, fasting and prayer which are preconditions of securing its favor.

The holy is the bearer of blessing or fortune. But a difference early developed between the ideas of the holy and the lucky, because of the different dispositions in which each was to be approached. A lucky object is something to be used. It is to be manipulated rather than approached with awe. It calls for incantations, spells, divinations rather than for supplication and humiliation. Moreover, the lucky thing tends to be a concrete and tangible object, while the holy one is not usually definitely localized; it is the more potent in the degree in which its habitation and form are vague. The lucky object is subject to pressure, at a pinch to coercion, to scolding and punishment. It might be discarded if it failed to bring luck. There developed a certain element of mastery in its use, in distinction from the dependence and subjection which remained the proper attitude toward the holy. Thus there was a kind of rhythm of domination and submission, of imprecation and supplication, of utilization and communion.

Such statements give, of course, a one-sided picture. Men at all times have gone about many things in a matter-of-fact way and have had their daily enjoyments. Even in the ceremonies of which we have spoken there entered the ordinary love of the dramatic as well as the desire for repetition, once routine is established. Primitive man early developed some tools and some modes of skill. With them went prosaic knowledge of the properties of ordinary things. But these beliefs were surrounded by others of an imaginative and emotional type, and were more or less submerged in the latter. Moreover, prestige attached to the latter. Just because some beliefs were matter-of-fact they did not have the weight and authority that belong to those about the extraordinary and unaccountable. We find the same phenomenon repeated to-day wherever religious beliefs have marked vitality.

Prosaic beliefs about verifiable facts, beliefs backed up by evidence of the senses and by useful fruits, had little glamour and prestige compared with the vogue of objects of rite and ceremony. Hence the things forming their subject-matter were felt to be lower in rank. Familiarity breeds a sense of equality if not of contempt. We deem ourselves on a par with things we daily administer. It is a truism to say that objects regarded with awe have perforce a superior status. Herein is the source of the fundamental dualism of human attention and regard. The distinction between the two attitudes of everyday control and dependence on something superior was finally generalized intellectually. It took effect in the conception of two distinct realms. The inferior was that in which man could foresee and in which he had instruments and arts by which he might expect a reasonable degree of control. The superior was that of occurrences so uncontrollable that they testified to the presence and operation of powers beyond the scope of everyday and mundane things.

The philosophical tradition regarding knowledge and practice, the immaterial or spiritual and the material, was not original and primitive. It had for its background the state of culture which has been sketched. It developed in a social atmosphere in which the division of the ordinary and extraordinary was domesticated. Philosophy reflected upon it and gave it a rational formulation and justification. The bodies of information that corresponded to the everyday arts, the store of matter-of-fact knowledge, were things men knew because of what they did. They were products and promises of utilities. They shared in the relatively low esteem belonging to such things in comparison with the extraordinary and divine. Philosophy inherited the realm with which religion had been concerned. Its mode of knowing was different from that accompanying the empirical arts, just because it dealt with a realm of higher Being. It breathed an air purer than that in which exist the making and doing that relate to livelihood, just as the activities which took the form of rites and ceremonies were nobler and nearer the divine than those spent in toil.

The change from religion to philosophy was so great in form that their identity as to content is easily lost from view. The form ceases to be that of the story told in imaginative and emotional style, and becomes that of rational discourse observing the canons of logic. It is well known that that portion of Aristotle's system which later generations have called metaphysics he called First Philosophy. It is possible to quote from him sentences descriptive of "First Philosophy" which make it seem that the philosophic enterprise is a coldly rational one, objective and analytic. Thus he says it is the most comprehensive of all branches of knowledge because it has for its subject-matter definition of the traits which belong to all forms of Being whatsoever, however much they may differ from one another in detail.

But when these passages are placed in the context they had in Aristotle's own mind, it is clear that the comprehensiveness and universality of first philosophy are not of a strictly analytic sort. They mark a distinction with respect to grade of value and title to reverence. For he explicitly identifies his first philosophy—or metaphysics—with theology; he says it is higher than other sciences. For these deal with generation and production, while its subject-matter permits of demonstrative, that is necessary, truth; and its objects are divine and such as are meet for God to occupy himself with. Again, he says that the objects of philosophy are such as are the causes of as much of the divine as is manifest to us, and that if the divine is anywhere present, it is present in things of the sort with which philosophy deals. The supremacy of worth and dignity of these objects are also made clear in the statement that the Being with which philosophy is occupied is primary, eternal and self-sufficient, because its nature is the Good, so that the Good is among the first principles which are philosophy's subject-matter:—yet not, it must be understood, the good in the sense in which it has meaning and standing in human life but the inherently and eternally perfect, that which is complete and self-sufficient.

Aristotle tells us that from remote antiquity tradition has handed down the idea, in story form, that the heavenly bodies are gods, and that the divine encompasses the entire natural world. This core of truth, he goes on to say in effect, was embroidered with myths for the benefit of the masses, for reasons of expediency, namely, the preservation of social institutions. The negative work of philosophy was then to strip away these imaginative accretions. From the standpoint of popular belief this was its chief work, and it was a destructive one. The masses only felt that their religion was attacked. But the enduring contribution was positive. The belief that the divine encompasses the world was detached from its mythical context and made the basis of philosophy, and it became also the foundation of physical science—as is suggested by the remark that the heavenly bodies are gods. Telling the story of the universe in the form of rational discourse instead of emotionalized imagination signified the discovery of logic as a rational science. Conformity on the part of supreme reality to the requirements of logic conferred upon its constitutive objects necessary and immutable characteristics. Pure contemplation of these forms was man's highest and most divine bliss, a communion with unchangeable truth.

The geometry of Euclid doubtless gave the clew to logic as the instrument of translation of what was sound in opinion into the forms of rational discourse. Geometry seemed to reveal the possibility of a science which owed nothing to observation and sense beyond mere exemplification in figures or diagrams. It seemed to disclose a world of ideal (or non-sensible) forms which were connected with one another by eternal and necessary relations which reason alone could trace. This discovery was generalized by philosophy into the doctrine of a realm of fixed Being which, when grasped by thought, formed a complete system of immutable and necessary truth.

If one looks at the foundations of the philosophies of Plato and Aristotle as an anthropologist looks at his material, that is, as cultural subject-matter, it is clear that these philosophies were systematizations in rational form of the content of Greek religious and artistic beliefs. The systematization involved a purification. Logic provided the patterns to which ultimately real objects had to conform, while physical science was possible in the degree in which the natural world, even in its mutabilities, exhibited exemplification of ultimate immutable rational objects. Thus, along with the elimination of myths and grosser superstitions, there were set up the ideals of science and of a life of reason. Ends which could justify themselves to reason were to take the place of custom as the guide of conduct. These two ideals form a permanent contribution to western civilization.

But with all our gratitude for these enduring gifts, we cannot forget the conditions which attended them. For they brought with them the idea of a higher realm of fixed reality of which alone true science is possible and of an inferior world of changing things with which experience and practical matters are concerned. They glorified the invariant at the expense of change, it being evident that all practical activity falls within the realm of change. It bequeathed the notion, which has ruled philosophy ever since the time of the Greeks, that the office of knowledge is to uncover the antecedently real, rather than, as is the case with our practical judgments, to gain the kind of understanding which is necessary to deal with problems as they arise.

In fixing this conception of knowledge it established also, as far as philosophies of the classic type are concerned, the special task of philosophic inquiry. As a form of knowledge it is concerned with the disclosure of the Real in itself, of Being in and of itself. It is differentiated from other modes of knowing by its preoccupation with a higher and more ultimate form of Being than that with which the sciences of nature are concerned. As far as it occupied itself at all with human conduct, it was to superimpose upon acts ends said to flow from the nature of reason. It thus diverted thought from inquiring into the purposes which experience of actual conditions suggest and from concrete means of their actualization. It translated into a rational form the doctrine of escape from the vicissitudes of existence by means of measures which do not demand an active coping with conditions. For deliverance by means of rites and cults, it substituted deliverance through reason. This deliverance was an intellectual, a theoretical affair, constituted by a knowledge to be attained apart from practical activity.

The realms of knowledge and action were each divided into two regions. It is not to be inferred that Greek philosophy separated activity from knowing. It connected them. But it distinguished activity from action—that is, from making and doing. Rational and necessary knowledge was treated, as in the celebrations of it by Aristotle, as an ultimate, self-sufficient and self-enclosed form of self-originated and self-conducted activity. It was ideal and eternal, independent of change and hence of the world in which men act and live, the world we experience perceptibly and practically. "Pure activity" was sharply marked off from practical action. The latter, whether in the industrial or the fine arts, in morals or in politics, was concerned with an inferior region of Being in which change rules, and which accordingly has Being only by courtesy, for it manifests deficiency of sure footing in Being by the very fact of change. It is infected with *non*-being.

On the side of knowledge, the division carried with it a difference between knowledge, in its full sense, and belief. The former is demonstrative, necessary—that is, sure. Belief on the contrary is only opinion; in its uncertainty and mere probability, it relates to the world of change as knowledge corresponds to the realm of true reality. This fact brings the discussion around once more to our special theme as far as it affects the conception of the office and nature of philosophy. That man has two modes, two dimensions, of belief, cannot be doubted. He has beliefs about actual existences and the course of events, and he has beliefs about ends to be striven for, policies to be adopted, goods to be attained and evils to be averted. The most urgent of all practical problems concerns the connection the subject-matter of these two kinds of beliefs sustain to each other. How shall our most authentic and dependable cognitive beliefs be used to regulate our practical beliefs? How shall the latter serve to organize and integrate our intellectual beliefs?

There is a genuine possibility that the true problem of philosophy is connected with precisely this type of question. Man has beliefs which scientific inquiry vouchsafes, beliefs about the actual structure and processes of things; and he also has beliefs about the values which should regulate his conduct. The question of how these two ways of believing may most effectively and fruitfully interact with one another is the most general and significant of all the problems which life presents to us. Some reasoned discipline, one obviously other than any science, should deal with this issue. Thus there is supplied one way of conceiving of the function of philosophy. But from this mode of defining philosophy we are estopped by the chief philosophical tradition. For according to it the realms of knowledge and of practical action have no inherent connection with each other. Here then is the focus to which the various elements in our discussion converge. We may then profitably recapitulate. The realm of the practical is the region of change, and change is always contingent;

it has in it an element of chance that cannot be eliminated. If a thing changes, its alteration is convincing evidence of its lack of true or complete Being. What *is*, in the full and pregnant sense of the word, is always, eternally. It is self-contradictory for that which *is* to alter. If it had no defect or imperfection in it how could it change? That which becomes merely *comes* to be, never truly is. It is infected with non-being; with privation of Being in the perfect sense. The world of generation is the world of decay and destruction. Wherever one thing comes into being something else passes out of being.

Thus the depreciation of practice was given a philosophic, an ontological, justification. Practical action, as distinct from self-revolving rational self-activity, belongs in the realm of generation and decay, a realm inferior in value as in Being. In form, the quest for absolute certainty has reached its goal. Because ultimate Being or reality is fixed, permanent, admitting of no change or variation, it may be grasped by rational intuition and set forth in rational, that is, universal and necessary, demonstration. I do not doubt that there was a feeling before the rise of philosophy that the unalterably fixed and the absolutely certain are one, or that change is the source from which comes all our uncertainties and woes. But in philosophy this inchoate feeling was definitely formulated. It was asserted on grounds held to be as demonstrably necessary as are the conclusions of geometry and logic. Thus the predisposition of philosophy toward the universal, invariant and eternal was fixed. It remains the common possession of the entire classic philosophic tradition.

All parts of the scheme hang together. True Being or Reality is complete; in being complete, it is perfect, divine, immutable, the "unmoved mover." Then there are things that change, that come and go, that are generated and perish, because of lack of the stability which participation in ultimate Being alone confers. These changes, however, have form and character and are knowable in the degree in which they tend toward an end which is the fulfillment and completion of the changes in question. Their instability is not absolute but is marked by aspiration toward a goal.

The perfect and complete is rational thought, the ultimate "end" or terminus of all natural movement. That which changes, which becomes and passes away, *is* material; change *defines* the physical. At most and best, it is a potentiality of reaching a stable and fixed end. To these two realms belong two sorts of knowledge. One of them is alone knowledge in the full sense, *science*. This has a rational, necessary and unchanging form. It is *certain*. The other, dealing with change, is belief or opinion; empirical and particular; it is contingent, a matter of probability, not of certainty. The most it can assert is that things are so and so "upon the whole," usually. Corresponding to the division in Being and in knowledge is that in activities. Pure activity is rational; it is theoretical, in the sense in which theory is apart from practical action. Then there is action in doing and making, occupied with the needs and defects of the lower realm of change in which, in his physical nature, man is implicated.

Although this Greek formulation was made long ago and much of it is now strange in its specific terms, certain features of it are as relevant to present thought as they were significant in their original formulation. For in spite of the great, the enormous changes in the subject-matter and method of the sciences and the tremendous expansion of practical activities by means of arts and technologies, the main tradition of western culture has retained intact this framework of ideas. Perfect certainty is what man wants. It cannot be found by practical doing or making; these take effect in an uncertain future, and involve peril, the risk of misadventure, frustration and failure. Knowledge, on the other hand, is thought to be concerned with a region of being which is fixed in itself. Being eternal and unalterable, human knowing is not to make any difference in it. It can be approached through the medium of the apprehensions and demonstrations of thought, or by some other organ of mind, which does nothing to the real, except just to know it.

There is involved in these doctrines a whole system of philosophical conclusions. The first and foremost is that there is complete correspondence between knowledge in its true meaning and what is real. What is known, what is true for cognition, is what is real in being. The objects of knowledge form the standards of measures of the reality of all other objects of experience. Are the objects of the affections, of desire, effort, choice, that is to say everything to which we attach value, real? Yes, if they can be warranted by knowledge; if we can *know objects* having these value properties, we are justified in thinking them real. But as objects of desire and purpose they have no sure place in Being until they are approached and validated through knowledge. The idea is so familiar that we overlook the unexpressed premise upon which it rests, namely that only the completely fixed and unchanging can be real. The quest for certitude has determined our basic metaphysics.

Secondly, the theory of knowledge has its basic premises fixed by the same doctrine. For knowledge to be certain must relate to that which has antecedent existence or essential being. There are certain things which are alone inherently the proper objects of knowledge and science. Things in the production of which we participate we cannot know in the true sense of the word, for such things succeed instead of preceding our action. What concerns action forms the realm of mere guesswork and probability, as distinct from the warrant of rational assurance which is the ideal of true knowledge. We are so accustomed to the separation of knowledge from doing and making that we fail to recognize how it controls our conceptions of mind, of consciousness and of reflective inquiry. For as relates to genuine knowledge, these must all be defined, on the basis of the premise, so as not to admit of the presence of any overt action that modifies conditions having prior and independent existence.

Special theories of knowledge differ enormously from one another. Their quarrels with one another fill the air. The din thus created makes us deaf to the way in which they say one thing in common. The controversies are familiar. Some theories ascribe the ultimate test of knowledge to impressions passively received, forced upon us whether we will or no. Others ascribe the guarantee of knowledge to synthetic activity of the intellect. Idealistic theories hold that mind and the object known are ultimately one; realistic doctrines reduce knowledge to awareness of what exists independently, and so on. But they all make one common assumption. They all hold that the operation of inquiry excludes any element of practical activity that enters into the construction of the object known. Strangely enough this is as true of idealism as of realism, of theories of synthetic activity as of those of passive receptivity. For according to them "mind" constructs the known object not in any observable way, or by means of practical overt acts having a temporal quality, but by some occult internal operation.

The common essence of all these theories, in short, is that what is known is antecedent to the mental act of observation and inquiry, and is totally unaffected by these acts; otherwise it would not be fixed and unchangeable. This negative condition, that the processes of search, investigation, reflection, involved in knowledge relate to something having prior being, fixes once for all the main characters attributed to mind, and to the organs of knowing. They *must* be outside what is known, so as not to interact in any way with the object to be known. If the word "interaction" be used, it cannot denote that overt production of change it signifies in its ordinary and practical use.

The theory of knowing is modeled after what was supposed to take place in the act of vision. The object refracts light to the eye and is seen; it makes a difference to the eye and to the person having an optical apparatus, but none to the thing seen. The real object is the object so fixed in its regal aloofness that it is a king to any beholding mind that may gaze upon it. A spectator theory of knowledge is the inevitable outcome. There have been theories which hold that mental activity intervenes, but they have retained the old premise. They have therefore concluded that it is impossible to know reality. Since mind intervenes, we know, according to them, only some modified semblance of the real object, some "appearance." It would be hard to find a more thoroughgoing confirmation than this conclusion provides of the complete hold possessed by the belief that the object of knowledge is a reality fixed and complete in itself, in isolation from an act of inquiry which has in it any element of production of change.

All of these notions about certainty and the fixed, about the nature of the real world, about the nature of the mind and its organs of knowing, are completely bound up with one another, and their consequences ramify into practically all important ideas entertained upon any philosophic question. They all flow—such is my basic thesis—from the separation (set up in the interest of the quest for absolute certainty) between theory and practice, knowledge and action. Consequently the latter problem cannot be attacked in isolation, by itself. It is too thoroughly entangled with fundamental beliefs and ideas in all sorts of fields.

In later chapters the theme will, therefore, be approached in relation to each of the above-mentioned points. We shall first take up the effect of the traditional separation upon the conception of the nature of philosophy, especially in connection with the question of the secure place of values in existence. We shall then pass on to an account of the way in which modern philosophies have been dominated by the problem of reconciling the conclusions of natural science with the objective validity of the values by which men live and regulate their conduct:—a problem which would have no existence were it not for the prior uncritical acceptance of the traditional notion that knowledge has a monopolistic claim to access to reality. The discussion will then take up various phases of the development of actual knowing as exemplified in scientific procedure, so as to show, by an analysis of experimental inquiry in its various phases, how completely the traditional assumptions, mentioned above, have been abandoned in concrete scientific procedure. For science in becoming experimental has itself become a mode of directed practical doing. There will then follow a brief statement of the effect of the destruction of the barriers which have divided theory and practice upon reconstruction of the basic ideas about mind and thought, and upon the solution of a number of long-standing problems as to the theory of knowledge. The consequences of substituting search for security by practical means for quest of absolute certainty by cognitive means will then be considered in its bearing upon the problem of our judgments regarding the values which control conduct, especially its social phases.

Study Questions

1.   What elements of their philosophies entitle historians of American philosophy to describe Peirce, James, and Dewey as pragmatists? Explain.

2.   What evidence do you find in the writings of Peirce and Dewey to suggest that the views of Darwinian biology are important to their philosophical thought and theories? Be specific and defend your answer.

3.   What are the distinctions between the methods of "fixing belief" in Peirce's work and what are the strengths and weaknesses of each method?

4.   What is the principal argument in Peirce's "How to Make Our Ideas Clear"? Does he succeed in making his case? Why or why not?

5.   Dewey had no patience with traditional dualism. What are his reasons for rejecting dualism of almost every kind, and what does his rejection of dualism tell you about his view of pragmatism and worldly action? Explain.

6.   In essays such as "The Will to Believe" and "The Dilemma of Determinism," James seems to allow people to adopt metaphysical hypotheses even if they are not supported by experience. How does he build a case for the surrender to belief when nothing in experience sustains it? Is this position convincing?

7.   Peirce and James try to tell us what pragmatism is and what it means. How are their explanations similar and how are they different? Explain.

Suggestions for Further Reading

Brent, Joseph. *Charles Sanders Peirce: A Life*. Bloomington: Indiana University Press, 1993.

Conkin, Paul K. *Puritans and Pragmatists: Eight Eminent American Thinkers*. New York: Dodd, Mead & Company, 1968.

Dewey, John. *Experience and Nature*. Chicago: Open Court, 1925.

Dewey, John. *The Quest for Certainty*. New York: G.P. Putnam's Sons, 1929.

Dewey, John. *Reconstruction in Philosophy*, second edition, Boston: Beacon Press, 1948.

Gale, Richard M. *The Divided Self of William James*. Cambridge: Cambridge University Press, 1999.

Geiger, George R. *John Dewey in Perspective*. New York: McGraw-Hill, 1964.

Hookway, Christopher. *Peirce*. London: Routledge, 1985.

Hookway, Christopher. *Truth, Rationality and Pragmatism: Themes from Peirce*. Oxford: Oxford University Press, 2000.

James, William. *"The Will to Believe," and Other Essays in Popular Philosophy*. New York: Longmans, Green and Company, 1897.

James, William. *The Varieties of Religious Experience: A Study in Human Nature*. New York: Longmans, Green and Company, 1902.

James, William. *Pragmatism and Other Writings*. Edited by Giles Gunn. New York: Penguin Books, 2000.

Menand, Louis. *The Metaphysical Club: A Story of Ideas in America*. New York: Farrar, Straus and Giroux, 2001.

Peirce, Charles Sanders. *Philosophical Writings*. Edited by Justus Buchler. New York: Dover Publications, 1955.

Peirce, Charles Sanders. *Selected Writings (Values in a Universe of Chance)*. Edited by Philip P. Wiener. New York: Dover Publications, 1966.

Perry, Ralph Barton. *The Thought and Character of William James: Briefer Version*. Cambridge, Mass.: Harvard University Press, 1948.

Putnam, Ruth Anna, ed. *The Cambridge Companion to William James*. Cambridge: Cambridge University Press, 1997.

Ratner, Joseph, ed. *Intelligence in the Modern World: John Dewey's Philosophy*. New York: Modern Library, 1939.

Simon, Linda. *Genuine Reality: A Life of William James*. New York: Harcourt Brace, 1998.

Wainwright, William J. *Reason and the Heart*. Ithaca: Cornell University Press, 1995.

Welchman, Jennifer. *Dewey's Ethical Thought*. Ithaca: Cornell University Press, 1995.

White, Morton. *Pragmatism and the American Mind: Essays and Reviews in Philosophy and Intellectual History*. New York: Oxford University Press, 1973.

Wiener, Philip P. *Evolution and the Founders of Pragmatism*. Cambridge, Mass.: Harvard University Press, 1949.

Chapter 6

Josiah Royce
*Idealism, Absolute Pragmatism,
and the Search for Unity*

Josiah Royce is the first philosopher in this anthology who grew up west of the Mississippi River. Born in 1855 in the mountains of northern California, he studied at the University of California, Berkeley, and earned his Ph.D. at Johns Hopkins University. In 1882 he was invited to lecture for a year at Harvard while William James was on academic leave. That year turned out to be the beginning of more than three decades in Harvard's remarkable Department of Philosophy. Although he and James were endlessly at odds intellectually, they became close friends and were, with George Santayana, the pillars of what historians call the "Golden Age" of Harvard philosophy. At his death in 1916, Royce had established himself as America's leading voice in philosophical idealism, as a seminal philosopher of religion, and as one of the finest lecturers at Harvard or any other university in the United States.

Royce's philosophy can be complex and in a few cases almost impenetrable. On the other hand, some of his very important writings such as *The Conception of God* (1898), *The Philosophy of Loyalty* (1908), and the posthumously published *Lectures on Modern Idealism* (1919) are straightforward enough to enable his first-time readers to understand what it means to describe Royce as an Anglo-American idealist and to see some points of convergence between his philosophy and that of the pragmatists. If one can understand Royce's conception of God or the Absolute, together with his quasi-religious epistemology, much of the rest that Royce says falls into place. Further, if readers also keep in view Royce's passion for unity—whether he is discussing the unity of all knowledge, the unity of being, or the less ethereal unity of some European and American communities—they can understand the connective tissue between Royce's metaphysics and his social views.

Readers will discover, for example, how different Royce is from a Transcendentalist like Thoreau, even though each of them speaks for individual autonomy and responsibility. Thoreau, as one can tell throughout the pages of *Walden*, finds these virtues best instantiated outside communities and beyond close-knit societies. Royce, despite growing up among the so-called "rugged individualists" of the West, insists that true individualism finds its purest expression within a community of sociable people.

The selections that follow must speak for themselves. But Royce's prose is sometimes turgid, and thus his philosophy can strike even his most serious followers as no less complex than its English and German antecedents. A curious reader must, therefore, be willing to cut through the underbrush and thickets of his arguments and style in order to discover the themes that justify regarding Royce as one of America's finest philosophers. Moreover, work and patience reward the effort, since, besides learning about Royce's philosophy, readers who stay with the task discover important ties between Royce's thought and the changes that America underwent leading up to the twentieth century. If, therefore, Royce's idealism is shaped by English and German thinkers, his rendering of these influences takes on an urgency that is not so remote from the problems of many twenty-first century Americans. Those who are estranged from other human beings, suffer from loneliness or alienation, worry about amoralism and the consequent erosion of traditional values, will find a sympathetic companion in Royce. They will also find that Royce, much like James and Dewey, believes these problems can be solved and that it is never too late to strive for a better world.

The Conception of God (1897)

. . . The Conception of God—this is our immediate topic. And I begin its consideration by saying that, to my mind, a really fruitful philosophical study of the conception of God is inseparable from an attempt to estimate what evidence there is for the existence of God. When one conceives of God, one does so because one is interested, not in the bare definition of a purely logical or mathematical notion, but in the attempt to make out what sort of real world this is in which you and I live. If it is worth while even to speak of God before the forum of the philosophical reason, it is so because one hopes to be able, in a measure, to translate into articulate terms the central mystery of our existence, and to get some notion about what is at the heart of the world. Therefore, when to-night I speak of the conception of God, I mean to do so in the closest relation to a train of thought concerning the philosophical proof that this conception corresponds to some living Reality. It is useless in this region to define unless one wishes to show that, corresponding to the definition, there is a reality. And, on the other hand, the proof that one can offer for God's presence at the heart of the world constitutes also the best exposition that one can suggest regarding what one means by the conception of God.

Yet, of course, some preliminary definition of what one has in mind when one uses the word "God" is of value, since our proof will then involve a development of the fuller meaning of just this preliminary definition. . . . I propose to define, in advance, what we mean under the name "God," by means . . . of the attribute of Omniscience, or of the Divine Wisdom. By the word "God" I shall mean, then, . . . a being who is conceived as possessing to the full all logically possible knowledge, insight, wisdom. Our problem, then, becomes at once this: Does there demonstrably exist an Omniscient Being? or is the conception of an Omniscient Being, for all that we can say, a bare ideal of the human mind?

Why I choose this so-called attribute of Omniscience as constituting for the purposes of this argument the primary attribute of the Divine Being, students of philosophy . . . will easily understand. . . . What we here need to see from the outset, however, is that this conceived attribute of Omniscience, if it were once regarded as expressing the nature of a real being, would involve as a consequence the concurrent presence, in such a being, of attributes that we could at pleasure express under other names; such, for instance, as what is rationally meant by Omnipotence, by Self-Consciousness, by Self-Possession— yes, I should unhesitatingly add, by Goodness, by Perfection, by Peace. For consider for an instant what must be meant by Omniscience if one undertakes for a moment to view an Omniscient Being as real.

An Omniscient Being would be one who simply found presented to him, not by virtue of fragmentary and gradually completed processes of inquiry, but by virtue of an all-embracing, direct, and transparent insight into his own truth,—who found thus presented to him, I say, the complete, the fulfilled answer to every genuinely rational question. Observe the terms used. I say, the answer to every question. The words are familiar. Consider their meaning. We mortals question. To question involves thinking of possible facts, or of what one may call possible experiences, that are not now present to us. Thinking of these conceived or possible experiences that we do not now possess, we question in so far as we ask either what it would be to possess them, or whether the world is such that, under given conditions, these experiences that we think of when we question could be presented to us. In other words, to question means to have ideas of what is not now present, and to ask whether these ideas do express, or could express, what some experience would verify. I question, on the country road: "Is it four miles to the railway station, or more, or less?" In this case I have ideas or thoughts about possible experiences not now present to me. I question in so far as I wonder whether these possible experiences, if I got them,—that is, if I walked or rode to yonder railway station and measured my way,—would fulfill or verify one or another of these my various thoughts or ideas about the distance. To be limited to mere questions, then,—and here is the essential point about questioning,—involves a certain divorce between your ideas and their objects, between facts conceived and facts directly experienced, between what you think about and what you regard as possibly to be presented to your direct experience. In this divorce of ideas or thought and experience or fact, lies the essence of the state of mind of a being who merely questions.

On the other hand, to answer to the full, and with direct insight, any question, means to get your ideas, just in so far as they turn out to be true ideas, fulfilled, confirmed, verified by your experiences. When with full and complete insight you answer a question, then you can get into the direct presence of facts, of experiences, which you behold as the confirmation or fulfillment of certain ideas, as the verification of certain thoughts. Take your mere ideas, as such, alone by themselves, and you have to question whether or no they are true accounts of facts. Answer your questions, wholly for yourself, without intermediation, and then you have got your ideas, your thoughts, somehow into the presence of experienced facts. There are thus two factors or elements in completed and genuine knowing, namely: fact, or something experienced, on the one hand; and mere idea, or pure thought about actual or possible experience, on the other hand. Divorce those two elements of knowledge, let the experienced fact, actual or possible, be remote from the idea or thought about it, and then the being who merely thinks, questions, and, so far, can only question. His state is such that he wonders: Is my idea true? But let the divorce be completely overcome, and then the being who fully knows answers questions, in so far as he simply sees his ideas fulfilled in the facts of his experience, and beholds his experiences as the fulfillment of his ideas.

Very well, then, an Omniscient Being is defined as one in whom these two factors of knowledge, so often divorced in us, are supposed to be fully and universally joined. . . .

These factors of his knowledge would, however, still remain distinguishable. He would think, or have ideas,—richer ideas than our present fragments of thought, I need not say; but he would think. And he would experience. That is, he would have, in perfect fullness, what we call feeling—a world of immediate data of consciousness, presented as facts. This his world of feeling, of presented fact, would be richer than our fragments of scattered sensation . . .; but he would experience. Only,—herein lies the essence of his conceived Omniscience,—in him and for him these facts would not be, as they often are in us, merely felt, but they would be seen as fulfilling his ideas; as answering what, were he not omniscient, would be his mere questions.

But now, in us, our ideas, our thoughts, our questions, not merely concern what experienced facts might come to us through our senses, but also concern the value, the worth, the relations, the whole significance, ethical or aesthetic, of our particular experiences themselves. . . . Misfortune comes to us, and we ask: What means this horror of my fragmentary experience?—why did this happen to me? The question involves the idea of an experience that, if present, would answer the question. Now such an experience, if it were present to us, would be an experience of a certain passing through pain to peace, of a certain winning of triumph through partial defeat, or a certain far more exceeding weight of glory that would give even this fragmentary horror its place in an experience of triumph and of self-possession. In brief, every time we are weak, downcast, horror-stricken, alone with our sin, the victims of evil fortune or of our own baseness, we stand, as we all know, not only in the presence of agonizing fragmentary experiences, but in presence of besetting problems, which in fact constitute the very heart of our calamity. We are beset by questions to which we now get no answers. Those questions could only be answered, those bitter problems that pierce our hearts with the keen edge of doubt and wonder,—when friends part, when lovers weep, when the lighting of fortune blasts our hopes, when remorse and failure make desolate the lonely hours of our private despair,—such questions, such problems, I say, could only be answered if the flickering ideas then present in the midst of our darkness shone steadily in the presence of some world of superhuman experience, of which ours would then seem to be only the remote hint. . . .

Well, then,—if the divorce of ideas and experience characterises every form of our human consciousness of finitude, of weakness, of evil, of sin, of despair,—you see that Omniscience, involving, by definition, the complete and final fulfillment of idea in experience, the unity of thought and fact, the illumination of feeling by comprehension, would be an attribute implying, for the being who possessed it, much more than a universally clear but absolutely passionless insight. An Omniscient Being could answer your bitter *Why?* when you mourn, with an experience that would not simply ignore your passion. For your passion, too, is a fact. It is experienced. The experience of the Omniscient Being would therefore include it. Only his insight, unlike yours, would comprehend it, and so would answer whatever is rational about your present question.

This is what I mean by saying that the definition of God by means of the attribute of Omniscience would involve far more than the phrase "mere omniscience" at first easily suggests. As a fact, in order to have the attribute of Omniscience, a being would necessarily be conceived as essentially world-possessing,—as the source and principle of the universe of truth,—not merely as an external observer of a world of foreign truth. As such, he would be conceived as omnipotent, and also in possession of just such experience as ideally ought to be; in other words, as good and perfect.

So much, then, for the mere preliminary definition. To this definition I should here add a word or two of more technical analysis. We mortals have an incomplete experience. This means that the ideas awakened in us by our experience far transcend what we are now able to verify. We think, then, of actual or of possible experience that is not now ours. But an Omniscient Being would have no genuine or logically permissible ideas of any experience actually beyond his own or remote from his own. We express this by saying, technically, that an Omniscient Being would express an Absolute Experience; that is, a wholly complete or self-contained experience, not a mere part of some larger whole. Again, the Omniscient Being would be, as we have said, a thinker. But we, as thinkers, are limited, both in so far as there is possible thought not yet attained by us, and in so far as we often do not know what ones amongst our thoughts or ideas have a genuine meaning, or correspond to what an absolute experience would fulfill. But the Omniscient Being would not be thus limited as to his thinking. Accordingly, he would possess what we may call an Absolute Thought; that is, a self-contained thought, sufficient unto itself, and needing no further comment, supplement, or correction. As the union of such an Absolute Thought and Absolute Experience, our Omniscient Being is technically to be named simply the Absolute; that is, the being sufficient unto himself. . . . I should also say that the experience and thought of this being might be called completely or fully *organized*. For us . . . facts come in a disjointed way . . . and our thoughts, equally, seek a connection which they do not now possess. (God's) experience . . . would form one whole. There would be endless variety in this whole, but the whole, as such, would fulfill an all-embracing unity, a single system of ideas.

This is what I mean by calling his Experience, as we here conceive it, an absolutely organized experience, his Thought an absolutely organized thought.

. . . The question is: Does such a being exist? We turn from the ideal to the hard fact that we mortals find ourselves very ignorant beings. What can such as we are hope to know of the Absolute? . . .

. . . Any finite experience either regards itself as suggesting some sort of truth, or does not so regard itself. If it does not regard itself as suggesting truth, it concerns us not here. Enough, one who thinks, who aims at truth, who means to know anything, is regarding his experience as suggesting truth. . . . [T]o regard our experience as suggesting truth is . . . to mean that our experience indicates what a higher or inclusive . . . experience would find presented . . . to itself. It is the meaning, this intent, this aim, this will to find in the moment the indication of what a higher experience directly grasps,—it is this that embodies for us the fact of which our hypothetical proposition aforesaid is the expression. . . .

. . . Grant hypothetically . . . that there is no universal experience of a concrete fact, but only the hope of it, the definition of it, the will to win it. . . . Well, what will that mean? This ultimate limitation, this finally imprisoned finitude, this absolute fragmentariness and error, of the actual experience that aims at the absolute experience when there is no absolute experience at which to aim,—this absolute finiteness and erroneousness of the real experience, I say, will itself be a fact, a truth, a reality, and, as such, just the absolute truth. But this supposed ultimate truth will exist for whose experience? For the finite experience? No. . . . For if any experience actually knew . . . itself to be the whole of experience, it would have to experience how and why it were so. And if it knew this, it would be *ipso facto* an absolute. . . . Only . . . an absolute experience could say with assurance: "Beyond my world there is no further experience actual." But if . . . there is to be no such experience, but only a limited collection of finite experiences, the question returns: The reality of this final limitation, the existence of no experience beyond the broken mass of finite fragments,—this is to be a truth,—but for whose experience is it to be a truth? Plainly . . . it will be a truth nowhere presented—a truth for nobody. But . . . to assert any absolute reality as real is simply to assert an experience—and . . . just in so far as the reality is absolute, an absolute experience—for which this reality exists. To assert a truth as more than possible is to assert the concrete reality of an experience that knows this truth. Hence, . . . the very effort hypothetically to assert that the whole world of experience is a world of fragmentary and finite experience is an effort involving a contradiction. Experience must constitute . . . one self-determined and consequently absolute and organized whole.

Otherwise put: All concrete or genuine, and not barely possible truth is, as such, a truth somewhere experienced. This is the inevitable result of the view with which we started when we said that without experience there is no knowledge. . . .

. . . Let us sum up . . . our whole argument. There is, for us as we are, experience. Our thought undertakes the interpretation of this experience. Every intelligent interpretation of an experience involves . . . the appeal from this experienced fragment to some more organised whole of experience, in whose unity this fragment is conceived as finding its organic place. To talk of any reality which this fragmentary experience indicates, is to conceive this reality as the content of the more organized experience. To assert that there is any absolutely real fact indicated by our experience, is to regard this reality as presented to an absolutely organized experience in which every fragment finds its place. . . .

Our result, then, is: There is an Absolute Experience, for which the conception of an absolute reality, *i.e.*, the conception of a system of ideal truth, is fulfilled by the very contents that get presented to this Experience. This Absolute Experience is related to our experience as an organic whole to its own fragments. It is an experience which finds fulfilled all that the completest thought can rationally conceive as genuinely possible. Herein lies its definition as an Absolute. For the Absolute Experience, as for ours, there are data, contents, facts. But these data, these contents, express, for the Absolute Experience, its own meaning, its thought, its ideas. Contents beyond these that it possesses, the Absolute Experience knows to be, in genuine truth, impossible. Hence its contents are indeed particular,—a selection from the world of bare or merely conceptual possibilities,—but they form a self-determined whole, than which nothing completer, more organic, more fulfilled, more transparent, or more complete in meaning, is concretely or genuinely possible. On the other hand, these contents are not foreign to those of our finite experience, but are inclusive of them in the unity of one life. . . .

The Philosophy of Loyalty (1908)

. . . Our age . . . is a good deal perplexed regarding its moral ideals and its standards of duty. It has doubts about what is really the best plan of human life. This perplexity is not wholly due to any peculiar waywardness of our time, or to any general lack of moral seriousness. It is just our moral leaders, our reformers, our prophets, who most perplex us. Whether these revolutionary moral teachers are right or wrong, they beset us, they give us no rest, they call in doubt our moral judgments, they undertake to "transmute values." And the result for many of us, is a practical result. It tends to deprive us of that confidence which we all need in order to be ready to do good works. It threatens to paralyze the effectiveness of many conscientious people. Hence any effort to reason calmly and constructively about the foundations of the moral life may serve, not merely to clarify our minds, but to give vigor to our deeds. . . . I shall ask you to think indeed about moral problems, but to think for the sake of action. I shall try to give you some fragments of a moral philosophy; but I shall try to justify the philosophy through its application to life. . . .

The phrase, "Philosophy of Loyalty," is intended to indicate first, that we are here to consider loyalty as an ethical principle. For philosophy deals with first principles. And secondly, my title means to suggest that we are to view the matter discriminatingly, as well as practically. For philosophy is essentially a criticism of life. Not everything, then, that calls itself loyalty, and not every form of loyalty, shall be put in our discussion on the same level with every other moral quality that uses or that deserves the ancient name in question. Moreover, the term "loyalty" comes to us as a good old popular word, without any exact definition. We are hereafter to define our term as precisely as possible, yet so as to preserve the spirit of the former usage. In estimating the place of loyalty in the moral life, we are, moreover, to follow neither traditional authority nor the voice of private prejudice. We are to use our reason as best we can; for philosophy is an effort to think out the reasons for our opinions. We are not to praise blindly, nor to condemn according to our moods. Where loyalty seems to be a good, we are to see why; when what men call loyalty leads them astray, we are to find wherein the fault lies. Since loyalty is a relative term, and always implies that there is some object, some cause, to which any given loyalty is to be shown, we must consider what are the fitting objects of loyalty. In attempting an answer to these various questions, our philosophy of loyalty must try to delve down to the roots of human conduct, the grounds for our moral standards. . . .

. . . *In loyalty, when loyalty is properly defined, is the fulfillment of the whole moral law.* You can truthfully center your entire moral world about a rational conception of loyalty. Justice, charity, industry, wisdom, spirituality, are all definable in terms of enlightened loyalty. And, as I shall maintain, this very way of viewing the moral world—this deliberate centralization of all the duties and of all the virtues about the one conception of rational loyalty—is of great service as a means of clarifying and simplifying the tangled moral problems of our lives and of our age. . . .

Loyalty shall mean, according to this preliminary definition: *The willing and practical and thoroughgoing devotion of a person to a cause.* A man is loyal when, first, he has some *cause* to which he is loyal; when, secondly, he *willingly* and *thoroughly* devotes himself to this cause; and when, thirdly, he expresses his devotion in some *sustained and practical way*, by acting steadily in the service of his cause. Instances of loyalty are: The devotion of a patriot to his country, when this devotion leads him actually to live and perhaps to die for his country; the devotion of a martyr to his religion; the devotion of a ship's captain to the requirements of his office when, after a disaster, he works steadily for his ship and for the saving of his ship's company until the last possible service is accomplished, so that he is the last man to leave the ship, and is ready if need be to go down with his ship. . . .

. . . Loyalty is never mere emotion. Adoration and affection may go with loyalty but can never alone constitute loyalty. Furthermore, the devotion of the loyal man involves a sort of restraint or submission of his natural desires to his cause. Loyalty without self-control is impossible. The loyal man serves. That is, he does not merely follow his own impulses. He looks to his cause for guidance. This cause tells him what to do, and he does it. His devotion, furthermore, is entire. He is ready to live or to die as the cause directs. . . .

. . . If one is loyal, he has a cause which he indeed personally values. Otherwise, how could he be devoted to it? He therefore takes interest in the cause, loves it, is well pleased with it. On the other hand, loyalty never means the mere emotion of love for your cause, and never means merely following your own pleasure, viewed *as* your private pleasure and interest. For if you are loyal, your cause is viewed by you as something outside of you. Or if, like your country, your cause includes yourself, it is still much larger than your private self. It has its own value, so you as a loyal person believe. This essential value it would keep (so you believe) even if your private interest were left out of account. Your cause you take, then, to be something objective—something that is not your private self. It does not get its value merely from your being pleased with it. You believe, on the contrary, that you love it just because of its own value, which it has by itself, even if you die. That is just why one may be ready to die for his cause. . . .

Moreover, the cause to which a loyal man is devoted is never something *wholly* impersonal. It concerns other men. Loyalty is social. If one is a loyal servant of a cause, one has at least possible fellow-servants. On the other hand, since a cause, in general, tends to unite the many fellow-servants in one service, it consequently seems to the loyal man to have a sort of impersonal or superpersonal quality about it. You can love an individual. But you can be loyal only to a tie that binds you and others into some sort of unity, and loyal to individuals only through the tie. The cause to which loyalty devotes itself has always this union of the personal and the seemingly superindividual about it. It binds many individuals into one service. . . .

What do we live for? What is our duty? What is the true ideal of life? What is the true difference between right and wrong? What is the true good which we all need? Whoever begins seriously to consider such questions as these soon observes certain great truths about the moral life which he must take into account if his enterprise is to succeed, that is, if he is ever to answer these questions.

The first truth is this: We all of us first learned about what we ought to do, about what our ideal should be, and in general about the moral law, through some authority external to our own wills. Our teachers, our parents, our playmates, society, custom, or perhaps some church. . . . The moral law came to us from without. It often seemed to us, in so far, something other than our will, something threatening or socially compelling, or externally restraining. In so far as our moral training is still incomplete, the moral law may at any moment have to assume afresh this air of an external authority merely in order to win our due attention. But if we have learned the moral law, or any part of it, and if we do not ask any longer how we first learned, or how we may still have to learn afresh our duty, but if, on the contrary, we rather ask: "What reason can I now give to myself why a given act is truly right? What reason can I give why my duty is my duty?"—then, indeed, we find that no external authority, viewed merely as external, can give one any reason why an act is truly right or wrong. Only a calm and reasonable view of what it is that I myself really will,—only this can decide such a question. My duty is simply my own will brought to my clear self-consciousness. . . .

If you want to find out, then, what is right and what is good for you, bring your own will to self-consciousness. Your duty is what you yourself will to do in so far as you clearly discover who you are, and what your place in the world is. This is, indeed, a first principle of all ethical inquiry. Kant called it the Principle of the Autonomy or self-direction of the rational will of each moral being.

But now there stands beside this first principle a second principle, equally inevitable and equally important. This principle is, that I can never find out what my own will is by merely brooding over my natural desires, or by following my momentary caprices. For by nature I am a sort of meeting place of countless streams of ancestral tendency. From moment to moment, if you consider me apart from my training, I am a collection of impulses. There is no one desire that is always consciousness, to make us more than ever determined to express our own will and more than ever sure of our own rights, of our own strength, of our dignity, of our power, of our value; (. . .) to make obvious to us that this our will has no purpose but to do the will of some fascinating social power. This social power is the cause to which we are loyal.

Loyalty, then, fixes our attention upon some one cause, bids us look without ourselves to see what this unified cause is, shows us thus some one plan of action, and then says to us, "In this cause is your life, your will, your opportunity, your fulfillment."

Thus loyalty, viewed merely as a personal attitude, solves the paradox of our ordinary existence, by showing us outside of ourselves the cause which is to be served, and inside of ourselves the will which delights to do this service, and which is not thwarted but enriched and expressed in such service. . . .

And again, the loyal have known what it was to be free from moral doubts and scruples. Their cause has been their conscience. It has told them what to do. They have listened and obeyed, not because of what they took to be blind convention, not because of a fear of external authority, not even because of what seemed to themselves any purely private and personal intuition, but because, when they have looked first outwards at their cause, and then inwards at themselves, they have found themselves worthless in their own eyes, except when viewed as active, as confidently devoted, as willing instruments of their cause. Their cause has forbidden them to doubt; it has said: "You are mine, you cannot do otherwise." And they have said to the cause: "I am, even of my own will, thine. I have no will except thy will." . . . That is again the speech of the devoted patriots, soldiers, mothers, and martyrs of our race. They have had the grace of this willing, this active loyalty.

Now, people loyal in this sense have surely existed in the world, and, as you all know, the loyal still exist among us. And I beg you not to object to me, at this point, that such devoted people have often been loyal to very bad causes; or that different people have been loyal to causes which were in deadly war with one another, so that loyal people must often have been falsely guided. I beg you, above all, not to interpose here the objection that our modern doubters concerning moral problems simply cannot at present see to what one cause they ought to be loyal, so that just herein, just in our ability to see a fitting and central object of loyalty, lies the root of our modern moral confusion and distraction. . . . But just now we are getting our first glimpse of our future philosophy of loyalty. All that you can say of the defects of loyalty leaves still untouched the one great fact that, if you want to find a way of living which surmounts doubts, and centralizes your powers, it must be some such a way as all the loyal in common have trodden, since first loyalty was known amongst men. . . .

But to repeat, perhaps in bewilderment, your question: "Where, in our distracted modern world, in this time when cause wars with cause, and when all old moral standards are remorselessly criticized and doubted, are we to find such a cause—a cause, all-embracing, definite, rationally compelling, supreme, certain, and fit to centralize life? What cause is there that for us would rationally justify a martyr's devotion?" I reply: "A perfectly simple consideration, derived from a study of the very spirit of loyalty itself, as this spirit is manifested by all the loyal, will soon furnish to us the unmistakable answer to this question. . . ."

. . . And so, a cause is good, not only for me, but for mankind, in so far as it is essentially a *loyalty to loyalty*, that is, is an aid and a furtherance of loyalty in my fellows. It is an evil cause in so far as, despite the loyalty that it arouses in me, it is destructive of loyalty in the world of my fellows. My cause is, indeed, always such as to involve some loyalty to loyalty, because, if I am loyal to any cause at all, I have fellow-servants whose loyalty mine supports. But in so far as my cause is a predatory cause, which lives by overthrowing the loyalties of others, it is an evil cause, because it involves disloyalty to the very cause of loyalty itself.

In view of these considerations, we are now able still further to simplify our problem by laying stress upon one more of those very features which seemed, but a moment since, to complicate the matter so hopelessly. Loyalty, as we have defined it, is the willing devotion of a self to a cause. In answering the ethical individualists, we have insisted that all of the higher types of loyalty involve autonomous choice. The cause that is to appeal to me at all must indeed have some elemental fascination for me. It must stir me, arouse me, please me, and in the end possess me. Moreover, it must, indeed, be set before me by my social order as a possible, a practically significant, a living cause, which binds many selves in the unity of one life. But, nevertheless, if I am really awake to the significance of my own moral choices, I must be in the position of accepting this cause. . . . My cause cannot be merely forced upon me. It is I who make it my own. . . . However much the cause may seem to be assigned to me by my social station, I must cooperate in the choice of the cause, before the act of loyalty is complete.

Since this is the case, since my loyalty never is my mere fate, but is always also my choice, I can of course determine my loyalty, at least to some extent, by the consideration of the actual good and ill which my proposed cause does to mankind. And since I now have the main criterion of the good and ill of causes before me, I can define a principle of choice which may so guide me that my loyalty shall become a good, not merely to myself, but to mankind.

This principle is now obvious. I may state it thus: In so far as it lies in your power, so choose your cause and so serve it, that, by reason of your choice and of your service, there shall be more loyalty in the world rather than less. And, in fact, so choose and so serve your individual cause as to secure thereby the greatest possible increase of loyalty amongst men. More briefly: *In choosing and in serving the cause to which you are to be loyal, be, in any case, loyal to loyalty.*

This precept, I say, will express how one should guide his choice of a cause, in so far as he considers not merely his own supreme good, but that of mankind. That such autonomous choice is possible, tends, as we now see, not to complicate, but to simplify our moral situation. For if you regard men's loyalty as their fate, if you think that a man must be loyal simply to the cause which tradition sets before him, without any power to direct his own moral attention, then indeed the conflict of loyalties seems an insoluble problem; so that, if men find themselves loyally involved in feuds, there is no way out. But if, indeed, choice plays a part,—a genuine even if limited part, in directing the individual's choice of the cause to which he is to be loyal, then indeed this choice may be so directed that loyalty to the universal loyalty of all mankind shall be furthered by the actual choices which each enlightened loyal person makes when he selects his cause. . . .

Where, in all our complex and distracted modern world, in which at present cause wars with cause, shall we find a cause that is certainly worthy of our loyalty? This question, at this very moment, has received in our discussion an answer which you may feel to be so far provisional,—perhaps unpractical,—but which you ought to regard as, at least in principle, somewhat simple and true to human nature. Loyalty is a good, a supreme good. If I myself could but find a worthy cause . . . then my highest human good, in so far as I am indeed an active being, would be mine. But this very good of loyalty is no peculiar privilege of mine; nor is it good only for me. It is an universally human good. For it is simply the finding of a harmony of the self and the world,—such a harmony as alone can content any human being. . . .

Loyalty, then, is contagious. It infects not only the fellow-servant of your own special cause, but also all who know of this act. Loyalty is a good that spreads. Live it and you thereby cultivate it in other men. Be faithful, then, so one may say, to the loyal man; be faithful over your few things, for the spirit of loyalty, secretly passing from you to many to whom you are a stranger, may even thereby make you unconsciously rule over many things. Loyalty to loyalty is then no unpractical cause. And you serve it not by becoming a mere citizen of the world, but by serving your own personal cause. We set before you, then, no unpractical rule when we repeat our moral formula in this form:

Find your own cause, your interesting, fascinating, personally engrossing cause; serve it with all your might and soul and strength; but so choose your cause, and so serve it, that thereby you show forth your loyalty to loyalty, so that because of your choice and service of your cause, there is a maximum of increase of loyalty amongst your fellow-men. . . .

Herewith we approach a thesis which is central in my whole philosophy of loyalty. I announced the thesis in other words in the opening lecture. My thesis is that *all those duties which we have learned to recognize as the fundamental duties of the civilized man, the duties that every man owes to every man, are to be rightly interpreted as special instance of loyalty to loyalty.* . . .

In trying to meet these questions so far as they here concern us, it is important next to note a few fundamental features which characterize the personal life of all of us. The first of these features appears if one, instead of stopping with the question, "What is my conscience?" goes deeper still and asks the question, "Who and what am I?" This latter question also has indeed countless aspects, and a complete answer to it would constitute an entire system of metaphysics. But for our present purpose it is enough to note that I cannot answer the question, "Who am I?" except in terms of some sort of statement of the plans and purposes of my life. In responding to the question, "Who are you?" a man may first mention his name. But his name is a mere tag. He then often goes on to tell where he lives, and where he comes from. His home and his birthplace, however, are already what one may call purposeful aspects of his personality. For dwelling-place, country, birthplace, and similar incidental facts about a man tend to throw light upon his personality mainly because they are of importance for a further knowledge of his social relations, and so of his social uses and activities.

But the answer to the question, "Who are you?" really begins in earnest when a man mentions his calling, and so actually sets out upon the definition of his purposes and of the way in which these purposes get expressed in his life. And when a man goes on to say, "I am the doer of these and these deeds, the friend of these friends, the enemy of these opposing purposes, the member of this family, the one whose ideals are such and such, and are so and so expressed in my life," the man expresses to you at length whatever is most expressible and worth knowing in answer to the question, "Who are you?"

To sum up, then, I should say that a person, an individual self, may be defined as a human life according to a plan. If a man could live with no plan at all, purposelessly and quite passively, he would in so far be an organism, and also, if you choose, he would be a psychological specimen, but he would be no personality. Wherever there is personality, there are purposes worked out in life. If, as often happens, there are many purposes connected with the life of this human creature, many plans in this life, but no discoverable unity and coherence of these plans, then in so far there are many glimpses of selfhood, many fragmentary selves present in connection with the life of some human organism. But there is so far no one self, no one person discoverable. You are one self just in so far as the life that goes on in connection with your organism has some one purpose running through it. By the terms "this person" and "this self," then, we mean this human life in so far as it expresses some one purpose. Yet, of course, this one purpose which is expressed in the life of a single self need not be one which is defined by this self in abstract terms. On the contrary, most of us are aware that our lives are unified, after a fashion, by the very effort that we more or less vaguely make to assert ourselves somehow as individuals in our world. Many of us have not yet found out how it would be best to assert ourselves. But we are trying to find out. This very effort to find out gives already a certain unity of purpose to our lives. . . .

Study Questions

1. In *The Conception of God*, Royce offers a proof for the existence of God. State this proof in your own words, and make clear the assumptions on which it rests. Defend or criticize this proof.
2. What is the basic moral law that Royce states and attempts to defend in *The Philosophy of Loyalty*? What does he mean by this moral law? Explain, and defend your claims.
3. In what way do Royce's absolutism and demand for unity show themselves throughout *The Philosophy of Loyalty*? Be specific, and defend your answer.

Suggestions for Further Reading

Clendenning, John. *The Life and Thought of Josiah Royce.* Madison: University of Wisconsin Press, 1985.

Kegley, Jacquelyn Ann. "Josiah Royce: Introduction." *In Pragmatism and Classical American Philosophy: Essential Readings and Interpretive Essays*, second edition. Edited by John J. Stuhr. New York: Oxford University Press, 2000.

Kucklick, Bruce. *The Rise of American Philosophy: Cambridge, Massachusetts, 1860–1930.* New Haven: Yale University Press, 1977.

McDermott, John J., ed. *The Basic Writings of Josiah Royce*, 2 vols. Chicago: University of Chicago Press, 1969.

Roth, John K., ed. *The Philosophy of Josiah Royce.* Indianapolis: Hackett Publishing, 1982.

Royce, Josiah. *The Conception of God.* New York: Macmillan, 1898.

Royce, Josiah. *The Philosophy of Loyalty.* New York: Macmillan, 1908.

Royce, Josiah. *Lectures on Modern Idealism.* New Haven: Yale University Press, 1919.

Chapter 7

George Santayana
Naturalism and Realism

George Santayana was born in Spain in 1836 and came with his family to the United States when he was only six years old. He lived in Boston, attended Harvard until 1889, and was hired in the same year to teach for the Harvard Department of Philosophy. He remained at Harvard until 1912, when he retired from teaching and left the United States to spend the balance of his long life in England and Europe. He departed Harvard because he was uncomfortable as an academic and never wished to remain one. He died in 1952.

Santayana is variously described as a realist, a materialist, and a naturalist. These titles, separately or together, apply well enough to his mature philosophy. He was a skeptic in religious matters and believed that the pervasiveness of religious beliefs and creeds is worth understanding but not accepting or practicing. This set him apart from James and Royce. As a naturalistic or "physicalist," Santayana sought and defended natural and physical accounts of mind and intelligence. He believed with Spinoza that the physical laws to which we appeal to explain the behavior that interests physicists, chemists, and biologists are the kind of laws to which we should appeal in accounting for human nature and behavior. Unlike Descartes and very much like Chauncey Wright, Santayana found no good reasons for thinking that human beings, unlike anything else in nature, are remarkable and inexplicable combinations of physical bodies and nonphysical minds. He was no less puzzled than Spinoza over why dualists and spiritualists actually believe that they can think of all people as supernatural "kingdoms within kingdoms."

Santayana wore many hats, most of them within the scope of his philosophy and a few of them outside it. He was an ethicist and in "Hypostatic Ethics" (1913) produced a compelling criticism of moral absolutism, together with a defense of ethical relativism. He was also a philosopher of the arts and, in *Scepticism and Animal Faith* (1923), he was an epistemologist who first defended and then retreated from classical skepticism. He was also a poet and one-novel novelist. *The Last Puritan: A Memoir in the Form of a Novel* (1936) allows its readers to enjoy insights into Santayana's character, shortcomings, and expectations. His four-volume *The Life of Reason* (1922) is a philosophical classic and is perhaps his most important work. For purposes of getting at the flavor of American philosophy and culture, his lecture "The Genteel Tradition in American Philosophy" is invaluable.

In the "Genteel Tradition" (1911) Santayana described and criticized the religious and philosophical gentility that he cannot accept on personal grounds.

We cannot be surprised that an atheist and naturalist is impatient with the marrow, influence, and remnants of Calvinism and New England Transcendentalism. But this lecture, later included in a collected titled *Winds of Doctrine* (1926), has a broader focus than Santayana's private preferences. In it he argued that there was in late nineteenth- and early twentieth-century America an antagonism between lingering, but moribund, spiritualism and the revolutionary changes that we find in the sciences, technology, and invention. The America that was once nurtured and dominated by Calvinism, like philosophies that were indebted to Transcendentalism, was history. From Santayana's perspective, the philosopher who deserves most credit for thoughtfully rejecting the genteel tradition was James. In fact, nearly half this famous lecture is a celebration of James's no-nonsense pragmatism and his direct, or sometimes indirect, rejection of philosophies that do not match the dreams, aspirations, and expectations of Americans in search of something more than they find in Edwards or Emerson.

In the final analysis, we can justifiably claim that whether one likes the message of the "Genteel Tradition" is one issue, and whether one is impressed by what it helps to lay bare in the history of American philosophy is a different issue. This lecture links Santayana to James and Emerson. It is a rich point of departure for anyone who wishes to know something about vintage Santayana, something about the ebb and flow of the tides in American thought at its best, and something else about a nation that Santayana understood so well but could not wait to leave.

The Genteel Tradition in American Philosophy (1911)

Ladies and Gentlemen,—The privilege of addressing you to-day is very welcome to me, not merely for the honour of it, which is great, nor for the pleasures of travel, which are many, when it is California that one is visiting for the first time, but also because there is something I have long wanted to say which this occasion seems particularly favourable for saying. America is still a young country, and this part of it is especially so; and it would have been nothing extraordinary if, in this young country, material preoccupations had altogether absorbed people's minds, and they had been too much engrossed in living to reflect upon life, or to have any philosophy. The opposite, however, is the case. Not only have you already found time to philosophise in California, as your society proves, but the eastern colonists from the very beginning were a sophisticated race. As much as in clearing the land and fighting the Indians they were occupied, as they expressed it, in wrestling with the Lord. The country was new, but the race was tried, chastened, and full of solemn memories. It was an old wine in new bottles; and America did not have to wait for its present universities, with their departments of academic philosophy, in order to possess a living philosophy—to have a distinct vision of the universe and definite convictions about human destiny.

Now this situation is a singular and remarkable one, and has many consequences, not all of which are equally fortunate. America is a young country with an old mentality: it has enjoyed the advantages of a child carefully brought up and thoroughly indoctrinated; it has been a wise child. But a wise child, an old head on young shoulders, always has a comic and an unpromising side. The wisdom is a little thin and verbal, not aware of its full meaning and grounds; and physical and emotional growth may be stunted by it, or even deranged. Or when the child is too vigorous for that, he will develop a fresh mentality of his own, out of his observations and actual instincts; and this fresh mentality will interfere with the traditional mentality, and tend to reduce it to something perfunctory, conventional, and perhaps secretly despised. A philosophy is not genuine unless it inspires and expresses the life of those who cherish it. I do not think the hereditary philosophy of America has done much to atrophy the natural activities of the inhabitants; the wise child has not missed the joys of youth or of manhood; but what has happened is that the hereditary philosophy has grown stale, and that the academic philosophy afterwards developed has caught the stale odour from it. America is not simply, as I said a moment ago, a young country with an old mentality: it is a country with two mentalities, one a survival of the beliefs and standards of the fathers, the other an expression of the instincts, practice, and discoveries of the younger generations. In all the higher things of the mind—in religion, in literature, in the moral emotions—it is the hereditary spirit that still prevails, so much so that Mr. Bernard Shaw finds that America is a hundred years behind the times. The truth is that one-half of the American mind, that not occupied intensely in practical affairs, has remained, I will not say high-and-dry, but slightly becalmed; it has floated gently in the back-water, while, alongside, in invention and industry and social organisation, the other half of the mind was leaping down a sort of Niagara Rapids. This division may be found symbolised in American architecture: a neat reproduction of the colonial mansion—with some modern comforts introduced surreptitiously—stands beside the sky-scraper. The American Will inhabits the sky-scraper; the American Intellect inhabits the colonial mansion. The one is the sphere of the American man; the other, at least predominantly, of the American woman. The one is all aggressive enterprise; the other is all genteel tradition.

Now, with your permission, I should like to analyse more fully how this interesting situation has arisen, how it is qualified, and whither it tends. And in the first place we should remember what, precisely, that philosophy was which the first settlers brought with them into the country. In strictness there was more than one; but we may confine our attention to what I will call Calvinism, since it is on this that the current academic philosophy has been grafted. I do not mean exactly the Calvinism of Calvin, or even of Jonathan Edwards; for in their systems there was much that was not pure philosophy, but rather faith in the externals and history of revelation. Jewish and Christian revelation was interpreted by these men, however, in the spirit of a

particular philosophy, which might have arisen under any sky, and been associated with any other religion as well as with Protestant Christianity. . . .
Calvinism, taken in this sense, is an expression of the agonised conscience. It
is a view of the world which an agonised conscience readily embraces, if it
takes itself seriously, as, being agonised, of course it must. Calvinism, essentially, asserts three things: that sin exists, that sin is punished, and that it is
beautiful that sin should exist to be punished. The heart of the Calvinist is
therefore divided between tragic concern at his own miserable condition,
and tragic exultation about the universe at large. He oscillates between a profound abasement and a paradoxical elation of the spirit. To be a Calvinist
philosophically is to feel a fierce pleasure in the existence of misery, especially of one's own, in that this misery seems to manifest the fact that the Absolute is irresponsible or infinite or holy. Human nature, it feels, is totally
depraved: to have the instincts and motives that we necessarily have is a
great scandal, and we must suffer for it; but that scandal is requisite, since
otherwise the serious importance of being as we ought to be would not have
been vindicated. . . .

Calvinism . . . lost its basis in American life. Some emotional natures, indeed, reverted in their religious revivals or private searchings of heart to the
sources of the tradition; for any of the radical points of view in philosophy
may cease to be prevalent, but none can cease to be possible. Other natures,
more sensitive to the moral and literary influences of the world, preferred to
abandon parts of their philosophy, hoping thus to reduce the distance which
should separate the remainder from real life.

Meantime, if anybody arose with a special sensibility or a technical genius, he was in great straits; not being fed sufficiently by the world, he was
driven in upon his own resources. The three American writers whose personal endowment was perhaps the finest—Poe, Hawthorne, and Emerson—had
all a certain starved and abstract quality. They could not retail the genteel tradition; they were too keen, too perceptive, and too independent for that. But
life offered them little digestible material, nor were they naturally voracious.
They were fastidious, and under the circumstances they were starved. Emerson, to be sure, fed on books. There was a great catholicity in his reading; and
he showed a fine tact in his comments, and in his way of appropriating what
he read. But he read transcendentally, not historically, to learn what he himself
felt, not what others might have felt before him. And to feed on books, for a
philosopher or a poet, is still to starve. Books can help him to acquire form, or
to avoid pitfalls; they cannot supply him with substance, if he is to have any.
Therefore the genius of Poe and Hawthorne, and even of Emerson, was employed on a sort of inner play, or digestion of vacancy. It was a refined labour,
but it was in danger of being morbid, or tinkling, or self-indulgent. . . . Their
manner, in a word, was subjective. In their own persons they escaped the
mediocrity of the genteel tradition, but they supplied nothing to supplant it in
other minds.

The churches, likewise, although they modified their spirit, had no philosophy to offer save a new emphasis on parts of what Calvinism contained. The theology of Calvin, we must remember, had much in it besides philosophical Calvinism. A Christian tenderness, and a hope of grace for the individual, came to mitigate its sardonic optimism; and it was these evangelical elements that the Calvinistic churches now emphasised, seldom and with blushes referring to hell-fire or infant damnation. Yet philosophic Calvinism, with a theory of life that would perfectly justify hell-fire and infant damnation if they happened to exist, still dominates the traditional metaphysics. It is an ingredient, and the decisive ingredient, in what calls itself idealism. But in order to see just what part Calvinism plays in current idealism, it will be necessary to distinguish the other chief element in that complex system, namely, transcendentalism.

Transcendentalism is the philosophy which the romantic era produced in Germany, and independently, I believe, in America also. Transcendentalism proper, like romanticism, is not any particular set of dogmas about what things exist; it is not a system of the universe regarded as a fact, or as a collection of facts. It is a method, a point of view, from which any world, no matter what it might contain, could be approached by a self-conscious observer. Transcendentalism is systematic subjectivism. It studies the perspectives of knowledge as they radiate from the self; it is a plan of those avenues of inference by which our ideas of things must be reached, if they are to afford any systematic or distant vistas. In other words, transcendentalism is the critical logic of science. Knowledge, it says, has a station, as in a watch-tower; it is always seated here and now, in the self of the moment. The past and the future, things inferred and things conceived, lie around it, painted as upon a panorama. They cannot be lighted up save by some centrifugal ray of attention and present interest, by some active operation of the mind.

This is hardly the occasion for developing or explaining this delicate insight; suffice it to say, lest you should think later that I disparage transcendentalism, that as a method I regard it as correct and, when once suggested, unforgettable. I regard it is as the chief contribution made in modern times to speculation. But it is a method only, an attitude we may always assume if we like and that will always be legitimate. . . . Yet the Germans who first gained the full transcendental insight were romantic people; they were more or less frankly poets; they were colossal egotists, and wished to make not only their own knowledge but the whole universe center about themselves. And full as they were of their romantic isolation and romantic liberty, it occurred to them to imagine that all reality might be a transcendental self and a romantic dreamer like themselves; nay, that it might be just their own transcendental self and their own romantic dreams extended indefinitely. Transcendental logic, the method of discovery for the mind, was to become also the method of evolution in nature and history. Transcendental method, so abused, produced transcendental myth. A conscientious critique of knowledge was turned into a sham system of nature. We must therefore distinguish sharply the transcendental grammar of the intellect, which is significant and potentially correct, from the various transcendental systems of the universe, which are chimeras.

In both its parts, however, transcendentalism had much to recommend it to American philosophers, for the transcendental method appealed to the individualistic and revolutionary temper of their youth, while transcendental myths enabled them to find a new status for their inherited theology, and to give what parts of it they cared to preserve some semblance of philosophical backing. . . .

. . . To embrace this philosophy was regarded as a sign of profound metaphysical insight, although the most mediocre minds found no difficulty in embracing it. In truth it was a sign of having been brought up in the genteel tradition, of feeling it weak, and of wishing to save it.

But the transcendental method, in its way, was also sympathetic to the American mind. It embodied, in a radical form, the spirit of Protestantism as distinguished from its inherited doctrines; it was autonomous, undismayed, calmly revolutionary; it felt that Will was deeper than Intellect; it focussed everything here and now, and asked all things to show their credentials at the bar of the young self, and to prove their value for this latest born moment. These things are truly American; they would be characteristic of any young society with a keen and discursive intelligence, and they are strikingly exemplified in the thought and in the person of Emerson. They constitute what he called self-trust. Self-trust, like other transcendental attitudes, may be expressed in metaphysical fables. The romantic spirit may imagine itself to be an absolute force, evoking and moulding the plastic world to express its varying moods. . . . Emerson was a shrewd Yankee, by instinct on the winning side; he was a cheery, child-like soul, impervious to the evidence of evil, as of everything that it did not suit his transcendental individuality to appreciate or to notice. More, perhaps than anybody that has ever lived, he practised the transcendental method in all its purity. He had no system. He opened his eyes on the world every morning with a fresh sincerity, marking how things seemed to him then, or what they suggested to his spontaneous fancy. . . .

Emerson had no system; and his coveting truth had another exceptional consequence: he was detached, unworldly, contemplative. When he came out of the conventicle or the reform meeting, or out of the rapturous close atmosphere of the lecture-room, he heard Nature whispering to him: "Why so hot, little sir?" No doubt the spirit or energy of the world is what is acting in us, as the sea is what rises in every little wave; but it passes through us, and cry out as we may, it will move on. Our privilege is to have perceived it as it moves. Our dignity is not in what we do, but in what we understand. The whole world is doing things. We are turning in that vortex; yet within us is silent observation, the speculative eye before which all passes, which bridges the distances and compares the combatants. On this side of his genius Emerson broke away from all conditions of age or country and represented nothing except intelligence itself.

There was another element in Emerson, curiously combined with transcendentalism, namely, his love and respect for Nature. Nature, for the transcendentalist, is precious because it is his own work, a mirror in which he looks at himself and says (like a poet relishing his own verses), "What a genius I am! Who would have thought there was such stuff in me?" And the philosophical egotist finds in his doctrine a ready explanation of whatever beauty and commodity Nature actually has. No wonder, he says to himself, that Nature is sympathetic, since I made it. . . . Just as some people are naturally enthralled and refreshed by music, so others are by landscape. Music and landscape make up the spiritual resources of those who cannot or dare not express their unfulfilled ideals in words. Serious poetry, profound religion (Calvinism, for instance), are the joys of an unhappiness that confesses itself; but when a genteel tradition forbids people to confess that they are unhappy, serious poetry and profound religion are closed to them by that; and since human life, in its depths, cannot then express itself openly, imagination is driven for comfort into abstract arts, where human circumstances are lost sight of, and human problems dissolve in a purer medium. The pressure of care is thus relieved, without its quietus being found in intelligence. To understand oneself is the classic form of consolation; to elude oneself is the romantic. In the presence of music or landscape human experience eludes itself; and thus romanticism is the bond between transcendental and naturalistic sentiment. The winds and clouds come to minister to the solitary ego.

Have there been, we may ask, any successful efforts to escape from the genteel tradition, and to express something worth expressing behind its back? This might well not have occurred as yet; but America is so precocious, it has been trained by the genteel tradition to be so wise for its years, that some indications of a truly native philosophy and poetry are already to be found. . . . So when Mark Twain says, "I was born of poor but dishonest parents," the humour depends on the parody of the genteel Anglo-Saxon convention that it is disreputable to be poor; but to hint at the hollowness of it would not be amusing if it did not remain at bottom one's habitual conviction.

The one American writer who has left the genteel tradition entirely behind is perhaps Walt Whitman. For this reason educated Americans find him rather an unpalatable person, who they sincerely protest ought not to be taken for a representative of their culture; and he certainly should not, because their culture is so genteel and traditional. . . . His work, for the very reason that it is so rudimentary, contains a beginning, or rather many beginnings, that might possibly grow into a noble moral imagination, a worthy filling for the human mind. An American in the nineteenth century who completely disregarded the genteel tradition could hardly have done more.

But there is another distinguished man, lately lost to this country, who has given some rude shocks to this tradition and who, as much as Whitman, may be regarded as representing the genuine, the long silent American mind—I mean William James. He and his brother Henry were as tightly swaddled in the genteel tradition as any infant geniuses could be, for they were born before 1850, and in a Swedenborgian household. Yet they burst those bands almost entirely. The ways in which the two brothers freed themselves, however, are interestingly different. Mr. Henry James has done it by adopting the point of view of the outer world, and by turning the genteel American tradition, as he turns everything else, into a subject-matter for analysis. For him it is a curious habit of mind, intimately comprehended, to be compared with other habits of mind, also well known to him. Thus he has overcome the genteel tradition in the classic way, by understanding it. With William James too this infusion of worldly insight and European sympathies was a potent influence, especially in his earlier days; but the chief source of his liberty was another. It was his personal spontaneity, similar to that of Emerson, and his personal vitality, similar to that of nobody else. Convictions and ideas came to him, so to speak, from the subsoil. He had a prophetic sympathy with the dawning sentiments of the age, with the moods of the dumb majority. His scattered words caught fire in many parts of the world. His way of thinking and feeling represented the true America, and represented in a measure the whole ultra-modern, radical world. Thus he eluded the genteel tradition in the romantic way, by continuing it into its opposite. The romantic mind, glorified in Hegel's dialectic (which is not dialectic at all, but a sort of tragi-comic history of experience), is always rendering its thoughts unrecognisable through the infusion of new insights, and through the insensible transformation of the moral feeling that accompanies them, till at last it has completely reversed its old judgments under cover of expanding them. Thus the genteel tradition was led a merry dance when it fell again into the hands of a genuine and vigorous romanticist like William James. He restored their revolutionary force to its neutralised elements, by picking them out afresh, and emphasising them separately, according to his personal predilections.

For one thing, William James kept his mind and heart wide open to all that might seem, to polite minds, odd, personal, or visionary in religion and philosophy. He gave a sincerely respectful hearing to sentimentalists, mystics, spiritualists, wizards, cranks, quacks, and impostors—for it is hard to draw the line, and James was not willing to draw it prematurely. He thought, with his usual modesty, that any of these might have something to teach him. The lame, the halt, the blind, and those speaking with tongues could come to him with the certainty of finding sympathy; and if they were not healed, at least they were comforted, that a famous professor should take them so seriously; and they began to feel that after all to have only one leg, or one hand, or one eye, or to have three, might be in itself no less beauteous than to have just two, like the stolid majority. Thus William James became the friend and helper of those groping, nervous, half-educated, spiritually disinherited, passionately hungry individuals of which America is full. He became, at the same time, their spokesman and representative before the learned world; and he made it a chief part of his vocation to recast what the learned world has to offer, so that as far as possible it might serve the needs and interests of these people.

Yet the normal practical masculine American, too, had a friend in William James. There is a feeling abroad now, to which biology and Darwinism lend some colour, that theory is simply an instrument for practice, and intelligence merely a help toward material survival. Bears, it is said, have fur and claws, but poor naked man is condemned to be intelligent, or he will perish. This feeling William James embodied in that theory of thought and of truth which he called pragmatism. Intelligence, he thought, is no miraculous, idle faculty, by which we mirror passively any or everything that happens to be true, reduplicating the real world to no purpose. Intelligence has its roots and its issue in the context of events; it is one kind of practical adjustment, an experimental act, a form of vital tension. It does not essentially serve to picture other parts of reality, but to connect them. This view was not worked out by William James in its psychological and historical details; unfortunately he developed it chiefly in controversy against its opposite, which he called intellectualism, and which he hated with all the hatred of which his kind heart was capable. Intellectualism, as he conceived it, was pure pedantry; it impoverished and verbalised everything, and tied up nature in red tape. Ideas and rules that may have been occasionally useful it put in the place of the full-blooded irrational movement of life which had called them into being; and these abstractions, so soon obsolete, it strove to fix and to worship for ever. Thus all creeds and theories and all formal precepts sink in the estimation of the pragmatist to a local and temporary grammar of action; a grammar that must be changed slowly by time, and may be changed quickly by genius. ... Ideas are not mirrors, they are weapons; their function is to prepare us to meet events, as future experience may unroll them. Those ideas that disappoint us are false ideas; those to which events are true are true themselves.

This may seem a very utilitarian view of the mind; and I confess I think it a partial one, since the logical force of beliefs and ideas, their truth or falsehood as assertions, has been overlooked altogether, or confused with the vital force of the material processes which these ideas express. It is an external view only, which marks the place and conditions of the mind in nature, but neglect its specific essence; as if a jewel were defined as a round hole in a ring. Nevertheless, the more materialistic the pragmatist's theory of the mind is, the more vitalistic his theory of nature will have to become. If the intellect is a device produced in organic bodies to expedite their processes, these organic bodies must have interests and a chosen direction in their life; otherwise their life could not be expedited, nor could anything be useful to it. In other words—and this is a third point at which the philosophy of William James has played havoc with the genteel tradition, while ostensibly defending it—nature must be conceived anthropomorphically and in psychological terms. Its purposes are not to be static harmonies, self-unfolding destinies, the logic of spirit, the spirit of logic, or any other formal method and abstract law; its purposes are to be concrete endeavours, finite efforts of souls living in an environment which they transform and by which they, too, are affected. A spirit, the divine spirit as much as the human, as this new animism conceives it, is a romantic adventurer. Its future is undetermined. Its scope, its duration, and the quality of its life are all contingent. This spirit grows; it buds and sends forth feelers, sounding the depths around for such other centres of force or life as may exist there. It has a vital momentum, but no predetermined goal. It uses its past as a stepping-stone, or rather as a diving-board, but has an absolutely fresh will at each moment to plunge this way or that into the unknown. The universe is an experiment; it is unfinished. It has no ultimate or total nature, because it has no end. It embodies no formula or statable law; any formula is at best a poor abstraction, describing what, in some region and for some time, may be the most striking characteristic of existence; the law is a description *a posteriori* of the habit things have chosen to acquire, and which they may possibly throw off altogether. What a day may bring forth is uncertain; uncertain even to God. Omniscience is impossible; time is real; what had been omniscience hitherto might discover something more to-day. "There shall be news," William James was fond of saying with rapture, quoting from the unpublished poem of an obscure friend, "there shall be news in heaven!" There is almost certainly, he thought, a God now; there may be several gods, who might exist together, or one after the other. We might, by our conspiring sympathies, help to make a new one. Much in us is doubtless immortal; we survive death for some time in a recognisable form; but what our career and transformations may be in the sequel we cannot tell, although we may help to determine them by our daily choices. Observation must be continual if our ideas are to remain true. Eternal vigilance is the price of knowledge; perpetual hazard, perpetual experiment keep quick the edge of life.

This is, so far as I know, a new philosophical vista; it is a conception never before presented, although implied, perhaps, in various quarters, as in Norse and even Greek mythology. It is a vision radically empirical and radically romantic; and as William James himself used to say, the visions and not the arguments of a philosopher are the interesting and influential things about him. . . .

. . . [M]y point is only that William James, in this genial evolutionary view of the world, has given a rude shock to the genteel tradition. What! The world a gradual improvisation? Creation unpremeditated? God a sort of young poet or struggling artist? William James is an advocate of theism; pragmatism adds one to the evidences of religion; that is excellent. But is not the cool abstract piety of the genteel getting more than it asks for? This empirical naturalistic God is too crude and positive a force; he will work miracles, he will answer prayers, he may inhabit distinct places, and have distinct conditions under which alone he can operate; he is a neighbouring being, whom we can act upon, and rely upon for specific aids, as upon a personal friend, or a physician, or an insurance company. How disconcerting! Is not this new theology a little like superstition? And yet how interesting, how exciting, if it should happen to be true! I am far from wishing to suggest that such a view seems to me more probable than conventional idealism or than Christian orthodoxy.

All three are in the region of dramatic system-making and myth to which probabilities are irrelevant. If one man says the moon is sister to the sun, and another that she is his daughter, the question is not which notion is more probable, but whether either of them is at all expressive. The so-called evidences are devised after-wards, when faith and imagination have prejudged the issue. The force of William James's new theology, or romantic cosmology, lies only in this: that it has broken the spell of the genteel tradition, and enticed faith in a new direction, which on second thoughts may prove no less alluring than the old. The important fact is not that the new fancy might possibly be true—who shall know that?—but that it has entered the heart of a leading American to conceive and to cherish it. The genteel tradition cannot be dislodged by these insurrections; there are circles to which it is still congenial, and where it will be preserved. But it has been challenged and (what is perhaps more insidious) it has been discovered. No one need be browbeaten any longer into accepting it. No one need be afraid, for instance, that his fate is sealed because some young prig may call him a dualist; the pint would call the quart a dualist, if you tried to pour the quart into him. We need not be afraid of being less profound, for being direct and sincere. The intellectual world may be traversed in many directions; the whole has not been surveyed; there is a great career in it open to talent. That is a sort of knell, that tolls the passing of the genteel tradition. Something else is now in the field; something else can appeal to the imagination, and be a thousand times more idealistic than academic idealism, which is often simply a way of white-washing and adoring things as they are. . . . An honest man has spoken, and the cant of the genteel tradition has become harder for young lips to repeat.

With this I have finished such a sketch as I am here able to offer you of the genteel tradition in American philosophy. The subject is complex, and calls for many an excursus and qualifying footnote; yet I think the main outlines are clear enough. The chief fountains of this tradition were Calvinism and transcendentalism. Both were living fountains; but to keep them alive they required, one an agonised conscience, and the other a radical subjective criticism of knowledge. When these rare metaphysical preoccupations disappeared—and the American atmosphere is not favourable to either of them—the two systems ceased to be inwardly understood; they subsisted as sacred mysteries only; and the combination of the two in some transcendental system of the universe (a contradiction in principle) was doubly artificial. . . .

Hypostatic Ethics (1913)

If Mr. Russell, in his essay on "The Elements of Ethics," had wished to propitiate the unregenerate naturalist, before trying to convert him, he could not have chosen a more skilful procedure; for he begins by telling us that "what is called good conduct is conduct which is a means to other things which are good on their own account; and hence . . . the study of what is good or bad on its own account must be included in ethics." Two consequences are involved in this: first, that ethics is concerned with the economy of all values, and not with "moral" goods only, or with duty; and second, that values may and do inhere in a great variety of things and relations, all of which it is the part of wisdom to respect, and if possible to establish. In this matter, according to our author, the general philosopher is prone to one error and the professed moralist to another. "The philosopher, bent on the construction of a system, is inclined to simplify the facts unduly . . . and to twist them into a form in which they can all be deduced from one or two general principles. The moralist, on the other hand, being primarily concerned with conduct, tends to become absorbed in means, to value the actions men ought to perform more than the ends which such actions serve. . . . Hence most of what they value in this world would have to be omitted by many moralists from any imagined heaven, because there such things as self-denial and effort and courage and pity could find no place. . . . Kant has the bad eminence of combining both errors in the highest possible degree, since he holds that there is nothing good except the virtuous will—a view which simplifies the good as much as any philosopher could wish, and mistakes means for ends as completely as any moralist could enjoin."

Those of us who are what Mr. Russell would call ethical sceptics will be delighted at this way of clearing the ground; it opens before us the prospect of a moral philosophy that should estimate the various values of things known and of things imaginable, showing what combinations of goods are possible in any one rational system, and (if fancy could stretch so far) what different rational systems would be possible in places and times remote enough from one another not to come into physical conflict. Such ethics, since it would express in reflection the dumb but actual interests of men, might have both influence and authority over them; two things which an alien and dogmatic ethics necessarily lacks. The joy of the ethical sceptic in Mr. Russell is destined, however, to be shortlived. Before proceeding to the expression of concrete ideals, he thinks it necessary to ask a preliminary and quite abstract question, to which his essay is chiefly devoted; namely, what is the right definition of the predicate "good," which we hope to apply in the sequel to such a variety of things? And he answers at once: The predicate "good" is indefinable. This answer he shows to be unavoidable, and so evidently unavoidable that we might perhaps have been absolved from asking the question; for, as he says, the so-called definitions of "good"—that it is pleasure, the desired, and so forth—are not definitions of the predicate "good," but designations of the things to which this predicate is applied by different persons. Pleasure, and its rivals, are not synonyms for the abstract quality "good," but names for classes of concrete facts that are supposed to possess that quality. From this correct, if somewhat trifling, observation, however, Mr. Russell, like Mr. Moore before him, evokes a portentous dogma. Not being able to define good, he hypostasises it. "Good and bad," he says, "are qualities which belong to objects independently of our opinions, just as much as round and square do; and when two people differ as to whether a thing is good, only one of them can be right, though it may be very hard to know which is right." "We cannot maintain that for me a thing ought to exist on its own account, while for you it ought not; that would merely mean that one of us is mistaken, since in fact everything either ought to exist, or ought not." Thus we are asked to believe that good attaches to things for no reason or cause, and according to no principles of distribution; that it must be found there by a sort of receptive exploration in each separate case; in other words, that it is an absolute, not a relative, thing, a primary and not a secondary quality.

That the quality "good" is indefinable is one assertion, and obvious; but that the presence of this quality is unconditioned is another, and astonishing. My logic, I am well aware, is not very accurate or subtle; and I wish Mr. Russell had not left it to me to discover the connection between these two propositions. Green is an indefinable predicate, and the specific quality of it can be given only in intuition; but it is a quality that things acquire under certain conditions, so much so that the same bit of grass, at the same moment, may have it from one point of view and not from another. Right and left are indefinable; the difference could not be explained without being invoked in the explanation; yet everything that is to the right is not to the right on no condition, but obviously on the condition that some one is looking in a certain direction; and if some one else at the same time is looking in the opposite direction, what is truly to the right will be truly to the left also. If Mr. Russell thinks this is a contradiction, I understand why the universe does not please him. The contradiction would be real, undoubtedly, if we suggested that the *idea* of good was at any time or in any relation the *idea* of evil, or the *intuition* of right that of left, or the *quality* of green that of yellow; these disembodied essences are fixed by the intent that selects them, and in that ideal realm they can never have any relations except the dialectical ones implied in their nature, and these relations they must always retain. But the contradiction disappears when, instead of considering the qualities in themselves, we consider the things of which those qualities are aspects; for the qualities of things are not compacted by implication, but are conjoined irrationally by nature, as she will; and the same thing may be, and is, at once yellow and green, to the left and to the right, good and evil, many and one, large and small; and whatever verbal paradox there may be in this way of speaking (for from the point of view of nature it is natural enough) had been thoroughly explained and talked out by the time of Plato, who complained that people should still raise a difficulty so trite and exploded. Indeed, while square is always square, and round round, a thing that is round may actually be square also, if we allow it to have a little body, and to be a cylinder.

But perhaps what suggests this hypostasis of good is rather the fact that what others find good, or what we ourselves have found good in moods with which we retain no sympathy, is sometimes pronounced by us to be bad; and far from inferring from this diversity of experience that the present good, like the others, corresponds to a particular attitude or interest of ours, and is dependent upon it, Mr. Russell and Mr. Moore infer instead that the presence of the good must be independent of all interests, attitudes, and opinions. They imagine that the truth of a proposition attributing a certain relative quality to an object contradicts the truth of another proposition, attributing to the same object an opposite relative quality. Thus if a man here and another man at the antipodes call opposite directions up, "only one of them can be right, though it may be very hard to know which is right."

To protect the belated innocence of this state of mind, Mr. Russell, so far as I can see, has only one argument, and one analogy. The argument is that "if this were not the case, we could not reason with a man as to what is right." "We do in fact hold that when one man approves of a certain act, while another disapproves, one of them is mistaken, which would not be the case with a mere emotion. If one man likes oysters and another dislikes them, we do not say that either of them is mistaken." In other words, we are to maintain our prejudices, however absurd, lest it should become unnecessary to quarrel about them! Truly the debating society has its idols, no less than the cave and the theatre. The analogy that comes to buttress somewhat this singular argument is the analogy between ethical propriety and physical or logical truth. An ethical proposition may be correct or incorrect, in a sense justifying argument, when it touches what is good as a means, that is, when it is not intrinsically ethical, but deals with causes and effects, or with matters of fact or necessity. But to speak of the truth of an ultimate good would be a false collocation of terms; an ultimate good is chosen, found, or aimed at; it is not opined. The ultimate intuitions on which ethics rests are not debatable, for they are not opinions we hazard but preferences we feel; and it can be neither correct nor incorrect to feel them. We may assert these preferences fiercely or with sweet reasonableness, and we may be more or less incapable of sympathising with the different preferences of others; about oysters we may be tolerant, like Mr. Russell, and about character intolerant. ...

I am not sure whether Mr. Russell thinks he has disposed of this view where he discusses the proposition that the good is the desired and refutes it on the ground that "it is commonly admitted that there are bad desires; and when people speak of bad desires, they seem to mean desires for what is bad." Most people undoubtedly call desires bad when they are generically contrary to their own desires, and call objects that disgust them bad, even when other people covet them. This human weakness is not, however, a very high authority for a logician to appeal to, being too like the attitude of the German lady who said that Englishmen called a certain object *bread*, and Frenchmen called it *pain*, but that it really was *Brod*. . . .

In a somewhat worthier sense, however, we may admit that there are desires for what is bad, since desire and will, in the proper psychological sense of these words, are incidental phases of consciousness, expressing but not constituting those natural relations that make one thing good for another. At the same time the words desire and will are often used, in a mythical or transcendental sense, for those material dispositions and instincts by which vital and moral units are constituted. It is in reference to such constitutional interests that things are "really" good or bad; interests which may not be fairly represented by any incidental conscious desire. No doubt any desire, however capricious, represents some momentary and partial interest, which lends to its objects a certain real and inalienable value; yet when we consider, as we do in human society, the interests of men, whom reflection and settled purposes have raised more or less to the ideal dignity of individuals, then passing fancies and passions may indeed have bad objects, and be bad themselves, in that they thwart the more comprehensive interests of the soul that entertains them. Food and poison are such only relatively, and in view of particular bodies, and the same material thing may be food and poison at once; the child, and even the doctor, may easily mistake one for the other. . . .

I cannot help thinking that a consciousness of the relativity of values, if it became prevalent, would tend to render people more truly social than would a belief that things have intrinsic and unchangeable values, no matter what the attitude of any one to them may be. If we said that goods, including the right distribution of goods, are relative to specific natures, moral warfare would continue, but not with poisoned arrows. Our private sense of justice itself would be acknowledged to have but a relative authority, and while we could not have a higher duty than to follow it, we should seek to meet those whose aims were incompatible with it as we meet things physically inconvenient, without insulting them as if they were morally vile or logically contemptible. . . .

The consequences of a hypostasis of the good are no less interesting than its causes. If the good were independent of nature, it might still be conceived as relevant to nature, by being its creator or mover; but Mr. Russell is not a theist after the manner of Socrates; his good is not a power. Nor would representing it to be such long help his case; for an ideal hypostasised into a cause achieves only a mythical independence. The least criticism dicloses that it is natural laws, zoological species, and human ideals, that have been projected into the empyrean; and it is no marvel that the good should attract the world where the good, by definition, is whatever the world is aiming at. The hypostasis accomplished by Mr. Russell is more serious, and therefore more paradoxical. If I understand it, it may be expressed as follows: In the realm of eternal essences, before anything exists, there are certain essences that have this remarkable property, that they ought to exist, or at least that, if anything exists, it ought to conform to them. What exists, however, is deaf to this moral emphasis in the eternal; nature exists for no reason. . . .

Ultimate Scepticism (1923)

Why should the mystic, in proportion as he dismisses the miscellany of experience as so much illusion, feel that he becomes one with reality and attains to absolute existence? I think that the same survival of vulgar presumptions which leads the romantic solipsist to retain his belief in his personal history and destiny, leads the mystic to retain, and fondly to embrace, the feeling of existence. His speculation is indeed inspired by the love of security: his grand objection to the natural world, and to mortal life, is that they are deceptive, that they cheat the soul that loves them, and prove to be illusions: the assumption apparently being that reality must be permanent, and that he who has hold on reality is safe for ever. In this the mystic, who so hates illusions, is the victim of an illusion himself: for the reality he has hold of is but the burden of a single moment, which in its solipsism thinks itself absolute. What is reality? As I should like to use the term, reality is being of any sort. If it means character or essence, illusions have it as much as substance, and more richly. If it means substance, then sceptical concentration upon inner experience, or ecstatic abstraction, seems to me the last place in which we should look for it. The immediate and the visionary are at the opposite pole from substance; they are on the surface or, if you like, at the top; whereas substance if it is anywhere is at the bottom. The realm of immediate illusion is as real as any other, and very attractive; many would wish it to be the only reality, and hate substance; but if substance exists (which I am not yet ready to assert) they have no reason to hate it, since it is the basis of those immediate feelings which fill them with satisfaction. Finally, if reality means existence, certainly the mystic and his meditation may exist, but not more truly than any other natural fact; and what would exist in them would be a pulse of animal being, kindling that momentary ecstasy, as animal life at certain intensities is wont to do. The theme of that meditation, its visionary object, need not exist at all; it may be incapable of existing if it is essentially timeless and dialectical. The animal mind treats its data as facts, or as signs of facts, but the animal mind is full of the rashest presumptions, positing time, change, a particular station in the midst of events yielding a particular perspective of those events, and the flux of all nature precipitating that experience at that place. None of these posited objects is a datum in which a sceptic could rest. Indeed, existence or fact, in the sense which I give to these words, cannot be a datum at all, because existence involves external relations and actual (not merely specious) flux: whereas, however complex a datum may be, with no matter what perspectives opening within it, it must be embraced in a single stroke of apperception, and nothing outside it can belong to it at all. The datum is a pure image; it is essentially illusory and unsubstantial, however thunderous its sound or keen its edge, or

From *The Works of George Santayana*, Vol. XIII. (New York: Dover Publications, 1955) pp. 33–40.

however normal and significant its presence may be. When the mystic asserts enthusiastically the existence of his immediate, ideal, unutterable object, Absolute Being, he is peculiarly unfortunate in his faith: it would be impossible to choose an image less relevant to the agencies that actually bring that image before him. The burden and glow of existence which he is conscious of come entirely from himself; his object is eminently empty, impotent, non-existent; but the heat and labour of his own soul suffuse that emptiness with light, and the very hum of change within him, accelerated almost beyond endurance and quite beyond discrimination, sounds that piercing note.

The last step in scepticism is now before me. It will lead me to deny existence to any datum, whatever it may be; and as the datum, by hypothesis, is the whole of what solicits my attention at any moment, I shall deny the existence of everything, and abolish that category of thought altogether. If I could not do this, I should be a tyro in scepticism. Belief in the existence of anything, including myself, is something radically incapable of proof, and resting, like all belief, on some irrational persuasion or prompting of life. Certainly, as a matter of fact, when I deny existence I exist; but doubtless many of the other facts I have been denying, because I found no evidence for them, were true also. To bring me evidence of their existence is no duty imposed on facts, nor a habit of theirs: I must employ private detectives. The point is, in this task of criticism, to discard every belief that is a belief merely; and the belief in existence, in the nature of the case, can be a belief only. The datum is an idea, a description; I may contemplate it without belief; but when I assert that such a thing exists I am hypostatising this datum, placing it in presumptive relations which are not internal to it, and worshipping it as an idol or thing. Neither its existence nor mine nor that of my belief can be given in any datum. These things are incidents involved in that order of nature which I have thrown over; they are no part of what remains before me.

Assurance of existence expresses animal watchfulness: it posits, within me and round me, hidden and imminent events. The sceptic can easily cast a doubt on the remoter objects of this belief; and nothing but a certain obduracy and want of agility prevents him from doubting present existence itself. For what could present existence mean, if the imminent events for which animal sense is watching failed altogether, failed at the very roots, so to speak, of the tree of intuition, and left nothing but its branches flowering *in vacuo*? Expectation is admittedly the most hazardous of beliefs: yet what is watchfulness but expectation? Memory is notoriously full of illusion; yet what would experience of the present be if the veracity of primary memory were denied, and if I no longer believed that anything had just happened, or that I had ever been in the state from which I suppose myself to have passed into this my present condition?

It will not do for the sceptic to take refuge in the confused notion that expectation *possesses* the future, or memory the past. As a matter of fact, expectation is like hunger; it opens its mouth, and something probably drops into it, more or less, very often, the sort of thing it expected; but sometimes a surprise comes, and sometimes nothing. Life involves expectation, but does not prevent death: and expectation is never so thoroughly stultified as when it is not undeceived, but cancelled. The open mouth does not then so much as close upon nothing. It is buried open. Nor is memory in a better case. As the whole world might collapse and cease at any moment, nullifying all expectation, so it might at any moment have sprung out of nothing: for it is thoroughly contingent, and might have begun to-day, with this degree of complexity and illusive memory, as well as long ago, with whatever energy or momentum it was first endowed with. The backward perspective of time is perhaps really an inverted expectation; but for the momentum of life forward, we might not be able to space the elements active in the present so as to assign to them a longer or a shorter history; for we should not attempt to discriminate amongst these elements such as we could still count on in the immediate future, and such as we might safely ignore: so that our conception of the past implies, perhaps, a distinction between the living and the dead. This distinction is itself practical, and looks to the future. In the absolute present all is specious; and to pure intuition the living are as ghostly as the dead, and the dead as present as the living.

In the sense of existence there is accordingly something more than the obvious character of that which is alleged to exist. What is this compliment? It cannot be a feature in the datum, since the datum by definition is the whole of what is found. Nor can it be, in my sense at least of the word existence, the intrinsic constitution or specific being of this object, since existence comports external relations, variable, contingent, and not discoverable in a given being when taken alone: for there is nothing that may not lose its existence, or the existence of which might not be conceivably denied. The complement added to the datum when it is alleged to exist seems, then, to be added by *me*; it is the finding, the occurrence, the assault, the impact of that being here and now; it is the experience of it. But what can experience be, if I take away from it the whole of what is experienced? And what meaning can I give to such words as impact, assault, occurrence, or finding, when I have banished and denied my body, my past, my residual present being, and everything except the datum which I find? The sense of existence evidently belongs to the intoxication, to the *Rausch*, of existence itself; it is the strain of life within me, prior to all intuition, that in its precipitation and terror, passing as it continually must from one untenable condition to another, stretches my attention absurdly over what is not given, over the lost and the unattained, the before and after which are wrapped in darkness, and confuses my breathless apprehension of the clear presence of all I can ever truly behold.

Indeed, so much am I a creature of movement, and of the ceaseless metabolism of matter, that I should never catch even these glimpses of the light, if there were not rhythms, pauses, repetitions, and nodes in my physical progress, to absorb and reflect it here and there: as the traveller, hurried in a cloud of smoke and dust through tunnel after tunnel in the Italian Riviera, catches and loses momentary visions of blue sea and sky, which he would like to arrest, but cannot; yet if he had not been rushed and whistled along these particular tunnels, even those snatches, in the form in which they come to him, would have been denied him. So it is the rush of life that, at its open moments, floods me with intuitions, partial and confused, but still revelations; the landscape is wrapped in the smoke of my little engine, and turned into a tantalising incident of my hot journey. What appears (which is an ideal object and not an event) is thus confused with the event of its appearance; the picture is identified with the kindling or distraction of my attention falling by chance upon it; and the strain of my material existence, battling with material accidents, turns the ideal object too into a temporal fact, and makes it seem substantial. But this fugitive existence which I egotistically attach to it, as if its fate was that of my glimpses of it, is no part of its true being, as even my intuition discerns it; it is a practical dignity or potency attributed to it by the irrelevant momentum of my animal life. Animals, being by nature hounded and hungry creatures, spy out and take alarm at any datum of sense or fancy, supposing that there is something substantial there, something that will count and work in the world. The notion of a moving world is brought implicitly with them; they fetch it out of the depths of their vegetating psyche, which is a small dark cosmos, silently revolving within. By being noticed, and treated as a signal for I know not what material opportunity or danger, the given image is taken up into the business world, and puts on the garment of existence. Remove this frame, strip off all suggestion of a time when this image was not yet present, or a time when it shall be past, and the very notion of existence is removed. The datum ceases to be an appearance, in the proper and pregnant sense of this word, since it ceases to imply any substance that appears or any mind to which it appears. It is an appearance only in the sense that its nature is wholly manifest, that it is a specific being, which may be mentioned, thought of, seen, or defined, if any one has the wit to do so. But its own nature says nothing of any hidden circumstances that shall bring it to light, or any adventitious mind that shall discover it. It lies simply in its own category. If a colour, it is just this colour; if a pain, just this pain. Its appearance is not an event: its presence is not an experience; for there is no surrounding world in which it can arise, and no watchful spirit to appropriate it. The sceptic has here withdrawn into the intuition of a surface form, without roots, without origin or environment, without a seat or a locus; a little universe, an immaterial absolute theme, rejoicing merely in its own quality. This theme, being out of all adventitious relations and not in the least threatened with not being the theme it is, has not the contingency nor the fortunes proper to an existence; it is simply that which it inherently, logically, and unchangeably is.

Existence, then, not being included in any immediate datum, is a fact always open to doubt. I call it a fact notwithstanding, because in talking about the sceptic I am positing his existence. If he has any intuition, however little the theme of that intuition may have to do with any actual world, certainly I who think of his intuition, or he himself thinking of it afterwards, see that this intuition of his must have been an event, and his existence at that time a fact;

but like all facts and events, this one can be known only by an affirmation which posits it, which may be suspended or reversed, and which is subject to error. Hence all this business of intuition may perfectly well be doubted by the sceptic: the existence of his own doubt (however confidently I may assert it for him) is not given to him then: all that is given is some ambiguity or contradiction in images; and if afterwards he is sure that he has doubted, the sole cogent evidence which that fact can claim lies in the psychological impossibility that, so long as he believes he has doubted, he should not believe it. But he may be wrong in harbouring this belief, and he may rescind it. For all an ultimate scepticism can see, therefore, there may be no facts at all, and perhaps nothing has ever existed.

Scepticism may thus be carried to the point of denying change and memory, and the reality of all facts. Such a sceptical dogma would certainly be false, because this dogma itself would have to be entertained, and that event would be a fact and an existence: and the sceptic in framing that dogma discourses, vacillates, and lives in the act of contrasting one assertion with another—all of which is to exist with a vengeance. Yet this false dogma that nothing exists is tenable intuitively and, while it prevails, is irrefutable. There are certain motives (to be discussed later) which render ultimate scepticism precious to a spiritual mind, as a sanctuary from grosser illusions. For the wayward sceptic, who regards it as no truer than any other view, it also has some utility: it accustoms him to discard the dogma which an introspective critic might be tempted to think self-evident, namely, that he himself lives and thinks. That he does so is true; but to establish that truth he must appeal to animal faith. If he is too proud for that, and simply stares at the datum, the last thing he will see is himself.

Study Questions

1. What exactly is the "genteel tradition" to which Santayana objects, and why does he object to it? Explain, and support your answer.

2. From a philosophical perspective what, for Santayana, are the chief flaws in Calvinism and New England Transcendentalism? Explain, and defend your answer.

3. Why does Santayana praise William James and his philosophy as significant alternatives to the "genteel tradition" of Edwards, Emerson, and their followers? Explain.

4. What are Santayana's principal objections to ethical absolutes, and how does he try in "Hypostatic Ethics" to establish that absolutism in ethics must take a back seat to moral relativism or naturalism?

5. In *Scepticism and Animal Faith*, Santayana produces arguments for nearly absolute skepticism. What are his arguments? Are they convincing?

Suggestions for Further Reading

McCormick, John. *George Santayana: A Biography*. New York: Alfred A. Knopf, 1987.

Santayana, George. *The Life of Reason*, 4 vols., second edition. New York: Charles Scribner's Sons, 1922.

Santayana, George. *Scepticism and Animal Faith*. New York: Charles Scribner's Sons, 1923.

Santayana, George. *Winds of Doctrine*. New York: Charles Scribner's Sons, 1926.

Santayana, George. *The Last Puritan: A Memoir in the Form of a Novel*. New York: Charles Scribner's Sons, 1936.

Sprigge, Timothy L. S. *George Santayana: An Examination of His Philosophy*. Boston: Routledge and Kegan Paul, 1974.

White, Morton. *Science and Sentiment in America*. New York: Oxford University Press, 1972.

White, Morton, and White, Lucia. "Provincialism and Alienation: An Aside on Josiah Royce and George Santayana." In *The Intellectual Versus the City: From Thomas Jefferson to Frank Lloyd Wright*. Cambridge, Mass: Harvard University Press and MIT Press, 1962.

Chapter 8

C. I. Lewis, W. V. O. Quine, and Richard Rorty
American Analytic Philosophy and Pragmatism Prolonged (1923)

As we advance to the middle decades of the twentieth century and from them into the present, an important question is whether there is anything specifically American about philosophy that has been recently crafted in America. When three important thinkers express trends in twentieth-century philosophy, we find ourselves trying to decide whether their views bear on anything we can link to *American* culture and history.

C. I. Lewis (1883–1964), the most significant American philosopher between the two World Wars, taught for almost twenty-five years at Harvard and there wrote his classic *Mind and the World-Order* (1929). Apart from working through complex issues in epistemology and theories of meaning, Lewis was also curious about the character of a priori knowledge and its source. He was persuaded that the objects of a priori knowledge are necessary truths that we—scientists and philosophers—stipulate for pragmatic ends. Lewis's "A Pragmatic Conception of the A Priori" (1923) sets out his conviction that an avid interest in the fruits of philosophical analysis is congruent with an equally vigorous commitment to the tenets of pragmatism.

Willard Van Orman Quine (1908–2000), for many years a distinguished Harvard professor, explored subtle problems in metaphysics, epistemology, and logic in essays. His books, *From a Logical Point of View* (1953) and *Word and Object* (1960), remain classics in the analytic tradition that concerns itself with unpacking and explicating concepts. The article "Two Dogmas of Empiricism" (1951) is Quine's most famous and influential short essay. In fact, it is one of the most widely known philosophical articles published in twentieth-century America. In it, Quine makes a case for the shortcomings of what many philosophers treated as almost self-evidently true, namely, that only two kinds of sentences amount to meaningful propositions and that one of these kinds, which Kant called "analytic," is more problematic than traditional empiricists have recognized.

Richard Rorty is, at least in the early years of the twenty-first century, America's best-known philosopher. Many philosophical analysts are turned aside by what he writes, but many other philosophers, as well as a host of literary critics, see him as one of their own. More than that, Rorty is sympathetic to a good deal of what he finds in the pragmatists. He praises John Dewey in *Philosophy and the Mirror of Nature* (1979). In *Consequences of Pragmatism*

(1982), he applauds William James for having the good sense and bravado to abandon the notion that truth somehow corresponds to what is real. Rorty, like the pragmatists, is impatient with the weight of philosophical traditions that—despite their flaws and untested assumptions—die hard and slowly. Analytic philosophy is, therefore, only one among various philosophies toward which Rorty directs his difficult arguments and unveiled displeasure.

In the selection from *Consequences of Pragmatism*, we read why Rorty believes that renewed attention to James rewards anyone who criticizes philosophy as it is and anyone who hopes that pragmatism may direct us to "a new form of intellectual life." Whether one agrees with Rorty or not, his generous attitudes toward the major pragmatists might suggest that philosophy in America still has a pulse and that reviving the best of pragmatism may prove a fruitful resource for philosophers to come. If Rorty's position can stand up against its critics, then slightly altered pragmatism might remain one of this country's most enduring intellectual products and exports.

A Pragmatic Conception of the A Priori (1951)

C. I. Lewis

The conception of the a priori points to two problems which are perennial in philosophy: the part played in knowledge by the mind itself, and the possibility of 'necessary truth' or of knowledge 'independent of experience.' But traditional conceptions of the a priori have proved untenable. That the mind approaches the flux of immediacy with some godlike foreknowledge of principles which are legislative for experience, that there is any natural light or any innate ideas, it is no longer possible to believe. ...

The difficulties of the conception are due, I believe, to two mistakes: whatever is a priori is necessary, but we have misconstrued the relation of necessary truth to mind; and the a priori is independent of experience, but in so taking it, we have misunderstood its relation to empirical fact. What is a priori is necessary truth not because it compels the mind's acceptance, but precisely because it does not. It is given experience, brute fact, the a posteriori element in knowledge which the mind must accept willy-nilly. The a priori represents an attitude in some sense freely taken, a stipulation of the mind itself, and a stipulation which might be made in some other way if it suited our bent or need. Such truth is necessary as opposed to contingent, not as opposed to voluntary. And the a priori is independent of experience not because it prescribes a form which the data of sense must fit, or anticipates some pre-established harmony

From C. I. Lewis, "A Pragmatic Conception of A Priori," *The Journal of Philosophy*, Vol. XX, No. 7 (March 29, 1923): 169–177. Reprinted with permission of the publisher.

of experience with the mind, but precisely because it prescribes nothing to experience. That is a priori which is true, no matter what. What it anticipates is not the given, but our attitude toward it: it concerns the uncompelled initiative of mind or, as Josiah Royce would say, our categorical ways of acting.

The traditional example of the a priori par excellence is the laws of logic. These cannot be derived from experience since they must first be taken for granted in order to prove them. They make explicit our general modes of classification. . . . What kind of experience could defy the principle that everything must either be or not be, that nothing can both be and not be, or that if x is y and y is z, then x is z? If anything imaginable or unimaginable could violate such laws, then the ever-present fact of change would do it every day. The laws of logic are purely formal; they forbid nothing but what concerns the use of terms and the corresponding modes of classification and analysis. The law of contradiction tells us that nothing can be both white and not-white, but it does not and cannot tell us whether black is not-white, or soft or square is not-white. To discover *what contradicts what* we must always consult the character of experience. Similarly, the law of the excluded middle formulates our decision that whatever is not designated by a certain term shall be designated by its negative. It declares our purpose to make, for every term, a complete dichotomy of experience, instead—as we might choose—of classifying on the basis of a tripartite division into opposites (as black and white) and the middle ground between the two. Our rejection of such tripartite division represents only our penchant for simplicity.

Further laws of logic are of similar significance. They are principles of procedure, the parliamentary rules of intelligent thought and speech. Such laws are independent of experience because they impose no limitations whatever upon it. They are legislative because they are addressed to ourselves—because definition, classification, and inference represent no operations of the objective world, but only our own categorical attitudes of mind.

And further, the ultimate criteria of the laws of logic are pragmatic. Those who suppose that there is, for example, *a* logic which everyone would agree to if he understood it and understood himself are more optimistic than those versed in the history of logical discussion have a right to be. The fact is that there are several logics, markedly different, each self-consistent in its own terms and such that whoever using it, if he avoids false premises, will never reach a false conclusion. Mr Russell, for example, bases *his* logic on an implication relation such that if twenty sentences be cut from a newspaper and put in a hat, and then two of these be drawn at random, one of them will certainly imply the other, and it is an even bet that the implication will be mutual. Yet upon a foundation so remote from ordinary modes of inference the whole structure of *Principia Mathematica* is built. This logic—and there are others even more strange—is utterly consistent and the results of it entirely valid. Over and above all questions of consistency, there are issues of logic which cannot be determined—nay, cannot even be argued—except on pragmatic grounds of conformity to human bent and intellectual convenience. That we have been blind to this fact, itself reflects traditional errors in the conception of the a priori.

We may note in passing one less important illustration of the a priori—the proposition 'true by definition'. Definitions and their immediate consequences, analytic propositions generally, are necessarily true, true under all possible circumstances. Definition is legislative because it is in some sense arbitrary. Not only is the meaning assigned to words more or less a matter of choice—that consideration is relatively trivial—but the manner in which the precise classifications which definition embodies shall be effected is something not dictated by experience. If experience were other than it is, the definition and its corresponding classification might be inconvenient, fantastic, or useless, but it could not be false. Mind makes classifications and determines meanings; in so doing it creates the a priori truth of analytic judgements. But that the manner of this creation responds to pragmatic considerations is so obvious that it hardly needs pointing out.

If the illustrations so far given seem trivial or verbal, that impression may be corrected by turning to the place which the a priori has in mathematics and in natural science. Arithmetic, for example, depends in toto upon the operation of counting or correlating, a procedure which can be carried out at will in any world containing identifiable things—even identifiable ideas—regardless of the further characters of experience. Mill challenged this a priori character of arithmetic. He asked us to suppose a demon sufficiently powerful and maleficent so that every time two things were brought together with two other things, this demon should always introduce a fifth. The implication which he supposed to follow is that under such circumstances $2 + 2 = 5$ would be a universal law of arithmetic. But Mill was quite mistaken. In such a world we should be obliged to become a little clearer than is usual about the distinction between arithmetic and physics; that is all. If two black marbles were put in the same urn with two white ones, the demon could take his choice of colors, but it would be evident that there were more black marbles or more white ones than were put in. The same would be true of all objects in any wise identifiable. We should simply find ourselves in the presence of an extraordinary physical law, which we should recognize as universal in our world, that whenever two things were brought into proximity with two others, an additional and similar thing was always created by the process. Mill's world would be physically most extraordinary. The world's work would be enormously facilitated if hats or locomotives or tons of coal could be thus multiplied by anyone possessed originally of two pairs. But the laws of mathematics would remain unaltered. It is because this is true that arithmetic is a priori. Its laws prevent *nothing*; they are compatible with anything which happens or could conceivably happen in nature. They would be true in any possible world. Mathematical addition is not a physical transformation. Physical changes which result in an increase or decrease of the countable things involved are matters of everyday occurrence. Such physical processes present us with phenomena in which the purely mathematical has to be separated out by abstraction. Those laws and those laws only have necessary truth which we are prepared to maintain, no matter what. It is because we shall always separate out that part of the phenomenon not in conformity with arithmetic and designate it by some other category—physical change, chemical reaction, optical illusion—that arithmetic is a priori.

The a priori element in science and in natural law is greater than might be supposed. In the first place, all science is based upon definitive concepts. The formulation of these concepts is, indeed, a matter determined by the commerce between our intellectual or our pragmatic interests and the nature of experience. Definition is classification. The scientific search is for such classification as will make it possible to correlate appearance and behaviour, to discover law, to penetrate to the 'essential nature' of things in order that behaviour may become predictable. In other words, if definition is unsuccessful, as early scientific definitions mostly have been, it is because the classification thus set up corresponds with no natural cleavage and does not correlate with any important uniformity of behaviour. A name itself must represent *some* uniformity in experience or it names nothing. What does not repeat itself or recur in intelligible fashion is not a thing. Where the definitive uniformity is a clue to other uniformities, we have successful scientific definition. Other definitions cannot be said to be false; they are merely useless. In scientific classification the search is, thus, for *things worth naming*. But the naming, classifying, defining activity is essentially prior to investigation. We cannot interrogate experience in general. Until our meaning is definite and our classification correspondingly exact, experience cannot conceivably answer our questions.

In the second place, the fundamental laws of any science—or those treated as fundamental—are a priori because they formulate just such definitive concepts or categorical tests by which alone investigation becomes possible. If the lightning strikes the railroad track at two places, A and B, how shall we tell whether these events are simultaneous?

> We . . . require a definition of simultaneity such that this definition supplies us with the method by means of which . . . [we] can decide whether or not both the lightning strokes occurred simultaneously. As long as this requirement is not satisfied, I allow myself to be deceived as a physicist (and of course the same applies if I am not a physicist), when I imagine that I am able to attach a meaning to the statement of simultaneity. . . .
>
> After thinking the matter over for some time you then offer the following suggestions with which to test simultaneity. By measuring along the rails, the connecting line AB should be measured up and an observer placed at the mid-point M of the distance AB. This observer should be supplied with an arrangement (e.g. two mirrors inclined at 90 degrees) which allows him visually to observe both places A and B at the same time. If the observer perceives the two flashes at the same time, then they are simultaneous.
>
> I am very pleased with this suggestion, but for all that I cannot regard the matter as quite settled, because I feel constrained to raise

the following objection: 'Your definition would certainly be right, if I only knew that the light by means of which the observer at M perceives the lightning flashes travels along the length A—M with the same velocity as along the length B—M. But an examination of this supposition would only be possible if we already had at our disposal the means of measuring time. It would thus appear as though we were moving here in a logical circle.'

After further consideration you cast a somewhat disdainful glance at me—and rightly so—and you declare: 'I maintain my previous definition, nevertheless, because in reality it assumes absolutely nothing about light. There is only *one* demand to be made of the definition of simultaneity, namely, that in every real case it must supply us with an empirical decision as to whether or not the conception which has to be defined is fulfilled. ... That light requires the same time to traverse the path A—M as for the path B—M is in reality *neither a supposition nor a hypothesis* about the physical nature of light, but a *stipulation* which I can make of my own free will in order to arrive at a definition of simultaneity.' ... We are thus led also to a definition of 'time' in physics.[1]

As this example from the theory of relativity well illustrates, we cannot even ask the questions which discovered law would answer until we have first by a priori stipulation formulated definitive criteria. Such concepts are not verbal definitions, nor classifications merely; they are themselves laws which prescribe a certain uniformity of behaviour to whatever is thus named. Such definitive laws are a priori; only so can we enter upon the investigation by which further laws are sought. Yet it should also be pointed out that such a priori laws are subject to abandonment if the structure which is built upon them does not succeed in simplifying our interpretation of phenomena. If, in the illustration given, the relation 'simultaneous with,' as defined, should not prove transitive—if event A should prove simultaneous with B, and B with C, but not A with C—this definition would certainly be rejected.

And thirdly, there is that a priori element in science—as in other human affairs—which constitutes the criteria of the real as opposed to the unreal in experience. An object itself is a uniformity. Failure to behave in certain categorical ways marks it as unreal. Uniformities of the type called 'natural law' are the clues to reality and unreality. A mouse which disappears where no hole is, is no real mouse; a landscape which recedes as we approach is but illusion. As the queen remarked in the episode of the wishing-carpet: 'if this were real, then it would be a miracle. But miracles do not happen. Therefore I shall wake presently.' That the uniformities of natural law are the only reliable criteria of the real is inescapable. But such a criterion is *ipso facto* a priori. No conceivable experience could dictate the alteration of a law so long as failure to obey that law marked the content of experience as unreal.

---

[1] Albert Einstein, *Relativity: The Special and General Theory*, trans. R. W. Lawson (New York, 1920), pp. 26–28; italics are the author's.

This is one of the puzzles of empiricism. We deal with experience: what any reality may be which underlies experience, we have to learn. What we desire to discover is natural law, the formulation of those uniformities which obtain amongst the real. But experience as it comes to us contains not only the real but all the content of illusion, dream, hallucination, and mistake. The *given* contains both real and unreal, confusingly intermingled. If we ask for uniformities of this unsorted experience, we shall not find them. Laws which characterize all experience, of real and unreal both, are non-existent and would in any case be worthless. What we seek are the uniformities of the *real*; but *until we have such laws, we cannot sift experience and segregate the real.*

The obvious solution is that the enrichment of experience, the separation of the real from the illusory or meaningless, and the formulation of natural law all grow up together. If the criteria of the real are a priori, that is not to say that no conceivable character of experience would lead to alteration of them. For example, spirits cannot be photographed. But if photographs of spiritistic phenomena, taken under properly guarded conditions, should become sufficiently frequent, this a priori dictum would be called in question. What we should do would be to redefine our terms. Whether 'spook' was spirit or matter, whether the definition of 'spirit' or of 'matter' should be changed—all this would constitute one interrelated problem. We should reopen together the question of definition or classification, of criteria for this sort of real, and of natural law. And the solution of one of these would mean the solution of all. Nothing could *force* a redefinition of spirit or of matter. A sufficiently fundamental relation to human bent, to human interests, would guarantee continuance unaltered even in the face of unintelligible and baffling experiences. In such problems, the mind finds itself uncompelled save by its own purposes and needs. I *may* categorize experience as I will; but *what* categorical distinctions will best serve my interests and objectify my own intelligence? What the mixed and troubled experience shall be—that is beyond me. But what I shall do with it—that is my own question, when the character of experience is sufficiently before me. I am coerced only by my own need to understand.

It would indeed be inappropriate to characterize as a priori a law which we are wholly prepared to alter in the light of further experience, even though in an isolated case we should discard as illusory any experience which failed to conform. But the crux of the situation lies in this: beyond such principles as those of logic, which we seem fully prepared to maintain no matter what, there must be further and more particular criteria of the real prior to any investigation of nature whatever. We cannot even interrogate experience without a network of categories and definitive concepts. And we must further be prepared to say what experimental findings will answer what questions, and how. Without tests which represent anterior principle, there is no question which experience could answer at all. Thus the most fundamental laws in any category—or those which we regard as most fundamental—are a priori, even though continued failure to render experience intelligible in such terms might result eventually in the abandonment of that category altogether. Matters so comparatively small as the behaviour of Mercury and of starlight passing the sun's limb may, if there be persistent failure to bring them within the field of previously accepted modes of explanation, result in the abandonment of the independent categories of space and time. But without the definitions, fundamental principles, and tests of the type which constitute such categories, no experience whatever could prove or disprove anything. And to that mind which should find independent space and time absolutely necessary conceptions, no possible experiment could prove the principles of relativity. . . .

At the bottom of all science and all knowledge are categories and definitive concepts which represent fundamental habits of thought and deep-lying attitudes which the human mind has taken in the light of its total experience. But a new and wider experience may bring about some alteration of these attitudes, even though by themselves they dictate nothing as to the content of experience, and no experience can conceivably prove them invalid.

Perhaps some will object to this conception on the ground that only such principles should be designated a priori as the human mind *must* maintain, no matter what; that if, for example, it is shown possible to arrive at a consistent doctrine of physics in terms of relativity even by the most arduous reconstruction of our fundamental notions, then the present conceptions are by that fact shown not to be a priori. Such objection is especially likely from those who would conceive the a priori in terms of an absolute mind or an absolutely universal human nature. We should readily agree that a decision by popular approval or a congress of scientists or anything short of such a test as would bring to bear the full weight of human capacity and interest would be ill-considered as having to do with the a priori. But we wish to emphasize two facts: first, that in the field of those conceptions and principles which have altered in human history, there are those which could neither be proved nor disproved by any experience, but represent the uncompelled initiative of human thought—that without this uncompelled initiative no growth of science, nor any science at all, would be conceivable; and second, that the difference between such conceptions as are, for example, concerned in the decision of relativity versus absolute space and time, and those more permanent attitudes such as are vested in the laws of logic, there is only a difference of degree. The dividing line between the a priori and the a posteriori is that between principles and definitive concepts which *can* be maintained in the face of all experience and those genuinely empirical generalizations which *might* be proven flatly false. The thought which both rationalism and empiricism have missed is that there are principles, representing the initiative of mind, which impose upon experience no limitations whatever, but that such conceptions are still subject to alteration on pragmatic grounds when the expanding boundaries of experience reveal their infelicity as intellectual instruments.

Neither human experience nor the human mind has a character which is universal, fixed, and absolute. 'The human mind' does not exist at all save in the sense that all humans are very much alike in fundamental respects, and that the language habit and the enormously important exchange of ideas has greatly increased our likeness in those respects which are here in question. Our categories and definitions are peculiarly social products, reached in the light of experiences which have much in common, and beaten out, like other pathways, by the coincidence of human purposes and the exigencies of human co-operation. Concerning the a priori there need be neither universal agreement nor complete historical continuity. Conceptions, such as those of logic, which are least likely to be affected by the opening of new ranges of experience, represent the most stable of our categories; but none of them is beyond the possibility of alteration.

Mind contributes to experience the element of order, of classification, categories, and definition. Without such, experience would be unintelligible. Our knowledge of the validity of these is simply consciousness of our own fundamental ways of acting and our own intellectual intent. Without this element, knowledge is impossible, and it is here that whatever truths are necessary and independent of experience must be found. But the commerce between our categorical ways of acting, our pragmatic interests, and the particular character of experience is closer than we have realized. No explanation of any one of these can be complete without consideration of the other two.

Pragmatism has sometimes been charged with oscillating between two contrary notions: the one, that experience is 'through and through malleable to our purpose'; the other, that facts are 'hard' and uncreated by the mind. We here offer a mediating conception: through all our knowledge runs the element of the a priori, which is indeed malleable to our purpose and responsive to our need. But throughout, there is also that other element of experience which is 'hard,' 'independent,' and unalterable to our will.

Two Dogmas of Empiricism

W. V. O. QUINE

Modern empiricism has been conditioned in large part by two dogmas. One is a belief in some fundamental cleavage between truths which are *analytic*, or grounded in meanings independently of matters of fact, and truths which are *synthetic*, or grounded in fact. The other dogma is *reductionism*: the belief that each meaningful statement is equivalent to some logical construct upon terms which refer to immediate experience. Both dogmas, I shall argue, are ill founded. . . .

I. BACKGROUND FOR ANALYTICITY

Kant's cleavage between analytic and synthetic truths was foreshadowed in Hume's distinction between relations of ideas and matters of fact, and in Leibniz's distinction between truths of reason and truths of fact. Leibniz spoke of the truths of reason as true in all possible worlds. Picturesqueness aside, this is to say that the truths of reason are those which could not possibly be false. In the same vein we hear analytic statements defined as statements whose denials are self-contradictory. But this definition has small explanatory value; for the notion of self-contradictoriness, in the quite broad sense needed for this definition of analyticity, stands in exactly the same need of clarification as does the notion of analyticity itself. The two notions are the two sides of a single dubious coin.

Kant conceived of an analytic statement as one that attributes to its subject no more than is already conceptually contained in the subject. This formulation has two shortcomings: it limits itself to statements of subject-predicate form, and it appeals to a notion of containment which is left at a metaphorical level. But Kant's intent, evident more from the use he makes of the notion of analyticity than from his definition of it, can be restated thus: a statement is analytic when it is true by virtue of meanings and independently of fact. Pursuing this line, let us examine the concept of *meaning* which is presupposed.

We must observe to begin with that meaning is not to be identified with naming, or reference. Consider Frege's example of 'Evening Star' and 'Morning Star.' Understood not merely as a recurrent evening apparition but as a body, the Evening Star is the planet Venus, and the Morning Star is the same. The two singular terms *name* the same thing. But the meanings must be treated as distinct, since the identity 'Evening Star = Morning Star' is a statement of fact established by astronomical observation. If 'Evening Star' and 'Morning Star' were alike in meaning, the identity 'Evening Star = Morning Star' would be analytic.

From *Philosophical Review* 60 (1951). Copyright 1951 Cornell University. Reprinted by permission of the publisher.

Again there is Russell's example of 'Scott' and 'the author of *Waverley*.' Analysis of the meanings of words was by no means sufficient to reveal to George IV that the person named by these two singular terms was one and the same.

The distinction between meaning and naming is no less important at the level of abstract terms. The terms '9' and 'the number of planets' name one and the same abstract entity but presumably must be regarded as unlike in meaning; for astronomical observation was needed, and not mere reflection on meanings, to determine the sameness of the entity in question.

Thus far we have been considering singular terms. With general terms, or predicates, the situation is somewhat different but parallel. Whereas a singular term purports to name an entity, abstract or concrete, a general term does not; but a general term is *true of* an entity, or of each of many, or of none. The class of all entities of which a general term is true is called the *extension* of the term. Now paralleling the contrast between the meaning of a singular term and the entity named, we must distinguish equally between the meaning of a general term and its extension. The general terms 'creature with a heart' and 'creature with a kidney', e.g., are perhaps alike in extension but unlike in meaning.

Confusion of meaning with extension, in the case of general terms, is less common than confusion of meaning with naming in the case of singular terms. It is indeed a commonplace in philosophy to oppose intension (or meaning) to extension, or, in a variant vocabulary, connotation to denotation. . . .

A felt need for meant entities may derive from an earlier failure to appreciate that meaning and reference are distinct. Once the theory of meaning is sharply separated from the theory of reference, it is a short step to recognizing as the business of the theory of meaning simply the synonymy of linguistic forms and the analyticity of statements; meanings themselves, as obscure intermediary entities, may well be abandoned.

The description of analyticity as truth by virtue of meanings started us off in pursuit of a concept of meaning. But now we have abandoned the thought of any special realm of entities called meanings. So the problem of analyticity confronts us anew.

Statements which are analytic by general philosophical acclaim are not, indeed, far to seek. They fall into two classes. Those of the first class, which may be called *logically true*, are typified by:

(1) No unmarried man is married.

The relevant feature of this example is that it is not merely true as it stands, but remains true under any and all reinterpretations of 'man' and 'married.' If we suppose a prior inventory of *logical* particles, comprising 'no,' 'un-,' 'not,' 'if,' 'then,' 'and,' etc., then in general a logical truth is a statement which is true and remains true under all reinterpretations of its components other than the logical particles.

But there is also a second class of analytic statements, typified by:

(2) No bachelor is married.

The characteristic of such a statement is that it can be turned into a logical truth by putting synonyms for synonyms; thus (2) can be turned into (1) by putting 'unmarried man' for its synonym 'bachelor.' We still lack a proper characterization of this second class of analytic statements, and therewith of analyticity generally, inasmuch as we have had in the above description to lean on a notion of "synonymy" which is no less in need of clarification than analyticity itself. . . .

II. DEFINITION

There are those who find it soothing to say that the analytic statements of the second class reduce to those of the first class, the logical truths, by *definition;* 'bachelor,' e.g., is *defined* as 'unmarried man.' But how do we find that 'bachelor' is defined as 'unmarried man'? Who defined it thus, and when? Are we to appeal to the nearest dictionary, and accept the lexicographer's formulation as law? Clearly this would be to put the cart before the horse. The lexicographer is an empirical scientist, whose business is the recording of antecedent facts; and if he glosses 'bachelor' as 'unmarried man' it is because of his belief that there is a relation of synonymy between these forms, implicit in general or preferred usage prior to his own work. The notion of synonymy presupposed here has still to be clarified, presumably in terms relating to linguistic behavior. Certainly the "definition" which is the lexicographer's report of an observed synonymy cannot be taken as the ground of the synonymy.

Definition is not, indeed, an activity exclusively of philologists. Philosophers and scientists frequently have occasion to "define" a recondite term by paraphrasing it into terms of a more familiar vocabulary. But ordinarily such a definition, like the philologist's, is pure lexicography, affirming a relationship of synonymy antecedent to the exposition in hand.

Just what it means to affirm synonymy, just what the interconnections may be which are necessary and sufficient in order that two linguistic forms be properly describable as synonymous, is far from clear; but, whatever these interconnections may be, ordinarily they are grounded in usage. Definitions reporting selected instances of synonymy come then as reports upon usage. . . .

There does, however, remain still an extreme sort of definition which does not hark back to prior synonymies at all; viz., the explicitly conventional introduction of novel notations for purposes of sheer abbreviation. Here the definiendum becomes synonymous with the definiens simply because it has been created expressly for the purpose of being synonymous with the definiens. Here we have a really transparent case of synonymy created by definition; would that all species of synonymy were as intelligible. For the rest, definition rests on synonymy rather than explaining it. . . .

III. INTERCHANGEABILITY

A natural suggestion, deserving close examination, is that the synonymy of two linguistic forms consists simply in their interchangeability in all contexts without change of truth value; interchangeability, in Leibniz's phrase, *salva veritate*. Note that synonyms so conceived need not even be free from vagueness, as long as the vaguenesses match.

But it is not quite true that the synonyms 'bachelor' and 'unmarried man' are everywhere interchangeable *salva veritate*. Truths which become false under substitution of 'unmarried man' for 'bachelor' are easily constructed with help of 'bachelor of arts' or 'bachelor's buttons.' Also with help of quotation, thus:

'Bachelor' has less than ten letters.

Such counterinstances can, however, perhaps be set aside by treating the phrases 'bachelor of arts' and 'bachelor's buttons' and the quotation "bachelor" each as a single indivisible word and then stipulating that the interchangeability *salva veritate* which is to be the touchstone of synonymy is not supposed to apply to fragmentary occurrences inside of a word. This account of synonymy, supposing it acceptable on other counts, has indeed the drawback of appealing to a prior conception of "word" which can be counted on to present difficulties of formulation in its turn. Nevertheless some progress might be claimed in having reduced the problem of synonymy to a problem of wordhood. Let us pursue this line a bit, taking "word" for granted.

The question remains whether interchangeability *salva veritate* (apart from occurrences within words) is a strong enough condition for synonymy, or whether, on the contrary, some nonsynonymous expressions might be thus interchangeable. Now let us be clear that we are not concerned here with synonymy in the sense of complete identity in psychological associations or poetic quality; indeed no two expressions are synonymous in such a sense. We are concerned only with what may be called *cognitive synonymy*. Just what this is cannot be said without successfully finishing the present study; but we know something about it from the need which arose for it in connection with analyticity in Section I. The sort of synonymy needed there was merely such that any analytic statement could be turned into a logical truth by putting synonyms for synonyms. Turning the tables and assuming analyticity, indeed, we could explain cognitive synonymy of terms as follows (keeping to the familiar example): to say that 'bachelor' and 'unmarried man' are cognitively synonymous is to say no more nor less than that the statement:

(3) All and only bachelors are unmarried men is analytic.

What we need is an account of cognitive synonymy not presupposing analyticity—if we are to explain analyticity conversely with help of cognitive synonymy as undertaken in Section I. And indeed such an independent account of cognitive synonymy is at present up for consideration, viz., interchangeability *salva veritate* everywhere except within words. The question before us, to resume the thread at last, is whether such interchangeability is a sufficient condition for cognitive synonymy. We can quickly assure ourselves that it is, by examples of the following sort. The statement:

(4) Necessarily all and only bachelors are bachelors

is evidently true, even supposing 'necessarily' so narrowly construed as to be truly applicable only to analytic statements. Then, *if* 'bachelor' and 'unmarried man' are interchangeable *salva veritate*, the result

(5) Necessarily, all and only bachelors are unmarried men

of putting 'unmarried man' for an occurrence of 'bachelor' in (4) must, like (4), be true. But to say that (5) is true is to say that (3) is analytic, and hence that 'bachelor' and 'unmarried men' are cognitively synonymous.

Let us see what there is about the above argument that gives it its air of hocus-pocus. The condition of interchangeability *salva veritate* varies in its force with variations in the richness of the language at hand. The above argument supposes we are working with a language rich enough to contain the adverb 'necessarily,' this adverb being so construed as to yield truth when and only when applied to an analytic statement. But can we condone a language which contains such an adverb? Does the adverb really make sense? To suppose that it does is to suppose that we have already made satisfactory sense of 'analytic.' Then what are we so hard at work on right now?

Our argument is not flatly circular, but something like it. It has the form, figuratively speaking, of a closed curve in space.

Interchangeability *salva veritate* is meaningless until relativized to a language whose extent is specified in relevant respects. Suppose now we consider a language containing just the following materials. There is an indefinitely large stock of one- and many-place predicates, mostly having to do with extralogical subject matter. The rest of the language is logical. The atomic sentences consist each of a predicate followed by one or more variables; and the complex sentences are built up of atomic ones by truth functions and quantification. In effect such a language enjoys the benefits also of descriptions and class names and indeed singular terms generally, these being contextually definable in known ways. Such a language can be adequate to classical mathematics and indeed to scientific discourse generally, except in so far as the latter involves debatable devices such as modal adverbs and contrary-to-fact conditionals. Now a language of this type is *extensional*, in this sense: any two predicates which *agree extensionally* (i.e., are true of the same objects) are interchangeable *salva veritate*.

In an extensional language, therefore, interchangeability *salva veritate* is no assurance of cognitive synonymy of the desired type. That 'bachelor' and 'unmarried man' are interchangeable *salva veritate* in an extensional language assures us of no more than that (3) is true. There is no assurance here that the extensional agreement of 'bachelor' and 'unmarried man' rests on meaning rather than merely on accidental matters of fact, as does extensional agreement of 'creature with a heart' and 'creature with a kidney.'

For most purposes extensional agreement is the nearest approximation to synonymy we need care about. But the fact remains that extensional agreement falls far short of cognitive synonymy of the type required for explaining analyticity in the manner of Section I. The type of cognitive synonymy required there is such as to equate the synonymy of 'bachelor' and 'unmarried man' with the analyticity of (3), not merely with the truth of (3).

So we must recognize that interchangeability *salva veritate*, if construed in relation to an extensional language, is not a sufficient condition of cognitive synonymy in the sense needed for deriving analyticity in the manner of Section I. If a language contains an intensional adverb 'necessarily' in the sense lately noted, or other particles to the same effect, then interchangeability *salva veritate* in such a language does afford a sufficient condition of cognitive synonymy; but such a language is intelligible only if the notion of analyticity is already clearly understood in advance. . . .

. . . Certain technical questions arise, indeed, over cases of ambiguity or homonymy; let us not pause for them, however, for we are already digressing. . . .

It is obvious that truth in general depends on both language and extralinguistic fact. The statement 'Brutus killed Caesar' would be false if the world had been different in certain ways, but it would also be false if the word 'killed' happened rather to have the sense of 'begat.' Hence the temptation to suppose in general that the truth of a statement is somehow analyzable into a linguistic component and a factual component. Given this supposition, it next seems reasonable that in some statements the factual component should be null; and these are the analytic statements. But, for all its a priori reasonableness, a boundary between analytic and synthetic statements simply has not been drawn. That there is such a distinction to be drawn at all is an unempirical dogma of empiricists, a metaphysical article of faith. . . .

Nineteenth-Century Idealism
and Twentieth-Century Textualism (1981)

Richard Rorty

I

In the last century there were philosophers who argued that nothing exists but ideas. In our century there are people who write as if there were nothing but texts. These people, whom I shall call "textualists," include for example the so-called "Yale school" of literary criticism centering around Harold Bloom, Geoffrey Hartmann, J. Hillis Miller, and Paul De Man, "post-structuralist" French thinkers like Jacques Derrida and Michel Foucault, historians like Hayden White, and social scientists like Paul Rabinow. Some of these people take their point of departure from Heidegger, but usually the influence of philosophers is relatively remote. The center of gravity of the intellectual movement in which these people figure is not philosophy, but literary criticism. In this paper I want to discuss some similarities and differences between this movement and nineteenth-century idealism.

The first similarity is that both movements adopt an antagonistic position to natural science. Both suggest that the natural scientist should not be the dominant cultural figure, that scientific knowledge is not what really matters. Both insist that there is a point of view other than, and somehow higher than, that of science. They warn us against the idea that human thought culminates in the application of "scientific method." Both offer to what C. P. Snow called "the literary culture" a self-image, and a set of rhetorical devices.

The second similarity is that both insist that we can never compare human thought or language with bare, unmediated reality. The idealists started off from Berkeley's claim that nothing can be like an idea except another idea. The textualists start off from the claim that all problems, topics, and distinctions are language-relative—the results of our having chosen to use a certain vocabulary, to play a certain language-game. Both use this point to put natural science in its place. The concepts of natural science, idealists pointed out, were shown by Kant to be merely instruments which the mind uses to synthesize sense-impressions; science, therefore, can know only a phenomenal world. In textualist terms, this becomes the claim that the vocabulary of science is merely one among others—merely the vocabulary which happens to be handy in predicting and controlling nature. It is not, as physicalism would have us think, Nature's Own Vocabulary. Both use the same point to exalt the function of art. For the idealists, art could put us in touch with that part of ourselves—the noumenal, free, spiritual part—which science cannot see. For the textualists, the literary artist's awareness that he is making rather than finding, and more specifically the ironic modernist's awareness that he is responding to texts rather than to things, puts him one up on the scientist. Both movements treat the scientist as naive in thinking that he is doing something *more* than putting together ideas, or constructing new texts.

I hope that these two similarities are enough to justify my attempt to view textualism as the contemporary counterpart of idealism—the textualists as spiritual descendants of the idealists, the species having adapted to a changed environment. The differences in environment, I shall claim, consist in the fact that in the early nineteenth century there was a well-defined and well-regarded discipline, philosophy, which had claims to be architectonic for culture, and within which metaphysical theses could be argued. In our culture there is no such discipline. Idealism was based upon a metaphysical thesis, but textualism is not. When philosophers like Derrida say things like "there is nothing outside the text" they are not making theoretical remarks, remarks backed up by epistemological or semantical arguments. Rather, they are saying, cryptically and aphoristically, that a certain framework of interconnected ideas—truth as correspondence, language as picture, literature as imitation—ought to be abandoned. They are not, however, claiming to have discovered the *real* nature of truth or language or literature. Rather, they say that the very notion of discovering the *nature* of such things is part of the intellectual framework which we must abandon—part of what Heidegger calls "the metaphysics of presence," or "the onto-theological tradition."

If one repudiates that tradition, one repudiates the notion which once held realists and idealists together in a single enterprise called "philosophy"—the notion that there is a nonempirical quasi-science which can weigh the considerations for and against a certain view of what reality or knowledge is like. When textualists claim that issues such as those between nineteenth-century idealists and positivists were created by an outdated vocabulary, and are to be dismissed rather than (as some contemporary analytic philosophers would wish) reformulated and made precise, they do not attempt to defend this claim by anything one could call a "philosophical argument." Textualists sometimes, it is true, claim that Heidegger ended metaphysics, just as positivists used to smugly claim that Carnap had. Smugness, however, is all the cases have in common. Heidegger did not announce a new philosophical discovery, in the way in which Carnap claimed to have discovered something about language. The whole idea of adopting a new vocabulary because *something has been discovered to be the case* is just one more element in that "metaphysics of presence" which Heidegger wants to deconstruct.

I have been saying, first, that idealism and textualism have in common an opposition to the claim of science to be a paradigm of human activity, and, second, that they differ in that one is a philosophical doctrine and the other an expression of suspicion about philosophy. I can put these two points together by saying that whereas nineteenth-century idealism wanted to substitute one sort of science (philosophy) for another (natural science) as the center of culture, twentieth-century textualism wants to place literature in the center, and to treat both science and philosophy as, at best, literary genres. The rest of my paper will be an attempt to refine this crude formula and to make it plausible. I shall begin by defining its component terms in the senses in which I wish to use them.

By 'science' I shall mean the sort of activity in which argument is relatively easy—in which one can agree on some general principles which govern discourse in an area, and then aim at consensus by tracing inferential chains between these principles and more particular and more interesting propositions. Philosophy since Kant has purported to be a science which could sit in judgment on all the other sciences. As the science of knowledge, the science of science, *Wissen-schaftslehre, Erkenntnistheorie*, it claimed to discover those general principles which made scientific discourse scientific, and thus to "ground" both the other sciences and itself.

It is a feature of a science that the vocabulary in which problems are posed is accepted by all those who count as contributing to the subject. The vocabulary may be changed, but that is only because a new theory has been discovered which explains the phenomena better by invoking a new set of theoretical terms. The vocabulary in which the *explananda* are described has to remain constant. It is a feature of what I shall call "literature" that one can achieve success by introducing a quite new genre of poem or novel or critical essay *without* argument. It succeeds simply by its success, not because there are good reasons why poems or novels or essays should be written in the new way rather than the old. There is no constant vocabulary in which to describe the values to be defended or objects to be imitated, or the emotions to be expressed, or whatever, in essays or poems or novels. The reason "literary criticism" is "unscientific" is just that whenever somebody tries to work up such a vocabulary he makes a fool of himself. We don't *want* works of literature to be criticizable within a terminology we already know; we want both those works and criticism of them to give us *new* terminologies. By 'literature,' then, I shall mean the areas of culture which, quite self-consciously, forego agreement on an encompassing critical vocabulary, and thus forego argumentation.

Though obviously crude, this way of separating science and literature has at least the merit of focusing attention on a distinction which is relevant to both idealism and textualism—the distinction between finding out whether a proposition is true and finding out whether a vocabulary is good. Let me call "romanticism" the thesis that what is most important for human life is not what propositions we believe but what vocabulary we use. Then I can say that romanticism is what unites metaphysical idealism and literary textualism. Both, as I said earlier, remind us that scientists do not bring a naked eye to nature, that the propositions of science are not simple transcriptions of what is present to the senses. Both draw the corollary that the current scientific vocabulary is one vocabulary among others, and that there is no need to give it primacy, nor to reduce other vocabularies to it. Both see the scientists' claim to discover the ways things really are as needing qualification, as a pretension which needs to be curbed. The scientist, they say, is discovering "merely scientific" or "merely empirical" or "merely phenomenal" or "merely positive" or "merely technical" truths. Such dismissive epithets express the suspicion that the scientist merely goes through mechanical procedures, checking off the truth-value of propositions—behaving like a glorified stockroom clerk inventorying the universe in accord with a predetermined scheme. The sense that science is banausic, except perhaps in those rare creative moments when a Galileo or a Darwin suddenly imposes a new scheme, is the essence of romanticism. Romanticism inverts the values which, in the third *Critique*, Kant assigned to the determinate and the reflective judgment. It sees the determinate judgment—the activity which ticks off instances of concepts by invoking common, public criteria—as producing merely *agreement*. Kant thought "knowledge," the name for the result of such activity, was a term of praise. Romanticism accepts Kant's point that objectivity is conformity to rule, but changes the emphasis, so that objectivity becomes *mere* conformity to rule, merely going along with the crowd, merely consensus. By contrast, romanticism sees the reflective judgment—the activity of operating without rules, of searching for concepts under which to group particulars (or, by extension, of constructing new concepts which are "transgressive" in that they do not fit under any of the old rules)—as what really matters. Kant, in saying that aesthetic judgment is noncognitive because it cannot be brought under rules, is assigning it a second-best status—the status which the scientific culture has always assigned to the literary culture. Romanticism, on the other hand, when it says that science is *merely* cognitive, is trying to turn the tables.

I can sum up by saying that post-Kantian metaphysical idealism was a specifically philosophical form of romanticism whereas textualism is a specifically post-philosophical form. In the next section I shall argue that philosophy and idealism rose and fell together. In section III I shall discuss the relation between textualism as post-philosophical romanticism and pragmatism, arguing that pragmatism is, to speak oxymoronically, post-philosophical philosophy. Finally, in section IV, I shall take up some criticisms which apply equally to textualism and to pragmatism.

II

. . . If you just spring the question "what is the ultimate nature of reality?" on somebody, he won't know where to begin. One needs a sense of what some possible answers might be. . . .

In order to have such a notion one needs an idea of what such an alternative view might be. Idealism—the view that the ultimate nature of reality is "revealed through those traits which distinguish man as a spiritual being" is not just *a* possibility; it is pretty much the *only* possibility which has ever been offered. But, in Berkeley and Kant, idealism becomes something very different from the tradition which starts with Anaxagoras and runs through Plato and various forms of Platonism. None of these various suggestions that the material world is unreal were presented as the outcome of scientific argumentation—as a solution to an outstanding scientific difficulty. For Berkeley, however, this is just what idealism was—a neat way of coping with the difficulty which had been created by the new and "scientific" doctrine that the mind perceives only its own ideas. As George Pitcher says, the "beautiful and extravagant" Berkeleian philosophy has among its roots a "sober, well-informed account of . . . sense-perception."[1] The problem which Berkeley confronted was raised by the fact that, as Hume put it "'tis universally allowed by philosophers that nothing is ever really present with the mind but its perceptions or impressions and ideas, and that external objects become known to us only by those perceptions they occasion."[2] The "philosophers" in question were people like Locke, who were doing what we would call psychology, and especially perceptual psychology. Berkeley took himself out of the running as a psychologist by proposing too "quick and dirty" a solution to the puzzle about which ideas resembled their objects—namely, that "*nothing* can be like an idea except an idea." This struck his contemporaries as the panpsychist suggestion that all matter is alive strikes present-day evolutionary biologists. The problem is not that it's a silly idea, but that it is so abstract and empty that it simply doesn't *help*.

Berkeley, however, is important for an understanding of why idealism was taken seriously, even though his own version is only a curiosity. Berkeley's idealism is not Platonic other-worldliness but a sober answer to a scientific question, Locke's question about the resemblance of ideas to their objects. Hume proceeded to generalize Locke's question into the question of whether we were entitled to speak of "objects" at all, and this enabled Kant to change a scientific question about psychophysiological mechanisms into a question about the legitimacy of science itself. He did so by making three points:

a. One can solve the problem of the nature of scientific truth only by saying that science corresponds to a world which is transcendentally idea, made rather than found[.]

b. One can explain the contrast between making and finding, transcendental ideality and transcendental reality, only by contrasting the use of *ideas* to *know* with the use of the *will* to *act*—science with morality[.]

c. Transcendental philosophy, as the discipline which can rise above both science and morality to allot their respective spheres, replaces science as the discipline which tells us about the ultimate nature of reality.

Kant thus finessed the Enlightenment notion of an opposition between science and religion, reason and superstition, by taking over an unsolved scientific problem—the nature of knowledge—and transmuting it into an issue about the *possibility* of knowledge. This transmutation was made possible by taking seriously Berkeley's suggestion that "nothing can be like an idea except an idea," while revising it to read "no idea can be true of anything except a world made of ideas." But this latter notion of a world made of ideas needs to be backed up with an explanation of whose ideas these are. Since Berkeley's God was not available to Kant, he had to create the transcendental ego to do the job. As Kant's successors were quick to point out, the only way we could make sense of the transcendental ego was to identify it with the thinkable but unknowable self who is a moral agent—the autonomous noumenal self.

At this point idealism ceases to be a mere intellectual curiosity. For now it offers us not *just* Berkeley's gimmicky *ad hoc* solution to the problem of the relation between sensations and external objects, but a solution to the problem of how to fit art, religion, and morality into the Galilean world-picture. Once one could see a solution to this slightly shamefaced spiritual difficulty as a corollary to the solution of a perfectly respectable scientific problem, one could see the discipline which offered both solutions as *replacing science*, and making respectable Rousseau's distrust of the Enlightenment. Philosophy thus gets to be both a *science* (for has it not solved a problem science was unable to solve?) and a way to regain what science had seemed to take away—morality and religion. Morality and religion could now be encompassed within the bounds of reason alone. For reason had been discovered by philosophy to be wider than science, and philosophy had thus shown itself to be a *super*-science.

So far I have been arguing that transcendental idealism was necessary to make sense of the notion that a discipline called "philosophy" could transcend both religion and science by giving you a third, decisive view about the ultimate nature of reality. The Kantian system, on my account, began by borrowing the prestige of science through its solution to a scientific problem, and then proceeded to demote science to the second rank of cultural activities. It promoted philosophy to the first rank by showing you how to have the best of both religion and science, while looking down on both. Idealism seemed a scientific thesis—a thesis for which one might actually *argue*—because of what Berkeley and Kant had in common, namely, a concern with Locke's psychological problem about the relation of sensations to their objects. Philosophy came to look like a super-science because of what Kant and Hegel had in common—namely, a solution to the problem of the relation of science to art, morality, and religion. One side of transcendental idealism is turned toward Newton, Locke, the way of ideas, and the problem of perception. The other faces toward Schiller, Hegel, and romanticism. This ambivalence helps explain why, in the first decades of the nineteenth century, transcendental idealism could look like demonstrable truth. It also helps explain why transcendental philosophy could seem as dramatically new and permanent an addition to culture as Newtonian science had seemed a century earlier. Both illusions were possible only because the prestige of one side of Kant was borrowed by the other side. The argumentative character which the first *Critique* shares with Newton's *Principia* and Locke's *Essay* created an aura of *Wissenschaftlichkeit* which stretched over the second and third *Critiques*, and even over Fichte.

The next step in the development of idealism, however, was the beginning of the end for both idealism and philosophy. Hegel decided that philosophy should be speculative rather than merely reflective, changed the name of the Transcendental Ego to "the Idea," and began treating the vocabulary of Galilean science as simply one among dozens of others in which the Idea chose to describe itself. If Kant had survived to read the *Phenomenology* he would have realized that philosophy had only managed to stay on the secure path of a science for about twenty-five years. Hegel kept the name of "science" without the distinctive mark of science—willingness to accept a neutral vocabulary in which to state problems, and thereby make argumentation possible. Under cover of Kant's invention, a new superscience called "philosophy," Hegel invented a literary genre which lacked any trace of argumentation, but which obsessively captioned itself *System der Wissenschaft* or *Wissenschaft der Logik*, or *Encyklopädie der philosophischen Wissenschaften*.

By the time of Marx and Kierkegaard, everybody was saying that the emperor had no clothes—that whatever idealism might be it was not a demonstrable, quasi-scientific thesis. By the end of the century (the time of Green and

Royce) idealism had been trimmed back to its Fichtean form—an assemblage of dusty Kantian arguments about the relation between sensation and judgment, combined with intense moral earnestness. But what Fichte had been certain was both demonstrable truth and the beginning of a new era in human history, Green and Royce disconsolately knew to be merely the opinion of a group of professors. . . .

III

What survived from the disappearance of metaphysical idealism as a scientific, arguable thesis was, simply, romanticism. In section I, I defined 'romanticism' as the thesis that the one thing needful was to discover not which propositions are true but rather what vocabulary we should use. This may sound both vague and innocuous, but I think that it is the best formula to express the sense of liberation from science which was Hegel's chief legacy to the nineteenth century. Hegel left Kant's ideal of philosophy-as-science a shambles, but he did, as I have said, create a new literary genre, a genre which exhibited the relativity of significance to choice of vocabulary, the bewildering variety of vocabularies from which we can choose, and the intrinsic instability of each. Hegel made unforgettably clear the deep self-certainty given by each achievement of a new vocabulary, each new genre, each new style, each new dialectical synthesis—the sense that now, at last, for the first time, we have grasped things as they truly are. He also made unforgettably clear why such certainty lasts but a moment. He showed how the passion which sweeps through each generation serves the cunning of reason, providing the impulse which drives that generation to self-immolation and transformation. He writes in that tone of belatedness and irony which is characteristic of the literary culture of the present day.

Hegel's romantic description of how thought works is appropriate for post-Hegelian politics and literature and almost entirely inappropriate for science. One can respond to this difference by saying "So much the worse for Hegel," or by saying "So much the worse for science." The choice between those responses is a choice between Snow's "two cultures" (and between "analytic" and "Continental" philosophy, which are, so to speak, the public relations agencies for those two cultures). From Hegel on, intellectuals who wished to transform the world or themselves, who wished for more than science could give, felt entitled simply to *forget* about science. Hegel had put the study of nature in its place—a relatively low one. Hegel had also shown that there can be a kind of rationality without argumentation, a rationality which works outside the bounds of what Kuhn calls a "disciplinary matrix," in an ecstasy of spiritual freedom. Reason cunningly employed Hegel, contrary to his own intentions, to write the charter of our modern literary culture. This is the culture which claims to have taken over and reshaped whatever is worth keeping in science, philosophy, and religion—looking down on all three from a higher standpoint. . . .

I would claim, then, that the principal legacy of metaphysical idealism is the ability of the literary culture to stand apart from science, to assert its spiritual superiority to science, to claim to embody what is most important for human beings. Kant's suggestion that using the vocabulary of *Verstand*, of science, was simply *one* of the good things human beings could do, was a first and absolutely crucial step in making a secular but nonscientific culture respectable. Hegel's inadvertent exemplification of what such a culture could offer—namely, the historical sense of the relativity of principles and vocabularies to a place and time, the romantic sense that everything can be changed by talking in new terms—was the second, no less necessary step. The romanticism which Hegel brought to philosophy reinforced the hope that literature might be the successor subject to philosophy—that what the philosophers had been seeking, the inmost secrets of the spirit, were to be discovered by the new literary genres which were emerging.

There was, however, a third step in the process of establishing the autonomy and supremacy of the literary culture. This was the step taken by Nietzsche and William James. Their contribution was to replace romanticism by pragmatism. Instead of saying that the discovery of vocabularies could bring hidden secrets to light, they said that new ways of speaking could help get us what we want. Instead of hinting that literature might succeed philosophy as discoverer of ultimate reality, they gave up the notion of truth as a correspondence to reality. Nietzsche and James said, in different tones of voice, that philosophy *itself* had only the status which Kant and Fichte had assigned to science—the creation of useful or comforting pictures. Nietzsche and James interpreted metaphysical idealism, and, more generally, the metaphysical urge to say something about "the ultimate nature of reality," in psychological terms. Marx, of course, had already done this, but unlike Marx, James and Nietzsche did not attempt to formulate a new philosophical position from which to look down on idealism. Instead, they self-consciously abandoned the search for an Archimedean point from which to survey culture. They abandoned the notion of philosophy as super-science. They applied Kant's and Hegel's metaphors of making (as opposed to traditional realist metaphors of finding) not only to Kant and Hegel but to *themselves*. As Nietzsche said, they were the first generation not to believe that they had the truth. So they were content to have *no* answer to the question "Where do you stand when you say all these terrible things about other people?" They were content to take the halo off words like 'truth' and 'science' and 'knowledge' and 'reality,' rather than offering a view about the nature of the things named by these words.

This replacement of romanticism by pragmatism within philosophy was paralleled by a change in the literary culture's self-conception. The great figures of that culture in our century—the great "modernists," if you like— have tried to show what our lives might be like if we had no hope of what

Nietzsche called "metaphysical comfort." The movement I am calling "textualism" stands to pragmatism and to this body of literature as the nineteenth-century attempt to make literature a discoverer of ultimate truth stood to metaphysical idealism and to Romantic poetry. I think we shall best understand the role of textualism within our culture if we see it as an attempt to think through a thorough-going pragmatism, a thorough-going abandonment of the notion of *discovering the truth* which is common to theology and science. . . .

I can summarize what I've been saying as follows. Metaphysical idealism was a momentary, though important, stage in the emergence of romanticism. The notion that philosophy might replace science as a secular substitute for religion was a momentary, though important, stage in the replacement of science by literature as the presiding cultural discipline. Romanticism was *aufgehoben* in pragmatism, the claim that the significance of new vocabularies was not their ability to decode but their mere utility. Pragmatism is the philosophical counterpart of literary modernism, the kind of literature which prides itself on its autonomy and novelty rather than its truthfulness to experience or its discovery of pre-existing significance. . . . The pragmatist reminds us that a new and useful vocabulary is just *that*, not a sudden unmediated vision of things or texts as they are.

As usual with pithy little formulae, the Derridean claim that "There is nothing outside the text" is right about what it implicitly denies and wrong about what it explicitly asserts. The *only* force of saying that texts do not refer to nontexts is just the old pragmatist chestnut that any specification of a referent is going to be in some vocabulary. Thus one is really comparing two descriptions of a thing rather than a description with the thing-in-itself. This chestnut, in turn, is just an expanded form of Kant's slogan that "Intuitions without concepts are blind," which, in turn, was just a sophisticated restatement of Berkeley's ingenuous remark that "nothing can be like an idea except an idea." These are all merely misleading ways of saying that we shall not see reality plain, unmasked, naked to our gaze. Textualism has nothing to add to this claim except a new misleading image—the image of the world as consisting of everything written in all the vocabularies used so far. The practices of the textualists have nothing to add save some splendid examples of the fact that the author of a text did not know a vocabulary in which his text can usefully be described. But this insight—that a person's own vocabulary of self-description is not necessarily the one which helps us understand him—does not need any metaphysical or epistemological or semantic back-up. It is the sort of claim which becomes convincing only through the accumulation of examples of the practices it inspires. Strong textualists like Bloom and Foucault are busy providing us with such examples.

I conclude, therefore, that textualism has nothing to add to romanticism and pragmatism save instances of what can be achieved once one stops being bothered by realistic questions such as "Is that what the text really *says*?" or "How could one *argue* that that is what the poem is really *about*?" or "How are we to distinguish between what is in the text from what the critic is imposing upon it?" The claim that the world is nothing but texts is simply the same sort of light-hearted extravagance as the claim that it is nothing but matter in motion, or a permanent possibility of sensation, or the sensible material of our duty. Taken in a strong and ironic sense, the claim that everything is texts can be read as saying: "It makes as much sense to say that atoms are simply Democritean texts as to say that Democritus is merely a collection of atoms. That is because both slogans are attempts to give one vocabulary a privileged status, and are therefore equally silly." Taken in a weakly literal-minded sense, however, this claim is just one more metaphysical thesis. There are, alas, people nowadays who owlishly inform us "philosophy has *proved*" that language does not refer to anything nonlinguistic, and thus that everything one can talk about is a text. This claim is on a par with the claim that Kant proved that we cannot know about things-in-themselves. Both claims rest on a phony contrast between some sort of nondiscursive unmediated vision of the real and the way we actually talk and think. Both falsely infer from "We can't think without concepts, or talk without words" to "We can't think or talk except about what has been created by our thought or talk."

The *weakest* way to defend the plausible claim that literature has now displaced religion, science, and philosophy as the presiding discipline of our culture is by looking for a philosophical foundation for the practises of contemporary criticism.[3] That would be like defending Galilean science by claiming that it can be found in the Scriptures, or defending transcendental idealism as the latest result of physiological research. It would be acknowledging the authority of a deposed monarch in order to buttress the claims of a usurper. The claims of a usurping discipline to preside over the rest of culture can only be defended by an exhibition of its ability to put the other disciplines in their places. This is what the literary culture has been doing recently, with great success. It is what science did when it displaced religion and what idealist philosophy did when it briefly displaced science. Science did not *demonstrate* that religion was false, nor philosophy that science was merely phenomenal, nor can modernist literature or textualist criticism *demonstrate* that the "metaphysics of presence" is an outdated genre. But each in turn has managed, without argument, to make its point. . . .

Notes

1. George Pitcher, *Berkeley* (London: Routledge, Kegan Paul, 1977), p. 4.
2. David Hume, *Treatise of Human Nature*, I, ii, 2.
3. Thus when Geoffrey Hartman says, in the preface to *Deconstruction and Criticism* (New York: The Seabury Press, 1979, p. 6) that it would be fruitful for literary criticism and philosophy to interact, he strikes me as simply being courteous to a defeated foe. But perhaps he may be read simply as

saying, quite rightly, that it would be useful if people who had read a lot of philosophy books would join with people who had read a lot of poetry and novels in relating these two streams of texts to one another.

Study Questions

1. What is the defining thesis of Lewis's "A Pragmatic Conception of the A Priori," and how well does he defend his thesis? Defend your answer.
2. Lewis is sometimes characterized as a Neo-pragmatist. What, if anything, do you find in "A Pragmatic Conception of the A Priori" to defend this characterization? Explain.
3. What, according to Quine, is the first of the "two dogmas of empiricism" and what does this first "dogma" entail or involve? Develop your answer fully.
4. What does Quine understand by the words "analytic" and "synthetic" as each applies to a certain class of sentences? Does Quine accept this distinction? Defend your claim.
5. In what sense does the central argument of "Two Dogmas of Empiricism" help to enrich one's understanding of empiricism and its problems? Explain.
6. What is the central thesis in Rorty's "Nineteenth-Century Idealism and Twentieth-Century Textualism"? Explain fully and carefully.
7. Do you agree with Rorty's description of the parallels between traditional idealism and what he calls "textualism"? Defend your answer.
8. For Rorty, what are some important similarities between textualism and the pragmatism of Nietzsche and William James? Be specific. Do you agree that these similarities are genuine? Defend your answer.
9. If Rorty's analysis is correct, what becomes of traditional philosophy and the traditional picture of philosophers? Explain, and defend your answer.

Suggestions for Further Reading

Ammerman, Robert R., ed. *Classics of Analytic Philosophy.* Indianapolis: Hackett Publishing, 1990.

Barrett, Robert B., and Gibson, Roger F., eds. *Perspectives on Quine.* Cambridge, Mass.: Basil Blackwell, 1990.

Caton, Charles E. *Philosophy and Ordinary Language.* Urbana: University of Illinois Press, 1963.

Harris, James F., and Severens, Richard H., eds. *Analyticity.* Chicago: Quadrangle Books, 1970.

Lewis, Clarence Irving. *Mind and World Order: Outline of a Theory of Knowledge*. New York: Charles Scribner's Sons, 1929.

Lewis, Clarence Irving. *An Analysis of Knowledge and Evaluation*. LaSalle, Ill.: Open Court, 1946.

Moser, Paul K., ed. *A Priori Knowledge*. Oxford: Oxford University Press, 1987.

Quine, Willard Van Orman. *Word and Object*. Cambridge, Mass.: MIT Press, 1960.

Quine, Willard Van Orman. *From a Logical Point of View*, revised edition. New York: Harper Torchbooks, 1961.

Rorty, Richard. *Philosophy and the Mirror of Nature*. Princeton: Princeton University Press, 1979.

Rorty, Richard. *Consequences of Pragmatism*. Minneapolis: University of Minnesota Press, 1982.

Rorty, Richard. *Contingency, Irony, and Solidarity*. Cambridge: Cambridge University Press, 1989.

Rosenthal, Sandra B. *The Pragmatic A Priori: A Study of the Epistemology of C. I. Lewis*. St. Louis, Mo.: W. H. Green, 1976.

Schilpp, Paul Arthur, ed. *The Philosophy of C. I. Lewis*. LaSalle, Ill.: Open Court, 1968.

White, Morton. "The Analytic and Synthetic: An Untenable Dualism." *In Pragmatism and the American Mind: Essays and Reviews in Philosophy and Intellectual History*. New York: Oxford University Press, 1973.

Part II
American Ethics, Social and Political Philosophy

Chapter 9

The New American Republic
Revolutionary Ideas and Canonical Documents

The works in this chapter represent the revolutionary thought of four of America's most celebrated statesmen and thinkers. Among the ideas and arguments they put forth are the justification for revolution, the distinction between natural rights and civil rights, the limits of government power, the way that government is to be established to protect and defend individuals' interests and rights, the appropriate division of powers of government, and the obligations of responsible democratic citizenship. Representative and seminal works from Thomas Paine (1737–1809), Thomas Jefferson (1743–1826), James Madison (1751–1836), and John Adams (1735–1826) appear in this chapter and form a backdrop of ideas for ethical, social, and political thought informing the new American republic and continuing to the present day.

The central ideas of these works are infused with the American spirit of democratic reform associated with a realistic and practical optimism regarding the possibility of meaningful and significant progress in American government and society. Such progress includes and depends upon a deep and abiding respect for the intelligence, autonomy, dignity, and rights of the individual citizen as a human being. Self-government requires such respect and in turn is designed to foster and nourish it. For these thinkers, then, the new American republic should be designed and organized so that the interests and aspirations of all individual citizens are taken into account in the workings of the political machinery and accorded their appropriate place in all social and political processes. From Thomas Paine's position on the distinction between government and society to Thomas Jefferson's thoughts on education, morality, and government, there is in these works an expression of the American tradition of impassioned reason leading to determinate action. There is the deep conviction that people must act decisively—from good reasons and with courage—to achieve the full potential of which human beings are capable in their personal and political lives.

There is no doubt that a spirit of reform manifests itself in the words of these representatives of early American social and political thought, all of whom risked their lives, reputations, and fortunes for the realization in practice of the great American experiment in self-government. By acting on principles leading to the creation of an independent American government constructed on ideals of fairness and liberty, the dignity and value of the individual are recognized and defended in a rejection of absolute monarchy, a defense of individual rights, and the determination of appropriate limits on government power. It is the spirit and intent of these American thinkers to further the cause of freedom through the light of reason. Whether it is Paine arguing against monarchy or Adams defending the American constitutions, Jefferson composing the Declaration of Independence or Madison expressing his position regarding the appropriate division of powers in government, the American political mind of the revolutionary era is bent on the establishment of government based on principles expressing and defending fairness, justice, equality, and respect for the individual human being.

There have been dismal failures (the persistence of slavery and oppression) and glorious triumphs in the democratic experiment begun by early theorists and framers of the U.S. Constitution and carried on in subsequent political thought developing from it. But a large part of the beauty, power, and significance of the American experiment is that it *is* an experiment. Because this is the case, failures can be rectified, but even success is not to be taken without question and accepted as a perfect solution. In the American political psyche there is always recognition that things can be done better, that they should be done better, and that it is the responsibility of the citizen, as an active and central participant in political life, to reach toward personal and political improvement. American citizens are guaranteed the right to change and amend the practices and processes upon which the continuing American experience finds its moving force—in the principles informing responsible democratic citizenship and the celebration, employment, and defense of the rights of the individual.

Common Sense (1776)

On the Origin and Design of Government in General

 THOMAS PAINE

Some writers have so confounded society with government as to leave little or no distinction between them; whereas they are not only different, but have different origins. Society is produced by our wants, and government by our wickedness; the former promotes our happiness *positively* by uniting our affections, the latter negatively by restraining our vices. The one encourages intercourse, the other creates distinctions. The first is a patron, the last a punisher.

Society in every state is a blessing, but Government, even in its best state, is but a necessary evil; in its worst state an intolerable one: for when we suffer, or are exposed to the same miseries *by a Government*, which we might expect in a country *without Government*, our calamity is heightened by reflecting that we furnish the means by which we suffer. Government, like dress, is the badge of lost innocence. . . . For were the impulses of conscience clear, uniform and irresistibly obeyed, man would need no other lawgiver; but that not being the case, he finds it necessary to surrender up a part of his property to furnish a means for the protection of the rest; and this he is induced to do by the same prudence which in every other case advises him, out of two evils, to choose the least. Wherefore, security being the true design and end of government, it unanswerably follows that whatever form thereof appears most likely to ensure it to us, with the least expence and greatest benefit, is preferable to all others.

In order to gain a clear and just idea of the design and end of government, let us suppose a small number of persons settled in some sequestered part of the earth, unconnected with the rest; they will then represent the first peopling of any country, or of the world. In this state of natural liberty, society will be their first thought. A thousand motives will excite them thereto; the strength of one man is so unequal to his wants, and his mind so unfitted for perpetual solitude, that he is soon obliged to seek assistance and relief of another, who in his turn requires the same. . . .

Thus necessity . . . would soon form our newly arrived emigrants into society, the reciprocal blessings of which would supersede, and render the obligations of law and government unnecessary while they remained perfectly just to each other; but as nothing but Heaven is impregnable to vice, it will unavoidably happen that in proportion as they surmount the first difficulties of emigration . . . they will begin to relax in their duty and attachment to each other: and this remissness will point out the necessity of establishing some form of government to supply the defect of moral virtue. . . .

But as the Colony encreases, . . . it will become necessary to augment the number of representatives, and that the interest of every part of the colony

From Thomas Paine, *Common Sense*, (New York: The Modern Library) © 1925, pp. 1–40.

may be attended to, it will be found best to divide the whole into convenient parts, each part sending its proper number: and that the *elected* might never form to themselves an interest separate from the *electors*, prudence will point out the propriety of having elections often: because as the *elected* might by that means return and mix again with the general body of the *electors* in a few months, their fidelity to the public will be secured by the prudent reflection of not making a rod for themselves. And as this frequent interchange will establish a common interest with every part of the community, they will mutually and naturally support each other, and on this, (not on the unmeaning name of king,) depends the *strength of government, and the happiness of the governed*.

Here then is the origin and rise of government; namely, a mode rendered necessary by the inability of moral virtue to govern the world; here too is the design and end of government, viz. Freedom and security. . . .

I draw my idea of the form of government from a principle in nature which no art can overturn, viz. that the more simple any thing is, the less liable it is to be disordered, and the easier repaired when disordered. . . .

THOUGHTS ON THE PRESENT STATE OF AMERICAN AFFAIRS

In the following pages I offer nothing more than simple facts, plain arguments, and common sense. . . .

Volumes have been written on the subject of the struggle between England and America. Men of all ranks have embarked in the controversy, from different motives, and with various designs; but all have been ineffectual, and the period of debate is closed. Arms as the last resource decide the contest; the appeal was the choice of the King and the Continent has accepted the challenge. . . .

The Sun never shined on a cause of greater worth. 'Tis not the affair of a City, a County, a Province, or a Kingdom; but of a Continent—of at least one eight part of the habitable Globe. 'Tis not the concern of a day, a year, or an age; posterity are virtually involved in the contest, and will be more or less affected even to the end of time, by the proceedings now. Now is the seed-time of Continental union, faith and honour. . . .

. . . We have boasted the protection of Great Britain, without considering that her motive was *interest*, not *attachment*; and that she did not protect us from *our enemies* on *our account*; but from *her enemies* on *her own account*, from those who had no quarrel with us on any *other account*, and who will always be our enemies on the *same account*. . . .

But Britain is the parent country, say some. Then the more shame upon her conduct. Even brutes do not devour their young, nor savages make war upon their families. Wherefore, the assertion, if true, turns to her reproach. . . . Europe, and not England, is the parent country of America. This new World hath been the asylum for the persecuted lovers of civil and religious liberty from *every part* of Europe. Hither they have fled, not from the tender embraces of the mother, but from the cruelty of the monster. . . .

But, admitting that we were all of English descent, what does it amount to? Nothing. Britain, being now an open enemy, extinguishes every other name and title: and to say that reconciliation is our duty, is truly farcical. The first king of England, of the present line (William the Conqueror) was a Frenchman, and half the peers of England are descendants from the same country; wherefore, by the same method of reasoning, England ought to be governed by France.

Much hath been said of the united strength of Britain and the Colonies, that in conjunction they might bid defiance to the world: But this is mere presumption; the fate of war is uncertain, neither do the expressions mean any thing. . . .

Besides, what have we to do with setting the world at defiance? Our plan is commerce, and that, well attended to, will secure us the peace and friendship of all Europe; because it is in the interest of all Europe to have America a free port. Her trade will always be a protection, and her barrenness of gold and silver secure her from invaders. . . .

I challenge the warmest advocate for reconciliation to show a single advantage that this continent can reap by being connected with Great Britain. . . . Our corn will fetch its price in any market in Europe, and our imported goods must be paid for, buy them where we will.

But the injuries and disadvantages which we sustain by that connection, are without number; and our duty to mankind at large, as well as to ourselves, instruct us to renounce the alliance: because, any submission to, or dependence on, Great Britain, tends directly to involve this Continent in European wars and quarrels, and set us at variance with nations who would otherwise seek our friendship, and against whom we have neither anger nor complaint. As Europe is our market for trade, we ought to form no partial connection with any part of it. . . .

Europe is too thickly planted with Kingdoms to be long at peace, and whenever a war breaks out between England and any foreign power, the trade of America goes to ruin, *because of her connection with Britain.* . . . Everything that is right or reasonable pleads for separation. The blood of the slain, the weeping voice of nature cries, 'TIS TIME TO PART. Even the distance at which the Almighty hath placed England and America is a strong and natural proof that the authority of the one over the other, was never the design of heaven. The time likewise at which the Continent was discovered, adds weight to the argument, and the manner in which it was peopled, encreases the force of it. The Reformation was preceded by the discovery of America: As if the Almighty graciously meant to open a sanctuary to the persecuted in future years, when home should afford neither friendship nor safety.

The authority of Great Britain over this continent, is a form of government, which sooner or later must have an end. . . . As parents, we can have no joy, knowing that this government is not sufficiently lasting to ensure any thing which we may bequeath to posterity. . . .

Small islands not capable of protecting themselves are the proper objects for government to take under their care; but there is something absurd, in supposing a Continent to be perpetually governed by an island. . . .

I am not induced by motives of pride, party, or resentment to espouse the doctrine of separation and independence; I am clearly, positively, and conscientiously persuaded that it is the true interest of this Continent to be so; that every thing short of *that* . . . can afford no lasting felicity,—that it is leaving the sword to our children, and shrinking back at a time when a little more, a little further, would have rendered this Continent the glory of the earth. . . .

. . . The most powerful of all arguments is, that nothing but independence, *i.e.* a Continental form of government, can keep the peace of the Continent and preserve it inviolate from civil wars. . . . For as in absolute governments the King is law, so in free countries the law ought to be king; and there ought to be no other. . . .

A government of our own is our natural right: and when a man seriously reflects on the precariousness of human affairs, he will become convinced, that it is infinitely wiser and safer, to form a constitution of our own in a cool deliberate manner, while we have it in our power, than to trust such an interesting event to time and chance. . . .

The U.S. Declaration of Independence (1776)

IN CONGRESS, July 4, 1776.

The unanimous Declaration of the thirteen united States of America,
When in the Course of human events, it becomes necessary for one people to dissolve the political bands which have connected them with another, and to assume among the powers of the earth, the separate and equal station to which the Laws of Nature and of Nature's God entitle them, a decent respect to the opinions of mankind requires that they should declare the causes which impel them to the separation.

We hold these truths to be self-evident, that all men are created equal, that they are endowed by their Creator with certain unalienable Rights, that among these are Life, Liberty and the pursuit of Happiness.—That to secure these rights, Governments are instituted among Men, deriving their just powers from the consent of the governed,—That whenever any Form of Government becomes destructive of these ends, it is the Right of the People to alter or to abolish it, and to institute new Government, laying its foundation on such principles and organizing its powers in such form, as to them shall seem most likely to effect their Safety and Happiness. Prudence, indeed, will dictate that Governments long established should not be changed for light and transient causes; and accordingly all experience hath shewn, that mankind are more disposed to suffer, while evils are sufferable, than to right themselves by abolishing the forms to which they are accustomed. But when a long train of abuses and usurpations, pursuing invariably the same Object evinces a design to reduce them under absolute Despotism, it is their right, it is their duty, to throw off such Government, and to provide new Guards for their future security.—Such has been the patient sufferance of these Colonies; and such is now the necessity which constrains them to alter their former Systems of Government. The history of the present King of Great Britain is a history of repeated injuries and usurpations, all having in direct object the establishment of an absolute Tyranny over these States. To prove this, let Facts be submitted to a candid world.

He has refused his Assent to Laws, the most wholesome and necessary for the public good.

He has forbidden his Governors to pass Laws of immediate and pressing importance, unless suspended in their operation till his Assent should be obtained; and when so suspended, he has utterly neglected to attend to them.

He has refused to pass other Laws for the accommodation of large districts of people, unless those people would relinquish the right of Representation in the Legislature, a right inestimable to them and formidable to tyrants only.

He has called together legislative bodies at places unusual, uncomfortable, and distant from the depository of their public Records, for the sole purpose of fatiguing them into compliance with his measures.

He has dissolved Representative Houses repeatedly, for opposing with manly firmness his invasions on the rights of the people.

He has refused for a long time, after such dissolutions, to cause others to be elected; whereby the Legislative powers, incapable of Annihilation, have returned to the People at large for their exercise; the State remaining in the mean time exposed to all the dangers of invasion from without, and convulsions within.

He has endeavoured to prevent the population of these States; for that purpose obstructing the Laws for Naturalization of Foreigners; refusing to pass others to encourage their migrations hither, and raising the conditions of new Appropriations of Lands.

He has obstructed the Administration of Justice, by refusing his Assent to Laws for establishing Judiciary powers.

He has made Judges dependent on his Will alone, for the tenure of their offices, and the amount and payment of their salaries.

He has erected a multitude of New Offices, and sent hither swarms of Officers to harrass our people, and eat out their substance.

He has kept among us, in times of peace, Standing Armies without the Consent of our legislatures.

He has affected to render the Military independent of and superior to the Civil power.

He has combined with others to subject us to a jurisdiction foreign to our constitution, and unacknowledged by our laws; giving his Assent to their Acts of pretended Legislation:

For Quartering large bodies of armed troops among us:

For protecting them, by a mock Trial, from punishment for any Murders which they should commit on the Inhabitants of these States:

For cutting off our Trade with all parts of the world:

For imposing Taxes on us without our Consent:

For depriving us in many cases, of the benefits of Trial by Jury:

For transporting us beyond Seas to be tried for pretended offences

For abolishing the free System of English Laws in a neighbouring Province, establishing therein an Arbitrary government, and enlarging its Boundaries so as to render it at once an example and fit instrument for introducing the same absolute rule into these Colonies:

For taking away our Charters, abolishing our most valuable Laws, and altering fundamentally the Forms of our Governments:

For suspending our own Legislatures, and declaring themselves invested with power to legislate for us in all cases whatsoever.

He has abdicated Government here, by declaring us out of his Protection and waging War against us.

He has plundered our seas, ravaged our Coasts, burnt our towns, and destroyed the lives of our people.

He is at this time transporting large Armies of foreign Mercenaries to compleat the works of death, desolation and tyranny, already begun with circumstances of Cruelty & perfidy scarcely paralleled in the most barbarous ages, and totally unworthy the Head of a civilized nation.

He has constrained our fellow Citizens taken Captive on the high Seas to bear Arms against their Country, to become the executioners of their friends and Brethren, or to fall themselves by their Hands.

He has excited domestic insurrections amongst us, and has endeavoured to bring on the inhabitants of our frontiers, the merciless Indian Savages, whose known rule of warfare, is an undistinguished destruction of all ages, sexes and conditions.

In every stage of these Oppressions We have Petitioned for Redress in the most humble terms: Our repeated Petitions have been answered only by repeated injury. A Prince whose character is thus marked by every act which may define a Tyrant, is unfit to be the ruler of a free people.

Nor have We been wanting in attentions to our British brethren. We have warned them from time to time of attempts by their legislature to extend an unwarrantable jurisdiction over us. We have reminded them of the circumstances of our emigration and settlement here. We have appealed to their native justice and magnanimity, and we have conjured them by the ties of our common kindred to disavow these usurpations, which, would inevitably interrupt our connections and correspondence. They too have been deaf to the voice of justice and of consanguinity. We must, therefore, acquiesce in the necessity, which denounces our Separation, and hold them, as we hold the rest of mankind, Enemies in War, in Peace Friends.

We, therefore, the Representatives of the united States of America, in General Congress, Assembled, appealing to the Supreme Judge of the world for the rectitude of our intentions, do, in the Name, and by Authority of the good People of these Colonies, solemnly publish and declare, That these United Colonies are, and of Right ought to be Free and Independent States; that they are Absolved from all Allegiance to the British Crown, and that all political connection between them and the State of Great Britain, is and ought to be totally dissolved; and that as Free and Independent States, they have full Power to levy War, conclude Peace, contract Alliances, establish Commerce, and to do all other Acts and Things which Independent States may of right do. And for the support of this Declaration, with a firm reliance on the protection of divine Providence, we mutually pledge to each other our Lives, our Fortunes and our sacred Honor.

Constitution of the United States of America (1787)

We the People of the United States, in Order to form a more perfect Union, establish Justice, insure domestic Tranquility, provide for the common defense, promote the general Welfare, and secure the Blessings of Liberty to ourselves and our Posterity, do ordain and establish this Constitution for the United States of America.

ARTICLE. I.

Section. 1.

All legislative Powers herein granted shall be vested in a Congress of the United States, which shall consist of a Senate and House of Representatives.

Section. 2.

The House of Representatives shall be composed of Members chosen every second Year by the People of the several States, and the Electors in each State shall have the Qualifications requisite for Electors of the most numerous Branch of the State Legislature.

No Person shall be a Representative who shall not have attained to the Age of twenty five Years, and been seven Years a Citizen of the United States, and who shall not, when elected, be an Inhabitant of that State in which he shall be chosen.

Representatives and direct Taxes shall be apportioned among the several States which may be included within this Union, according to their respective Numbers, which shall be determined by adding to the whole Number of free

Persons, including those bound to Service for a Term of Years, and excluding Indians not taxed, three fifths of all other Persons. The actual Enumeration shall be made within three Years after the first Meeting of the Congress of the United States, and within every subsequent Term of ten Years, in such Manner as they shall by Law direct. The Number of Representatives shall not exceed one for every thirty Thousand, but each State shall have at Least one Representative; and until such enumeration shall be made, the State of New Hampshire shall be entitled to chuse three, Massachusetts eight, Rhode-Island and Providence Plantations one, Connecticut five, New-York six, New Jersey four, Pennsylvania eight, Delaware one, Maryland six, Virginia ten, North Carolina five, South Carolina five, and Georgia three.

When vacancies happen in the Representation from any State, the Executive Authority thereof shall issue Writs of Election to fill such Vacancies.

The House of Representatives shall chuse their Speaker and other Officers; and shall have the sole Power of Impeachment.

Section. 3.

The Senate of the United States shall be composed of two Senators from each State, chosen by the Legislature thereof for six Years; and each Senator shall have one Vote.

Immediately after they shall be assembled in Consequence of the first Election, they shall be divided as equally as may be into three Classes. The Seats of the Senators of the first Class shall be vacated at the Expiration of the second Year, of the second Class at the Expiration of the fourth Year, and of the third Class at the Expiration of the sixth Year, so that one third may be chosen every second Year; and if Vacancies happen by Resignation, or otherwise, during the Recess of the Legislature of any State, the Executive thereof may make temporary Appointments until the next Meeting of the Legislature, which shall then fill such Vacancies.

No Person shall be a Senator who shall not have attained to the Age of thirty Years, and been nine Years a Citizen of the United States, and who shall not, when elected, be an Inhabitant of that State for which he shall be chosen.

The Vice President of the United States shall be President of the Senate, but shall have no Vote, unless they be equally divided.

The Senate shall chuse their other Officers, and also a President pro tempore, in the Absence of the Vice President, or when he shall exercise the Office of President of the United States.

The Senate shall have the sole Power to try all Impeachments. When sitting for that Purpose, they shall be on Oath or Affirmation. When the President of the United States is tried, the Chief Justice shall preside: And no Person shall be convicted without the Concurrence of two thirds of the Members present.

Judgment in Cases of Impeachment shall not extend further than to removal from Office, and disqualification to hold and enjoy any Office of honor, Trust or Profit under the United States: but the Party convicted shall nevertheless be liable and subject to Indictment, Trial, Judgment and Punishment, according to Law.

Section. 4.

The Times, Places and Manner of holding Elections for Senators and Representatives, shall be prescribed in each State by the Legislature thereof; but the Congress may at any time by Law make or alter such Regulations, except as to the Places of chusing Senators.

The Congress shall assemble at least once in every Year, and such Meeting shall be on the first Monday in December, unless they shall by Law appoint a different Day.

Section. 5.

Each House shall be the Judge of the Elections, Returns and Qualifications of its own Members, and a Majority of each shall constitute a Quorum to do Business; but a smaller Number may adjourn from day to day, and may be authorized to compel the Attendance of absent Members, in such Manner, and under such Penalties as each House may provide.

Each House may determine the Rules of its Proceedings, punish its Members for disorderly Behaviour, and, with the Concurrence of two thirds, expel a Member.

Each House shall keep a Journal of its Proceedings, and from time to time publish the same, excepting such Parts as may in their Judgment require Secrecy; and the Yeas and Nays of the Members of either House on any question shall, at the Desire of one fifth of those Present, be entered on the Journal.

Neither House, during the Session of Congress, shall, without the Consent of the other, adjourn for more than three days, nor to any other Place than that in which the two Houses shall be sitting.

Section. 6.

The Senators and Representatives shall receive a Compensation for their Services, to be ascertained by Law, and paid out of the Treasury of the United States. They shall in all Cases, except Treason, Felony and Breach of the Peace, be privileged from Arrest during their Attendance at the Session of their respective Houses, and in going to and returning from the same; and for any Speech or Debate in either House, they shall not be questioned in any other Place.

No Senator or Representative shall, during the Time for which he was elected, be appointed to any civil Office under the Authority of the United States, which shall have been created, or the Emoluments whereof shall have been encreased during such time; and no Person holding any Office under the United States, shall be a Member of either House during his Continuance in Office.

Section. 7.

All Bills for raising Revenue shall originate in the House of Representatives; but the Senate may propose or concur with Amendments as on other Bills.

Every Bill which shall have passed the House of Representatives and the Senate, shall, before it become a Law, be presented to the President of the

United States: If he approve he shall sign it, but if not he shall return it, with his Objections to that House in which it shall have originated, who shall enter the Objections at large on their Journal, and proceed to reconsider it. If after such Reconsideration two thirds of that House shall agree to pass the Bill, it shall be sent, together with the Objections, to the other House, by which it shall likewise be reconsidered, and if approved by two thirds of that House, it shall become a Law. But in all such Cases the Votes of both Houses shall be determined by Yeas and Nays, and the Names of the Persons voting for and against the Bill shall be entered on the Journal of each House respectively. If any Bill shall not be returned by the President within ten Days (Sundays excepted) after it shall have been presented to him, the Same shall be a Law, in like Manner as if he had signed it, unless the Congress by their Adjournment prevent its Return, in which Case it shall not be a Law.

Every Order, Resolution, or Vote to which the Concurrence of the Senate and House of Representatives may be necessary (except on a question of Adjournment) shall be presented to the President of the United States; and before the Same shall take Effect, shall be approved by him, or being disapproved by him, shall be repassed by two thirds of the Senate and House of Representatives, according to the Rules and Limitations prescribed in the Case of a Bill.

Section. 8.

The Congress shall have Power To lay and collect Taxes, Duties, Imposts and Excises, to pay the Debts and provide for the common Defence and general Welfare of the United States; but all Duties, Imposts and Excises shall be uniform throughout the United States;

To borrow Money on the credit of the United States;

To regulate Commerce with foreign Nations, and among the several States, and with the Indian Tribes;

To establish an uniform Rule of Naturalization, and uniform Laws on the subject of Bankruptcies throughout the United States;

To coin Money, regulate the Value thereof, and of foreign Coin, and fix the Standard of Weights and Measures;

To provide for the Punishment of counterfeiting the Securities and current Coin of the United States;

To establish Post Offices and post Roads;

To promote the Progress of Science and useful Arts, by securing for limited Times to Authors and Inventors the exclusive Right to their respective Writings and Discoveries;

To constitute Tribunals inferior to the supreme Court;

To define and punish Piracies and Felonies committed on the high Seas, and Offences against the Law of Nations;

To declare War, grant Letters of Marque and Reprisal, and make Rules concerning Captures on Land and Water;

To raise and support Armies, but no Appropriation of Money to that Use shall be for a longer Term than two Years;

To provide and maintain a Navy;

To make Rules for the Government and Regulation of the land and naval Forces;

To provide for calling forth the Militia to execute the Laws of the Union, suppress Insurrections and repel Invasions;

To provide for organizing, arming, and disciplining the Militia, and for governing such Part of them as may be employed in the Service of the United States, reserving to the States respectively, the Appointment of the Officers, and the Authority of training the Militia according to the discipline prescribed by Congress;

To exercise exclusive Legislation in all Cases whatsoever, over such District (not exceeding ten Miles square) as may, by Cession of particular States, and the Acceptance of Congress, become the Seat of the Government of the United States, and to exercise like Authority over all Places purchased by the Consent of the Legislature of the State in which the Same shall be, for the Erection of Forts, Magazines, Arsenals, dock-Yards, and other needful Buildings;—And

To make all Laws which shall be necessary and proper for carrying into Execution the foregoing Powers, and all other Powers vested by this Constitution in the Government of the United States, or in any Department or Officer thereof.

Section. 9.

The Migration or Importation of such Persons as any of the States now existing shall think proper to admit, shall not be prohibited by the Congress prior to the Year one thousand eight hundred and eight, but a Tax or duty may be imposed on such Importation, not exceeding ten dollars for each Person.

The Privilege of the Writ of Habeas Corpus shall not be suspended, unless when in Cases of Rebellion or Invasion the public Safety may require it.

No Bill of Attainder or ex post facto Law shall be passed.

No Capitation, or other direct, Tax shall be laid, unless in Proportion to the Census or enumeration herein before directed to be taken.

No Tax or Duty shall be laid on Articles exported from any State.

No Preference shall be given by any Regulation of Commerce or Revenue to the Ports of one State over those of another; nor shall Vessels bound to, or from, one State, be obliged to enter, clear, or pay Duties in another.

No Money shall be drawn from the Treasury, but in Consequence of Appropriations made by Law; and a regular Statement and Account of the Receipts and Expenditures of all public Money shall be published from time to time.

No Title of Nobility shall be granted by the United States: And no Person holding any Office of Profit or Trust under them, shall, without the Consent of the Congress, accept of any present, Emolument, Office, or Title, of any kind whatever, from any King, Prince, or foreign State.

Section. 10.

No State shall enter into any Treaty, Alliance, or Confederation; grant Letters of Marque and Reprisal; coin Money; emit Bills of Credit; make any Thing but gold and silver Coin a Tender in Payment of Debts; pass any Bill of Attainder, ex post facto Law, or Law impairing the Obligation of Contracts, or grant any Title of Nobility.

No State shall, without the Consent of the Congress, lay any Imposts or Duties on Imports or Exports, except what may be absolutely necessary for executing its inspection Laws: and the net Produce of all Duties and Imposts, laid by any State on Imports or Exports, shall be for the Use of the Treasury of the United States; and all such Laws shall be subject to the Revision and Controul of the Congress.

No State shall, without the Consent of Congress, lay any Duty of Tonnage, keep Troops, or Ships of War in time of Peace, enter into any Agreement or Compact with another State, or with a foreign Power, or engage in War, unless actually invaded, or in such imminent Danger as will not admit of delay.

ARTICLE. II.

Section. 1.

The executive Power shall be vested in a President of the United States of America. He shall hold his Office during the Term of four Years, and, together with the Vice President, chosen for the same Term, be elected, as follows:

Each State shall appoint, in such Manner as the Legislature thereof may direct, a Number of Electors, equal to the whole Number of Senators and Representatives to which the State may be entitled in the Congress: but no Senator or Representative, or Person holding an Office of Trust or Profit under the United States, shall be appointed an Elector.

The Electors shall meet in their respective States, and vote by Ballot for two Persons, of whom one at least shall not be an Inhabitant of the same State with themselves. And they shall make a List of all the Persons voted for, and of the Number of Votes for each; which List they shall sign and certify, and transmit sealed to the Seat of the Government of the United States, directed to the President of the Senate. The President of the Senate shall, in the Presence of the Senate and House of Representatives, open all the Certificates, and the Votes shall then be counted. The Person having the greatest Number of Votes shall be the President, if such Number be a Majority of the whole Number of Electors appointed; and if there be more than one who have such Majority, and have an equal Number of Votes, then the House of Representatives shall immediately chuse by Ballot one of them for President; and if no Person have a Majority, then from the five highest on the List the said House shall in like Manner chuse the President. But in chusing the President, the Votes shall be taken by States, the Representation from each State having one Vote; A quorum for this purpose shall consist of a Member or Members from two thirds of the States, and a Majority of all the States shall be necessary to a Choice. In every Case, after the Choice of the President, the Person having the greatest Number of Votes of the Electors shall be the Vice President. But if there should remain two or more who have equal Votes, the Senate shall chuse from them by Ballot the Vice President.

The Congress may determine the Time of chusing the Electors, and the Day on which they shall give their Votes; which Day shall be the same throughout the United States.

No Person except a natural born Citizen, or a Citizen of the United States, at the time of the Adoption of this Constitution, shall be eligible to the Office of President; neither shall any Person be eligible to that Office who shall not have attained to the Age of thirty five Years, and been fourteen Years a Resident within the United States.

In Case of the Removal of the President from Office, or of his Death, Resignation, or Inability to discharge the Powers and Duties of the said Office, the Same shall devolve on the Vice President, and the Congress may by Law provide for the Case of Removal, Death, Resignation or Inability, both of the President and Vice President, declaring what Officer shall then act as President, and such Officer shall act accordingly, until the Disability be removed, or a President shall be elected.

The President shall, at stated Times, receive for his Services, a Compensation, which shall neither be increased nor diminished during the Period for which he shall have been elected, and he shall not receive within that Period any other Emolument from the United States, or any of them.

Before he enter on the Execution of his Office, he shall take the following Oath or Affirmation:—"I do solemnly swear (or affirm) that I will faithfully execute the Office of President of the United States, and will to the best of my Ability, preserve, protect and defend the Constitution of the United States."

Section. 2.

The President shall be Commander in Chief of the Army and Navy of the United States, and of the Militia of the several States, when called into the actual Service of the United States; he may require the Opinion, in writing, of the principal Officer in each of the executive Departments, upon any Subject relating to the Duties of their respective Offices, and he shall have Power to grant Reprieves and Pardons for Offences against the United States, except in Cases of Impeachment.

He shall have Power, by and with the Advice and Consent of the Senate, to make Treaties, provided two thirds of the Senators present concur; and he shall nominate, and by and with the Advice and Consent of the Senate, shall appoint Ambassadors, other public Ministers and Consuls, Judges of the supreme Court, and all other Officers of the United States, whose Appointments are not herein otherwise provided for, and which shall be established by Law: but the Congress may by Law vest the Appointment of such inferior Officers, as they think proper, in the President alone, in the Courts of Law, or in the Heads of Departments.

The President shall have Power to fill up all Vacancies that may happen during the Recess of the Senate, by granting Commissions which shall expire at the End of their next Session.

Section. 3.

He shall from time to time give to the Congress Information of the State of the Union, and recommend to their Consideration such Measures as he shall judge necessary and expedient; he may, on extraordinary Occasions, convene both Houses, or either of them, and in Case of Disagreement between them, with Respect to the Time of Adjournment, he may adjourn them to such Time as he shall think proper; he shall receive Ambassadors and other public Ministers; he shall take Care that the Laws be faithfully executed, and shall Commission all the Officers of the United States.

Section. 4.

The President, Vice President and all civil Officers of the United States, shall be removed from Office on Impeachment for, and Conviction of, Treason, Bribery, or other high Crimes and Misdemeanors.

ARTICLE. III.

Section. 1.

The judicial Power of the United States shall be vested in one supreme Court, and in such inferior Courts as the Congress may from time to time ordain and establish. The Judges, both of the supreme and inferior Courts, shall hold their Offices during good Behaviour, and shall, at stated Times, receive for their Services a Compensation, which shall not be diminished during their Continuance in Office.

Section. 2.

The judicial Power shall extend to all Cases, in Law and Equity, arising under this Constitution, the Laws of the United States, and Treaties made, or which shall be made, under their Authority;—to all Cases affecting Ambassadors, other public Ministers and Consuls;—to all Cases of admiralty and maritime Jurisdiction;—to Controversies to which the United States shall be a Party;—to Controversies between two or more States;—between a State and Citizens of another State;—between Citizens of different States;—between Citizens of the same State claiming Lands under Grants of different States, and between a State, or the Citizens thereof, and foreign States, Citizens or Subjects.

In all Cases affecting Ambassadors, other public Ministers and Consuls, and those in which a State shall be Party, the supreme Court shall have original Jurisdiction. In all the other Cases before mentioned, the supreme Court shall have appellate Jurisdiction, both as to Law and Fact, with such Exceptions, and under such Regulations as the Congress shall make.

The Trial of all Crimes, except in Cases of Impeachment, shall be by Jury; and such Trial shall be held in the State where the said Crimes shall have been committed; but when not committed within any State, the Trial shall be at such Place or Places as the Congress may by Law have directed.

Section. 3.

Treason against the United States, shall consist only in levying War against them, or in adhering to their Enemies, giving them Aid and Comfort. No Person shall be convicted of Treason unless on the Testimony of two Witnesses to the same overt Act, or on Confession in open Court.

The Congress shall have Power to declare the Punishment of Treason, but no Attainder of Treason shall work Corruption of Blood, or Forfeiture except during the Life of the Person attainted.

ARTICLE. IV.

Section. 1.

Full Faith and Credit shall be given in each State to the public Acts, Records, and judicial Proceedings of every other State. And the Congress may by general Laws prescribe the Manner in which such Acts, Records and Proceedings shall be proved, and the Effect thereof.

Section. 2.

The Citizens of each State shall be entitled to all Privileges and Immunities of Citizens in the several States.

A Person charged in any State with Treason, Felony, or other Crime, who shall flee from Justice, and be found in another State, shall on Demand of the executive Authority of the State from which he fled, be delivered up, to be removed to the State having Jurisdiction of the Crime.

No Person held to Service or Labour in one State, under the Laws thereof, escaping into another, shall, in Consequence of any Law or Regulation therein, be discharged from such Service or Labour, but shall be delivered up on Claim of the Party to whom such Service or Labour may be due.

Section. 3.

New States may be admitted by the Congress into this Union; but no new State shall be formed or erected within the Jurisdiction of any other State; nor any State be formed by the Junction of two or more States, or Parts of States, without the Consent of the Legislatures of the States concerned as well as of the Congress.

The Congress shall have Power to dispose of and make all needful Rules and Regulations respecting the Territory or other Property belonging to the United States; and nothing in this Constitution shall be so construed as to Prejudice any Claims of the United States, or of any particular State.

Section. 4.

The United States shall guarantee to every State in this Union a Republican Form of Government, and shall protect each of them against Invasion; and on Application of the Legislature, or of the Executive (when the Legislature cannot be convened), against domestic Violence.

ARTICLE. V.

The Congress, whenever two thirds of both Houses shall deem it necessary, shall propose Amendments to this Constitution, or, on the Application of the Legislatures of two thirds of the several States, shall call a Convention for proposing Amendments, which, in either Case, shall be valid to all Intents and Purposes, as Part of this Constitution, when ratified by the Legislatures of three fourths of the several States, or by Conventions in three fourths thereof, as the one or the other Mode of Ratification may be proposed by the Congress; Provided that no Amendment which may be made prior to the Year One thousand eight hundred and eight shall in any Manner affect the first and fourth Clauses in the Ninth Section of the first Article; and that no State, without its Consent, shall be deprived of its equal Suffrage in the Senate.

ARTICLE. VI.

All Debts contracted and Engagements entered into, before the Adoption of this Constitution, shall be as valid against the United States under this Constitution, as under the Confederation.

This Constitution, and the Laws of the United States which shall be made in Pursuance thereof; and all Treaties made, or which shall be made, under the Authority of the United States, shall be the supreme Law of the Land; and the Judges in every State shall be bound thereby, any Thing in the Constitution or Laws of any State to the Contrary notwithstanding.

The Senators and Representatives before mentioned, and the Members of the several State Legislatures, and all executive and judicial Officers, both of the United States and of the several States, shall be bound by Oath or Affirmation, to support this Constitution; but no religious Test shall ever be required as a Qualification to any Office or public Trust under the United States.

ARTICLE. VII.

The Ratification of the Conventions of nine States, shall be sufficient for the Establishment of this Constitution between the States so ratifying the Same.

The Word, "the," being interlined between the seventh and eighth Lines of the first Page, the Word "Thirty" being partly written on an Erazure in the fifteenth Line of the first Page, The Words "is tried" being interlined between the thirty second and thirty third Lines of the first Page and the Word "the" being interlined between the forty third and forty fourth Lines of the second Page. Attest William Jackson Secretary

Done in Convention by the Unanimous Consent of the States present the Seventeenth Day of September in the Year of our Lord one thousand seven hundred and Eighty seven and of the Independence of the United States of America the Twelfth In witness whereof We have hereunto subscribed our Names. . . .

AMENDMENT I

Congress shall make no law respecting an establishment of religion, or prohibiting the free exercise thereof; or abridging the freedom of speech, or of the press; or the right of the people peaceably to assemble, and to petition the Government for a redress of grievances.

AMENDMENT II

A well regulated Militia, being necessary to the security of a free State, the right of the people to keep and bear Arms, shall not be infringed.

AMENDMENT III

No Soldier shall, in time of peace be quartered in any house, without the consent of the Owner, nor in time of war, but in a manner to be prescribed by law.

AMENDMENT IV

The right of the people to be secure in their persons, houses, papers, and effects, against unreasonable searches and seizures, shall not be violated, and no Warrants shall issue, but upon probable cause, supported by Oath or affirmation, and particularly describing the place to be searched, and the persons or things to be seized.

AMENDMENT V

No person shall be held to answer for a capital, or otherwise infamous crime, unless on a presentment or indictment of a Grand Jury, except in cases arising in the land or naval forces, or in the Militia, when in actual service in time of War or public danger; nor shall any person be subject for the same offence to be twice put in jeopardy of life or limb; nor shall be compelled in any criminal case to be a witness against himself, nor be deprived of life, liberty, or property, without due process of law; nor shall private property be taken for public use, without just compensation.

AMENDMENT VI

In all criminal prosecutions, the accused shall enjoy the right to a speedy and public trial, by an impartial jury of the State and district wherein the crime shall have been committed, which district shall have been previously ascertained by law, and to be informed of the nature and cause of the accusation; to be confronted with the witnesses against him; to have compulsory process for obtaining witnesses in his favor, and to have the Assistance of Counsel for his defence.

AMENDMENT VII

In suits at common law, where the value in controversy shall exceed twenty dollars, the right of trial by jury shall be preserved, and no fact tried by a jury, shall be otherwise reexamined in any Court of the United States, than according to the rules of the common law.

AMENDMENT VIII

Excessive bail shall not be required, nor excessive fines imposed, nor cruel and unusual punishments inflicted.

AMENDMENT IX

The enumeration in the Constitution, of certain rights, shall not be construed to deny or disparage others retained by the people.

AMENDMENT X

The powers not delegated to the United States by the Constitution, nor prohibited by it to the States, are reserved to the States respectively, or to the people.

AMENDMENT XI

Passed by Congress March 4, 1794. Ratified February 7, 1795.

Note: Article III, section 2, of the Constitution was modified by amendment 11.

The Judicial power of the United States shall not be construed to extend to any suit in law or equity, commenced or prosecuted against one of the United States by Citizens of another State, or by Citizens or Subjects of any Foreign State.

AMENDMENT XII

Passed by Congress December 9, 1803. Ratified June 15, 1804.

Note: A portion of Article II, section 1 of the Constitution was superseded by the 12th amendment.

The Electors shall meet in their respective states and vote by ballot for President and Vice President, one of whom, at least, shall not be an inhabitant of the same state with themselves; they shall name in their ballots the person voted for as President, and in distinct ballots the person voted for as Vice President, and they shall make distinct lists of all persons voted for as President, and of all persons voted for as Vice President, and of the number of votes for each, which lists they shall sign and certify, and transmit sealed to the seat of the government of the United States, directed to the President of the Senate;—the President of the Senate shall, in the presence of the Senate and House of Representatives, open all the certificates and the votes shall then be counted;—The person having the greatest number of votes for President, shall be the President, if such number be a majority of the whole number of Electors appointed; and if no person have such majority, then from the persons having the highest numbers not exceeding three on the list of those voted for as President, the House of Representatives shall choose immediately, by ballot, the President. But in choosing the President, the votes shall be taken by states, the representation from each state having one vote; a quorum for this purpose shall consist of a member or members from two-thirds of the states, and a majority of all the states shall be necessary to a choice. [And if the House of Representatives shall not choose a President whenever the right of choice shall devolve upon them, before the fourth day of March next following, then the Vice President shall act as President, as in case of the death or other constitutional disability of the President.—]* The person having the greatest number of votes as Vice President, shall be the Vice President, if such number be a majority of the whole number of Electors appointed, and if no person have a majority, then from the two highest numbers on the list, the Senate shall

---

* Superseded by section 3 of the 20th amendment.

choose the Vice President; a quorum for the purpose shall consist of two-thirds of the whole number of Senators, and a majority of the whole number shall be necessary to a choice. But no person constitutionally ineligible to the office of President shall be eligible to that of Vice President of the United States.

AMENDMENT XIII

Passed by Congress January 31, 1865. Ratified December 6, 1865.

Note: A portion of Article IV, section 2, of the Constitution was superseded by the 13th amendment.

Section 1.

Neither slavery nor involuntary servitude, except as a punishment for crime whereof the party shall have been duly convicted, shall exist within the United States, or any place subject to their jurisdiction.

Section 2.

Congress shall have power to enforce this article by appropriate legislation.

AMENDMENT XIV

Passed by Congress June 13, 1866. Ratified July 9, 1868.

Note: Article I, section 2, of the Constitution was modified by section 2 of the 14th amendment.

Section 1.

All persons born or naturalized in the United States, and subject to the jurisdiction thereof, are citizens of the United States and of the State wherein they reside. No State shall make or enforce any law which shall abridge the privileges or immunities of citizens of the United States; nor shall any State deprive any person of life, liberty, or property, without due process of law; nor deny to any person within its jurisdiction the equal protection of the laws.

Section 2.

Representatives shall be apportioned among the several States according to their respective numbers, counting the whole number of persons in each State, excluding Indians not taxed. But when the right to vote at any election for the choice of electors for President and Vice President of the United States, Representatives in Congress, the Executive and Judicial officers of a State, or the members of the Legislature thereof, is denied to any of the male inhabitants of such State, being twenty-one years of age,* and citizens of the United States, or in any way abridged, except for participation in rebellion, or other crime, the basis of representation therein shall be reduced in the proportion which the number of such male citizens shall bear to the whole number of male citizens twenty-one years of age in such State.

Section 3.

No person shall be a Senator or Representative in Congress, or elector of President and Vice President, or hold any office, civil or military, under the United States, or under any State, who, having previously taken an oath, as a member of Congress, or as an officer of the United States, or as a member of any State legislature, or as an executive or judicial officer of any State, to support the Constitution of the United States, shall have engaged in insurrection or rebellion against the same, or given aid or comfort to the enemies thereof. But Congress may by a vote of two-thirds of each House, remove such disability.

Section 4.

The validity of the public debt of the United States, authorized by law, including debts incurred for payment of pensions and bounties for services in suppressing insurrection or rebellion, shall not be questioned. But neither the United States nor any State shall assume or pay any debt or obligation incurred in aid of insurrection or rebellion against the United States, or any claim for the loss or emancipation of any slave; but all such debts, obligations and claims shall be held illegal and void.

Section 5.

The Congress shall have the power to enforce, by appropriate legislation, the provisions of this article.

AMENDMENT XV

Passed by Congress February 26, 1869. Ratified February 3, 1870.

Section 1.

The right of citizens of the United States to vote shall not be denied or abridged by the United States or by any State on account of race, color, or previous condition of servitude—

Section 2.

The Congress shall have the power to enforce this article by appropriate legislation.

---

* Changed by section 1 of the 26th amendment.

AMENDMENT XVI

Passed by Congress July 2, 1909. Ratified February 3, 1913.

Note: Article I, section 9, of the Constitution was modified by amendment 16.

The Congress shall have power to lay and collect taxes on incomes, from whatever source derived, without apportionment among the several States, and without regard to any census or enumeration.

AMENDMENT XVII

Passed by Congress May 13, 1912. Ratified April 8, 1913.

Note: Article I, section 3, of the Constitution was modified by the 17th amendment.

The Senate of the United States shall be composed of two Senators from each State, elected by the people thereof, for six years; and each Senator shall have one vote. The electors in each State shall have the qualifications requisite for electors of the most numerous branch of the State legislatures.

When vacancies happen in the representation of any State in the Senate, the executive authority of such State shall issue writs of election to fill such vacancies: *Provided,* That the legislature of any State may empower the executive thereof to make temporary appointments until the people fill the vacancies by election as the legislature may direct.

This amendment shall not be so construed as to affect the election or term of any Senator chosen before it becomes valid as part of the Constitution.

AMENDMENT XVIII

Passed by Congress December 18, 1917. Ratified January 16, 1919. Repealed by amendment 21.

Section 1.

After one year from the ratification of this article the manufacture, sale, or transportation of intoxicating liquors within, the importation thereof into, or the exportation thereof from the United States and all territory subject to the jurisdiction thereof for beverage purposes is hereby prohibited.

Section 2.

The Congress and the several States shall have concurrent power to enforce this article by appropriate legislation.

Section 3.

This article shall be inoperative unless it shall have been ratified as an amendment to the Constitution by the legislatures of the several States, as provided in the Constitution, within seven years from the date of the submission hereof to the States by the Congress.

AMENDMENT XIX

Passed by Congress June 4, 1919. Ratified August 18, 1920.

The right of citizens of the United States to vote shall not be denied or abridged by the United States or by any State on account of sex.
Congress shall have power to enforce this article by appropriate legislation.

AMENDMENT XX

Passed by Congress March 2, 1932. Ratified January 23, 1933.

Note: Article I, section 4, of the Constitution was modified by section 2 of this amendment. In addition, a portion of the 12th amendment was superseded by section 3.

Section 1.

The terms of the President and the Vice President shall end at noon on the 20th day of January, and the terms of Senators and Representatives at noon on the 3d day of January, of the years in which such terms would have ended if this article had not been ratified; and the terms of their successors shall then begin.

Section 2.

The Congress shall assemble at least once in every year, and such meeting shall begin at noon on the 3d day of January, unless they shall by law appoint a different day.

Section 3.

If, at the time fixed for the beginning of the term of the President, the President elect shall have died, the Vice President elect shall become President. If a President shall not have been chosen before the time fixed for the beginning of his term, or if the President elect shall have failed to qualify, then the Vice President elect shall act as President until a President shall have qualified; and the Congress may by law provide for the case wherein neither a President elect nor a Vice President shall have qualified, declaring who shall then act as President, or the manner in which one who is to act shall be selected, and such person shall act accordingly until a President or Vice President shall have qualified.

Section 4.

The Congress may by law provide for the case of the death of any of the persons from whom the House of Representatives may choose a President whenever the right of choice shall have devolved upon them, and for the case of the death of any of the persons from whom the Senate may choose a Vice President whenever the right of choice shall have devolved upon them.

Section 5.

Sections 1 and 2 shall take effect on the 15th day of October following the ratification of this article.

Section 6.

This article shall be inoperative unless it shall have been ratified as an amendment to the Constitution by the legislatures of three-fourths of the several States within seven years from the date of its submission.

AMENDMENT XXI

Passed by Congress February 20, 1933. Ratified December 5, 1933.

Section 1.

The eighteenth article of amendment to the Constitution of the United States is hereby repealed.

Section 2.

The transportation or importation into any State, Territory, or Possession of the United States for delivery or use therein of intoxicating liquors, in violation of the laws thereof, is hereby prohibited.

Section 3.

This article shall be inoperative unless it shall have been ratified as an amendment to the Constitution by conventions in the several States, as provided in the Constitution, within seven years from the date of the submission hereof to the States by the Congress.

AMENDMENT XXII

Passed by Congress March 21, 1947. Ratified February 27, 1951.

Section 1.

No person shall be elected to the office of the President more than twice, and no person who has held the office of President, or acted as President, for more than two years of a term to which some other person was elected President shall be elected to the office of President more than once. But this Article shall not apply to any person holding the office of President when this Article was proposed by Congress, and shall not prevent any person who may be holding the office of President, or acting as President, during the term within which this Article becomes operative from holding the office of President or acting as President during the remainder of such term.

Section 2.

This article shall be inoperative unless it shall have been ratified as an amendment to the Constitution by the legislatures of three-fourths of the several States within seven years from the date of its submission to the States by the Congress.

AMENDMENT XXIII

Passed by Congress June 16, 1960. Ratified March 29, 1961.

Section 1.

The District constituting the seat of Government of the United States shall appoint in such manner as Congress may direct:

A number of electors of President and Vice President equal to the whole number of Senators and Representatives in Congress to which the District would be entitled if it were a State, but in no event more than the least populous State; they shall be in addition to those appointed by the States, but they shall be considered, for the purposes of the election of President and Vice President, to be electors appointed by a State; and they shall meet in the District and perform such duties as provided by the twelfth article of amendment.

Section 2.

The Congress shall have power to enforce this article by appropriate legislation.

AMENDMENT XXIV

Passed by Congress August 27, 1962. Ratified January 23, 1964.

Section 1.

The right of citizens of the United States to vote in any primary or other election for President or Vice President, for electors for President or Vice President, or for Senator or Representative in Congress, shall not be denied or abridged by the United States or any State by reason of failure to pay poll tax or other tax.

Section 2.

The Congress shall have power to enforce this article by appropriate legislation.

AMENDMENT XXV

Passed by Congress July 6, 1965. Ratified February 10, 1967.

Note: Article II, section 1, of the Constitution was affected by the 25th amendment.

Section 1.

In case of the removal of the President from office or of his death or resignation, the Vice President shall become President.

Section 2.

Whenever there is a vacancy in the office of the Vice President, the President shall nominate a Vice President who shall take office upon confirmation by a majority vote of both Houses of Congress.

Section 3.

Whenever the President transmits to the President pro tempore of the Senate and the Speaker of the House of Representatives his written declaration that he is unable to discharge the powers and duties of his office, and until he transmits to them a written declaration to the contrary, such powers and duties shall be discharged by the Vice President as Acting President.

Section 4.

Whenever the Vice President and a majority of either the principal officers of the executive departments or of such other body as Congress may by law provide, transmit to the President pro tempore of the Senate and the Speaker of the House of Representatives their written declaration that the President is unable to discharge the powers and duties of his office, the Vice President shall immediately assume the powers and duties of the office as Acting President.

Thereafter, when the President transmits to the President pro tempore of the Senate and the Speaker of the House of Representatives his written declaration that no inability exists, he shall resume the powers and duties of his office unless the Vice President and a majority of either the principal officers of the executive department or of such other body as Congress may by law provide, transmit within four days to the President pro tempore of the Senate and the Speaker of the House of Representatives their written declaration that the President is unable to discharge the powers and duties of his office. Thereupon Congress shall decide the issue, assembling within forty-eight hours for that purpose if not in session. If the Congress, within twenty-one days after receipt of the latter written declaration, or, if Congress is not in session, within twenty-one days after Congress is required to assemble, determines by two-thirds vote of both Houses that the President is unable to discharge the powers and duties of his office, the Vice President shall continue to discharge the same as Acting President; otherwise, the President shall resume the powers and duties of his office.

AMENDMENT XXVI

Passed by Congress March 23, 1971. Ratified July 1, 1971.

Note: Amendment 14, section 2, of the Constitution was modified by section 1 of the 26th amendment.

Section 1.

The right of citizens of the United States, who are eighteen years of age or older, to vote shall not be denied or abridged by the United States or by any State on account of age.

Section 2.

The Congress shall have power to enforce this article by appropriate legislation.

AMENDMENT XXVII

Originally proposed Sept. 25, 1789. Ratified May 7, 1992.

No law, varying the compensation for the services of the Senators and Representatives, shall take effect, until an election of representatives shall have intervened.

The Federalist Papers, Federalist 10

The Union as a Safeguard Against Domestic Faction and Insurrection (1787)

JAMES MADISON

Among the numerous advantages promised by a well constructed Union, none deserves to be more accurately developed than its tendency to break and control the violence of faction. The friend of popular governments never finds himself so much alarmed for their character and fate, as when he contemplates their propensity to this dangerous vice. He will not fail, therefore, to set a due value on any plan which, without violating the principles to which he is attached, provides a proper cure for it. The instability, injustice, and confusion introduced into the public councils, have, in truth, been the mortal diseases under which popular governments have everywhere perished; as they continue to be the favorite and fruitful topics from which the adversaries to liberty derive their most specious declamations. The valuable improvements made by the American constitutions on the popular models, both ancient and modern, cannot certainly be too much admired; but it would be an unwarrantable partiality, to contend that they have as effectually obviated the danger on this side, as was wished and expected. Complaints are everywhere heard from our most considerate and virtuous citizens, equally the friends of public and private faith, and of public and personal liberty, that our governments are too unstable, that the public good is disregarded in the conflicts of rival parties, and that measures are too often decided, not according to the rules of justice and the rights of the minor party, but by the superior force of an interested and overbearing majority. However anxiously we may wish that these complaints had no foundation, the evidence, of known facts will not permit us to deny that they are in some degree true. It will be found, indeed, on a candid review of our situation, that some of the distresses under which we labor have been erroneously charged on the operation of our governments; but it will be found, at the same time, that other causes will not alone account for many of our heaviest misfortunes; and, particularly, for that prevailing and increasing distrust of public engagements, and alarm for private rights, which are echoed from one end of the continent to the other. These must be chiefly, if not wholly, effects of the unsteadiness and injustice with which a factious spirit has tainted our public administrations.

By a faction, I understand a number of citizens, whether amounting to a majority or a minority of the whole, who are united and actuated by some common impulse of passion, or of interest, adverse to the rights of other citizens, or to the permanent and aggregate interests of the community.

There are two methods of curing the mischiefs of faction: the one, by removing its causes; the other, by controlling its effects.

There are again two methods of removing the causes of faction: the one, by destroying the liberty which is essential to its existence; the other, by giving to every citizen the same opinions, the same passions, and the same interests.

It could never be more truly said than of the first remedy, that it was worse than the disease. Liberty is to faction what air is to fire, an aliment without which it instantly expires. But it could not be less folly to abolish liberty, which is essential to political life, because it nourishes faction, than it would be to wish the annihilation of air, which is essential to animal life, because it imparts to fire its destructive agency.

The second expedient is as impracticable as the first would be unwise. As long as the reason of man continues fallible, and he is at liberty to exercise it, different opinions will be formed. As long as the connection subsists between his reason and his self-love, his opinions and his passions will have a reciprocal influence on each other; and the former will be objects to which the latter will attach themselves. The diversity in the faculties of men, from which the rights of property originate, is not less an insuperable obstacle to a uniformity of interests. The protection of these faculties is the first object of government. From the protection of different and unequal faculties of acquiring property, the possession of different degrees and kinds of property immediately results; and from the influence of these on the sentiments and views of the respective proprietors, ensues a division of the society into different interests and parties.

The latent causes of faction are thus sown in the nature of man; and we see them everywhere brought into different degrees of activity, according to the different circumstances of civil society. A zeal for different opinions concerning religion, concerning government, and many other points, as well of speculation as of practice; an attachment to different leaders ambitiously contending for pre-eminence and power; or to persons of other descriptions whose fortunes have been interesting to the human passions, have, in turn, divided mankind into parties, inflamed them with mutual animosity, and rendered them much more disposed to vex and oppress each other than to co-operate for their common good. So strong is this propensity of mankind to fall into mutual animosities, that where no substantial occasion presents itself, the most frivolous and fanciful distinctions have been sufficient to kindle their unfriendly passions and excite their most violent conflicts. But the most common and durable source of factions has been the various and unequal distribution of property. Those who hold and those who are without property have ever formed distinct interests in society. Those who are creditors, and those who are debtors, fall under a like discrimination. A landed interest, a manufacturing interest, a mercantile interest, a moneyed interest, with many lesser interests, grow up of necessity in civilized nations, and divide them into different classes, actuated by different sentiments and views. The regulation of these various and interfering interests forms the principal task of modern legislation, and involves the spirit of party and faction in the necessary and ordinary operations of the government.

No man is allowed to be a judge in his own cause, because his interest would certainly bias his judgment, and, not improbably, corrupt his integrity. With equal, nay with greater reason, a body of men are unfit to be both judges and parties at the same time; yet what are many of the most important acts of legislation, but so many judicial determinations, not indeed concerning the rights of single persons, but concerning the rights of large bodies of citizens? And what are the different classes of legislators but advocates and parties to the causes which they determine? Is a law proposed concerning private debts? It is a question to which the creditors are parties on one side and the debtors on the other. Justice ought to hold the balance between them. Yet the parties are, and must be, themselves the judges; and the most numerous party, or, in other words, the most powerful faction must be expected to prevail. Shall domestic manufactures be encouraged, and in what degree, by restrictions on foreign manufactures? are questions which would be differently decided by the landed and the manufacturing classes, and probably by neither with a sole regard to justice and the public good. The apportionment of taxes on the various descriptions of property is an act which seems to require the most exact impartiality; yet there is, perhaps, no legislative act in which greater opportunity and temptation are given to a predominant party to trample on the rules of justice. Every shilling with which they overburden the inferior number, is a shilling saved to their own pockets.

It is in vain to say that enlightened statesmen will be able to adjust these clashing interests, and render them all subservient to the public good. Enlightened statesmen will not always be at the helm. Nor, in many cases, can such an adjustment be made at all without taking into view indirect and remote considerations, which will rarely prevail over the immediate interest which one party may find in disregarding the rights of another or the good of the whole.

The inference to which we are brought is, that the CAUSES of faction cannot be removed, and that relief is only to be sought in the means of controlling its EFFECTS.

If a faction consists of less than a majority, relief is supplied by the republican principle, which enables the majority to defeat its sinister views by regular vote. It may clog the administration, it may convulse the society; but it will be unable to execute and mask its violence under the forms of the Constitution. When a majority is included in a faction, the form of popular government, on the other hand, enables it to sacrifice to its ruling passion or interest both the public good and the rights of other citizens. To secure the public good and private rights against the danger of such a faction, and at the same time to preserve the spirit and the form of popular government, is then the great object to which our inquiries are directed. Let me add that it is the great desideratum by which this form of government can be rescued from the opprobrium under which it has so long labored, and be recommended to the esteem and adoption of mankind.

By what means is this object attainable? Evidently by one of two only. Either the existence of the same passion or interest in a majority at the same time must be prevented, or the majority, having such coexistent passion or interest, must be rendered, by their number and local situation, unable to concert and carry into effect schemes of oppression. If the impulse and the opportunity be suffered to coincide, we well know that neither moral nor religious motives can be relied on as an adequate control. They are not found to be such on the injustice and violence of individuals, and lose their efficacy in proportion to the number combined together, that is, in proportion as their efficacy becomes needful.

From this view of the subject it may be concluded that a pure democracy, by which I mean a society consisting of a small number of citizens, who assemble and administer the government in person, can admit of no cure for the mischiefs of faction. A common passion or interest will, in almost every case, be felt by a majority of the whole; a communication and concert result from the form of government itself; and there is nothing to check the inducements to sacrifice the weaker party or an obnoxious individual. Hence it is that such democracies have ever been spectacles of turbulence and contention; have ever been found incompatible with personal security or the rights of property; and have in general been as short in their lives as they have been violent in their deaths. Theoretic politicians, who have patronized this species of government, have erroneously supposed that by reducing mankind to a perfect equality in their political rights, they would, at the same time, be perfectly equalized and assimilated in their possessions, their opinions, and their passions.

A republic, by which I mean a government in which the scheme of representation takes place, opens a different prospect, and promises the cure for which we are seeking. Let us examine the points in which it varies from pure democracy, and we shall comprehend both the nature of the cure and the efficacy which it must derive from the Union.

The two great points of difference between a democracy and a republic are: first, the delegation of the government, in the latter, to a small number of citizens elected by the rest; secondly, the greater number of citizens, and greater sphere of country, over which the latter may be extended. The effect of the first difference is, on the one hand, to refine and enlarge the public views, by passing them through the medium of a chosen body of citizens, whose wisdom may best discern the true interest of their country, and whose patriotism and love of justice will be least likely to sacrifice it to temporary or partial considerations. Under such a regulation, it may well happen that the public voice, pronounced by the representatives of the people, will be more consonant to the public good than if pronounced by the people themselves, convened for the purpose. On the other hand, the effect may be inverted. Men of factious tempers, of local prejudices, or of sinister designs, may, by intrigue, by corruption, or by other means, first obtain the suffrages, and then betray the interests, of the people. The question resulting is, whether small or extensive republics are more favorable to the election of proper guardians of the public weal; and it is clearly decided in favor of the latter by two obvious considerations:

In the first place, it is to be remarked that, however small the republic may be, the representatives must be raised to a certain number, in order to guard against the cabals of a few; and that, however large it may be, they must be limited to a certain number, in order to guard against the confusion of a multitude. Hence, the number of representatives in the two cases not being in proportion to that of the two constituents, and being proportionally greater in the small republic, it follows that, if the proportion of fit characters be not less in the large than in the small republic, the former will present a greater option, and consequently a greater probability of a fit choice.

In the next place, as each representative will be chosen by a greater number of citizens in the large than in the small republic, it will be more difficult for unworthy candidates to practice with success the vicious arts by which elections are too often carried; and the suffrages of the people being more free, will be more likely to centre in men who possess the most attractive merit and the most diffusive and established characters.

It must be confessed that in this, as in most other cases, there is a mean, on both sides of which inconveniences will be found to lie. By enlarging too much the number of electors, you render the representatives too little acquainted with all their local circumstances and lesser interests; as by reducing it too much, you render him unduly attached to these, and too little fit to comprehend and pursue great and national objects. The federal Constitution forms a happy combination in this respect; the great and aggregate interests being referred to the national, the local and particular to the State legislatures.

The other point of difference is, the greater number of citizens and extent of territory which may be brought within the compass of republican than of democratic government; and it is this circumstance principally which renders factious combinations less to be dreaded in the former than in the latter. The smaller the society, the fewer probably will be the distinct parties and interests composing it; the fewer the distinct parties and interests, the more frequently will a majority be found of the same party; and the smaller the number of individuals composing a majority, and the smaller the compass within which they are placed, the more easily will they concert and execute their plans of oppression. Extend the sphere, and you take in a greater variety of parties and interests; you make it less probable that a majority of the whole will have a common motive to invade the rights of other citizens; or if such a common motive exists, it will be more difficult for all who feel it to discover their own strength, and to act in unison with each other. Besides other impediments, it may be remarked that, where there is a consciousness of unjust or dishonorable purposes, communication is always checked by distrust in proportion to the number whose concurrence is necessary.

Hence, it clearly appears, that the same advantage which a republic has over a democracy, in controlling the effects of faction, is enjoyed by a large over a small republic,—is enjoyed by the Union over the States composing it. Does the advantage consist in the substitution of representatives whose enlightened views and virtuous sentiments render them superior to local prejudices and schemes of injustice? It will not be denied that the representation of the Union will be most likely to possess these requisite endowments. Does it consist in the greater security afforded by a greater variety of parties, against the event of any one party being able to outnumber and oppress the rest? In an equal degree does the increased variety of parties comprised within the Union, increase this security. Does it, in fine, consist in the greater obstacles opposed to the concert and accomplishment of the secret wishes of an unjust and interested majority? Here, again, the extent of the Union gives it the most palpable advantage.

The influence of factious leaders may kindle a flame within their particular States, but will be unable to spread a general conflagration through the other States. A religious sect may degenerate into a political faction in a part of the Confederacy; but the variety of sects dispersed over the entire face of it must secure the national councils against any danger from that source. A rage for paper money, for an abolition of debts, for an equal division of property, or for any other improper or wicked project, will be less apt to pervade the whole body of the Union than a particular member of it; in the same proportion as such a malady is more likely to taint a particular county or district, than an entire State.

In the extent and proper structure of the Union, therefore, we behold a republican remedy for the diseases most incident to republican government. And according to the degree of pleasure and pride we feel in being republicans, ought to be our zeal in cherishing the spirit and supporting the character of Federalists.

PUBLIUS.

The Federalist Papers, Federalist 51

The Structure of the Government Must Furnish the Proper Checks and Balances Between the Different Departments (1788)

JAMES MADISON

To what expedient, then, shall we finally resort, for maintaining in practice the necessary partition of power among the several departments, as laid down in the Constitution? The only answer that can be given is, that as all these exterior provisions are found to be inadequate, the defect must be supplied, by so contriving the interior structure of the government as that its several constituent parts may, by their mutual relations, be the means of keeping each other in their proper places. Without presuming to undertake a full development of this important idea, I will hazard a few general observations, which may perhaps place it in a clearer light, and enable us to form a more correct judgment of the principles and structure of the government planned by the convention. In order to lay a due foundation for that separate and distinct exercise of the different powers of government, which to a certain extent is admitted on all hands to be essential to the preservation of liberty, it is evident that each department should have a will of its own; and consequently should be so constituted that the members of each should have as little agency as possible in the appointment of the members of the others. Were this principle rigorously adhered to, it would require that all the appointments for the supreme executive, legislative, and judiciary magistracies should be drawn from the same fountain of authority, the people, through channels having no communication whatever with one another. Perhaps such a plan of constructing the several departments would be less difficult in practice than it may in contemplation appear. Some difficulties, however, and some additional expense would attend the execution of it. Some deviations, therefore, from the principle must be admitted. In the constitution of the judiciary department in particular, it might be inexpedient to insist rigorously on the principle: first, because peculiar qualifications being essential in the members, the primary consideration ought to be to select that mode of choice which best secures these qualifications; secondly, because the permanent tenure by which the appointments are held in that department, must soon destroy all sense of dependence on the authority conferring them. It is equally evident, that the members of each department should be as little dependent as possible on those of the others, for the emoluments annexed to their offices. Were the executive magistrate, or the judges, not independent of the legislature in this particular, their independence in every other would be merely nominal. But the great security against a gradual concentration of the several powers in the same department, consists in giving to those who administer each department the necessary constitutional means and personal motives to resist encroachments of the others. The provision for defense must in this, as in all other cases, be made commensurate to the danger of attack. Ambition must be made to counteract ambition. The interest of the man must be connected with the constitutional rights of the place. It may be a reflection on human nature, that such devices should be necessary to control the abuses of government. But what is government itself, but the greatest of all reflections on human nature? If men were angels, no government would be necessary. If angels were to govern men, neither external nor internal controls on government would be necessary. In framing a government which is to be administered by men over men, the great difficulty lies in this: you must first enable the government to control the governed; and in the next place oblige it to control itself. A dependence on the people is, no doubt, the primary control on the government; but experience has taught mankind the necessity of auxiliary precautions. This policy of supplying, by opposite and rival interests, the defect of better motives, might be traced through the whole system of human affairs, private as well as public. We see it particularly displayed in all the subordinate distributions of power, where the constant aim is to divide and arrange the several offices in such a manner as that each may be a check on the other that the private interest of every individual may be a sentinel over the public rights. These inventions of prudence cannot be less requisite in the distribution of the supreme powers of the State. But it is not possible to give to each department an equal power of self-defense. In republican government, the legislative authority necessarily predominates. The remedy for this inconveniency is to divide the legislature into different branches; and to render them, by different modes of election and different principles of action, as little connected with each other as the nature of their common functions and their common dependence on the society will admit. It may even be necessary to guard against dangerous encroachments by still further precautions. As the weight of the legislative authority requires that it should be thus divided, the weakness of the executive may require, on the other hand, that it should be fortified. An absolute negative on the legislature appears, at first view, to be the natural defense with which the executive magistrate should be armed. But perhaps it would be neither altogether safe nor alone sufficient. On ordinary occasions it might not be exerted with the requisite firmness, and on extraordinary occasions it might be perfidiously abused. May not this defect of an absolute negative be supplied by some qualified connection between this weaker department and the weaker branch of the stronger department, by which the latter may be led to support the constitutional rights of the former, without being too much detached from the rights of its own department? If the principles on which these observations are founded be just, as I persuade myself they are, and they be applied as a criterion to the several State constitutions, and to the federal Constitution it will be found that if the latter does not perfectly correspond with them, the former are infinitely less able to bear such a test. There are, moreover, two considerations particularly applicable to the federal system of America, which place that system in a very interesting point of view. First. In a single republic, all the power surrendered by the people is submitted to the administration of a single government; and the usurpations are guarded against by a division of the government into distinct and separate departments. In the compound republic of America, the power surrendered by the people is first divided between two distinct governments, and then the portion allotted to each subdivided among distinct and separate departments. Hence a double security arises to the rights of the people. The different governments will control each other, at the same time that each will be controlled by itself. Second. It is of great importance in a republic not only to guard the society against the oppression of its rulers, but to guard one part of the society against the injustice of the other part. Different interests necessarily exist in different classes of citizens. If a majority be united by a common interest, the rights of the minority will be insecure. There are but two methods of providing against this evil: the one by creating a will in the community independent of the majority that is, of the society itself; the other, by comprehending in the society so many separate descriptions of citizens as will render an unjust combination of a majority of the whole very improbable, if not impracticable. The first method prevails in all governments possessing an hereditary or self-appointed authority. This, at best, is but a precarious security; because a power independent of the society may as well espouse the unjust views of the major, as the rightful interests of the minor party, and may possibly be turned against both parties. The second method will be exemplified in the federal republic of the United States. Whilst all authority in it will be derived from and dependent on the society, the society itself will be broken into so many parts, interests, and classes of citizens, that the rights of individuals, or of the minority, will be in little danger from interested combinations of the majority. In a free government the security for civil rights must be the same as that for religious rights. It consists in the one case in the multiplicity of interests, and in the other in the multiplicity of sects. The degree of security in both cases will depend on the number of interests and sects; and this may be presumed to depend on the extent of country and number of people comprehended under the same government. This view of the subject must particularly recommend a proper federal system to all the sincere and considerate friends of republican government, since it shows that in exact proportion as the territory of the Union may be formed into more circumscribed Confederacies, or States oppressive combinations of a majority will be facilitated: the best security, under the republican forms, for the rights of every class of citizens, will be diminished: and consequently the stability and independence of some member of the government, the only other security, must be proportionately increased. Justice is the end of government. It is the end of civil society. It ever has been and ever will be pursued until it be obtained, or until liberty be lost in the pursuit. In a society under the forms of which the stronger faction can readily unite and oppress the weaker, anarchy may as truly be said to reign as in a state of nature, where the weaker individual is not secured against the violence of the stronger; and as, in the latter state, even the stronger individuals are prompted, by the uncertainty of their condition, to submit to a government which may protect the weak as well as themselves; so, in the former state, will the more powerful factions or parties be gradually induced, by a like motive, to wish for a government which will protect all parties, the weaker as well as the more powerful. It can be little doubted that if the State of Rhode Island was separated from the Confederacy and left to itself, the insecurity of rights under the popular form of government within such narrow limits would be displayed by such reiterated oppressions of factious majorities that some power altogether independent of the people would soon be called for by the voice of the very factions whose misrule had proved the necessity of it. In the extended republic of the United States, and among the great variety of interests, parties, and sects which it embraces, a coalition of a majority of the whole society could seldom take place on any other principles than those of justice and the general good; whilst there being thus less danger to a minor from the will of a major party, there must be less pretext, also, to provide for the security of the former, by introducing into the government a will not dependent on the latter, or, in other words, a will independent of the society itself. It is no less certain than it is important, notwithstanding the contrary opinions which have been entertained, that the larger the society, provided it lie within a practical sphere, the more duly capable it will be of self-government. And happily for the REPUBLICAN CAUSE, the practicable sphere may be carried to a very great extent, by a judicious modification and mixture of the FEDERAL PRINCIPLE.

PUBLIUS.

The Rights of Man, Part I (1791–1792)

THOMAS PAINE

. . . The error of those who reason by precedents drawn from antiquity, respecting the rights of man, is that . . . they do not go the whole way. They stop in some of the intermediate stages of an hundred or a thousand years, and produce what was then done, as a rule for the present day. This is no authority at all. If we travel still farther into antiquity, we shall find a direct contrary opinion and practice prevailing; and if antiquity is to be an authority, a thousand such authorities may be produced, successively contradicting each other; but if we proceed on, we shall at last come out right; we shall come to the time when man came from the hand of his Maker. What was he then? Man. Man was his high and only title, and a higher cannot be given him. . . .

. . . If the mere name of antiquity is to govern in the affairs of life, the people who are to live an hundred or a thousand years hence, may as well take us for a precedent, as we make a precedent of those who lived an hundred or a thousand years ago. The fact is, that portions of antiquity, by proving everything, establish nothing. It is authority against authority all the way, till we come to the divine origin of the rights of man at the creation. Here our enquiries find a resting-place, and our reason finds a home. . . .

. . . The illuminating and divine principle of the equal rights of man . . . relates, not only to the living individuals, but to generations of men succeeding each other. Every generation is equal in rights to generations which preceded it, by the same rule that every individual is born equal in rights with his contemporary.

Every history of the creation, and every traditionary account . . . , however they may vary in their opinion or belief of certain particulars, all agree in establishing one point, *the unity of man*; by which I mean that men are all of *one degree*, and consequently that all men are born equal, and with natural right, in the same manner as if posterity had been continued by *creation* instead of *generation*, the latter being the only mode by which the former is carried forward; and consequently every child born into the world must be considered as deriving its existence from God. The world is as new to him as it was to the first man that existed, and his natural right in it is of the same kind. . . .

. . . We have now to consider the civil rights of man, and to show how the one originates from the other. Man did not enter into society to become *worse* than he was before, nor to have fewer rights than he had before, but to have those rights better secured. His natural rights are the foundation of all his civil rights. . . .

. . . Natural rights are those which appertain to man in right of his existence. Of this kind are all the intellectual rights, or rights of the mind, and

From Thomas Paine, *The Rights of Man*. (New York: The Modern Library) © 1925, pp. 128–165.

also all those rights of acting as an individual for his own comfort and happiness, which are not injurious to the natural rights of others. Civil rights are those which appertain to man in right of his being a member of society. Every civil right has for its foundation some natural right pre-existing in the individual, but to the enjoyment of which his individual power is not, in all cases, sufficiently competent. Of this kind are all those which relate to security and protection.

From this sort of review it will be easy to distinguish between that class of natural rights which man retains after entering into society and those which he throws into the common stock as a member of society.

The natural rights which he retains are all those in which the *power* to execute is as perfect in the individual as the right itself. Among this class . . . are all the intellectual rights, or rights of mind; consequently religion is one of those rights. The natural rights which are not retained, are all those in which, though the right is perfect in the individual, the power to execute them is defective. They answer not his purpose. A man, by natural right, has a right to judge in his own cause; and so far as the right of the mind is concerned, he never surrenders it. But what availeth it him to judge, if he has not power to redress? He therefore deposits this right in the common stock of society, and takes the arm of society, of which he is a part, in preference and in addition to his own. Society *grants* him nothing. Every man is a proprietor in society, and draws on the capital as a matter of right.

From these premises . . . certain conclusions will follow:

First, That every civil right grows out of a natural right; or, in other words, is a natural right exchanged.

Secondly, That civil power properly considered as such is made up of the aggregate of that class of the natural rights of man, which becomes defective in the individual in point of power, and answers not his purpose, but when collected to focus becomes competent to the purpose of every one.

Thirdly, That the power produced from the aggregate of natural rights, imperfect in power in the individual, cannot be applied to invade the natural rights which are retained in the individual, and in which the power to execute is as perfect as the right itself.

We have now, in a few words, traced man from a natural individual to a member of society, and shewn, or endeavoured to shew, the quality of the natural rights retained, and of those which are exchanged for civil rights. Let us now apply these principles to governments.

. . . It is extremely easy to distinguish the governments which have arisen out of society, or out of the social compact, from those which have not; but to place this in a clearer light . . . it will be proper to take a review of the several sources from which governments have arisen and on which they have been founded.

They may all be comprehended under three heads. First, Superstition. Secondly, Power. Thirdly, the common interest of society and the common rights of man.

The first was a government of priestcraft, the second of conquerors, and the third of reason.

When a set of artful men pretended, through the medium of oracles, to hold intercourse with the Deity . . . the world was completely under the government of superstition. . . . This sort of government lasted as long as this sort of superstition lasted.

After these a race of conquerors arose, whose government, like that of William the Conqueror, was founded in power, and the sword assumed the name of a scepter. Governments thus established last as long as the power to support them lasts; but that they might avail themselves of every single engine in their favor, they united fraud to force, and set up an idol which they called *Divine Right*, and which . . . twisted itself afterwards into an idol of another shape, called *Church and State*. . . .

When I contemplate the natural dignity of man, when I feel (for Nature has not been kind enough to me to blunt my feelings) for the honour and happiness of its character, I become irritated at the attempt to govern mankind by force and fraud, as if they were all knaves and fools. . . .

We now have to review the governments which arise out of society, in contradistinction to those which arose out of superstition and conquest.

It has been thought a considerable advance towards establishing the principles of Freedom to say that Government is a compact between those who govern and those who are governed; but this cannot be true, because it is putting the effect before the cause; for as man must have existed before governments existed, there necessarily was a time when governments did not exist, and consequently there could originally exist no governors to form such a compact with.

The fact therefore must be that the *individuals themselves*, each in his own personal and sovereign right, *entered into a compact with each other* to produce a government: and this is the only mode in which governments have a right to arise, and the only principle on which they have a right to exist.

To possess ourselves of a clear idea of what government is, or ought to be, we must trace it to its origin. In doing this we shall easily discover that governments must have arisen either *out* of the people or *over* the people. . . .

But it will be first necessary to define what is meant by a *Constitution*. . . .

A constitution is not a thing in name only, but in fact. It has not an ideal, but a real existence; and wherever it cannot be produced in a visible form, there is none. A constitution is a thing *antecedent* to a government, and a government is only the creature of a constitution. The constitution of a country is not the act of its government, but of the people constituting its government. It is the body of elements, to which you can refer, and quote article by article; and which contains the principles on which the government shall be established, the manner in which it shall be organized, the powers it shall have, the mode of elections, the duration of Parliaments, or by what other name such bodies may be called; the powers which the executive part of the government shall have; and in fine, everything that relates to the complete organization of a civil government, and the principles on which it shall act, and by which it shall be bound. A constitution, therefore, is to a government what the laws made afterwards by that government are to a court of judicature. The court of judicature does not make the laws, neither can it alter them; it only acts in conformity to the laws made: and the government is in like manner governed by the constitution. . . .

PART II

. . . The independence of America, considered merely as a separation from England, would have been a matter but of little importance, had it not been accompanied by a revolution in the principles and practices of governments. She made a stand, not for herself only, but for the world, and looked beyond the advantages herself could receive. Even the Hessian, though hired to fight against her, may live to bless his defeat; and England, condemned in the viciousness of its government, rejoice in its miscarriage.

As America was the only spot in the political world where the principle of universal reformation could begin, so also was it the best in the natural world. An assemblage of circumstances conspired, not only to give birth, but to add gigantic maturity to its principles. The scene which that country presents to the eye of a spectator, has something in it which generates and encourages great ideas. Nature appears to him in magnitude. The mighty objects he beholds, act upon his mind by enlarging it, and he partakes of the greatness he contemplates.—Its first settlers were emigrants from different European nations, and of diversified professions of religion, retiring from the governmental persecutions of the old world, and meeting in the new, not as enemies, but as brothers. The wants which necessarily accompany the cultivation of a wilderness produced among them a state of society, which countries long harassed by the quarrels and intrigues of governments, had neglected to cherish. In such a situation man becomes what he ought. He sees his species, not with the inhuman idea of a natural enemy, but as kindred; and the example shews to the artificial world, that man must go back to Nature for information. . . .

If systems of government can be introduced less expensive and more productive of general happiness than those which have existed, all attempts to oppose their progress will in the end be fruitless. Reason, like time, will make its own way, and prejudice will fall in a combat with interest. If universal peace, civilization, and commerce are ever to be the happy lot of man, it cannot be accomplished but by a revolution in the system of governments. . . .

The revolutions which formerly took place in the world had nothing in them that interested the bulk of mankind. They extended only to a change of persons and measures, but not of principles, and rose or fell among the common transactions of the moment. What we now behold may not improperly be called a *"counter revolution."* Conquest and tyranny, at some earlier period, dispossessed man of his rights, and he is now recovering them. . . . Government founded on a *moral theory, on a system of universal peace, on the indefeasible hereditary Right of Man*, is now revolving from west to east by a stronger impulse than the government of the sword revolved from east to west. It interests not particular individuals, but nations in its progress, and promises a new era to the human race.

The danger to which the success of revolution is most exposed is that of attempting them before the principles on which they proceed, and the advantages to result from them, are sufficiently seen and understood. Almost everything appertaining to the circumstances of a nation, has been absorbed and confounded under the general and mysterious word *government*. Though it avoids taking to its account the errors it commits, and the mischiefs it occasions, it fails not to arrogate to itself whatever has the appearance of prosperity. It robs industry of its honours, by pedanticly making itself the cause of its effects; and purloins from the general character of man, the merits that appertain to him as a social being.

It may therefore be of use in this day of revolutions to discriminate between those things which are the effect of government, and those things which are not. This will best be done by taking a review of society and civilization, and the consequences resulting therefrom, as things distinct from what are called governments. By beginning with this investigation, we shall be able to assign effects to their proper causes and analise the mass of common errors.

Great part of that order which reigns among mankind is not the effect of government. It has its origin in the principles of society and the natural constitution of man. It existed prior to government, and would exist if the formality of government was abolished. The mutual dependence and reciprocal interest which man has upon man, and all the parts of civilized community upon each other, create that great chain of connection which holds it together. The landholder, the farmer, the manufacturer, the merchant, the tradesman, and every occupation, prospers by the aid which each receives from the other, and from the whole. Common interest regulates their concerns, and forms their law; and the laws which common usage ordains, have a greater influence than the laws of government. In fine society performs for itself almost everything which is ascribed to government.

To understand the nature and quantity of government proper for man, it is necessary to attend to his character. As Nature has created him for social life, she fitted him for the station she intended. In all cases she made his natural wants greater than his individual powers. No one man is capable, without the aid of society, of supplying his own wants; and those wants, acting upon every individual, impel the whole of them into society, as naturally as gravitation acts to a center.

But she has gone further. She has not only forced man into society by a diversity of wants which the reciprocal aid of each other can supply, but she has implanted in him a system of social affections, which, though not necessary to his existence, are essential to his happiness. There is no period in life when his love for society ceases to act. It begins and ends with our being.

If we examine with attention into the composition and constitution of man, the diversity of his wants, and the diversity of talents in different men for reciprocally accommodating the wants of each other, his propensity to society, and consequently to preserve the advantages resulting from it, we shall easily discover, that a great part of what is called government is mere imposition.

Government is no farther necessary than to supply the few cases to which society and civilization are not conveniently competent; and instances are not wanting to show, that everything which government can usefully add thereto, has been performed by the common consent of society, without government. . . .

. . . There is a natural aptness in man, and more so in society, because it embraces a greater variety of abilities and resource, to accommodate itself to whatever situation it is in. The instant formal government is abolished, society begins to act: a general association takes place, and common interest produces common security.

So far is it from being true, as has been pretended, that the abolition of any formal government is the dissolution of society, that it acts by a contrary impulse, and brings the latter the closer together. All that part of its organization which it had committed to its government, devolves again upon itself, and acts through its medium. When men, as well from natural instinct as from reciprocal benefits, have habituated themselves to social and civilized life, there is always enough of its principles in practice to carry them through any changes they may find necessary or convenient to make in their government. In short, man is so naturally a creature of society that it is almost impossible to bring him out of it. . . .

The more perfect civilization is, the less occasion has it for government, because the more does it regulate its own affairs, and govern itself; but so contrary is the practice of old governments to the reason of the case, that the expences of them increase in proportion they ought to diminish. It is but few general laws that civilized life requires, and those of such common usefulness, that whether they are enforced by the forms of government or not, the effect will be nearly the same. If we consider what the principles are that first condense men into society, and what are the motives that regulate their mutual intercourse afterwards, we shall find, by the time we arrive at what is called government, that nearly the whole of the business is performed by the natural operation of the parts upon each other.

. . . All the great laws of society are laws of nature. Those of trade and commerce, whether with respect to the intercourse of individuals or of nations, are laws of mutual and reciprocal interest. They are followed and obeyed, because it is the interest of the parties so to do, and not on account of any formal laws their governments may impose or interpose.

But how often is the natural propensity of society disturbed or destroyed by the operations of government! When the latter, instead of being ingrafted on the principles of the former, assumes to exist for itself, and acts by partialities of favour and oppression, it becomes the cause of the mischiefs it ought to prevent. . . .

. . . If there is a country in the world where concord, according to common calculation, would be least expected, it is in America. Made up as it is of people from different nations, accustomed to different forms and habits of government, speaking different languages, and more different in their modes of worship, it would appear that the union of such a people was impracticable; but by the simple operation of constructing government on the principles of society and the rights of man, every difficulty retires, and all the parts are brought into cordial unison. There the poor are not oppressed, the rich are not privileged. Industry is not mortified by the splendid extravagance of a court rioting at its expence. Their taxes are few, because their government is just: and as there is nothing to render them wretched, there is nothing to engender riots and tumults. . . .

That men mean distinct and separate things when they speak of constitutions and of governments, is evident: or why are those terms distinctly and separately used? A constitution is not the act of government, but of a people constituting a government; and government without a constitution, is power without a right.

All power exercised over a nation, must have some beginning. It must either be delegated or assumed. There are no other sources. All delegated power is trust, and all assumed power is usurpation. Time does not alter the nature and quality of either. . . .

. . . One of the greatest improvements that have been made for the perpetual security and progress of constitutional liberty, is the provision which the new constitutions make for occasionally revising, altering, and amending them. . . .

The constitutions of America, and also that of France, have either affixed a period for their revision, or laid down the mode by which improvement shall be made. . . . To prevent inconveniences from accumulating, till they discourage reformations or provoke revolutions, it is best to provide the means of regulating them as they occur. The Rights of Man are the rights of all generations of men, and cannot be monopolized by any. That which is worth following, will be followed for the sake of its worth, and it is in this that its security lies, and not in any conditions with which it may be encumbered. When a man leaves property to his heirs, he does not connect it with an obligation that they shall accept it. Why, then, should we do otherwise with respect to constitutions? The best constitution that could now be devised, consistent with the condition of the present moment, may be far short of that excellence which a few years may afford. There is a morning of reason rising upon man on the subject of government, that has not appeared before. As the barbarism of the present old governments expires, the moral conditions of nations with respect to each other will be changed. Man will not be brought up with the savage idea of considering his species as his enemy, because the accident of his birth gave the individuals existence in countries distinguished by different names; and as constitutions have always some relation to external as well as to domestic circumstances, the means of benefiting by every change, foreign or domestic, should be a part of every constitution. . . . Government ought to be as much open to improvement as anything which appertains to man, instead of which it has been monopolized from age to age, by the most ignorant and vicious of the human race. Need we any other proof of their wretched management, than the excess of debts and taxes with which every nation groans, and the quarrels into which they have precipitated the world? Just emerging from such a barbarous condition, it is too soon to determine to what extent of improvement government may yet be carried. For what we can foresee, all Europe may form but one great Republic, and man be free of the whole.

A Defence of the Constitutions of Government of the United States of America (1786–1787)

JOHN ADAMS

. . . It is become a kind of fashion among writers, to admit, as a maxim, that if you could be always sure of a wise, active, and virtuous prince, monarchy would be the best of governments. But this is so far from being admissible, that it will forever remain true, that a free government has a great advantage over a simple monarchy. The best and wisest prince, by means of a freer communication with his people, and the greater opportunities to collect the best advice from the best of his subjects, would have an immense advantage in a free state over a monarchy. A senate consisting of all that is most noble, wealthy, and able in a nation, with a right to counsel the crown at all times, is a check to ministers, and a security against abuses, such as a body of nobles who never meet, and have no such right, can never supply. Another assembly, composed of representatives chosen by the people in all parts, gives free access to the whole nation, and communicates all wants, knowledge and projects, and wishes to government; it excites emulation among all classes, removes complaints, redresses grievances, affords opportunities of exertion to genius, though in obscurity, and gives full scope to all faculties of man; it opens a passage for every speculation to the legislature, to administration, and to the public; it gives a universal energy to the human character, in every part of the state, such as never can be obtained in monarchy.

There is a third particular which deserves attention both from governments and people. In a simple monarchy, the ministers of state can never know their friends from their enemies; secret cabals undermine their influence, and blast their reputation. This occasions jealousy ever anxious and irritated, which never thinks the government safe without an encouragement of informers and spies, throughout every part of the state, who interrupt the tranquility of private life, destroy the confidence of families in their own domestics and in one another, and poison freedom in its sweetest retirements. In a free government, on the contrary, the ministers can have no enemies of consequences but among the members of the great or little council, where every man is obliged to take his side, and declare his opinion, upon every question. This circumstance alone . . . would be sufficient to decide the preference in favor of a free government. Even secrecy, where the executive is entire on one hand, is as easily and surely preserved in a free government, as in a simple monarchy; and as to dispatch, all the simple monarchies of the whole universe may be defied to produce greater or more numerous examples of it than are to be found in English history. . . .

There can be no free government without a democratical branch in the constitution. Monarchies and aristocracies are in possession of the voice and influence of every university and academy in Europe. Democracy, simple democracy, never had a patron among men of letters. Democratical mixtures in government have lost almost all the advocates they ever had out of England and America. Men of letters must have a great deal of praise, and some of the necessaries, conveniences, and ornaments of life. Monarchies and aristocracies pay well and applaud liberally. The people have almost always expected to be served gratis, and to be paid for the honor of serving them; and their applauses and adorations are bestowed too often on artifices and tricks, on hypocrisy and superstition, on flattery, bribes, and largesses. It is no wonder then that democracies and democratical mixtures are annihilated all over Europe, except on a barren rock, a paltry fen, an inaccessible mountain, or an impenetrable forest. The people of England, to their immortal honor, are hitherto an exception; but, to the humiliation of human nature, they show very often that they are like other men. The people in America have now the best opportunity and the greatest trust in their hands, that Providence ever committed to so small a number, since the transgression of the first pair; if they betray their trust, their guilt will merit even greater punishment than other nations have suffered, and the indignation of Heaven. If there is one certain truth to be collected from the history of all ages, it is this; that the people's rights and liberties, and the democratical mixture in a constitution, can never be preserved without a strong executive, or, in other words, without separating the executive from the legislative power. . . .

The rich, the well-born, and the able, acquire influence among the people that will soon be too much for simple honesty and plain sense, in a house of representatives. The most illustrious of them must, therefore, be separated from the mass, and placed by themselves in a senate; this is, to all honest and useful intents, an ostracism. A member of a senate, of immense wealth, the most respected birth, and transcendent abilities, has no influence in the nation, in comparison of what he would have in a single representative assembly. When a senate exists, the most powerful man in the state may be safely admitted into the house of representatives, because the people have it in their power to remove him into the senate as soon as his influence becomes dangerous. The senate becomes the great object of ambition; and the richest and the most sagacious wish to merit an advancement to it by services to the public in the house. When he has obtained the object of his wishes, you may still hope for the benefits of his exertions, without dreading his passions; for the executive power being in other hands, he has lost much of his influence with the people, and can govern very few votes more than his own among the senators. . . .

The United States of America have exhibited, perhaps, the first example of governments erected on the simple principles of nature; and if men are now sufficiently enlightened to disabuse themselves of artifice, imposture, hypocrisy, and superstition, they will consider this event as an era in their history. Although the detail of the formation of the American governments is at present little known or regarded either in Europe or in America, it may hereafter become an object of curiosity. It will never be pretended that any persons employed in that service had interviews with the gods, or were in any degree under the inspiration of Heaven, more than those at work upon ships or houses, or laboring in merchandise or agriculture; it will forever be acknowledged that these governments were contrived merely by the use of reason and the senses. . . . Neither the people, nor their conventions, committees, or sub-committees, considered legislation in any other light than as ordinary arts and sciences, only more important. . . .

. . . The people were universally too enlightened to be imposed on by artifice; and their leaders, or more properly followers, were men of too much honor to attempt it. Thirteen governments thus founded on the natural authority of the people alone, without a pretence of miracle or mystery, and which are destined to spread over the northern part of that whole quarter of the globe, are a great point gained in favor of the rights of mankind. The experiment is made, and has completely succeeded; it can no longer be called in question, whether authority in magistrates and obedience of citizens can be grounded on reason, morality, and the Christian religion, without the monkery of priests, or the knavery of politicians. As the writer was personally acquainted with most of the gentlemen in each of the states, who had the principal share in the first draughts, the following work was really written to lay before the public a specimen of that kind of reading and reasoning which produced the American constitutions. . . .

. . . As we have taken a cursory view of those countries in Europe where the government may be called, in any reasonable construction of the word, republican, let us now pause a few moments, and reflect upon what we have seen.

Among every people, and in every species of republics, we have con-stantly found *a first magistrate, a head, a chief*, under various denominations, in-deed, and with different degrees of authority, . . . in every nation we have met with a distinguished officer. If there is no example, then, in any free govern-ment, any more than in those which are not free, of a society without a princi-pal personage, we may fairly conclude that the body politic cannot subsist, any more than the animal body, without a head. . . .

In every form of government we have seen a *senate*, or *little council*, a composition, generally, of those officers of state who have the most experience and power, and of a few other members selected from the highest ranks and most illustrious reputations. On these lesser councils, with the first magistrate at their head, generally rests the principal burden of administration, a share in the legislative, as well as executive and judicial authority of government. The admission of such senates to a participation of these three kinds of power, has been generally observed to produce in the minds of their members an ardent aristocratical ambition, grasping equally at the prerogatives of the first magis-trate, and the privileges of the people, and ending in the nobility of a few fam-ilies, and a tyrannical oligarchy. But in those states, where the senates have been debarred from all executive power, and confined to the legislative, they have been observed to be firm barriers against the encroachments of the crown, and often great supporters of the liberties of the people. The Ameri-cans, then, who have carefully confined their senates to the legislative power, have done wisely in adopting them.

We have seen, in every instance, another and a larger assembly, com-posed of the body of the people, in some little states; of representatives chosen by the people, in others; of members appointed by the senate, and supposed to represent the people, in a third sort; and of persons appointed by themselves or the senate, in certain aristocracies; to prevent them from becoming oli-garchies. The Americans, then, whose assemblies are the most adequate, pro-portional, and equitable representations of the people, that are known in the world, will not be thought mistaken in appointing houses of representatives.

In every republic,—in the smallest and most popular, in the larger and more aristocratical, as well as in the largest and most monarchical,—we have observed a multitude of curious and ingenious inventions to balance, in their turn, all those powers, to check the passions peculiar to them, and to control them from rushing into those exorbitancies to which they are most addicted. The Americans will then be no longer censured for endeavoring to introduce an equilibrium, which is much more profoundly meditated, and much more effectual for the protection of the laws, than any we have seen, except in Eng-land. We may even question whether that is an exception.

In every country we have found a variety of *orders*, with very great dis-tinctions. In America, there are different orders of *offices*, but none of *men*. Out of office, all men are of the same species, and of one blood; there is neither a greater nor a lesser nobility. Why, then, are the Americans accused of estab-lishing different orders of men? . . .

Wherever we have seen a territory somewhat larger, arts and sciences more cultivated, commerce flourishing, or even agriculture improved to any great degree, an aristocracy has risen up in a course of time, consisting of a few rich and honorable families, who have united with each other against both the people and the first magistrate; who have wrested from the former, by art and by force, all their participation in the government; and have even inspired them with so mean an esteem of themselves, and so deep a veneration and strong attachment to their rulers, as to believe and confess them a superior order of beings.

We have seen these noble families, although necessitated to have a head, extremely jealous of his influence, anxious to reduce his power, and to constrain him to as near a level as possible with themselves; always endeavoring to establish a rotation, by which they may all equally be entitled in turn to the preeminence, and likewise anxious to preserve to themselves as large a share as possible of power in the executive and judicial, as well as the legislative departments of the state.

These patrician families have also appeared in every instance to be equally jealous of each other, and to have contrived, by blending lot and choice, by mixing various bodies in the elections to the same offices, and even by a resort to the horrors of an inquisition, to guard against the sin that so easily besets them, of being wholly influenced and governed by a junto or oligarchy of a few among themselves.

We have seen no one government in which is a distinct separation of the legislative from the executive power, and of the judicial from both, or in which any attempt has been made to balance these powers with one another, or to form an equilibrium between the one, the few, and the many, for the purpose of enacting and executing equal laws, by common consent, for the general interest, excepting in England.

Shall we conclude, from these melancholy observations, that human nature is incapable of liberty, that no honest equality can be preserved in society, and that such forcible causes are always at work as must reduce all men to a submission to despotism, monarchy, oligarchy, or aristocracy?

By no means. We have seen one of the first nations in Europe, possessed of ample and fertile territories at home and extensive dominions abroad, of a commerce with the whole world, immense wealth, and the greatest naval power which ever belonged to any nation, which has still preserved the power of the people by the equilibrium we are contending for, by the trial by jury, and by constantly refusing a standing army. The people of England alone, by preserving their share in the legislature, at the expense of the blood of heroes and patriots, have enabled their king to curb the nobility, without giving him a standing army.

After all, let us compare every constitution we have seen with those of the United States of America, and we shall have no reason to blush for our country. On the contrary, we shall feel the strongest motives to fall upon our knees, in gratitude from heaven for having been graciously pleased to give us birth and education in that country, and for having destined us to live under her laws! We shall have reason to exult, if we make our comparison with England and the English constitution. Our people are undoubtedly sovereign; all the landed and other property is in the hands of the citizens; not only their representatives, but their senators and governors, are annually chosen; there are no hereditary titles, honors, offices, or distinctions; the legislative, executive, and judicial powers are carefully separated from each other; the powers of the one, the few, and the many are nicely balanced in the legislatures; trials by jury are preserved in all their glory, and there is no standing army; the *habeus corpus* is in full force; the press is the most free in the world. Where all these circumstances take place, it is necessary to add that the laws alone can govern. . . .

By the authorities and examples already recited, you will be convinced that three branches of power have unalterable foundation in nature; that they exist in every society natural and artificial; and that if all of them are not acknowledged in any constitution of government, it will be found to be imperfect, unstable, and soon enslaved; that the legislative and executive authorities are naturally distinct; and that liberty and the laws depend entirely on a separation of them in the frame of government; that the legislative power is naturally and necessarily sovereign and supreme over the executive; and, therefore, that the latter must be made an essential branch of the former, even with a negative, or it will not be able to defend itself, but will be soon invaded, undermined, attacked, or in some way or other totally ruined and annihilated by the former. This is applicable to every state in America, in its individual capacity; but is it equally applicable to the United States in their federal capacity? . . .

Notes on the State of Virginia

Thomas Jefferson

AN ACT FOR ESTABLISHING RELIGIOUS FREEDOM [1779], PASSED IN THE ASSEMBLY OF VIRGINIA IN THE BEGINNING OF THE YEAR 1786

Well aware that Almighty God hath created the mind free; that all attempts to influence it by temporal punishments or burdens, or by civil incapacitations, tend only to beget habits of hypocrisy and meanness, and are a departure from the plan of the Holy Author of our religion, who being Lord both of body and mind, yet chose not to propagate it by coercions on either, as was in his Almighty power to do; that the impious presumption of legislators and rulers, civil as well as ecclesiastical, who, being themselves but fallible and uninspired men have assumed dominion over the faith of others, setting up their own opinions and modes of thinking as the only true and infallible, and as such endeavoring to impose them on others, hath established and maintained false religions over the greatest part of the world, and through all time; that to compel a man to furnish contributions of money for the propagation of opinions which he disbelieves, is sinful and tyrannical; that even the forcing him to support this or that teacher of his own religious persuasion, is depriving him of the comfortable liberty of giving his contributions to the particular pastor whose morals he would make his pattern, and whose powers he feels most persuasive to righteousness, and is withdrawing from the ministry those temporal rewards, which proceeding from an approbation of their personal conduct, are an additional incitement to earnest and unremitting labors for the instruction of mankind; that our civil rights have no dependence on our religious opinions, more than our opinions in physics or geometry; that, therefore, the proscribing any citizen as unworthy the public confidence by laying upon him an incapacity of being called to the offices of trust and emolument, unless he profess or renounce this or that religious opinions, is depriving him injuriously of those privileges and advantages to which in common with his fellow citizens he has a natural right; that it tends also to corrupt the principles of that very religion it is meant to encourage, by bribing, with a monopoly of worldly honors and emoluments, those who will externally profess and conform to it; that though indeed these are criminal who do not withstand such temptation, yet neither are those innocent who lay the bait in their way; that to suffer the civil magistrate to intrude his powers into the field of opinion and to restrain

From *The Life and Selected Writings of Thomas Jefferson*, edited by Adrienne Koch and William Peden (New York: Modern Library) © 1944.

the profession or propagation of principles, on the supposition of their ill tendency, is a dangerous fallacy, which at once destroys all religious liberty, because he being of course judge of that tendency, will make his opinions the rule of judgment, and approve or condemn the sentiments of others only as they shall square with or differ from his own; that it is time enough for the rightful purposes of civil government, for its offices to interfere when principles break out into overt acts against peace and good order; and finally, that truth is great and will prevail if left to herself, that she is the proper and sufficient antagonist to error, and has nothing to fear from the conflict, unless by human interposition disarmed of her natural weapons, free argument and debate, errors ceasing to be dangerous when it is permitted freely to contradict them.

Be it therefore enacted by the General Assembly, That no man shall be compelled to frequent or support any religious worship, place or ministry whatsoever, nor shall be enforced, restrained, molested, or burthened in his body or goods, nor shall otherwise suffer on account of his religious opinions or belief; but that all men shall be free to profess, and by argument to maintain, their opinions in matters of religion, and that the same shall in nowise diminish, enlarge, or affect their civil capacities. . . .

MESSRS. NEHEMIAH DODGE, EPHRAIM ROBBINS, AND STEPHEN S. NELSON, A COMMITTEE OF THE DANBURY BAPTIST ASSOCIATION, IN THE STATE OF CONNECTICUT. WASHINGTON, JANUARY 1, 1802

Gentlemen:—The affectionate sentiments of esteem and approbation which you are so good as to express towards me, on behalf of the Danbury Baptist Association, give me the highest satisfaction. My duties dictate a faithful and zealous pursuit of the interests of my constituents, and in proportion as they are persuaded of my fidelity to those duties, the discharge of them becomes more and more pleasing.

Believing with you that religion is a matter which lies solely between man and his God, that he owes account to none other for his faith or his worship, that the legislative powers of government reach actions only, and not opinions, I contemplate with sovereign reverence that act of the whole American people which declared that their legislature should "make no law respecting an establishment of religion, or prohibiting the free exercise thereof," thus building a wall of separation between Church and State. Adhering to this expression of the supreme will of the nation in behalf of the rights of conscience, I shall see with sincere satisfaction the progress of those sentiments which tend to restore to man all his natural rights, convinced he has not natural rights in opposition to his social duties.

I reciprocate your kind prayers for the protection and blessing of the common Father and Creator of man, and tender you for yourselves and your religious association, assurances of my high respect and esteem.

Study Questions

1. In *Common Sense*, what is Paine's distinction between government and so-
    ciety? How does this distinction affect or inform his views on the limits,
    power, legitimacy, and function of government? In your view, are his
    arguments and claims well supported? Justify your answer.
2. Paine answers objections regarding the American Revolution that it
    would be unjustified because Britain is America's mother country. What is
    Paine's argument with respect to this claim? Is his argument compelling?
    Justify your claims.
3. According to Madison in *Federalist 10*, what is "faction" and what are the
    two methods by which the causes of faction may be removed? Why is the
    first remedy, destruction of liberty, worse than faction itself? Why is
    the second remedy insufficient or inappropriate for controlling factions?
    Since the causes of faction cannot be removed, Madison proposes control-
    ling the effects of faction. What is the method by which the effects of fac-
    tion may be controlled? Do you agree with Madison's position and
    proposal regarding this issue? Why or why not? Defend your answer.
4. What is Madison's position in *Federalist 51* with respect to the divisions of
    power within government? In what way will the division of power be
    conducive to the maintenance of justice?
5. What is Paine's primary argument regarding the origin of the rights of
    man? What is the significance of his claim that there is a distinction
    between natural rights and civil rights, and what is this distinction?
6. In your view, what is it about the notion that government arising from the
    interest of society and the common rights of man maintains and respects
    the dignity of humanity, but governments arising from superstition and
    power do not?
7. How does Paine justify the claim that subjects/citizens do not have a con-
    tract or compact with government? What, in your view, is the most signif-
    icant aspect of this concept? What is Paine's view? Do you agree with his
    reasoning? Why or why not? Defend your position.
8. In Part II of *The Rights of Man*, Paine puts forth an argument concerning
    the limitations on the power and necessity of government based at least in
    part on the notion that a more perfect civilization has less need for gov-
    ernment. How does this position fit with Paine's position in *Common Sense*
    regarding the distinction between government and society? In your view,
    are Paine's claims regarding the diversity of immigrants in America a sup-
    port for his distinction between government and society and his views of
    limited government?
9. In "A Defense of the Constitutions of Government of the United States of
    America," John Adams argues for the necessity of a balance of powers in a
    democratic republic. What are his main arguments for this balance of
    separate powers? Are his arguments sound? Defend your claims.

10. What is Jefferson's argument for religious liberty? Does his position include the right to adhere to no religious tenets at all? Why is it important, in your view and in Jefferson's, to ensure that there is no establishment of state religion?

Suggestions for Further Reading

Adams, John. *The Political Writings of John Adams*. Edited by George W. Carey. Washington, D.C.: Regnery Publishing, 2000.

Bailyn, Bernard. *The Ideological Origins of the American Revolution*. Cambridge: Belknap Press of Harvard University Press, 1967.

Brinkley, Alan, Poslby, Nelson W., and Sullivan, Kathleen M. *The New Federalist Papers: Essays in Defense of the Constitution*. New York: W. W. Norton, 1997.

Hobbes, Thomas. *Leviathan*. Edited by Michael Oakeshott. Oxford: Basil Blackwell, 1946.

Jefferson, Thomas. *The Life and Selected Writings of Thomas Jefferson*. Edited, and with Introduction by Adrienne Koch and William Peden. New York: Modern Library, 1944.

Kammen, Michael, ed. *The Origins of the American Constitution*. New York: Penguin, 1986.

Kerber, Linda. "The Republican Ideology of the Revolutionary Generation." *American Quarterly 37* (1985): 474–495.

Lemisch, Jesse L., ed. *Benjamin Franklin: The Autobiography and Other Writings*. New York: New American Library, 1961.

Levy, Leonard W., ed. *Essays on the Making of the Constitution*. 2d ed. New York: Oxford University Press, 1987.

Locke, John. *Second Treatise of Government*. Edited, and with Introduction by C. B. MacPherson. Indianapolis: Hackett Publishing, 1980.

Matthews, Richard K. *The Radical Politics of Thomas Jefferson: A Revisionist View*. Lawrence: University Press of Kansas, 1984.

Quinn, Frederick, ed. *The Federalist Papers Reader and Historical Documents of Our American Heritage*. Santa Ana, Calif.: Seven Locks Press, 1997.

Storing, Herbert J. *What the Anti-Federalists Were For: The Political Thought of the Opponents of the Constitution*. Chicago: University of Chicago Press, 1981.

Wood, Gordon S. *The Creation of the American Republic, 1776–1787*. Chapel Hill: University of North Carolina Press, 1969.

Chapter 10

The Continuing Revolution
American Women's Rights and Civil Rights

The American revolutionaries succeeded in establishing a new representative government founded on belief in the inalienable rights to life, liberty, and the pursuit of happiness. What they did not succeed in creating was a government and society intent upon securing those rights to all people living under it. The founders had a vision of what it is to be a participating democratic citizen and what it means to be a possessor of effective individual rights. To be a possessor of the inalienable rights to life, liberty, and the pursuit of happiness was, unfortunately, the domain of only a select few. American women, slaves, and other nonwhite male people were often left out of the American dream and lived some version of an American nightmare. Slaves were systematically deprived of opportunities for personal fulfillment and a meaningful life; they were beaten and killed, deprived of the fruits of their labor and the basic necessities central to a life of human dignity. They were denied education and protection of the laws; they were relegated to the status of things in American law and practice.

The condition of white women in American society before and after the Revolution of 1775 was in most cases materially better than the condition of American slaves, but even here, the American ideals of liberty and happiness were not given their fullest expression. Women were considered the property of their husbands, absorbed into their husbands' existences and deprived not only of the right to vote, but also, legally, deprived of the fruits of their own labor if their husbands, fathers, brothers, or other male "protectors" saw fit to appropriate them. The custom in American society was to consider a woman both irrational and childlike, ironically to be considered an object of affection and devotion by her male counterparts while simultaneously being subject to the degradation inherent in the notion of the "defect of sex." White American women and African American slaves were relegated essentially to the status of things and property, afforded little or no respect and deprived of the most basic rights essential to existence as a human being.

If revolutionary thought were to be taken to its logical conclusions and the practices and principles of American revolutionary thought were applied to all people, African Americans and American women would have to be recognized as full participants in the American political process and equal partners in the community of citizens. But achieving such recognition would prove to be a long and difficult process, requiring an intertwining of ideals and actions of America's early agitators for, and defenders of, American women's rights and civil rights for disenfranchised people. Whether the writers included in this chapter are speaking about issues of slavery or women's subordination, their shared conception of the ideals of America rest largely on the conviction that the words written in the Declaration of Independence and the Constitution apply to all human beings, not simply to white men or persons of privilege.

The works in this chapter come from a wide variety of sources, beginning with William Lloyd Garrison's (1805–1879) "Declaration of Sentiments of the American Anti-Slavery Society" in the early 1830s and moving through the work of Marilyn Frye (1941–) in the late twentieth century. There are common themee running through the arguments illuminating the ideals of Garrison, the Grimké sisters—Angelina (1805–1879) and Sarah (1792–1873), Elizabeth Cady Stanton (1815–1902), Frederick Douglass (1817–1895), Martin Luther King, Jr. (1929–1968), and Marilyn Frye. These thinkers and activists are committed to showing that we have a right to live our lives according to principles that are more than mere slogans and that securing this right requires respect, action, and belief in the power of humanity to apply American ideals to all people. If there is any part of the American moral and political experience that is alive with devotion to extending American ideals and interests and applying them fairly, it is the American women's rights and civil rights movements.

Perhaps it is these thinkers' manner of presenting arguments that makes all the difference in our recognition of the strength and truth of their claims. The early American revolutionaries pointed out the unfairness and injustice of British policy against American colonists and acted in the only way they thought sufficient to right the wrongs against them. In doing so, they created their own unique political existence as a government and society separate from their British oppressors. Enslaved African Americans, abolitionists, and white American women took up the cause of freedom and righting of wrongs using the same principles enlisted by the early revolutionaries. However, they were required to go further in producing arguments and reforming American society than the early revolutionaries because of the one significant difference in their fight for freedom and recognition of rights. The British government never questioned the humanity of the American colonists as the colonists questioned the humanity of women and all African Americans. Early abolitionists and women's rights activists thus needed to appeal to the ideals of the Declaration of Independence and the rights recognized and guaranteed in the U.S. Constitution while simultaneously arguing for recognition of slaves and women as human beings.

As the women's rights and civil rights movements progressed, the arguments began to change and focus not so squarely on constitutional guarantees, but on the simple fact that there is a difference between a written guarantee and what actually takes place in practice. In the work of Elizabeth Cady Stanton, Martin Luther King, Jr., and Marilyn Frye, the women's rights and civil rights movements go beyond the original arguments contending that slaves and women are human beings and are therefore to be afforded the rights guaranteed in the Constitution. These revolutionary thinkers try to right social wrongs caused by deeply ingrained practices of oppression that mere corrective formalization and codification in law cannot change. For example, recognition of equality and insistence upon personal responsibility lead these writers, especially Elizabeth Cady Stanton in "Solitude of Self," to impress upon us the importance of the fullest development of which a human being is capable for his or her journey through the loneliness of life's struggles. Reverence for an Emersonian sort of self-reliance is found in Stanton's work, existing in conjunction with her fervently stated desire that the legal and customary bonds to which women are subject should be loosened to realize the value of the individual. Martin Luther King, Jr., puts forth arguments for the necessity of direct action against racism and oppression in "Letter from the Birmingham Jail," appealing to the reason of his adversaries for redress of grievances and substantial change in social attitudes. Marilyn Frye, building on the concept of oppression and power wielded over others, examines the philosophical and psychosocial factors involved in the oppression and enslavement of women in male-dominated societies.

Undaunted by persecution or fear, American abolitionists, women's rights activists, civil rights activists, writers, and orators present compelling arguments for the emancipation of slaves and women from the bonds that hold them in subjection and leave them open to the cruelties and dangers of oppression. Sarah Grimké puts it best in "Social Intercourse of the Sexes" when she says that she wishes that men would take their feet off the necks of women and allow them to stand and take their rightful place in the intellectual, moral, and political worlds, to have a voice in the workings of their own affairs, and to realize the potential of all human beings to live freely and well. Similarly, American civil rights activists argued that white Americans needed to remove the shackles from the necks of African Americans and recognize their rights as American citizens, as responsible persons, and as human beings.

Notes on the State of Virginia (1781)

Thomas Jefferson

THE ADMINISTRATION OF JUSTICE
AND THE DESCRIPTION OF THE LAWS

. . . Many of the laws which were in force during the monarchy being relative merely to that form of government, or inculcating principles inconsistent with republicanism, the first assembly which met after the establishment of the commonwealth appointed a committee to revise the whole code, to reduce it into proper form and volume, and report it to the assembly. This work has been executed . . . ; but probably will not be taken up till a restoration of peace shall leave to the legislature leisure to go through such a work.

The plan of the revisal was this. The common law of England, by which is meant, that part of the English law which was anterior to the date of the oldest statutes extant, is made the basis of the work. It was thought dangerous to attempt to reduce it to a text; it was therefore left to be collected from the usual monuments of it. Necessary alterations in that and so much of the whole body of the British statutes, and of acts of assembly, as were thought proper to be retained, were digested into one hundred and twenty-six new acts, in which simplicity of style was aimed at, as far as was safe. The following are the most remarkable alterations proposed: . . .

To make slaves distributable among the next of kin, as other movables. . . .

To emancipate all slaves born after passing the act. The bill reported by the revisers does not itself contain this proposition; but an amendment containing it was prepared, to be offered to the legislature whenever the bill should be taken up, and farther directing, that they should continue with their parents to a certain age, then to be brought up, at public expense, to tillage, arts, or sciences, according to their geniuses, till the females should be eighteen, and the males twenty-one years of age, when they should be colonized to such place as the circumstances of the time should render most proper, sending them out with arms, implements of household and of the handicraft arts, seeds, pairs of the useful domestic animals, &c., to declare them a free and independent people, and extend to them our alliance and protection, till they have acquired strength; and to send vessels at the same time to other parts of the world for an equal number of white inhabitants; to induce them to migrate hither proper encouragements were to be proposed. It will probably be asked, Why not retain and incorporate the blacks into the State, and thus save the expense of supplying by importation of white settlers, the vacancies they will

From *The Life and Selected Writings of Thomas Jefferson*, edited by Adrienne Koch and William Peden (New York: Modern Library) © 1944.

leave? Deep-rooted prejudices entertained by the whites; ten thousand recollections, by the blacks, of the injuries they have sustained; new provocations; the real distinctions which nature has made; and many other circumstances, will divide us into parties, and produce convulsions, which will probably never end but in the extermination of the one or the other race. To these objections, which are political, may be added others, which are physical and moral. The first difference which strikes us is that of color. Whether the black of the Negro resides in the recticular membrane between the skin and the scarf-skin, or in the scarf-skin itself; whether it proceeds from the color of the blood, the color of the bile, or from that of some other secretion, the difference is fixed in nature, and is as real as if its seat and cause were better known to us. And is this difference of no importance? Is it not the foundation of a greater or less share of beauty in the two races? Are not the fine mixtures of red and white, the expressions of every passion by greater or less suffusions of color in the one, preferable to that eternal monotony, which reigns in the countenances, that immovable veil of black, which covers the emotions of the other race? Add to these, flowing hair, a more elegant symmetry of form, their own judgment in favor of the whites, declared by their preference of them, as uniformly as is the preference of the Oran-utan for the black woman over those of his own species. The circumstances of superior beauty, is thought worthy attention in the propagation of our horses, dogs, and other domestic animals; why not in that of man? Besides those of color, figure, and hair, there are other physical distinctions proving a difference of race. They have less hair on the face and body. They secrete less by the kidneys, and more than by the glands of the skin, which gives them a very strong and disagreeable odor. This greater degree of transpiration, renders them more tolerant of heat, and less so of cold than the whites. Perhaps, too, a difference of structure in the pulmonary apparatus, which a late ingenious experimentalist has discovered to be the principal regulator of animal heat, may have disabled them from extricating, in the act of inspiration, so much of that fluid from the outer air, or obliged them in expiration, to part with more of it. They seem to require less sleep. A black after hard labor through the day, will be induced by the slightest amusements to sit up till midnight, or later, though knowing he must be out with the first dawn of the morning. They are at least as brave, and more adventuresome. But this may perhaps proceed from a want of forethought, which prevents their seeing a danger till it be present. When present, they do not go through it with more coolness or steadiness than the whites. They are more ardent after their female; but love seems with them to be more an eager desire, than a tender delicate mixture of sentiment and sensation. Their griefs are transient. Those numberless afflictions, which render it doubtful whether heaven has given life to us in mercy or in wrath, are less felt, and sooner forgotten with them. In general, their existence appears to participate more of sensation than reflection. To this must be ascribed their disposition to sleep when abstracted from their diversions, and unemployed in labor. An animal whose body is at rest, and who does not reflect must be disposed to sleep of course. Comparing them by their faculties of memory, reason, and imagination, it appears to me that in memory they are equal to the whites; in reason much inferior, as I think one could scarcely be found capable of tracing and comprehending the investigations of Euclid; and that in imagination they are dull, tasteless, and anomalous. . . . We will consider them here, on the same stage with the whites, and where the facts are not apocryphal on which a judgment is to be formed. It will be right to make great allowances for the difference of condition, of education, of conversation, of the sphere in which they move. Many millions of them have been brought to, and born in America. Most of them, indeed, have been confined to tillage, to their own homes, and their own society; yet many have been so situated, that they might have availed themselves of the conversation of their masters; many have been brought up to the handicraft arts, and from that circumstance have always been associated with the whites. Some have been liberally educated, and all have lived in countries where the arts and sciences are cultivated to a considerable degree, and all have had before their eyes samples of the best works from abroad. The Indians, with no advantages of this kind, will often carve figures on their pages not destitute of design and merit. They will crayon out an animal, a plant, or a country, so as to prove the existence of a germ in their minds which only wants cultivation. They astonish you with strokes of the most sublime oratory; such as prove their reason and sentiment strong, their imagination glowing and elevated. But never yet could I find that a black had uttered a thought above the level of plain narration; never saw even an elementary trait of painting or sculpture. In music they are more generally gifted than the whites with accurate ears for tune and time, and they have been found capable of imagining a small catch. Whether they will be equal to the composition of a more extensive run of melody, or of complicated harmony, is yet to be proved. Misery is often the parent of the most affecting touches in poetry. Among the blacks is misery enough, God knows, but no poetry. Love is the peculiar oestrum of the poet. Their love is ardent, but it kindles the senses only, not the imagination. . . .

. . . The opinion that they are inferior in the faculties of reason and imagination, must be hazarded with great diffidence. To justify a general conclusion, requires many observations, even where the subject may be submitted to the anatomical knife, to optical glasses, to analysis by fire or by solvents. How much more then where it is a faculty, not a substance, we are examining. . . . I advance it, therefore, as a suspicion only, that the blacks, whether originally a distinct race, or made distinct by time and circumstances, are inferior to the whites in the endowments both of body and mind. It is not against experience to suppose that different species of the same genus, of varieties of the same species, may possess different qualifications. Will not a lover of natural history then, one who views the gradations in all the races of animals with the eye of philosophy, excuse an effort to keep those in the department of man as distinct as nature has formed them? This unfortunate difference of color, and perhaps of faculty, is a powerful obstacle to the emancipation of these people. Many of their advocates, while they wish to vindicate the liberty of human nature, are anxious also to preserve its dignity and beauty. Some of these, embarrassed by the question, "What further is to be done with them?" join themselves in opposition with those who are actuated by sordid avarice only. Among the Romans emancipation required but one effort. The slave, when made free, might mix with, without staining the blood of his master. But with us a second is necessary, unknown to history. When freed, he is to be removed beyond the reach of mixture. . . .

Declaration of Sentiments
of the American Anti-Slavery Convention (1833)

WILLIAM LLOYD GARRISON

The Convention assembled in the city of Philadelphia, to organize a National Anti-Slavery Society, promptly seize the opportunity to promulgate the following Declaration of Sentiments, as cherished by them in relation to the enslavement of one-sixth portion of the American people.

More than fifty-seven years have elapsed, since a band of patriots convened in this place, to devise measures for the deliverance of this country form a foreign yoke. The corner-stone upon which they founded the Temple of Freedom was broadly this—'that all men are created equal; that they are endowed by their Creator with certain inalienable rights; that among these are life, LIBERTY, and the pursuit of happiness.' At the sound of their trumpet-call, three millions of people rose up as from the sleep of death, and rushed to the strife of blood; deeming it more glorious to die instantly as freemen, than desirable to live one hour as slaves. They were few in number—poor in resources; but the honest conviction that Truth, Justice and Right were on their side, made them invincible.

We have met together for the achievement of an enterprise, without which that of our fathers is incomplete; and which, for its magnitude, solemnity, and probable results upon the destiny of the world, as far transcends theirs as moral truth does physical force.

In purity of motive, in earnestness of zeal, in decision of purpose, in intrepidity of action, in steadfastness of faith, in sincerity of spirit, we would not be inferior to them.

Their principles led them to wage war against their oppressors, and to spill human blood like water, in order to be free. Ours forbid the doing of evil that good may come, and lead us to reject, and to entreat the oppressed to reject, the use of all carnal weapons for deliverance from bondage; relying solely upon those which are spiritual, and mighty through God to the pulling down of strong holds.

Their measures were physical resistance—the marshalling in arms—the hostile array—the mortal encounter. Ours shall be such only as the opposition of moral purity to moral corruption—the destruction of error by the potency of truth—the overthrow of prejudice by the power of love—and the abolition of slavery by the spirit of repentance.

Their grievances, great as they were, were trifling in comparison with the wrongs and sufferings of those for whom we plead. Our fathers were never slaves—never bought and sold like cattle—never shut out from the light of knowledge and religion—never subjected to the lash of brutal taskmasters.

But those, for whose emancipation we are striving—constituting at the present time at least one-sixth part of our countrymen—are recognized by law, and treated by their fellow-beings, as marketable commodities, as goods and chattels, as brute beasts; are plundered daily of the fruits of their toil without redress; really enjoy no constitutional nor legal protection from licentious and murderous outrages upon their persons; and are ruthlessly torn asunder—the tender babe from the arms of its frantic mother—the heartbroken wife from her weeping husband—at the caprice or pleasure of irresponsible tyrants. For the crime of having a dark complexion, they suffer the pangs of hunger, the infliction of stripes, the ignominy of brutal servitude. They are kept in heathenish darkness by laws expressly enacted to make their instruction a criminal offence.

These are the prominent circumstances in the condition of more than two millions of our people, the proof of which may be found in the thousands of indisputable facts, and in the laws of the slaveholding States.

Hence we maintain—that, in view of the civil and religious privileges of this nation, the guilt of its oppression is unequalled by any other on the face of the earth; and, therefore, that it is bound to repent instantly, to undo the heavy burdens, and to let the oppressed go free.

We further maintain—that no man has a right to enslave or imbrute his brother—to hold or acknowledge him, for one moment, as a piece of merchandize—to keep back his hire by fraud—or to brutalize his mind, by denying him the means of intellectual, social and moral improvement.

The right to enjoy liberty is inalienable. . . . Every man has a right to his own body—to the products of his own labor—to the protection of law—and to the common advantages of society. It is piracy to buy or steal a native African, and subject him to servitude. Surely, the sin is as great to enslave an American as an African.

Therefore we believe and affirm—that there is no difference, in principle, between the African slave trade and American slavery:

That every American citizen, who detains a human being in involuntary bondage as his property, is, according to Scripture, (Ex. xxi. 16,) a man-stealer:

That the slaves ought instantly to be set free, and brought under the protection of law:

That if they had lived from the time of Pharaoh down to the present period, and had been entailed through successive generations, their right to be free could never have been alienated, but their claims would have constantly risen in solemnity:

That all those laws which are now in force, admitting the right of slavery, are therefore, before God, utterly null and void; being an audacious usurpation of the Divine prerogative, a daring infringement on the law of nature, a base overthrow of the very foundations of the social compact, a complete extinction of all the relations, endearments and obligations of mankind, and a presumptuous transgression of all the holy commandments; and that therefore they ought instantly to be abrogated.

We further believe and affirm—that all persons of color, who possess the qualifications which are demanded of others, ought to be admitted forthwith to the enjoyment of the same privileges, and the exercise of the same prerogatives, as others; and that the paths of preferment, of wealth, and of intelligence, should be opened as widely to them as to persons of a white complexion.

We maintain that no compensation should be given to the planters emancipating their slaves:

Because it would be a surrender of the great fundamental principle, that man cannot hold property in man:

Because slavery is a crime, and therefore is not an article to be sold:

Because the holders of slaves are not the just proprietors of what they claim; freeing the slave is not depriving them of property, but restoring it to its rightful owner; it is not wronging the master, but righting the slave—restoring him to himself:

Because immediate and general emancipation would only destroy nominal, not real property; it would not amputate a limb or break a bone of the slaves, but by infusing motives into their breasts, would make them doubly valuable to the masters as free laborers; and

Because, if compensation is to be given at all, it should be given to the outraged and guiltless slaves, and not to those who have plundered and abused them.

We regard as delusive, cruel and dangerous, any scheme of expatriation which pretends to aid, either directly or indirectly, in the emancipation of the slaves, or to be a substitute for the immediate and total abolition of slavery.

We fully and unanimously recognize the sovereignty of each State, to legislate exclusively on the subject of the slavery which is tolerated within its limits; we concede that Congress, under the present national compact, has no right to interfere with any of the slave States, in relation to this momentous subject:

But we maintain that Congress has a right, and is solemnly bound, to suppress the domestic slave trade between the several States, and to abolish slavery in those portions of our territory which the Constitution has placed under its exclusive jurisdiction.

We also maintain that there are, at the present time, the highest obligations resting upon the people of the free States to remove slavery by moral and political action, as prescribed in the Constitution of the United States. They are now living under a pledge of their tremendous physical force, to fasten the galling fetters of tyranny upon the limbs of millions in the Southern States; they are liable to be called at any moment to suppress a general insurrection of the slaves; they authorize the slave owner to vote for three-fifths of his slaves as property, and thus enable him to perpetuate his oppression; they support a standing army at the South for its protection; and they seize the slave, who has escaped into their territories, and send him back to be tortured by an enraged master or a brutal driver. This relation to slavery is criminal, and full of danger: IT MUST BE BROKEN UP.

These are our views and principles—these our designs and measures. With entire confidence in the overruling justice of God, we plant ourselves upon the Declaration of our Independence and the truths of Divine Revelation, as upon the Everlasting Rock.

We shall organize Anti-Slavery Societies . . . in every city, town and village in our land.

We shall send forth agents to lift up the voice of remonstrance, of warning, of entreaty, and of rebuke.

We shall circulate, unsparingly and extensively, anti-slavery tracts and periodicals.

We shall enlist the pulpit and the press in the cause of the suffering and the dumb.

We shall aim at purification of the churches from all participation in the guilt of slavery.

We shall encourage the labor of freemen rather than that of slaves, by giving a preference to their productions: and

We shall spare no exertions nor means to bring the whole nation to speedy repentance.

Our trust for victory is solely in God. We may be personally defeated, but our principles never! Truth, Justice, Reason, Humanity, must and will gloriously triumph. Already a host is coming up to the help of the Lord against the mighty, and the prospect before us is full of encouragement.

Submitting this Declaration to the candid examination of the people of this country, and of the friends of liberty throughout the world, we hereby affix our signatures to it; pledging ourselves that, under the guidance and by the help of Almighty God, we will do all that in us lies, consistently with this Declaration of our principles, to overthrow the most execrable system of slavery that has ever been witnessed upon earth; to deliver our land from its deadliest curse; to wipe out the foulest stain which rests upon our national escutcheon; and to secure to the colored population of the United States, all the rights and privileges which belong to them as men, and as Americans—come what may to our persons, our interests, or our reputation—whether we live to witness the triumph of Liberty, Justice and Humanity, or perish untimely as martyrs in this great, benevolent, and holy cause.

Appeal to the Christian Women of the South (1836)

ANGELINA GRIMKÉ

. . . Moral, like natural light, is so extremely subtle in its nature as to overlap all human barriers, and laugh at the puny efforts of man to control it. All the excuses and palliations of this system must inevitably be swept away. . . . It will be, and that very soon, clearly perceived and fully acknowledged by all the virtuous and the candid, that in principle it is as sinful to hold a human being in bondage who has been born in Carolina, as one who has been born in Africa. All that sophistry of argument which has been employed to prove, that although it is sinful to send to Africa to procure men and women as slaves, who have never been in slavery, that still, it is not sinful to keep those in bondage who have come down by inheritance, will be utterly overthrown. We must come back to the good old doctrine of our forefathers who declared to the world, "this self evident truth that *all* men are created equal, and that they have certain *inalienable* rights among which are life, *liberty*, and the pursuit of happiness." . . . If then, we have no right to enslave an African, surely we can have none to enslave an American; if it is a self evident truth that *all* men, every where and of every color are born equal, and have an *inalienable right to liberty*, then it is equally true that *no* man can be born a slave, and no man can ever *rightfully* be reduced to *involuntary* bondage and held as a slave. . . .

But after all, it may be said, our fathers were certainly mistaken, for the Bible sanctions Slavery, and that is the highest authority. Now the Bible is my ultimate appeal in all matters of faith and practice, and it is to *this test* I am anxious to bring the subject at issue between us. Let us then begin with Adam and examine the charter of privileges which was given to him. "Have dominion over the fish of the sea, and over the fowl of the air, and over every living thing that moveth upon the earth." In the eighth Psalm we have a still fuller description of the charter which through Adam was given to all mankind. "Thou madest him to have dominion over the works of thy hands; thou hast put all things under his feet. All sheep and oxen, yea, and the beasts of the field, the fowl of the air, the fish of the sea, and whatsoever passeth through the paths of the seas." And after the flood when this charter of human rights was renewed, we find *no additional* power vested in man. . . . In this charter, although the different kinds of *irrational* beings are so particularly enumerated, and supreme dominion over *all of them* is granted, yet man is *never* vested with this dominion *over his fellow man*. . . . *Man* then, I assert *never* was put *under the feet of man*, by that first charter of human rights which was given by God. . . .

But it may be argued, that in the very chapter of Genesis from which I have last quoted, will be found the curse pronounced upon Canaan, by which his posterity was consigned to servitude under his brothers Shem and Japeth. . . . I do not know that prophecy does *not* tell us what *ought to be*, but what actually does take place, ages after it has been delivered, and that if we justify America for enslaving the children of Africa, we must also justify Egypt for reducing the children of Israel to bondage, for the latter was foretold as explicitly as the former. I am well aware that prophecy has often been urged as an excuse for Slavery, but be not deceived, the fulfillment of prophecy will *not cover one sin* in the awful days of account. . . .

But it has been urged that the patriarchs held slaves, and therefore, slavery is right. Do you really believe that patriarchal servitude was like American slavery? Can you believe it? If so, read the history of these primitive fathers of the church and be undeceived. Look at Abraham, though so great a man, going to the herd himself and fetching a calf from thence and serving it up with his own hands, for the entertainment of his guests. Look at Sarah, that princess as her name signifies, baking cakes upon the hearth. If the servants they had were like Southern slaves, would they have performed such comparatively menial offices for themselves? Hear too the plaintive lamentation of Abraham when he feared he should have no son to bear his name down to posterity. "Behold thou hast given me no seed, &c, one born in my house *is mine* heir." From this it appears that one of his *servants* was to inherit his immense estate. Is this like Southern slavery? . . . Besides, such was the footing upon which Abraham was with *his* servants, that he trusted them with arms. Are slaveholders willing to put swords and pistols into the hands of their slaves? He was as a father among his servants; what are planters and masters generally among theirs? . . .

Where, . . . I would ask, is the warrant, the justification, or the palliation of American Slavery from Hebrew servitude? How many of the southern slaves would be in bondage according to the laws of Moses; Not one. You may observe that I have carefully avoided using the term *slavery* when speaking of Jewish servitude; and simply for this reason, that *no such thing* existed among that people; the word translated servant does *not* mean *slave*, it is the same that is applied to Abraham, to Moses, to Elisha and the prophet generally. *Slavery* then *never* existed under the Jewish Dispensation at all. . . . If slaveholders are determined to hold slaves as long as they can, let them not dare say that the God of mercy and truth *ever* sanctioned such a system of cruelty and wrong. It is blasphemy against Him.

We have seen that the code of laws framed by Moses with regard to servants was designed to *protect them* as *men and women*, to secure to them their *rights* as *human beings*, to guard them from oppression and defend them from violence of every kind. Let us now turn to the Slave laws of the South and West and examine them too. . . .

1. *Slavery* is hereditary and perpetual, to the last moment of the slave's earthly existence, and to all his descendants to the latest posterity.

2. The labor of the slave is compulsory and uncompensated; while the kind of labor, the amount of toil, the time allowed for rest, are dictated solely by the master. No bargain is made, no wages given. . . .

3. The slave being considered a personal chattel may be sold or pledged, or leased at the will of his master. . . .

4. Slaves can make no contracts and have no *legal* right to any property, real or personal. Their own honest earnings and the legacies of friends belong in point of law to their masters.

5. Neither a slave nor a free colored person can be a witness against any *white*, or free person, in a court of justice, however atrocious may have been the crimes they have seen him commit, if such testimony would be for the benefit of a *slave*; but they may give testimony *against a fellow slave*, or free colored man, even in cases affecting life, if the *master* is to reap the advantage of it.

6. The slave may be punished at his master's discretion—without trial—without any means of legal redress; whether his offence be real or imaginary; and the master can transfer the same despotic power to any person or persons, he may choose to appoint.

7. The slave is not allowed to resist any free man under *any* circumstances, *his* only safety consists in the fact that his *owner* may bring suit and recover the price of his body, in case his life is taken, or his limbs rendered unfit for labor.

8. Slaves cannot redeem themselves, or obtain a change of masters, though cruel treatment may have rendered such a change necessary for their personal safety.

9. The slave is entirely unprotected in his domestic relations.

10. The laws greatly obstruct the manumission of slaves, even where the master is willing to enfranchise them.

11. The operation of the laws tends to deprive slaves of religious instruction and consolation.

12. The whole power of the laws is exerted to keep slaves in a state of the lowest ignorance.

13. There is in this country a monstrous inequality of law and right. What is a trifling fault in the *white* man, is considered highly criminal in the *slave*; the same offences which cost a white man a few dollars only, are punished in the negro with death.

14. The laws operate most oppressively upon free people of color. . . .

. . . The Code Noir of the South, *robs the slave of all his rights* as a *man*, reduces him to a chattel personal, and defends the *master* in the exercise of the most unnatural and unwarrantable power over his slave. . . . Truly it was wise in the slaveholders of the South to declare their slaves to be "chattels personal"; for before they could be robbed of wages, wives, children, and friends, it was absolutely necessary to deny they were human beings. It is wise in them, to keep them in abject ignorance, for the strong man armed must be bound before we can spoil his house—the powerful intellect of man must be bound down with the iron chains of nescience before we can rob him of his rights as a man; we must reduce him to a *thing* before we can claim the right to set our feet upon his neck, because it was only *all things* which were originally *put under the feet of man* by the Almighty. . . .

But some have even said that Jesus Christ did not condemn slavery. To this I reply that our Holy Redeemer lived and preached among the Jews only. The laws which Moses had enacted fifteen hundred years previous to his appearance among them, had never been annulled, and those laws protected every servant in Palestine. If then He did not condemn Jewish servitude this does not prove that he would not have condemned such a monstrous system as that of American *slavery*. . . . But did not Jesus condemn slavery? Let us examine some of his precepts. "*Whatsoever* ye would that men should do to you, do *ye even so to them*." Let every slaveholder apply these queries to his own heart; Am *I* willing to see *my* wife the slave of another—Am *I* willing to see my mother a slave, or my father, my sister or my brother? If *not*, then in holding others as slaves, I am doing what I would *not* wish to be done to me or any relative I have; and thus have I broken this rule which was given *me* to walk by.

But some slaveholders have said, "we were never in bondage to any man," and therefore the yoke of bondage would be insufferable to us, but slaves are accustomed to it, their backs are fitted to the burden. Well, I am willing to admit that you who have lived in freedom would find slavery even more oppressive than the poor slave does, but then you may try this question in another form—Am I willing to reduce *my little child* to slavery? You know that *if it is brought up a slave* it will never know any contrast, between freedom and bondage, its back will become fitted to the burden just as the Negro child's does—*not by nature*—but by daily, violent pressure. . . . It has been justly remarked that "*God never made a slave*," he made man upright; his back was *not* made to carry burdens, nor his neck to wear a yoke, and the *man* must be crushed within him, before his *back* can be *fitted* to the burden of perpetual slavery. . . . I appeal to you, my friends, as mothers; Are you willing to enslave *your* children? You start back with horror and indignation at such a question. But why, if slavery is *no wrong* to those upon whom it is imposed? Why, if as has often been said, slaves are happier than their masters, free from the cares and perplexities of providing for themselves and their families? Why not place *your* children in the way of being supported without your having the trouble to provide for them, or they for themselves? Do you not perceive that as soon as this golden rule of action is applied to *yourselves* that you involuntarily shrink from the test; as soon as *your* actions are weighed in *this* balance of the sanctuary that *you are found wanting*? Try yourselves by another of the Divine precepts, "Thou shalt love thy neighbor as thyself." Can we love a man *as* we love *ourselves* if we do, and continue to do unto him, what we would not wish any one to do to us? . . .

But perhaps you will be ready to query, why appeal to *women* on this subject? *We* do not make the laws which perpetuate slavery. *No* legislative power is vested in *us; we* can do nothing to overthrow the system, even if we wished to do so. To this I reply, I know you do not make the laws, but I also know that *you are the wives and mothers, the sisters and daughters of those who do*; and if you really suppose *you* can do nothing to overthrow slavery, you are greatly mistaken. You can do much in every way: four things I will name. 1st. You can read on this subject. 2d. You can pray over this subject. 3d. You can speak on this subject. 4th. You can *act* on this subject. I have not placed reading before praying because I regard it more important, but because, in order to pray aright, we must understand what we are praying for; it is only then we can "pray with the understanding and the spirit also."

1. Read then on the subject of slavery. Search the Scriptures daily, whether the things I have told you are true. . . . The *Bible* . . . is the book I want you to read in the spirit of inquiry, and the spirit of prayer. . . .

2. Pray over this subject. . . . Pray to your father, who seeth in secret, that he would open your eyes to see whether slavery is *sinful*; and if it is, that he would enable you to bear a faithful, open and unshrinking testimony against it, and to do whatsoever your hands find to do, leaving the consequences entirely to him, who still says to us whenever we try to reason away duty from the fear of consequences, *"What is that to thee, follow thou me."* Pray also for that poor slave.

3. Speak on this subject. It is through the tongue, the pen, and the press, that truth is principally propagated. Speak then to your relatives, your friends, your acquaintances on the subject of slavery; be not afraid if you are conscientiously convinced it is *sinful*, to say so openly, but calmly, and to let your sentiments be known. If you are served by the slaves of others, try to ameliorate their condition as much as possible. . . .

4. Act on this subject. Some of you *own* slaves yourselves. If you believe slavery is *sinful*, set them at liberty. . . . If they wish to remain with you, pay them wages, if not let them leave you. Should they remain teach them, and have them taught the common branches of an English education; they have minds and those minds, *ought to be improved.* So precious a talent as intellect, never was given to be wrapt in a napkin and buried in the earth. . . .

5. But some of you will say, we can neither free our slaves nor teach them to read, for the laws of our state forbid it. Be not surprised when I say such wicked laws *ought to be no barrier* in the way of your duty. . . .

But some of you may say, if we free our slaves, they will be taken up and sold, therefore there will be no use in doing it. Peter and John might just as well have said, we will not preach the gospel, for if we do, we shall be taken up and put in prison, therefore there will be no use in our preaching. *Consequences*, my friends, belong no more to *you*, than they did to these apostles. Duty is ours and events are God's. If you think slavery is sinful, all *you* have to do is to set your slaves at liberty, do all you can to protect them, and in humble faith and fervent prayer, commend them to your common Father. . . .

I know that this doctrine of obeying *God*, rather than man, will be considered as dangerous, and heretical by many, but I am not afraid openly to avow it, because it is the doctrine of the Bible; but I would not be understood to advocate resistance to any law however oppressive, if, in obeying it, I was not obliged to commit *sin*. If for instance, there was a law, which imposed imprisonment or a fine upon me if I manumitted a slave, I would on no account resist that law, I would set the slave free, and then go to prison or pay the fine. If a law commands me to *sin I will break it*; if it calls me to *suffer*, I will let it take its course *unresistingly*. The doctrine of blind obedience and unqualified submission to *any human* power, whether civil or ecclesiastical, is the doctrine of despotism, and ought to have no place among Republicans and Christians.

But you will perhaps say, such a course of conduct would inevitably expose us to great suffering. Yes! My Christian friends, I believe it would, but this will *not* excuse you or any one else for the neglect of *duty*. . . .

Letters on the Equality of the Sexes

The Original Equality of Women (1837)

SARAH GRIMKÉ

. . . In attempting to comply with thy request to give my views on the Province of Woman, I feel that I am venturing on nearly untrodden ground, and that I shall advance arguments in opposition to a corrupt public opinion, and the perverted interpretations of Holy Writ, which has so universally obtained. But I am in search of truth; and no obstacle shall prevent my prosecuting that search, because I believe the welfare of the world will be materially advanced by every new discovery we make of the designs of Jehovah in the creation of woman. It is impossible that we can answer the purpose of our being, unless we understand that purpose. It is impossible that we should fulfill our duties, unless we comprehend them; or live up to our privileges, unless we know what they are.

In examining this important subject, I shall depend solely on the bible to designate the sphere of woman, because I believe almost every thing that has been written on the subject, has been the result of a misconception on the simple truths revealed in the Scriptures, in consequence of the false translation of many passages of Holy Writ. . . .

We must first view woman at the period of her creation. . . . God created man in his own image, in the image of God created he him, male and female created he them." In all this sublime description of the creation of man (which

From *The Public Years of Sarah and Angelina Grimké*, ed. Larry Ceplair (New York: Columbia University Press) 1989, pp. 204–210, 216–219. Reprinted with permission.

is a generic term including man and woman), there is not one particle of difference intimated as existing between them. They were both made in the image of God; dominion was given to both over every other creature, but not over each other. Created in perfect equality, they were expected to exercise the viceregency intrusted to them by their Maker, in harmony and love.

Let us pass on now to the recapitulation of the creation of man. . . . All creation swarmed with animated beings capable of natural affection, as we know they still are; it was not, therefore, merely to give man a creature susceptible of loving, obeying, and looking up to him, for all that the animals could do and did do. It was to give him a companion, *in all respects* his equal; one who was like himself *a free agent*, gifted with intellect and endowed with immortality; not a partaker merely of his animal gratifications, but able to enter into all his feelings as a moral and responsible being. If this had not been the case, how could she have been a help meet for him? I understand this as applying not only to the parties entering into the marriage contract, but to all men and women, because I believe God designed woman to be a help meet for man in every good and perfect work. . . .

This Blissful condition was not long enjoyed by our first parents. Eve, it would seem from the history, was wandering alone amid the bowers of Paradise, when the serpent met with her. . . .

We next find Adam involved in the same sin, not through the instrumentality of a super-natural agent, but through that of his equal, a being whom he must have known was liable to transgress the divine command, because he must have felt that he was himself a free agent, and that he was restrained from disobedience only by the exercise of faith and love towards his Creator. Had Adam tenderly reproved his wife, and endeavored to lead her to repentance instead of sharing in her guilt, I should be much more ready to accord to man that superiority which he claims; but as the facts stand disclosed by the sacred historian, it appears to me that to say the least, there was as much weakness exhibited by Adam as by Eve. They both fell from innocence, and consequently from happiness, *but not from equality*.

Let us next examine the conduct of this fallen pair, when Jehovah interrogated them respecting their fault. They both frankly confessed their guilt. "The man said, the woman whom thou gavest to be with me, she gave me of the tree and I did eat. And the woman said, the serpent beguiled me and I did eat." And the Lord God said unto the woman, "thou wilt be subject unto thy husband, and he will rule over thee." That this did not allude to the subjection of woman to man is manifest, because the same mode of expression is used in speaking to Cain of Abel. . . . They had incurred the penalty of sin, they were shorn of their innocence, but they stood on the same platform side by side, acknowledging *no superior* but their God. Notwithstanding what has been urged, woman I am aware stands charged to the present day with having brought sin into the world. I shall not repel the charge by any counter assertions, although, as was before hinted, Adam's ready acquiescence with his wife's proposal, does not savor much of that superiority *in strength of mind,* which is arrogated by man. Even admitting that Eve was the greater sinner, it seems to me man might be satisfied with the dominion he has claimed and exercised for nearly six thousand years, and that more true nobility would be manifested by endeavoring to raise the fallen and invigorate the weak, than by keeping woman in subjection. . . .

The lust of dominion was probably the first effect of the fall; and as there was no other intelligent being over whom to exercise it, woman was the first victim of this unhallowed passion. . . . All history attests that man has subjected woman to his will, used her as a means to promote his selfish gratification, to minister to his sensual pleasures, to be instrumental in promoting his comfort; but never has he desired to elevate her to that rank she was created to fill. He has done all he could to debase and enslave her mind; and now he looks triumphantly on the ruin he has wrought, and says, the being he has thus deeply injured is his inferior.

Woman has been placed by John Quincy Adams, side by side with the slave, whilst he was contending for the right side of petition. I thank him for ranking us with the oppressed; for I shall not find it difficult to show, that in all ages and countries, not even excepting enlightened republic America, woman has more or less been made a *means* to promote the welfare of man, without due regard to her own happiness, and the glory of god as the end of her creation. . . .

The cupidity of man soon led him to regard woman as property, and hence we find them sold to those, who wished to marry them, as far as appears, without any regard to those sacred rights which belong to woman, as well as to man in the choice of a companion. . . .

Social Intercourse of the Sexes

. . . Before I proceed with the account of that oppression which woman has suffered in every age and country from her *protector*, man, permit me to offer for your consideration, some views relative to the social intercourse of the sexes. Nearly the whole of this intercourse is, in my apprehension, derogatory to man and woman, as moral and intellectual beings. We approach each other, and mingle with each other, under the constant pressure of a feeling that we are of different sexes; and, instead of regarding each other only in the light of immortal creatures, the mind is fettered by the idea which is early and industriously infused into it, that we must never forget the distinction between male and female. Hence our intercourse, instead of being elevated and refined, is generally calculated to excite and keep alive the lowest propensities of our nature. Nothing, I believe, has tended more to destroy the true dignity of woman, than the fact that she is approached by man in the character of a female. The idea that she is sought as an intelligent and heaven-born creature, whose society will cheer, refine and elevate her companion, and that she will receive the same blessings she confers, is rarely held up to her view. On the contrary, man almost always addresses himself to the weakness of woman. By flattery, by an appeal to her passions, he seeks access to her heart; and when he has gained her affections, he uses her as the instrument of his pleasure—the minister of his temporal comfort. He furnishes himself with a housekeeper, whose chief business is in the kitchen, or the nursery. And whilst he goes abroad and enjoys the means of improvement afforded by collision of intellect with cultivated minds, his wife is condemned to draw nearly all her instruction from books, if she has time to peruse them. . . .

Surely no one who contemplates, with the eye of a Christian philosopher, the design of God in the creation of woman, can believe that she is now fulfilling that design. The literal translation of the word "helpmeet" is a helper like unto himself . . . and manifestly signifies a companion. Now I believe it will be impossible for woman to fill the station assigned to her by God, until her brethren mingle with her as an equal, as a moral being; and lose, in the dignity of her immortal nature, and in the fact of her bearing like himself the image of superscription of her God, the idea of her being a female. . . . Until our intercourse is purified by the forgetfulness of sex,—until we rise above the present low and sordid views which entwine themselves around our social and domestic interchange of sentiment and feelings, we never can derive that benefit from each other's society which it is the design of our Creator that we should. Man has inflicted an unspeakable injury upon woman, by holding up to her view her animal nature, and placing in the background her moral and intellectual being. Woman has inflicted an injury upon herself by submitting to be thus regarded; and she is now called upon to rise from the station where *man*, not God, has placed her, and claim those sacred and inalienable rights, as a moral and responsible being, with which her Creator has invested her. . . .

The First Convention Ever Called to Discuss the Civil and Political Rights of Women

Seneca Falls, NY (1848)

ELIZABETH CADY STANTON

When, in the course of human events, it becomes necessary for one portion of the family of man to assume among the people of the earth a position different from that which they have hitherto occupied, but one to which the laws of nature and of nature's God entitle them, a decent respect to the opinions of mankind requires that they should declare the causes that impel them to such a course.

We hold these truths to be self-evident: that all men and women are created equal; that they are endowed by their Creator with certain inalienable rights, that among these are life, liberty, and the pursuit of happiness; that to secure these rights governments are instituted, deriving their just powers from the consent of the governed. Whenever any form of government becomes destructive of those ends, it is the right of those who suffer from it to refuse allegiance to it, and to insist upon the institution of a new government, laying its foundation on such principles, and organizing its powers in such form as to them shall seem most likely to effect their safety and happiness. Prudence, indeed, will dictate that governments long established should not be changed for light and transient causes; and accordingly, all experience hath shown that mankind are more disposed to suffer, while evils are sufferable, than to right themselves by abolishing the forms to which they were accustomed. But when a long train of abuses and usurpations, pursuing invariably the same object evinces a design to reduce them under absolute despotism, it is their duty to throw off such government, and to provide new guards for their future security. Such has been the patient sufferance of the women under this government, and such is now the necessity which constrains them to demand the equal station to which they are entitled.

The history of mankind is a history of repeated injuries and usurpations on the part of man toward woman, having in direct object the establishment of an absolute tyranny over her. To prove this, let facts be submitted to a candid world.

He has never permitted her to exercise her inalienable right to the elective franchise.

He has compelled her to submit to laws, in the formation of which she had no voice.

He has withheld from her rights which are given to the most ignorant and degraded men—both natives and foreigners.

Having deprived her of this first right of a citizen, the elective franchise, thereby leaving her without representation in the halls of legislation, he has oppressed her on all sides.

He has made her, if married, in the eye of the law, civilly dead.

He has taken from her all right in property, even to the wages she earns.

He has made her, morally, an irresponsible being, as she can commit many crimes with impunity, provided they be done in the presence of her husband. In the covenant of marriage, she is compelled to promise obedience to her husband, he becoming to all intents and purposes, her master—the law giving him power to deprive her of her liberty, and to administer chastisement.

He has so framed the laws of divorce, as to what shall be the proper causes of divorce; in case of separation, to whom the guardianship of the children shall be given; as to be wholly regardless of the happiness of women—the law, in all cases, going upon a false supposition of the supremacy of man, and giving all power into his hands.

After depriving her of all rights as a married woman, if single and the owner of property, he has taxed her to support a government which recognizes her only when her property can be made profitable to it.

He has monopolized nearly all the profitable employments, and from those she is permitted to follow, she receives but a scanty remuneration.

He closes against her all the avenues to wealth and distinction, which he considers most honorable to himself. As a teacher of theology, medicine, or law, she is not known.

He has denied her all the facilities for obtaining a thorough education—all colleges being closed against her.

He allows her in Church, as well as State, but a subordinate position, claiming Apostolic authority for her exclusion from the ministry, and, with some exceptions, from any public participating in the affairs of the Church.

He has created a false public sentiment, by giving to the world a different code of morals for men and women, by which moral delinquencies which exclude women from society, are not only tolerated but deemed of little account in man.

He has usurped the prerogative of Jehovah himself, claiming it as his right to assign for her a sphere of action, when that belongs to her conscience and to her god.

He has endeavored, in every way that he could, to destroy her confidence in her own powers, to lessen her self-respect, and to make her willing to lead a dependent and abject life.

Now, in view of this entire disfranchisement of one-half the people of this country, their social and religious degradation,—in view of the unjust laws above mentioned, and because women do feel themselves aggrieved, oppressed, and fraudulently deprived of their most sacred rights, we insist that they have immediate admission to all the rights and privileges which belong to them as citizens of the United States.

In entering upon the great work before us, we anticipate no small amount of misconception, misrepresentation, and ridicule; but we shall use every instrumentality within our power to effect our object. We shall employ agents, circulate tracts, petition the state and national legislatures, and endeavor to enlist the pulpit and the press in our behalf. We hope this Convention will be followed by a series of Conventions, embracing every part of the country.

Firmly relying upon the final triumph of the Right and the True, we do this day affix our signatures to this declaration. . . .

This Declaration was unanimously adopted and signed by 32 men and 68 women.

RESOLUTIONS

Whereas the great precept of nature is conceded to be, "that man shall pursue his own true and substantial happiness," Blackstone, in his Commentaries, remarks, that this law of Nature being coeval with mankind, and dictated by God himself, is of course superior in obligation to any other. It is binding over all the globe, in all countries, and at all times; no human laws are of any validity if contrary to this, and such of them as are valid, derive all their force, and all their validity, and all their authority, mediately and immediately, from this original; therefore,

Resolved, That such laws as conflict, in any way, with the true and substantial happiness of woman, are contrary to the great precept of nature, and of no validity; for this is "superior in obligation to any other."

Resolved, That all laws which prevent woman from occupying such a station in society as her conscience shall dictate, or which place her in a position inferior to that of man, are contrary to the great precept of nature, and therefore of no force or authority.

Resolved, That woman is man's equal—was intended to be so by the Creator—and the highest good of the race demands that she should be recognized as such.

Resolved, That the women of this country ought to be enlightened in regard to the laws under which they live, that they may no longer publish their degradation, by declaring themselves satisfied with their present position, nor their ignorance, by asserting that they have all the rights they want.

Resolved, That inasmuch as man, while claiming for himself intellectual superiority, does accord to woman moral superiority, it is pre-eminently his duty to encourage her to speak, and teach, as she has an opportunity, in all religious assemblies.

Resolved, That the same amount of virtue, delicacy, and refinement of behavior, that is required of woman in the social state, should also be required of man, and the same transgressions should be visited with equal severity on both man and woman.

Resolved, That the objection of indelicacy and impropriety, which is so often brought against woman when she addresses a public audience, comes with a very ill grace from those who encourage, by their attendance, her appearance on the stage, in the concert, or in feats of the circus.

Resolved, That woman has too long rested satisfied in the circumscribed limits which corrupt customs and a perverted application of the Scriptures have marked out for her, and that it is time she should move in the enlarged sphere which her great Creator assigned her.

Resolved, That it is the duty of the women of this country to secure to themselves their sacred right to the elective franchise.

Resolved, That the equality of human rights results necessarily from the fact of the identity of the race in capabilities and responsibilities.

Resolved, therefore, That, being invested by the Creator with the same capabilities, and the same consciousness of responsibility for their exercise, it is demonstrably the right and duty of woman, equally with man, to promote every righteous cause, by every righteous means; and especially in regard to the great subjects of morals and religion, it is self-evidently her right to participate with her brother in teaching them, both in private and in public, by writing and by speaking, by any instrumentalities proper to be used, and in any assemblies proper to be held; and this being a self-evident truth, growing out of the divinely implanted principles of human nature, any custom or authority adverse to it, whether modern or wearing the hoary sanction of antiquity, is to be regarded as a self-evident falsehood, and at war with the interests of mankind. . . .

THE FIRST AND CLOSING PARAGRAPHS OF MRS. STANTON'S ADDRESS, DELIVERED AT SENECA FALLS, NY, JULY 19, 20, 1848

I should feel exceedingly diffident to appear before you at this time, having never before spoken in public, were I not nerved by a sense of right and duty, did I not feel the time had fully come for the question of woman's wrongs to be laid before the public, did I not believe that woman herself must do this work; for woman alone can understand the height, the depth, the length, and the breadth of her own degradation. Man cannot speak for her, because he has been educated to believe that she differs from him so materially, that he cannot judge of her thoughts, feelings and opinions by his own. Moral beings can only judge of others by themselves. The moment they assume a different nature for any of their own kind, they utterly fail. . . .

Let a man once settle the question that a woman does not think and feel like himself, and he may as well undertake to judge the amount of intellect and sensation of any of the animal creation as of woman's nature. He can know but little with certainty, and that but by observation.

Among the many important questions which have been brought before the public, there is none that more vitally affects the whole human family than that which is technically called Woman's Rights. Every allusion to the degraded and inferior position occupied by women all over the world has been met by scorn and abuse. From the man of highest mental cultivation to the most degraded wretch who staggers in the streets do we meet ridicule, and coarse jests, freely bestowed upon those who dare assert that woman stands by the side of man, his equal, placed here by her God, to enjoy with him the beautiful earth, which is her home as it is his, having the same sense of right and wrong and looking to the same Being for guidance and support. So long has man exercised tyranny over her, injurious to himself and benumbing to her faculties, that few can nerve themselves to meet the storm; and so long has the chain been about her that she knows not there is a remedy.

The whole social, civil and religious condition of woman is a subject too vast to be brought within the limits of one short lecture. Suffice it to say, for the present, wherever we turn, the history of woman is sad and dark, without any alleviating circumstances, nothing from which we can draw consolation. . . .

What to the Slave Is the Fourth of July? (1852)

FREDERICK DOUGLASS

Fellow-Citizens—Pardon me, and allow me to ask, why am I called upon to speak here to-day? What have I, or those I represent, to do with your national independence? Are the great principles of political freedom and of natural justice, embodied in that Declaration of Independence, extended to us? And am I, therefore, called upon to bring our humble offering to the national altar, and to confess the benefits, and express devout gratitude for the blessings, resulting from your independence to us?

Would to God, both for your sakes and ours, that an affirmative answer could be truthfully returned to these questions! Then would my task be light, and my burden easy and delightful. For who is there so cold that a nation's sympathy could not warm him? Who so obdurate and dead to the claims of gratitude, that would not thankfully acknowledge such priceless benefits? Who so stolid and selfish, that would not give his voice to swell the hallelujahs of a nation's jubilee, when the chains of servitude had been torn from his limbs? I am not that man. . . .

. . . I am not included within the pale of this glorious anniversary! Your high independence only reveals the immeasurable distance between us. The blessings in which you this day rejoice, are not enjoyed in common. The rich inheritance of justice, liberty, prosperity, and independence, bequeathed by your fathers, is shared by you, not by me. The sunlight that brought light and healing to you, has brought stripes and death to me. This Fourth of July is *yours*, not *mine*. *You* may rejoice, *I* must mourn. To drag a man in fetters into the grand illuminated temple of liberty, and call upon him to join you in joyous anthems, were inhuman mockery and sacrilegious irony. Do you mean, citizens, to mock me, by asking me to speak to-day? If so, there is a parallel to

From *My Bondage and My Freedom* by Frederick Douglass. (New York: Dover Publications, Inc., 1855) pp. 130–146.

your conduct. And let me warn you that it is dangerous to copy the example of a nation whose crimes, towering up to heaven, were thrown down by the breath of the Almighty, burying that nation in irrecoverable ruin! I can today make up the plaintive lament of the peeled and woe-smitten people. . . .

Fellow-citizens, above your national, tumultuous joy, I hear the mournful wail of millions, whose chains, heavy and grievous yesterday, are to-day rendered more intolerable by the jubilant shouts that reach them. If I do forget, if I do not faithfully remember those bleeding children of sorrow this day, "may my right hand forget her cunning, and may my tongue cleave to the roof of my mouth!" To forget them, to pass lightly over their wrongs, and to chime in with the popular theme, would be treason most scandalous and shocking, and would make me a reproach before God and the world. My subject, then, fellow-citizens, is AMERICAN SLAVERY. I shall see this day and its popular characteristics from the slave's point of view. Standing there, identified with the American bondman, making his wrongs mine, I do not hesitate to declare, with all my soul, that the character and conduct of this nation never looked blacker to me than on this Fourth of July. Whether we turn to the declarations of the past, or to the professions of the present, the conduct of the nation seems equally hideous and revolting. America is false to the past, false to the present, and solemnly binds herself to be false to the future. Standing with God and the crushed and bleeding slave on this occasion, I will, in the name of humanity which is outraged, in the name of liberty which is fettered, in the name of the constitution and the bible, which are disregarded and trampled upon, dare to call in question and to denounce, with all the emphasis I can command, everything that serves to perpetuate slavery—the great sin and shame of America! "I will not equivocate; I will not excuse"; I will use the severest language I can command; and yet not one word shall escape me that any man, whose judgment is not blinded by prejudice, or who is not at heart a slaveholder, shall not confess to be right and just.

But I fancy I hear some of my audience say, it is just in this circumstance that you and your brother abolitionists fail to make a favorable impression on the public mind. Would you argue more, and denounce less, would you persuade more and rebuke less, your cause would be much more likely to succeed. But, I submit, where all is plain there is nothing to be argued. What point in the anti-slavery creed would you have me argue? On what branch of the subject do the people of this country need light? Must I undertake to prove that the slave is a man? That point is conceded already. Nobody doubts it. The slaveholders themselves acknowledge it when they punish disobedience on the part of the slave. There are seventy-two crimes in the state of Virginia, which, if committed by a black man (no matter how ignorant he be,) subject him to the punishment of death; while only two of these same crimes will subject a white man to the like punishment. What is this but the acknowledgement that the slave is a moral, intellectual, and responsible being. The manhood of the slave is conceded. It is admitted in the fact that southern statute books are covered with enactments forbidding, under severe fines and penalties, the teaching of the slave to read or write. When you can point to any such laws, in reference to the beasts of the field, then I may consent to argue the manhood of the slave. . . .

For the present, it is enough to affirm the equal manhood of the Negro race. Is it not astonishing that, while we are plowing, planting, and reaping, using all kinds of mechanical tools, erecting houses, constructing bridges, building ships, working in metals of brass, iron, copper, silver, and gold; that, while we are reading, writing and ciphering, acting as clerks, merchants, and secretaries, having among us lawyers, doctors, ministers, poets, authors, editors, orators, and teachers; that, while we are engaged in all manner of enterprises common to other men—digging gold in California, capturing the whale in the Pacific, feeding sheep and cattle on the hillside, living, moving, acting, thinking, planning, living in families as husbands, wives, and children, and above all, confessing and worshiping the christian's God, and looking hopefully for life and immortality beyond the grave,—we are called upon to prove that we are men!

Would you have me argue that man is entitled to liberty? That he is the rightful owner of his own body? You have already declared it. Must I argue the wrongfulness of slavery? Is that a question for republicans? Is it to be settled by the rules of logic and argumentation, as a matter beset with great difficulty, involving a doubtful application of the principle of justice hard to be understood? How should I look to-day in the presence of Americans, dividing and subdividing a discourse, to show that men have a natural right to freedom, speaking of it relatively and positively, negatively and affirmatively? To do so, would be to make myself ridiculous, and to offer an insult to your understanding. There is not a man beneath the canopy of heaven that does not know that slavery is wrong *for him.*

What! Am I to argue that it is wrong to make men brutes, to rob them of their liberty, to work them without wages, to keep them ignorant of their relations to their fellow men, to beat them with sticks, to flay their flesh with the lash, to load their limbs with irons, to hunt them with dogs, to sell them at auction, to sunder their families, to knock out their teeth, to burn their flesh, to starve them into obedience and submission to their masters? Must I argue that a system, thus marked with blood and stained with pollution, is wrong? No; I will not. I have better employment for my time and strength than such arguments would imply.

What, then remains to be argued? Is it that slavery is not divine; that God did not establish it; that our doctors of divinity are mistaken? There is blasphemy in this thought. That which is inhuman cannot be divine. Who can reason on such proposition! They that can, may; I cannot. The time for such argument is past.

At a time like this, scorching irony, not convincing argument, is needed. Oh! Had I the ability, and could I reach the nation's ear, I would to-day pour out a fiery stream of biting ridicule, blasting reproach, withering sarcasm, and stern rebuke. For it is not light that is needed, but fire; it is not the gentle shower, but thunder. We need the storm, the whirlwind, the earthquake. The feeling of the nation must be quickened; the conscience of the nation must be roused; the propriety of the nation must be startled; the hypocrisy of the nation must be exposed; and its crimes against God and man must be proclaimed and denounced.

What to the American slave is your Fourth of July? I answer, a day that reveals to him, more than all other days in the year, the gross injustice and cruelty to which he is the constant victim. To him, your celebration is a sham; your boasted liberty, an unholy license; your national greatness, swelling vanity; your sounds of rejoicing are empty and heartless; your denunciation of tyrants, brass-fronted impudence; your shouts of liberty and equality, hollow mockery; your prayers and hymns, your sermons and thanksgivings, with all your religious parade and solemnity, are to him mere bombast, fraud, deception, impiety, and hypocrisy—a thin veil to cover up crimes which would disgrace a nation of savages. There is not a nation on the earth guilty of practices more shocking and bloody, than are the people of these United States, at this very hour.

Go where you may, search where you will, roam through all the monarchies and despotisms of the old world, travel through South America, search out every abuse, and when you have found the last, lay your facts by the side of every-day practices of this nation, and you will say with me, that, for revolting barbarity and shameless hypocrisy, America reigns without rival.

Solitude of Self (1892)

Elizabeth Cady Stanton

Mr. Chairman and gentlemen of the committee . . . The point I wish plainly to bring before you on this occasion is the individuality of each human soul; our Protestant idea, the right of individual conscience and judgment—our republican idea, individual citizenship. In discussing the rights of woman, we are to consider, first, what belongs to her as an individual, in a world of her own, the arbiter of her own destiny, an imaginary Robinson Crusoe with her woman Friday on a solitary island. Her rights under such circumstances are to use all her faculties for her own safety and happiness.

Secondly, if we consider her as a citizen, as a member of a great nation, she must have the same rights as all other members, according to the fundamental principles of our government.

Thirdly, viewed as a woman, an equal factor in civilization, her rights and duties are still the same—individual happiness and development.

Fourthly, it is only the incidental relations of life, such as mother, wife, sister, daughter, that may involve some special duties and training. In the usual discussion in regard to woman's sphere, such as men as Herbert Spencer, Frederic Harrison, and Grant Allen uniformly subordinate her rights and duties as an individual, as a citizen, as a woman, to the necessities of these incidental relations, some of which a large class of woman may never assume. In discussing the sphere of man we do not decide his rights as an individual, as a citizen, as a man by his duties as a father, a husband, a brother, or a son, relations some of which he may never fill. Moreover he would be better fitted for these very relations and whatever special work he might choose to do to earn his bread by the complete development of all his faculties as an individual.

Just so with woman. The education that will fit her to discharge the duties in the largest sphere of human usefulness will best fit her for whatever special work she may be compelled to do.

The isolation of every human soul and the necessity of self-dependence must give each individual the right, to choose his own surroundings.

"Nature never repeats herself, and the possibilities of one human soul will never be found in another." The strongest reason for giving woman all the opportunities for higher education, for the full development of her faculties, forces of mind and body; for giving her the most enlarged freedom of thought and action; a complete emancipation from all forms of bondage, of custom, dependence, superstition; from all the crippling influences of fear, is the solitude and personal responsibility of her own individual life. The strongest reason why we ask for woman a voice in the government under which she lives; in

Excerpted from *The Search for Self Sovereignty*, ed. by Beth Waggenspack (Westport, CT: Greenwood Press) © 1989, pp. 159–167, Reproduced with permission of Greenwood Publishing Group Inc.

the religion she is asked to believe; equality in social life, where she is the chief factor; a place in the trades and professions, where she may earn her bread, is because of her birthright to self-sovereignty; because, as an individual, she must rely on herself. No matter how much women prefer to lean, to be protected and supported, nor how much men desire to have them do so, they must make the voyage of life alone, and for safety in an emergency they must know something of the laws of navigation. To guide our own craft, we must be captain, pilot, engineer; with chart and compass to stand at the wheel; to match the wind and waves and know when to take in the sail, and to read the signs in the firmament over all. It matters not whether the solitary voyager is man or woman.

Nature having endowed them equally, leaves them to their own skill and judgment in the hour of danger, and, if not equal to the occasion, alike they perish.

To appreciate the importance of fitting every human soul for independent action, think for a moment of the immeasurable solitude of self. We come into the world alone, unlike all who have gone before us; we leave it alone under circumstances peculiar to ourselves. No mortal ever has been, no mortal over will be like the soul just launched on the sea of life. There can never again be just such environments as make up the infancy, youth and manhood of this one. Nature never repeats herself, and the possibilities of one human soul will never be found in another. No one has ever found two blades of ribbon grass alike, and no one will ever find two human beings alike. Seeing, then, what must be the infinite diversity in human character, we can in a measure appreciate the loss to a nation when any large class of the people is uneducated and unrepresented in the government. We ask for the complete development of every individual, first, for his own benefit and happiness. In fitting out an army we give each soldier his own knapsack, arms, powder, his blanket, cup, knife, fork and spoon. We provide alike for all their individual necessities, then each man bears his own burden.

Again we ask complete individual development for the general good; for the consensus of the competent on the whole round of human interest; on all questions of national life, and here each man must bear his share of the general burden. It is sad to see how soon friendless children are left to bear their own burdens before they can analise their feelings; before they can even tell their joys and sorrows, they are thrown on their own resources. The great lesson that nature seems to teach us at all ages is self-dependence, self-protection, self-support. What a touching instance of a child's solitude; of that hunger of heart for love and recognition, in the case of the little girl who helped to dress a Christmas tree for the children of the family in which she served. On finding there was no present for herself she slipped away in the darkness and spent the night in an open field sitting on a stone, and when found in the morning was weeping as if her heart would break. No mortal will ever know the thoughts that passed through the mind of that friendless child in the long hours of that cold night, with only the silent stars to keep her company. The mention of her case in the daily papers moved many generous hearts to send her presents, but in the hours of her keenest sufferings she was thrown wholly on herself for consolation.

In youth our most bitter disappointments, our brightest hopes and ambitions are known only to otherwise, even our friendship and love we never fully share with another; there is something of every passion in every situation we conceal. Even so in our triumphs and our defeats.

The successful candidate for Presidency and his opponent each have a solitude peculiarly his own, and good form forbid either to speak of his pleasure or regret. The solitude of the king on his throne and the prisoner in his cell differs in character and degree, but it is solitude nevertheless.

We ask no sympathy from others in the anxiety and agony of a broken friendship or shattered love. When death sunders our nearest ties, alone we sit in the shadows of our affliction. Alike mid the greatest triumphs and darkest tragedies of life we walk alone. On the divine heights of human attainments, eulogized land worshiped as a hero or saint, we stand alone. In ignorance, poverty, and vice, as a pauper or criminal, alone we starve or steal; alone we suffer the sneers and rebuffs of our fellows; alone we are hunted and hounded thro dark courts and alleys, in by-ways and highways; alone we stand in the judgment seat; alone in the prison cell we lament our crimes and misfortunes; alone we expiate them on the gallows. In hours like these we realize the awful solitude of individual life, its pains, its penalties, its responsibilities; hours in which the youngest and most helpless are thrown on their own resources for guidance and consolation. Seeing then that life must ever be a march and a battle, that each soldier must be equipped for his own protection, it is the height of cruelty to rob the individual of a single natural right.

To throw obstacles in the way of a complete education is like putting out the eyes; to deny the rights of property, like cutting off the hands. To deny political equality is to rob the ostracised of all self-respect; of credit in the market place; of recompense in the world of work; of a voice among those who make and administer the law; a choice in the jury before whom they are tried, and in the judge who decides their punishment. Shakespeare's play of Titus and Andronicus contains a terrible satire on woman's position in the nineteenth century—"Rude men" (the play tells us) "seized the king's daughter, cut out her tongue, cut off her hands, and then bade her go call for water and wash her hands." What a picture of woman's position. Robbed of her natural rights, handicapped by law and custom at every turn, yet compelled to fight her own battles, and in the emergencies of life to fall back on herself for protection.

The girl of sixteen, thrown on the world to support herself, to make her own place in society, to resist the temptations that surround her and maintain a spotless integrity, must do all this by native force or superior education. She does not acquire this power by being trained to trust others and distrust herself. If she wearies of the struggle, finding it hard work to swim upstream, and allows herself to drift with the current, she will find plenty of company, but not one to share her misery in the hour of her deepest humiliation. If she tried to retrieve her position, to conceal the past, her life is hedged about with fears lest willing hands should tear the veil from what she fain would hide. Young and friendless, she knows the bitter solitude of self.

How the little courtesies of life on the surface of society, deemed so important from man towards woman, fade into utter insignificance in view of the deeper tragedies in which she must play her part alone, where no human aid is possible.

The young wife and mother, at the head of some establishment with a kind husband to shield her from the adverse winds of life, with wealth, fortune and position, has a certain harbor of safety, occurs against the ordinary ills of life. But to manage a household, have a desirable influence in society, keep her friends and the affections of her husband, train her children and servants well, she must have rare common sense, wisdom, diplomacy, and a knowledge of human nature. To do all this she needs the cardinal virtues and the strong points of character that the most successful statesman possesses.

An uneducated woman, trained to dependence, with no resources in herself must make a failure of any position in life. But society says women do not need a knowledge of the world, the liberal training that experience in public life must give, all the advantages of collegiate education; but when for the lack of all this, the woman's happiness is wrecked, alone she bears her humiliation; and the attitude of the weak and the ignorant is indeed pitiful in the wild chase for the price of life they are ground to powder.

In age, when the pleasures of youth are passed, children grown up, married and gone, the hurry and hustle of life in a measure over, when the hands are weary of active service, when the old armchair and the fireside are the chosen resorts, then men and women alike must fall back on their own resources. If they cannot find companionship in books, if they have no interest in the vital questions of the hour, no interest in watching the consummation of reforms, with which they might have been identified, they soon pass into their dotage. The more fully the faculties of the mind are developed and kept in use, the longer the period of vigor and active interest in all around us continues. If from a lifelong participation in public affairs a woman feels responsible for the laws regulating our system of education, the discipline of our jails and prisons, the sanitary conditions of our private homes, public buildings, and thoroughfares, an interest in commerce, finance, or foreign relations, in any or all of these questions, here solitude will at least be respectable, and she will not be driven to gossip or scandal for entertainment.

The chief reason for opening to every soul the doors to the whole round of human duties and pleasures is the individual development thus attained, the resources thus provided under all circumstances to mitigate the solitude that at times must come to everyone. I once asked Prince Krapotkin, the Russian nihilist, how he endured his long years in prison, deprived of books, pen, ink, and paper. "Ah," he said, "I thought out many questions in which I had a deep interest. In the pursuit of an idea I took no note of time. When tired of solving knotty problems I recited all the beautiful passages in prose or verse

I have ever learned. I became acquainted with myself and my own resources. I had a world of my own, a vast empire, that no Russian jailor or Czar could invade." Such is the value of liberal thought and broad culture when shut off from all human companionship, bringing comfort and sunshine within even the four walls of a prison cell.

As women of times share a similar fate, should they not have all the consolation that the most liberal education can give? Their suffering in the prisons of St. Petersburg; in the long, weary marches to Siberia, and in the mines, working side by side with men, surely call for all the self-support that the most exalted sentiments of heroism can give. When suddenly roused at midnight, with the startling cry of "fire! fire!" to find the house over their heads in flames, do women wait for men to point the way to safety? And are the men, equally bewildered and half suffocated with smoke, in a position to more than try to save themselves?

At such times the most timid women have shown a courage and heroism in saving their husbands and children that has surprised everybody. Inasmuch, then, as woman shares equally the joys and sorrows of time and eternity, is it not the height of presumption in man to propose to represent her at the ballot box and the throne of grace, do her voting in the state, her praying in the church, and to assume the position of priest at the family altar?

Nothing strengthens the judgment and quickens the conscience like individual responsibility. Nothing adds such dignity to character as the recognition of one's self-sovereignty; the right to an equal place, every where conceded; a place earned by personal merit, not an artificial attainment, by inheritance, wealth, family, and position. Seeing then, that the responsibilities of life rest equally on man and woman, that their destiny is the same, they need the same preparation for time and eternity. The talk of sheltering woman from the fierce storms of life is the sheerest mockery, for they beat on her from every point of the compass, just as they do on man, and with more fatal results, for he has been trained to protect himself, to resist, to conquer. Such are the facts in human experience, the responsibilities of individual sovereignty. Rich and poor, intelligent and ignorant, wise and foolish, virtuous and vicious, man and woman . . . , each soul must depend wholly on itself.

Whatever the theories may be of woman's dependence on man, in the supreme moments of her life he can not bear her burdens. Alone she goes to the gates of death to give life to every man that is born into the world. No one can share her fears, no one mitigate her pangs; and if her sorrow is greater than she can bear, alone she passes beyond the gates into the vast unknown.

From the mountain tops of Judea, long ago, a heavenly voice bade His disciples, "Bear ye one another's burdens," but humanity has not yet risen to that point of self-sacrifice, and if ever so willing, how few the burdens are that one soul can bear for another. In the highways of Palestine; in prayer and fasting on the solitary mountain top; in the Garden of Gethsemane; before the judgment seat of Pilate; betrayed by one of His trusted disciples at His last supper; in His agonies on the cross, even Jesus of Nazareth, in these last sad days on earth, felt the awful solitude of self. Deserted by man, in agony he cries, "My God! My God! why hast Thou forsaken me?" And so it ever must be in the conflicting scenes of life, on the long weary march, each one walks alone. We may have many friends, love, kindness, sympathy and charity to smooth our pathway in everyday life, but in the tragedies and triumphs of human experience each mortal stands alone.

But when all artificial trammels are removed, and women are recognized as individuals, responsible for their own environments, thoroughly educated for all the positions in life they may be called to fill; with all the resources in themselves that liberal thought and broad culture can give; guided by their own conscience and judgment; trained to self-protection by a healthy development of the muscular system and skill in the use of weapons of defense, and stimulated to self-support by the knowledge of the business world and the pleasure that pecuniary independence must ever give; when women are trained in this way they will, in a measure, be fitted for those hours of solitude that come alike to all, whether prepared or otherwise. As in our extremity we must depend on ourselves, the dictates of wisdom point to complete individual development.

In talking of education how shallow the argument that each class must be educated for the special work it proposed to do, and all those faculties not needed in this special walk must lie dormant and utterly wither for want of use, when, perhaps, these will be the very faculties needed in life's greatest emergencies. Some say, Where is the use of drilling girls in the languages, the sciences, in law, medicine, theology? As wives, mothers, housekeepers, cooks, they need a different curriculum from boys who are to fill all positions. The chief cooks in our great hotels and ocean steamers are men. In large cities men run the bakeries; they make our bread, cake and pies. They manage the laundries; they are now considered our best milliners and dressmakers. Because some men fill these departments of usefulness, shall we regulate the curriculum in Harvard and Yale to their present necessities? If not why this talk in our best colleges of a curriculum for girls who are crowding into the trades and professions; teachers in all our public schools rapidly filling many lucrative and honorable positions in life? They are showing too, their calmness and courage in the most trying hours of human experience.

You have probably all read in the daily papers of the terrible storm in the Bay of Biscay when a tidal wave made such havoc on the shore, wrecking vessels, unroofing houses and carrying destruction everywhere. Among other buildings the women's prison was demolished. Those who escaped saw men struggling to reach the shore. They promptly by clasping hands made a chain of themselves and pushed out into the sea, again and again, at the risk of their lives until they had brought six men to shore, carried them to a shelter, and did all in their power for their comfort and protection.

What special school of training could have prepared these women for this sublime moment of their lives? In times like this humanity rises above all college curriculums and recognises Nature as the greatest of all teachers in the hour of danger and death. Women are already the equals of men in the whole realm of thought, in art, science, literature, and government. With telescope vision they explore the starry firmament, and bring back the history of the planetary world. With chart and compass they pilot ships across the mighty deep, and with skillful finger send electric messages around the globe. In galleries of art the beauties of nature and the virtues of humanity are immortalized by them on their canvas and by their inspired touch dull blocks of marble are transformed into angels of light.

In music they speak again the language of Mendelssohn, Beethoven, Chopin, Schumann, and are worthy interpreters of their great thoughts. The poetry and novels of the century are theirs, and they have touched the keynote of reform in religion, politics, and social life. They fill the editor's and professor's chair, and plead at the bar of justice, walk the wards of the hospital, and speak from the pulpit and the platform; such is the type of womanhood that an enlightened public sentiment welcomes today, and such the triumph of the facts of life over the false theories of the past.

Is it, then, consistent to hold the developed woman of this day within the same narrow political limits as the dame with the spinning wheel and knitting needle occupied in the past? No! no! Machinery has taken the labors of woman as well as man on its tireless shoulders; the loom and the spinning wheel are but dreams of the past; the pen, the brush, the easel, the chisel, have taken their places, while the hopes and ambitions of women are essentially changed.

We see reason sufficient in the outer conditions of human beings for individual liberty and development, but when we consider the self dependence of every human soul we see the need of courage, judgment, and the exercise of every faculty of mind and body, strengthened and developed by use, in woman as well as man.

Whatever may be said of man's protecting power in ordinary conditions, mid all the terrible disasters by land and sea, in the supreme moments of danger, alone, woman must ever meet the horrors of the situation; the Angel of Death even makes no royal pathway for her. Man's love and sympathy enter only into the sunshine of our lives. In that solemn solitude of self, that links us with the immeasurable and the eternal, each soul lives alone forever. A recent writer says:

I remember once, in crossing the Atlantic, to have gone upon the deck of the ship at midnight, when a dense black cloud enveloped the sky, and the great deep was roaring madly under the lashes of demoniac winds. My feeling was not of danger or fear (which is a base surrender of the immortal soul), but of utter desolation and loneliness; a little speck of life shut in by a tremendous darkness. Again I remember to have climbed the slopes of the Swiss Alps, up beyond the point where vegetation ceases, and the stunted conifers no longer struggle against the unfeeling blasts. Around me lay a huge confusion of rocks, out of which the gigantic ice peaks shot into the measureless blue of the heavens, and again my only feeling was the awful solitude.

And yet, there is a solitude, which each and every one of us has always carried with him, more inaccessible than the ice-cold mountains, more profound than the midnight sea; the solitude of self. Our inner being, which we call ourself, no eye nor touch of man or angel has ever pierced. It is more hidden than the caves of the gnome; the sacred adytum of the oracle; the hidden chamber of eleusinian mystery, for to it only omniscience is permitted to enter.

Such is individual life. Who, I ask you, can take, dare take, on himself the rights, the duties, the responsibilities of another human soul?

The Woman's Bible (1898)

Introduction

Elizabeth Cady Stanton

From the inauguration of the movement for woman's emancipation the Bible has been used to hold her in the "divinely ordained sphere," prescribed in the Old and New Testaments.

The canon and civil law; church and state; priests and legislators; all political parties and religious denominations have alike taught that woman was made after man, of man, and for man, an inferior being, subject to man. Creeds, codes, Scriptures and statutes, are all based on this idea. The fashions, forms, ceremonies and customs of society, church ordinances and discipline all grow out of this idea. . . .

The Bible teaches that woman brought sin and death into the world, that she precipitated the fall of the race, that she was arraigned before the judgment seat of Heaven, tried, condemned and sentenced. Marriage for her was to be a condition of bondage, maternity a period of suffering and anguish, and in silence and subjection, she was to play the role of a dependent on man's bounty for all her material wants, and for all the information she might desire on the vital questions of the hour, she was commanded to ask her husband at home. Here is the Bible position of woman briefly summed up.

Those who have the divine insight to translate, transpose and transfigure this mournful object of pity into an exalted, dignified personae, worthy our worship as the mother of the race, are to be congratulated as having a share of the occult mystic power of the eastern Mahatmas.

The plain English to the ordinary mind admits of no such liberal interpretation. The unvarnished texts speak for themselves. The canon law, church ordinances, and Scriptures, are homogeneous, and all reflect the same spirit and sentiments.

These familiar texts are quoted by clergymen in their pulpits, by statesmen in the halls of legislation, by lawyers in the courts, and are echoed by the press of all civilized nations, and accepted by woman herself as "The Word of

God." So perverted is the religious element in her nature, that with faith and works she is the chief support of the church and clergy; the very powers that make her emancipation impossible. When, in the early part of the Nineteenth Century, women began to protest against their civil and political degradation, they were referred to the Bible for an answer. When they protested against their unequal position in the church, they were referred to the Bible for an answer.

This led to a general and critical study of the Scriptures. Some, having made a fetish of these books and believing them to be the veritable "Word of God," with liberal translations, interpretations, allegories and symbols, glossed over the most objectionable features of the various books and clung to them as divinely inspired. Others, seeing the family resemblance between the Mosaic code, the canon law, and the old English common law, came to the conclusion that all alike emanated from the same source; wholly human in their origin and inspired by the natural love of domination in the historians. Others, bewildered with their doubts and fears, came to no conclusion. While their clergymen told them on the one hand, that they owed all the blessings and freedom they enjoyed to the Bible, on the other, they said it clearly marked out their circumscribed sphere of action: that the demands for political and civil rights were irreligious, dangerous to the stability of the home, the state and the church. Clerical appeals were circulated from time to time conjuring members of their churches to take no part in the anti-slavery or woman suffrage movements, as they were infidel in their tendencies, undermining the very foundations of society. No wonder the majority of women stood still and with bowed heads, accepted the situation. . . .

If the Bible teaches the equality of Woman, why does the church refuse to ordain women to preach the gospel, to fill the offices of deacons and elders, and to administer the Sacraments, or to admit them as delegates to the Synods, General Assemblies and Conferences of the different denominations? They have never yet invited a woman to join one of their Revising Committees, nor tried to mitigate the sentence pronounced on her by changing one count in the indictment served on her in Paradise.

. . . But we have the usual array of objectors to meet and answer. One correspondent conjures us to suspend the work, as it is "ridiculous" for "women to attempt the revision of the Scriptures." I wonder if any man wrote to the late revising committee of Divines to stop their work on the ground that it was ridiculous for men to revise the Bible. Why is it more ridiculous for women to protest against her present status in the Old and New Testament, in the ordinances and discipline of the church, than in the statutes and constitution of the state? Why is it more ridiculous to arraign ecclesiastics for their false teaching and acts of injustice to women, than members of Congress and the House of Commons? Why is it more audacious to review Moses than Blackstone, the Jewish code of laws, than the English system of jurisprudence? Women have compelled their legislators in every state in the Union to so modify their statutes for women that the old common law is now almost a dead letter. Why not compel Bishops and Revising Committees to modify their creeds and dogmas? Forty years ago it seemed as ridiculous to timid, time-serving and retrograde folk for women to demand an expurgated edition of the laws, as it now does to demand an expurgated edition of the Liturgies and the Scriptures. Come, come, my conservative friend, wipe the dew off your spectacles, and see that the world is moving. Whatever your views may be as to the importance of the proposed work, your political and social degradation are but an outgrowth of your status in the Bible. When you express your aversion, based on a blind feeling of reverence in which reason has no control, to the revision of the Scriptures, you do but echo Cowper, who, when asked to read Paine's "Rights of Man," exclaimed, "No man shall convince me that I am improperly governed while I *feel* the contrary."

Others say it is not *politic* to rouse religious opposition. This much-lauded policy is but another word for *cowardice*. How can woman's position be changed from that of a subordinate to an equal, without opposition, without the broadest discussion of all the questions involved in her present degradation? For so far-reaching and momentous a reform as her complete independence, an entire revolution in all existing institutions is inevitable.

Let us remember that all reforms are interdependent, and that whatever is done to establish one principle on a solid basis, strengthens all. Reformers who are always compromising, have not yet grasped the idea that truth is the only safe ground to stand upon. The object of an individual life is not to carry one fragmentary measure in human progress, but to utter the highest truth clearly seen in all directions, and thus to round out and perfect a well balanced character. . . .

Bible historians claim special inspiration for the Old and New Testaments containing most contradictory records of the same events, of miracles opposed to all known laws, of customs that degrade the female sex of all human and animal life, stated in most questionable language that could not be read in a promiscuous assembly, and call all this "The Word of God."

The only points in which I differ from all ecclesiastical teaching is that I do not believe that any man ever saw or talked with God, I do not believe that God inspired the Mosaic code, or told the historians what they say he did about woman, for all the religions on the face of the earth degrade her, and so long as woman accepts the position that they assign her, her emancipation is impossible. Whatever the Bible may be made to do in Hebrew or Greek, in plain English it does not exalt and dignify woman. . . . But the verbal criticism in regard to woman's position amounts to little. The spirit is the same in all periods and languages, hostile to her as an equal.

There are some general principles in the holy books of all religions that teach love, charity, liberty, justice and equality for all the human family, there are many grand and beautiful passages, the golden rule has been echoed and re-echoed around the world. There are lofty examples of good and true men and women, all worthy our acceptance and imitation whose luster cannot be dimmed by the false sentiments and vicious characters bound up in the same volume. The Bible cannot be accepted or rejected as a whole. Its teachings are varied and its lessons differ widely from each other. ... The canon law, the Scripture, the creeds and codes of church discipline and the leading religions bear the impress of fallible man, and not of our ideal great first cause. ...

Letter from the Birmingham Jail (1963)

Martin Luther King, Jr.

My dear fellow clergymen,

... I am in Birmingham now because injustice is here. ... I am compelled to carry the gospel of freedom beyond my particular hometown. ...

Moreover, I am cognizant of the interrelatedness of all communities and states. I cannot sit idly by in Atlanta and not be concerned about what happens in Birmingham. Injustice anywhere is a threat to justice everywhere. We are caught in an inescapable network of mutuality, tied in a single garment of destiny. Whatever affects one directly affects all indirectly. Never again can we afford to live with the narrow, provincial "outside agitator" idea. Anyone who lives in the United States can never be considered an outsider anywhere in this country.

You deplore the demonstrations that are presently taking place in Birmingham. But I am sorry that your statement did not express a similar concern for the conditions that brought the demonstrations into being. I am sure that each of you would want to go beyond the superficial social analyst who looks merely at effects, and does not grapple with underlying causes. I would not hesitate to say that it is unfortunate that so-called demonstrations are taking place in Birmingham at this time, but I would say in more emphatic terms that it is even more unfortunate that the white power structure of this city left the Negro community with no other alternative.

In any nonviolent campaign there are four basic steps: (1) collection of the facts to determine whether injustices are alive, (2) negotiation, (3) self-purification, and (4) direct action. We have gone through all of these steps in Birmingham. There can be no gainsaying of the fact that racial injustice engulfs this community. ...

Then came the opportunity last September to talk with some of the leaders of the economic community. In these negotiating sessions certain promises were made by the merchants—such as the promise to remove the humiliating racial signs from the stores. On the basis of these promises Rev. Shuttlesworth and the leaders of the Alabama Christian Movement for Human Rights agreed to call a moratorium on any type of demonstrations. As the weeks and months unfolded we realized that we were the victims of a broken promise. The signs remained. Like so many experiences of the past we were confronted with blasted hopes, and the dark shadow of a deep disappointment settled upon us. So we had no alternative except that of preparing for direct action, whereby we would present our very bodies as a means of laying our case before the conscience of the local and national community. We were not unmindful of the difficulties involved. So we decided to go through a process of self-purification. We started having workshops on nonviolence and repeatedly asked ourselves the questions, "Are you able to accept blows without retaliating?" "Are you able to endure the ordeals of jail?" . . .

You may well ask, "Why direct action? Why sit-ins, marches, etc.? Isn't negotiation a better path?" You are exactly right in your call for negotiation. Indeed, this is the purpose of direct action. Nonviolent direct action seeks to create such a crisis and establish such creative tension that a community that has constantly refused to negotiate is forced to confront the issue. It seeks so to dramatize the issue that it can no longer be ignored. I just referred to the creation of tension as a part of the work of the nonviolent resister. This may sound rather shocking. But I must confess that I am not afraid of the word *tension*. I have earnestly worked and preached against violent tension, but there is a type of constructive nonviolent tension that is necessary for growth. Just as Socrates felt that it was necessary to create a tension in the mind so that individuals could rise from the bondage of myths and half-truths to the unfettered realm of creative analysis and objective appraisal, we must see the need of having nonviolent gadflies to create the kind of tension in society that will help men to rise from the dark depths of prejudice and racism to the majestic heights of understanding and brotherhood. So the purpose of the direct action is to create a situation so crisis-packed that it will inevitably open the door to negotiation. . . .

. . . Some have asked, "Why didn't you give the new administration time to act?" The only answer that I can give to this inquiry is that the new administration must be prodded about as much as the outgoing one before it acts. . . . My friends, I must say to you that we have not made a single gain in civil rights without determined legal and nonviolent pressure. History is the long and tragic story of the fact that privileged groups seldom give up their privileges voluntarily. Individuals may see the moral light and voluntarily give up their unjust posture; but . . . groups are more immoral than individuals.

We know through painful experience that freedom is never voluntarily given by the oppressor; it must be demanded by the oppressed. Frankly, I have never yet engaged in a direct action movement that was "well-timed," according to the timetable of those who have not suffered unduly from the disease of segregation. For years now I have heard the word "Wait!" It rings in the ear of every Negro with a piercing familiarity. This "Wait" has almost always meant "Never." . . . We have waited for more than 340 years for our constitutional and God-given rights. The nations of Asia and Africa are moving with jet-like speed toward the goal of political independence, and we still creep at horse and buggy pace toward the gaining of a cup of coffee at a lunch counter. I guess it is easy for those who have never felt the stinging darts of segregation to say, "Wait." But when you have seen vicious mobs lynch your mothers and fathers at will and drown your sisters and brothers at whim; when you have seen hate-filled policemen curse, kick, brutalize and even kill your black brothers and sisters with impunity; when you see the vast majority of your twenty million Negro brothers smothering in an air-tight cage of poverty in the midst of an affluent society; when you suddenly find your tongue twisted and your speech stammering as you seek to explain to your six-year-old daughter why she can't go to the public amusement park that has just been advertised on television, and see tears welling up in her little eyes when she is told that Funtown is closed to colored children, and see the depressing clouds of inferiority begin to form in her little mental sky, and see her begin to distort her little personality by unconsciously developing a bitterness toward white people; when you have to concoct an answer for a five-year-old son asking in agonizing pathos; "Daddy, why do white people treat colored people so mean?"; when you take a cross-country drive and find it necessary to sleep night after night in the uncomfortable corners of your automobile because no motel will accept you; when you are humiliated day in and day out by nagging signs reading "white" and "colored"; when your first name becomes "nigger" and your middle name becomes "boy" (however old you are) and your last name becomes "John," and when your wife and mother are never given the respected title "Mrs."; when you are harried by day and haunted by night by the fact that you are a Negro, living constantly at tiptoe stance never quite knowing what to expect next, and plagued with inner fears and outer resentments; when you are forever fighting a degenerating sense of "nobodiness"; then you will understand why we find it difficult to wait. There comes a time when the cup of endurance runs over, and men are no longer willing to be plunged into an abyss of injustice where they experience the blackness of corroding despair. . . .

You express a great deal of anxiety over our willingness to break laws. This is certainly a legitimate concern. Since we so diligently urge people to obey the Supreme Court's decision of 1954 outlawing segregation in the public schools, it is rather strange and paradoxical to find us consciously breaking laws. One may well ask, "How can you advocate breaking some laws and obeying others?" The answer is found in the fact that there are two types of laws: there are *just* and there are *unjust* laws. I would agree with Saint Augustine that "An unjust law is no law at all."

Now what is the difference between the two? How does one determine when a law is just or unjust? A just law is a man-made code that squares with the moral law or the law of God. An unjust law is a code that is out of harmony with the moral law. To put it in the terms of Saint Thomas Aquinas, an unjust law is a human law that is not rooted in eternal and natural law. Any law that uplifts human personality is just. Any law that degrades human personality is unjust. All segregation statutes are unjust because segregation distorts the soul and damages the personality. It gives the segregator a false sense of superiority, and the segregated a false sense of inferiority. To use the words of Martin Buber, the great Jewish philosopher, segregation substitutes an "I-it" relationship for the "I-thou" relationship, and ends up relegating persons to the status of things. So segregation is not only politically, economically and sociologically unsound, but it is morally wrong and sinful. . . . So I can urge men to disobey segregation ordinances because they are morally wrong.

Let us turn to a more concrete example of just and unjust laws. An unjust law is a code that a majority inflicts on a minority that is not binding on itself. This is difference made legal. On the other hand a just law is a code that a majority compels a minority to follow that it is willing to follow itself. This is sameness made legal.

Let me give another explanation. An unjust law is a code inflicted upon a minority which that minority had no part in enacting or creating because they did not have the unhampered right to vote. Who can say that the legislature of Alabama which set up the segregation laws was democratically elected? Throughout the state of Alabama all types of conniving methods are used to prevent Negroes from becoming registered voters and there are some counties without a single Negro registered to vote despite the fact that the Negro constitutes a majority of the population. Can any law set up in such a state be considered democratically structured?

These are just a few examples of unjust and just laws. There are some instances when a law is just on its face and unjust in its application. For instance, I was arrested Friday on a charge of parading without a permit. Now there is nothing wrong with an ordinance which requires a permit for a parade, but when the ordinance is used to preserve segregation and to deny citizens the First Amendment privilege of peaceful assembly and peaceful protest, then it becomes unjust.

I hope you can see the distinction I am trying to point out. In no sense do I advocate evading or defying the law as the rabid segregationist would do. This would lead to anarchy. One who breaks an unjust law must do it *openly, lovingly* . . . and with a willingness to accept the penalty. I submit that an individual who breaks a law that conscience tells him is unjust, and willingly accepts the penalty by staying in jail to arouse the conscience of the community over its injustice, is in reality expressing the very highest respect for law. . . .

We can never forget that everything Hitler did in Germany was "legal" and everything the Hungarian freedom fighters did in Hungary was "illegal." It was "illegal" to aid and comfort a Jew in Hitler's Germany. But I am sure that if I had lived in Germany during that time I would have aided and comforted my Jewish brothers even though it was illegal. If I lived in a Communist country today where certain principles dear to the Christian faith are suppressed, I believe I would openly advocate disobeying these anti-religious laws. I must make two honest confessions to you, my Christian and Jewish brothers. First, I must confess that over the last few years I have been gravely disappointed with the white moderate. I have almost reached the regrettable conclusion that the Negro's great stumbling block in the stride toward free-dom is not the White Citizens Counciler or the Ku Klux Klanner, but the white moderate who is more devoted to "order" than to justice; who prefers a nega-tive peace which is the absence of tension to a positive peace which is the pres-ence of justice; who constantly says, "I agree with you in the goal you seek, but I can't agree with your methods of direct action"; who paternalistically feels that he can set the timetable for another man's freedom; who lives by the myth of time and who constantly advised the Negro to wait until a "more conve-nient season." Shallow understanding from people of good will is more frus-trating than absolute misunderstanding from people of ill will. Lukewarm acceptance is much more bewildering than outright rejection.

I had hoped that the white moderate would understand that law and order exist for the purpose of establishing justice, and that when they fail to do this they become dangerously structured dams that block the flow of social progress. I hoped that the white moderate would understand that the present tension of the South is merely a necessary phase of the transition from an ob-noxious negative peace, where the Negro passively accepted his unjust plight, to a substance-filled positive peace, where all men will respect the dignity and worth of human personality. Actually, we who engage in nonviolent direct ac-tion are not the creators of tension. We merely bring to the surface the hidden tension that is already alive. We bring it out in the open where it can be seen and dealt with. . . .

In your statement you asserted that our actions, even though peaceful, must be condemned because they precipitate violence. But can this assertion be logically made? Isn't this like condemning the robbed man because his possession of money precipitated the evil act of robbery? Isn't this like con-demning Socrates because his unswerving commitment to truth and his philo-sophical delvings precipitated the misguided popular mind to make him drink the hemlock? Isn't this like condemning Jesus because His unique God-consciousness and never-ceasing devotion to his will precipitated the evil act of crucifixion? We must come to see, as federal courts have consistently affirmed, that it is immoral to urge an individual to withdraw his efforts to gain his basic constitutional rights because the quest precipitates violence. Society must protect the robbed and punish the robber.

I had also hoped that the white moderate would reject the myth of time. I received a letter this morning from a white brother in Texas which said: "All Christians know that the colored people will receive equal rights eventually, but it is possible that you are in too great of a religious hurry. It has taken Christianity almost two thousand years to accomplish what it has. The teach-ings of Christ take time to come to earth." All that is said here grows out of a tragic misconception of time. It is the strangely irrational notion that there is something in the very flow of time that will inevitably cure all ills. Actually time is neutral. It can be used either destructively or constructively. I am com-ing to feel that the people of ill will have used time much more effectively than the people of good will. We will have to repent in this generation not merely for the vitriolic words and actions of the bad people, but for the appalling silence of the good people. We must come to see that human progress never rolls in on the wheels of inevitability. It comes through the tireless efforts and persistent work of men willing to be co-workers with God, and without this hard work time itself becomes an ally of the forces of social stagnation. We must use time creatively, and forever realize that the time is always ripe to do right. . . .

You spoke of our activity in Birmingham as extreme. At first I was rather disappointed that fellow clergymen would see my nonviolent efforts as those of the extremist. I started thinking about the fact that I stand in the middle of two opposing forces in the Negro community. One is the force of complacency made up of Negroes who, as a result of long years of oppression, have been so completely drained of self-respect and a sense of "somebodies" that they have adjusted to segregation and, of a few Negroes in the middle class who, because of a degree of academic and economic security, and because at points they profit by segregation, have unconsciously become insensitive to the problems of the masses. The other force is one of bitterness and hatred, and comes perilously close to advocating violence. It is expressed in the various black nationalist groups that are springing up over the nation, the largest and best known being Elijah Muhammad's Muslim movement. This movement is nourished by the contemporary frustration over the continued existence of racial discrimination. It is made up of people who have lost faith in America, who have absolutely repudiated Christianity, and who have concluded that the white man is an incurable "devil." I have tried to stand between these two forces, saying that we need not follow the "do-nothingism" of the complacent or the hatred and despair of the black nationalist. There is the more excellent way of love and nonviolent protest. . . .

Oppressed people cannot remain oppressed forever. The urge for freedom will eventually come. This is what happened to the American Negro. Something within has reminded him of his birthright of freedom; something without has reminded him that he can gain it. Consciously and unconsciously, he has been swept in by what the Germans call the *Zeitgeist*, and with his black brothers of Africa, his brown and yellow brothers of Asia, South America and the Caribbean, he is moving with a sense of cosmic urgency toward the promised land of racial justice. Recognizing this vital urge that has engulfed the Negro community, one should readily understand public demonstrations. The Negro has many pent-up resentments and latent frustrations. He has to let them out. . . . If his repressed emotions do not come out in these nonviolent ways, they will come out in ominous expressions of violence. This is not a threat; it is a fact of history. So I have not said to my people "get rid of your discontent." But I have tried to say that this normal and healthy discontent can be channelized through the creative outlet of nonviolent direct action. Now this approach is being dismissed as extremist. I must admit that I was initially disappointed in being so categorized.

But as I continued to think about the matter I gradually gained a bit of satisfaction from being considered an extremist. Was not Jesus an extremist in love. . . . Was not Paul an extremist for the gospel of Jesus Christ. . . . Was not Martin Luther an extremist. . . . Was not Abraham Lincoln an extremist. . . . So the question is not whether we will be extremist but what kind of extremist will we be. Will we be extremists for hate or will we be extremists for love? Will we be extremists for the cause of justice? . . .

. . . One day the South will know that when . . . disinherited children of God sat down at lunch counters they were in reality standing up for the best in the American dream and the most sacred values in our Judeo-Christian heritage, and thusly, carrying our whole nation back to those great wells of democracy which were dug deep by the Founding Fathers in the formulation of the Constitution and the Declaration of Independence. . . . Let us all hope that the dark clouds of racial prejudice will soon pass away and the deep fog of misunderstanding will be lifted from our fear-drenched communities and in some not too distant tomorrow the radiant stars of love and brotherhood will shine over our great nation with all of their scintillating beauty. . . .

In and Out of Harm's Way: Arrogance and Love (1983)

MARILYN FRYE

INTRODUCTION

Most of this essay is devoted to constructing an account of some of the mechanisms of the exploitation and enslavement of women by men in phallocratic culture. Understanding such things is obviously important in a general way to feminist theory and strategies: it is essential, as they say, to know your enemy. But there is a more specific need of feminist theorists and activists which these analyses also address, at another level. This is the need to locate a point of purchase for a radical feminist vision.

The accounts here of the mechanisms of exploitation and enslavement yield up a vivid picture of a kind of harm characteristically done the victims of these operations. Seeing these things as *harmful* is fundamental to my belief that women's being subjected to such machinations is an evil. This is a place

In working out the materials in this essay, I benefited from discussion with C. Shafer in many ways and to a degree which cannot be reflected in particular footnotes to particular points.

From Marilyn Frye, "In and Out of Harm's Way: Arrogance and Love," in *The Politics of Reality* (Freedom, CA: The Crossing Press) 1983, pp. 52–83. Reprinted with permission of the author.

where a feminist politics can begin; but it cannot end here. When we see the effects of these machinations as harm, we implicitly invoke a contrast between the victims and the female human animal unharmed (unharmed, at least, by these particular processes). Although such an animal may be unknown in contemporary human experience, we are committed at least to an abstract conception of her. More than an abstract conception is needed if we are not simply to condemn but to resist effectively or escape. For that we need a revolutionary vision, which in turn requires that we have rich images of such an animal. . . .

. . . If it is important to imagine women untouched by phallocratic machinations, then we must take care to discover what we can know here and now on which that imagining can be fed.

The analyses in the body of this essay tell us some of what we need to know. . . . They enhance our understanding of the harm done women by the processes of subordination and enslavement, and so facilitate our understanding of the creature who is harmed. The harm lies in what these processes do to women; the analyses make clearer what these processes produce, as product. Understanding something of the stages and goals of the processing, one can see what shapes and qualities it imposes. This, in turn, suggests something of the nature of the being which is processed: one can reason that this being would not have had those shapes and those qualities if left unmolested. This sort of thinking back through phallocratic process turns out to provide valuable clues for the feminist visionary.

COERCION

To coerce is to make or force someone to do something. This seems pretty straightforward, but some of the uses of this concept are not, and one might get confused. The law in some states and general opinion in most places would have it, for instance, that an act is not rape unless the woman's engagement in sexual intercourse is coerced, and will not count the act as coerced unless the alleged victim of the alleged crime is literally physically overcome to the point where the rapist (or rapists) literally physically controls the movements of the victim's limbs and the location and position of her body. In any other case she is seen as choosing intercourse over other alternatives and thus as not being coerced. The curious thing about this interpretation of coercion is that it has the consequence that there is no such thing as a person being coerced into *doing* something. For if the movements of one's limbs and the location and position of one's body are not physically under one's control, one surely cannot be said to have *done* anything, except perhaps at the level of flexing one's muscles in resistance to the force. Given this way of thinking, one could reason that if one did anything (beyond the level of flexing muscles), then it would follow that one was not coerced, and in the sense of 'free' that only means *not coerced*, all actions and all choices would be free.

Sartre took this economical route to freedom and embraced the absurd conclusion as profundity:

> If I am mobilized in a war, this war is *my* war; it is in my image and I deserve it. I deserve it first because I could always get out of it by suicide or by desertion. . . . For lack of getting out of it, I have *chosen* it. This can be due to inertia, to cowardice in the face of public opinion, or because I prefer certain other values to the value of the refusal to join the war. . . . Any way you look at it, it is a matter of choice. . . . Therefore we must agree with the statement by J. Romains, "In war there are no innocent victims." If therefore I have preferred war to death or to dishonor, everything takes place as if I bore the entire responsibility for this war. . . . There was no compulsion here.[1]

It should not be surprising that the same small mind, embracing a foolish consistency, cannot recognize rape when he sees it and employs a magical theory of "bad faith" to account for its evidence. . . .

It is by this kind of reasoning that we are convinced that women's choices to enter and remain within the institutions of heterosexuality, marriage and motherhood are free choices, that prostitution is a freely chosen life, and that all slaves who have not risen up and killed their masters or committed suicide have freely chosen their lots as slaves.

But choice and action obviously can take place under coercion. The paradigm of coercion is *not* the direct and over-powering application of force to move or arrange someone's body and limbs. The situation of coercion must be one in which choice and action do take place and in which the victim's body and limbs are moved under the victim's own steam, their motions determined by the victim's own perception and judgment. Hence, in the standard case, the force involved in coercion is applied at some distance, and the will of the coerced agent must somehow be engaged in the determination of the bodily movements.

The general strategy involved in all coercion is exemplified in the simple case of armed robbery. You point a gun at someone and demand that she hand over her money. A moment before this she had no desire to unburden herself of her money, no interest in transferring her money from her possession to that of another; but the situation has changed, and now, of all the options before her, handing over her money seems relatively attractive. Under her own steam, moving her own limbs, she removes her money from her pocket and hands it to you. Her situation did not just change, of course. *You changed it.*

What you did (and I think this is the heart of coercion) was to arrange things so that of the options available, the one that was the least unattractive or the most attractive was the very act you wanted the victim to perform. *Given* those options, and the victim's judgments and priorities, she chooses and acts. Nobody else controls her limbs or makes that judgment for her. The elements of coercion lie not in her person, mind or body, but in the manipulation of the circumstances and manipulation of the options.*

It will be noted by the clever would-be robber that it does not matter in such a situation whether the gun is loaded or not, or whether or not the robber really would or could pull the trigger. It has only to be credible *to the victim* that the gun is loaded and that the person holding it will fire; and dying has to be perceived *by that victim* at that moment as more undesireable than handing over her money. If she thinks the person wouldn't shoot, or if she is feeling cheerfully suicidal, this will not work. If it works, she has been coerced.

The structure of coercion, then, is this: to coerce someone into doing something, one has to manipulate the situation so that the world as perceived by the victim presents the victim with a range of options the least unattractive of which (or the most attractive of which) in the judgment of the victim is the act one wants the victim to do. Given the centrality of the victim's perception and judgment, the plotting coercer might manipulate the physical environment but usually would proceed, at least in part, by manipulating the intended victim's perception and judgment through various kinds of influence and deception.

I assume that free and healthy humans would do much that would cohere with and contribute to the satisfaction of each other's interests and the enhancement of each other's capacities for pursuit of those interests. But for many reasons and by many causes, many people want more and different contributions and on very different terms than is consistent with the health and the will of those they want them from, however amiable, benevolent and naturally cooperative the latter may be. Hence, there is coercion. . . . But if you want another to perform for you frequently or regularly, your operation must be more complex. People don't like being coerced, and setting up a situation which is reliably and adaptably coercive requires doing something more about resistance and attempts to escape the imposed dilemma than a simple robber has to do. Hence coercion is extended, ramified and laminated as systems of oppression and exploitation.

EXPLOITATION AND OPPRESSION

Conjure for yourself an image of someone felling a tree with an ax. The ax is a tool; the tree a resource. The ax, properly used, will last for many years. The tree, properly felled, ceases to be; a log comes into being. A tool is by nature or manufacture so constituted and shaped that it is suited to a user's interest in

---

* What the coercer does is deliberately to create just the sort of situation Aristotle agonizes over in *Nichomachean Ethics*, III. 1., wherein "the initiative in moving the parts of the body which act as instruments rests with the agent himself," but the agent does something which "nobody would choose to do . . . for its own sake." (*Nichomachean Ethics*, translated by Martin Ostwald, (The Library of Liberal Arts, 1962.) Thanks to Claudia Card for reminding me of this passage.)

bringing about a certain sort of effect, and so its being put to use does not require its alteration. The case is otherwise with resources or materials; their uses or exploitations typically transform them. Trees become wood which becomes pulp which becomes paper. At each stage the relations of the parts, the composition, and the condition of the thing used are significantly altered in or by the use. The parts and properties of the thing or stuff were not initially organized with reference to a certain purpose or *telos*; they are altered and rearranged so that they *are* organized with reference to that *telos*. A transforming manipulation is characteristic of this kind of using, of the exploitation of resources or materials.

Analogues of this occur in the exploitation of animate beings. In the case of nonhuman animals, their shapes, the relations of their parts, their constitutions and conditions, and the ways these change or move in the absence of human intervention generally suit them and their behavior to human interests in few and undependable ways. To make much use of such animals, one generally has to do some manipulation and alteration of them. . . . To get nonhuman animals (draft animals, for instance) to work for them, human animals breed certain species to configurations, tempers and capacities to respond to training, and they train individuals of those species from a very young age to tolerate various bindings and harnesses and the bearing of various weights. . . . In the end, by its "second" nature, acquired through processes appropriately called "breaking" and "training" and by the physical restraints placed on it, such a beast can do very little which does *not* serve some human purpose.[2]

Some analogue of this "breaking" must be developed if a person is to exploit another person or group of persons. . . . If you would harness someone else to your wagon, the other must be remodelled. Like any animal, the other is not in the nature of things ready-made to suit anyone's interests but its own. But unlike nonhuman animals, this one matches the exploiter in intelligence and fineness of physical abilities, and this one is capable of self-respect, righteousness and resentment. The human exploiter may not so easily win or outwit the human victim.

Exploitation and oppression are in tension with each other, as one would expect of things which harmonize. Efficient exploitation requires that those exploited be relatively mobile, self-animating and self-maintaining—the more so as the work in question requires greater intelligence, attention or ingenuity. But it also requires that they not be free enough, strong enough or willful enough to resist, escape or significantly misfit the situation of exploitation. While oppressive structures provide for the latter, those which consist mainly of variations on bondage and confinement are inefficient. A system which relies heavily on physical restriction both presupposes and generates resistance and attempts to escape. These in turn exacerbate the need for bondage and containment. This cycle leads to a situation in which the exploited are subjected to maximal limitation and maximal damage, including the passivity of a broken spirit. . . .

. . . Efficient exploitation of "human resources" requires that the structures that refer the others' actions to the exploiter's ends must extend beneath the victim's skin. The exploiter has to bring about the partial disintegration and

re(mis)integration of the others' matter, parts and properties so that as organized systems the exploited are oriented to some degree by habits, skills,
schedules, values and tastes to the exploiter's ends rather than, as they would
otherwise be, to ends of their own. In particular, the manipulations which
adapt the exploited to a niche in another's economy must accomplish a great
reduction of the victim's intolerance of coercion.

The best solutions to the problem are those which dissolve it. What the
exploiter needs is that the will and intelligence of the victim be disengaged
from the projects of resistance and escape but that they not be simply broken
or destroyed. Ideally, the dis-integration and mis-integration of the victim
should accomplish the detachment of the victim's will and intelligence from
the victim's own interests and their attachment to the interests of the exploiter.
This will effect a displacement or dissolution of self-respect and will undermine the victim's intolerance of coercion. With that, the situation transcends
the initial paradigmatic form or structure of coercion; for if people don't mind
doing what you want them to do, then, in a sense, you can't really be *making*
them do it. In the limiting case, the victim's will and intelligence are wholly
transferred to a full engagement in the pursuit of the dominating person's
interests. The "problem" had been that there were two parties with divergent
interests; this sort of solution (which is very elegant, as that word is used in
logic) is to erase the conflict by reducing the number of interested parties to
one.* This radical solution can properly be called "enslavement."

ENSLAVEMENT

The mechanisms of enslavement, in cases where it is deliberately and self-
consciously carried out, have been studied and documented in, among other
cases, European colonization of Africa and the enslavement of Blacks and
indigenous peoples in the "New World." Kathleen Barry has documented
them in her book, *Female Sexual Slavery*,[3] in the case of what has been called by
the misnomer "white slavery" . . . I want to draw on this latter work here because this is the category of slavery that is specific to the system of oppression
which subordinates women to men.

Many feminists have found it illuminating to compare the situations of
women in general to enslavement, or have seen the situations of women as
forms of enslavement. For people in the United States, the use of the concept
of slavery can usually be heard only as a reference to the experience and institutions of enslavement of Blacks by whites in the United States. For many reasons, such a comparison between women generally and Blacks in pre-Civil

---

* The foregoing discussion may seem to present a picture of exploiters which exaggerates
their inhumanity. I recommend one read or re-read such texts as Machiavelli's *The Prince*,
Orwell's *1984* and *The Report From Iron Mountain on the Possibility and Desirability of Peace*
(Dell, New York, 1967), to recover a suitable sense of proportion.

War enslavement is misleading and politically suspect.[4] But the literal enslavement of women for sexual service (frequently for both sexual and domestic service) is a venerated, vigorous, current and universal institution of male-dominated cultures which routinely victimizes girls and women of all racial, economic and ethnic affiliations all over the world. It is this institution that is the appropriate object of reference when one explores the ways in which women's situations are like, or are forms of, slavery.

According to Barry, the strategy for converting a half-grown willful girl or a reasonably independent and competent woman to a servile prostitute or a passive concubine has three stages: Abduction, Seasoning and Criminalization.

Under the heading of Abduction come kidnapping and seduction, or any other act by which the abductor can remove the girl or woman from a setting which is familiar to her to a setting which is totally unfamiliar to her, where she has no allies and no knowledge of what resources are potentially available. ... The abductor has stripped her of the most ordinary powers and resources which even the most socially powerless people usually retain.* She is frightened and oriented to escape, but he has imposed on her by force a condition in which she can do almost nothing in her own behalf.

The next stage is Seasoning.

While he holds her in captivity and isolation, he brutalizes the victim in as many ways as there are to brutalize. Rape. Beatings. Verbal and physical degradation. Deprivation. Intense and enduring discomfort. Credible threats of murder.

The abductor's brutality functions in several ways. By placing the victim in a life-threatening and absolutely aversive situation, he maximizes the urgency of the victim's taking action in her own behalf while making it utterly impossible for her to do so. This puts maximum force into the processes of alienating her from herself through total helplessness. The result is radical loss of self-esteem, self-respect and any sense of capacity or agency.[†] The brutality also establishes intimacy, both by being invasive and by the intensity of the one-on-one contact. At a certain point, the abductor shifts from unabating brutality to intermittent and varying brutality. This creates occasions for positive feeling on the part of the victim. She is now in a world of distorted moral proportion where not being beaten, not being under threat of imminent death, being permitted to urinate when she needs to, etc., have become occasions for gratitude. Gratitude is a positive and a binding affect. The intimacy is intensified. From now on, any time the man is not torturing her she feels herself to be relatively well treated. The process of reconstructing the elements of the person into the shape of a slave has begun.

---

* Except, in many cases, those in "mental institutions" or prisons.

† It is interesting to note that in *Story of O*, a classic of sado-masochistic pornography, O is forbidden at this point in her "training" and ever after to touch her own genitals or breasts, which she is inclined to do to comfort herself. She is instructed that they belong to the men. (*Story of O*, by Pauline Reage [Grove Press, New York, 1965.])

The shift to less constant abuse is also a perverse kind of empowerment of the victim. After having been in a situation where her presence as agent has been reduced to nothing, she now has the opportunity to try to act in support of her physical survival. She can try to discover what pleases and what displeases the man, and try to please him and avoid displeasing him, thereby avoiding or postponing beatings and degradation, or being killed. She had been annihilated as an agent; when she is restored to agency, it is kept at a remove from her own interests and self-preservation. She can act indirectly and negatively in the interest of her physical survival and freedom from pain by trying to behave in ways which will forestall or avoid the man's abuse, but any direct presence of herself to herself, any directly self-preserving or self-serving behavior, will displease him and thus be counterproductive.

If he is any good at this, the man will make it a point to be arbitrary and capricious in his pleasures and displeasures and to be very brutal when he is brutal. This will make the victim's task of anticipating his will extremely difficult and keep the stakes high. All of this draws her closer to him: her attention will be on him constantly and exclusively; her every resource of intelligence, will and sensitivity will be drawn into the most intense engagement with and focus upon him. She is likely to become "clinging" and "possessive"—not wanting to let him out of her sight. All of the will and resources she would draw upon to survive are thus channeled to the service of his interests.

The final stage, Criminalization, is necessary in order for the abductor to return the woman and his relationship with her to a more public sphere where he can turn the newly-wrought relationship to his economic benefit. He forces the woman or girl to engage in or be an accomplice to some criminal act or acts—larceny, drug traffic, murder, prostitution, kidnapping. By this she becomes and knows she becomes a criminal, part of the "underworld." Now she cannot return to family or friends, or turn to the police. As a female and a criminal she has nowhere to escape to and a great deal to be protected from. Her procurer and his associates become her protectors from the violence and scorn of the straight society. She now depends on him for protection from fates worse than he: he who is familiar, in whose domain she probably can survive by being and doing whatever he wants, and in whose world she will find the only acceptance, economic viability or social interaction and emotional life now available to her.

She is now his. . . .

. . . Although the slave is not engaged in "surpassing herself," she *is* engaged in surpassing: she is engaged in the master's "surpassing" *him*self. Her substance is organized toward his "transcendence."

THE ARROGANT EYE

. . . The Bible says that all of nature (including woman) exists for man. Man is invited to subdue the earth and have dominion over every living thing on it, all of which is said to exist "to you" "for meat."[5] Woman is created to be man's helper. This captures in myth Western Civilization's primary answer to the philosophical question of man's place in nature: everything that is is resource for man's exploitation. With this world view, men see with arrogant eyes which organize everything seen with reference to themselves and their own interests. The arrogating perceiver is a teleologist, a believer that everything exists and happens for some purpose, and he tends to animate things, imagining attitudes toward himself as the animating motives. Everything is either "for me" or "against me." This is the kind of vision that interprets the rock one trips on as hostile, the bolt one cannot loosen as stubborn, the woman who made meatloaf when he wanted spaghetti as "bad" (though he didn't say what he wanted). The arrogant perceiver does not countenance the possibility that the Other is independent, indifferent. The feminist separatist can only be a man-hater; Nature is called "Mother."

The arrogant perceiver falsifies—the Nature who makes both green beans and *Bacillus botulinus* doesn't give a passing damn whether humans live or die[6]—but he also coerces the objects of his perception into satisfying the conditions his perception imposes. He tries to accomplish in a glance what the slave masters and batterers accomplish by extended use of physical force, and to a great extent he succeeds. . . .

How one sees another and how one expects the other to behave are in tight interdependence, and how one expects another to behave is a large factor in determining how the other does behave. . . .

. . . Women experience the coerciveness of this kind of "influence" when men perversely impose sexual meanings on our every movement. We know the palpable pressure of a man's reduction of our objection to an occasion for our instruction. Women do not so often experience ourselves imposing expectations on situations and making them stick, but some of the most awesome stories of women's successful resistance to male violence involve a woman's expecting the male assailant into the position of a little boy in the power of his mother.* The power of expectations is enormous; it should be engaged and responded to attentively and with care. The arrogant perceiver engages it with the same unconsciousness with which he engages his muscles when he writes his name.

The arrogant perceiver's expectation creates in the space about him a sort of vacuum mold into which the other is sucked and held. But the other is not sucked into his structure always, nor always without resistance. In the absence of his manipulation, the other *is* not organized primarily with reference to his interests. To the extent that she is not shaped to his will, does not fit the conformation he imposes, there is friction, anomaly or incoherence in his world. To the extent that he notices this incongruity, he can experience it in no other way than as something wrong with her. His perception is arrogating; his

* I refer here to some experience of my own, and to such stories as the Success Stories included in "Do It Yourself-Self-Defense," by Pat James, in *Fight Back: Feminist Resistance to Male Violence*, edited by Frederique Delacoste & Felice Newman (Cleis Press, 1981), p. 205.

senses tell him that the world and everything in it (with the occasional exception of other men) is in the nature of things there *for* him, that she is by her constitution and *telos* his servant. He believes his senses. If woman does not serve man, it can only be because he is not a sufficiently skilled master or because there is something wrong with the woman. ...

Though anyone might wish, for any of many reasons, to contribute to another's pursuit of her or his interests, the health and integrity of an organism is a matter of its being organized largely toward its own interests and welfare. The arrogant perceiver knows this in his own case, but he *arrogates* everything to himself and thus perceives as healthy or "right" everything that relates to him as his own substance does when he is healthy. But what's sauce for the gander is sauce for the goose. *She* is healthy and "working right" when *her* substance is organized primarily on principles which align it to *her* interests and welfare. Cooperation is essential, of course, but it will not do that I arrange everything so that you get enough exercise: for me to be healthy, *I* must get enough exercise. My being adequately exercised is logically independent of your being so.

The arrogant perceiver's perception of the other's normalcy or defectiveness is not only dead wrong, it is coercive. It manipulates the other's perception and judgment at the root by mislabeling the unwholesome as healthy, and what is wrong as right. One judges and chooses within a framework of values—notions as to what 'good' and 'good for you' pertain to. ... But what we have in the case of the arrogant perceiver is the mis-defining of 'good' and 'healthy.' If one has the cultural and institutional power to make the misdefinition stick, one can turn the whole other person right around to oneself by this one simple trick. This is the sort of thing that makes the "reversals" Mary Daly talks about in *Gyn/Ecology* so evil and so dangerous.[7] If one does not get the concepts *right* and *wrong, healthy* and *unhealthy* right, and in particular, if one gets them wrong in the specific way determined by the arrogant eye, one *cannot* take care of oneself. This is the most fundamental kind of harm. It is, in effect, *mayhem*: a maiming which impairs a person's ability to defend herself.[8] Mayhem is very close kin both morally and logically to murder.

The procurer-enslaver, working with overt force, constructs a situation in which the victim's pursuit of her own survival or health and her attempt to be good always require, as a matter of practical fact in that situation, actions which serve him. In the world constructed by the arrogant eye, this same connection is established not by terror but by definition.*

---

* Neither the arrogant perceiver nor the procurer works in a vacuum, of course. They are supported by a culture which in many ways "softens up" their victims for them, an economy which systematically places women in positions of economic dependence on men, and a community of men which threatens women with rape at every turn. Also, the existence of the procurers supports the arrogant perceiver by making him seem benign by comparison. The arrogant perceiver, in addition, has the support of a community of arrogant perceivers, among whom are all or most of the most powerful members of the community at large.

The official story about men who batter women is that they do so in large part because they suffer "low self-esteem." What this suggests to me is that they suffer a lack of arrogance and cannot fully believe in themselves as centers about which all else (but some other men) revolves and to which all else refers. Because of this they cannot effectively exercise the power of that expectation. But as men they "know" they are supposed to be centers of universes, so they are reduced to trying to create by force what more successful men, men who can carry off masculinity better, create by arrogant perception. This is, perhaps, one reason why some of the men who do not batter have contempt for men who do.

Western philosophy and science have for the most part been built on the presumption of the Intelligibility of the Universe. This is the doctrine that everything in the universe and the universe itself can, at least in principle, be understood and comprehended by human intelligence, reason and understanding.

Western philosophy and science have for the most part been committed to the Simplicity Theory of Truth: the simplest theory that accounts for the data is the true theory. (Theories are simplest which postulate the fewest entities, require the fewest hypotheses, generate predictions by the fewest calculations, etc.)

The connection seems clear: only if the truth is simple can the universe be intelligible.

But why believe either of these principles?

If someone believes that the world is made for him to have dominion over and he is made to exploit it, he must believe that he and the world are so made that he *can*, at least in principle, achieve and maintain dominion over everything. But you can't put things to use if you don't know how they work. So he must believe that he can, at least in principle, understand everything. If the world exists for man, it must be usably intelligible, which means it must be simple enough for him to understand. A usable universe is an intelligible universe is a simple universe.

If something seems to be unintelligible, you can decide it is unnatural or unreal. Or you can decide *it* is what is *really* real and then declare that you have discovered the Problem of Knowledge. Or, having declared what seems unintelligible to be the *really* real, you can claim it is, after all, intelligible, but only to the extraordinary few (who, in spite of being so few somehow can be normative of what Man really is).

. . . and so it goes with the philosophy and the science of The Arrogant Eye.

THE LOVING EYE

The attachment of the well-broken slave to the master has been confused with love. Under the name of Love, a willing and unconditional servitude has been promoted as something ecstatic, noble, fulfilling and even redemptive. All praise is sung for the devoted wife who loves the husband and children she is willing to live for, and of the brave man who loves the god he is willing to kill for, the country he is willing to die for.

We can be taken in by this equation of servitude with love because we make two mistakes at once: we think, of both servitude and love, that they are selfless or unselfish. We tend to think of them as attachments in which the person is not engaged because of self-interest and does not pursue self-interest. The wife who married for money did not marry for love, we think; the mercenary soldier is despised by the loyal patriot. And the slave, we think, is selfless because she *can* do nothing but serve the interests of another. But this is wrong. Neither is the slave selfless, nor is the lover.

It is one mark of a voluntary association that the one person can survive displeasing the other, defying the other, dissociating from the other. The slave, the battered wife, the not-so-battered wife, is constantly in jeopardy. She is in a situation where she cannot, or reasonably believes she cannot, survive without the other's provision and protection, and where experience has made it credible to her that the other may kill her or abandon her if and when she displeases him. . . . In her situation of utter dependence and peril, every detail of the other's action, interests and wishes are ineluctably and directly, as a matter of empirical fact, connected to her interest in survival. She does not see the other as, or expect the other to be, organized to the service of her interests (quite the contrary), but she cannot fail to interpret the other always with an eye to what will keep her from being killed or abandoned. Her eye is not arrogating, but it is the furthest thing from disinterested; she does not have the option of setting her interests aside, of not calculating them. . . . On the other hand, the victim may survive, as *Story of O* presents her or as she is pictured in the old Geritol commercials, solely because the other wishes it. In *Story of O*, the master would be most displeased to find that O was interested in her survival for any reason other than that he wanted her to survive; that would be a last vestige of "willfulness," a telltale sign of the imperfection of her "love" for him.[9] In the Geritol commercial, the woman "takes care of herself" because her family needs her; her husband will "keep her" because she serves so devotedly. In this latter case, if it ever really is the case (as I am pessimistic enough to think it is), the slave/wife really is not motivated by self-interest, but her behavior toward and perception of the other is still not disinterested. She has assumed *his* interest. She now sees with *his* eye, his arrogant eye. . . .

One who loves is not selfless either. If the loving eye is in any sense disinterested, it is not that the seer has lost herself, has no interests, or ignores or denies her interests. Any of these would seriously incapacitate her as a perceiver. What *is* the case, surely, is that unlike the slave or the master, the loving perceiver can see without the presupposition that the other poses a constant threat or that the other exists for the seer's service; nor does she see with the other's eye instead of her own. Her interest does not blend the seer and the seen, either empirically by terror or *a priori* by conceptual links forged by the arrogant eye. One who sees with a loving eye is separate from the other whom she sees. There are boundaries between them; she and the other are two; their interests are not identical; they are not blended in vital parasitic or symbiotic relations, nor does she believe they are or try to pretend they are.

The loving eye is a contrary of the arrogant eye.

The loving eye knows the independence of the other. It is the eye of a seer who knows that nature is indifferent. It is the eye of one who knows that to know the seen, one must consult something other than one's own will and interests and fears and imagination. One must look at the thing. One must look and listen and check and question.

The loving eye is one that pays a certain sort of attention. This attention can require a discipline but *not* a self-denial. The discipline is one of self-knowledge, knowledge of the scope and boundary of the self. What is required is that one know what are one's interests, desires and loathings, one's projects, hungers, fears and wishes, and that one know what is and what is not determined by these. In particular, it is a matter of being able to tell one's own interests from those of others and of knowing where one's self leaves off and another begins. . . .

The loving eye . . . knows the complexity of the other as something which will forever present new things to be known. The science of the loving eye would favor The Complexity Theory of Truth and presuppose The Endless Interestingness of the Universe.

The loving eye seems generous to its object, though it means neither to give nor to take, for not-being-invaded, not-being-coerced, not-being-annexed must be felt in a world such as ours as a great gift.

THE BELOVED

We who would love women, and well, who would change ourselves and change the world so that it is possible to love women well, we need to imagine the possibilities for what women might be if we lived lives free of the material and perceptual forces which subordinate women to men. The point is not to imagine a female human animal unaffected by the other humans around it, uninfluenced by its own and others' perceptions of others' interests, unaffected by culture. The point is only to imagine women not enslaved, to imagine these intelligent, willful and female bodies not subordinated in service to males, individually or via institutions (or to anybody, in any way); not pressed into a shape that suits an arrogant eye.

The forces which we want to imagine ourselves free of are a guide to what we might be when free of them. They mark the shape they mold us to, but they also suggest by implication the shapes we might have been without that molding. One can guess something of the magnitude and direction of the tendencies the thing would exhibit when free by attending to the magnitudes and directions of the forces required to confine and shape it. For instance, much pressure is applied at the point of our verbal behavior, enforcing silence or limiting our speech.[10] One can reason that without that force we might show ourselves to be loquacious and perhaps prone to oratory, not to mention prone to saying things unpleasant to male ears. . . .

But to speak most generally: the forces of men's material and perceptual violence mold Woman to dependence upon Man, in every meaning of 'dependence': contingent upon; conditional upon; necessitated by; defined in terms of; incomplete or unreal without; requiring the support or assistance of; being a subordinate part of; being an appurtenance to.

Dependence is forced upon us. It is not rash to speculate that without this force, much, most or all of what most or all of us are and do would not be contingent upon, conditional upon, necessitated by, or subordinate to any man or what belongs to or pertains to a man, men or masculinity. What we are and how we are, or what we would be and how we would be if not molded by the arrogating eye, is: *not molded to man, not dependent.*

I do not speak here of a specious absolute independence that would mean never responding to another's need and never needing another's response. I conceive here simply of a being whose needs and responses are not *bound* by concepts or by terror in a dependence upon those of another. The loving eye makes the correct assumption: the object of the seeing is *another* being whose existence and character are logically independent of the seer and who may be practically or empirically independent in any particular respect at any particular time.

It is not an easy thing to grasp the meaning or the truth of this "independence," nor is a clear or secure belief in it at all common, even among those who identify themselves as feminists. The inability to think it is one of the things that locks men in eternal infantilism; it is one of the things that makes women endlessly susceptible to deep uncertainty in our political and epistemological claims, and to nearly fatal indecisiveness in our actions. . . .

We have to a great extent learned the arrogant boychild's vocabulary, and to identify with him and see with his eye; we have learned to think of agency and power very much as he does. What we may do when we try to imagine ourselves independent is just slip ourselves slyly into his shoes and imagine *ourselves* the center of the universe, the darlings of Mother Nature and the cherished sisters of all other women. . . .

. . . The woman who wants "equality" in many cases simply wants to be in there *too*, as one of the men for whom men's God made everything "for meat."

It has been suggested to me that we fail in these efforts of imagination partly because we insist on reinventing the wheel. We might give womankind some credit: we might suppose that not all women lead and have led male-mediated lives, and that the lives of the more independent women could provide material for the stimulation and correction of our imaginations. Women of exceptional gifts and creative achievements there are, and women whose lives do not follow the beaten path. But also, when one looks closely at the lives of the women presented by history or in one's own experience as exceptional, one often sees both some not-so-exceptional causal factors like the patronage of exceptional men (for which one must assume the women pay in some coin or other), and signs of peculiar fears and strange lapses of imagination. . . .

. . . [T]here is in the fabric of our lives, not always visible but always affecting its texture and strength, a mortal dread of being outside the field of vision of the arrogant eye. That eye gives all things meaning by connecting all things to each other by way of their references to one point—Man. . . .

This is a terrible disability. If we have no intuition of ourselves as independent, unmediated beings in the world, then we cannot conceive ourselves surviving our liberation; for what our liberation will do is dissolve the structures and dismantle the mechanisms by which Woman is mediated by Man. If we cannot imagine ourselves surviving this, we certainly will not make it happen.

There probably is really no distinction, in the end, between imagination and courage. We can't imagine what we can't face, and we can't face what we can't imagine. To break out of the structures of the arrogant eye we have to dare to rely on ourselves to make meaning and we have to imagine ourselves beings capable of that. . . .

We have correctly intuited that the making of meaning is social and requires a certain community of perception. We also are individually timid and want "support." So it is only against a background of an imagined community of ultimate harmony and perfect agreement that we dare to think it possible to make meaning. This brings us into an arrogance of our own, for we make it a prerequisite for our construction of meaning that other women be what we need them to be to constitute the harmonious community of agreement we require. Some women refuse to participate at all in this meaning construction "because feminists are divided and can't agree among themselves." . . . In other words, we threaten to fail in imagination and courage like all the other exceptional and ordinary women, if our sisters do not or will not harmonize and agree with us. . . .

. . . The community required for meaning, however, is precisely *not* a homogenous herd, for without difference there is no meaning. Meaning is a system of connections and distinctions among different and distinguishable things. The hypothetical homogeneous community which we imagine we need *could* not be the community in which we can make ourselves intelligible, im-mediately, to and for ourselves. . . .

We need to know women as independent: subjectively in our own beings, and in our appreciations of others. If we are to know it in ourselves, I think we may have to be under the gaze of a loving eye, the eye which presupposes our independence. The loving eye does not prohibit a woman's experiencing the world directly, does not force her to experience it by way of the interested interpretations of the seer in whose visual field she moves. In this situation, she *can* experience directly in her bones the contingent character of her relations to all others and to Nature. If we are to know women's independence in the being of others, I think we may have to cast a loving eye toward them . . . and wait, and see.

Notes

1. *Being and Nothingness,* translated by Hazel E. Barnes (Philosophical Library, New York, 1956), p. 553.
2. I am indebted to Carolyn Shafer both for information about the breeding and training of domestic animals and for political interpretation of it. See also, *Woman And Nature: The Roaring Inside Her,* by Susan Griffin (Harper and Row, New York, 1978).
3. Prentice-Hall, Englewood Cliffs, New Jersey, 1979.
4. Cf., *Ain't I A Woman: Black Women and Feminism,* by bell hooks (South End Press, Boston, 1981), p. 143 and all of Chapter IV, "Racism and Feminism."
5. Genesis 1:29.
6. Due to Catherine Madsen, from her review of *Wanderground,* by Sally Gearhart (Persephone Press, Watertown, Massachusetts, 1979), in *Conditions No. 7,* p. 138.
7. *Gyn/Ecology: the Metaethics of Radical Feminism,* by Mary Daly (Boston, Beacon, 1990), pp. 2, 30 and elsewhere throughout the book.
8. *Webster's Third New International Dictionary* and *The Shorter Oxford English Dictionary.*
9. *Story of O,* by Pauline Reage (Grove Press, New York, 1965). See also *Woman Hating,* by Andrea Dworkin (E.P. Dutton, New York, 1974), Chapter 3, "Woman as Victim: *Story of O.*"
10. Cf., *Man-Made Language,* by Dale Spender (Routledge & Kegan Paul, London, 1980), pp. 43–50.

Study Questions

1. In his essay concerning the emancipation of slaves, what is Jefferson's attitude toward African American intelligence, abilities (emotional, artistic, and intellectual), and the possibility of intermarriage of whites and African Americans?
2. Briefly outline William Lloyd Garrison's arguments against slavery, and explain why there should be no compensation to slaveholders upon slaves' emancipation. In what way(s) might you be able to improve upon the arguments put forth by Garrison? Explain.

3. What are Angelina Grimké's arguments against the notion that the Bible sanctions slavery? How does she use the anti-abolitionist's claim that African Americans are fit for slavery because they have already been in bondage and the slave's condition is tolerable?

4. What are Angelina Grimké's seven major conclusions in *The Appeal to the Christian Women of the South?* What are her reasons put forth to justify these conclusions?

5. Angelina Grimké argued that it is up to the individual to work toward human treatment and emancipation of slaves. What are her proposals for achieving these goals? In what sense, in your considered view, are Grimké's arguments dependent upon the notion of duty without consideration of consequences for those working toward the abolition of slavery?

6. What are Sarah Grimké's arguments from scripture regarding the equality of women and men with each other? Do you agree with her claims? Why or why not? Defend your position. With respect to the notion that Eve was responsible for original sin, what is Grimké's attitude toward the subjection of women? What are her arguments regarding the equality of men and women with particular respect to the concept of moral responsibility? Are you convinced by her references to scriptural claims of the equality of the sexes? Are there other arguments you might put forth that would strengthen Grimké's position? Explain.

7. Writing regarding the "social intercourse of the sexes," Sarah Grimké claims that men almost always address themselves to the weakness of women. What are those weaknesses, and how does Grimké attempt to show that men and women are equal as moral beings to men?

8. Comparing the words of the Declaration of Independence to Elizabeth Cady Stanton's speech at the first woman's rights convention, why do you believe that she used that document to put forth her position on the equality of women? What is the significance of the resolutions made at the convention? In your view, have all of those resolutions found adequate fulfillment in our time? Defend your claims.

9. Frederick Douglass claimed that the Fourth of July does not mean the same thing to slaves in America as it does to American nonslaves. What is his explanation of this position? Do you believe that emancipated people would or should feel differently about the Fourth of July and its "meaning"? Defend your answer.

10. In "The Solitude of Self," Elizabeth Cady Stanton expresses the conviction that all human beings are alone in the world and are ultimately responsible for themselves. How does she justify this claim, how is it especially relevant to women, and how is it connected to her arguments concerning the necessity for adequate education for women? In what ways, in your considered view, is Stanton's position an expression of the same sort of sentiment regarding the equality of the sexes put forth in Sarah Grimké's letters?

11. In the "Introduction" to the *Woman's Bible*, Elizabeth Cady Stanton outlines a position on the subordination of women as it manifests itself in scripture. Do you agree with her claims, especially regarding translation of scripture and women's right to comment on the Bible? Why? Defend your answer.

12. In "The Letter from the Birmingham Jail," Martin Luther King, Jr. focuses his attention on the indignity and inhumanity of racial segregation and racism. What are the means by which King proposes to fight against such injustice? What is his concept of "direct action"? Are his arguments for the necessity of direct action compelling? Why is he justified in engaging in acts of civil disobedience? Do you agree with King's claims and his proposals? Why? Defend your answer.

13. What is Marilyn Frye's conception of coercion and how does she show that under the traditional way of understanding the term, it is impossible to coerce anyone into *doing* anything? How does Frye use the analogy of the training of domestic animals to show that exploitation and oppression are part of coercion? What are the three stages of the conversion of a girl or a woman into a servile or passive person? How does Frye distinguish between the "arrogant eye" and the "loving eye," and what is it incumbent upon women to do to avoid the attitude within themselves of the arrogant perceiver?

Suggestions for Further Reading

Bass, Jonathan S. *Blessed are the Peacemakers: Martin Luther King, Jr., Eight White Religious Leaders, and the "Letter from Birmingham Jail."* Baton Rouge: Louisiana State University Press, 2001.

Boxill, Bernard. *Blacks and Social Justice, Revised Edition.* Totowa, N.J.: Rowman & Allenheld, 1984.

Boxill, Bernard. *Race and Racism.* New York: Oxford University Press, 2001.

Douglass, Frederick. *The Frederick Douglass Papers.* Edited by John W. Blassingame. New Haven: Yale University Press, 1979.

Douglass, Frederick. *Narrative of the Life of Frederick Douglass, An American Slave.* Edited by William L. Andrews and William S. McFeely. New York: W. W. Norton, 1997.

Frye, Marilyn. *The Politics of Reality: Essays in Feminist Theory.* Freedom, Calif.: Crossing Press, 1983.

Frye, Marilyn. *Willful Virgin: Essays in Feminism, 1976–1992.* Freedom, Calif.: Crossing Press, 1992.

Goodman, Paul. *Of One Blood: Abolitionism and the Origins of Racial Equality.* Berkeley: University of California Press, 1998.

Jaggar, Alison M. "Feminist Ethics." In L. Becker and C. Becker, eds. *Encyclopedia of Ethics.* New York: Garland Press, 1992, 361–370.

Kern, Kathi. *Mrs. Stanton's Bible*. Ithaca: Cornell University Press, 2001.

King, Martin Luther, Jr. *A Call to Conscience: The Landmark Speeches of Dr. Martin Luther King, Jr.* Edited by Clayborne Carson and Kris Shephard. New York: IPM in Association with Warner Books, 2001.

Lerner, Gerda. *The Feminist Thought of Sarah Grimké*. New York: Oxford University Press, 1998.

Mayer, Henry. *All on Fire: William Lloyd Garrison and the Abolition of Slavery*. New York: St. Martin's Press, 1998.

Miller, Bradford. *Returning to Seneca Falls: The First Woman's Rights Convention & its Meaning for Men & Women Today*. Hudson, N.Y.: Lindisfarne Press, 1995.

Rogers, William B. *"We are All Together Now": Frederick Douglass, William Lloyd Garrison, and the Prophetic Tradition*. New York: Garland, 1995.

Stanton, Elizabeth Cady. *Eighty Years and More: Reminiscences, 1815–1897*. New Introduction by Gail Parker. New York: Schocken Books, 1971.

Stanton, Elizabeth Cady. *Elizabeth Cady Stanton, Susan B. Anthony: Correspondence, Writings, Speeches*. Edited by Ellen Carol DuBois. New York: Schocken Books, 1981.

Stanton, Elizabeth Cady, and Anthony, Susan B. *The Selected Papers of Elizabeth Cady Stanton and Susan B. Anthony*. Edited by Ann D. Gordon. New Brunswick, N.J.: Rutgers University Press, 1997.

Waggenspack, Beth Marie. *The Search for Self-Sovereignty: The Oratory of Elizabeth Cady Stanton*. New York: Greenwood Press, 1989.

Chapter 11

American Ethics and Politics
The Individual and the Community

American ethical and political thought after the American Revolution takes many turns and is often difficult to characterize in simple or singular terms. The works in this chapter are but a small sample of the rich and varied ideas and interests expressed in the tapestry of works that are American ethical and political thought. Representative works from New England Transcendentalists (Emerson and Henry David Thoreau), pragmatists (James and Dewey), contemporary American analytical political theorists (Rawls and Nozick), the communitarianism of Sandel, and the feminism of Held are included here. These thinkers continue the revolutionary ideals of the constitutionalist founders in the wide-ranging interests and concerns associated with individual rights and responsibilities, individualism and its connection with community, and suggestions and proposals for more inclusive and diverse conceptions of ethics and politics in American society in particular, but also for human societies in general.

Ralph Waldo Emerson (1803–1882) and Henry David Thoreau (1817–1862) present views on individual responsibility and moral greatness through the lenses of their unique brands of American thought. Being fully entrenched in the romantic tradition, one finds less argumentation in their works than is so often found in the history of philosophy. Nonetheless, their positions regarding our responsibilities to ourselves and to others in society are given clear, perceptive, and vigorous literary defense in Emerson's "Politics" and Thoreau's "Civil Disobedience."

The views of Emerson and Thoreau regarding the responsibilities of human beings to themselves and others are expressed in a style in which reasons and argumentation are subordinated to a feeling for the truth of the claims they present. They present ideas with a level of conviction more sentimental than intellectual, more from feeling than from reason. Emerson makes this explicit in his conviction that we ought not to worry ourselves over creating grand schemes of logical perfection and consistency. The point instead is to live one's life authentically, to be the unique, responsible, moral individual that every human being has the capacity to become.

Building from this sort of view, Emerson and Thoreau embrace the notion that the best government is the government that governs least. Emerson and Thoreau both hold with an unremitting optimism concerning the ability of human beings to go beyond the limitations of government and enforced and false conformity. Just as Emerson said in "Self-Reliance" that "to be great is to be misunderstood" and that "a foolish consistency is the hobgoblin of little minds," so also does Thoreau make a case for the courage of the individual to live his life based on personal convictions without regard for transitory and unimportant personal consequences. Emerson holds that the rise of the "wise man" would make government unnecessary. This is what Emerson has in mind when he contends in "Politics" that the purpose or goal of the state is to educate its citizens not simply in traditional and customary ways, but also to educate them for proper citizenship. The notion of proper education for an effective and responsible democratic citizenry, to be developed later in a new way by John Dewey's instrumentalist pragmatism, is part and parcel of the American commitment to innovation that begins and continues only with individual action.

Thus it is that Thoreau is able to say with a clear conscience that he wishes to be a good neighbor as much as he wishes to be a bad subject, expressing the obligation of the individual to develop good character through the community in which he lives, but not to be held back or stifled by customs or traditions that are themselves unjustified or unjustifiable, and not to allow himself an excuse for immorality. As a movement in American thought, New England Transcendentalism is one of the clearest expressions of the American spirit of individualism in its conviction that the individual be responsible not only for the development of his own conscience, but also for taking direct action (e.g., in the case of Thoreau, to refuse to pay taxes to an immoral government supporting slavery) to improve the world in which he lives by refusing to do something wrong. As such, the Transcendentalist is a living tribute to the commitment always to do better, to achieve more, to be more, and to live authentically.

William James (1842–1910) writes of the value of human life and of the importance of moral inquiry in this regard, expressing the notion that ethics is not to be characterized by ultimate truth or a conception of a final good. A position very similar to this, held by John Dewey (1859–1952), is that our moral inquiries are not to be understood as quests for certainty or absolute truth, but as practical inquiries subject to the vagaries of experience and the changing tides of human societies.

William James's "What Makes a Life Significant" is a celebration of the value of individual lives and the influence of our philosophical temperament on them. The optimism of James's moral conceptions shines brightly in his passionate portrait of the distinction between the realization of our overriding ideals and an understanding of the notion of ideals for a particular person. In holding views skeptical of the value of grand schemes of moral and political philosophy, James and Dewey are optimistic regarding the value of the individual and the importance of individual lives to and in the progress of the societies in which they live. In fact, Dewey's view of progress and his confidence in the possibilities for progress that are realizable through properly used technologies and innovations in communication are strangely prophetic. Although it is not much in vogue today to have such a high level of confidence in the power of technology to cure social ills, Dewey's optimism regarding the necessity of communication to enhance and empower a democratic citizenry could be embodied in our time in the proliferation of information arising through advances in communication technology. Unfortunately, however, there is probably as much mis-information as information available to us. Yet it is still part of the Deweyan landscape to see that we have responsibilities as democratic citizens to be informed and be able to differentiate between "news" that is simple novelty and "news" that is relevant to our time, society, culture and values and how the events of our lives are shaped by the cultural milieu in which we live.

John Rawls (1921–2002) and Robert Nozick (1938–2002), two of America's premier political theorists, present differing accounts of the nature of justice with respect to the distribution of social goods, possession of property, and the rights of individuals. Their positions, different as they are, represent the rich and varied structure of the society from which they come, and the freedom of thought and opinion regarding the appropriate way to structure the society in which one lives.

Rawls presents a "redistributional" theory of justice in which principles of justice would be chosen by rationally self-interested human beings who are concerned to further their own interests, but who also recognize obligations to others stemming from opportunities and successful endeavors that a particular society makes available to its members. Rawls argues for patterned principles of justice, often understood as leading to a kind of welfare state in which the distribution of social goods is constrained by principles such that no system of appropriation and distribution is fair unless it is to the benefit either of all members of society, or to its least advantaged member. Furthermore, Rawls argues, it is in no person's interest to be oppressed, so the priority of liberty over any distributional principle must be acknowledged because no one would rationally give up freedom for economic security.

Robert Nozick argues, against Rawls's position and against any and all patterned principles of justice, for an entitlement theory of justice, an historical approach to the acquisition of goods not composed of patterned principles. His argument depends upon the notion that there is no central distributional "facility" in any society from which social goods may be distributed to any of its members. Instead, things become the property of individual people through transfers such as inheritance and gift, labor and luck. Nozick takes the view of John Locke that a person is entitled to what he possesses when he has obtained it through a just process (for example, through labor) and that it is the right of the individual to determine how he wishes to distribute his possessions. Utilizing the example of Wilt Chamberlain (a basketball player who enjoyed a level of fame much like that of Michael Jordan in the 21st century) acquiring more "goods" (money) than his teammates when spectators voluntarily give him money to see him play, Nozick attempts to show that even when we attempt to set up a system from some supposedly "fair" or "equal" starting point, the free exercise of a person's right to distribute what is his own as he sees fit will upset the patterned principles upon which an original starting point was based. In sum, Nozick argues for a minimal state and for minimal state interference in the rights and property of individuals.

The lively debate engendered by the conflicting views of Rawls and Nozick is not likely to end soon. Both theorists take their lead from the social contract tradition embodied in the works of European philosophers like Thomas Hobbes, John Locke, and Immanuel Kant and later expressed in American philosophy by Thomas Paine, Thomas Jefferson, and others. The philosophical positions of Rawls and Nozick make it clear that it is the individual human being who is the guarantor of the legitimacy of government and government action, and that it is the individual human being whose interests are to be served. Regardless of their differences, Rawls and Nozick are deeply concerned with issues of social justice, with distribution of social goods, and with the creation of a good and meaningful life for all people.

Michael Sandel, reacting against the rationalistic political thought exemplified in the work of Rawls and Nozick, helps to resurrect the tradition of moral and political thought embodied in the Aristotelian ideal of community. A communitarian/virtue theorist, Sandel challenges the notion that it is either possible or desirable for people to attempt to found social and political institutions and processes on a model of pure procedural justice and a conception of an unencumbered, isolated, or atomistic individual. Building on the contention that we are fully entrenched in communities and societies that influence who we are, what we prefer, and what we will become, Sandel presents compelling arguments against the Enlightenment-based, rationalistic notion embodied in modern political theories that there is an isolated individual whose interests are always to be understood in terms of his individual rationality and individual, negative rights.

Concluding this chapter is Virginia Held's "Feminist Transformations of Moral Theory." In this work, Held discusses the ways in which traditional ethical theories have failed to capture the experience of women. She considers three areas of inquiry (the distinctions between the public and the private, between reason and emotion, and the concept of self) in which feminist theorists are making progress in improving theory to include substantially the experience of women. Traditional moral and political theories have either completely or practically omitted women from the moral and political realms. For example, the family (the realm of the private) has been conceived as a non-moral region in which animal functions and the reproduction of human beings takes place, but not a place in which any sort of political activity or moral growth exists. Held challenges this notion (among many others), arguing along lines similar to the position of Sandel, that it is precisely in the family and in caring relationships that morality begins and in which moral human beings are created. Held's work closes the content of *Philosophy in America: Primary Readings* not as its last word, or as American social thought's last word, but as a hopeful note for the improvement of the present and future that characterizes the American philosophical experience.

Politics (1844)

Ralph Waldo Emerson

In dealing with the state, we ought to remember that its institutions are not aboriginal, though they existed before we were born: that they are not superior to the citizen: that every one of them was once the act of a single man: every law and usage was a man's expedient to meet a particular case; that they all are imitable, all alterable; we may make as good; we may make better. Society is an illusion to the young citizen. It lies before him in rigid repose, with certain names, men, and institutions, rooted like oak-trees to the center, round which all arrange themselves the best they can. But the old statesman knows that society is fluid; there are no such roots and centers; but any particle may suddenly become the center of the movement, and compel the system to gyrate round it. . . . But politics rest on necessary foundations and cannot be treated with levity. Republics abound in young civilians, who believe that the laws make the city, that grave modifications of the policy and modes of living, and employments of the population, that commerce, education, and religion, may be voted in or out; and that any measure, though it were absurd, may be imposed on a people, if only you can get sufficient voices to make it a law. But the wise know that foolish legislation is a rope of sand, which perishes in the twisting; that the State must follow, and not lead the character and progress of the citizen; the strongest usurper is quickly got rid of; and they only who built on Ideas, build for eternity; and that the form of government which prevails, is the expression of what cultivation exists in the population which permits it. The law is only a memorandum. We are superstitious, and esteem the statute somewhat: so much life as it has in the character of living men, is its force. The statute stands there to say, yesterday we agreed so and so, but how feel ye this article to-day? Our statute is a currency, which we stamp with our own portrait: it soon becomes unrecognizable, and in process of time will return to the mint. Nature is not democratic, nor limited monarchical, but despotic, and will not be fooled or abated of any jot of her authority, by the protest of her sons: and as fast as the public mind is opened to more intelligence, the code is seen to be brute and stammering. It speaks not articulately, and must be made to. Meantime the education of the general mind never stops. The reveries of the true and simple are prophetic. What the tender poetic youth dreams, and prays, and paints to-day, but shuns the ridicule of saying aloud, shall presently be the resolutions of public bodies, then shall be carried as grievance and bill of rights through conflict and war, and then shall be triumphant law and establishment for a hundred years, until it gives place, in turn, to new prayers and pictures. The history of the State sketches in coarse outline the progress of thought, and follows at a distance the delicacy of culture and aspiration.

The theory of politics, which has possessed the mind of men, and which they have expressed the best they could in their laws and in their revolutions, considers persons and property as the two objects for whose protection government exists. Of persons, all have equal rights, in virtue of being identical in nature. This interest, of course, with its whole power demands a democracy. Whilst the rights of all as persons are equal, in virtue of their access to reason, their rights in property are very unequal. One man owns his clothes, and another owns a county. This accident, depending, primarily, on the skill and virtue of the parties, of which there is every degree, and secondarily, on patrimony, falls unequally, and its rights, of course, are unequal. Personal rights, universally the same, demand a government framed on the ratio of the census: property demands a government framed on the ratio of owners and of owning. . . .

In the earliest society the proprietors made their own wealth, and so long as it comes to the owners in the direct way, no other opinion would arise in any equitable community, than that property should make the law for property, and persons the law for persons.

But property passes through donation or inheritance to those who do not create it. Gift, in one case, makes it as really the new owner's, as labor made it the first owner's: in the other case, of patrimony, the law makes an ownership, which will be valid in each man's view according to the estimate which he sets on the public tranquility.

It was not, however, found easy to embody the readily admitted principle, that property should make law for property, and persons for persons: since persons and property mixed themselves in every transaction. At last it seems settled, that the rightful distinction was, that the proprietors should have more elective franchise than non-proprietors, on the Spartan principle of "calling that which is just, equal; not that which is equal, just."

That principle no longer looks so self evident as it appeared in former times, partly, because doubts have arisen whether too much weight had not been allowed in the laws, to property, and such a structure given to our usages, as allowed the rich to encroach on the poor, and to keep them poor; but mainly, because there is an instinctive sense, however obscure and yet inarticulate, that the whole constitution of property, on its present tenures, is injurious, and its influence on persons deteriorating and degrading; that truly, the only interest for the consideration of the State, is persons; that property will always follow persons; that the highest end of government is the culture of men: and if men can be educated, the institutions will share their improvement, and the moral sentiment will write the law of the land.

If it be not easy to settle with equity of this question, the peril is less when we take note of our natural defences. We are kept by better guards than the vigilance of such magistrates as we commonly elect. Society always consists, in greatest part, of young and foolish persons. The old, who have seen through the hypocrisy of courts and statesmen, die, and leave no wisdom to their sons. They believe their own newspaper, as their fathers did at their age. With such an ignorant and deceivable majority, states would soon run to ruin, but that there are limitations beyond which the folly and ambition of governors cannot go. Things have their laws, as well as men; and things refuse to be

trifled with. Property will be protected. Corn will not grow, unless it is planted and manured; but the farmer will not plant or hoe it, unless the chances are
a hundred to one, that he will cut and harvest it. Under any forms, persons
and property must and will have their just sway. . . .

The boundaries of personal influence it is impossible to fix, as persons
are organs of moral or supernatural force. Under the dominion of an idea . . . as
civil freedom, or the religious sentiment, the powers of persons are no longer
subjects of calculation. A nation of men unanimously bent on freedom, or conquest, can easily confound the arithmetic of statists, and achieve extravagant
actions, out of all proportion to their means; as, the Greeks, the Saracens, the
Swiss, the Americans, and the French have done.

In like manner, to every particle of property belongs its own attraction. A
cent is the representative of a certain quantity of corn or other commodity. Its
value is in the necessities of the animal man. It is so much warmth, so much
bread, so much water, so much land. The law may do what it will with the
owner of property, its just power will still attach to the cent. The law may in a
mad freak say, that all shall have power except the owners of property: they
shall have no vote. Nevertheless, by a higher law, the property will, year after
year, write every statute that respects property. The non-proprietor will be the
scribe of the proprietor. What the owners wish to do, the whole power of
property will do, either through the law, or else in defiance of it. Of course, I
speak of all the property, not merely of the great estates. When the rich are out-
voted, as frequently happens, it is the joint treasury of the poor which exceeds
their accumulations. Every man owns something, if it is only a cow, or a
wheelbarrow, or his arms, and so has that property to dispose of.

The same necessity which secures the rights of person and property
against the malignity or folly of the magistrate, determines the form and
methods of governing, which are proper to each nation, and to its habit of
thought, and nowise transferable to other states of society. In this country, we
are very vain of our political institutions, which are singular in this, that they
sprung, within the memory of living men, from the character and condition of
the people, which they still express with sufficient fidelity,—and we ostenta-
tiously prefer them to any other in history. They are not better, but only fitter
for us. We may be wise in asserting the advantage in modern times of the democratic form, but to other states of society, in which religion consecrated the
monarchical, that and not this was expedient. Democracy is better for us, because the religious sentiment of the present time accords better with it. Born
democrats, we are nowise qualified to judge of monarchy, which, to our fathers living in the monarchical idea, was also relatively right. But our institutions, though in coincidence with the spirit of the age, have not any exemption
from the practical defects which have discredited other forms. Every actual
State is corrupt. Good men must not obey the laws too well. . . .

The same benign necessity and the same practical abuse appear in the
parties into which each State divides itself of opponents and defenders of the
administration of the government. Parties are also founded on instincts, and

have better guides to their own humble aims than the sagacity of their leaders. They have nothing perverse in their origin, but rudely mark some real and lasting relation. We might as wisely reprove the east wind, or the frost, as a political party, whose members, for the most part, could give no account of their position, but stand for the defence of those interests in which they find themselves. Our quarrel with them begins, when they quit this deep natural ground at the bidding of some leader, and, obeying personal considerations, throw themselves into the maintenance and defence of points, nowise belonging to their system. A party is perpetually corrupted by personality. Whilst we absolve the association from dishonesty, we cannot extend the same character to their leaders. They reap the rewards of the docility and zeal of the masses which they direct. Ordinarily, our parties are parties of circumstance, and not of principle; as, the planting interest in conflict with the commercial; the party of capitalists, and that of operatives; parties which are identical in their moral character, and which can easily change ground with each other, in the support of many of their measures. Parties of principle, as, religious sects, or the party of free-trade, of universal suffrage, of abolition of slavery, of abolition of capital punishment, degenerate into personalities, or would inspire enthusiasm. The vice of our leading parties in this country . . . is, that they do not plant themselves on the deep and necessary grounds to which they are respectively entitled, but lash themselves to fury in the carrying of some local and momentary measure, nowise useful to the commonwealth. Of the two great parties, which, at this hour, almost share the nation between them, I should say, that, one has the best cause, and the other contains the best men. The philosopher, the poet, or the religious man will, of course, wish to cast his vote with the democrat, for free-trade, for wide suffrage, for the abolition of legal cruelties in the penal code, and for facilitating in every manner the access of the young and the poor to the sources of wealth and power. But he can rarely accept the persons whom the so-called popular party propose to him as representatives of these liberalities. They have got at heart the ends which give to the name of democracy what hope and virtue are in it. The spirit of our American radicalism is destructive and aimless: it is not loving, it has no ulterior and divine ends; but is destructive only out of hatred and selfishness. On the other side, the conservative party, composed of the most moderate, able, and cultivated part of the population, is timid, and merely defensive of property. It vindicates no right, it aspires to no real good, it brands no crime, it proposes no generous policy, it does not build, nor write, nor cherish the arts, nor foster religion, nor establish schools, nor encourage science, nor emancipate the slave, nor befriend the poor, or the Indian, or the immigrant. From neither party, when in power, has the world any benefit to expect in science, art, or humanity, at all commensurate with the resources of the nation.

I do not for these defects despair of our republic. We are not at the mercy of any waves of chance. In the strife of ferocious parties, human nature always finds itself cherished, as the children of the convicts at Botany Bay are found to have as healthy a moral sentiment as other children. Citizens of feudal states are alarmed at our democratic institutions lapsing into anarchy; and the older and more cautious among ourselves are learning from Europeans to look with some terror at our turbulent freedom. It is said that in our license of construing the Constitution and in the despotism of public opinion, we have no anchor. . . . No forms can have any dangerous importance, whilst we are befriended by the laws of things. It makes no difference how many tons weight of atmosphere presses on our heads, so long as the same pressure resists it within the lungs. Augment the mass a thousand fold, it cannot begin to crush us, as long as reaction is equal to action. . . . Wild liberty develops iron conscience. Want of liberty, by strengthening law and decorum, stupefies conscience. "Lynch-law" prevails only where there is greater hardihood and self-subsistency in the leaders. A mob cannot be a permanency; everybody's interest requires that it should not exist, and only justice satisfies all.

We must trust infinitely to the beneficent necessity which shines through all laws. . . . Governments have their origin in the moral identity of men. Reason for one is seen to be reason for another, and for every other. There is a middle measure which satisfies all parties, be they never so many, or so resolute for their own. Every man finds a sanction for his simplest claims and deeds in decisions of his own mind, which he calls Truth and Holiness. In these decisions all the citizens find a perfect agreement, and only in these; not in what is good to eat, good to wear, good use of time, or what amount of land, or of public aid, each is entitled to claim. This truth and justice men presently endeavor to make application of, to the measuring of land, the apportionment of service, the protection of life and property. Their first endeavors, no doubt, are very awkward. Yet absolute right is the first governor; or, every government is an impure theocracy. The idea, after which each community is aiming to make and mend its law, is, the will of the wise man. The wise man, it cannot find in nature, and it makes awkward but earnest efforts to secure his government by contrivance. . . . All forms of government symbolize an immortal government, common to all dynasties and independent of numbers, perfect where two men exist, perfect where there is only one man.

Every man's nature is a sufficient advertisement to him of the character of his fellows. My right and my wrong, is their right and their wrong. Whilst I do what is fit for me, and abstain from what is unfit, my neighbor and I shall often agree in our means, and work together for a time to one end. But whenever I find my dominion over myself not sufficient for me, and undertake the direction of him also, I overstep the truth, and come into false relations to him. I may have so much more skill or strength than he, that he cannot express adequately his sense of wrong, but it is a lie, and hurts like a lie both him and me. Love and nature cannot maintain the assumption: it must be executed by a practical lie, namely, by force. This undertaking for another, is the blunder which stands in colossal ugliness in the governments of the world. . . . I can see well enough a great difference between my setting myself down to a self-control, and my going to make somebody else act after my views: but when a quarter of the human race assume to tell me what I must do, I may be too much disturbed by the circumstances to see so clearly the absurdity of their command. Therefore, all public ends look vague and quixotic beside private ones. For, any laws but those which men make for themselves, are laughable. . . . This is the history of governments,—one man does something which is to bind another. A man who cannot be acquainted with me, taxes me; looking from afar at me, ordains that a part of my labor shall go to this or that whimsical end, not as I, but as he happens to fancy. Behold the consequence. Of all debts, men are least willing to pay the taxes. What a satire is this on government! Everywhere they think they get their money's worth, except for these.

Hence, the less government we have, the better,—the fewer laws, and the less confided power. The antidote to this abuse of formal Government, is, the influence of private character, the growth of the Individual the appearance of the wise man, of whom the existing government, is, it must be owned, but a shabby imitation. That which all things tend to educe, which freedom, cultivation, intercourse, revolutions, go to form and deliver, is character; that this is the end of nature, to reach unto this coronation, of her king. To educate the wise man, the State exists; and with the appearance of the wise man, the State expires. The appearance of character makes the State unnecessary. The wise man is the State. He needs no army, fort, or navy,—he loves men too well; no bribe, or feast, or palace, to draw friends to him; no vantage ground, no favorable circumstance. He needs no library, for he has not done thinking; no church, for he is a prophet; no statute book, for he is the law-giver; no money, for he is value; no road, for he is at home where he is; no experience, for the life of the creator shoots through him and looks from his eyes. He has no personal friends, for he who has the spell to draw the prayer and piety of all men unto him, needs not husband and educate a few, to share with him a select and poetic life. . . .

We think our civilization near its meridian, but we are yet only at the cock-crowing and the morning star. In our barbarous society the influence of character is in its infancy. . . . Every thought which genius and piety throw into the world, alters the world. The gladiators in the lists of power feel, through all their frocks of force and simulation, the presence of worth. I think the very strife of trade and ambition are confession of this divinity; and successes in those fields are the poor amends, the fig-leaf with which the shamed soul attempts to hide its nakedness. I find the like unwilling homage in all quarters. It is because we know how much is due from us that we are impatient to show some petty talent as a substitute for worth. . . . But each of us has some talent, can do somewhat useful, or graceful, or formidable, or amusing, or lucrative. That we do, as an apology to others and to ourselves, for not reaching the mark of a good and equal life. But it does not satisfy us, whilst we thrust it on the notice of our companions. It may throw dust in their eyes, but does not smooth our own brow, or give us the tranquility of the strong when we walk abroad. We do penance as we go. Our talent is a sort of expiation, and we are constrained to reflect on our splendid moment, with a certain humiliation, as somewhat too fine, and not as one act of many acts, a fair expression of our permanent energy. . . .

The tendencies of the times favor the idea of self-government, and leave the individual, for all code, to the rewards and penalties of his own constitution, which work with more energy than we believe, whilst we depend on artificial restraints. The movement in this direction has been very marked in modern history. Much has been blind and discreditable, but the nature of the revolution is not affected by the vices of the revolters; for this is a purely moral force. . . . A man has a right to be employed, to be trusted, to be loved, to be revered. The power of love, as the basis of the State, has never been tried. . . . For, according to the order of nature, which is quite superior to our will, it stands thus; there will always be a government of force, where men are selfish; and when they are pure enough to abjure the code of force, they will be wise enough to see how these public ends of the post-office, of the highway, of commerce, and the exchange of property, of museums and libraries, of institutions of art and science, can be answered.

We live in a very low state of the world, and pay unwilling tribute to governments founded on force. There is not, among the most religious and civil nations, a reliance on the moral sentiment, and a sufficient belief in the unity of things to persuade them that society can be maintained without artificial restraints, as well as the solar system; or that the private citizen might be reasonable, and a good neighbor, without the hint of a jail or a confiscation. What is strange too, there never was in any man sufficient faith in the power of rectitude, to inspire him with the broad design of renovating the State on the principle of right and love. All those who have pretended this design, have been partial reformers, and have admitted in some manner the supremacy of the bad State. I do not call to mind a single human being who has steadily denied the authority of the laws, on the simple ground of his own moral nature. Such designs, full of genius and full of fate as they are, are not entertained except avowedly as air-pictures. If the individual who exhibits them, dare to think them practicable, he disgusts scholars and churchmen; and men of talent, and women of superior sentiments, cannot hide their contempt. Not the less does nature continue to fill the heart of youth with suggestions of this enthusiasm, and there are now men,—if indeed I can speak in the plural number,—more exactly, I will say, I have just been conversing with one man, to whom no weight of adverse experience will make it for moment appear impossible, that thousands of human beings might exercise towards each other the grandest and simplest sentiments, as well as a knot of friends, or a pair of lovers.

Civil Disobedience (1849)

HENRY DAVID THOREAU

I heartily accept the motto,—"That government is best which governs least"; and I should like to see it acted up to more rapidly and systematically. Carried out, it finally amounts to this, which also I believe,—"That government is best which governs not at all"; and when men are prepared for it, that will be the kind of government which they will have. Government is at best but an expedient; but most governments are usually, and all governments are sometimes, inexpedient. The objections which have been brought against a standing army . . . may also at last be brought against a standing government. The standing army is only an arm of the standing government. The government itself, which is only the mode which the people have chosen to execute their will, is equally liable to be abused and perverted before the people can act through it. . . .

This American government,—what is it but a tradition, though a recent one, endeavoring to transmit itself unimpaired to posterity, but each instant losing some of its integrity? It has not the vitality and force of a single living man; for a single man can bend it to his will. . . . But it is not the less necessary for this; for the people must have some complicated machinery or other, and hear its din, to satisfy the idea of government which they have. Governments thus show us how successfully men can be imposed on, even impose on themselves, for their own advantage. It is excellent, we must all allow. Yet this government never of itself furthered any enterprise. . . . *It* does not keep the country free. *It* does not settle the West. *It* does not educate. The character inherent in the American people has done all that has been accomplished; and it would have done somewhat more, if the government had not sometimes got in its way. For government is an expedient by which men would fain succeed in letting one another alone; and, as has been said, when it is most expedient, the governed are most let alone by it. . . .

. . . I ask for, not at once no government, but *at once* a better government. Let every man make known what kind of government would command his respect, and that will be one step toward obtaining it.

After all, the practical reason why . . . a majority are permitted . . . to rule is not because they are most likely to be in the right, nor because this seems fairest to the minority, but because they are physically the strongest. But a government in which the majority rule in all cases cannot be based on justice. . . . Can there not be a government in which majorities do not virtually decide right and wrong, but conscience?—in which majorities decide only those questions to which the rule of expediency is applicable? Must the citizen ever for a moment, or in the least degree, resign his conscience to the legislator? Why has every man a conscience, then? I think that we should be men first, and subjects afterward. It is not desirable to cultivate a respect for the law, so

Courtesy of Houghton Mifflin Company, New York.

much as for the right. The only obligation which I have a right to assume is to do at any time what I think right. . . . Law never made men a whit more just. . . .

The mass of men serve the state . . . not as men mainly, but as machines, with their bodies. They are the standing army, the militia, jailers, constables, posse comitatus, etc. In most cases there is no free exercise whatever of the judgment or of the moral sense; but they put themselves on a level with wood and earth and stones; and wooden men can perhaps be manufactured that will serve the purpose as well. Such command no more respect than men of straw or a lump of dirt. . . . Yet such as these even are commonly esteemed good citizens. Others—as most legislators, politicians, lawyers, ministers, and office-holders—serve the state chiefly with their heads; and, as they rarely make any moral distinctions, they are as likely to serve the Devil, without *intending* it, as God. A very few, as heroes, patriots, martyrs, reformers in the great sense . . . serve the state with their consciences also, and so necessarily resist it for the most part; and they are commonly treated as enemies by it. . . .

How does it become a man to behave toward this American government to-day? I answer, that he cannot without disgrace be associated with it. I cannot for an instant recognize that political organization as *my* government which is the *slave's* government also.

All men recognize the right of revolution; that is, the right to refuse allegiance to, and to resist, the government, when its tyranny or its inefficiency are great and unendurable. But almost all say that such is not the case now. But such was the case, they think, in the Revolution of '75. If one were to tell me that this was a bad government because it taxed certain foreign commodities brought to its ports, it is most probable that I should not make an ado about it, for I can do without them. . . . At any rate, it is a great evil to make a stir about it. But when the friction comes to have its machine, and oppression and robbery are organized, I say, let us not have such a machine any longer. In other words, when a sixth of the population of a nation which has undertaken to be the refuge of liberty are slaves, and a whole country is unjustly overrun and conquered by a foreign army, and subjected to military law, I think that it is not too soon for honest men to rebel and revolutionize. What makes this duty the more urgent is the fact that the country so overrun is not our own, but ours is the invading army.

Paley, a common authority with many on moral questions, in his chapter on the "Duty of Submission to Civil Government," resolves all civil obligation into expediency; and he proceeds to say, "that so long as the interest of the whole society requires it, that is, so long as the established government cannot be resisted or changed without public inconveniency, it is the will of God that the established government be obeyed, and no longer. . . . This principle being admitted, the justice of every particular case of resistance is reduced to a computation of the quantity of the danger and grievance on the one side, and of the probability and expense of redressing it on the other." Of this, he says, every man shall judge for himself. But Paley appears never to have contemplated those cases to which the rule of expediency does not apply, in which people, as well as an individual, must do justice, cost what it may. . . . This people must cease to hold slaves, and to make war on Mexico, though it cost them their existence as a people.

In their practice, nations agree with Paley; but does any one think that Massachusetts does exactly what is right at the present crisis? . . . Practically speaking, the opponents to a reform in Massachusetts are not a hundred thousand politicians at the South, but a hundred thousand merchants and farmers here, who are more interested in commerce and agriculture than they are in humanity, and are not prepared to do justice to the slave and to Mexico, *cost what it may*. I quarrel not with far-off foes, but with those who, near at home, cooperate with, and do the bidding of, those far away, and without whom the latter would be harmless. . . . There are thousands who are *in opinion* opposed to slavery and to the war, who yet in effect do nothing to put an end to them. . . . They will wait, well disposed, for others to remedy the evil, that they may no longer have it to regret. At most, they give only a cheap vote, and a feeble countenance and God-speed, to the right, as it goes by them. . . .

All voting is a sort of gaming . . . with a slight moral tinge to it, a playing with right and wrong, with moral questions; and betting naturally accompanies it. The character of the voters is not staked. I cast my vote, perchance, as I think right; but I am not vitally concerned that the right should prevail. I am willing to leave it to the majority. Its obligation, therefore, never exceeds that of expediency. Even voting *for the right* is *doing* nothing for it. It is only expressing to men feebly your desire that it should prevail. A wise man will not leave the right to the mercy of chance, nor wish it to prevail through the power of the majority. There is but little virtue in the action of masses of men. When the majority shall at length vote for the abolition of slavery, it will be because they are indifferent to slavery, or because there is but little slavery left to be abolished by their vote. *They* will then be the only slaves. Only *his* vote can hasten the abolition of slavery who asserts his own freedom by his vote.

. . . O for a man who is a *man*, and, as my neighbor says, has a bone in his back which you cannot pass your hand through! Our statistics are at fault: the population has been returned too large. How many *men* are there to a square thousand miles in this country? Hardly one. Does not America offer any inducement for men to settle here? The American has dwindled into an Odd Fellow,—one who may be known by the development of his organ of gregariousness, and a manifest lack of intellect and cheerful self-reliance. . . .

It is not a man's duty, as a matter of course, to devote himself to the eradication of any, even the most enormous wrong; he may still properly have other concerns to engage him; but it is his duty, at least, to wash his hands of it, and, if he gives it no thought longer, not to give it practically his support. . . .

The broadest and most prevalent error requires the most disinterested virtue to sustain it. The slight reproach to which the virtue of patriotism is commonly liable, the noble are most likely to incur. Those who, while they disapprove of the character and measures of a government, yield to it their allegiance and support are undoubtedly its most conscientious supporters, and so frequently the most serious obstacles to reform. Some are petitioning the state to dissolve the Union, to disregard the requisitions of the President. Why do they not dissolve it themselves,—the union between themselves and the state,—and refuse to pay their quota into its treasury? Do not they stand in the same relation to the state that the state does to the Union? And have not the same reasons prevented the state from resisting the Union which have prevented them from resisting the state?

How can a man be satisfied to entertain an opinion merely, and enjoy *it?* Is there any enjoyment in it, if his opinion is that he is aggrieved? If you are cheated out of a single dollar by your neighbor, you do not rest satisfied with knowing that you are cheated . . . ; but you take effectual steps at once to obtain the full amount, and see that you are never cheated again. Action from principle, the perception and the performance of right, changes things and relations; it is essentially revolutionary, and does not consist wholly with anything which was. It not only divides states and churches, it divides families; nay, it divides the *individual*, separating the diabolical in him from the divine.

Unjust laws exist: shall we be content to obey them, or shall we endeavor to amend them, and obey them until we have succeeded, or shall we transgress them at once? Men generally, under such government as this, think that they ought to wait until they have persuaded the majority to alter them. They think that, if they should resist, the remedy would be worse than the evil. But it is the fault of the government itself that the remedy *is* worse than the evil. *It* makes it worse. Why is it not more apt to anticipate and provide for reform? Why does it not cherish its wise minority? Why does it cry and resist before it is hurt? Why does it not encourage its citizens to be on the alert to point out its faults, and *do* better than it would have them? Why does it always crucify Christ, and excommunicate Copernicus and Luther, and pronounce Washington and Franklin rebels? . . .

If the injustice is part of the necessary friction of the machine of government, let it go, let it go: perchance it will wear smooth,—certainly the machine will wear out. If the injustice has a spring, or a pulley, or a rope, or a crank, exclusively for itself, then perhaps you may consider whether the remedy will not be worse than the evil; but if it is of such a nature that it requires you to be the agent of injustice to another, then, I say, break the law. Let your life be a counter friction to stop the machine. What I have to do is to see, at any rate, that I do not lend myself the wrong which I condemn.

As for adopting the ways which the state has provided for remedying the evil, I know not of such ways. They take too much time, and a man's life will be gone. . . . I came into this world, not chiefly to make this a good place to live in, but to live in it, be it good or bad. A man has not everything to do, but something; and because he cannot do *everything*, it is not necessary that he should do *something* wrong. . . .

. . . Those who call themselves abolitionists should at once effectually withdraw their support, both in person and property, from the government of Massachusetts, and not wait till they constitute a majority of one, before they suffer the right to prevail through them. I think that it is enough if they have God on their side, without waiting for that other one. Moreover, any man more right than his neighbors constitutes a majority of one already.

I meet this American government, or its representative, the state government, directly, and face to face, once a year . . . in the person of its tax-gatherer. . . . It then says distinctly, Recognize me; and the simplest, the most effectual, and, in the present posture of affairs, the indispensablest mode of treating with it on this head, of expressing your little satisfaction with and love for it, is to deny it then. My civil neighbor, the tax-gatherer, is the very man I have to deal with,—for it is, after all, with men and not with parchment that I quarrel,—and he has voluntarily chosen to be an agent of the government. How shall he ever know well what he is and does as an officer of the government, or as a man, until he is obliged to consider whether he shall treat me, his neighbor, for whom he has respect, as a neighbor and well-disposed man, or as a maniac and disturber of the peace, and see if he can get over this obstruction to his neighborliness without a ruder and more impetuous thought or speech corresponding with his action. I know this well, that if one thousand, if one hundred, if ten men whom I could name,—if ten *honest* men only,—nay, if *one* HONEST man, in this State of Massachusetts, *ceasing to hold slaves*, were actually to withdraw from this copartnership, and be locked up in the county jail therefore, it would be the abolition of slavery in America. For it matters not how small the beginning may seem to be: what is once well done is done forever. . . .

Under a government which imprisons any unjustly, the true place for a just man is also a prison. . . . It is there that the fugitive slave, and the Mexican prisoner on parole, and the Indian come to plead the wrongs of his race should find them; on that separate, but more free and honorable ground, where the State places those who are not *with* her, but *against* her,—the only house in a slave State in which a free man can abide with honor. . . . Cast your whole vote, not a strip of paper merely, but your whole influence. A minority is powerless while it conforms to the majority; it is not even a minority then; but it is irresistible when it clogs by its whole weight. If the alternative is to keep all just men in prison, or give up war and slavery, the State will not hesitate which to choose. If a thousand men were not to pay their tax-bills this year, that would not be a violent and bloody measure, as it would be to pay them, and enable the State to commit violence and shed innocent blood. This is, in fact, the definition of a peaceable revolution. . . . If the tax-gatherer, or any other public officer, asks me, as one has done, "But what shall I do?" my answer is, "If you really wish to do anything, resign your office." When the subject has refused allegiance, and the officer has resigned his office, then the revolution is accomplished. But even suppose blood should flow. Is there not a sort of blood shed when the conscience is wounded? . . .

I have contemplated the imprisonment of the offender, rather than the seizure of his goods,—though both will serve the same purpose,—because they who assert the purest right, and consequently are most dangerous to a corrupt State, commonly have not spent much time in accumulating property. To such the State renders comparatively small service, and a slight tax is wont to appear exorbitant, particularly if they are obliged to earn it by special labor with their hands. If there were one who lived wholly without the use of money, the State itself would hesitate to demand it of him. But the rich man—not to make any invidious comparison—is always sold to the institution which makes him rich. Absolutely speaking, the more money, the less virtue; for money comes between a man and his objects, and obtains them for him; and it was certainly no great virtue to obtain it. . . . Thus his moral ground is taken from under his feet. The opportunities of living are diminished in proportion as what are called the "means" are increased. The best thing a man can do for his culture when he is rich is to endeavor to carry out those schemes which he entertained when he was poor. . . .

When I converse with the freest of my neighbors, I perceive that, whatever they may say about the magnitude and seriousness of the question, and their regard for the public tranquility, the long and short of the matter is, that they cannot spare the protection of the existing government, and they dread the consequences of their property and families of disobedience to it. For my own part, I should not like to think that I ever rely on the protection of the State. But, if I deny the authority of the State when it presents its tax-bill, it will soon take and waste all my property, and so harass me and my children without end. This is hard. This makes it impossible for a man to live honestly, and at the same time comfortably, in outward respects. It will not be worth the while to accumulate property; that would be sure to go again. You must hire or squat somewhere, and raise but a small crop, and eat that soon. You must live within yourself, and depend upon yourself always tucked up and ready for a start, and not have many affairs. . . . It costs me less in every sense to incur the penalty of disobedience to the State than it would to obey. I should feel as if I were worth less in that case. . . .

I have paid no poll-tax for six years. I was put into a jail once on this account, for one night; and, as I stood considering the walls of solid stone, two or three feet thick, the door of wood and iron, a foot thick, and the iron grating which strained the light, I could not help being struck with the foolishness of that institution which treated me as if I were mere flesh and blood and bones, to be locked up. . . . I did not for a moment feel confined, and the walls seemed a great waste of stone and mortar. I felt as if I alone of all my townsmen had paid my tax. . . . In every threat and in every compliment there was a blunder; for they thought that my chief desire was to stand the other side of that stone wall. I could not but smile to see how industriously they locked the door on my meditations, which followed them out again without let or hindrance, and *they* were really all that was dangerous. As they could not reach me, they had resolved to punish my body; just as boys, if they cannot come at some person against whom they have a spite, will abuse his dog. I saw that the State was half-witted, that it was timid . . . and that it did not know its friends from its foes, and I lost all my remaining respect for it, and pitied it.

Thus the State never intentionally confronts a man's sense, intellectual or moral, but only his body, his senses. It is not armed with superior wit or honesty, but with superior physical strength. I was not born to be forced. I will breathe after my own fashion. . . . They only can force me who obey a higher law than I. . . . I perceive that, when an acorn and a chestnut fall side by side, the one does not remain inert to make way for the other, but both obey their own laws, and spring and grow and flourish as best they can, till one, perchance, overshadows and destroys the other. If a plant cannot live according to its nature, it dies: and so a man.

When I came out of prison,—for some one interfered, and paid that tax,—I did not perceive that great changes had taken place on the common, such as he observed who went in a youth and emerged a tottering and grayheaded man; and yet a change had to my eyes come over the scene,—the town, and State, and country,—greater than any that mere time could effect. I saw yet more distinctly the State in which I lived. I saw to what extent the people among whom I lived could be trusted as good neighbors and friends; that their friendship was for summer weather only; that they did not greatly propose to do right; that they were a distinct race from me by their prejudices and superstitions, . . . that in their sacrifices to humanity they ran no risks. . . .

I have never declined paying the highway tax, because I am as desirous of being a good neighbor as I am of being a bad subject; and as for supporting schools, I am doing my part to educate my fellow-countrymen now. It is for no particular item in the tax-bill that I refuse to pay it. I simply wish to refuse allegiance to the State, to withdraw and stand aloof from it effectually. I do not care to trace the course of my dollar, if I could, till it buys a man or a musket to shoot one with,—the dollar is innocent,—but I am concerned to trace the effects of my allegiance. In fact, I quietly declare war with the State, after my fashion. . . .

If others pay the tax which is demanded of me, from a sympathy with the State, they do but what they have already done in their own case, or rather they abet injustice to a greater extent than the State requires. If they pay the tax from a mistaken interest in the individual taxed, to save his property, or prevent his going to jail, it is because they have not considered wisely how far they let their private feelings interfere with the public good. . . .

I do not wish to quarrel with any man or nation. I do not wish to split hairs, to make fine distinctions, or set myself up as better than my neighbors. I seek rather, I may say, even an excuse for conforming to the laws of the land. I am but too ready to conform to them. Indeed, I have reason to suspect myself on this head; and each year, as the tax-gatherer comes round, I find myself disposed to review the acts and position of the general and State governments, and the spirit of the people, to discover a pretext for conformity. . . . I believe that the State will soon be able to take all my work of this sort out of my hands, and then I shall be no better a patriot than my fellow-countrymen. Seen from a lower point of view, the Constitution, with all its faults, is very good; the law and the courts are very respectable; even this State and this American government are, in many respects, very admirable, and rare things, to be thankful for, such as a great many have described them; but seen from a point of view a little higher, they are what I have described them; seen from a higher still, and the highest, who shall say what they are, or that they are worth looking at or thinking of at all?

However, the government does not concern me much, and I shall bestow the fewest possible thoughts on it. It is not many moments that I live under a government, even in this world. If a man is thought-free, fancy-free, imagination-free, that which *is not* never for a long time appearing *to be* to him, unwise rulers or reformers cannot fatally interrupt him. . . .

No man with a genius for legislation has appeared in America. They are rare in the history of the world. There are orators, politicians, and eloquent men, by the thousand; but the speaker has not yet opened his mouth to speak who is capable of settling the much-vexed questions of the day. We love eloquence for its own sake, and not for any truth which it may utter, or any heroism it may inspire. . . .

The authority of government, even such as I am willing to submit to,— for I will cheerfully obey those who know and can do better than I, and in many things even those who neither know nor can do so well,—is still an impure one: to be strictly just, it must have the sanction and consent of the governed. It can have no pure right over my person and property but what I concede to it. The progress from an absolute to a limited monarchy, from a limited monarchy to a democracy, is a progress toward a true respect for the individual. . . . There will never be a really free and enlightened State until the State comes to recognize the individual as a higher and independent power, from which all its own power and authority are derived, and treats him accordingly. I please myself with imagining a State at last which can afford to be just to all men, and to treat the individual with respect as a neighbor. . . .

What Makes a Life Significant (1892)

WILLIAM JAMES

In my previous talk, 'On a Certain Blindness,' I tried to make you feel how soaked and shot-through life is with values and meanings which we fail to realize because of our external and insensible point of view. The meanings are there for the others, but they are not there for us. There lies more than a mere interest of curious speculation in understanding this. It has the most tremendous practical importance. I wish that I could convince you of it as I feel it myself. It is the basis of all our tolerance, social, religious, and political. The forgetting of it lies at the root of every stupid and sanguinary mistake that rulers over subject-peoples make. The first thing to learn in intercourse with others is non-interference with their own peculiar ways of being happy, provided those ways do not assume to interfere by violence with ours. No one has insight into all the ideals. No one should presume to judge them off-hand. The pretension to dogmatize about them in each other is the root of most human injustices and cruelties and the trait in human character most likely to make the angels weep. . . .

A few summers ago I spent a happy week at the famous Assembly Grounds on the borders of Chautauqua Lake. The moment one treads that sacred enclosure, one feels one's self in an atmosphere of success. Sobriety and industry, intelligence and goodness, orderliness and ideality, prosperity and cheerfulness, pervade the air. It is a serious and studious picnic on a gigantic scale. Here you have a town of many thousands of inhabitants, beautifully laid out in the forest and drained, and equipped with means for satisfying all the necessary lower and most of the superfluous higher wants of man. You have magnificent music . . . every sort of athletic exercise, . . . kindergartens and model secondary schools. You have general religious services and special club-houses for the several sects. You have perpetually running soda-water fountains, and daily public lectures by distinguished men. You have the best of company, and yet no effort. You have no zymotic diseases, no poverty, no drunkenness, no crime, no police. You have culture, . . . kindness, . . . cheapness, . . . the best fruits of what mankind has fought and bled and striven for under the name of civilization for centuries. You have, in short, a foretaste of what human society might be, were it all in the light, with no suffering and no dark corners.

I went in curiosity for a day. I stayed for a week, held spell-bound by the charm and ease of everything, by the middle-class paradise, without a sin, without a victim, without a blot, without a tear.

And yet what was my own astonishment, on emerging into the dark and wicked world again, to catch myself quite unexpectedly and involuntarily

From *Talks to Teachers on Psychology and to Students on Some of Life's Ideals*, by William James, Dover Publications, Inc., pp. 136–146.

saying: "Ouf! What a relief! Now for something primordial and savage . . . to set the balance straight again. This order is too tame, this culture too second-rate, this goodness too uninspiring. This human drama without a villain or a pang; this community so refined that ice-cream soda-water is the utmost offering it can make to the brute animal in man; this city simmering in the tepid lakeside sun; this atrocious harmlessness of all things,—I cannot abide with them. Let me take my chances again in the big outside worldly wilderness with all its sins and sufferings. There are the heights and depths, the precipices and the steep ideals, the gleams of the awful and the infinite; and there is more hope and help a thousand times than in this dead level and quintessence of every mediocrity."

. . . There had been spread before me the realization—on a small, sample scale of course—of all the ideals for which our civilization has been striving: security, intelligence, humanity, and order; and here was the instinctive hostile reaction, not of the natural man, but of a so-called cultivated man upon such a Utopia. There seemed thus to be a self-contradiction and paradox somewhere. . . .

. . . I asked myself what the thing was that was so lacking in this Sabbatical city, and the lack of which kept one forever falling short of the higher sort of contentment. And soon I recognized that it was the element that gives to the wicked outer world all its moral style, expressiveness and picturesqueness,—the element of precipitousness, so to call it, of strength and strenuousness, intensity and danger. What excites and interests the looker-on at life, what the romances and the statues celebrate and the grim civic monuments remind us of, is the everlasting battle of the powers of light with those of darkness; with heroism, reduced to its bare chance, yet ever and anon snatching victory from the jaws of death. But in this unspeakable Chautauqua there was no potentiality of death in sight anywhere, and no point on the compass visible from which danger might possibly appear. The ideal was so completely victorious already that no sign of any previous battle remained, the place just resting on its oars. . . .

Such absence of human nature *in extremis* anywhere seemed, then, a sufficient explanation for Chautauqua's flatness and lack of zest.

But was not this paradox well calculated to fill one with dismay? It looks indeed, thought I, as if the romantic idealists with their pessimism about our civilization were, after all, quite right. An irremediable flatness is coming over the world. Bourgeoisie and mediocrity, church sociables and teachers' conventions, are taking the place of the old heights and depths and romantic chiaroscuro. And, to get human life in its wild intensity, we must in future turn more and more away from the actual, and forget it, if we can, in the romancer's or the poet's pages. The whole world, delightful and sinful as it may still appear for a moment to one just escaped from the Chautauquan enclosure, is nevertheless obeying more and more just those ideals that are sure to make of it in the end a mere Chautauqua Assembly on an enormous scale. . . . Even now . . . correctness, fairness, and compromise for every small advantage are crowding out all other qualities. The higher heroisms and the old rare flavors are passing out of life.

If there *were* any ... morally exceptional individuals, ... what made them different from the rest? It can only have been this,—that their souls worked and endured in obedience to some inner *ideal*. ... These ideals of other lives are among those secrets that we can almost never penetrate, although something about the man may often tell us when they are there. ...

The barrenness and ignobleness of the more usual laborer's life consist in the fact that it is moved by no such ideal inner springs. The backache, the long hours, the danger, are patiently endured—for what? To gain a quid of tobacco, a glass of beer, a cup of coffee, a meal, and a bed, and to begin again the next day and shirk as much as one can. This really is why we raise no monument to the laborers in the Subway, even though they be our conscripts, and even though after a fashion our city is indeed based upon their patient hearts and enduring backs and shoulders. And this is why we do raise monuments to our soldiers, whose outward conditions were even brutaller still. The soldiers are supposed to have followed an ideal, and the laborers are supposed to have followed none.

You see, my friends, how the plot thickens; and how strangely the complexities of this wonderful human nature of ours begin to develop under our hands. We have seen the blindness and deadness to each other which are our natural inheritance; and, in spite of them, we have been led to acknowledge an inner meaning which passeth show, and which may be present in the lives of others where we least descry it. And now we are led to say that such inner meaning can be *complete* and *valid for us also*, only when the inner joy, courage, and endurance are joined with an ideal.

But what, exactly, do we mean by an ideal? ...

... An ideal, for instance, must be something intellectually conceived, something of which we are not unconscious, if we have it; and it must carry with it that sort of outlook, uplift, and brightness that go with all intellectual facts. Secondly, there must be *novelty* in an ideal,—novelty at least for him whom the ideal grasps. Sodden routine is incompatible with ideality, although what is sodden routine for one person may be ideal novelty for another. This shows that there is nothing absolutely ideal: ideals are relative to the lives that entertain them. To keep out of the gutter is for us here no part of consciousness at all, yet for many of our brethren it is the most legitimately engrossing of ideals.

Now, taken nakedly, abstractly, and immediately, you see that mere ideals are the cheapest things in life. Everybody has them in some shape or other, personal or general, sound or mistaken, low or high; and the most worthless sentimentalists and dreamers, drunkards, shirks and verse-makers, who never show a grain of effort, courage, or endurance, possibly have them on the most copious scale. Education, enlarging as it does our horizon and perspective, is a means of multiplying our ideals, of bringing new ones into view. And your college professor, with a starched shirt and spectacles, would, if a stock of ideals were all alone by itself enough to render a life significant, be the most absolutely and deeply significant of men. Tolstoi would be completely blind in despising him for a prig, a pedant and a parody; and all our new insight into the divinity of muscular labor would be altogether off the track of truth.

But such consequences as this, you instinctively feel, are erroneous. The more ideals a man has, the more contemptible, on the whole, do you continue to deem him, if the matter ends there for him, and if none of the laboring man's virtues are called into action on his part,—no courage shown, no privations undergone, no dirt or scars contracted in the attempt to get them realized. It is quite obvious that something more than the mere possession of ideals is required to make a life significant in any sense that claims the spectator's admiration. Inner joy, to be sure, it may *have*, with its ideals; but that is its own private sentimental matter. To extort from us, outsiders as we are, with our own ideals to look after, the tribute of our grudging recognition, it must back its ideal visions with what the laborers have, the sterner stuff of manly virtue; it must multiply their sentimental surface by the dimension of the active will, if we are to have *depth*, if we are to have anything cubical and solid in the way of character.

The significance of a human life for communicable and publicly recognizable purposes is thus the offspring of a marriage of two different parents, either of whom alone is barren. The ideals taken by themselves give no reality, the virtues by themselves no novelty. And let the orientalists and pessimists say what they will, the thing of deepest—or, at any rate, of comparatively deepest—significance in life does seem to be its character of *progress*, or that strange union of reality with ideal novelty which it continues from one moment to another to present. To recognize ideal novelty is the task of what we call intelligence. Not every one's intelligence can tell which novelties are ideal. For many the ideal thing will always seem to cling still to the older and more familiar good. In this case character, though not significant totally, may be still significant pathetically. . . .

But with all this beating and tacking on my part, I fear you take me to be reaching a confused result. I seem to be just taking things up and dropping them again. First I took up Chautauqua, and dropped that; then Tolstoi and the heroism of common toil, and dropped them; finally, I took up ideals, and seem now almost dropping those. But please observe in what sense it is that I drop them. It is when they pretend *singly* to redeem life from insignificance. Culture and refinement all alone are not enough to do so. Ideal aspirations are not enough, when uncombined with pluck and will. But neither are pluck and will, dogged endurance and insensibility to danger enough, when taken all alone. There must be some sort of fusion, some chemical combination among these principles, for a life objectively and thoroughly significant to result.

Of course, this is a somewhat vague conclusion. But in a question of significance, of worth, like this, conclusions can never be precise. The answer of appreciation, of sentiment, is always a more or a less, a balance struck by sympathy, insight, and good will. But it is an answer, all the same, a real conclusion. And, in the course of getting it, it seems to me that our eyes have been opened to many important things. Some of you are, perhaps, more livingly aware than you were an hour ago of the depths of worth that lie around you, hid in alien lives. And, when you ask how much sympathy you ought to bestow, although the amount is, truly enough, a matter of ideal on your own part, yet in this notion of the combination of ideals with active virtues you have a rough standard for shaping your decision. In any case, your imagination is extended. You divine in the world about you matter for a little more humility on your own part, and tolerance, reverence, and love for others; and you gain a certain inner joyfulness at the increased importance of our common life. Such joyfulness is a religious inspiration and an element of spiritual health, and worth more than large amounts of that sort of technical and accurate information which we professors are supposed to be able to impart.

To show the sort of thing I mean by these words, I will just make one brief practical illustration. . . .

We are suffering to-day in America from what is called the labor-question; and, when you go out into the world, you will . . . be caught up in its perplexities. I use the brief term labor-question to cover all sorts of anarchistic discontents and socialistic projects, and the conservative resistances which they provoke. So far as this conflict is unhealthy and regrettable,—and I think it is so only to a limited extent,—the unhealthiness consists solely in the fact that one-half of our fellow-countrymen remain entirely blind to the internal significance of the lives of the other half. They miss the joys and sorrows, they fail to feel the moral virtue, and they do not guess the presence of the intellectual ideals. They are at cross-purposes all along the line, regarding each other as they might regard a set of dangerously gesticulating automata, or, if they seek to get at the inner motivation, making the most horrible mistakes. Often all the poor man can think of in the rich man is a cowardly greediness for safety, luxury, and effeminacy, and a boundless affectation. What he is, is not a human being, but a pocket-book, a bank-account. And a similar greediness, turned by disappointment into envy, is all that many rich men can see in the state of mind of the dissatisfied poor. And, if the rich man begins to do the sentimental act over the poor man, what senseless blunders does he make, pitying him for just those very duties and those very immunities which, rightly taken, are the condition of his most abiding and characteristic joys! Each, in short, ignores the fact that happiness and unhappiness and significance are a vital mystery; each pins them absolutely on some ridiculous feature of the external situation; and everybody remains outside of everybody else's sight.

Society has, with all this, undoubtedly got to pass toward some newer and better equilibrium, and the distribution of wealth has doubtless slowly got to change: such changes have always happened, and will happen to the end of time. But if, after all that I have said, any of you expect that they will make any *genuine vital difference* on a large scale, to the lives of our descendants, you will have missed the significance of my entire lecture. The solid meaning of life is always the same eternal thing,—the marriage, namely, of some habitual ideal, however special, with some fidelity, courage, and endurance; with some man's or woman's pains.—And, whatever or wherever life may be, there will always be the chance for that marriage to take place.

. . . With each new ideal that comes into life, the chance for a life based on some old ideal will vanish; and he would needs be a presumptuous calculator who should with confidence say that the total sum of significances is positively and absolutely greater at any one epoch than at any other of the world.

. . . *There are compensations*: and no outward changes of condition in life can keep the nightingale of its eternal meaning from singing in all sorts of different men's hearts. That is the main fact to remember. If we could not only admit it with our lips, but really and truly believe it, how our convulsive insistencies, how our antipathies and dreads of each other, would soften down! If the poor and the rich could look at each other in this way, *sub specie aeternitatis*, how gentle would grow their disputes! What tolerance and good humor, what willingness to live and let live, would come into the world!

Search for the Great Community (1927)

JOHN DEWEY

We have had occasion to refer in passing to the distinction between democracy as a social idea and political democracy as a system of government. The two are, of course, connected. The idea remains barren and empty save as it is incarnated in human relationships. Yet in discussion they must be distinguished. The idea of democracy is a wider and fuller idea than can be exemplified in the state even at its best. To be realized it must affect all modes of human association, the family, the school, industry, religion. . . . The old saying that the cure for the ills of democracy is more democracy is not apt if it means that the evils may be remedied by introducing more machinery of the same kind as that which already exists, or by refining and perfecting that machinery. But the phrase may also indicate the need of returning to the idea itself, of clarifying and deepening our apprehension of it, and of employing our sense of its meaning to criticize and remake its political manifestations.

Confining ourselves . . . to political democracy, we must . . . renew our protest against the assumption that the idea has itself produced the governmental practices which obtain in democratic states: General suffrage, elected representatives, majority rule, and so on. The idea has influenced the concrete

From *The Collected Works of John Dewey, Later Works, Volume Two,* 1925–1927. © 1984 by the Center for Dewey Studies, reprinted by permission of Southern Illinois University Press.

political movement, but it has not caused it. . . . The forms to which we are accustomed in democratic governments represent the cumulative effect of a multitude of events, unpremeditated as far as political effects were concerned and having unpredictable consequences. There is no sanctity in universal suffrage, frequent elections, majority rule, congressional and cabinet government. These things are devices evolved in the direction in which the current was moving, each wave of which involved at the time of its impulsion a minimum of departure from antecedent custom and law. The devices served a purpose; but the purpose was rather that of meeting existing needs which had become too intense to be ignored, than that of forwarding the democratic idea. In spite of all defects, they served their own purpose well.

Looking back, with the aid which *ex post facto* experience can give, it would be hard for the wisest to devise schemes which, under the circumstances, would have met the needs better. In this retrospective glance, it is possible, however, to see how the doctrinal formulations which accompanied them were inadequate, one-sided and positively erroneous. In fact they were hardly more than political war-cries adopted to help in carrying on some immediate agitation or in justifying some particular practical polity struggling for recognition, even though they were asserted to be absolute truths of human nature or of morals. The doctrines served a particular local pragmatic need. But often their very adaptation to immediate circumstances unfitted them, pragmatically, to meet more enduring and more extensive needs. They lived to cumber the political ground, obstructing progress, all the more so because they were uttered and held not as hypotheses with which to direct social experimentation but as final truths, dogmas. No wonder they call urgently for revision and displacement.

Nevertheless the current has set steadily . . . toward democratic forms. That government exists to serve its community, and that this purpose cannot be achieved unless the community itself shares in selecting its governors and determining their policies, are a deposit of fact left . . . permanently in the wake of doctrines and forms, however transitory the latter. They are not the whole of the democratic idea, but they express it in its political phase. Belief in this political aspect is not a mystic faith. . . . It marks a well-attested conclusion from historic facts. We have every reason to think that whatever changes may take place in existing democratic machinery, they will be of a sort to make the interest of the public a more supreme guide and criterion of governmental activity, and to enable the public to form and manifest its purposes still more authoritatively. In this sense the cure for the ailments of democracy is more democracy. The prime difficulty, as we have seen, is that of discovering the means by which a scattered, mobile and manifold public may so recognize itself as to define and express its interests. This discovery is necessarily precedent to any fundamental change in the machinery. We are not concerned therefore to set forth counsels as to advisable improvements in the political forms of democracy. . . . The problem lies deeper; it is in the first instance an intellectual problem: the search for the conditions under which the Great Society may become the Great Community. When these conditions are brought into being they will make their own forms. Until they have come about, it is somewhat futile to consider what political machinery will suit them.

In a search for the conditions under which the inchoate public now extant may function democratically, we may proceed from a statement of the nature of the democratic idea in its generic social sense. From the standpoint of the individual, it consists in having a responsible share according to capacity in forming and directing the activities of the groups to which one belongs and in participating according to need in the values which the groups sustain. From the standpoint of the groups, it demands liberation of the potentialities of members of a group in harmony with the interests and goods which are common. Since every individual is a member of many groups, this specification cannot be fulfilled except when different groups interact flexibly and fully in connection with other groups. A member of a robber band may express his powers in a way consonant with belonging to that group and be directed by the interest common to its members. But he does so only at the cost of repression of those of his potentialities which can be realized only through membership in other groups. The robber band cannot interact flexibly with other groups; it can act only through isolating itself. It must prevent the operation of all interests save those which circumscribe it in its separateness. But a good citizen finds his conduct as a member of a political group enriching and enriched by his participating in family life, industry, scientific and artistic associations. There is a free give-and-take: fullness of integrated personality is therefore possible of achievement, since the pulls and responses of different groups reinforce one another and their values accord.

Regarded as an idea, democracy is not an alternative to other principles of associated life. It is the idea of community life itself. It is an ideal in the only intelligible sense of an idea: namely, the tendency and movement of some thing which exists carried to its final limit, viewed as completed, perfected. Since things do not attain such fulfillment but are in actuality distracted and interfered with, democracy in this sense is not a fact and never will be. But neither in this sense is there or has there ever been anything which is a community in its full measure, a community unalloyed by alien elements. The idea or ideal of a community presents, however, actual phases of associated life as they are freed from restrictive and disturbing elements, and are contemplated as having attained their limit of development. Wherever there is a conjoint activity whose consequences are appreciated as good by all singular persons who take part in it, and where the realization of the good is such as to effect an energetic desire and effort to sustain it in being just because it is a good shared by all, there is in so far a community. The clear consciousness of a communal life, in all its implications, constitutes the idea of democracy.

Only when we start from a community as a fact, grasp the fact in thought so as to clarify and enhance its constituent elements, can we reach an idea of democracy which is not utopian. . . . Fraternity, liberty and equality isolated from communal life are hopeless abstractions. Their separate assertion leads to mushy sentimentalism or else to extravagant and fanatical violence which in the end defeats its own aims. Equality then becomes a creed of mechanical identity which is false to facts and impossible of realization. Effort to attain it is divisive of the vital bonds which hold men together; as far as it puts forth issue, the outcome is mediocrity in which good is common only in the sense of being average and vulgar. Liberty is then thought of as independence of social ties, and ends in dissolution and anarchy. It is more difficult to sever the idea of brotherhood from that of a community, and hence it is either practically ignored in the movements which identify democracy with Individualism, or else it is a sentimentally appended tag. In its just connections with communal experience, fraternity is another name for the consciously appreciated goods which accrue from an association in which all share, and which give direction to the conduct of each. Liberty is that secure release and fulfillment of personal potentialities which take place only in rich and manifold association with others: the power to be an individualized self making a distinctive contribution and enjoying in its own way the fruits of association. Equality denotes the unhampered share which each individual member of the community has in the consequences of associated action. It is equitable because it is measured only by need and capacity to utilize, not by extraneous factors which deprive one in order that another may take and have. . . . Equality does not signify that kind of mathematical or physical equivalence in virtue of which any one element may be substituted for another. It denotes effective regard for whatever is distinctive and unique in each, irrespective of physical and psychological inequalities. It is not a natural possession but is a fruit of the community when its action is directed by its character as a community.

Associated or joint activity is a condition of the creation of a community. But association itself is physical and organic, while communal life is moral, that is emotionally, intellectually, consciously sustained. Human beings combine in behavior as directly and unconsciously as do atoms, stellar masses and cells; as directly and unknowingly as they divide and repel. . . . They do so from external circumstances. . . . Associated activity needs no explanation; things are made that way. But no amount of aggregated collective action of itself constitutes a community. For beings who observe and think, and whose ideas are absorbed by impulses and become sentiments and interests, "we" is as inevitable as "I." But "we" and "our" exist only when the consequences of combined action are perceived and become an object of desire and effort, just as "I" and "mine" appear on the scene only when a distinctive share in mutual action is consciously asserted or claimed. Human associations may be ever so organic in origin and firm in operation, but they develop into societies in a human sense only as far as their consequences, being known, are esteemed and sought for. Even if "society" were as much an organism as some writers have held, it would not on that account be society. Interactions, transactions, occur *de facto* and the results of interdependence follow. But participation in activities and sharing in results are additive concerns. They demand *communication* as a prerequisite.

. . . Only when there exist *signs* or *symbols* of activities and of their outcome can the flux be viewed as from without, be arrested for consideration and esteem, and be regulated. . . . But when phases of the process are represented by signs, a new medium is interposed. As symbols are related to one another, the important relations of a course of events are recorded and are preserved as meanings. Recollection and foresight are possible; the new medium facilitates calculation, planning, and a new kind of action which intervenes in what happens to direct its course in the interest of what is foreseen and desired.

Symbols in turn depend upon and promote communication. The results of conjoint experience are considered and transmitted. Events cannot be passed from one to another, but meanings may be shared. . . . Wants and impulses are then attached to common meanings. They are thereby transformed into desires and purposes, which, since they implicate a common or mutually understood meaning, present new ties, converting a conjoint activity into a community of interest and endeavor. Thus there is generated what, metaphorically, may be termed a general will and social consciousness: desire and choice on the part of individuals in behalf of activities that, by means of symbols, are communicable and shared by all concerned. A community thus presents an order of energies transmuted into one of the meanings which are appreciated and mutually referred by each to every other on the part of those engaged in combined action. "Force" is not eliminated but is transformed in use and direction by ideas and sentiments made possible by means of symbols. . . .

. . . We are born organic beings associated with others, but we are not born members of a community. The young have to be brought within the traditions, outlook and interests which characterize a community by means of education: by unremitting instruction and by learning in connection with the phenomena of overt association. Everything which is distinctively human is learned, not native, even though it could not be learned without native structures which mark man off from other animals. To learn in a human way and to human effect is not just to acquire added skill through refinement of original capacities.

To learn to be human is to develop through the give-and-take of communication an effective sense of being an individually distinctive member of a community; one who understands and appreciates its beliefs, desires and methods, and who contributes to a further conversion of organic powers into human resources and values. But this translation is never finished. . . . It manifests itself . . . subtly, pervasively and effectually when knowledge of the instrumentalities of skill which are the product of communal life are employed in the service of wants and impulses which have not themselves been modified by reference to a shared interest. . . .

. . . What are the conditions under which it is possible for the Great Society to approach more closely and vitally the status of a Great Community, and thus take form in genuinely democratic societies and states? What are the conditions under which we may reasonably picture the Public emerging from its eclipse?

The study will be an intellectual and hypothetical one. . . . The object of the analysis will be to show that *unless* ascertained specifications are realized, the Community cannot be organized as a democratically effective public. . . .

Two essential constituents in that older theory . . . were the notions that each individual is of himself equipped with the intelligence needed, under the operation of self-interest, to engage in political affairs; and that general suffrage, frequent elections of officials and majority rule are sufficient to ensure the responsibility of elected rulers to the desires and interests of the public. As we shall see, the second conception is logically bound up with the first and stands or falls with it. At the basis of the scheme lies what Lippmann has well called the idea of the "omnicompetent" individual: competent to frame policies, to judge their results; competent to know in all situations demanding political action what is for his own good, and competent to enforce his idea of good and the will to effect it against contrary forces. Subsequent history has proved that the assumption involved illusion. . . . [K]knowledge is a function of association and communication; it depends upon tradition, upon tolls and methods socially transmitted, developed and sanctioned. Faculties of effectual observation, reflection and desire are habits acquired under the influence of the culture and institutions of society, not ready-made inherent powers. The fact that man acts from crudely intelligized emotion and from habit rather than from rational consideration, is now so familiar that it is not easy to appreciate that the other idea was taken seriously as the basis of economic and political philosophy.

Habit is the mainspring of human action, and habits are formed for the most part under the influence of the customs of a group. The organic structure of man entails the formation of habit, for, whether we wish it or not, whether we are aware of it or not, every act effects a modification of attitude and set which directs future behavior. . . .

The influence of habit is decisive because all distinctively human action has to be learned, and the very heart, blood and sinews of learning is creation of habitudes. Habits bind us to orderly and established ways of action because they generate ease, skill and interest in things to which we have grown used and because they instigate fear to walk in different ways, and because they leave us incapacitated for the trial of them. Habit does not preclude the use of thought, but it determines the channels within which it operates. Thinking is secreted in the interstices of habits. The sailor, miner, fisherman and farmer think, but their thoughts fall within the framework of accustomed occupations and relationships. We dream beyond the limits of use and wont, but only rarely does revery become a source of acts which break bounds; so rarely that we name those in whom it happens demonic geniuses and marvel at the spectacle. Thinking itself becomes habitual along certain lines; a specialized occupation. Scientific men, philosophers, literary persons, are not men and women who have so broken the bonds of habits that pure reason and emotion undefiled by use and wont speak through them. They are persons of a specialized infrequent habit. Hence the idea that men are moved by an intelligent and calculated regard for their own good is pure mythology. Even if the principle of self-love actuated behavior, it would still be true that the *objects* in which men find their love manifested, the objects which they take as constituting their peculiar interests, are set by habits reflecting social customs.

These facts explain why the social doctrinaires of the new industrial movement had so little prescience of what was to follow in consequence of it. These facts explain why the more things changed, the more they were the same; they account, that is, for the fact that instead of the sweeping revolution which was expected to result from democratic political machinery, there was in the main but a transfer of vested power from one class to another. . . .

. . . When a certain state of accumulated knowledge, of techniques and instrumentalities is attained, the process of change is so accelerated, that, as to-day, it appears externally to be the dominant trait. But there is a marked lag in any corresponding change of ideas and desires. Habits of opinion are the toughest of all habits; when they have become second nature . . . they creep in again as stealthily and surely as does first nature. And as they are modified, the alteration first shows itself negatively, in the disintegration of old beliefs, to be replaced by floating, volatile and accidentally snatched up opinions. Of course, there has been an enormous increase in the amount of knowledge possessed by mankind, but it does not equal, probably, the increase in the amount of errors and half-truths which have got into circulation. In social and human matters, especially, the development of a critical sense and methods of discriminating judgment has not kept pace with the growth of careless reports and of motives for positive misrepresentation.

What is more important, however, is that so much of knowledge is not knowledge in the ordinary sense of the word, but is "science." The quotation marks are not used disrespectfully, but to suggest the technical character of scientific material. The layman takes certain conclusions which get into circulation to be science. But the scientific inquirer knows that they constitute science only in connection with the methods by which they are reached. Even when true, they are not science in virtue of their correctness, but by reason of the apparatus which is employed in reaching them. This apparatus is so highly specialized that it requires more labor to acquire ability to use and understand it than to get skill in any other instrumentalities possessed by man. Science, in other words, is a highly specialized language. . . .

For most men . . . science is a mystery in the hands of initiates, who have become adept in virtue of following ritualistic ceremonies from which the profane herd is excluded. They are fortunate who get as far as a sympathetic appreciation of the methods which give pattern to the complicated apparatus. . . . For most persons, the reality of the apparatus is found only in its embodiments in practical affairs, in mechanical devices and in techniques which touch life as it is lived. For them, electricity is *known* by means of the telephones, bells and lights they use. . . . The physiology and biology they are acquainted with is that they have learned in taking precautions against germs and from the physicians they depend on for health. The science of what might be supposed to be closest to them, of human nature, was for them an esoteric mystery until it was applied in advertising, salesmanship and personnel selection and management, and until, through psychiatry, it spilled over into life and popular consciousness. . . .

Meanwhile the technological application of the complex apparatus which is science has revolutionized the conditions under which associated life goes on. . . . But it is not known in the sense that men understand it. They do not know it as they know some machine which they operate, or as they know electric light and steam locomotives. They do not understand *how* the change has gone on nor *how* it affects their conduct. Not understanding its "how," they cannot use and control its manifestations. They undergo the consequences, they are affected by them. They cannot manage them, though some are fortunate enough—what is commonly called good fortune—to be able to exploit some phase of the process for their own personal profit. . . . Skill and ability work within a framework which we have not created and do not comprehend. . . . But such knowledge goes relatively but little further than that of the competent skilled operator who manages a machine. It suffices to employ the conditions which are before him. Skill enables him to turn the flux of events this way or that in his own neighborhood. It gives him no control of the flux.

Why should the public and its officers, even if the latter are termed statesmen, be wiser and more effective? The prime condition of a democratically organized public is a kind of knowledge and insight which does not yet exist. In its absence, it would be the height of absurdity to try to tell what it would be like if it existed. But some of the conditions which must be fulfilled if it is to exist can be indicated. . . . An obvious requirement is freedom of social inquiry and of distribution of its conclusions. The notion that men may be free in their thought even when they are not in its expression and dissemination has been sedulously propagated. It had its origin in the idea of a mind complete in itself, apart from actions and from objects. Such a consciousness presents in fact the spectacle of mind deprived of its normal functioning, because it is baffled by the actualities in connection with which alone it is truly mind, and is driven back into secluded and impotent revery.

There can be no public without full publicity in respect to all consequences which concern it. Whatever obstructs and restricts publicity, limits and distorts public opinion and checks and distorts thinking on social affairs. Without freedom of expression, not even methods of social inquiry can be developed. For tools can be evolved and perfected only in operation; in application to observing, reporting and organizing actual subject-matter; and the application cannot occur save through free and systematic communication. . . .

The belief that thought and communication are now free simply because legal restrictions which once obtained have been done away with is absurd. Its currency perpetuates the infantile state of social knowledge. For it blurs recognition of our central need to possess conceptions which are used as tools of directed inquiry and which are tested, rectified and caused to grow in actual use. No man and no mind was ever emancipated merely by being left alone. Removal of formal limitations is but a negative condition; positive freedom is not a state but an act which involves methods and instrumentalities for control of conditions. Experience shows that sometimes the sense of external oppression, as by censorship, acts as a challenge and arouses intellectual energy and excites courage. But a belief in intellectual freedom where it does not exist contributes only to complacency in virtual enslavement, to sloppiness, superficiality and recourse to sensations and a substitute for ideas: marked traits of our present estate with respect to social knowledge. . . .

Emotional habituations and intellectual habitudes on the part of the mass of men create conditions of which the exploiters of sentiment and opinion only take advantage. Men have got used to an experimental method in physical and technical matters. They are still afraid of it in human concerns. The fear is the more efficacious because like all deep-lying fears it is covered up and disguised by all kinds of rationalizations. One of its commonest forms is a truly religious idealization of, and reverence for, established institutions; for example in our own politics, the Constitution, the Supreme Court, private property, free contract and so on. The words "sacred" and "sanctity" come readily to our lips when such things come under discussion. . . .

The backwardness of social knowledge is marked in its division into independent and insulated branches of learning. Anthropology, history, sociology, morals, economics, political science, go their own ways without constant and systematized fruitful interaction. Only in appearance is there a similar division in physical knowledge. There is continuous cross-fertilization between astronomy, physics, chemistry and the biological sciences. Discoveries and improved methods are so recorded and organized that constant exchange and intercommunication take place. The isolation of the humane subjects from one another is connected with their aloofness from physical knowledge. The mind still draws a sharp separation between the world in which man lives and the life of man in and by that world, a cleft reflected in the separation of man himself into a body and a mind, which, it is currently supposed, can be known and dealt with apart. . . .

Nevertheless, the course of development has left us of this age in a plight. When we say that a subject of science is technically specialized, or that it is highly "abstract," what we practically mean is that it is not conceived in terms of its bearing upon human life. All *merely* physical knowledge is technical, couched in a technical vocabulary communicable only to the few. Even physical knowledge which does not affect human conduct . . . is also technical and remote to the degree in which its bearings are not understood and used. The sunlight, rain, air and soil have always entered in visible ways into human experience; atoms and molecules and cells and most other things with which the sciences are occupied affect us, but not visibly. Because they enter life and modify experience in imperceptible ways, and their consequences are not realized, speech about them is technical. . . . One would think, then, that a fundamental and ever-operating aim would be to translate knowledge of the subject-matter of physical conditions into terms which are generally understood, into signs denoting human consequences of services and disservices rendered. . . . One would think, then, that any state of affairs which tends to render the things of the environment unknown and incommunicable by human beings in terms of their own activities and sufferings would be deplored as a disaster. . . .

But the facts are to the contrary. Matter and the material are words which in the minds of many convey a note of disparagement. They are taken to be foes of whatever is of ideal value in life, instead of as conditions of its manifestation and sustained being. In consequence of this division, they do become in fact enemies. . . . There are even some who regard the materialism and dominance of commercialism of modern life as fruits of undue devotion to physical science, not seeing that the split between man and nature, artificially made by a tradition which originated before there was understanding of the physical conditions that are the medium of human activities, is the benumbing factor. . . . What is applied and employed as the alternative to knowledge in regulation of society is ignorance, prejudice, class-interest and accident. Science is converted into knowledge in its honorable and emphatic sense *only* in application. Otherwise it is truncated, blind, distorted. When it is then applied, it is in ways which explain the unfavorable sense so often attached to "application" and the "utilitarian": namely, use for pecuniary ends to the profit of a few.

. . . [T]he use of science to regulate industry and trade has gone on steadily. The scientific revolution of the seventeenth century was the precursor of the industrial revolution of the eighteenth and nineteenth. In consequence, man has suffered the impact of an enormously enlarged control of physical energies without any corresponding ability to control himself and his own affairs. Knowledge divided against itself, a science to whose incompleteness is added an artificial split, has played its part in generating enslavement of men, women and children in factories in which they are animated machines to tend inanimate machines. It has maintained sordid slums, flurried and discontented careers, grinding poverty and luxurious wealth, brutal exploitation of nature and man in times of peace and high explosives and noxious gases in times of war. Man, a child in understanding of himself, has placed in his hands physical tools of incalculable power. He plays with them like a child, and whether they work harm or good is largely a matter of accident. The instrumentality becomes master and works fatally as if possessed of a will of its own—not because it has a will but because man has not.

The glorification of "pure" science under such conditions is a rationalization of an escape; it marks a construction of an asylum of refuge, a shirking of responsibility. The true purity of knowledge exists not when it is uncontaminated by contact with use and service. It is wholly a moral matter. . . . Humanity is not, as was once thought, the end for which all things were formed; it is but a slight and feeble thing, perhaps an episodic one, in the vast stretch of the universe. But for man, man is the center of interest and the measure of importance. ... The ultimate harm is that the understanding by man of his own affairs and his ability to direct them are sapped at their root when knowledge of nature is disconnected from its human function. ...

Record and communication are indispensable to knowledge. ... Dissemination is something other than scattering at large. Seeds are sown, not by virtue of being thrown out at random, but by being so distributed as to take root and have a chance of growth. Communication of the results of social inquiry is the same thing as the formation of public opinion. This marks one of the first ideas framed in the growth of political democracy as it will be one of the last to be fulfilled. For public opinion is judgment which is formed and entertained by those who constitute the public and is about public affairs. Each of the two phases imposes for its realization conditions hard to meet.

Opinions and beliefs concerning the public presuppose effective and organized inquiry. Unless there are methods for detecting the energies which are at work and tracing them through an intricate network of interactions to their consequences, what passes as public opinion will be "opinion" in its derogatory sense rather than truly public, no matter how widespread the opinion is. ... Opinion casually formed and formed under the direction of those who have something at stake in having a lie believed can be *public* opinion only in name. Calling it by this name, acceptance of the name as a kind of warrant, magnifies its capacity to lead action estray. The more who share it, the more injurious its influence. Public opinion, even if it happens to be correct, is intermittent when it is not the product of methods of investigation and reporting constantly at work. It appears only in crises. Hence its "rightness" concerns only an immediate emergency. ... Only continuous inquiry, continuous in the sense of being connected as well as persistent, can provide the material of enduring opinion about public matters. ...

A glance at the situation shows that the physical and external means of collecting information in regard to what is happening in the world have far outrun the intellectual phase of inquiry and organization of its results. Telegraph, telephone, and now the radio, cheap and quick mails, the printing press, capable of swift reduplication of material at low cost, have attained a remarkable development. But when we ask what sort of material is recorded and how it is organized when we ask about the intellectual form in which the material is presented, the tale to be told is very different. "News" signifies something which has just happened, and which is new just because it deviates from the old and regular. But its *meaning* depends upon relation to what it imports, to what its social consequences are. This import cannot be determined unless the new is placed in relation to the old, to what has happened and been integrated into the course of events. Without coordination and consecutiveness, events are not events, but mere occurrences, intrusions. ...

... The political forms of democracy and quasi-democratic habits of thought on social matters have compelled a certain amount of public discussion and at least the simulation of general consultation in arriving at political decisions. Representative government must at least seem to be founded on public interests as they are revealed to public belief. The days are past when government can be carried on without any pretense of ascertaining the wishes of the governed. In theory, their assent must be secured. . . .

The smoothest road to control of political conduct is by control of opinion. As long as interests of pecuniary profit are powerful, and a public has not located and identified itself, those who have this interest will have an unresisted motive for tampering with the springs of political action in all that affects them. . . .

. . . It is often said, and with a great appearance of truth, that the freeing and perfecting of inquiry would not have any especial effect. For, it is argued, the mass of the reading public is not interested in learning and assimilating the results of accurate investigation. Unless they are read, they cannot seriously affect the thought and action of members of the public; they remain in secluded library alcoves, and are studied and understood only by a few intellectuals. The objection is well taken save as the potency of art is taken into account. A technical high-brow presentation would appeal only to those technically high-brow; it would not be news to the masses. Presentation is fundamentally important, and presentation is a question of art. . . . Men's conscious life of opinion and judgment often proceeds on a superficial and trivial plane. But their lives reach a deeper level. The function of art has always been to break through the crust of conventionalized routine and consciousness. . . .

We have but touched lightly and in passing upon the conditions which must be fulfilled if the Great Society is to become a Great Community; a society in which the ever-expanding and intricately ramifying consequences of associated activities shall be known in the full sense of that word, so that an organized, articulate Public comes into being. . . . When the machine age has thus perfected its machinery it will be a means of life and not its despotic master. Democracy will come into its own, for democracy is a name for a life of free and enriching communion. It had its seer in Walt Whitman. It will have its consummation when free social inquiry is indissolubly wedded to the art of full and moving communication. . . .

Justice as Fairness (1958)

JOHN RAWLS

1. It might seem at first sight that the concepts of justice and fairness are the same, and that there is no reason to distinguish them, or to say that one is more fundamental than the other. I think that this impression is mistaken. In this paper I wish to show that the fundamental idea in the concept of justice is fairness; and I wish to offer an analysis of the concept of justice from this point of view. To bring out the force of this claim, and the analysis based upon it, I shall then argue that it is this aspect of justice for which utilitarianism, in its classical form, is unable to account, but which is expressed, even if misleadingly, by the idea of the social contract.

To start with I shall develop a particular conception of justice by stating and commenting upon two principles which specify it, and by considering the circumstances and conditions under which they may be thought to arise. ...

Throughout I consider justice only as a virtue of social institutions, or what I shall call practices. The principles of justice are regarded as formulating restrictions as to how practices may define positions and offices, and assign thereto powers and liabilities, rights and duties. Justice as a virtue of particular actions or of persons I do not take up at all. It is important to distinguish these various subjects of justice, since the meaning of the concept varies according to whether it is applied to practices, particular actions, or persons. These meanings are, indeed, connected, but they are not identical. I shall confine my discussion to the sense of justice as applied to practices, since this sense is the basic one. Once it is understood, the other senses should go quite easily.

Justice is to be understood in its customary sense as representing but *one* of the many virtues of social institutions, for these may be antiquated, inefficient, degrading, or any number of other things, without being unjust. Justice is not to be confused with an all-inclusive vision of a good society; it is only one part of any such conception. It is important, for example, to distinguish that sense of equality which is an aspect of the concept of justice from that sense of equality which belongs to a more comprehensive social ideal. There may well be inequalities which one concedes are just, or at least not unjust, but which, nevertheless, one wishes, on other grounds, to do away with. I shall focus attention, then, on the usual sense of justice in which it is essentially the elimination of arbitrary distinctions and the establishment, within the structure of a practice, of a proper balance between competing claims.

Finally, there is no need to consider the principles discussed below as *the* principles of justice. For the moment it is sufficient that they are typical of a family of principles normally associated with the concept of justice. ...

Excerpted from John Rawls, "Justice as Fairness," in *The Philosophical Review*, Vol. 67, Issue 2 (Apr. 1958) pp. 164–194. Reprinted by permission of the publisher.

2. The conception of justice which I want to develop may be stated in the form of two principles as follows: first, each person participating in a practice, or affected by it, has an equal right to the most extensive liberty compatible with a like liberty for all; and second, inequalities are arbitrary unless it is reasonable to expect that they will work out for everyone's advantage, and provided the positions and offices to which they attach, or from which they may be gained, are open to all. These principles express justice as a complex of three ideas: liberty, equality, and reward for services contributing to the common good.

The term "person" is to be construed variously depending on the circumstances. On some occasions it will mean human individuals, but in others it may refer to nations, provinces, business firms, churches, teams, and so on. The principles of justice apply in all these instances, although there is a certain logical priority to the case of human individuals. As I shall use the term "person," it will be ambiguous in the manner indicated.

The first principle holds, of course, only if other things are equal: that is, while there must always be a justification for departing from the initial position of equal liberty (which is defined by the pattern of rights and duties, powers and liabilities, established by a practice), and the burden of proof is placed on him who would depart from it, nevertheless, there can be, and often there is, a justification for doing so. Now, that similar particular cases, as defined by a practice, should be treated similarly as they arise, is part of the very concept of a practice; it is involved in the notion of an activity in accordance with rules. The first principle expresses an analogous conception, but as applied to the structure of practices themselves. It holds, for example, that there is a presumption against the distinctions and classifications made by legal systems and other practices to the extent that they infringe on the original and equal liberty of the persons participating in them. The second principle defines how this presumption may be rebutted.

It might be argued at this point that justice requires only an equal liberty. If, however, a greater liberty were possible for all without loss or conflict, then it would be irrational to settle on a lesser liberty. There is no reason for circumscribing rights unless their exercise would be incompatible, or would render the practice defining them less effective. Therefore no serious distortion of the concept of justice is likely to follow from including within it the concept of the greatest equal liberty.

The second principle defines what sorts of inequalities are permissible; it specifies how the presumption laid down by the first principle may be put aside. Now by inequalities it is best to understand not *any* differences between offices and positions, but differences in the benefits and burdens attached to them either directly or indirectly, such as prestige and wealth, or liability to taxation and compulsory services. Players in a game do not protest against there being different positions, such as batter, pitcher, catcher, and the like, nor to there being various privileges and powers as specified by the rules; nor do the citizens of a country object to there being the different offices of government such as president, senator, governor, judge, and so on, each with their special rights and duties. It is not differences of this kind that are normally thought of as inequalities, but differences in the resulting distribution established by a practice, or made possible by it, of the things men strive to attain or avoid. Thus they may complain about the pattern of honors and rewards set up by a practice (e.g., the privileges and salaries of government officials) or they may object to the distribution of power and wealth which results from the various ways in which men avail themselves of the opportunities allowed by it (e.g., the concentration of wealth which may develop in a free price system allowing large entrepreneurial or speculative gains).

It should be noted that the second principle holds that an inequality is allowed only if there is reason to believe that the practice with the inequality, or resulting in it, will work for the advantage of *every* party engaging in it. Here it is important to stress that *every* party must gain from the inequality. Since the principle applies to practices, it implies that the representative man in every office or position defined by a practice, when he views it as a going concern, must find it reasonable to prefer his condition and prospects with the inequality to what they would be under the practice without it. The principle excludes, therefore, the justification of inequalities on the grounds that the disadvantages of those in one position are outweighed by the greater advantages of those in another position. This rather simple restriction is the main modification I wish to make in the utilitarian principle as usually understood. ...

Further, it is also necessary that the various offices to which special benefits or burdens attach are open to all. It may be, for example, to the common advantage, as just defined, to attach special benefits to certain offices. Perhaps by doing so the requisite talent can be attracted to them and encouraged to give its best efforts. But any offices having special benefits must be won in a fair competition in which contestants are judged on their merits. If some offices were not open, those excluded would normally be justified in feeling unjustly treated, even if they benefited from the greater efforts of those who were allowed to compete for them. Now if one can assume that offices are open, it is necessary only to consider the design of practices themselves and how they jointly, as a system, work together. It will be a mistake to focus attention on the varying relative positions of particular persons, who may be known to us by their proper names, and to require that each such change, as a once for all transaction viewed in isolation, must be in itself just. It is the system of practices which is to be judged, and judged from a general point of view: unless one is prepared to criticize it from the standpoint of a representative man holding some particular office, one has no complaint against it. ...

Imagine a society of persons amongst whom a certain system of practices is *already* well established. Now suppose that by and large they are mutually self-interested; their allegiance to their established practices is normally founded on the prospect of self-advantage. One need not assume that, in all senses of the term "person," the persons in this society are mutually self-interested. If the characterization as mutually self-interested applies when the line of division is the family, it may still be true that members of families are bound by ties of sentiment and affection and willingly acknowledge duties in contradiction to self-interest. Mutual self-interestedness in the relations be- tween families, nations, churches, and the like, is commonly associated with intense loyalty and devotion on the part of individual members. Therefore, one can form a more realistic conception of this society if one thinks of it as consisting of mutually self-interested families, or some other association. . . .

Now suppose also that these persons are rational: they know their own interests more or less accurately; they are capable of tracing out the likely con- sequences of adopting one practice rather than another; they are capable of adhering to a course of action once they have decided upon it; they can resist present temptations and the enticements of immediate gain; and the bare knowledge or perception of the difference between their condition and that of others is not, within certain limits and in itself, a source of great dissatisfac- tion. Only the last point adds anything to the usual definition of rationality. This definition should allow, I think, for the idea that a rational man would not be greatly downcast from knowing, or seeing, that others are in a better position than himself, unless he thought their being so was the result of injus- tice, or the consequence of letting chance work itself out for no useful common purpose, and so on. So if these persons strike us as unpleasantly egoistic, they are at least free in some degree from the fault of envy.

Finally, assume that these persons have roughly similar needs and inter- ests, or needs and interests in various ways complementary, so that fruitful cooperation amongst them is possible; and suppose that they are sufficiently equal in power and ability to guarantee that in normal circumstances none is able to dominate the others. This condition (as well as the others) may seem excessively vague; but in view of the conception of justice to which the argu- ment leads, there seems no reason for making it more exact here.

Since these persons are conceived as engaging in their common practices, which are already established, there is no question of our supposing them to come together to deliberate as to how they will set these practices up for the first time. Yet we can imagine that from time to time they discuss with one an- other whether any of them has a legitimate complaint against their established institutions. Such discussions are perfectly natural in any normal society. Now suppose that they have settled on doing this in the following way. They first try to arrive at the principles by which complaints, and so practices them- selves, are to be judged. Their procedure for this is to let each person propose the principles upon which he wishes his complaints to be tried with the un- derstanding that, if acknowledged, the complaints of others will be similarly tried, and that no complaints will be heard at all until everyone is roughly of one mind as to how complaints are to be judged. They each understand fur- ther that the principles proposed and acknowledged on this occasion are bind- ing on future occasions. Thus each will be wary of proposing a principle which would give him a peculiar advantage, in his present circumstances, supposing it to be accepted. Each person knows that he will be bound by it in future circumstances the peculiarities of which cannot be known, and which might well be such that the principle is then to his disadvantage. The idea is that everyone should be required to make *in advance* a firm commitment, which others also may reasonably be expected to make, and that no one be given the opportunity to tailor the canons of a legitimate complaint to fit his own special condition, and then to discard them when they no longer suit his purpose. Hence each person will propose principles of a general kind which will, to a large degree, gain their sense from the various applications to be made of them, the particular circumstances of which being as yet unknown. These principles will express the conditions in accordance with which each is the least unwilling to have his interests limited in the design of practices, given the competing interests of the others, on the supposition that the interests of others will be limited likewise. The restrictions which would so arise might be thought of as those a person would keep in mind if he were designing a practice in which his enemy were to assign him his place.

The two main parts of this conjectural account have a definite significance. The character and respective situations of the parties reflect the typical circumstances in which questions of justice arise. The procedure whereby principles are proposed and acknowledged represents constraints, analogous to those of having a morality, whereby rational and mutually self-interested persons are brought to act reasonably. Thus the first part reflects the fact that questions of justice arise when conflicting claims are made upon the design of a practice and where it is taken for granted that each person will insist, as far as possible, on what he considers his rights. It is typical of cases of justice to involve persons who are pressing on one another their claims, between which a fair balance or equilibrium must be found. On the other hand, as expressed by the second part, having a morality must at least imply the acknowledgment of principles as impartially applying to one's own conduct as well as to another's, and moreover principles which may constitute a constraint, or limitation, upon the pursuit of one's own interests. There are, of course, other aspects of having a morality: the acknowledgment of moral principles must show itself in accepting a reference to them as reasons for limiting one's claims, in acknowledging the burden of providing a special explanation, or excuse, when one acts contrary to them, or else in showing shame and remorse and a desire to make amends, and so on. It is sufficient to remark here that having a morality is analogous to having made a firm commitment in advance; for one must acknowledge the principles of morality even when to one's disadvantage. A man whose moral judgments always coincided with his interests could be suspected of having no morality at all.

Thus the two parts of the foregoing account are intended to mirror the kinds of circumstances in which questions of justice arise and the constraints which having a morality would impose upon persons so situated. In this way one can see how the acceptance of the principles of justice might come about, for given all these conditions as described, it would be natural if the two principles of justice were to be acknowledged. Since there is no way for anyone to win special advantages for himself, each might consider it reasonable to acknowledge equality as an initial principle. There is, however, no reason why they should regard this position as final; for if there are inequalities which satisfy the second principle, the immediate gain which equality would allow can be considered as intelligently invested in view of its future return. If, as is quite likely, these inequalities work as incentives to draw out better efforts, the members of this society may look upon them as concessions to human nature: they, like us, may think that people ideally should want to serve one another. But as they are mutually self-interested, their acceptance of these inequalities is merely the acceptance of the relations in which they actually stand, and a recognition of the motives which lead them to engage in their common practices. *They* have no title to complain of one another. And so provided that the conditions of the principle are met, there is no reason why they should not allow such inequalities. Indeed, it would be short-sighted of them to do so, and could result, in most cases, only from their being dejected by the bare knowledge, or perception, that others are better situated. Each person will, however, insist on an advantage to himself, and so on a common advantage, for none is willing to sacrifice anything for the others.

These remarks are not offered as a proof that persons so conceived and circumstanced would settle on the two principles, but only to show that these principles could have such a background, and so can be viewed as those principles which mutually self-interested and rational persons, when similarly situated and required to make in advance a firm commitment, could acknowledge as restrictions governing the assignment of rights and duties in their common practices, and thereby accept as limiting their rights against one another. The principles of justice may, then, be regarded as those principles which arise when the constraints of having a morality are imposed upon parties in the typical circumstances of justice. . . .

. . . [I]n contrast to the various conceptions of the social contract, the several parties do not establish any particular society or practice; they do not covenant to obey a particular sovereign body or to accept a given constitution. . . . What the parties do is to *jointly* acknowledge certain *principles* of appraisal relating to their common *practices* either as already established or merely proposed. They accede to standards of judgment, not to a given practice; they do not make any specific agreement, or bargain, or adopt a particular strategy. The subject of their acknowledgment is, therefore, very general indeed; it is simply the acknowledgment of certain principles of judgment, fulfilling certain general conditions, to be used in criticizing the arrangement of their common affairs. . . .

Finally, I do not, of course, conceive the several parties as necessarily coming together to establish their common practices for the first time. Some institutions may, indeed, be set up *de novo*; but I have framed the preceding account so that it will apply when the full complement of social institutions already exists and represents the result of a long period of development. Nor is the account in any way fictitious. In any society where people reflect on their institutions they will have an idea of what principles of justice would be acknowledged under the conditions described, and there will be occasions when questions of justice are actually discussed in this way. Therefore if their practices do not accord with these principles, this will affect the quality of their social relations. For in this case there will be some recognized situations wherein the parties are mutually aware that one of them is being forced to accept what the other would concede is unjust. The foregoing analysis may then be thought of as representing the actual quality of relations between persons as defined by practices accepted as just. In such practices the parties will acknowledge the principles on which it is constructed, and the general recognition of this fact shows itself in the absence of resentment and in the sense of being justly treated. Thus one common objection to the theory of the social contract, its apparently historical and fictitious character, is avoided.

5. That the principles of justice may be regarded as arising in the manner described illustrates an important fact about them. Not only does it bring out the idea that justice is a primitive moral notion in that it arises once the concept of morality is imposed on mutually self-interested agents similarly circumstanced, but it emphasizes that, fundamental to justice, is the concept of fairness which relates to right dealing between persons who are cooperating with or competing against one another, as when one speaks of fair games, fair competition, and fair bargains. The question of fairness arises when free persons, who have no authority over one another, are engaging in a joint activity and amongst themselves settling or acknowledging the rules which define it and which determine the respective shares in its benefits and burdens. A practice will strike the parties as fair if none feels that, by participating in it, they or any of the others are taken advantage of, or forced to give in to claims which they do not regard as legitimate. This implies that each has a conception of legitimate claims which he thinks it reasonable for others as well as himself to acknowledge. . . . A practice is just or fair, then, when it satisfies the principles which those who participate in it could propose to one another for mutual acceptance under the afore-mentioned circumstances. Persons engaged in a just, or fair, practice can face one another openly and support their respective positions, should they appear questionable, by reference to principles which it is reasonable to expect each to accept.

It is this notion of the possibility of mutual acknowledgment of principles by free persons who have no authority over one another which makes the concept of fairness fundamental to justice. Only if such acknowledgment is possible can there be true community between persons in their common practices; otherwise their relations will appear to them as founded to some extent on force. . . .

Now if the participants in a practice accept its rules as fair, and so have no complaint to lodge against it, there arises a prima facie duty (and a corresponding prima facie right) of the parties to each other to act in accordance with the practice when it falls upon them to comply. When any number of persons engage in a practice, or conduct a joint undertaking according to rules, and thus restrict their liberty, those who have submitted to these restrictions when required have the right to a similar acquiescence on the part of those who have benefited by their submission. These conditions will obtain if a practice is correctly acknowledged to be fair, for in this case all who participate in it will benefit from it. . . . It is not, however, an obligation which presupposes a deliberate performative act in the sense of a promise, or contract, and the like. An unfortunate mistake of proponents of the idea of the social contract was to suppose that political obligation does require some such act, or at least to use language which suggests it. It is sufficient that one has knowingly participated in and accepted the benefits of a practice acknowledged to be fair. This prima facie obligation may, of course, be overridden: it may happen, when it comes one's turn to follow a rule, that other considerations will justify not doing so. But one cannot, in general, be released from this obligation by denying the justice of the practice only when it falls on one to obey. If a person rejects a practice, he should, so far as possible, declare his intention in advance, and avoid participating in it or enjoying its benefits.

This duty I have called that of fair play, but it should be admitted that to refer to it in this way is, perhaps, to extend the ordinary notion of fairness. Usually acting unfairly is not so much the breaking of any particular rule, even if the infraction is difficult to detect (cheating), but taking advantage of loop-holes or ambiguities in rules, availing oneself of unexpected or special circumstances which make it impossible to enforce them, insisting that rules be enforced to one's advantage when they should be suspended, and more generally, acting contrary to the intention of a practice. It is for this reason that one speaks of the sense of fair play: acting fairly requires more than simply being able to follow rules; what is fair must often be felt, or perceived, one wants to say. It is not, however, an unnatural extension of the duty of fair play to have it include the obligation which participants who have knowingly accepted the benefits of their common practice owe to each other to act in accordance with it when their performance falls due; for it is usually considered unfair if someone accepts the benefits of a practice but refuses to do his part in maintaining it. . . .

. . . As with any moral duty, that of fair play implies a constraint on self-interest in particular cases; on occasion it enjoins conduct which a rational egoist strictly defined would not decide upon. So while justice does not require of anyone that he sacrifice his interests in that *general position* and procedure whereby the principles of justice are proposed and acknowledged, it may happen that in particular situations, arising in the context of engaging in a practice, the duty of fair play will often cross his interests in the sense that he will be required to forego particular advantages which the peculiarities of his circumstances might permit him to take. . . .

Now the acknowledgment of this constraint in particular cases, which is manifested in acting fairly or wishing to make amends, feeling ashamed, and the like, when one has evaded it, is one of the forms of conduct by which participants in a common practice exhibit their recognition of each other as persons with similar interests and capacities. . . .

Similarly, the acceptance of the duty of fair play by participants in a common practice is a reflection in each person of the recognition of the aspirations and interests of the others to be realized by their joint activity. . . . To recognize another as a person one must respond to him and act towards him in certain ways; and these ways are intimately connected with the various prima facie duties. Acknowledging these duties in *some* degree, and so having the elements of morality, is not a matter of choice, or of intuiting moral qualities, or a matter of the expression of feelings or attitudes (the three interpretations between which philosophical opinion frequently oscillates); it is simply the possession of one of the forms of conduct in which the recognition of others as persons is manifested. . . .

. . . A practice is just if it is in accordance with the principles which all who participate in it might reasonably be expected to propose or to acknowledge before one another when they are similarly circumstanced and required to make a firm commitment in advance without knowledge of what will be their peculiar condition, and thus when it meets standards which the parties could accept as fair should occasion arise for them to debate its merits. Regarding the participants themselves, once persons knowingly engage in a practice which they acknowledge to be fair and accept the benefits of doing so, they are bound by the duty of fair play to follow the rules when it comes their turn to do so, and this implies a limitation on their pursuit of self-interest in particular cases. . . .

. . . No study of the development of moral ideas and of the differences between them is more sound than the analysis of the fundamental moral concepts upon which it must depend. I have tried, therefore, to give an analysis of the concept of justice which should apply generally, however large a part the concept may have in a given morality, and which can be used in explaining the course of men's thoughts about justice and its relations to other moral concepts. How it is to be used for this purpose is a large topic which I cannot, of course, take up here. I mention it only to emphasize that I have been dealing with the concept of justice itself and to indicate what use I consider such an analysis to have.

Distributive Justice

From Anarchy, State, and Utopia (1974)

ROBERT NOZICK

The minimal state is the most extensive state that can be justified. Any state more extensive violates people's rights. Yet many persons have put forth reasons purporting to justify a more extensive state. . . . In this chapter we consider the claim that a more extensive state is justified, because necessary (or the best instrument) to achieve distributive justice. . . .

The term "distributive justice" is not a neutral one. Hearing the term "distribution," most people presume that some thing or mechanism uses some principle or criterion to give out a supply of things. Into this process of distributing shares some error may have crept. So it is an open question, at least, whether *re*distribution should take place; whether we should do again what has already been done once, though poorly. However, we are not in the position of children who have been given portions of pie by someone who now makes last minute adjustments to rectify careless cutting. There is no *central* distribution, no person or group entitled to control all the resources, jointly deciding how they are to be doled out. What each person gets, he gets from others who give to him in exchange for something, or as a gift. In a free society, diverse persons control different resources, and new holdings arise out of the voluntary exchanges and actions of persons. There is no more a distributing or distribution of shares than there is a distributing of mates in a society in which persons choose whom they shall marry. The total result is the product of many individual decisions which the individuals involved are entitled to make. . . . We shall speak of people's holdings; a principle of justice in holdings describes (part of) what justice tells us (requires) about holdings. . . .

THE ENTITLEMENT THEORY

The subject of justice in holdings consists of three major topics. The first is the *original acquisition of holdings*, the appropriation of unheld things. This includes the issues of how unheld things may come to be held, the process, or processes, by which unheld things may come to be held, the things that may come to be held by these processes, the extent of what comes to be held by a particular process, and so on. We shall refer to the complicated truth about this topic . . . as the principle of justice in acquisition. The second topic concerns the *transfer of holdings* from one person to another. By what processes may a person transfer holdings to another? How may a person acquire a holding

From Robert Nozick, *Anarchy, State, and Utopia*, NY: Basic Books Inc., © 1974, pp. 149–165. Reprinted by permission of Basic Books, a member of Perseus Books, L.L.C.

from another who holds it? Under this topic come general descriptions of voluntary exchange, and gift and (on the other hand) fraud, as well as reference to particular conventional details fixed upon a given society. The complicated truth about this subject . . . we shall call the principle of justice in transfer. (And we shall suppose it also includes principles governing how a person may divest himself of a holding, passing it into an unheld state.)

If the world were wholly just, the following inductive definition would exhaustively cover the subject of justice in holdings.

1. A person who acquires a holding in accordance with the principle of justice in acquisition is entitled to that holding.

2. A person who acquires a holding in accordance with the principle of justice in transfer, from someone else entitled to the holding, is entitled to the holding.

3. No one is entitled to a holding excepted by (repeated) applications of 1 and 2.

The complete principle of distributive justice would say simply that a distribution is just if everyone is entitled to the holdings they possess under the distribution.

A distribution is just if it arises from another just distribution by legitimate means. The legitimate means of moving from one distribution to another are specified by the principle of justice in transfer. The legitimate first "moves" are specified by the principle of justice in acquisition. Whatever arises from a just situation by just steps is itself just. The means of change specified by the principle of justice in transfer preserve justice. As correct rules of inference are truth-preserving, and any conclusion deduced via repeated application of such rules from only true premises is itself true, so the means of transition from one situation to another specified by the principle of justice in transfer are justice-preserving, and any situation actually arising from repeated transitions in accordance with the principle from a just situation is itself just. The parallel between justice-preserving transformations and truth-preserving transformations illuminates where it fails as well as where it holds. That a conclusion could have been deduced by truth-preserving means from premises that are true suffices to show its truth. That from a just situation a situation *could* have arisen via justice-preserving means does *not* suffice to show its justice. The fact that a thief's victims voluntarily *could* have presented him with gifts does not entitle the thief to his ill-gotten aims. Justice in holdings is historical; it depends upon what actually has happened. . . .

Not all actual situations are generated in accordance with the two principles of justice in holdings: the principle of justice in acquisition and the principle of justice in transfer. Some people steal from others, or defraud them, or enslave them, seizing their product and preventing them from living as they choose, or forcibly exclude others from competing in exchanges. None of these are permissible modes of transition from one situation to another. And some persons acquire holdings by means not sanctioned by the principle of justice in acquisition. The existence of past injustice (previous violations of the first two principles of justice in holdings) raises the third major topic under justice in holdings: the rectification of injustice in holdings. If past injustice has shaped present holdings in various ways, some identifiable and some not, what now, if anything, ought to be done to rectify these injustices? What obligations do the performers of injustice have toward those whose position is worse than it would have been had the injustice not been done? Or, than it would have been had compensation been paid promptly? How, if at all, do things change if the beneficiaries and those made worse off are not the direct parties in the act of injustice, but, for example, their descendants? Is an injustice done to someone whose holding was itself based upon an unrectified injustice? How far back must one go in wiping clean the historical slate of injustices? What may victims of injustice permissibly do in order to rectify the injustices being done to them, including the many injustices done by persons acting through their government? I do not know of a thorough or theoretically sophisticated treatment of such issues. Idealizing greatly, let us suppose theoretical investigation will produce a principle of rectification. This principle uses historical information about previous situations and injustices done in them (as defined by the first two principles of justice and rights against interference), and information about the actual course of events that flowed from these injustices, until the present, and it yields a description (or descriptions) of holdings in the society. The principle of rectification presumably will make use of its best estimate of subjunctive information about what would have occurred (or a probability distribution over what might have occurred, using the expected value) if the injustice had not taken place. If the actual description of holdings turns out not to be one of the descriptions yielded by the principle, then one of the descriptions yielded must be realized.

The general outlines of the theory of justice in holdings are that the holdings of a person are just if he is entitled to them by the principles of justice in acquisition and transfer, or by the principle of rectification of injustice (as specified by the first two principles). If each person's holdings are just, then the total set (distribution) of holdings is just. . . .

HISTORICAL PRINCIPLES AND END-RESULT PRINCIPLES

The general outlines of the entitlement theory illuminate the nature and defects of other conceptions of distributive justice. The entitlement theory of justice in distribution is *historical*; whether a distribution is just depends upon how it came about. In contrast, *current time-slice principles* of justice hold that the justice of a distribution is determined by how things are distributed (who has what) as judged by some *structural* principle(s) of just distribution. A utilitarian who judges between any two distributions by seeing which has the greater sum of utility and, if the sums tie, applies some fixed equality criterion to choose the more equal distribution, would hold a current time-slice principle of justice. As would someone who had a fixed schedule of trade-offs between the sum of happiness and equality. According to a current time-slice principle, all that needs to be looked at, in judging the justice of a distribution, is who ends up with what; in comparing any two distributions one need look only at the matrix presenting the distributions. No further information need be fed into a principle of justice. It is a consequence of such principles of justice that any two structurally identical distributions are equally just. (Two distributions are structurally identical if they present the same profile, but perhaps have different persons occupying the particular slots. My having ten and your having five, and my having five and your having ten are structurally identical distributions.) Welfare economics is the theory of current time-slice principles of justice. The subject is conceived as operating on matrices representing only current information about distribution. This, as well as some of the usual conditions (for example, the choice of distribution is invariant under relabeling of columns), guarantees that welfare economics will be a current time-slice theory, with all of its inadequacies.

Most persons do not accept current time-slice principles as constituting the whole story about distributive shares. They think it relevant in assessing the justice of a situation to consider not only the distribution it embodies, but also how that distribution came about. If some persons are in prison for murder or war crimes, we do not say that to assess the justice of the distribution in the society we must look only at what this person has, and that person has, and that person has, . . . at the current time. We think it relevant to ask whether someone did something so that he *deserved* to be punished, deserved to have a lower share. Most will agree to the relevance of further information with regard to punishments and penalties. Consider also desired things. One traditional socialist view is that workers are entitled to the product and full fruits of their labor; they have earned it; a distribution is unjust if it does not give the workers what they are entitled to. Such entitlements are based upon some past history. . . . [The] socialist rightly, in my view, holds onto the notions of earning, producing, entitlement, desert, and so forth, and he rejects current time-slice principles that look only to the structure of the resulting set of holdings. (The set of holdings resulting from what? Isn't it implausible that how holdings are produced and come to exist has no effect at all on who should hold what?) His mistake lies in his view of what entitlements arise out of what sorts of productive processes.

We construe the position we discuss too narrowly by speaking of *current* time-slice principles. Nothing is changed if structural principles operate upon a time sequence of current time-slice profiles and, for example, give someone more now to counterbalance the less he has had earlier. A utilitarian or an egalitarian or any mixture of the two over time will inherit the difficulties of his more myopic comrades. He is not helped by the fact that *some* of the information others consider relevant in assessing a distribution is reflected, unrecoverably, in past matrices. Henceforth, we shall refer to such unhistorical principles of distributive justice, including the current time-slice principles, as *end-result principles* or *end-state principles.*

In contrast to end-result principles of justice, *historical principles* of justice hold that past circumstances or actions of people can create differential entitlements or differential deserts to things. An injustice can be worked by moving from one distribution to another structurally identical one, for the second, in profile the same, may violate people's entitlements or deserts; it may not fit the actual history.

PATTERNING

The entitlement principles of justice in holdings that we have sketched are historical principles of justice. To better understand their precise character, we shall distinguish them from another subclass of the historical principles. Consider, as an example, the principle of distribution according to moral merit. This principle requires that total distributive shares vary directly with moral merit; no person should have a greater share than anyone whose moral merit is greater. (If moral merit could be not merely ordered but measured on an interval or ratio scale, stronger principles could be formulated. . . . Let us call a principle of distribution *patterned* if it specifies that a distribution is to vary along with some natural dimension, weighted sum of natural dimensions, or lexicographic ordering of natural dimensions. And let us say a distribution is patterned if it accords with some patterned principle. . . .

Almost every suggested principle of distributive justice is patterned: to each according to his moral merit, or needs, or marginal product, or how hard he tries, or the weighted sum of the foregoing, and so on. The principle of entitlement we have sketched is *not* patterned. There is no one natural dimension or weighted sum or combination of a small number of natural dimensions that yields the distributions generated in accordance with the principle of entitlement. The set of holdings that results when some persons receive their marginal products, others win at gambling, others receive a share of their mate's income, others receive gifts from foundations, others receive interest on loans, others receive gifts from admirers, others receive returns on investment, others make for themselves much of what they have, others find things, and so on, will not be patterned. Heavy strands of patterns will run through it; significant portions of the variance in holdings will be accounted for by pattern-variables. If most people most of the time choose to transfer some of their entitlements to others only in exchange for something from them, then a large part of what many people hold will vary with what they held that others wanted. . . . But gifts to relatives, charitable donations, bequests to children, and the like, are not best conceived, in the first instance, in this manner. . . . Though the resulting set of holdings will be unpatterned, it will not be incomprehensible, for it can be seen as arising from the operation of a small number of principles. These principles specify how an initial distribution may arise (the principle of acquisition of holdings) and how distributions may be transformed into others (the principle of transfer of holdings). The process whereby the set of holdings is generated will be intelligible, though the set of holdings itself that results from this process will be unpatterned. . . .

. . . No doubt people will not long accept a distribution they believe is *unjust*. People want their society to be and to look just. But must the look of justice reside in a resulting pattern rather than in the underlying generating principles? We are in no position to conclude that the inhabitants of a society embodying an entitlement conception of justice in holdings will find it unacceptable. Still, it must be granted that were people's reasons for transferring some of their holdings to others always irrational or arbitrary, we would find this disturbing. (Suppose people always determined what holdings they would transfer, and to whom, by using a random device.) We feel more comfortable upholding the justice of an entitlement system if most of the transfers under it are done for reasons. This does not mean necessarily that all deserve what holdings they receive. It means only that there is a purpose or point to someone's transferring a holding to one person rather than to another; that usually we can see what the transferrer thinks he's gaining, what cause he thinks he's serving, and what goals he thinks he's helping to achieve, and so forth. . . . The system of entitlements is defensible when constituted by the individual aims of individual transactions. No overarching aim is needed, no distributional pattern is required.

To think that the task of a theory of distributive justice is to fill in the blank in "each according to his _____" is to be predisposed to search for a pattern; and the separate treatment of "from each according to his _____" treats production and distribution as two separate and independent issues. On an entitlement view these are *not* two separate questions. Whoever makes something, having bought or contracted for all other held resources used in the process (transferring some of his holdings for these cooperating factors), is entitled to it. The situation is *not* one of something's getting made, and there being an open question of who is to get it. Things come into the world already attached to people having entitlements over them. From the point of view of the historical entitlement conception of justice in holdings, those who start afresh to complete "to each according to his _____" treat objects as if they appeared from nowhere, out of nothing. . . .

So entrenched are maxims of the usual form that perhaps we should present the entitlement conception as a competitor. Ignoring acquisition and rectification, we might say: From each according to what he chooses to do, to each according to what he makes for himself (perhaps with the contracted aid of others) and what others choose to do for him and choose to give him of what they've been given previously (under this maxim) and haven't yet expended or transferred.

This, the discerning reader will have noticed, has its defects as a slogan. So as a summary and great simplification (and not as a maxim with any independent meaning) we have:

From each as they choose, to each as they are chosen.

HOW LIBERTY UPSETS PATTERNS

It is not clear how those holding alternative conceptions of distributive justice can reject the entitlement conception of justice in holdings. For suppose a distribution favored by one of these non-entitlement conceptions is realized. Let us suppose it is your favorite one and let us call this distribution D_1; perhaps everyone has an equal share, perhaps shares vary in accordance with some dimension you treasure. Now suppose that Wilt Chamberlain is greatly in demand by basketball teams, being a great gate attraction. (Also suppose contracts run only for a year, with players being free agents.) He signs the following sort of contract with a team: In each home game, twenty-five cents from the price of each ticket of admission goes to him. (We ignore the question of whether he is "gouging" the owners, letting them look out for themselves.) The season starts, and people cheerfully attend his team's games; they buy their tickets, each time dropping a separate twenty-five cents of their admission price into a special box with Chamberlain's name on it. They are excited about seeing him play; it is worth the total admission price to them. Let us suppose that in one season one million persons attend his home games, and Wilt Chamberlain winds up with $250,000, a much larger sum than the average income and larger even than anyone else has. Is he entitled to the income? Is this new distribution D_2, unjust? If so, why? There is *no* question about whether each of the people was entitled to the control over the resources they held in D_1; because that was the distribution (your favorite) that (for purposes of argument) we assumed was acceptable. Each of these persons *chose* to give twenty-five cents of their money to Chamberlain. They could have spent it on going to the movies, or on candy bars, or on copies of *Dissent* magazine, or of *Monthly Review*. But they all, at least one million of them, converged on giving it to Wilt Chamberlain in exchange for watching him play basketball. If D_1 was a just distribution, and people voluntarily moved from it to D_2, transferring parts of their shares they were given under D_1 (what was it for if not to do something with?), isn't D_2 also just? If the people were entitled to dispose of the resources to which they were entitled . . . , didn't this include their being entitled to give it to, or exchange it with, Wilt Chamberlain? Can anyone else complain on the grounds of justice? Each other person already has his legitimate share under D_1. Under D_1, there is nothing that anyone has that anyone else has a claim of justice against. After someone transfers something to Wilt Chamberlain, third parties *still* have their legitimate shares; *their* shares are not changed. By what process could such a transfer among two persons give rise to a legitimate claim of distributive justice on a portion of what was transferred, by a third party who had no claim of justice on any holding of the others *before* the transfer? To cut off objections irrelevant here, we might imagine the exchanges occurring in a socialist society, after hours. After playing whatever basketball he does in his daily work, or doing whatever other daily work he does, Wilt Chamberlain decides to put in *overtime* to earn additional money. (First his work quota is set; he works time over that.) Or imagine it is a skilled juggler people like to see, who puts on shows after hours.

Why might someone work overtime in a society in which it is assumed their needs are satisfied? Perhaps because they care about things other than needs. . . .

The general point illustrated by the Wilt Chamberlain example . . . is that no end-state principle or distributional patterned principle of justice can be continuously realized without continuous interference with people's lives. . . . To maintain a pattern one must either continually interfere to stop people from transferring resources as they wish to, or continually (or periodically) interfere to take from some persons resources that others for some reason chose to transfer to them. (But if some time limit is to be set on how long people may keep resources others voluntarily transfer to them, why let them keep these resources for *any* period of time? Why not have immediate confiscation?) It might be objected that all persons voluntarily will choose to refrain from actions which would upset the pattern. This presupposes unrealistically (1) that all will most want to maintain the pattern (are those who don't, to be "reeducated" or forced to undergo "self-criticism"?), (2) that each can gather enough information about his own actions and the ongoing activities of others to discover which of his actions will upset the pattern, and (3) that diverse and far-flung persons can coordinate their actions to dovetail into the pattern. . . .

. . . Any distributional pattern with any egalitarian component is overturnable by the voluntary actions of individual persons over time; as is every patterned condition with sufficient content so as actually to have been proposed as presenting the central core of distributive justice. . . .

The Procedural Republic
and the Unencumbered Self (1984)

Michael J. Sandel

Political philosophy seems often to reside at a distance from the world. Principles are one thing, politics another, and even our best efforts to "live up" to our ideals typically founder on the gap between theory and practice.[1]

But if political philosophy is unrealizable in one sense, it is unavoidable in another. This is the sense in which philosophy inhabits the world from the start; our practices and institutions are embodiments of theory. To engage in a political practice is already to stand in relation to theory.[2] For all our uncertainties about ultimate questions of political philosophy—of justice and value and the nature of the good life—the one thing we know is that we live *some* answer all the time.

In this essay I will try to explore the answer we live now, in contemporary America. What is the political philosophy implicit in our practices and institutions? How does it stand, as philosophy? And how do tensions in the philosophy find expression in our present political condition?

It may be objected that it is a mistake to look for a single philosophy, that we live no "answer," only answers. But a plurality of answers is itself a kind of answer. And the political theory that affirms this plurality is the theory I propose to explore.

THE RIGHT AND THE GOOD

We might begin by considering a certain moral and political vision. It is a liberal vision, and like most liberal visions gives pride of place to justice, fairness, and individual rights. Its core thesis is this: a just society seeks not to promote any particular ends, but enables its citizens to pursue their own ends, consistent with a similar liberty for all; it therefore must govern by principles that do not presuppose any particular conception of the good. What justifies these regulative principles above all is not that they maximize the general welfare, or cultivate virtue, or otherwise promote the good, but rather that they conform to the concept of *right*, a moral category given prior to the good, and independent of it.

This liberalism says, in other words, that what makes the just society just is not the *telos* or purpose or end at which it aims, but precisely its refusal to choose in advance among competing purposes and ends. In its constitution and its laws, the just society seeks to provide a framework within which its

From *Political Theory*, Vol. 12, No. 1 (Feb. 1984), pp. 81–96. Reprinted by permission of Sage Publications, Inc.

citizens can pursue their own values and ends, consistent with a similar liberty for others.

The ideal I've described might be summed up in the claim that the right is prior to the good, and in two senses: The priority of the right means first, that individual rights cannot be sacrificed for the sake of the general good (in this it opposes utilitarianism), and second, that the principles of justice that specify these rights cannot be premised on any particular vision of the good life. (In this it opposes teleological conceptions in general.)

This is the liberalism of much contemporary moral and political philosophy, most fully elaborated by Rawls, and indebted to Kant for its philosophical foundations.[3] But I am concerned here less with the lineage of this vision than with what seem to me three striking facts about it.

First, it has a deep and powerful philosophical appeal. Second, despite its philosophical force, the claim for the priority of the right over the good ultimately fails. And third, despite its philosophical failure, this liberal vision is the one by which we live. For us in late twentieth century America, it is our vision, the theory most thoroughly embodied in the practices and institutions most central to our public life. And seeing how it goes wrong as philosophy may help us to diagnose our present political condition. So first, its philosophical power; second, its philosophical failure; and third, however briefly, its uneasy embodiment in the world.

But before taking up these three claims, it is worth pointing out a central theme that connects them. And that is a certain conception of the person, of what it is to be a moral agent. Like all political theories, the liberal theory I have described is something more than a set of regulative principles. It is also a view about the way the world is, and the way we move within it. At the heart of this ethic lies a vision of the person that both inspires and undoes it. As I will try to argue now, what make this ethic so compelling, but also, finally, vulnerable, are the promise and the failure of the unencumbered self.

KANTIAN FOUNDATIONS

The liberal ethic asserts the priority of right, and seeks principles of justice that do not presuppose any particular conception of the good.[4] This is what Kant means by the supremacy of the moral law, and what Rawls means when he writes that "justice is the first virtue of social institutions."[5] Justice is more than just another value. It provides the framework that *regulates* the play of competing values and ends; it must therefore have a sanction independent of those ends. But it is not obvious where such a sanction could be found.

Theories of justice, and for that matter, ethics, have typically founded their claims on one or another conception of human purposes and ends. Thus Aristotle said the measure of a *polis* is the good at which it aims, and even J. S. Mill, who in the nineteenth century called "justice the chief part, and incomparably the most binding part of all morality," made justice an instrument of utilitarian ends.[6]

This is the solution Kant's ethic rejects. Different persons typically have different desires and ends, and so any principle derived from them can only be contingent. But the moral law needs a *categorical* foundation, not a contingent one. Even so universal a desire as happiness will not do. People still differ in what happiness consists of, and to install any particular conception as regulative would impose on some the conceptions of others, and so deny at least to some the freedom to choose their *own* conceptions. In any case, to govern ourselves in conformity with desires and inclinations, given as they are by nature or circumstance, is not really to be *self*-governing at all. It is rather a refusal of freedom, a capitulation to determinations given outside us.

According to Kant, the right is "derived entirely from the concept of freedom in the external relationships of human beings, and has nothing to do with the end which all men have by nature [i.e., the aim of achieving happiness] or with the recognized means of attaining this end."[7] As such, it must have a basis prior to all empirical ends. Only when I am governed by principles that do not presuppose any particular ends am I free to pursue my own ends consistent with a similar freedom for all.

But this still leaves the question of what the basis of the right could possibly be. If it must be a basis prior to all purposes and ends, unconditioned even by what Kant calls "the special circumstances of human nature,"[8] where could such a basis conceivably be found? Given the stringent demands of the Kantian ethic, the moral law would seem almost to require a foundation in nothing, for any empirical precondition would undermine its priority. "Duty!" asks Kant at his most lyrical, "What origin is there worthy of thee, and where is to be found the root of thy noble descent which proudly rejects all kinship with the inclinations?"[9]

His answer is that the basis of the moral law is to be found in the *subject*, not the object of practical reason, a subject capable of an autonomous will. No empirical end, but rather "a subject of ends, namely a rational being himself, must be made the ground for all maxims of action."[10] Nothing other than what Kant calls "the subject of all possible ends himself" can give rise to the right, for only this subject is also the subject of an autonomous will. Only this subject could be that "something which elevates man above himself as part of the world of sense" and enables him to participate in an ideal, unconditioned realm wholly independent of our social and psychological inclinations. And only this thoroughgoing independence can afford us the detachment we need if we are ever freely to choose for ourselves, unconditioned by the vagaries of circumstance.[11]

Who or what exactly *is* this subject? It is, in a certain sense, *us*. The moral law, afterall, is a law we give *ourselves*: we don't *find* it, we *will* it. That is how it (and we) escape the reign of nature and circumstance and merely empirical ends. But what is important to see is that the "we" who do the willing are not "we" qua particular persons, you and me, each for ourselves—the moral law is not up to us as individuals—but "we" qua participants in what Kant calls "pure practical reason," "we" qua participants in a transcendental subject.

Now what is to guarantee that I *am* a subject of this kind, capable of exercising pure practical reason? Well, strictly speaking, there *is* no guarantee; the transcendental subject is only a possibility. But it is a possibility I must *presuppose* if I am to think of myself as a free moral agent. Were I wholly an empirical being, I would not be capable of freedom, for every exercise of will would be conditioned by the desire for some object. All choice would be heteronomous choice, governed by the pursuit of some end. My will could never be a first cause, only the effect of some prior cause, the instrument of one or another impulse or inclination. "When we think of ourselves as free," writes Kant, "we transfer ourselves into the intelligible world as members and recognize the autonomy of the will."[12] And so the notion of a subject prior to and independent of experience, such as the Kantian ethic requires, appears not only possible but indispensible, a necessary presupposition of the possibility of freedom.

How does all of this come back to politics? As the subject is prior to its ends, so the right is prior to the good. Society is best arranged when it is governed by principles that do not presuppose any particular conception of the good, for any other arrangement would fail to respect persons as being capable of choice; it would treat them as objects rather than subjects, as means rather than ends in themselves.

We can see in this way how Kant's notion of the subject is bound up with the claim for the priority of right. But for those in the Anglo-American tradition, the transcendental subject will seem a strange foundation for a familiar ethic. Surely, one may think, we can take rights seriously and affirm the primacy of justice without embracing the *Critique of Pure Reason*. This, in any case, is the project of Rawls.

He wants to save the priority of right from the obscurity of the transcendental subject. Kant's idealist metaphysic, for all its moral and political advantage, cedes too much to the transcendent, and wins for justice its primacy only by denying it its human situation. "To develop a viable Kantian conception of justice," Rawls writes, "the force and content of Kant's doctrine must be detached from its background in transcendental idealism" and recast within the "canons of a reasonable empiricism."[13] And so Rawls' project is to preserve Kant's moral and political teaching by replacing Germanic obscurities with a domesticated metaphysic more congenial to the Anglo-American temper. This is the role of the original position.

FROM TRANSCENDENTAL SUBJECT TO UNENCUMBERED SELF

The original position tries to provide what Kant's transcendental argument cannot—a foundation for the right that is prior to the good, but still situated in the world. Sparing all but essentials, the original position works like this: It invites us to imagine the principles we would choose to govern our society if we were to choose them in advance, before we knew the particular persons we would be—whether rich or poor, strong or weak, lucky or unlucky—before we knew even our interests or aims or conceptions of the good. These principles—the ones we would choose in that imaginary situation—are the principles of justice. What is more, if it works, they are principles that do not presuppose any particular ends.

What they *do* presuppose is a certain picture of the person, of the way we must be if we are beings for whom justice is the first virtue. This is the picture of the unencumbered self, a self understood as prior to and independent of purposes and ends.

Now the unencumbered self describes first of all the way we stand toward the things we have, or want, or seek. It means there is always a distinction between the values I *have* and the person I *am*. To identify any characteristics as *my* aims, ambitions, desires, and so on, is always to imply some subject "me" standing behind them, at a certain distance, and the shape of this "me" must be given prior to any of the aims or attributes I bear. One consequence of this distance is to put the self *itself* beyond the reach of its experience, to secure its identity once and for all. Or to put the point another way, it rules out the possibility of what we might call *constitutive* ends. No role or commitment could define me so completely that I could not understand myself without it. No project could be so essential that turning away from it would call into question the person I am.

For the unencumbered self, what matters above all, what is most essential to our personhood, are not the ends we choose but our capacity to choose them. The original position sums up this central claim about us. "It is not our aims that primarily reveal our nature," writes Rawls, "but rather the principles that we would acknowledge to govern the background conditions under which these aims are to be formed. We should therefore reverse the relation between the right and the good proposed by teleological doctrines and view the right as prior."[14]

Only if the self is prior to its ends can the right be prior to the good. Only if my identity is never tied to the aims and interests I may have at any moment can I think of myself as a free and independent agent, capable of choice.

This notion of independence carries consequences for the kind of community of which we are capable. Understood as unencumbered selves, we are of course free to join in voluntary association with others, and so are capable of community in the cooperative sense. What is denied to the unencumbered self is the possibility of membership in any community bound by moral ties antecedent to choice; he cannot belong to any community where the self *itself* could be at stake. Such a community—call it constitutive as against merely cooperative—would engage the identity as well as the interests of the participants, and so implicate its members in a citizenship more thoroughgoing than the unencumbered self can know.

For justice to be primary, then, we must be creatures of a certain kind, related to human circumstance in a certain way. We must stand to our circumstance always at a certain distance, whether as transcendental subject in the case of Kant, or as unencumbered selves in the case of Rawls. Only in this way can we view ourselves as subjects as well as objects of experience, as agents and not just instruments of the purposes we pursue.

The unencumbered self and the ethic it inspires, taken together, hold out a liberating vision. Freed from the dicates of nature and the sanction of social roles, the human subject is installed as sovereign, cast as the author of the only moral meanings there are. As participants in pure practical reason, or as parties to the original position, we are free to construct principles of justice unconstrained by an order of value antecedently given. And as actual, individual selves, we are free to choose our purposes and ends unbound by such an order, or by custom or tradition or inherited status. So long as they are not unjust, our conceptions of the good carry weight, whatever they are, simply in virtue of our having chosen them. We are, in Rawls' words, "self-originating sources of valid claims."[15]

This is an exhilarating promise, and the liberalism it animates is perhaps the fullest expression of the Enlightenment's quest for the self-defining subject. But is it true? Can we make sense of our moral and political life by the light of the self-image it requires? I do not think we can, and I will try to show why not by arguing first within the liberal project, then beyond it.

JUSTICE AND COMMUNITY

We have focused so far on the foundations of the liberal vision, on the way it derives the principles it defends. Let us turn briefly now to the substance of those principles, using Rawls as our example. Sparing all but essentials once again, Rawls' two principles of justice are these: first, equal basic liberties for all, and second, only those social and economic inequalities that benefit the least-advantaged members of society (the difference principle).

In arguing for these principles, Rawls argues against two familiar alternatives—utilitarianism and libertarianism. He argues against utilitarianism that it fails to take seriously the distinction between persons. In seeking to maximize the general welfare, the utilitarian treats society as [a] whole as if it were a single person; it conflates our many, diverse desires into a single system of desires, and tries to maximize. It is indifferent to the distribution of satisfactions among persons, except insofar as this may affect the overall sum. But this fails to respect our plurality and distinctness. It uses some as means to the happiness of all, and so fails to respect each as an end in himself. While utilitarians may sometimes defend individual rights, their defense must rest on the calculation that respecting those rights will serve utility in the long run. But this calculation is contingent and uncertain. So long as utility is what Mill said it is, "the ultimate appeal on all ethical questions,"[16] individual rights can never be secure. To avoid the danger that their life prospects might one day be sacrificed for the greater good of others, the parties to the original position therefore insist on certain basic liberties for all, and make those liberties prior.

If utilitarians fail to take seriously the distinctness of persons, libertarians go wrong by failing to acknowledge the arbitrariness of fortune. They define as just whatever distribution results from an efficient market economy, and oppose all redistribution on the grounds that people are entitled to whatever they get, so long as they do not cheat or steal or otherwise violate someone's rights in getting it. Rawls opposes this principle on the ground that the distribution of talents and assets and even efforts by which some get more and others get less is arbitrary from a moral point of view, a matter of good luck. To distribute the good things in life on the basis of these differences is not to do justice, but simply to carry over into human arrangements the arbitrariness of social and natural contingency. We deserve, as individuals, neither the talents our good fortune may have brought, nor the benefits that flow from them. We should therefore regard these talents as common assets, and regard one another as common beneficiaries of the rewards they bring. "Those who have been favored by nature, whoever they are, may gain from their good fortune only on terms that improve the situation of those who have lost out. In justice as fairness, men agree to share one another's fate."[17]

This is the reasoning that leads to the difference principle. Notice how it reveals, in yet another guise, the logic of the unencumbered self. I cannot be said to deserve the benefits that flow from, say, my fine physique and good looks, because they are only accidental, not essential facts about me. They describe attributes I *have*, not the person I *am*, and so cannot give rise to a claim of desert. Being an unencumbered self, this is true of *everything* about me. And so I cannot, as an individual, deserve anything at all.

However jarring to our ordinary understandings this argument may be, the picture so far remains intact; the priority of right, the dental of desert, and the unencumbered self all hang impressively together.

But the difference principle requires more, and it is here that the argument comes undone. The difference principle begins with the thought, congenial to the unencumbered self, that the assets I have are only accidentally mine. But it ends by assuming that these assets are therefore *common* assets and that society has a prior claim on the fruits of their exercise. But this assumption is without warrant. Simply because I, as an individual, do not have a privileged claim on the assets accidentally residing "here," it does not follow that everyone in the world collectively does. For there is no reason to think that their location in society's province or, for that matter, within the province of humankind, is any *less* arbitrary from a moral point of view. And if their arbitrariness within *me* makes them ineligible to serve *my* ends, there seems no obvious reason why their arbitrariness within any particular society should not make them ineligible to serve that society's ends as well.

To put the point another way, the difference principle, like utilitarianism, is a principle of sharing. As such, it must presuppose some prior moral tie among those whose assets it would deploy and whose efforts it would enlist in a common endeavor. Otherwise, it is simply a formula for using some as means to others' ends, a formula this liberalism is committed to reject.

But on the cooperative vision of community alone, it is unclear what the moral basis for this sharing could be. Short of the constitutive conception, deploying an individual's assets for the sake of the common good would seem an offense against the "plurality and distinctness" of individuals this liberalism seeks above all to secure.

If those whose fate I am required to share really are, morally speaking, *others*, rather than fellow participants in a way of life with which my identity is bound, the difference principle falls prey to the same objections as utilitarianism. Its claim on me is not the claim of a constitutive community whose attachments I acknowledge, but rather the claim of a concatenated collectivity whose entanglements I confront.

What the difference principle requires, but cannot provide, is some way of identifying those *among* whom the assets I bear are properly regarded as common, some way of seeing ourselves as mutually indebted and morally engaged to begin with. But as we have seen, the constitutive aims and attachments that would save and situate the difference principle are precisely the ones denied to the liberal self; the moral encumbrances and antecedent obligations they imply would undercut the priority of right.

What, then, of those encumbrances? The point so far is that we cannot be persons for whom justice is primary, and also be persons for whom the difference principle is a principle of justice. But which must give way? Can we view ourselves as independent selves, independent in the sense that our identity is never tied to our aims and attachments?[18]

I do not think we can, at least not without cost to those loyalties and convictions whose moral force consists partly in the fact that living by them is inseparable from understanding ourselves as the particular persons we are—as members of this family or community or nation or people, as bearers of that history, as citizens of this republic. Allegiances such as these are more than values I happen to have, and to hold, at a certain distance. They go beyond the obligations I voluntarily incur and the "natural duties" I owe to human beings as such. They allow that to some I owe more than justice requires or even permits, not by reason of agreements I have made but instead in virtue of those more or less enduring attachments and commitments that, taken together, partly define the person I am.

To imagine a person incapable of constitutive attachments such as these is not to conceive an ideally free and rational agent, but to imagine a person wholly without character, without moral depth. For to have character is to know that I move in a history I neither summon nor command, which carries consequences nonetheless for my choices and conduct. It draws me closer to some and more distant from others; it makes some aims more appropriate, others less so. As a self-interpreting being, I am able to reflect on my history and in this sense to distance myself from it, but the distance is always precarious and provisional, the point of reflection never finally secured outside the history itself. But the liberal ethic puts the self beyond the reach of its experience, beyond deliberation and reflection. Denied the expansive self-understandings

that could shape a common life, the liberal self is left to lurch between detachment on the one hand, and entanglement on the other. Such is the fate of the
unencumbered self, and its liberating promise.

THE PROCEDURAL REPUBLIC

But before my case can be complete, I need to consider one powerful reply.
While it comes from a liberal direction, its spirit is more practical than philosophical. It says, in short, that I am asking too much. It is one thing to seek
constitutive attachments in our private lives; among families and friends, and
certain tightly knit groups, there may be found a common good that makes
justice and rights less pressing. But with public life—at least today, and probably always—it is different. So long as the nation-state is the primary form of
political association, talk of constitutive community too easily suggests a
darker politics rather than a brighter one; amid echoes of the moral majority,
the priority of right, for all its philosophical faults, still seems the safer hope.

This is a challenging rejoinder, and no account of political community in
the twentieth century can fail to take it seriously. It is challenging not least because it calls into question the status of political philosophy and its relation to
the world. For if my argument is correct, if the liberal vision we have considered is not morally self-sufficient but parasitic on a notion of community it of-
ficially rejects, then we should expect to find that the political practice that
embodies this vision is not *practically* self-sufficient either—that it must draw
on a sense of community it cannot supply and may even undermine. But is
that so far from the circumstance we face today? Could it be that through the
original position darkly, on the far side of the veil of ignorance, we may
glimpse an intimation of our predicament, a refracted vision of ourselves?

How does the liberal vision—and its failure—help us make sense of our
public life and its predicament? Consider, to begin, the following paradox in the
citizen's relation to the modern welfare state. In many ways, we in the 1980s
stand near the completion of a liberal project that has run its course from the
New Deal through the Great Society and into the present. But notwithstanding
the extension of the franchise and the expansion on individual rights and entitlements in recent decades, there is a widespread sense that, individually and
collectively, our control over the forces that govern our lives is receding rather
than increasing. This sense is deepened by what appear simultaneously as the
power and the powerlessness of the nation-state. [On] the one hand, increasing
numbers of citizens view the state as an overly intrusive presence, more likely to
frustrate their purposes than advance them. And yet, despite its unprecedented
role in the economy and society, the modern state seems itself disempowered,
unable effectively to control the domestic economy, to respond to persisting
social ills, or to work America's will in the world.

This is a paradox that has fed the appeals of recent politicians (including
Carter and Reagan), even as it has frustrated their attempts to govern. To sort

it out, we need to identify the public philosophy implicit in our political practice, and to reconstruct its arrival. We need to trace the advent of the procedural republic, by which I mean a public life animated by the liberal vision and self-image we've considered.

The story of the procedural republic goes back in some ways to the founding of the republic, but its central drama begins to unfold around the turn of the century. As national markets and large-scale enterprise displaced a decentralized economy, the decentralized political forms of the early republic became outmoded as well. If democracy was to survive, the concentration of economic power would have to be met by a similar concentration of political power. But the Progressives understood, or some of them did, that the success of democracy required more than the centralization of government; it also re-quired the nationalization of politics. The primary form of political communi-ty had to be a recast on a national scale. For Herbert Croly, writing in 1909, the "nationalizing of American political, economic, and social life" was "an essen-tially formative and enlightening political transformation." We would become more of a democracy only as we became "more of a nation in ideas, in institu-tions, and in spirit."[19]

This nationalizing project would be consummated in the New Deal, but for the democratic tradition in America, the embrace of the nation was a deci-sive departure. From Jefferson to the populists, the party of democracy in American political debate had been, roughly speaking, the party of the provinces, of decentralized power, of small-town and small-scale America. And against them had stood the party of the nation—first Federalists, then Whigs, then the Republicans of Lincoln—a party that spoke for the consolida-tion of the union. It was thus the historic achievement of the New Deal to unite, in a single party and political program, what Samuel Beer has called "liberalism and the national idea."[20]

What matters for our purpose is that, in the twentieth century, liberalism made its peace with concentrated power. But it was understood at the start that the terms of this peace required a strong sense of national community, morally and politically to underwrite the extended involvements of a modern industrial order. If a virtuous republic of small-scale, democratic communities was no longer a possibility, a national republic seemed democracy's next best hope. This was still, in principle at least, a politics of the common good. It looked to the nation, not as a neutral framework for the play of competing interests, but rather as a formative community, concerned to shape a common life suited to the scale of modern social and economic forms.

But this project failed. By the mid- or late twentieth century, the national republic had run its course. Except for extraordinary moments, such as war, the nation proved too vast a scale across which to cultivate the shared self-understandings necessary to community in the formative, or constitutive sense. And so the gradual shift, in our practices and institutions, from a public philosophy of common purposes to one of fair procedures, from a politics of good to a politics of right, from the national republic to the procedural republic.

OUR PRESENT PREDICAMENT

A full account of this transition would take a detailed look at the changing shape of political institutions, constitutional interpretation, and the terms of political discourse in the broadest sense. But I suspect we would find in the *practice* of the procedural republic two broad tendencies foreshadowed by its philosophy: first, a tendency to crowd out democratic possibilities; second, a tendency to undercut the kind of community on which it nonetheless depends.

Where liberty in the early republic was understood as a function of democratic institutions and dispersed power,[21] liberty in the procedural republic is defined in opposition to democracy, as an individual's guarantee against what the majority might will. I am free insofar as I am the bearer of rights, where rights are trumps.[22] Unlike the liberty of the early republic, the modern version permits—in fact even requires—concentrated power. This has to do with the universalizing logic of rights. Insofar as I have a right, whether to free speech or a minimum income, its provision cannot be left to the vagaries of local preferences but must be assured at the most comprehensive level of political association. It cannot be one thing in New York and another in Alabama. As rights and entitlements expand, politics is therefore displaced from smaller forms of association and relocated at the most universal form—in our case, the nation. And even as politics flows to the nation, power shifts away from democratic institutions (such as legislatures and political parties) and toward institutions designed to be insulated from democratic pressures, and hence better equipped to dispense and defend individual rights (notably the judiciary and bureaucracy).

These institutional developments may begin to account for the sense of powerlessness that the welfare state fails to address and in some ways doubtless deepens. But it seems to me a further clue to our condition recalls even more directly the predicament of the unencumbered self—lurching, as we left it, between detachment on the one hand, the entanglement on the other. For it is a striking feature of the welfare state that it offers a powerful promise of individual rights, and also demands of its citizens a high measure of mutual engagement. But the self-image that attends the rights cannot sustain the engagement.

As bearers of rights, where rights are trumps, we think of ourselves as freely choosing, individual selves, unbound by obligations antecedent to rights, or to the agreements we make. And yet, as citizens of the procedural republic that secures these rights, we find ourselves implicated willy-nilly in a formidable array of dependencies and expectations we did not choose and increasingly reject.

In our public life, we are more entangled, but less attached, than ever before. It is as though the unencumbered self presupposed by the liberal ethic had begun to come true—less liberated than disempowered, entangled in a network of obligations and involvements unassociated with any act of will, and yet unmediated by those common identifications or expansive self-definitions that would make them tolerable. As the scale of social and political organization has become more comprehensive, the terms of our collective identity have become more fragmented, and the forms of political life have outrun the common purpose needed to sustain them.

Something like this, it seems to me, has been unfolding in America for the past half-century or so. I hope I have said at least enough to suggest the shape a fuller story might take. And I hope in any case to have conveyed a certain view about politics and philosophy and the relation between them—that our practices and institutions are themselves embodiments of theory, and to unravel their predicament is, at least in part, to seek after the self-image of the age.

Notes

1. An excellent example of this view can be found in Samuel Huntington, *American Politics: The Promise of Disharmony* (Cambridge: Harvard University Press, 1981). See especially his discussion of the "ideals versus institutions" gap, pp. 10–12, 39–41, 61–84, 221–262.

2. See, for example, the conceptions of a "practice" advanced by Alasdair MacIntyre and Charles Taylor. MacIntyre, *After Virtue* (Notre Dame: University of Notre Dame Press, 1981), pp. 175–209. Taylor, "Interpretation and the Sciences of Man," *Review of Metaphysics* 25, (1971), pp. 3–51.

3. John Rawls, *A Theory of Justice* (Oxford: Oxford University Press, 1971). Immanuel Kant, *Groundwork of the Metaphysics of Morals*, trans. H. J. Paton (1785; New York: Harper and Row, 1956). Kant, *Critique of Pure Reason*, trans. Norman Kemp Smith (1781, 1787; London: Macmillan, 1929). Kant, *Critique of Practical Reason*, trans. L. W. Beck (1788; Indianapolis: Bobbs-Merrill, 1956). Kant, "On the Common Saying: 'This May Be True in Theory, But It Does Not Apply in Practice,' " in Hans Reiss, ed., *Kant's Political Writings* (1793; Cambridge: Cambridge University Press, 1970). Other recent versions of the claim for the priority of the right over good can be found in Robert Nozick, *Anarchy, State and Utopia* (New York: Basic Books, 1974); Ronald Dworkin, *Taking Rights Seriously* (London: Duckworth, 1977); Bruce Ackerman, *Social Justice in the Liberal State* (New Haven: Yale University Press, 1980).

4. This section, and the two that follow, summarize arguments developed more fully in Michael Sandel, *Liberalism and the Limits of Justice* (Cambridge: Cambridge University Press, 1982).

5. Rawls (1971), p. 3.

6. John Stuart Mill, *Utilitarianism, in The Utilitarians* (1893; Garden City: Doubleday, 1973), p. 465. Mill, *On Liberty, in The Utilitarians*, p. 485 (originally published 1849).

7. Kant (1793), p. 73.

8. Kant (1785), p. 92.

9. Kant (1788), p. 89.

10. Kant (1785), p. 105.

11. Kant (1788), p. 89.

12. Kant (1785), p. 121.

13. Rawls, "The Basic Structure as Subject," *American Philosophical Quarterly* (1977), p. 165.

14. Rawls (1971), p. 560.

15. Rawls, "Kantian Constructivism in Moral Theory," *Journal of Philosophy* 77 (1980), p. 543.

16. Mill (1849), p. 485.

17. Rawls (1971), pp. 101–102.

18. The account that follows is a tentative formulation of themes requiring more detailed elaboration and support.

19. Croly, *The Promise of American Life* (Indianapolis: Bobbs-Merrill, 1965), pp. 270–273.

20. Beer, "Liberalism and the National Idea," *The Public Interest*, Fall (1966), pp. 70–82.

21. See, for example, Laurence Tribe, *American Constitutional Law* (Mineola: The Foundation Press, 1978), pp. 2–3.

22. See Ronald Dworkin, "Liberalism," in Stuart Hampshire, ed., *Public and Private Morality* (Cambridge: Cambridge University Press, 1978), p. 136.

Feminist Transformations of Moral Theory (1990)

Virginia Held

The history of philosophy, including the history of ethics, has been constructed from male points of view, and has been built on assumptions and concepts that are by no means gender-neutral. Feminists characteristically begin with different concerns and give different emphases to the issues we consider than do non-feminist approaches. . . . Within philosophy, feminists often start with, and focus on, quite different issues than those found in standard philosophy and ethics, however "standard" is understood. Far from providing mere additional insights which can be incorporated into traditional theory, feminist explorations often require radical transformations of existing fields of inquiry and theory. From a feminist point of view, moral theory along with almost all theory will have to be transformed to take adequate account of the experience of women.

I shall in this paper begin with a brief examination of how various fundamental aspects of the history of ethics have not been gender-neutral. And I shall discuss three issues where feminist rethinking is transforming moral concepts and theories.

Excerpted from *Philosophy and Phenomenological Research*, Vol. I, Supplement, Fall 1990, pp. 321–344. Reprinted with permission of the publisher.

THE HISTORY OF ETHICS

Consider the ideals embodied in the phrase "the man of reason." As Genevieve Lloyd has told the story, what has been taken to characterize the man of reason may have changed from historical period to historical period, but in each, the character ideal of the man of reason has been constructed in conjunction with a rejection of whatever has been taken to be characteristic of the feminine. ...

This has of course fundamentally affected the history of philosophy and of ethics. The split between reason and emotion is one of the most familiar of philosophical conceptions. And the advocacy of reason "controlling" unruly emotion, of rationality guiding responsible human action against the blindness of passion, has a long and highly influential history. ... We should certainly now be alert to the ways in which reason has been associated with male endeavor, emotion with female weakness, and the ways in which this is of course not an accidental association. ...

Reason, in asserting its claims and winning its status in human history, was thought to have to conquer the female forces of Unreason. Reason and clarity of thought were early associated with maleness. ... In later Greek philosophical thought, the form/matter distinction was articulated, and with a similar hierarchical and gendered association. Maleness was aligned with active, determinate, and defining form; femaleness with mere passive, indeterminate, and inferior matter. ...

The associations, between Reason, form, knowledge, and maleness, have persisted in various guises, and have permeated what has been thought to be moral knowledge as well as what has been thought to be scientific knowledge, and what has been thought to be the practice of morality. The associations between the philosophical concepts and gender cannot be merely dropped, and the concepts retained regardless of gender, because gender has been built into them in such a way that without it, they will have to be different concepts. As feminists repeatedly show, if the concept of "human" were built on what we think about "woman" rather than what we think about "man," it would be a very different concept. Ethics, thus, has not been a search for universal, or truly human guidance, but a gender-biased enterprise.

Other distinctions and associations have supplemented and reinforced the identification of reason with maleness, and of the irrational with the female; on this and other grounds "man" has been associated with the human, "woman" with the natural. Prominent among distinctions reinforcing the latter view has been that between the public and the private. ... It has been supposed that in the public realm, man transcends his animal nature and creates human history. As citizen, he creates government and law; as warrior, he protects society by his willingness to risk death; and as artist or philosopher, he overcomes his human mortality. Here, in the public realm, morality should guide human decision. In the household, in contrast, it has been supposed that women merely "reproduce" life as natural, biological matter. Within the household, the "natural" needs of man for food and shelter are served, and new instances of the biological creature that man is are brought into being. But what is distinctively human, and what transcends any given level of development to create human progress, are thought to occur elsewhere.

This contrast was made highly explicit in Aristotle's conceptions of polis and household; it has continued to affect the basic assumptions of a remarkably broad swath of thought ever since. In ancient Athens, women were confined to the household; the public sphere was literally a male domain. In more recent history, though women have been permitted to venture into public space, the associations of the public, historically male sphere with the distinctively human, and of the household, historically a female sphere, with the merely natural and repetitious, have persisted. These associations have deeply affected moral theory, which has often supposed the transcendent, public domain to be relevant to the foundations of morality in ways that the natural behavior of women in the household could not be. . . . Without feminist insistence on the relevance for morality of the experience in mothering, this context is largely ignored by moral theorists. And yet, from a gender-neutral point of view, how can this vast and fundamental domain of human experience possibly be imagined to lie "outside morality"?

The result of the public/private distinction, as usually formulated, has been to privilege the points of view of men in the public domains of state and law, and later in the marketplace, and to discount the experience of women. Mothering has been conceptualized as a primarily biological activity, even when performed by humans, and virtually no moral theory in the history of ethics has taken mothering, as experienced by women, seriously as a source of moral insight, until feminists in recent years have begun to. Women have been seen as emotional rather than as rational beings, and thus as incapable of full moral personhood. Women's behavior has been interpreted as either "natural" and driven by instinct, and thus as irrelevant to morality and to the construction of moral principles, or it has been interpreted as, at best, in need of instruction and supervision by males better able to know what morality requires and better able to live up to its demands. . . .

These images, of the feminine as what must be overcome if knowledge and morality are to be achieved, of female experience as naturally irrelevant to morality, and of women as inherently deficient moral creatures, are built into the history of ethics. Feminists examine these images, and see that they are not the incidental or merely idiosyncratic suppositions of a few philosophers whose views on many topics depart far from the ordinary anyway. Such views are the nearly uniform reflection in philosophical and ethical theory of patriarchal attitudes pervasive throughout human history. Or they are exaggerations even of ordinary male experience, which exaggerations then reinforce rather than temper other patriarchal conceptions and institutions. They distort the actual experience and aspirations of many men as well as of women. . . .

As feminists, we deplore the patriarchal attitudes that so much of philosophy and moral theory reflect. But we recognize that the problem is more serious even than changing those attitudes. For moral theory as so far developed is incapable of correcting itself without an almost total transformation. It cannot simply absorb the gender that has been "left behind," even if both genders would want it to. To continue to build morality on rational principles opposed to the emotions and to include women among the rational will leave no one to reflect the promptings of the heart, which promptings can be moral rather than merely instinctive. To simply bring women into the public and male domain of the polis will leave no one to speak for the household. Its values have been hitherto unrecognized, but they are often moral values. Or to continue to seek contractual restraints on the pursuits of self-interest by atomistic individuals, and to have women join men in devotion to these pursuits, will leave no one involved in the nurturance of children and cultivation of social relations, which nurturance and cultivation can be of greatest moral import.

There are very good reasons for women not to want simply to be accorded entry as equals into the enterprise of morality as so far developed. ... Women should clearly not agree, as the price of admission to the masculine realm of traditional morality, to abandon our own moral concerns as women.

And so we are groping to shape new moral theory. Understandably, we do not yet have fully worked out feminist moral theories to offer. ...

Not all feminists, by any means, agree that there are distinctive feminist virtues or values. Some are especially skeptical of the attempt to give positive value to such traditional "feminine virtues" as a willingness to nurture, or an affinity with caring, or reluctance to seek independence. They see this approach as playing into the hands of those who would confine women to traditional roles. Other feminists are skeptical of all claims about women as such, emphasizing that women are divided by class and race and sexual orientation in ways that make any conclusions drawn from "women's experience" dubious.

Still, it is possible, I think, to discern various important focal points evident in current feminist attempts to transform ethics into a theoretical and practical activity that could be acceptable from a feminist point of view. In the glimpse I have presented of bias in the history of ethics, I focused on what, from a feminist point of view, are three of its most questionable aspects: 1) the split between reason and emotion and the devaluation of emotion; 2) the public/private distinction and the relegation of the private to the natural; and 3) the concept of the self as constructed from a male point of view. In the remainder of this article, I shall consider further how some feminists are exploring these topics. We are showing how their previous treatment has been distorted, and we are trying to reenvision the realities and recommendations with which these aspects of moral theorizing do and should try to deal.

I. REASON AND EMOTION

In the area of moral theory in the modern era, the priority accorded to reason has taken two major forms. A) On the one hand has been the Kantian, or Kantian-inspired search for very general, abstract, deontological, universal moral principles by which rational beings should be guided. Kant's Categorical Imperative is a foremost example: it suggests that all moral problems can be handled by applying an impartial, pure, rational principle to particular cases. It requires that we try to see what the general features of the problem before us are, and that we apply an abstract principle, or rules derivable from it, to this problem. On this view, this procedure should be adequate for all moral decisions. We should thus be able to act as reason recommends, and resist yielding to emotional inclinations and desires in conflict with our rational wills.

B) On the other hand, the priority accorded to reason in the modern era has taken a Utilitarian form. The Utilitarian approach, reflected in rational choice theory, recognizes that persons have desires and interests, and suggests rules of rational choice for maximizing the satisfaction of these. While some philosophers in this tradition espouse egoism, especially of an intelligent and long-term kind, many do not. They begin, however, with assumptions that what are morally relevant are gains and losses of utility to theoretically isolatable individuals, and that the outcome at which morality should aim is the maximization of the utility of individuals. Rational calculation about such an outcome will, in this view, provide moral recommendations to guide all our choices. As with the Kantian approach, the Utilitarian approach relies on abstract general principles or rules to be applied to particular cases. And it holds that although emotion is, in fact, the source of our desires for certain objectives, the task of morality should be to instruct us on how to pursue those objectives most rationally. Emotional attitudes toward moral issues themselves interfere with rationality and should be disregarded. Among the questions Utilitarians can ask can be questions about which emotions to cultivate, and which desires to try to change, but these questions are to be handled in the terms of rational calculation, not of what our feelings suggest.

Although the conceptions of what the judgments of morality should be based on, and of how reason should guide moral decision, are different in Kantian and in Utilitarian approaches, both share a reliance on a highly abstract, universal principle as the appropriate source of moral guidance, and both share the view that moral problems are to be solved by the application of such an abstract principle to particular cases. Both share an admiration for the rules of reason to be appealed to in moral contexts, and both denigrate emotional responses to moral issues. . . .

A genuinely universal or gender-neutral moral theory would be one which would take account of the experience and concerns of women as fully as it would take account of the experience and concerns of men. When we focus on the experience of women, however, we seem to be able to see a set of moral concerns becoming salient that differs from those of traditional or standard moral theory. Women's experience of moral problems seems to lead us to be especially concerned with actual relationships between embodied persons, and with what these relationships seem to require. Women are often inclined to attend to rather than to dismiss the particularities of the context in which a moral problem arises. And we often pay attention to feelings of empathy and caring to suggest what we ought to do rather than relying as fully as possible on abstract rules of reason. . . .

. . . One should not equate tendencies women in fact display with feminist views, since the former may well be the result of the sexist, oppressive conditions in which women's lives have been lived. But many feminists see our own consciously considered experience as lending confirmation to the view that what has come to be called "an ethic of care" needs to be developed. Some think it should supercede "the ethic of justice" of traditional or standard moral theory. Others think it should be integrated with the ethic of justice and rules.

In any case, feminist philosophers are in the process of reevaluating the place of emotion in morality in at least two respects. First, many think morality requires the development of the moral emotions, in contrast to moral theories emphasizing the primacy of reason. . . .

Secondly, emotion will be respected rather than dismissed by many feminist moral philosophers in the process of gaining moral understanding. The experience and practice out of which feminist moral theory can be expected to be developed will include embodied feeling as well as thought. . . . Among the elements being reevaluated are feminine emotions. The "care" of the alternative feminist approach to morality appreciates rather than rejects emotion. The caring relationships important to feminist morality cannot be understood in terms of abstract rules or moral reasoning. And the "weighing" so often needed between the conflicting claims of some relationships and others cannot be settled by deduction or rational calculation. A feminist ethic will . . . embrace emotion as providing at least a partial basis for morality itself, and for moral understanding.

. . . Achieving and maintaining trusting, caring relationships is quite different from acting in accord with rational principles, or satisfying the individual desires of either self or other. Caring, empathy, feeling with others, being sensitive to each other's feelings, all may be better guides to what morality requires in actual contexts than may abstract rules of reason, or rational calculation, or at least they may be necessary components of an adequate morality.

The fear that a feminist ethic will be a relativistic "situation ethic" is misplaced. Some feelings can be as widely shared as are rational beliefs. . . .

The liberal tradition in social and moral philosophy argues that in pluralistic society and even more clearly in a pluralistic world, we cannot agree on our visions of the good life, on what is the best kind of life for humans, but we can hope to agree on the minimal conditions for justice, for coexistence within a framework allowing us to pursue our visions of the good life. Many feminists contend that the commitment to justice needed for agreement *in actual conditions* on even minimal requirements of justice is as likely to demand relational feelings as a rational recognition of abstract principles. Human beings can and do care, and are capable of caring far more than at present, about the sufferings of children quite distant from them, about the prospects for future generations, and about the well-being of the globe. The liberal tradition's mutually disinterested rational individualists would seem unlikely to care enough to take the actions needed to achieve moral decency at a global level, or environmental sanity for decades hence, as they would seem unable to represent caring relationships within the family and among friends. . . .

The possibilities as well as the problems (and we are well aware of some of them) in a feminist reenvisioning of emotion and reason need to be further developed, but we can already see that the views of nonfeminist moral theory are unsatisfactory.

II. THE PUBLIC AND THE PRIVATE

The second questionable aspect of the history of ethics on which I focused was its conception of the distinction between the public and the private. As with the split between reason and emotion, feminists are showing how gender-bias has distorted previous conceptions of these spheres, and we are trying to offer more appropriate understandings of "private" morality and "public" life.

Part of what feminists have criticized has been the way the distinction has been accompanied by a supposition that what occurs in the household occurs as if on an island beyond politics, whereas the personal is highly affected by the political power beyond, from legislation about abortion to the greater earning power of men, to the interconnected division of labor by gender both within and beyond the household, to the lack of adequate social protection for women against domestic violence. Of course we recognize that the family is not identical to the state, and we need concepts for thinking about the private or personal, and the public or political. But they will have to be very different from the traditional concepts.

Feminists have also criticized deeper assumptions about what is distinctively human and what is "natural" in the public and private aspects of human life, and what is meant by "natural" in connection with women. Consider the associations that have traditionally been built up: the public realm is seen as the distinctively human realm in which man transcends his animal nature, while the private realm of the household is seen as the natural region in which women merely reproduce the species. . . .

Dominant patterns of thought have seen women as primarily mothers, and mothering as the performance of a primarily biological function. Then it has been supposed that while engaging in political life is a specifically human activity, women are engaged in an activity which is not specifically human. Women accordingly have been thought to be closer to nature than men, to be enmeshed in a biological function involving processes more like those in which other animals are involved than like the rational discussion of the citizen in the polis, or the glorious battles of noble soldiers, or the trading and rational contracting of "economic man." The total or relative exclusion of women from the domain of public life has then been seen as either inevitable or appropriate.

The view that women are more determined by biology than are men is still extraordinarily prevalent. It is as questionable from a feminist perspective as many other traditional misinterpretations of women's experience. Human mothering is an extremely different activity from the mothering engaged in by other animals. The work and speech of men is recognized as very different from what might be thought of as the "work" and "speech" of other animals. Human mothering is fully as different from animal mothering. Of course all human beings are animal as well as human. But to whatever extent it is appropriate to recognize a difference between "man" and other animals, so would it be appropriate to recognize a comparable difference between "woman" and other animals, and between the activities—including mothering—engaged in by women and the behavior of other animals.

Human mothering shapes language and culture, it forms human social personhood, it develops morality. ... In creating human social persons, human mothering is different in kind from merely propagating a species. And human mothering can be fully as creative an activity as those activities traditionally thought of as distinctively human, because to create *new* persons, and new types of *persons*, can surely be as creative as to make new objects, products, or institutions. *Human* mothering is no more "natural" or "primarily biological" than is any other human activity.

Consider nursing an infant, often thought of as the epitome of a biological process with which mothering is associated and women are identified. There is no reason to think of human nursing as any more simply biological than there is to think of, say, a businessmen's lunch this way. Eating is a biological process, but what and how and with whom we eat are thoroughly cultural. Whether and how long and with whom a woman nurses an infant, are also human, cultural matters. ...

We are continually being presented with images of the humanly new and creative as occurring in the public realm of the polis, or the realms of marketplace or of art and science outside the household. The very term 'reproduction' suggests mere repetition, the "natural" bringing into existence of repeated instances of the same human animal. But human reproduction is not repetition. This is not to suggest that bringing up children in the interstices of patriarchal society, in society structured by institutions supporting male dominance, can achieve the potential of transformation latent in the activity of human mothering. But the activity of creating new social persons and new kinds of persons is potentially the most transformative human activity of all. And it suggests that morality should concern itself first of all with this activity, with what its norms and practices ought to be, and with how the institutions and arrangements throughout society and the world ought to be structured to facilitate the right kinds of development of the best kinds of new persons. The flourishing of children ought to be at the very center of moral and social and political and economic and legal thought, rather than, as at present, at the periphery, if attended to at all. ...

Clearly, a reconceptualization is needed of the ways in which every human life is entwined with personal and with social components. Feminist theorists are contributing imaginative work to this project.

III. THE CONCEPT OF SELF

Let me turn now to the third aspect of the history of ethics which I discussed and which feminists are re-envisioning: the concept of self. One of the most important emphases in a feminist approach to morality is the recognition that more attention must be paid to the domain between, on the one hand, the self as ego, as self-interested individual, and, on the other hand, the universal, everyone, others in general. Traditionally, ethics has dealt with these poles of individual self and universal all. Usually, it has called for impartiality against the partiality of the egoistic self; sometimes it has defended egoism against claims for a universal perspective. But most standard moral theory has hardly noticed as morally significant the intermediate realm of family relations and relations of friendship, of group ties and neighborhood concerns, especially from the point of view of women. When it has noticed this intermediate realm it has often seen its attachments as threatening to the aspirations of the Man of Reason, or as subversive of "true" morality. In seeing the problems of ethics as problems of reconciling the interests of the self with what would be right or best for "everyone," standard ethics has neglected the moral aspects of the concern and sympathy which people actually feel for particular others, and what moral experience in this intermediate realm suggests for an adequate morality.

The region of "particular others" is a distinct domain, where what can be seen to be artificial and problematic are the very egoistic "self" and the universal "all others" of standard moral theory. In the domain of particular others, the self is already constituted to an important degree by relations with others, and these relations may be much more salient and significant than the interests of any individual self in isolation. The "others" in the picture, however, are not the "all others," or "everyone," of traditional moral theory. ... They are, characteristically, actual flesh and blood other human beings for whom we have actual feelings and with whom we have real ties.

From the point of view of much feminist theory, the individualistic assumptions of liberal theory and of most standard moral theory are suspect. Even if we would be freed from the debilitating aspects of dominating male power to "be ourselves" and to pursue our own interests, we would, as persons, still have ties to other persons, and we would at least in part be constituted by such ties. Such ties would be part of what we inherently are. We are, for instance, the daughter or son of given parents, or the mother or father of given children, and we carry with us at least some ties to the racial or ethnic or national group within which we developed into the persons we are.

If we look, for instance, at the realities of the relation between mothering person (who can be female or male) and child, we can see that what we value in the relation cannot be broken down into individual gains and losses for the individual members in the relation. Nor can it be understood in universalistic terms. Self-development apart from the relation may be much less important than the satisfactory development of the relation. What matters may often be the health and growth of and the development of the relation-and-its-members in ways that cannot be understood in the individualistic terms of standard moral theories designed to maximize the satisfaction of self-interest. The universalistic terms of moral theories grounded in what would be right for "all rational beings" or "everyone" cannot handle, either, what has moral value in the relation between mothering person and child.

Feminism is of course not the only locus of criticism of the individualistic and abstractly universalistic features of liberalism and of standard moral theory. Marxists and communitarians also see the self as constituted by its social relations. But in their usual form, Marxist and communitarian criticisms pay no more attention than liberalism and standard moral theory to the experience of women, to the context of mothering, or to friendship as women experience it. . . .

Relationships can be evaluated as trusting or mistrustful, mutually considerate or selfish, harmonious or stressful, and so forth. Where trust and consideration are appropriate, which is not always, we can find ways to foster them. But understanding and evaluating relationships, and encouraging them to be what they can be at their best, require us to look at relationships between actual persons, and to see what both standard moral theories and their nonfeminist critics often miss. To be adequate, moral theories must pay attention to the neglected realm of particular others in the actual relationships and actual contexts of women's experience. In doing so, problems of individual self-interest vs. universal rules may recede to a region more like background, out-of-focus insolubility or relative unimportance. The salient problems may then be seen to be how we ought best to guide or to maintain or to reshape the relationships . . . with actual other human beings. . . .

I have examined three topics on which feminist philosophers and feminists in other fields are thinking anew about where we should start and how we should focus our attention in ethics. Feminist reconceptualizations and recommendations concerning the relation between reason and emotion, the distinction between public and private, and the concept of the self, are providing insights deeply challenging to standard moral theory. The implications of this work are that we need an almost total reconstruction of social and political and economic and legal theory in all their traditional forms as well as a reconstruction of moral theory and practice at more comprehensive, or fundamental, levels.

Study Questions

1. What is the meaning of Emerson's claim that the state must follow and not lead its citizens? How is this related to his notion that less government is best? Notice that both Emerson and Thoreau hold the position that government ought to be limited, and perhaps not to govern at all. Are they trying to justify absolute moral and political anarchy? Explain.

2. In Emerson's view, what is the highest end of government? What does this have to do with his convictions regarding the cure for the abuse of government?

3. In what sense is it the case that Thoreau's position puts primary emphasis on moral right over law? Note, for example, his claim that he wishes to be a bad subject as much as to be a good neighbor. Do his claims justify civil disobedience? Why?

4. What is the meaning of Thoreau's claim that the move toward democracy is progress toward "a true respect for the individual"? In your view, what is the role of the individual in government and society for the New England Transcendentalists?

5. How does Thoreau define a "peacable" revolution? What is his view regarding violent revolution? Was he right to refuse to pay his taxes? Did it make a difference? Explain.

6. What, in your view, are the most important claims made for the value of life in William James's "What Makes a Life Significant"?

7. According to James, what is it in particular that constitutes a morally superior individual? What does this notion have to do with James's recounting of the story of his visit to Chautauqua and his claim that "ideals taken by themselves give no reality, the virtues by themselves no novelty"? Explain.

8. How does Dewey's conception of democracy extend beyond simply that of a system or form of government? How is this notion of democracy related to the concept of a community? What does Dewey mean by the claim that liberty, fraternity, and equality separated from community life are simply abstractions? Do you agree with Dewey? Defend your answer.

9. What is the meaning of Dewey's conception of habit in human action? Explain the significance of his explanation of the way in which public and free communication are essential to the growth of human knowledge and the creation of community.

10. What is Dewey's distinction between the Great Society and the Great Community? How is the Great Community to be achieved? Are you convinced by Dewey's reasons and reasoning? Defend your position.

11. What are the two principles of justice developed by John Rawls? In what way do they capture Rawls's conception of "justice as fairness"?

12. Rawls claims that the parties to the development of the conception of justice he has in mind will not formulate or create a government or society, but instead will agree on principles by which to order the arrangements and practices already in place. Given what you already know about the notion of constitution and a contractarian theory of government form the works of Paine, Adams, and American political documents, do you believe that Rawls's conception of the development of principles of justice is more, or less, realistic and practically applicable than that of Paine? Why do you hold this position?

13. What are the founding ideas behind Robert Nozick's development of an entitlement theory? What, in particular, is an entitlement theory and how is it related to the subject of "justice in holdings"?

14. Why and how does Nozick argue against patterned principles of justice? In what way are Rawls's principles "patterned"? Whose position (that of Rawls or that of Nozick) do you find most convincing, just, and applicable to actual social arrangements? Why do you hold this view? Defend your claims.

15. In your view, does the example of Wilt Chamberlain suffice to show that liberty upsets patterns?

16. What, for Michael Sandel, is an "unencumbered self" and how is this notion related to his critique of political and moral theories such as those of Kant, Rawls, and Nozick? Does Sandel hold that we are "unencumbered" selves? How does he develop his view? Do you agree with Sandel's position? Defend your answer.

17. According to Virginia Held, what has been the effect in the history of ethics and political theory of the distinction between reason and emotion as it is related to the male/female distinction? Why is it that traditional moral theories utilizing this distinction do not "apply" to women's concerns, or even to generally human concerns?

18. What are Held's conclusions regarding the problems of traditional moral theories (the reason/emotion and public/private distinctions and the concept of the self), and how is feminist ethics capable of challenging those problems and creating more inclusive ethical theories? Do you agree that traditional moral theories do not include the experience of women? Do you agree with Held's conclusions? Why? Defend your answer.

Suggestions for Further Reading

Avineri, Shlomo, and de-Shalit, Avner. *Communitarianism and Individualism.* New York: Oxford University Press, 1992.

Barbour, Brian M., ed. *American Transcendentalism: An Anthology of Criticism.* Notre Dame: University of Notre Dame Press, 1973.

Bar On, Ami-Bat, and Ferguson, Ann. *Daring to be Good: Essays in Feminist Ethico-Politics.* New York: Routledge, 1998.

Barish, Evelyn. *Emerson: The Roots of Prophecy*. Princeton: Princeton University Press, 1989.

Bell, Daniel A. *Communitarianism and Its Critics*. Oxford: Clarendon Press, 1993.

Boydston, Jo Ann, ed. *Guide to the Works of John Dewey*. Carbondale: Southern Illinois University Press, 1970.

Brennen, Bernard P. *The Ethics of William James*. New York: Bookman Associates, 1961.

Bushnell, Dana E. *"Nagging" Questions: Feminist Ethics in Everyday Life*. Lanham, Md.: Rowman & Littlefield, 1995.

Cahn, Steven, ed. *New Studies in the Philosophy of John Dewey*. Hanover, N.H.: University Press of New England, 1977.

Clement, Grace. *Care, Autonomy and Justice: Feminism and the Ethic of Care*. Boulder, Colo.: Westview Press, 1996.

Corlett, Angelo J., ed. *Equality and Liberty: Analyzing Rawls and Nozick*. New York: St. Martin's Press, 1991.

Cotkin, George. *William James, Public Philosopher*. Baltimore and London: Johns Hopkins University Press, 1990.

Daniels, Norman A. *Reading Rawls: Critical Studies on Rawls's A Theory of Justice*. New York: Basic Books, 1975.

Davion, Victoria, and Wolf, Clark. *The Idea of a Political Liberalism: Essays on Rawls*. Lanham, Md.: Rowman & Littlefield, 2000.

Dewey, John. *The Public and its Problems*. Chicago: Swallow Press, 1927.

Dewey, John. *The Early Works: 1882–1898*. Edited by Jo Ann Boydston. 5 vols. Carbondale: Southern Illinois University Press, 1967–72.

Dewey, John. *The Later Works: 1925–1953*. Edited by Jo Ann Boydston. 17 vols. Carbondale: Southern Illinois University Press, 1976–83.

DiQuinzio, Patrice, and Young, Iris Marion. *Feminist Ethics and Social Policy*. Bloomington: Indiana University Press, 1997.

Dykhuizen, George. *The Life and Mind of John Dewey*. Carbondale: Southern Illinois University Press, 1973.

Emerson, Ralph Waldo. *The Collected Works of Ralph Waldo Emerson*. Cambridge: Belknap Press of Harvard University Press, 1971.

Emerson, Ralph Waldo. *Emerson's Prose and Poetry: Authoritative Texts, Contexts, Criticisms*. Edited by Joel Porte and Saundra Morris. New York: Norton, 2001.

Hailwood, Simon A. *Exploring Nozick: Beyond Anarchy, State, and Utopia*. Brookfield, Vt.: Avebury Press, 1996.

Held, Virginia. *Justice and Care: Essential Readings in Feminist Ethics*. Boulder, Colo.: Westview Press, 1995.

James, William. *The Works of William James*. Edited by Frederick H. Burkhardt, Fredson Bowers, and Ignas K. Skrupskelis. Cambridge: Harvard University Press, 1975–1988.

Konitz, Milton R. and Wilcher, Stephen, eds. *Emerson: A Collection of Critical Essays*. New York: Prentice Hall, 1962.

Kukathas, Chandran, and Petit, Phillip. *Rawls: A Theory of Justice and Its Critics*. Stanford: Stanford University Press, 1990.

Kuklick, Bruce. *Churchmen and Philosophers: From Jonathan Edwards to John Dewey*. New Haven: Yale University Press, 1985.

Martin, Rex. *Rawls and Rights*. Lawrence: University Press of Kansas, 1985.

MacIntyre, Alasdair C. *After Virtue: A Study in Moral Theory*. 2d ed. Notre Dame: University of Notre Dame Press, 1984.

Mackaye, James, ed. *Thoreau: Philosopher of Freedom: Writings on Liberty*. New York: Vanguard Press, 1930.

Moore, Edward C. *American Pragmatism: Peirce, James and Dewey*. New York: Columbia University Press, 1961.

Nozick, Robert. *Anarchy, State, and Utopia*. New York: Basic Books, 1974.

Padover, Saul K. "Ralph Waldo Emerson: The Moral Voice in Politics." *Political Science Quarterly* 74 (1959): 334–350.

Paul, Ellen Frankel, Miller, Fred D. and Paul, Jeffrey, eds. *The Communitarian Challenge to Liberalism*. New York: Cambridge University Press, 1996.

Paul, Jeffrey. *Reading Nozick: Essays on Anarchy, State, and Utopia*. Totowa, N.J.: Rowman and Littlefield, 1981.

Perry, Ralph Barton. *The Thought and Character of William James*. Nashville, Tenn.: Vanderbilt University Press, 1996.

Putnam, Ruth Anna, ed. *The Cambridge Companion to William James*. New York: Cambridge University Press, 1997.

Rawls, John. *A Theory of Justice*. Cambridge: Harvard University Press, 1971.

Rawls, John. *Political Liberalism*. New York: Columbia University Press, 1996.

Sandel, Michael J. *Liberalism and the Limits of Justice*. New York: Cambridge University Press, 1998.

Simon, Myron. "Thoreau and Anarchism." *Michigan Quarterly Review* 23 (1984): 360–384.

Singer, Marcus G., ed. *American Philosophy*. New York: Cambridge University Press, 1985.

Sleeper, R.W. *The Necessity of Pragmatism: John Dewey's Conception of Philosophy*. New Haven: Yale University Press, 1986.

Thoreau, Henry David. *A Yankee in Canada, with Anti-Slavery and Reform Papers*. New York: Greenwood Press, 1969.

Thoreau, Henry David. *The Portable Thoreau*. Edited by Carl Bode. New York: Penguin, 1982.

Wolff, Jonathan. *Robert Nozick: Property, Justice and the Minimal State*. Stanford: Stanford University Press, 1991.